New Business Ventures and the Entrepreneur

Sixth Edition

Michael J. Roberts
Senior Lecturer and Executive
Director, Arthur Rock Center
for Entrepreneurship

Howard H. Stevenson
Sarofim-Rock Professor of Business
Administration

William A. Sahlman
Dimitri V. d'Arbeloff—Class of 1955
Professor of Business Administration

Paul W. Marshall
MBA Class of 1960 Professor
of Management

Richard G. Hamermesh
Professor of Management

All of the Harvard Business School

 **McGraw-Hill
Irwin**

Boston   Burr Ridge, IL   Dubuque, IA   Madison, WI   New York   San Francisco   St. Louis
Bangkok   Bogotá   Caracas   Kuala Lumpur   Lisbon   London   Madrid   Mexico City
Milan   Montreal   New Delhi   Santiago   Seoul   Singapore   Sydney   Taipei   Toronto

McGraw-Hill
Irwin

NEW BUSINESS VENTURES AND THE ENTREPRENEUR
Published by McGraw-Hill/Irwin, a business unit of The McGraw-Hill Companies, Inc., 1221 Avenue of the Americas, New York, NY, 10020. Copyright © 2007 by The McGraw-Hill Companies, Inc. All rights reserved. No part of this publication may be reproduced or distributed in any form or by any means, or stored in a database or retrieval system, without the prior written consent of The McGraw-Hill Companies, Inc., including, but not limited to, in any network or other electronic storage or transmission, or broadcast for distance learning.

Some ancillaries, including electronic and print components, may not be available to customers outside the United States.

This book is printed on acid-free paper.

1 2 3 4 5 6 7 8 9 0 DOC/DOC 0 9 8 7 6

ISBN-13: 978-0-07-340497-4
ISBN-10: 0-07-340497-7

Editorial director: *John E. Biernat*
Senior sponsoring editor: *Ryan Blankenship*
Editorial coordinator: *Allison J. Belda*
Associate marketing manager: *Margaret A. Beamer*
Producer, Media technology: *Janna Martin*
Project manager: *Jim Labeots*
Production supervisor: *Debra R. Sylvester*
Designer: *Jillian Lindner*
Supplement producer: *Ira C. Roberts*
Typeface: *10/12 Times New Roman*
Compositor: *Interactive Composition Corporation*
Printer: *R. R. Donnelley*

Library of Congress Cataloging-in-Publication Data

New business ventures and the entrepreneur / Michael J. Roberts . . . [et al.].—6th ed.
        p. cm.
    Includes bibliographical references and index.
    ISBN-13: 978-0-07-340497-4 (alk. paper)
    ISBN-10: 0-07-340497-7 (alk. paper)
    1. New business enterprises. 2. New business enterprises--United States. I. Roberts, Michael J.
    HD62.5.S75 2007
    658.1'1--dc22

                                            2006042006

www.mhhe.com

To Patrick Rooney Liles (1937–1983)

Teacher
Scholar of Entrepreneurship
Business Leader
Athlete
Friend

Introduction: What Is Entrepreneurship?

Entrepreneurship is often defined as the creation of new enterprises. We agree that the formation of a new venture is typically an entrepreneurial act. However, we find it more useful to define entrepreneurship around "the pursuit of opportunity."[1]

This focus, in our view, puts the spotlight on the key dimension of entrepreneurship: the identification and evaluation of opportunity and the marshalling of resources required to pursue it. This view expands our lens on the phenomenon of entrepreneurship and allows us to examine entrepreneurial behavior in the context of existing businesses. Moreover, our focus is on the tasks and skills needed to exercise general manager responsibilities as an entrepreneur. Our exclusive focus on the entrepreneur and entrepreneurial management reflects two considerations. The first is the growing recognition of the critical importance of entrepreneurial activities in capitalistic economies. As Joseph Schumpeter argued almost 60 years ago:

> This process of *Creative Destruction* is the essential fact about Capitalism . . . In other words, the problem that is usually being visualized is how capitalism administers *existing structures,* whereas the *relevant problem is how it creates and destroys them . . .* In capitalist reality as distinguished from its textbook picture, it is not [price] competition which counts, but competition from the *new commodity, the new technology, the new source of supply, and the new type of organization.*[2] (*Emphasis added*)

Data of many sorts confirms this point of view. For example in the United States, over the past twenty years small companies have accounted for two-thirds of all new jobs created in the private sector. During the same period, employment in the Fortune 500 has declined by 5 million jobs. Globally, a recent study by researchers from the Global Entrepreneurship Monitor found that one third of the differential in national economic growth rates was due to the extent of entrepreneurial activity.[3] The pace of entrepreneurship also seems to be accelerating. For example, in the 1960s fewer than 10 new companies appeared each year on the Fortune 500 list. In recent years, roughly 50 new companies have been making the list each year.

The second reason for our focus on the entrepreneur is that it is a position a large group of MBA graduates aspire to occupy. In our view, MBAs share this aspiration for good reason. The satisfaction that comes from building something out of nothing, from harnessing the creative impulse to meet a customer need, from building an organization of people that reflects our own ideals—all of these are worthy goals.

Thus, this text focuses on a particular type of general management job that plays a critical role in market-based economies and to which many of you aspire and will eventually occupy. With this in mind, the text aims to convey the approach entrepreneurs use in identifying opportunity and creating new ventures; the analytic skills that are needed to practice this approach; and the background knowledge and managerial skills that are

---

[1] Howard Stevenson, "A Perspective on Entrepreneurship," HBS Case No. 384-131 (Boston: Harvard Business School Publishing, 1983).

[2] Joseph A. Schumpeter, *Capitalism, Socialism and Democracy,* New York: Harper, 1950: pp. 83–84.

[3] Global Entrepreneurship Monitor: 1999 Executive Report, p. 39.

necessary for dealing with the recurring issues involved in starting, growing, and harnessing the value of new ventures. The cases used in the text focus on new business opportunities in start-ups, growing companies, large corporations, and nonprofit enterprises. The underlying notion is that it is possible to manage as an entrepreneur in a variety of settings. Finally, the cases focus on the entrepreneur who, in the face of great uncertainty, still needs to make decisions and to take actions.

Our Viewpoint

The text is designed to focus on the Entrepreneur as a manager and the processes and techniques he or she uses to manage. In practice this means that in every case there is a person who must make some decisions and take the necessary actions to implement those decisions. The issues facing the entrepreneur are typically multifaceted and require an integrative perspective. There is a very important role for analytical tools and conceptual frameworks, but they are to be applied only to the extent that they help the manager make good decisions and develop realistic action plans that can be implemented and communicated to employees and investors. You should be prepared to think and act like the manager in the case. You will need to present the analysis that leads you to make a particular decision and to explain the plan you have for implementing your decision. Your goal should be to persuade your classmates that this is the appropriate plan and decision for the situation at hand. Entrepreneurs have a bias to take action, and this course is intended to help you develop this attitude.

Our Objectives

Because the text focuses on the entrepreneur, it is important to recognize the nature of the setting or context in which this type of manager operates and some of the special characteristics of the entrepreneurial manager.

Context and Characteristics of the Entrepreneur

In general, there are four distinguishing characteristics of the entrepreneurs' environment. The first is great uncertainty. Because they are undertaking something new, entrepreneurs face a tremendous range of uncertainty surrounding technological breakthroughs, potential demand, speed of acceptance, competitive response, availability of human and financial capital, etc. The next characteristic is rapid growth. Precisely because there is so much uncertainty, the expected return from a new venture is unlikely to be high enough unless it is in a field where rapid growth can be anticipated. While there are some exceptions to this, such as most leveraged buyouts and some industry roll-ups, annual revenue growth rates of 30%–60% are typical. This requires the entrepreneur to deal with such issues as attracting sufficient people, assuring adequate supply and distribution of the product or service, and developing enough infrastructure to prevent the venture from spinning out of control. Third, entrepreneurs are creators of fundamental and radical change. The source of this change may be in product or process technology, or in distribution, or in the basic business model and type of organization, or by changing the structure of an industry or creating new industries and markets. But it always involves moving from something that is known and familiar to something that is only conceived in the mind. Finally, entrepreneurs operate under conditions of extremely limited resources. The main reason for this is that because of the tremendous uncertainty, investors typically will commit only limited resources to a venture, preferring to invest in smaller, successive rounds of financing as events suggest an increasing probability of success.

This context—*high uncertainty, rapid growth, radical change, and limited resources*—is worth careful consideration on two levels. First and very personally, a career as an entrepreneur requires that you be comfortable with all four characteristics. Not all people can operate under conditions of great uncertainty, ambiguity, and limited resources. The pursuit of radical change often requires faith and belief that cannot be justified by analysis alone and is often accompanied by the doubts and resistance of skeptics. And rapid growth requires a pace and level of work effort that not everyone can or is willing to sustain. Second, because these four elements define a distinct reality in which entrepreneurs operate which is different from that of most general managers in large established companies, they require a distinct approach to management. This approach is described in the article by Howard Stevenson, "A Perspective on Entrepreneurship."[4] Below we underscore some of the key management approaches used by entrepreneurs and discuss how these differ from the approach of managers in existing organizations:

- *Entrepreneurs are opportunity driven.* Whereas most managers are constrained by their companies' current capabilities and the risk of cannibalizing existing products and businesses, the entrepreneur is motivated solely to pursue opportunity. For the entrepreneur, constraints are inconveniences to be overcome, not reasons for restraint.

- *Entrepreneurs are tremendously focused on cash and the need to conserve resources.* Some of this characteristic is due to the way investors typically prefer to invest in smaller incremental steps. But at the same time, entrepreneurs seek to maximize their personal returns by accepting less financing in order to protect their own ownership positions. The result is an intense need to husband cash and to rent or contract for resources rather than to buy or hire them.

- *Entrepreneurs have a tremendous sense of urgency.* Because they are opportunity driven, because they need to show tangible progress to attract funding, and because the mere passage of time consumes cash, entrepreneurs have a sense of urgency seldom experienced in established businesses.

- *Entrepreneurs have a singular focus and tremendous sense of ownership.* In an established company, any opportunity is part of a portfolio. A new, risky project is compared with investments in proven businesses and the company pursues multiple opportunities. As a result, even start-ups within large companies seldom have the same sense of focus and ownership as the efforts of independent entrepreneurs whose entire future rests on the success of their venture.

---

[4]Howard Stevenson, "A Perspective on Entrepreneurship," HBS Case No. 384-131 (Boston: Harvard Business School Publishing, 1983).

- *Entrepreneurs use flexible organization structures and approaches.* Precisely because their companies are growing rapidly and using many, disparate resources, rigid hierarchical structures are anathema to the entrepreneur. Instead flat organizations, informal relationships and networks, and frequent changes are the norm.

Underlying Goals and Themes

- *The text will help you to understand how entrepreneurs think about and approach the challenge of new venture creation.* The tasks of conceiving and obtaining resources for a new venture are at the core of what entrepreneurial managers do. Given the new and uncertain nature of the environments in which they operate, the tools and approaches used by entrepreneurs extend beyond typical industry and strategic analyses. Conceiving a new venture requires the ability to see new patterns emerging in the environment, new ways to conceptualize an industry's structure and boundaries, and careful analysis of the venture's underlying business model. Similarly, the approach to funding a new venture is different from traditional capital budgeting, which places a premium on forecasting total capital needs and rates of returns. In contrast, the entrepreneurial manager seeks financing in several stages. Finally, because new ventures contain so many risks and uncertainties, it is critical to manage in a way that systematically reduces the most significant uncertainties.

- *The text will familiarize you with the broad range of settings in which entrepreneurs operate.* Entrepreneurship is not limited to a few heroic figures who start grand high-technology enterprises. It is much more commonplace and can be practiced by any manager willing to pursue opportunity without regard to the resources they currently control. The settings of our cases range from fruit juice to genomics, from real estate to software, from manufacturing to services, from start-ups to leveraged buyouts, from ventures backed by sophisticated investors to those funded with credit card debt. As a result, we will come to see entrepreneurship as potentially accessible to all of us.

- *The text will familiarize you with the major sources of capital available to entrepreneurs and the expectations of those investors.* Because entrepreneurs are so dependent on capital to grow their enterprises, it is essential for them to know how to tap into all potential sources of funding: friends and family, angel investors, venture capital firms, commercial lending institutions, and regional and global investment bankers. Through a variety of cases, we will see the expectations of each of these investor groups, as well as the benefits and drawbacks of each.

- *The text will identify the major managerial issues entrepreneurs face when growing their businesses.* An entrepreneur must do more than just conceive and start a business. Some of the greatest challenges come in growing the business and the managerial tasks of expanding and systematizing the organization and its processes. The text will provide an overview of these issues, as well as some approaches for managing them.

- *The text will cause you to look introspectively at whether and how you want entrepreneurship to play a role in your career.* Some of you are considering joining a start-up upon graduation and many of you foresee working for an early-stage company at some point in your career. By virtue of your exposure to a variety of entrepreneurial issues, it will be only natural for you to consider if you can really excel in that environment and if you are ready for it now or need more managerial experience. Others may decide that they are more interested in the capital-provider side of the entrepreneurial equation. And some may be drawn to the challenge of being an entrepreneurial manager within a larger, established company or in a nonprofit institution.

Acknowledgments

Patrick R. Liles taught the New Ventures course at Harvard Business School from 1969 to 1977, and wrote the first edition of this text. In a very real sense, his early work in this field, his first edition of this book, and his vision of the entrepreneur provided a strong foundation upon which to build. Pat died—far too young—in 1983, and we dedicate this book to him out of respect and affection.

Since then, many others have shaped the work in entrepreneurship at HBS. In the 1980s and 1990s, this work primarily took place under the umbrella of a series of second-year elective courses. Bill Sahlman was an early pioneer in developing a very popular second-year elective course called "Entrepreneurial Finance." Bill developed a lot of important ideas that have informed much of the course development work in the entrepreneurship field here and elsewhere, and we are glad to welcome him as a co-author. Since 2000, HBS has required that all first-year students in the MBA program take, as part of the core curriculum, a course in entrepreneurship called "The Entrepreneurial Manager." Paul Marshall, and then Richard Hamermesh, were the heads of this course during its first five years and led the effort to build what is today one of the most popular courses at HBS. We are pleased to welcome Paul and Richard as co-authors to this edition of the book.

Thanks to our colleagues Irv Grousbeck and Amar Bhide for their work and contributions to previous editions of this book. Irv continues to be MBA Class of 1980 Consulting Professor of Management and Director of the Center for Entrepreneurial Studies at Stanford's Graduate School of Business, and Amar is now Lawrence D. Glaubinger Professor of Business Management at Columbia Business School.

Thanks to these faculty colleagues at HBS who allowed us to use cases they authored or co-authored in this text: Kash Rangan for Aravind Eye Hospital; Ashish Nanda for Vermeer Technologies; Myra Hart for Zipcar, Linda Cyr for NanoGene Technologies; Joe Lassiter for Room For Dessert; Kent Bowen for Jim Sharpe; Stig Leschly for Kipp National; and Dwight Crane for Kendle International.

All of the cases and chapters in this book were written with support from the Harvard Business School. Former Deans John McArthur and Kim Clark as well as our current acting Dean, Jay Light, have all been wonderful supporters of this work—and more—in the entrepreneurship domain at HBS, and we are grateful for all they have done.

The depth of alumni support for our work has been remarkable. Arthur Rock and Fayez Sarofim gave the first chair at Harvard to reestablish sustained work in entrepreneurship. Arthur expanded on this foundation with a wonderfully generous gift establishing the Arthur Rock Center for Entrepreneurship. Frank Batten and others have provided substantial funds to support the research and teaching of entrepreneurship at HBS.

Finally, all of these cases are based on real entrepreneurs—in many cases identified, in some cases disguised, who allowed us to tell their stories. We are indebted to these entrepreneurs who gave so willingly of their time, energy, and ideas so that we could compile these cases.

Table of Contents

Introduction: What Is Entrepreneurship?   iv

Introduction: What Is Entrepreneurship?

1 A Perspective on Entrepreneurship   3

   Case 1.1 The Aravind Eye Hospital, Madurai, India: In Service for Sight   17

   Case 1.2 R&R   45

   Case 1.3 Vermeer Technologies (A): A Company Is Born   63

   Case 1.4 Endeavor—Determining a Growth Strategy   73

Recognizing and Analyzing Opportunity

2 Some Thoughts on Business Plans   115

3 Note on Business Model Analysis for the Entrepreneur   149

4 Valuation, Financing and Capitalization Tables in the New Venture Context   163

5 How Venture Capitalists Evaluate Potential Venture Opportunities   169

   Case 2.1 Beta Golf   191

   Case 2.2 Zipcar: Refining the Business Model   213

   Case 2.3 Keurig   233

   Case 2.4 Crunch   257

Assembling Intellectual, Human, and Financial Resources

6 The Legal Protection of Intellectual Property   283

7 New Venture Financing   291

8 Deal Structure and Deal Terms   305

   Case 3.1 Sheila Mason & Craig Shepherd   315

   Case 3.2 NanoGene Technologies, Inc.   331

   Case 3.3 Business Plan for Room For Dessert™: Adding Unique Ingredients to Life's Balancing Act   343

   Case 3.4 Walnut Venture Associates (D): RBS Deal Terms   379

   Case 3.5 Jim Sharpe: Extrusion Technology, Inc. (Abridged)   389

Managing the Early-Stage Venture

9 Managing Risk and Reward in the Entrepreneurial Venture   417

10 The Legal Forms of Organization   425

   Case 4.1 ONSET Ventures   435

   Case 4.2 E Ink: Financing Growth   465

   Case 4.3 Valhalla Partners Due Diligence   483

   Case 4.4 MAC Development Corporation   499

Managing Growth and Realizing Value

11 Managing the Growing Venture   527

   Case 5.1 KIPP National (A) (Abridged)   537

   Case 5.2 Innocent Drinks   563

   Case 5.3 Shurgard Self-Storage: Expansion to Europe   585

   Case 5.4 Kendle International Inc.   617

   Case 5.5 RightNow Technologies   645

   Case 5.6 Jamie Dimon and Bank One (A)   667

Index   691

PART 1

Introduction: What Is Entrepreneurship?

The word "entrepreneurship" is used to mean many different things. To some, it suggests the starting of any business; to others, the development of a new and novel idea, whether that development takes place in the context of a start-up or an existing business. Some believe you need an "entrepreneur" for a business to behave entrepreneurially, others think a set of good managers in a large corporation can behave in a way that produces an entrepreneurial result. In this section, we argue that the key attribute of entrepreneurship is the pursuit of opportunity. This contrasts with the approach of "leveraging existing skills, capabilities, resources and core competencies," which is so often the mantra of the larger corporation (but which is rarely an option for a start-up, which has little or no resources to begin with). The chapters in this section articulate this idea more fully, and the cases provide an opportunity to see how the entrepreneurial process plays out in new and existing businesses, as well as in the for-profit and not-for-profit settings.

A Perspective on Entrepreneurship

The term "entrepreneurship" has entered the business vocabulary as the 1980s' equivalent of "professionalism," the managerial buzzword of the 1970s. Many individuals aspire to be entrepreneurs, enjoying the freedom, independence and wealth such a career seems to suggest. And larger corporations want to become more "entrepreneurial," their shorthand for the innovative and adaptive qualities they see in their smaller—and often more successful—competitors.

Our purpose in this chapter is to shed some light on the concept of entrepreneurship. We will define entrepreneurship as a management process, and will discuss why we believe encouraging entrepreneurial behavior is critical to the long-term vitality of our economy. Finally, we will suggest that the practice of entrepreneurship is as important— if not more important—to established companies as it is to start-ups.

Increasing Interest in Entrepreneurship

It would be difficult to overstate the degree to which there has been an increase in the level of interest in entrepreneurship. A strong indicator of such interest is provided by the unprecedented rise in the rate of new business formation. The number of annual new business incorporations has doubled in the last ten years, from annual rates of about 300,000 to over 600,000.

These trends are mirrored in the capital markets that fund these start-ups. The decade 1975–1984 saw explosive growth in the amount of capital committed to venture capital firms in the United States. There was a concurrent dramatic increase in the amount of money raised in the public capital markets by young companies.

In addition to interest on the part of individuals who wish to become entrepreneurs and investors who wish to back them, there has been a wave of interest in what some refer to as "Intrepreneurship," or entrepreneurship in the context of the larger corporation. In addition to the wealth of books and articles on the subject, some large firms

Professor Howard H. Stevenson prepared this case as the basis for class discussion.

seem to have recognized their shortcomings on certain critical dimensions of performance, and have structured themselves in an attempt to be more innovative.

Indeed, we believe that the strengthening of entrepreneurship is a critically important goal of American society. The first thirty years of the postwar period in the United States were characterized by an abundance of opportunity, brought about by expanding markets, high investment in the national infrastructure, mushrooming debt. In this environment, it was relatively easy to achieve business success, but this is no longer true. Access to international resources is not as easy as it once was; government regulation has brought a recognition of the full costs of doing business, many of which had previously been hidden; competition from overseas has put an end to American dominance in numerous industries; technological change has reduced product life in other industries; and so forth. In short, a successful firm is one that is either capable of rapid response to changes that are beyond its control, or is so innovative that it contributes to change in the environment. Entrepreneurship is an approach to management that offers these benefits.

Defining Entrepreneurship

As we have discussed, there has been a striking increase in the level of attention paid to the subject of entrepreneurship. However, we've not yet defined what the term means.

As a starting point, it may be helpful to review some of the definitions scholars have historically applied to entrepreneurship. There are several schools of thought regarding entrepreneurship, which may roughly be divided into those that define the term as an economic function and those that identify entrepreneurship with individual traits.

The functional approach focuses upon the role of entrepreneurship within the economy. In the 18th century, for instance, Richard Cantillon argued that entrepreneurship entailed bearing the risk of buying at certain prices and selling at uncertain prices. Jean Baptiste Say broadened the definition to include the concept of bringing together the factors of production. Schumpeter's work in 1911 added the concept of innovation to the definition of entrepreneurship. He allowed for many kinds of innovation including process innovation, market innovation, product innovation, factor innovation, and even organizational innovation. His seminal work emphasized the role of the entrepreneur in creating and responding to economic discontinuities.

While some analysts have focused on the economic function of entrepreneurship, still others have turned their attention to research on the personal characteristics of entrepreneurs. Considerable effort has gone into understanding the psychological and sociological sources of entrepreneurship—as Kent refers to it, "supply-side entrepreneurship." These studies have noted some common characteristics among entrepreneurs with respect to need for achievement, perceived locus of control, and risk-taking propensity. In addition, many have commented upon the common—but not universal—thread of childhood deprivation and early adolescent experiences as typifying the entrepreneur. These studies—when taken as a whole—are inconclusive and often in conflict.

We believe, however, that neither of these approaches is sound. Consider, for example, the degree to which entrepreneurship is synonymous with "bearing risk," "innovation," or even founding a company. Each of these terms focuses upon *some* aspect of *some* entrepreneurs. But, if one has to be the founder to be an entrepreneur, then neither

Thomas Watson of IBM nor Ray Kroc of McDonald's will qualify; yet, few would seriously argue that both these individuals were not entrepreneurs. And, while risk bearing is an important element of entrepreneurial behavior, it is clear that many entrepreneurs bear risk grudgingly and only after they have made valiant attempts to get the capital sources and resource providers to bear the risk. As one extremely successful entrepreneur said: "My idea of risk and reward is for me to get the reward and others to take the risks." With respect to the "supply side" school of entrepreneurship, many questions can be raised. At the heart of the matter is whether the psychological and social traits are either necessary or sufficient for the development of entrepreneurship.

Finally, the search for a single psychological profile of the entrepreneur is bound to fail. For each of the traditional definitions of the entrepreneurial type, there are numerous counter-examples that disprove the theory. We simply are not dealing with one kind of individual or behavior pattern, as even a cursory review of well-known entrepreneurs will demonstrate. Nor has the search for a psychological model proven useful in teaching or encouraging entrepreneurship.

Entrepreneurship as a Behavioral Phenomenon

Thus, it does not seem useful to delimit the entrepreneur by defining those economic functions that are "entrepreneurial" and those that are not. Nor does it appear particularly helpful to describe the traits that seem to engender entrepreneurship in certain individuals. From our perspective, entrepreneurship is an approach to management that we define as follows: the pursuit of opportunity without regard to resources currently controlled.

This summary description of entrepreneurial behavior can be further refined by examining six critical dimensions of business practice. These six dimensions are the following: strategic orientation, the commitment to opportunity, the resource commitment process, the concept of control over resources, the concept of management, and compensation policy.

We shall define these dimensions by examining a range of behavior between two extremes. At one extreme is the "*promoter*" who feels confident of his or her ability to seize opportunity regardless of the resources under current control. At the opposite extreme is the "*trustee*" who emphasizes the efficient utilization of existing resources. While the promoter and trustee define the end points of this spectrum, there is a spectrum of managerial behavior that lies between these end points, and we define (overlapping) portions of this spectrum as entrepreneurial and administrative behavior. Thus, entrepreneurial management is not an extreme example, but rather a range of behavior that consistently falls at the end of the spectrum.

The remainder of this chapter defines these key business dimensions in more detail, discusses how entrepreneurial differs from administrative behavior, and describes the factors that pull individuals and firms towards particular types of behavior.

Strategic Orientation

Strategic orientation is the business dimension that describes the factors that drive the firm's formulation of strategy. A promoter is truly opportunity-driven. His or her

FIGURE 1

Promoter	STRATEGIC ORIENTATION		Trustee
Driven by perception of opportunity	Entrepreneurial Domain ⟵⟶ ⟵⟶ Administrative Domain		Driven by resources currently controlled
Pressures toward this side			**Pressures toward this side**

Diminishing opportunity streams
 Rapidly changing:
  Technology
  Consumer economics
  Social values
  Political rules
			Social contracts
			 Performance measurements criteria
			 Planning systems and cycles

orientation is to say, "As I define a strategy, I am going to be driven only by my perception of the opportunities that exist in my environment, and I will not be constrained by the resources at hand." A trustee, on the other hand, is resource-driven and tends to say, "How do I utilize the resources that I control?"

Within these two poles, the administrator's approach recognizes the need to examine the environment for opportunities, but is still constrained by a trustee-like focus on resources: "I will prune my opportunity tree based on the resources I control. I will not try to leap very far beyond my current situation." An entrepreneurial orientation places the emphasis on opportunity: "I will search for opportunity, and my fundamental task is to acquire the resources to pursue that opportunity." These perspectives are represented on **Figure 1.**

It is this dimension that has led to one of the traditional definitions of the entrepreneur as opportunistic or—more favorably—creative and innovative. But the entrepreneur is not necessarily concerned with breaking new ground; opportunity can also be found in a new mix of old ideas or in the creative application of traditional approaches. We do observe, however, that firms tend to look for opportunities where their resources are. Even those firms that start as entrepreneurial by recognizing opportunities often become resource-driven as more and more resources are acquired by the organization.

The pressures that pull a firm towards the entrepreneurial range of behavior include the following:

- Diminishing opportunity streams: old opportunity streams have been largely played out. It is no longer possible to succeed merely by adding new options to old products.

- Rapid changes in:
  — Technology: creates new opportunities at the same time it obsoletes old ones.
  — Consumer economics: changes both ability and willingness to pay for new products and services.
  — Social values: defines new styles and standards and standards of living.
  — Political roles: affects competition through deregulation, product safety and new standards.

Pressures which pull a firm to become more "administrative" than entrepreneurial include the following:

- The "social contract": the responsibility of managers to use and employ people, plant, technology and financial resources once they have been acquired.
- Performance criteria: how many executives are fired for not pursuing an opportunity, compared with the number that are punished for not meeting return on investment targets? Capacity utilization and sales growth are the typical measures of business success.
- Planning systems and cycles: opportunities do not arrive at the start of a planning cycle and last for the duration of a three- or five-year plan.

Commitment to Opportunity

As we move on to the second dimension, it becomes clear that the definition of the entrepreneur as creative or innovative is not sufficient. There are innovative thinkers who never get anything done; it is necessary to move beyond the identification of opportunity to its pursuit.

The promoter is a person willing to act in a very short time frame and to chase an opportunity quickly. Promoters may be more or less effective, but they are able to engage in commitment in a rather revolutionary fashion. The duration of their commitment, not the ability to act, is all that is in doubt. Commitment for the trustee is time-consuming, and, once made, of long duration. Trustees move so slowly that it sometimes appears they are stationary; once there, they seem frozen. This spectrum of behavior is shown on **Figure 2.**

It is the willingness to get in and out quickly that has led to the entrepreneur's reputation as a gambler. However, the simple act of taking a risk does not lead to success. More critical to the success of the entrepreneurs is knowledge of the territory they operate in. Because of familiarity with their chosen field, they have the ability to recognize patterns as they develop, and the confidence to assume the missing elements of the pattern will take shape as they foresee. This early recognition enables them to get a jump on others in commitment to action.

Pressures which pull a business towards this entrepreneurial end of the spectrum include:

- Action orientation: enables a firm to make first claim to customers, employees and financial resources.

FIGURE 2

Promoter	COMMITMENT TO OPPORTUNITY		Trustee
Revolutionary with short duration	Entrepreneurial Domain ←——————→ ←——————→ Administrative Domain		Evolutionary of long duration
Pressures toward this side		**Pressures toward this side**	
Action orientation Short decision windows Risk management Limited decision constituencies		Acknowledgment of multiple constituencies Negotiation of strategy Risk reduction Management of fit	

- Short decision windows: due to the high costs of late entry, including lack of competitive costs and technology.
- Risk management: involves managing the firm's revenues in such a way that they can be rapidly committed to or withdrawn from new projects. As George Bernard Shaw put it, "Any fool can start a love affair, but it takes a genius to end one successfully."
- Limited decision constituencies: requires a smaller number of responsibilities and permits greater flexibility.

In contrast, administrative behavior is a function of other pressures:

- Multiple decision constituencies: a great number of responsibilities, necessitating a more complex, lengthier decision process.
- Negotiation of strategy: compromise in order to reach consensus and resultant evolutionary rather than revolutionary commitment.
- Risk reduction: study and analysis to reduce risk slows the decision-making process.
- Management of fit: to assure the continuity and participation of existing players, only those projects which "fit" existing corporate resources are acceptable.

Commitment of Resources

Another characteristic we observe in good entrepreneurs is a multistaged commitment of resources with a minimum commitment at each stage or decision point. The promoters, those wonderful people with blue shoes and diamond pinky rings on their left hands, say, "I don't need any resources to commence the pursuit of a given opportunity. I will

FIGURE 3

Promoter	COMMITMENT OF RESOURCES		Trustee
Multistaged with minimal exposure at each stage	← Entrepreneurial Domain → ← Administrative Domain →		Single-staged with complete commitment upon decision
Pressures toward this side		**Pressures toward this side**	
Lack of predictable resource needs Lack of long-term control Social needs for more opportunity per resource unit International pressure for more efficient resource use		Personal risk reduction Incentive compensation Managerial turnover Capital allocation systems Formal planning systems	

bootstrap it." The trustee says, "Since my object is to use my resources, once I finally commit I will go in very heavily at the front end."

The issue for the entrepreneur is: what resources are necessary to pursue a given opportunity? There is a constant tension between the amount of resources committed and the potential return. The entrepreneur attempts to maximize value creation by minimizing the resource set, and must, of course, accept more risk in the process. On the other hand, the trustee side deals with this challenge by careful analysis and large-scale commitment of resources after the decision to act. Entrepreneurial management requires that you learn to do a little more with a little less. **Figure 3** addresses this concept.

On this dimension we have the traditional stereotype of the entrepreneur as tentative, uncommitted, or temporarily dedicated—an image of unreliability. In times of rapid change, however, this characteristic of stepped, multistaged commitment of resources is a definite advantage in responding to changes in competition, the market, and technology.

The process of committing resources is pushed towards the entrepreneurial domain by several factors:

- Lack of predictable resource needs: forces the entrepreneurs to commit less up front so that more will be available later on, if required.

- Lack of long-term control: requires that commitment match exposure. If control over resources can be removed by environmental, political or technological forces, resource exposure should also be reduced.

- Social needs: multistaged commitment of resources brings us closer to the "small is beautiful" formulation of E. F. Schumacher, by allowing for the appropriate level of resource intensity for the task.

- International demands—pressures that we use no more than our "fair share" of the world's resources, e.g., not the 35% of the world's energy that the United States was using in the early 1970s.

The pressures within the large corporation, however, are in the other direction—toward resource intensity. This is due to:

- Personal risk reduction: any individual's risk is reduced by having excess resources available.
- Incentive compensation: excess resources increase short-term returns and minimize the period of cash and profit drains—typically the objects of incentive compensation systems.
- Managerial turnover: creates pressures for steady cash and profit gains, which encourages short-term, visible success.
- Capital allocation systems: generally designed for one-time decision making, these techniques assume that a single decision point is appropriate.
- Formal planning systems: once a project has begun, a request for additional resources returns the managers to the morass of analysis and bureaucratic delays; managers are inclined to avoid this by committing the maximum amount of resources up front.

Control of Resources

When it comes to the control of resources, the promoter mentality says, "All I need from a resource is the ability to use it." These are the people who describe the ideal business as the post office box to which people send money. For them, all additional overhead is a compromise of a basic value. On the other hand, we all know companies that believe they do not adequately control a resource unless they own it or have it on their permanent payroll.

Entrepreneurs learn to use other people's resources well; they learn to decide, over time, what resources they need to bring in-house. They view this as a time-phased sequence of decisions. Good managers also learn that there are certain resources you should never own or employ. For instance, very few good real estate firms employ an architect. They may need the best, but they do not want to employ him or her, because the need for that resource, although critical to the success of the business, is temporary. The same is true of good lawyers. They are useful to have when you need them, but most firms cannot possibly afford to have the necessary depth of specialization of legal professionals constantly at their beck and call. **Figure 4** illustrates this dimension.

The stereotype of the entrepreneur as exploitative derives from this dimension: the entrepreneur is adept at using the skills, talents, and ideas of others. Viewed positively, this ability has become increasingly valuable in the changed business environment; it need not be parasitic in the context of a mutually satisfying relationship. Pressures towards this entrepreneurial side come from:

- Increased resource specialization: an organization may have a need for a specialized resource like a VLSI design engineer, hi-tech patent attorney or state-of-the-art

FIGURE 4

Promoter	CONTROL OF RESOURCES	Trustee
Episodic use of rent of required resources	← Entrepreneurial Domain → ← Administrative Domain →	Ownership or employment of required resources

Pressures toward this side		Pressures toward this side
Increased resource specialization Long resource life compared to need Risk of obsolescence Risk inherent in any new venture Inflexibility of permanent commitment to resources		Power, status and financial rewards Coordination Efficiency measures Inertia and cost of change Industry structures

circuit test equipment, but only for a short time. By using, rather than owning, a firm reduces its risk and its fixed costs.

- Risk of obsolescence: reduced by merely using, rather than owning, an expensive resource.
- Increased flexibility: the cost of exercising the option to quit is reduced by using, not owning, a resource.

Administrative practices are the product of pressures in the other direction, such as:

- Power, status and financial rewards: determined by the extent of resources ownership and control in many corporations.
- Coordination: the speed of execution is increased because the executive has the right to request certain action without negotiation.
- Efficiency: enables the firm to capture, at least in the short run, all of the profits associated with an operation.
- Inertia and cost of change: it is commonly believed that it is good management to isolate the technical core of production from external shocks. This requires buffer inventories, control of raw materials, and control of distribution channels. Ownership also creates familiarity and an identifiable chain of command, which become stabilized wit time.
- Industry structures—encourage ownership to prevent being preempted by the competition.

FIGURE 5

Promoter	MANAGEMENT STRUCTURE	Trustee
Flat with multiple informal networks	Entrepreneurial Domain ◀━━━━━━━▶ Administrative Domain ◀━━━━━━━▶	Formalized hierarchy
Pressures toward this side		**Pressures toward this side**
Coordination of noncontrolled resources Challenge to legitimacy of owner's control Employees' desire for independence		Need for clearly defined authority and responsibility Organizational culture Reward systems Management theory

Management Structure

The promoter wants knowledge of his/her progress via direct contact with all of the principal actors. The trustee views relationships more formally, with specific rights and responsibilities assigned through the delegation of authority. The decision to use and rent resources and not to own or employ them will require the development of an informal information network. Only in systems where the relationship with resources is based on ownership or employment can resources be organized in a hierarchy. Informal networks arise when the critical success elements cannot be contained within the bounds of the formal organization. **Figure 5** illustrates this range of behavior.

Many people have attempted to distinguish between the entrepreneur and the administrator by suggesting that being a good entrepreneur precludes being a good manager. The entrepreneur is stereotyped as egocentric and idiosyncratic and thus unable to manage. However, though the managerial task is substantially different for the entrepreneur, management skill is nonetheless essential. The variation lies in the choice of appropriate tools.

More entrepreneurial management is a function of several pressures:

- Need for coordination of key noncontrolled resources results in need to communicate with, motivate, control and plan for resources *outside* the firm.
- Flexibility: maximized with a flat and informal organization.
- Challenge to owner's control: classic questions about the rights of ownership as well as governmental environmental, health and safety restrictions undermine the legitimacy of control.
- Employees' desire for independence—creates an environment where employees are unwilling to accept hierarchical authority in place of authority based on competence and persuasion.

On the other side of the spectrum, pressures push the firm towards more administrative behavior. These include:

- Need for clearly defined authority and responsibility: to perform the increasingly complex planning, organizing, coordinating, communicating and controlling required in a business.
- Organizational culture—which often demands that events be routinized.
- Reward systems—which encourage and reward breadth and span of control.

Reward Philosophy

Finally, entrepreneurial firms differ from administratively managed organizations in their philosophy regarding reward and compensation. First, entrepreneurial firms are more explicitly focused on the creation and harvesting of value. In start-up situations, the financial backers of the organization—as well as the founders themselves—have invested cash, and want cash out. As a corollary of this value-driven philosophy, entrepreneurial firms tend to base compensation on performance (where performance is closely related to value creation). Entrepreneurial firms are also more comfortable rewarding teams.

As a recent spate of take-overs suggests, more administratively managed firms are less often focused on maximizing and distributing value. They are more often guided in their decision making by the desire to protect their own positions and security. Compensation is often based on individual responsibility (assets or resources under control) and on performance relative to short-term profit targets. Reward in such firms is often heavily oriented towards promotion to increasing responsibility levels. **Figure 6** describes this dimension.

FIGURE 6

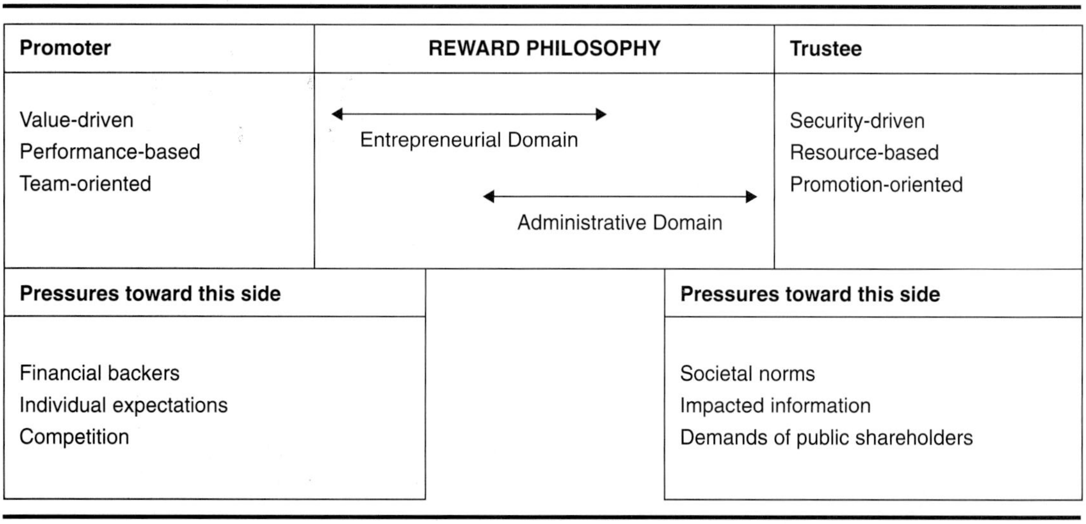

Promoter	REWARD PHILOSOPHY		Trustee
Value-driven Performance-based Team-oriented	← Entrepreneurial Domain → ← Administrative Domain →		Security-driven Resource-based Promotion-oriented
Pressures toward this side		**Pressures toward this side**	
Financial backers Individual expectations Competition		Societal norms Impacted information Demands of public shareholders	

FIGURE 7 | A Perspective on Entrepreneurship—Summary

Pressures toward This Side	Promoter	Key Business Dimension	Trustee	Pressures toward This Side
Diminishing opportunity streams Rapidly changing: Technology Consumer economics Social values	Driven by perception of opportunity	Entrepreneurial Domain ↑↓ Administrative Domain STRATEGIC ORIENTATION	Driven by resources currently controlled	Social contracts Performance measurement criteria Planning systems and cycle
Action orientation Short decisions windows Risk management Limited decision constituencies	Revolutionary with short duration	Entrepreneurial Domain ↑↓ Administrative Domain COMMITMENT TO OPPORTUNITY	Evolutionary of long duration	Acknowledgment of multiple constituencies Negotiation of strategy Risk reduction Management of fit
Lack of predictable resource needs Lack of long-term control Social need for more opportunity per resource unit Interpersonal pressure for more efficient resource use	Multistaged with minimal exposure at each stage	Entrepreneurial Domain ↑↓ Administrative Domain COMMITMENT OF RESOURCES	Single-staged with complete commitment upon decision	Personal risk reduction Incentive compensation Managerial turnover Capital allocation systems Formal planning systems
Increased resource specialization Long resource life compared to need Risk obsolescence Risk inherent in any new venture Inflexibility of permanent commitment to resources	Episodic us or rent of required resources	Entrepreneurial Domain ↑↓ Administrative Domain CONTROL OF RESOURCES	Ownership or employment of required resources	Power, status, and financial rewards Coordination Efficiency measures Inertia and cost of change Industry structures
Coordination of key noncontrolled resources Challenge to legitimacy of owner's control Employees' desire for independence	Flat with multiple informal networks	Entrepreneurial Domain ↑↓ Administrative Domain MANAGEMENT STRUCTURE	Formalized hierarchy	Need for clearly defined authority and responsibility Organizational culture Reward systems Management theory
Individual expectations Competition Increased perception of personal wealth creation possibilities	Value-based Team-based Unlimited	Entrepreneurial Domain ↑↓ Administrative Domain COMPENSATION/REWARD POLICY	Resource-based Driven by short-term data Promotion Limited amount	Societal norms IRS regulations Impacted information Search for simple solutions for complex problems Demands of public shareholders

The pressures that pull firms toward the promoter end of the spectrum include:

- Individual expectations: increasingly, individuals expect to be compensated in proportion to their contribution, rather than merely as a function of their performance relative to an arbitrary peer group. In addition, individuals seemingly have higher levels of aspiration for personal wealth.

- Investor demands: financial backers invest cash and expect cash back, and the sooner the better. Increasingly, shareholders in publicly held firms are starting to press with a similar orientation.

- Competition: increased people competition for talent creates pressure for firms to reward these individuals in proportion to their contributions.

On the other side, a variety of pressures pull firms toward more trustee-like behavior:

- Societal norms: we still value loyalty to the organization, and find it difficult to openly discuss compensation.

- Impacted information: it is often difficult to judge the value of an individual's contributions, particularly within the frame of the annual compensation cycle performance review that most firms use.

- Demands of public shareholders: many public shareholders are simply uncomfortable with compensation that is absolutely high, even if it is in proportion to contribution.

Summary

These characteristics have been gathered onto one summary chart (see **Figure 7**). In developing a behavioral theory of entrepreneurship, it becomes clear that entrepreneurship is defined by more than a set of individual traits and is different from an economic function. It is a cohesive pattern of managerial behavior.

This perspective on entrepreneurship highlights what we see as a false dichotomy: the distinction drawn between entrepreneurship and intrapreneurship. Entrepreneurship is an approach to management that can be applied in start-up situations as well as within more established businesses. As our definition suggests, the accumulation of resources that occurs as a firm grows is a powerful force that makes entrepreneurial behavior more difficult in a larger firm. But the fundamentals of the behavior required remain the same.

Still, our primary focus will be on the start-up. The situational factors that define a start-up situation do much to encourage entrepreneurship. As we look at the start-up process, however, it is worth keeping in mind that many of these lessons can be applied equally well in the large corporate setting.

The Aravind Eye Hospital, Madurai, India: In Service for Sight

I (the casewriter) arrived early at 7:00 a.m. at the outpatient department of the Aravind Eye Hospital at Madurai, India. My sponsor, Thulasi (R.D. Thulasiraj, hospital administrator), was expecting me at 8:00 o'clock, but I came early to observe the patient flow. More than 100 people formed two lines. Two young women, assisted by a third, were briskly registering the patients at the reception counter. They asked a few key questions: "Which village do you come from?" "Where do you live?" "What's your age?" and a few more, but it all took less than two minutes per patient. The women seemed very comfortable with the computer and its data-entry procedures.

Their supervisor, a somewhat elderly man with grey hair, was hunched over, gently nudging and helping them along with the registration process. He looked up and spotted me. I was the only man in that crowd who wore western-style trousers and shoes. The rest wore the traditional South Indian garment ("dhoti" or "veshti"), and many were barefooted because they could not afford "slippers." The old man hobbled from the registration desk and made his way toward me. The 50-foot distance must have taken him 10 minutes to make because he paused every now and then to answer a question here or help a patient there. I took a step forward, introduced myself, and asked to be guided to Thulasi's office. "Yes, we were expecting you," he said with an impish smile and walked me to the right wing of the hospital where all the administrative offices were. He ushered me into his office and pointed me to the couch across from his desk. It was only when I noticed his crippled fingers that I realized this grand old man was Dr. Venkataswamy himself, the 74-year-old ophthalmic surgeon who had founded the Aravind Eye Hospital and built it from 20 beds in 1976 to one of the biggest hospitals of its kind in the world in 1992, with 1,224 beds.

Professor V. Kasturi Rangan prepared this case as the basis for class discussion rather than to illustrate either effective or ineffective handling of an administrative situation.

Dr. V. spoke slowly and with a childlike sense of curiosity and excitement:

Tell me, can cataract surgery be marketed like hamburgers? Don't you call it social marketing or something? See, in America, McDonald's and Dunkin' Donuts and Pizza Hut have all mastered the art of mass marketing. We have to do something like that to clear the backlog of 20 million blind eyes in India. We perform only one million cataract surgeries a year. At this rate we cannot catch up. Modern communication through satellites is reaching every nook and corner of the globe. Even an old man like me from a small village in India knows of Michael Jackson and Magic Johnson. [At this point, Dr. V. knew that he had surprised me. He suppressed a smile and proceeded.]

Why can't we bring eyesight to the masses of poor people in India, Asia, Africa, and all over the world? I would like to do that in my lifetime. How do you think we should do it?

"I'm not sure," I responded, completely swept away and exhausted by the grand vision of this giant human being. But I don't think he wanted an answer that did not match his immense enthusiasm. He wanted a way to further his goal, not a real debate on whether the goal was feasible.

The Blindness Problem

As of 1992, there were 30 million blind people in the world—6 million in Africa, 20 million in Asia, 2 million in Latin America, and the rest in Europe, the former Soviet Union, Oceania, and North America.[1] The prevalence of blindness in most industrialized countries of Europe and North America varied between 0.15% to 0.25%, compared with blindness rates of nearly 1.5% for the developing countries in Africa, Asia, and Latin America. While age-related macular degeneration, diabetic retinopathy, and glaucoma were the dominant causes in developed countries, cataract was the major cause of blindness in the developing countries, accounting for nearly 75% of all cases in Asia. Of the several types of cataracts, more than 80% were age-related, generally occurring in people over 45 years (and increasing dramatically in the over-65 age group).

Cataract

As illustrated in **Figure A,** the natural lens of the eye, which is normally clear, helps to focus light on the retina. The lens becomes clouded in a cataract eye and light is not easily transmitted to the retina. The clouding process takes three to ten years to reach maturity and surgical removal of the clouded lens is the only proven treatment. Ophthalmic surgeons in some developing countries usually preferred to remove cataracts only when they were mature (i.e., when they significantly diminished sight.)

---

[1]A distance of 20 feet (or 6 meters) is used as a minimum standard in measuring the eye's ability to recognize certain sizes/profiles/shapes of objects. A less-than-normal eye would only be able to recognize objects at this minimum distance, which a normal eye could distinguish at a further distance (e.g., 40 feet or 12 meters). Such a vision, 20/40 or 6/12, would then have to be corrected with glasses. According to the World Health Organization, sight worse than 20/400 or 3/60 (even after correction with glasses) is considered blind.

FIGURE A

Cross Section of a normal eye

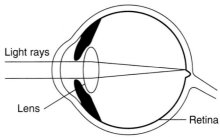

The lens focuses light on the retina

Cross Section of a cataract eye

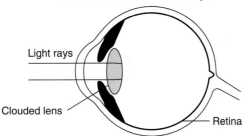

As a cataract forms, the lens becomes opaque
and light cannot easily be transmitted to the retina.

Cataract removal was considered a fairly routine operation, usually performed under local anaesthesia, with a higher than 95% chance of improved vision. Two principal surgical techniques were used: intracapsular surgery without intraocular lens (ICCE), and extracapsular surgery with intraocular lens (ECCE). ICCE remained the most widely used procedure in the developing countries. The surgery, almost always performed without an operating microscope, used fairly simple instruments and could be completed in under 20 minutes. Some three to five weeks after surgery, after the eyeball returned to its original shape, the patient was fitted with aphakic spectacles (rather thick lenses that improved vision to an acceptable level). In contrast, the ECCE technique was always performed under an operating microscope. This surgery often required close to 30 minutes, because the surgeon left the posterior capsule intact when removing the natural lens, and then inserted a tiny transparent plastic intraocular lens (IOL) in the posterior chamber. Patients often therefore did not require corrective spectacles to restore vision. Moreover, the quality of the restored sight was near-natural and free of distortion or magnification. Unlike ICCE patients, ECCE patients usually experienced significant improvement in sight within days of the operation. ICCE patients, on the other hand, usually experienced gradual improvement over a three- to five-week period.

India

India's population of 850 million in 1991 was the second-highest in the world, after China. Although there were nearly 20 million blind eyes in India, with another two million being added annually, only 12 million people were classified as blind because the rest had better than 20/200 or 6/60 vision in one eye. Cataract was the main cause in 75% to 80% of the cases. The annual per-capita income of an Indian citizen was Rs. 6,800 ($275), with over 70% below the Rs. 2,500 ($100) poverty line; the incidence of cataract blindness, however, was fairly uniformly distributed across the various socioeconomic groups. Although India's 8,000 ophthalmologists[2] (eye doctors) performed nearly 1.2 million cataract operations a year, the medical infrastructure to clear the backlog of cataract cases was woefully inadequate in making maximal use of existing resources. The United States, for instance, had twice as many ophthalmologists for a population of only about 250 million. India had about 42,000 eye hospital beds,[3] and the medical resources and infrastructure were two-thirds skewed to the urban areas where less than one-third of the nation's population lived. The government, through its Ministry of Health and Family Welfare, took an active role in blindness prevention programs. Its 425 district hospitals (about one for every two million people) offered free eye care and cataract surgery to people who could not afford private treatment. About 30% of all cataract surgeries in India were performed in the government sector (both central and state), free of cost to the patients. Another 40% were performed in the private sector for a fee, and the remaining 30% were performed free of cost by volunteer groups and NGOs (nongovernment organizations). The government currently allocated about Rs. 60 million ($2 million) annually for blindness prevention programs. A recent report to the World Bank estimated that nearly $200 million (Rs. 6,000 million) would be required immediately to build the infrastructure for training personnel, purchasing equipment, and building facilities to overcome the country's blindness problem.

Dr. V. and the Aravind Eye Hospital

The eldest son of a well-to-do farmer, Dr. Govindappa Venkataswamy was born in 1918 in a small village near Madurai in South India. After his education in local schools and colleges, Dr. V. graduated with a bachelor's degree in medicine from Madras University in 1944. During his university years, and immediately thereafter, he was deeply influenced by Mahatma (meaning "great man") Gandhi, who united the country in a nonviolent movement to seek independence from British rule. Dr. V. reasoned that the best way to serve his country in the struggle for freedom would be in the capacity he was best

---

[2]Ophthalmologists are trained eye doctors with medical degrees. They examined patients and prescribed treatment; if the treatment involved corrective glasses, the patients could get them from an optician. Unlike in the United States, there were very few optometrists (professionals who measured eyesight and prescribed glasses) in the Indian medical system.

[3]These were located in government hospitals, medical college hospitals, mobile hospitals, eye hospitals, and private nursing homes.

trained for—as a doctor. So he joined the Indian Army Medical Corps in 1945, but was discharged in 1948 because of severe rheumatoid arthritis. Dr. V. recalled,

> I developed severe rheumatoid arthritis and almost all the joints were severely swollen and painful. I was bedridden in a Madras hospital for over a year. The arthritis crippled me badly and for years I could not walk long distances, which I was accustomed to doing as a village boy. In the acute stage, for several months I could not stand on my feet and I was confined to bed for over a year. I still remember the day I was able to stand on my feet. A relative of mine had come to see me in the hospital ward and I struggled hard to keep my feet on the ground and stand close to the bed without holding it. When I did, it felt as though I was on top of the Himalayas. Then, for several years, I used to struggle to walk a few yards or squat down on the floor. Even now in villages we normally squat on the floor when we eat, and I find it difficult. I could not hold a pen with my fingers to write in the acute stage of arthritis. We normally eat food with our fingers. I found it difficult to handle the food with my swollen fingers. Later I trained slowly to hold the surgeon's scalpel and cut the eye for cataract operations. After some years, I could stand for a whole day and perform 50 operations or more at a stretch. Then I learned to use the operating microscope and do good, high-quality cataract and other eye surgeries.

By the time of his retirement in 1976, Dr. V. had risen to head the Department of Ophthalmology at the Government Madurai Medical College and also to head Eye Surgery at the Government Erskine Hospital, Madurai. After retirement, in order to fulfill a long-cherished dream—the creation of a private, nonprofit eye hospital that would provide quality eye care—Dr. V. founded the Aravind Eye Hospital, named after an Indian philosopher and saint, Sri Aurobindo. Dr. V. noted:

> What I learnt from Mahatma Gandhi and Swami [saint] Aurobindo was that all of us through dedication in our professional lives can serve humanity and God. Achieving a sense of spirituality or higher consciousness is a slow, gradual process. It is wrong to think that unless you are a mendicant or a martyr you can't be a spiritual person. When I go to the meditation room at the hospital every morning, I ask God that I be a better tool, a receptacle for the divine force. We can all serve humanity in our normal professional lives by being more generous and less selfish in what we do. You don't have to be a "religious" person to serve God. You serve God by serving humanity.

History

The 20-bed Aravind Eye Hospital opened in 1976 and performed all types of eye surgery; its goal was to offer quality eye care at reasonable cost. The first three surgeons were Dr. V.; his sister, Dr. G. Natchiar; and her husband, Dr. P. Namperumalswamy (Dr. Nam). A 30-bed annex was opened in 1977 to accommodate patients convalescing after surgery. It was not until 1978 that a 70-bed free hospital was opened to provide the poor with free eye care. It had a four-table operating theater with rooms for scrubbing, changing, and sterilization of instruments.

A main hospital (for paying patients), commenced in 1977 and completed in 1981, had 250 beds with 80,000 square feet of space in five floors, four major operating theaters (two tables per theater), and a minor one for septic care. There were specialty clinics in the areas of retina and vitreous diseases, cornea, glaucoma, and squint corrections, diabetic retinopathy, and pediatric ophthalmology; the heads of all but one of these clinics were family members of Dr. V., and all had received training in the United States. The Main Hospital was well-equipped with modern, often imported, equipment to provide the best possible eye care for its patients. (In 1992, there were about 240 people on the hospital's staff, including about 30 doctors, 120 nurses, 60 administrative personnel, and 30 housekeeping and maintenance workers.)

In 1984 a new 350-bed free hospital was opened. A "bed" here was equivalent to a $6' \times 3'$ mattress spread out on the floor. This five-story hospital had nearly 36,000 square feet of space and its top story accommodated the nurses' quarters for the entire Aravind group of hospitals. The hospital had two major operating theaters and a minor theater for septic cases. On the ground floor were facilities for treating outpatients; in-patients were housed in large wards on the upper floors. The Free Hospital was largely staffed with medical personnel from the Main Hospital. Doctors and nurses were posted in rotation so that they served both facilities, thereby ensuring that nonpaying and paying patients all received the same quality of eye care.

Until 1989, all the patients in the Free Hospital were attracted from eye camps. In 1990, Aravind opened its Free Hospital to walk-in patients. Every Saturday and Sunday, teams of doctors and support staff with diagnostic equipment fanned out to several rural sites to screen the local population. Eye camps were sponsored events, where a local businessman or a social service organization mobilized resources to inform the local public within about a 25- to 50-mile radius of the forthcoming screening camp. Camps were usually held in towns that served as the commercial hub for a number of neighboring villages. Local schools, colleges, or marriage halls often served as campsites. Patients from surrounding villages who traveled by bus to the central (downtown) bus stand were transported to the campsite by the sponsors. Several patients from the local area came directly to the campsite. The Aravind team screened patients at the camp, and those selected for surgery were transported the same afternoon by bus to the Free Hospital at Madurai. They were returned three days later, after surgery and recuperation, back to the campsite where their family members picked them up. Patients who came from nearby villages were taken to the central bus stand and provided return tickets to their appropriate destinations. A clinical team from Aravind went back to the campsite after three months for a follow-up evaluation of the discharged patients. Patients were informed of the dates for the follow-up camps well in advance—in many cases, at the time of the initial discharge after surgery. Aravind provided the services of its clinical staff and free treatment for the patients selected for surgery; the camp sponsors bore all other administrative, logistical, and food costs associated with the camp. (**Exhibit 1** shows the location of the various Aravind hospitals; **Exhibits 2** and **3** show the inpatient ward at the Aravind Main Hospital, Free Hospital, and some typical eye camp activities.)

As the Aravind Eye Hospital grew from a 20-bed to a 600-bed hospital, many members of Dr. V.'s family joined in support of his ideals. His brother, G. Srinivasan, a civil engineering contractor, constructed all the hospital buildings at cost and later became the hospital's finance manager. A nephew, R.D. Thulasiraj (Thulasi), gave up a management job in the private sector to join as the hospital's administrator. Thulasi, at Dr. V.'s insistence, trained at the University of Michigan in public health management before assuming administrative duties at Aravind. Thirteen ophthalmologists on the hospital's staff were related to Dr. V. In order to provide continuous training to its ophthalmic personnel, Aravind had research and training collaborations with St. Vincent's Hospital in New York City and the University of Illinois' Eye and Ear Infirmary in Chicago; both institutions also regularly sent their own ophthalmologists for residency training to Aravind. Aravind was also actively involved in training ophthalmic personnel in charge of administering blindness prevention projects in other parts of Asia and Africa. Explaining the unfailing support of his family members, Dr. V. recalled:

> We have always been a joint family through thick and thin. I was 32 when my father died. I was the eldest in the family, and in a family system like ours, I was responsible for educating my two younger brothers and two younger sisters, for organizing and fixing their marriages—that is the usual custom we have—for finding suitable partners for them. I was the head of the family and looked after all of them. But that was not a problem. I was not married, because of my arthritis trouble. Now it has become a boon. My brother takes care of me, and I stay with him all the time. His children are as much attached to me as they are to him.

Dr. Natchiar, Dr. V.'s sister and now the hospital's senior medical officer, elaborated:

> When Brother retired from government service, he seemed awfully impatient to serve society in a big way. He asked me and my husband [Dr. Nam] if we would give up our government jobs to join him. Usually in India, when one leaves government service to enter private practice, incomes go up threefold. In this case, we were told that our salaries would be about Rs. 24,000 a year (approximately $1,500 in 1980). And worse still, Brother always believed in pushing the mind and body to its highest effort levels. So we would have to work twice as hard for half the salary. My husband and I talked it over and said yes. We did not have the heart to say no. But what we lost in earnings was made up by the tremendous professional support that Brother gave us. We were encouraged to attend conferences, publish papers, buy books, and do anything to advance our professional standing in the field. It is only in the last five years that our senior surgeons' salaries are reasonably consistent with their reputation in the field.

On his insistence that the hospital staff be totally committed and dedicated to the mission of the Aravind Hospital, Dr. V. expressed his philosophy:

> We have a lot of very capable and intelligent people, all very well trained in theoretical knowledge. But knowledge by itself is not going to save the world. Look at Christ; you cannot call him a scholar, he was a spiritual man. What we need is dedication and devotion to the practice. When doctors join us for residencies, we gradually condition them physically for long hours of concentrated work. Most believe they need work only for a few hours and that, too, for four days a week. In government hospitals, rarely do surgeons work for more than 30 hours a week; we normally expect our doctors to go 60 hours. Moreover, in the government hospitals there is a lot of bureaucracy and corruption. Patients feel obliged to tip the support staff to get even routine things done. Worse still, poor villagers feel totally intimidated. We want to make all sorts of people feel at ease, and this can only come if the clinical staff and their support staff view the entire exercise as a spiritual experience.

Aravind Eye Hospital: 1992

By 1988, in addition to the 600 beds at Madurai, a 400-bed hospital at Tirunelveli, a bustling rural town 75 miles south of Madurai, and a 100-bed hospital at Theni, a small town 50 miles west of Madurai, were also started (see **Exhibit 1**). There were plans afoot to set up a 400-bed (Rs. 10 million) hospital at Coimbatore, a city 125 miles north of Madurai. Coimbatore, like Madurai, was the hub of its district and was bigger than Madurai in population and commerce. Dr. Ravindran, a family member who currently headed the Tirunelveli Hospital, was slated to run the Coimbatore Hospital. Succession plans for the Tirunelveli Hospital would then have to be worked out. Managing the Theni Hospital, which was located in Dr. Nam's home town, was not a big problem: first, because the facility was small, and second, because of the informal supervision it received whenever Dr. Nam visited his home town. In fact, Dr. Nam had been instrumental in setting up this facility to serve his community.

In Madurai, by adding a block of 50,000 square feet to the Main Hospital and some reorganization in the Free Hospital, another 124 beds were added in 1991—74 in the Main Hospital and 50 in the Free Hospital, respectively.

By 1992, the Aravind group of hospitals had screened 3.65 million patients and performed some 335,000 cataract operations—nearly 70% of them free of cost for the poorest of India's blind population. (See **Exhibit 4** for a performance summary since the hospital's inception in 1976, **Exhibit 5** for details of its 1991 performance.) All this was achieved with very little outside aid or donations. According to Dr. V.:

> When we first started in 1976, we went around asking for donations, but we didn't have the credibility. A few friends promised to help us, but even they preferred to avoid monetary assistance. It was simple: we had to get started. So I mortgaged my house and raised enough money to start. Then one thing led to another and suddenly we were able to plan the ground floor of the Main Hospital. From the revenue generated from operations there, we built the next floor, and so on until we had a nice five-story facility. And then with the money generated there, we built the Free Hospital. Almost 90% of our annual budget is self-generated. The other 10% comes from sources around the world, such as the Royal Commonwealth Society for the Blind [U.K.] and the SEVA Foundation [USA]. We expend all our surplus on modernizing and updating our equipment and facilities. We have enough credibility now to raise a lot of money, but we don't plan to. We have always accepted the generosity of the local business community, but by and large, our spiritual approach has sustained us.

(See **Exhibit 6** for a 1991–1992 statement of income and expenses, and **Exhibit 7** for a historical financial summary.)

Having grown from strength to strength, Aravind in 1991 made a bold move to set up a facility for manufacturing intraocular lenses (IOLs).

IOL factory   IOLs, which were an integral part of ECCE surgery, cost about $30 (Rs. 800) apiece to import from the United States. At a cost of Rs. 8 million, in 1991, Aravind had therefore set up a modern IOL manufacturing facility. Called the Auro Lab, it could produce up to 60,000 IOLs a year. Currently, Auro Lab production yielded about 50% defect-free lenses, quality rated on par with imported lens. Mr. Balakrishnan, a family member with extensive engineering experience and doctoral education in the United States, had returned to manage Auro Lab. Dr. V. reasoned that within a year or two when the factory yield improved, it would be possible to bring down the manufacturing costs from approximately Rs. 200 per lens to approximately Rs. 100:

> People come for cataract surgery very late in life, because the quality of regained vision after intra-cap surgery is so-so, but not excellent. With extra-cap surgery and IOL implants, the situation is dramatically different. People would opt for surgery earlier, because they can go back to their professions and be productive right away. My aim is to offer 100% IOL surgeries for all our patients, paying and free. That is the better-quality solution, and we should provide it to all our patients.

Thulasi, Aravind's hospital's administrator, explained the challenges ahead (see **Exhibit 8** for occupancy statistics):

> Yes, our expansion projects are all very exciting but we cannot take our eye off the ball. We have to concentrate on the things that made us good in the first place. For instance, my biggest concern is the occupancy rate in the free hospital. On Monday, Tuesday, and Wednesday we are choked and overflowing with patients. Our systems have all got to work at peak efficiency to get by. But on Thursday and Friday, we suddenly have a slack. We need some continuity to keep our staff motivated and systems tuned.

Dr. Ravindran, head of the Tirunelveli hospital, concurred:

> We have some fundamental management problems to sort out. While our cash flows and margins look all right at Tirunelveli, I am unable to repay the cost-of-capital. Thank God, Madurai buys all the equipment on our behalf. We started the Tirunelveli hospital with a lot of hope and experience. Even the physical design was an improvement over our Madurai facility. We have integrated the paying and free hospitals for economies of scale. The wards and patient examination rooms in the free section are far more spacious than at Madurai. Moreover, in order to better utilize operating room capacity, we have a central surgical facility which the free and paying sections of the hospital jointly utilize. Yet, after four years, we are not yet financially self-sufficient at Tirunelveli.

Thulasi mentioned another issue:

> When we expand so fast, we have to keep in mind that we need to attract quality people. Fortunately our salary scales are now reasonable in comparison with the private sector, but we are still not there. For example, an ophthalmologist at Aravind would today, on an average, make Rs. 80,000 annually. Not bad, compared to government sector salaries of about Rs. 60,000. Of course, in private practice, some ophthalmologists can make Rs. 300,000. But not everyone has the up-front capital to get top-notch equipment to facilitate such practice. Our nurses are paid Rs. 12,000 a year on average, which is not bad at all given that our staff is recruited and trained from scratch by us. They don't come from nursing school; we provide the training for them. It is like getting a prestigious degree and job training all in one.

A Visit to the Aravind Eye Hospital

The Main Hospital

Located one block from the Free Hospital, the Main Hospital functioned very much independently. Complicated cases from the Free Hospital were brought in when necessary for diagnosis and treatment, but by and large all patients at this hospital paid for the hospital's services. Patients came to this hospital from all over Madurai district (i.e., towns and villages surrounding the city). The cost of a normal cataract surgery (ICCE), inclusive of three to four days' post-operative recovery, was about Rs. 500 to Rs. 1,000. If the patient required an IOL implant (ECCE), the total cost of the surgery was Rs. 1,500 to Rs. 2,500. The hospital provided A, B, and C class rooms, each with somewhat different levels of privacy and facilities and appropriately different price levels.

The morning rush was usually very heavy, and by early afternoon, most people divided into two groups for a sequential series of evaluations. First, ophthalmic assistants recorded each person's vision. The patient then moved to the next room for a preliminary eye examination by an eye doctor. There were several eye doctors on duty, and ophthalmic assistants noted the preliminary diagnosis on the patient's medical record. Ophthalmic assistants then tested patients for ocular tension and tear duct function, followed by refraction tests. The final examination was always conducted by a senior medical officer. Not all patients passed through every step; for example, those referred to specialty clinics (such as retina and vitreous diseases) would directly move to the specialty section of the hospital on the first floor. Similarly, patients diagnosed as needing only corrective lenses would move to the optometry room for measurement and prescription of glasses. Those diagnosed as requiring cataract surgery would be advised in-patient admission, usually within three days. Most such patients followed up on the advice.

On the day of the surgery, the patient was usually awakened early, and after a light breakfast, was readied for surgery. On a visit to the operating theater, I noticed about 20 patients seated in the hallway, all appropriately prepared by the medical staff to enter into surgery, and another 20 in the adjacent room in the process of being readied by the nursing staff. The procedure involved cleaning and sterilizing the eye and injecting a local anaesthetic. The operating theater had two active operating tables and a third bed for the patient to be prepared prior to surgery.

I (the casewriter) watched several operations performed by Dr. Natchiar. She and her assistants took no more than 15 minutes for each ECCE cataract surgery. She generously offered me the east port of the operating microscope to observe the surgical procedure. She operated from the north port, directly behind the patient's head. A resident in training from the University of Illinois occupied the west port. I had never seen a cataract surgery before, but was amazed at the dexterity of her fingers as she made the incision and gently removed the clouded lens, leaving the posterior chamber in place. Then she inserted the IOL [intraocular lens], and carefully sutured the incision. Even while she was operating, she explained to me in a methodical step-by-step fashion the seven critical things she had to do to ensure a successful operation and recovery. When she was done, she simply moved on to the adjacent operating table, where the next patient and a second supporting team were all ready to go. Meanwhile, the previous surgical team helped the patient off the operating table to walk to the recovery room and prepared the next patient, who was already waiting in the third bed for the next surgery. Dr. Natchiar had started that day at about 7:30 a.m., and when I left at about 10:30 a.m., was still going strong in a smooth, steady, uninterrupted fashion. The whole team carried on about their tasks in a well-paced, routine way. There was none of the drama I had expected to encounter in an operating theater.

In contrast, Dr. Nam was performing a retina detachment repair in the adjoining operating theater. Without looking up from his task, Dr. Nam told me that he was in the midst of a particularly difficult procedure and it would probably be another hour before he could comfortably converse. His surgical team bent over the operating table in deep concentration, reflecting the nonroutine nature of their task.

The Free Hospital

The outpatient facilities at the Free Hospital were not as organized as the Main Hospital's. There was a temporary shelter at the Free Hospital's entrance where patients waited to register. Those who came for a return visit were directed to a different line from those who came for the first time. The patient flow inside also seemed somewhat crowded. The sequence, however, remained the same: registration; vision recording; preliminary examination; testing of tension and tear duct function; refraction test; and final examination.

The people in the hallways and waiting rooms appeared significantly poorer than those I had seen at the Main Hospital. A handful of administrative assistants in blue uniforms moved around in the crowd, helping patients and guiding them along in the sequential flow. As I walked up to the operating theaters on the next floor, patients from the previous day's "eye camp" were awaiting their turn to be prepared for surgery. Some older patients, clearly tired, had spread themselves out on the floor and against the walls. There was a lot more commotion here than at the Main Hospital.

Almost all the surgeries at the Free Hospital were of the intracapsular (ICCE) type. An extracapsular (ECCE) procedure with IOL was performed only when medical reasons dictated against an intracapsular surgery.

The operating theaters also appeared more crowded and cramped. The uniforms of the supporting staff here were green, whereas they were blue at the Main Hospital, and only one of the other operating tables was equipped with an operating microscope. The patient preparation for surgery and flow was similar to that at the Main Hospital. Two surgeons operated in the same theater, and each had two operating tables and one staging bed to organize the workflow. Historically, at Aravind, a team of five surgeons and 15 nurses could operate on about 150 cases in about five hours.

Dr. Narendran, who was in the midst of a cataract operation, invited me to the operating table. The critical steps in surgery here were essentially the same as I had seen in the Main Hospital except that the intact clouded lens, along with its supporting membrane capsule, was removed here with a cryogenic device and the incision was sutured. An IOL was not inserted. These patients would be fitted with aphakic glasses three days later. Dr. Narendran had the following conversation with his patient:

DOCTOR: Old man, what do you do for a living?
PATIENT: I don't do anything. I just sit at home.
DOCTOR: Does your wife provide you with food?

PATIENT: No, my wife died long ago. My daughter-in-law takes care of me.

DOCTOR: Does she take good care of you?

PATIENT: No, but she does the best she can. Once a day she gives me "kanji" [boiled rice and salt]. That, with some water, takes care of my needs.

DOCTOR: What will you do after you regain your eyesight?

PATIENT: I will go back to tending a herd of sheep. I used to know the owner [rancher]. He used to pay me a small fee.

DOCTOR: What will you do with that money?

PATIENT: Oh, I can then buy some meat once in a while. And I can also take my grand-daughter to the temple fair next year.

Unlike the Main Hospital, patients in the Free Hospital did not have "beds" in which to recuperate and recover, but rather were taken to big rooms on the upper floors and each was provided with a 6' × 3' bamboo/coir mat, which was spread out on the floor as a bed, and a small-sized pillow. There were several such rooms, each accommodating 20 to 30 patients. Each room had self-contained bathroom facilities. People from the same or nearby villages were usually accommodated in the same room. They moved together as a cohort, both before and after surgery. The post-operative recovery period was usually three days, when the bandage was removed, patients' eyes checked and, if all was well, aphakic glasses fitted. Patients were advised to come back in three months for follow-up evaluation.

At the Free Hospital, detailed records were kept of all post-operative complications (see **Exhibit 9**). Some complications, such as iritis, were considered minor and easily treatable, while others required extra care and additional hospital stay. Such complications were directly traced to the operating team, even to the level of the individual surgeon. Senior medical officers reviewed the data with the individuals concerned and offered coaching and advice to rectify operating techniques, if necessary.

At the records room in the Free Hospital, I pulled out six patient records at random to get a sense of the improvement in sight after surgery. A summary is provided below.

	Preoperative Sight Recording	Post-operative Sight Recording
Patient 1	No vision. Can register hand movements	6/12 [20/40]
Patient 2	No vision. Can register hand movements	6/12 [20/40]
Patient 3	No vision. Cannot register hand movements Can perceive light	6/36 [20/120]
Patient 4	No vision. Can register hand movements	6/06 [20/20]
Patient 5	No vision. Can register hand movements	6/18 [20/60]
Patient 6	6/60 [20/200]	6/12 [20/40]

The Eye Camp

I visited a typical eye camp, at Dindigul, a semi-urban town about 100 miles east of Madurai. These screening camps were almost always conducted with the help of local community support, with either a local business enterprise or a social service organization taking the lead role in organizing them.

The local sponsors provided information regarding the eye camp to all the neighboring communities (about a 25-mile radius). Public announcements in marketplaces, newspaper advertisements, information pamphlets, and other publicity material were prepared and distributed one to three weeks in advance of the camp. The camp was usually promoted under the sponsor's name, with the Aravind service playing only a supporting role. The sponsor not only paid all the publicity costs but also the direct costs associated with organizing the camp—patient transportation, food, and aphakic glasses. In addition, the sponsors also paid for the costs of transporting, feeding, and bringing back the patients selected for surgery. This portion was estimated at Rs. 200 per patient. Aravind bore the costs of surgery and medicines.

The camp at Dindigul was sponsored by a local textile mill owner. There were three other Aravind-associated camps in other parts of the Tamil-Nadu state that day. One was sponsored by a religious charity (Sathya Sai Baba Devotee's Association), one by a popular movie actor fan club (Rajni Kanth Appreciation Club), and the third by the Lion's Club. According to Dr. V.:

> The concept of eye camp is not new. As the head of the government hospital, I used to go out with a team of doctors and support staff several times a year to screen patients in their own villages. Many of my colleagues in other parts of India also use this idea as part of their outreach programs. We were somewhat fortunate in the sense that we invested in the infrastructure, such as the vans and the equipment and committed doctors to support the demand we got from philanthropic individuals and organizations.

In the formative years of Aravind, patients attending the screening camps were examined and those needing surgery were appropriately advised. Even though surgery was free, the patients had to come to Aravind at their own expense. The response rate was less than 15%. Concerned by the low turnout, a research team from Aravind conducted in-depth home interviews with a randomly selected group of 65 patients for whom surgery was recommended but who didn't respond for over six months. The study revealed the following constraints:

- Still have vision, however diminished   26%
- Cannot afford food and transportation   25
- Cannot leave family   13
- Fear of surgery   11
- No one to accompany   10
- Family opposition   5
- Others   10

As a consequence, Aravind requested and the camp sponsors readily agreed to bear the costs of food, transportation and, in many cases, the cost of aphakic glasses to be worn by the patient after surgery. In order to reduce the fear of surgery, as well as to encourage a support group, patients were transported to Madurai as a group by buses. Patients were asked to bring a small travel bag in case it was necessary to go to Madurai. The sequence of screening steps matched those at the base hospitals:

1. Registration
2. Vision recording
3. Preliminary examination
4. Testing of tension and tear duct function
5. Refraction
6. Final examination by a senior medical officer
7. Optical shop (for those that needed it)

In addition, those selected for surgery had to undergo tests for blood pressure and urine sugar and, if qualified, their surgery papers were prepared on the campsite. In addition, Aravind camp organizers, as well as local community elders, explained and reassured the patients regarding the importance of the surgery and the other logistics involved. Bus trips were so organized that individuals from the same or nearby villages were always clustered in the same bus trip, which reduced the need for anyone to accompany the patients. They were all returned together after three or four days. This established a support group during their recovery phase. A team from Aravind returned for follow-up after three months.

The Dindigul camp was very well run. Soundararaja Mills (the sponsors) had organized bus shuttles from the central town bus stand to transport passengers to the campsite. About 1,000 people came from villages within a 25-mile radius of the town. The mill owner had sought the cooperation of a local college, of which he was a trustee and a significant donor, for providing the physical facilities. At the campsite, the college principal was actively supervising the arrangements. He brought me a chart of the historical performance of the Soundararaja camp for the last five years. Many volunteer students were helping the Aravind staff organize the patient flow. The mill owner's son, also its finance manager, walked around the camp constantly inquiring about the arrangements. There was a sense of festivity in the air, as recorded "nadaswaram"[4] music was being played over the public address system. A packed lunch was provided for those selected for surgery, and refreshments and a sit-in lunch for all the doctors and support staff participating in the camp. One of the school teachers who had organized the marketing of the camp explained:

> My students simply worked flat out in the last one week. Soundararaja Mills provided us transportation to cover over 1,000 driving miles. Our "propaganda" was effected through handbills, wall posters, and traveling megaphone announcements. Last Thursday night, they were mounting publicity posters on every public bus. We could not do it earlier because buses in this town are all scrubbed and cleaned every Wednesday night.

The camp had commenced on a Sunday morning at 8:00 a.m., and when I left at about 2:00 p.m., about 800 people had been screened and nearly 150 selected for

---

[4]Nadaswaram, a wind instrument much like a clarinet, was often played at auspicious occasions such as weddings in South India.

surgery. The first group of patients were ready to leave for Madurai. Dr. Nam and his team were working away at a steady pace. He explained to me that nearly two-thirds of the work was done, but the turnout was a little lower than expected, because just two months prior to this camp, another organization had conducted an eye camp in the same area. (**Exhibit 10** provides a history of Aravind's "eye camp" performance. **Exhibit 11** provides further detail by type of sponsor for the 1991 eye camps.)

In the past, Aravind had also conducted several surgical camps. That is, patients identified as needing surgery would be provided the requisite treatment on-site. Recently, however, there was a conscious effort to move away from surgery camps because of the higher cost as well as lower quality of service they provided. For example, the makeshift operating theaters were not air-conditioned, cleanliness and hygiene were often not up to hospital standards, patient amenities were inferior, and post-operative complications were difficult to monitor.

The Aravind organization included a 10-person team of camp organizers. These individuals reported to Meenakshisunadaram (Sundar), the camp manager. Camp organizers were responsible for working closely with the camp sponsors, helping and guiding them with directions for mounting publicity, organizing the logistics, and arranging physical facilities for the eye camp. In addition to working closely with the sponsors who needed help, camp organizers also guided new sponsors who approached Aravind for their expertise and help in bringing eye-care to certain targeted communities. Camp organizers were aligned by district as shown in the territory map (**Exhibit 12**) and traveled extensively within their assigned territories. They all met at Aravind's headquarters at Madurai, once a week under the chairmanship of Dr. V. At one such meeting which I attended, Dr. V. went around the table from person to person asking for territory plans and every once in a while urged a camp organizer, "Why was the camp yield so poor in your territory? We could get only 14 surgery cases from a catchment population of nearly 100,000! Something is not right. Brother, find out what is going on! Work with the sponsor to improve propaganda." (See **Exhibit 13** for districtwide camp particulars.)

According to Sundar, the camp manager:

> We really don't have to sell the idea of an eye camp to anyone. There are far more individuals, businesses, and social organizations that need our services than what we can effectively offer. The prestige and goodwill that our sponsors earn, in their communities, far outweighs the financial burden. What they really need help on is how to organize the camp, how to create propaganda, and how to organize the logistics. That is where we are trying to put together a consistent set of procedures and a common set of principles.

Conclusion

I asked Dr. V. what his biggest challenge for the next three years was. His reply:

> My goal is to spread the Aravind model to every nook and corner of India, Asia, Africa; wherever there is blindness, we want to offer hope. Tell me, what is this concept of franchising? Can't we do what McDonald's and Burger King have done in the United States?

EXHIBIT 1 | Aravind Eye Hospital Locations

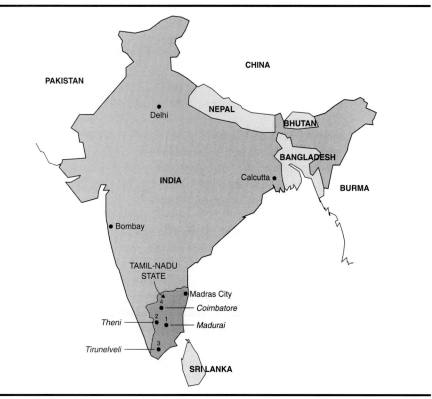

The four Aravind locations are shown in italics.

EXHIBIT 2 | Inpatient Ward at the Aravind Main Hospital

EXHIBIT 3 | Eye Camp Activities

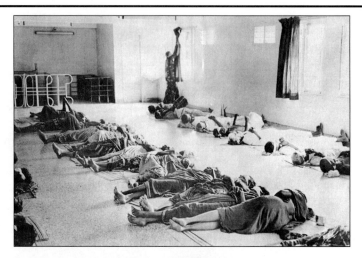

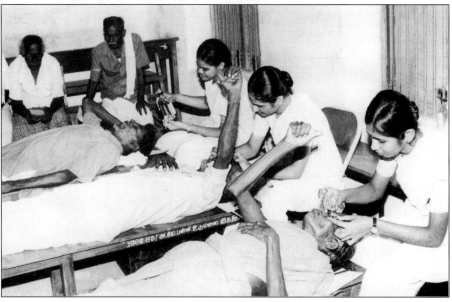

EXHIBIT 4 | Historical Patient Statistics (Consolidated)

	Paying		Free and Camp[a]	
Year	Outpatient Visits	Surgery	Outpatient Visits	Surgery
1976	—	248	—	—
1977	15,381	980	2,366	—
1978	15,781	1,320	18,251	1,045
1979	19,687	1,612	47,351	2,430
1980	31,334	2,511	65,344	5,427
1981	39,470	3,139	75,727	8,172
1982	46,435	4,216	79,367	8,747
1983	56,540	4,889	101,469	11,220
1984	69,419	5,796	103,177	11,954
1985	89,441	7,194	153,037	17,586
1986	111,546	8,202	164,977	19,623
1987	121,828	9,971	180,181	21,562
1988	182,274	12,702	232,838	23,635
1989	203,907	15,103	290,859	25,867
1990	227,243	17,896	338,407	31,162
1991	241,643	19,511	327,692	31,979
Total	1,471,929	115,290	2,184,043	220,409

Source: Aravind Eye Hospital.

[a]The 1990 and 1991 outpatient visits data includes camp patients as well as walk-in patients. See **Exhibit 10** for camp details.

EXHIBIT 5 | Patient Statistics: 1991

		Madurai	Tirunelveli	Theni	Total
Outpatient visits	– Paying	167,884	50,802	22,957	241,643
	– Free	212,809	91,482	23,401	327,692
Surgery	– Paying	16,447	2,572	492	19,511
	– Free	23,110	7,339	1,530	31,979
Hospital outpatient visits		263,518	84,360	30,457	378,335
Eye camp outpatient visits		117,175	57,924	15,901	191,000
Total outpatient visits		380,693	142,284	46,358	569,335
Screening camps		331	293	83	707
Surgery Details:					
Cataract and other lens removal procedures (without IOL)		23,321	6,618	1,535	31,474
Intraocular lens (IOL)		7,846	1,466	227	9,539
Trabeculectomy		359	80	13	452
Retinal detachment		401	1	—	402
Vitreous surgery		331	—	—	331
Membranectomy		61	2	—	63
Squint correction		262	—	—	262
Keratoplasty and therapeutic grafting		65	—	—	65
Ptosis		27	—	—	27
DCR, DCT and other septic operations		1,347	669	158	2,174
Pterygium		297	181	14	492
Laser and xenon photocoagulation		1,467	—	—	1,467
Nd Yag iridotomy		787	133	—	920
Nd Yag capsulotomy		806	201	—	1,007
Argon laser trabeculoplasty		43	—	—	43
Other surgical procedures		2,137	560	75	2,772
Total Surgery		39,557	9,911	2,022	51,490

Source: Aravind Eye Hospital.

EXHIBIT 6 | Income and Expenditures for 1991–1992 (Rupees)

	Cumulative Total	Percentage
Revenue:		
1. Medical services	3,380,985.00	9.57%
2. Operation charges	23,235,389.00	65.77
3. Treatment charges	2,225,609.25	6.30
4. Consulting fees	3,424,728.35	9.69
5. Laboratory charges	857,265.49	2.43
6. X-ray charges	206,890.00	0.59
7. Donations	771,474.80	2.18
8. Interest	1,062,889.50	3.01
9. Miscellaneous, course and others	129,666.65	0.37
10. Sale of ophthalmology books	33,835.00	0.10
Total Revenue	35,328,733.04	100.00%
Operating Expenses:		
1. Medicine and cotton	1,307,968.00	3.70%
2. Hospital linen	148,848.30	0.42
3. Library and subscription	66,519.40	0.19
4. Building maintenance	1,117,550.04	3.16
5. Electricity charges	1,667,964.01	4.72
6. Installation and equipment maintenance	774,129.46	2.19
7. Electric items and bulbs	196,195.55	0.56
8. Printing and stationery	564,841.48	1.60
9. Postage and telephone charges	447,750.30	1.27
10. Building rent	7,980.00	0.02
11. Cleaning and sanitation	356,515.70	1.01
12. Stipends and staff salaries	4,285,017.70	12.13
13. Employer's PF contribution	190,208.50	0.54
14. Bank commission	9,748.08	0.03
15. Traveling expenses	758,876.91	2.15
16. Miscellaneous expenses	236,508.18	0.67
17. Photography	181,316.90	0.51
18. Resident doctors' hostel expenses	54,338.10	0.15
19. Camp expenses	1,347,457.90	3.81
20. Vehicle maintenance	459,361.43	1.30
21. IOL	2,926,520.00	8.28
Expenditure Total	17,105,615.94	48.41%
Costs Offset by:		
1. W.H.O., Ford Foundation and Jain Hospital	96,246.00	
Actual Expenditure Total	17,009,369.94	48.41%
Percentage		
Net Surplus	18,319,363.10	51.59%

Source: Aravind Eye Hospital.

EXHIBIT 7 | Historical Financial Summary (Rupees)

Year	Income	Expenditure	Percentage of Expenditure Over Income
1979–1980	933,306.62	131,641.80	14.10
1980–1981	979,991.18	242,968.70	24.80
1981–1982	2,936,440.45	1,385,642.50	47.20
1982–1983	3,546,240.27	2,142,939.20	60.36
1983–1984	4,334,257.49	2,688,550.23	62.03
1984–1985	5,971,711.49	3,526,423.49	59.05
1985–1986	6,614,342.74	5,018,583.94	75.87
1986–1987	9,325,540.79	5,349,419.00	57.36
1987–1988	12,694,531.22	9,268,150.96	73.00
1988–1989	17,840,116.84	10,987,700.44	61.58
1989–1990	21,054,621.30	12,669,999.79	60.18
1990–1991	29,320,202.61	15,837,644.93	54.02

Source: Aravind Eye Hospital.

Note: One U.S. dollar was convertible to Rs. 12–Rs. 15 during 1979 to 1984; Rs. 18–Rs. 20 during 1985 to 1989; and Rs. 25–Rs. 28 during 1990 and 1991.

EXHIBIT 8 | January–July 1992 Performance Summary

	Paying				Free								Grand
					Madurai:		Tirunelveli:		Theni:		Total:		
	Madurai	Tirunelveli	Theni	Total	Direct	Camp	Direct	Camp	Direct	Camp	Direct	Camp	Total
Outpatients:													
New cases	50,498	14,710	5,669	70,877	30,662	65,669	8,900	30,863	3,662	7,312	43,224	103,844	217,945
Review cases	57,428	16,831	4,196	78,455	28,912	0	11,215	0	2,797	0	42,924	0	121,379
Total Patients	107,926	31,541	9,865	149,332	59,574	65,669	20,115	30,863	6,459	7,312	86,148	103,844	339,324
Cataract operations	7,382	1,211	228	8,821	5,192	8,290	1,195	2,739	402	551	6,726	11,580	27,127
Other major surgery	905	55	1	961	278	15	23	9	0	0	301	24	1,286
Other minor surgery	3,171	761	75	4,007	1,236	319	378	318	83	30	1,697	667	6,371
Total Surgery	11,458	2,027	304	13,789	6,706	8,624	1,596	3,066	485	581	8,724	12,271	34,784
Bed capacity	324	200	40	564	**400**		**200**		**60**		**660**		1,224
Beds occupied per day (six-month average)	265	51	10	326	167	229	62	92	14	14	243	335	903

Source: Aravind Eye Hospital.

EXHIBIT 9 | Free Section Complication Details for the Patients Operated on in the Month of October 1992

Complications	Pre-operative		Post-operative		Total	
	(#)	(%)	(#)	(%)	(#)	(%)
A/C shallow	0	0.0	39	2.7	39	2.7
Accidental extra	2	0.1	0	0.0	2	0.1
Blood clot	1	0.0	113	7.8	114	7.9
Cornea oedema	0	0.0	55	3.8	55	3.8
Cortex	2	0.1	36	2.4	38	2.6
Endophthalmitis	0	0.0	1	0.0	1	0.0
Exudate in pupil area	0	0.0	8	0.5	8	0.5
Flap turn	0	0.0	6	0.4	6	0.4
Hyphema	2	0.1	34	2.3	36	2.4
Hypopyon	0	0.0	10	0.6	10	0.6
Hypotony	0	0.0	1	0.0	1	0.0
Iridodialysis	1	0.0	1	0.0	2	0.1
Iris prolapse	0	0.0	1	0.0	1	0.0
Iritis	0	0.0	226	15.6	226	15.6
P.A.S.	1	0.0	0	0.0	1	0.0
Posterior synechiae	1	0.0	0	0.0	1	0.0
Pupillary block (air in PC)	0	0.0	2	0.1	2	0.1
S.K. (straight keratitis)	0	0.0	55	3.8	55	3.8
Vitreous bulge	0	0.0	1	0.0	1	0.0
Vitreous disturbance	5	0.3	0	0.0	5	0.3
Vitreous loss	2	0.1	0	0.0	2	0.1
Wound leak	0	0.0	1	0.0	1	0.0

Source: Aravind Eye Hospital.

EXHIBIT 10 | Eye Camp Performance

Year	Screening Camps	Operating Camps	Outpatients Seen	Operations
1978	118	—	18,251	1,045
1979	215	—	47,351	2,430
1980	198	10	65,344	5,427
1981	140	13	75,727	8,172
1982	205	9	79,367	8,747
1983	204	9	101,469	10,975
1984	247	21	103,177	11,796
1985	475	18	153,037	17,586
1986	516	13	164,977	19,623
1987	506	12	180,181	21,562
1988	536	9	232,838	23,635
1989	818	2	290,859	25,867
1990	884	3	203,805	20,852
1991	707	3	191,000	20,818
	5,769	122	1,907,383	198,535

EXHIBIT 11 | 1991 Eye Camps[a]

Name or Organization	No. of Camps	Total Outpatients	Surgery		
			Cataract	Others	Total
Lions Clubs	105	42,439	5,071	139	5,210
Rotary Clubs	42	17,629	1,941	69	2,010
Vivekananda Kendra	190	30,899	2,657	240	2,897
Bhagavan Sri Sathya Sai Seva Org.	20	7,114	1,472	47	1,519
Jaycees	18	3,823	309	10	319
Banks	27	4,854	371	18	389
Mills and factories	28	10,543	966	53	1,019
ASSEFA	6	900	104	5	109
Schools and colleges	50	8,577	475	17	492
Hospitals	12	4,291	974	57	1,031
Trusts	16	6,329	1,224	34	1,258
Youth and fans associations	37	6,291	365	27	392
Other religious organizations	41	12,696	1,315	47	1,362
Other voluntary service organizations	75	23,356	1,913	68	1,981
Others	40	11,259	791	39	830
Total	707	191,000	19,948	870	20,818

Source: Aravind Eye Hospital.

[a]These statistics include the work of all three hospitals. For example, in 1991, the breakdown by hospital was as follows:

	Total Camps	Outpatients	Operations
Madurai	331	117,175	14,951
Tirunelveli	293	57,924	4,922
Theni	83	15,901	945
Total	707	191,000	20,818

EXHIBIT 12 | Camp Organizer Territories

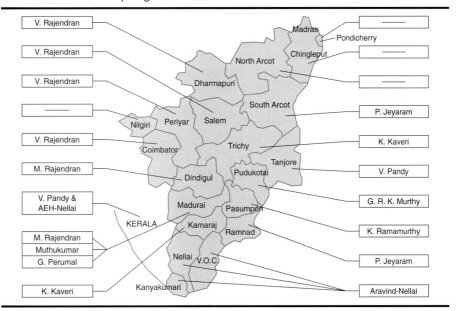

Source: Aravind Eye Hospital.

EXHIBIT 13 | Districtwise Camp Particulars—1991

#	District	Population (millions)	# of Camps	# of Cases Screened	# Advised Surgery	# Accepting Surgery
1.	Madras City	3.795	—	—	—	—
2.	Chingleput	4.621	—	—	—	—
3.	North Arcot	3.000	—	—	—	—
4.	South Arcot	4.871	4	4,491	1,058	1,009
5.	Dharmapuri	2.396	5	4,495	657	609
6.	Salem	3.914	17	14,026	3,333	3,179
7.	Periyar	2.323	21	12,760	2,145	2,064
8.	Nilgiris	0.705	2	465	22	19
9.	Coimbatore	3.531	19	11,836	2,114	2,002
10.	Trichy	4.114	12	7,029	654	592
11.	Tanjore	4.527	23	9,264	1,208	1,095
12.	Pudukottai	1.322	12	2,432	231	201
13.	Madurai	3.448	119	19,992	1,693	1,184
14.	Dindigul	1.769	45	9,399	991	828
15.	Pasumpon	1.075	32	5,514	583	427
16.	Kamaraj	1.554	44	8,800	1,185	1,004
17.	Ramnad	1.136	46	6,402	769	647
18.	Nellai	2.493	123	18,031	2,680	1,795
19.	Kanyakumari	1.591	60	8,994	796	529
20.	VOC	1.156	75	11,066	1,678	1,174
21.	Pondicherry	0.500	4	2,893	288	258
22.	Kerala State[a]	12.000	44	33,111	2,912	2,202
	Total		707	191,000	24,997	20,818

Source: Aravind Eye Hospital.

[a]The first 21 districts listed in the above exhibit are part of the Tamil-Nadu state. Kerala is a neighboring state. Statistics for Kerala have been aggregated for its 10 districts.

R&R

During the summer of 1983, Bob Reiss observed with interest the success in the Canadian market of a new board game called "Trivial Pursuit." His years of experience selling games in the U.S. had taught him a rough rule of thumb: the sales of a game in the U.S. tended to be approximately ten times those of sales in Canada. Since "Trivial Pursuit" had sold 100,000 copies north of the border, Reiss thought that trivia games might soon boom in the U.S., and that this might represent a profitable opportunity for him.

Reiss' Background

After his graduation from Harvard Business School in 1956, Reiss began working for a company that made stationery products. His main responsibility was to build a personalized pencil division, and he suggested that he be paid a low salary and a high sales commission. He was able to gain an excellent understanding of that market, and by 1959 could start on his own as an independent manufacturer's representative in the same industry. His direct contact with stores that sold stationery products revealed that many of them were beginning to sell adult games. He decided to specialize in those products.

In 1973, Reiss sold his representative business to a small American Stock Exchange company in the needlecraft business in exchange for shares. He then set up a game manufacturing division and ran it for that company, building sales to $12,000,000 in three years.

Reiss decided to go into business for himself again in 1979 and left the company. He incorporated under the name of R&R and worked with the help of a secretary from a rented office in New York; Reiss promised himself that he would keep overhead very low, even in good years, and never own or be responsible for a factory. In addition to being a traditional manufacturer's representative, he did some consulting for toy manufacturers, using his extensive knowledge of the market.

This case was prepared by Research Assistant Jose-Carlos Jarillo Mossi, under the supervision of Professor Howard H. Stevenson, as the basis for class discussion rather than to illustrate either effective or ineffective handling of an administrative situation.

The Toy and Game Industry

One of the main characteristics of the toy industry was that products generally had very short life cycles, frequently of no more than two years. "Fads" extended to whole categories of items: one class of toys would sell well for a couple of years and then fade away. Products that were part of categories tended to ride with the fate of that category, regardless, to some extent, of their intrinsic merit. Many new products were introduced every year, which made the fight for shelf space aggressive.

Promotional plans for a new product were a key factor in buy or no-buy decisions of the major retailers. At the same time, fewer and fewer retailers were dominating more of the market every year. The largest one, Toys "R" Us, for example, had 14% of the entire market in 1984. The success of a product was often based on less than a dozen retailers.

A few large manufacturers were also becoming dominant in the industry, because they could afford the expensive TV promotional campaigns that retailers demanded of the products they purchased. Billing terms to retailers were extremely generous compared to other industries, thus increasing the need for financial strength. Financing terms ran from a low of 90 days to 9 to 12 months. In general, major retailers were reluctant to buy from new vendors with narrow product lines unless they felt that the volume potential was enormous. On the other hand, the large manufacturers tended to require a long lead time for introducing new products, typically on the order of 18 to 24 months.

The industry was also highly seasonal. Most final sales to the public were made in the four weeks prior to Christmas. Retailers decided what to carry for the Christmas season during the preceding January through March. There was a growing tendency among them, however, not to accept delivery until the goods were needed, in effect using the manufacturer as their warehouse.

The Trivia Game Opportunity

"Trivial Pursuit" was developed in Canada, and introduced there in 1980. Its 1983 sales were exceptionally strong, especially for a product that had been promoted primarily via word of mouth. The game was introduced in the U.S. at the Toy Fair in February, 1983 by Selchow & Righter, makers of "Scrabble," under license from Horn & Abbot in Canada. Earlier, the game had been turned down by Parker Bros. and Bradley, the two largest game manufacturers in the United States.

"Trivial Pursuit" in the U.S. had a $19.00 wholesale price, with a retail price varying from $29.95 to $39.95, about 200% to 300% more expensive than comparable board games. Selchow was not known as a strong marketer and had no TV advertising or public relations budget for the game. The initial reaction at the Toy Fair in February had been poor. Yet, by August the game had started moving at retail.

Reiss thought that if the success of "Trivial Pursuit" in Canada spilled over to the U.S., the large game companies would eventually produce and market their own similar products. This would generate popular interest in trivia games in general and constitute a window of opportunity for him. The only trivia game in the market as of September 1983 was "Trivial Pursuit." Two small firms had announced their entries and were taking orders for the next season. Bob Reiss decided to design and market his own trivia game.

Developing the Concept

Reiss' first task was to find an interesting theme, one that would appeal to as broad an audience as possible. On one hand, he wanted to capitalize on the new "trivia" category that "Trivial Pursuit" would create; on the other, he wanted to be different, and therefore could not use a topic already covered by that game, such as movies or sports. Further, his game would have its own rules, yet be playable on the "Trivial Pursuit" board.

As was his custom, Reiss discussed these ideas with some of his closest friends in the manufacturer's representative business. Over the years, he had found them a source of good ideas. One of the reps suggested television as a topic. Reiss saw immediately that this had great potential: not only did it have a broad appeal (the average American family watches over seven hours of TV per day), it offered a great PR opportunity. A strong PR campaign would be needed since Reiss knew clearly that he was not going to be able to even approach the advertising budgets of the large manufacturers, which would probably surpass $1 million just for their own trivia games.

Because licensing was common in the toy industry and was a way to obtain both an easily recognizable name and a partner who could help promote the product, Reiss realized he could add strength and interest to his project if he could team up with the publishers of *TV Guide*. This magazine had the highest diffusion in the U.S., approaching 18 million copies sold each week. It reached more homes than any other publication and could be called a household name.

On October 17, 1983, Reiss sent a letter, printed below, to Mr. Eric Larson, publisher of *TV Guide*.

Mr. Eric Larson, Publisher   October 17, 1983
T.V. GUIDE
P.O. Box 500
Radnor, PA 19088

Dear Mr. Larson:

I am a consultant in the game industry and former owner of a game company.

Briefly, I would like to talk to you about creating a game and marketing plan for a 'T.V. GUIDE TRIVIA GAME'.

In 1984, trivia games will be a major classification of the Toy Industry. I'm enclosing copy of a forthcoming ad that will introduce a game based upon the 60 years of *Time Magazine*. I am the marketer of this game and have received a tremendous response to the game, both in orders and future publicity.

This project can benefit both of us, and I would like to explore the opportunities.

Sincerely,

Robert S. Reiss

In a follow-up phone conversation, Mr. Bill Deitch, assistant to the publisher of the magazine, asked Reiss for some detailed explanation on the idea. Reiss sent the following proposal:

Mr. Bill Deitch   November 14, 1983
T.V. GUIDE
P.O. Box 500
Radnor, PA 19088

Dear Mr. Deitch:

In response to our phone conversation, I will attempt to briefly outline a proposal to do a TV Trivia Game by *TV Guide*.

WHY A TV GAME? It is a natural follow up to the emerging craze of Trivia Games that is sweeping the country. This category should be one of the 'Hot' categories in the Toy/Game industry in 1984. This type of game got its start in Canada three years ago with the introduction of Trivial Pursuit. It continues to be the rage in Canada and was licensed in the U.S. this year. It is currently the top selling non-electronic game. It retails from $24.95 to $39.95 and is projected to sell 1,000,000 units. It is not TV promoted. The 'Time Game', with 8,000 questions covering six general subject areas, only began to ship two weeks ago and had an unprecedented initial trade buy, particularly with no finished sample available for prior inspection.

WILL TV GUIDE BE JUST ANOTHER TRIVIA GAME? No. The next step is to do specialty subjects. Trivial Pursuit has just done a Motion Picture Game with excellent success. Our research tells us that a TV oriented game would have the broadest national appeal.

THE MARKETS - This type of game has wide appeal in that it is non-sexual and is of interest to adults and children. We feel we can place it in over 10,000 retail outlets ranging from upscale retailers like Bloomingdale's and Macy's to mass merchants like Toys "R" Us, Sears, Penney, Kmart, Target, etc. There is also a good mail-order market. The market is particularly receptive to good playing, social interactive games at this time. Video games are in a state of decline as their novelty has worn off. (To say nothing about profits.)

WHO WILL DEVELOP THE GAME? Alan Charles, a professional game developer who did the 'Time Game', is free at this moment to do work on the project. He has satisfied the strict standards 'Time' has set for putting its name on a product and mine for play value and product graphics in a highly competitive market . . . No easy task.

WHO WILL PRODUCE & MARKET THE GAME? There are two options for producing the game.

1. Give it to an established game company who would assume all financial risk as well as production and distribution responsibilities. Under this set-up, *TV Guide* would get a royalty on all goods sold.

2. *TV Guide* assume all financial responsibilities to game. Production and shipping would be handled by a contract manufacturer. Bob Reiss would be responsible for

hiring and supervising a national sales force to sell the game. This is not an unusual option, and I do have experience in this. All sales are on a commission basis. This way, *TV Guide* gets the major share of the profits.

Attached exhibit explores some rough profit numbers for *TV Guide,* via both options.

POSITIONING OF GAME - We see the game as non-competitive to Trivial Pursuit and Time Magazine. It can be developed to retail at $14.95, as opposed to $39.95 for Trivial Pursuit and $29.95 for Time. (Mass merchants generally discount from these list prices.) The TV Game should be able to be played by owners of both games as well as on its own. The name 'TV Guide' is important to the credibility of the product. Sales of licensed products have been growing at geometric rates in the last decade. Consumers are more comfortable buying a product with a good name behind it.

PROMOTION OF GAME - Pricing of the product will have an ad allowance built into it. This will allow the retailers to advertise in their own catalog, tabloids and/or newspaper ads. An important part of promotion should be ads in *TV Guide.* Ads can be handled two ways: one, with mail order coupon and profits accruing to *TV Guide;* the other, with listing of retailers carrying the item, as you have so many regional splits, the listing could be rather extensive. Financially, you would probably opt for the first option on a royalty arrangement and the second if you owned the product.

This product lends itself perfectly to an extensive public relations program. This is an excellent product for radio stations to promote. This should be pursued vigorously.

BENEFITS TO TV GUIDE

• Profits from royalties or manufacturing

• Extensive publicity through wide distribution on U.S. retail counter, including the prestigious retailers as well as the volume ones. This is the unique type of product that can bridge this gap.

• Good premium for your clients. Can be excellent premium for TV Stations. Can be used as a circulation builder. In projecting profits, I have not included premiums. The numbers can be big, but they are difficult to count on.

TIMING To effectively do business in 1984, all contracts must be done and a prototype developed for the American Toy Fair, which takes place in early February, 1984. Shipments need not be made until late spring.

WHO IS BOB REISS? He is a graduate of Columbia College and Harvard Business School who started his own national rep firm in 1959, specializing in adult games, when it became a distinct category in 1968. He sold his company in 1973 to an American Stock Exchange Company. He remained there for five years and built Reiss Games to a dominant position in the adult-game field. For the last three years, he has been consulting in the game/toy industry and recently acted as broker in the sale of one of his clients, Pente Games, to Parker Bros.

I am enclosing some articles that have a bearing on the subject matter. I think what is needed, as soon as possible, is a face-to-face meeting, where we can discuss in greater detail all aspects of this proposal as well as responsibilities for all parties.

Sincerely,

RSR/ck   Robert S. Reiss

encl.

ROUGH PROFIT POTENTIALS TO TV GUIDE

ASSUMPTIONS

1. Average wholesale cost of $7.15 after all allowances. (This would allow Department Stores and Mail Order to sell at $15.00. Discounters would sell at $9.95 to $11.95.)

2. Cost to manufacture, $3.00 each.

3. Royalty rate of 10% - (Range is 6% to 10%, depending on licensor support and name. Assuming 10%, based on fact you would run No Cost ads in *TV Guide*.)

4. Mail order retail in *TV Guide* is $14.95, and you would pay $4.00 for goods. Postage and Handling would be a wash with small fee charged to customer.

OPTION I - ROYALTY BASIS

Projected Retail Sales - 500,000 units.
   * Royalty to *TV Guide* of $357,500

Mail Order Sales - 34,000 units (.002 pull on 17,000,000 circulation). Based on full-page ad with coupon. It is extremely difficult to project mail order sales without testing—too many variables. However, this is a product that is ideal for your audience.
   * Profit to *TV Guide* of $372,300

OPTION II - YOU OWN GOODS

Costs: (Rough Estimate)

Manufacture	$3.00
Royalties to inventor	.36
Fulfillment	.30
Sales Costs	1.43
Amortization of start-up costs	.10
TOTAL COST	$5.19
Profit per unit	$1.96

Profit on 500,000 units = $980,000.00
(Does not include cost of money.)

Another phone conversation followed in which *TV Guide* showed a clear interest in pursuing the subject. Reiss answered with a new letter on December 12, 1983, that outlined clearly the steps that had to be followed by both parties should they want to go ahead with the venture. Reiss had to send still another letter with a long list of personal references that *TV Guide* could contact. *TV Guide* finally opted to be a licensor, not a manufacturer. They would give Bob Reiss a contract for him to manufacture the game or farm it out to an established manufacturer, provided he stayed involved with the project. *TV Guide* would receive a royalty that would escalate with volume. Royalties were normally paid quarterly, over shipments; Reiss, however, proposed to pay over money collected, which *TV Guide* accepted. As part of the final deal, *TV Guide* would insert, at no cost, five ads in the magazine worth $85,000 each. These would be "cooperative ads"; that is, the name of the stores selling the game in the area of each edition would also be displayed. Reiss thought that including the name of the stores at no cost to them would be a good sales argument and would help insure a wide placement of the product.

Developing the TV Guide Trivia Game

The actual game was designed by a professional inventor, whom Reiss knew, in exchange for a royalty of 5%—decreasing to 3% with volume—per game sold. No upfront monies were paid or royalties guaranteed. Although the inventor delivered the package design in just a few weeks, the questions to be asked were not yet formulated, and Reiss realized he could not do this alone. *TV Guide*'s management insisted that their employees should develop them. Reiss would pay per question for each of the 6,000 questions he needed; employees could moonlight on nights and weekends. Reiss felt it was important to put questions and answers in books rather than cards, like "Trivial Pursuit." The cost would be considerably lower, and the most serious bottleneck in manufacturing—collating the cards—would be eliminated. The game also lent itself well to this approach, as the question books imitated the appearance of *TV Guide* magazine **(Exhibit 1)**. Overall, the presentation of the game tried to capitalize on the well-known *TV Guide* name **(Exhibit 2).**

Initially, Reiss had not wanted to include a board with the game; he wanted people to use "Trivial Pursuit's" board and had made sure that the rules of the new game would take this into account. However, *TV Guide* wanted a complete game of its own, not just supplementary questions to be played on someone else's game. Another advantage of including a board, Reiss realized, was that a higher price could be charged.

Since *TV Guide* had opted for being merely a licensor, it was Reiss' responsibility to set up all the operations needed to take the game to market in time for the 1984 season, and there were only two months left until the February Toy Fair, where the game had to be introduced.

His first consideration was financial. He estimated that the fixed cost of developing the product would be between $30,000 and $50,000, but some $300,000 would be needed to finance the first production run. Those funds would be needed until the initial payments from sales arrived a few months later.

Reiss seriously considered raising the required money from the strongest among his manufacturer's representatives in the toy business, thinking they would push hard to sell the game to every account. Eventually, he decided against this approach: not only would it not contribute that much to the venture, reps could be motivated to sell in other ways. Perhaps more important, Reiss feared the prospect of perhaps 20 partners who "would be every day on the phone asking how things are going."

Another option that passed through his mind, which he dismissed promptly, was venture capital. He realized that he would have to give up too much and, even worse, that venture capitalists would not understand this kind of deal—one that had very attractive short-term profits but few long-term prospects.

Trivia, Inc.

With the agreement with *TV Guide* in hand, Reiss called Sam Kaplan—a long-time friend who lived in Chicago. Kaplan, 65 years old, had a sizeable personal net worth, yet kept working at his small but successful advertising agency (25 employees) "for the fun of it," as he liked to say. Reiss thought that teaming up could be an important help, and Kaplan was indeed enthusiastic about the idea.

Reiss proposed to establish a company, Trivia Inc., that would develop the project. The equity would be split evenly among the two partners. Kaplan, besides lending his line of credit to purchase supplies for the initial run, would use his office to handle day-to-day details. (In fact, Trivia Inc. ended up having only one full-time employee.) Also, because of his vast knowledge of printing and his contacts, Kaplan could secure press time and paper supplies on short notice, and he would supervise the product's manufacturing. This was especially important, since the special paper stock on which the game was printed was then in short supply, and long lead times were generally needed to obtain it. Kaplan would also produce all the ads and the catalog sheets. Reiss would take responsibility for sales and marketing of the product and would pay all reps and coordinate the publicity and the relations with *TV Guide*. An important part of the agreement was that R&R (Reiss' company) would have the exclusive rights to market the game and would receive a commission of 20% of the wholesale price from which it would pay the commissions to the reps.

Production, Shipping and Billing

From the beginning, Reiss' intention was not to be a manufacturer. Through Kaplan's connections, they found not only good suppliers for the question books, the board and the boxes, they even got lower costs than expected. But, they still had to tackle the problem of assembly and shipping. Kaplan was a long-time consultant to Swiss Colony, a manufacturer of cheese based in Madison, Wisconsin. This company specialized in mail sales and had developed a strong capability to process mail orders. As a result, Swiss Colony's management had decided several years earlier to offer that fulfillment capability to other companies. They took the orders, shipped the product, and billed to the retailer.

In the deal ultimately reached, Trivia Inc. would have the components sent by the different suppliers to Madison on a "just in time" basis, and Swiss Colony would put the boards, dice, and questions in the boxes, package and ship them. Swiss Colony would charge $.25 per box, including billing for the games, and would send complete daily information on sales to Trivia Inc. Trivia Inc. would pay $2,500 for a customized computer program. With all these measures, Reiss and Kaplan were able to lower their estimated costs by 30% and attained the flexibility they wanted. The final cost of manufacturing, assembling and shipping was about $3.10, not including the royalties paid to the inventor and to *TV Guide.*

A final point was financing the accounts receivable, once the sales started rolling in, and collecting the debts. Reiss was somewhat afraid that the bills of some of the smaller stores carrying the game would be very difficult to collect, since R&R did not have the resources to follow up closely on its collections; moreover, Trivia Inc. needed the leverage of a factor in order to collect from the larger retailers on time. He and Kaplan decided to use Heller Factoring to check credit, guarantee payment, collect the money, and pay Trivia Inc., all for a fee of 1% over sales. Trivia Inc. would not need any financing for operations: after 45 days of shipping, Trivia Inc. would always be in a positive cashflow. Thanks to Heller and Swiss Colony, Trivia Inc. had practically no administrative work left to itself.

Selling the Game

Selling was the most important issue for Reiss. He knew that placing the goods in the stores and selling them to the public (selling through) were two distinct, many times unrelated, problems. In any case, however, he thought that the game needed to be priced below "Trivial Pursuit" to make up for both their lack of a complete national advertising campaign that major manufacturers would launch, and their lack of the kind of brand recognition that "Trivial Pursuit" was achieving. Accordingly, the wholesale price was set at $12.50, with a retail list price of $25.

Reiss distinguished carefully between two different channels: the mass merchandisers and the department/gift stores. An important part of the overall strategy was to sell quickly to upscale retailers who would establish a full retail mark-up (50%). These were mainly department stores, such as Bloomingdale's or Marshall Field's, and mail order gift catalogs and specialty gift stores. This, it was hoped, would help sell mass merchandisers and give them a price from which to discount. Such a two-tiered approach was not common in the industry. On long-life products, many times only the full-margin retailers got the product the first year. But Reiss felt that this could not be done with his product, because it could well be only a one-year product. Mass merchandisers, however, had to be reached, since they accounted for at least 75% of the market. (**Exhibit 3** shows some of the stores Reiss thought had to be reached.)

Two different sets of reps were employed for the two different channels; on average, they received a 7% commission on sales. Reiss' personal knowledge of buyers for the major chains proved invaluable. He was able to obtain quick access to the important decision-makers at the major chains. They also followed, when possible, the distribution pattern of *TV Guide* magazine. It was soon apparent that the statistics on demographics reached by *TV Guide,* which Reiss made sure all buyers saw (**Exhibit 4),** had a major impact. As Reiss said, "It appeared that every outlet's customers read *TV Guide.*" The cooperative ads in the magazine, with the possibility of including the store's name, were also a powerful attraction for different buyers, as Reiss had expected: the name of their stores would be displayed in far more homes than it would with a conventional advertising campaign in national magazines. The stores would not be charged to have their name in the ads, but minimum purchase orders would be requested. Many large customers, such as Kmart and Sears, placed large orders before the product was even finished. (**Exhibit 5** shows a cover letter that was sent to supermarket buyers.)

Promotion

In order to promote the game to the public, Trivia Inc. had a four-part plan, beginning with the five ads in *TV Guide*. (**Exhibit 6**) The first ad broke in mid-September, 1984, and was strictly for upscale retailers, with $25.00 as the price of the game. *TV Guide* had eight regional issues, and different stores were listed in each area with a total of about 120, including Bloomingdale's, Marshall Field's, Jordan Marsh and J.C. Penney. They all had to place minimum orders. The second ad, shown on October 6th, was just for Sears. The third, on November 10th, was devoted to mass merchandisers and did not include a retail price. The fourth, two weeks later, listed four of the most important toy chains: Toys "R" Us, Child World, Lionel Leisure and Kay Bee. The appeal to the public, then, was not just the ad: Reiss knew that showing well-known upscale stores carrying the game initially was the best way to obtain instant credibility for the product. Finally, Kmart, the largest U.S. chain, gave Trivia Inc. an opening order to all their 2,100 stores, even before the game went into production, in exchange for the exclusivity in the fifth ad to be run in *TV Guide* on December 8, 1984. In that ad, Kmart offered a three-day sale at $16.97.

The second part of the plan also tried to give credibility to the game. Trivia Inc. offered the department stores a 5% ad allowance (a 5% discount from wholesale price) if they put the product in newspaper ads, tabloids or catalogs. For similar reasons, Reiss wanted to have the game placed in mail order gift catalogs. Their sales in the toy-game business were only moderate, but catalogs gave a lot of product exposure because of their large circulation figures.

The final part of the plan was to obtain free media publicity. The publisher of *TV Guide* magazine wrote a letter to be sent to the producers of such shows as "Good Morning, America," "CBS Morning News," "The Tonight Show," and to 25 top TV personalities, together with a sample of the game. Through *TV Guide*'s P.R. agency and the joint efforts of *TV Guide* and Trivia Inc., many newspapers, radio and TV stations were reached. In all, more than 900 press kits were sent to media organizations. As a result, the game was mentioned on many talk shows (TV and radio), and news of it was published in many newspapers (**Exhibit 7**). The cost of this campaign was split between Trivia Inc. and *TV Guide*.

The Results

By October 1983, Selchow, manufacturer of "Trivial Pursuit," started falling behind trying to meet the demand. By Christmas, when sales exploded, there was no hope of keeping up—and one of the most serious manufacturing problems was the bottleneck of collating the cards. By the February, 1984 Toy Fair, most of the major manufacturers offered trivia games, which was projected to be the hottest category for the year.

R&R sold 580,000 units of the *TV Guide* game in 1984 at the full wholesale price of $12.50. There were few reorders after mid-October, as the market became saturated with trivia games (over 80 varieties) and "Trivial Pursuit" flooded the market. By Christmas 1984, all trivia games became heavily discounted; many retailers ran sales on "Trivial Pursuit" at $14.95, having paid $19.00.

Bad debts for Trivia Inc. were about $30,000 on approximately $7,000,000 billings, with hope of recovering $15,000. Losses from final inventory disposal (it was decided to close-out the game) were less than $100,000.

TV Guide was extremely pleased with the royalty collected from the venture. Kaplan, through his 50% ownership in Trivia Inc., made over $1,000,000 net. The total cost of designing and launching the product had been $50,000.

Commenting on the whole deal, Reiss said:

> I think the critical aspects of success in being a contract manufacturer are to take care of your suppliers and to take care of your sales representatives. We want our suppliers to charge us full mark-up, so that we are a good customer to them, and we try hard to give them enough lead time to deliver. We pay on time always, no matter what happens. In exchange, we demand perfect work from them. They understand and like this relationship. We need their cooperation, because we are completely dependent on them.
>
> The other aspect is how to deal with your customers, which for us are the manufacturer's representatives and the buyers of major chains. The manufacturer's reps are used to the fact that, when sales really do pick up in any product and they can make a lot of money, many manufacturers try to "shave" their commissions, perhaps feeling that they are making too much money. I never do that: I am happy if they make millions, and they know it. I also pay on time always. With this, I have developed a loyal and experienced work force and have no fixed or up-front sales cost.
>
> All of these factors allowed us to move quickly. My contacts enabled me to print and manufacture the game for the same cost as a big company. But, a Parker Bros. or Milton Bradley would have incurred fixed costs of roughly $250,000 just for design and development and would then have committed to an advertising and promotion budget of at least $1 million.

The Future

According to Reiss, the big question at the end of 1984 was, "Do we add on a new version of the *TV Guide* game, do a new trivia game, or go onto something new in spite of the great market penetration and success of our game?"

He had been doing some planning for a new game to be called "WHOOZIT?" and, instead of questions, it would show photographs of famous people that the players would have to recognize. He had a preliminary royalty deal with Bettman Archives, who had the exclusive marketing rights to all the photographs of the news service UPI, in addition to their own extensive archives. But, he was unsure about what the best follow-up for the success of 1984 could be.

The market, however, did not seem to be in the best condition. The 1984 Christmas season had ended with large unsold inventories of "Trivial Pursuit" and other trivia games. Some major companies, like Parker Bros., Lakeside, and Ideal, had closed out their games at low prices, further flooding the market. Many buyers were saying that trivia games, as a category, were over, although they seemed to accept Selchow's estimate of 7,000,000 units of "Trivial Pursuit" sold in 1985. That figure was well below the 20,000,000 units sold in 1984 but was still an exceptionally high figure compared with other board games. Selchow had also announced a plan to spend $5,000,000 to promote the game in 1985. Some upscale retailers, however, had announced their intention to abandon "Trivial Pursuit" and other trivia games, mostly because of the heavy discounting.

Reiss thought that one of the reasons why the public seemed to have lost interest in trivia games is that they were hard to play; too often, none of the players knew the answers. In retrospect, he thought that the *TV Guide* game had had the same problem. But, that would be different with "WHOOZIT?." He was thinking of making easier questions and giving several chances to each player and really expected the new game to be enjoyable.

In addition to improving the intrinsic playability of the game, Reiss wanted to have more flexibility selling it. He planned to offer three different price points, one of the versions having only the questions so it could be played on the "Trivial Pursuit" board. In spite of all these improvements, however, he was not sure whether he should try to replicate the success obtained with the *TV Guide* game and wondered what his best strategy for a follow-up could be.

EXHIBIT 1 | Box of the Game

EXHIBIT 2 | Book with the Questions

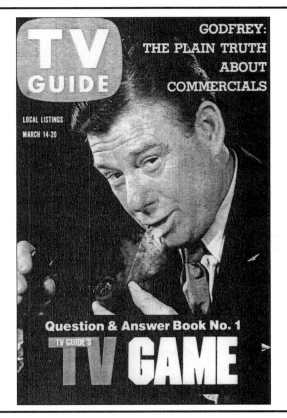

EXHIBIT 3 | Stores to Be Reached

Sears	879
Penney	450
Federated	451
Dayton Hudson	1149
R.H. Macy	96
Allied Stores	596
Carter Hawley Hale	268
Associated Dry Goods	332
Mercantile	79
Kmart	2174
Woolworth	N/A
Wal-Mart	751
T.G.&Y.	754
Zayre	848
Bradlees	132
Murphy	386
Rose's	195
Kay Bee	500
Spencer Gifts	450
Hook's Drug	120
Toys "R" Us	200

Bob Reiss thought that some 5,000 independent stores would be suitable targets, too.

EXHIBIT 4 | Data on *TV Guide*'s Audience

February 3, 1984

Mr. Robert Reiss
President
R & R
230 Fifth Avenue
New York, New York 10001

Dear Bob:

I had our Research Department pull together some statistics about *TV Guide* that should be useful in discussing the audience dimensions of our magazine with major department stores and mass merchandisers.

First off, *TV Guide*'s circulation averages over 17,000,000 copies each week.

Included in *TV Guide*'s average issue audience are:

1. 37,838,000 adult readers age 18 and over.
2. 8,829,000 teenage readers 12–17.
3. 46,667,000 total readers age 12 and over.
4. 19,273,000 readers age 18–34.
5. 28,085,000 readers 18–49.
6. 10,312,000 adult readers in homes with one or more children 10–17 years of age.
7. 16,334,000 adult readers in homes with $25,000+ household income.
8. 11,815,000 adult readers with one or more years of college.
9. 4,344,000 adult readers who bought games or toys for children 12–17 in the past year.
10. 3,688,000 adult readers who bought games or toys for adults 18+ in the past year.

EXHIBIT 5 | Letter to Supermarket Buyers

TRIVIA
INCORPORATED
Exclusive Marketing Agent
R & R
230 Fifth Avenue, New York, NY 10001
1-212-686-6003 Telex 238131-RR UR

June 29, 1984

Mr. Lamar Williams
General Mdse. Buyer
JITNEY JUNGLE STORES of AMERICA
P.O. Box 3409
453 N. Mill St.
Jackson, MI 39207

Dear Mr. Williams:

Once every decade a product comes along that is just right!

We think we have that product for you. It has two key elements:

1- It is licensed by TV GUIDE. I'm sure we don't have to tell
   you about the sales strength of TV GUIDE with its 17,000,000+
   weekly circulation, 46,000,000 readers, etc.. If your supermarket is typical, TV GUIDE is one of your best sellers and has
   earned its exalted position next to the cash registers.

2- The Trivia Game explosion has taken America by storm and
   duplicated its Canadian heritage, where Trivia games have
   reigned for four years.

We have put these two elements together and with TV GUIDE'S help,
developed a TV GUIDE Trivia Game with over 6,000 questions and
answers. The enclosed catalog sheet gives full description and
pricing. All our sales are final. We will advertise the game in
5 full page color ads in TV GUIDE this fall and will reach your
customers.

We feel this game is ideally suited to be sold in your stores.
We would be happy to send you a sample and/or answer any
questions you may have.

We look forward to the opportunity of working with you.

Sincerely,

Robert S. Reiss

RSR/ck
encl.

EXHIBIT 6 | Ads in *TV Guide* Magazine

*Party Fun
For Everyone...
2 to 20 Players!*

**Over 6,000
TV Trivia
Questions**

The Exciting New TV Trivia Game YOU Play at Home!

· Drama · Sports · Comedy · News
· Soaps · Kid's · Specials · Movies
· Talk Shows · Quiz Shows and More!

Nothing mirrors our life and times like the electronic eye of television. For over 30 years, TV GUIDE has been writing the book on television every week. The TV GAME is both a nostalgic trip through the days of Lucy and Uncle Miltie, and an exciting journey through today's video environment...its people, its programs, and the world we all experience.
The TV GAME will provide endless hours of fun for you, your family, and your friends.

TV Guide's TV Game At These Fine Stores

Sears | Available at Most Larger Sears Stores and Sears 1984 Christmas Catalog.

Copyright © 1984 Triangle Publications, Inc. Manufactured in USA by Trivia, Inc., Chicago, IL 60602

*Party Fun
For Everyone...
2 to 20 Players!*

**Over 6,000
TV Trivia
Questions**

The Exciting New TV Trivia Game YOU Play at Home!

· Drama · Sports · Comedy · News
· Soaps · Kid's · Specials · Movies
· Talk Shows · Quiz Shows and More!

Nothing mirrors our life and times like the electronic eye of television. For over 30 years, TV GUIDE has been writing the book on television every week. The TV GAME is both a nostalgic trip through the days of Lucy and Uncle Miltie, and an exciting journey through today's video environment...its people, its programs, and the world we all experience.
The TV GAME will provide endless hours of fun for you, your family, and your friends.

TV Guide's TV Game At These Fine Stores

Store Name Goes Here   Store Name Goes Here   Store Name Goes Here
Store Name Goes Here   Store Name Goes Here   Store Name Goes Here
Store Name Goes Here   Store Name Goes Here   Store Name Goes Here
Store Name Goes Here   Store Name Goes Here   Store Name Goes Here
Store Name Goes Here   Store Name Goes Here   Store Name Goes Here
Store Name Goes Here   Store Name Goes Here   Store Name Goes Here
Store Name Goes Here   Store Name Goes Here   Store Name Goes Here

Copyright © 1984 Triangle Publications, Inc. Manufactured in USA by Trivia, Inc. Chicago, IL 60602

STYLE NO. 048

Copyright © 1984 Triangle Publications, Inc.

OVER 6000 TV TRIVIA QUESTIONS

**· Drama · Sports · Comedy · News
· Soaps · Kid's · Specials · Movies
· Talk Shows · Quiz Shows and More!**

Nothing mirrors our life and times like the electronic eye of television. For over 30 years, TV GUIDE has been writing the book on television every week. The TV GAME is both a nostalgic trip through the days of Lucy and Uncle Miltie, and an exciting journey through today's video environment...its people, its programs, and the world we all experience.

TRIVIA
INCORPORATED
230 Fifth Avenue, Suite 1104
New York, NY 10001   1-212-686-6003

EXHIBIT 7 | Press Releases on the Game

The Indianapolis Star
INDIANAPOLIS, IND.
D. 225,148 SUN. 370.356

BURRELLE'S

The trivia edge

Walter Cronkite, reportedly a trivia game enthusiast, will have an edge if he plays *TV Guide's TV Game,* due in stores in June. The former *CBS Evening News* anchorman figures in more than a dozen of the 6,000-plus TV trivia questions in the new game.

MAY 26 1984

DAILY☉NEWS
NEW YORK'S PICTURE NEWSPAPER®

★★★★ 30¢   Tuesday, June 12, 1984   Mostly sunny. Less humid. 85-90. Details p. 2

TV, too, gets into the trivia act

By BRUCE CHADWICK

SO YOU KNOW who was the only vice president to resign. So what? Okay, you know who threw the ball that Babe Ruth hit into the seats for his 60th home run. Big deal. And you know the name of the drummer in Glen Miller's band. Who cares?

Think you're so smart at trivia? All right, in addition to Matt Dillon, who was the only other character seen during the entire run of "Gunsmoke"? What business did John Walton and his father run in "The Waltons"? In the early days of "All in the Family," what was the name of the company where Archie Bunker worked?

Gotcha, didn't we? Well, to find out all the answers, see below, and also see "TV Guide's TV Game," the latest in the avalanche of trivia games that are flooding stores.

What's different about this one, though, is' that it is limited to television.

It's a board game with cards and dice. You land on squares that have questions in seven categories: drama, sports, comedy, news, kids, movies and other TV (questions are divided into three levels of difficulty and many are aimed at today's youngsters and yes, there is a Mr. T question). Whoever gets the most right answers wins. The game is designed for individual or team play.

"Trivia games are hot because peo-

Milburn Stone

ple are tired of video games and computer games in which the player is isolated," said Bob Reese, head of Trivia Inc. and the game's founder. "People want to play games with other people and match wits with talking faces, not TV screens. That, plus the yen for nostalgia, is making all trivia games, not just ours, big sellers."

Reese wanted to get into trivia games when Trivial Pursuit became a best seller last fall. He needed something different and turned to television.

"Everyone watches television, so

Mary Tyler Moore

everyone will be interested in playing and, in fact, everyone will do reasonably well at this game," he said.

Reese turned to TV Guide because the magazine specializes in television coverage and has an extensive research department and library.

Researchers at TV Guide, led by Teresa Hagen, compiled a list of over 6,000 questions from over 20,000 submitted by writers there. Each question/answer had to have two written sources. Those that did not were dropped.

"It was harder than you'd think,"

said .Hagen. "We needed a good balance of questions, easy to very difficult, and wanted a game that everyone, regardless of age, had a decent chance of winning."

The real research problems came in early television history.

"We had a very difficult time finding out firsts—the first comedy show, soap opera, president on TV, baseball game on TV—because early records were destroyed or sketchy."

They uncovered some unusual facts about television. As an example, the "Armed Forces Hour," an early '50's musical variety show, was only a half hour long. Dr. Ed Diethrich, owner of the USFL Arizona Wranglers, once performed open-heart surgery on live TV. Mary Tyler Moore's first major TV show was not "The Dick Van Dyke Show," but "Richard   Diamond,   Private Detective."

Hagen thinks the game is more than trivia. "We found that in playing it, we'd slide into conversations about what our own lives were like in relation to TV, like who our own heroes were, and our attitudes about things 20 years ago," she said. "We hope the game triggers conversations about life as well as TV."

The other continuing character on "Gunsmoke" was Doc Adams, played by Milburn Stone; the Waltons ran a lumber mill and Archie Bunker worked at Prendergast Tool and Die Co.

Vermeer Technologies (A): A Company Is Born

Charles Ferguson was exhilarated as he hung up the telephone after talking with Andy Marcuvitz, co-leader of the venture capital (VC) consortium that was considering financing Vermeer Technologies, Ferguson's startup for developing software for the Internet. It was the first week of January 1995. Marcuvitz had called Ferguson to tell him that the group was prepared to make an initial infusion of $4 million.

The moment was an unparalleled one for Ferguson. After years of dispensing advice as a consultant, he had finally realized his ambition of owning his own company—and at a juncture in information technology that he believed was revolutionary. It had been only eighteen months since Ferguson had first had the idea for Vermeer.

And yet, Ferguson was having second thoughts about proceeding further with the VCs. Marcuvitz had made the funding decision contingent on some rather onerous conditions. Delighted though he was with the VCs' decision to back him, Ferguson was nevertheless wondering whether he should pull back from the deal.

Founding the Company

The thinking that led to Vermeer began late in 1993, shortly after Ferguson had completed a consulting project for Apple on electronic publishing and on-line services. As he thought about his findings over the subsequent months, Ferguson concluded that there were fundamental problems with existing offerings. These services were based on a centralized design and used proprietary technology. Consequently, not only were these services extremely expensive to develop (costs ran up to $50 million for complex systems), but they were also incompatible with other services. As a result, businesses using these services found themselves locked into a limited set of subscriber-customers. They found it difficult to link into their own internal data-bases because of technological incompatibilities. Besides, they had to pay high fees for the privilege of using the services.

Research Associate Takia Mahmood and Professor Ashish Nanda prepared this case as the basis for class discussion rather than to illustrate either effective or ineffective handling of an administrative situation.

Of course, businesses could develop their own customized on-line services. However, they still faced stiff development and operational costs, the resulting systems were isolated technologically, and they provided access to only a limited set of customers.

Ferguson conceptualized that the solution to these problems with on-line services lay in providing a standardized, shrink-wrapped, inexpensive, and easy-to-use software package that would allow anybody to develop and operate an on-line service—without using a complicated programming language. Moreover, the software would enable businesses and professionals to develop these services based on local and real-time use of hardware resources, data, and applications. In Ferguson's view, such an innovation would spark the widespread development and deployment of on-line services, and dramatically alter the $12 billion industry, currently growing at 10% per year.

Someone could produce the software in three parts: a server[1] for disseminating information, a browser for retrieving and processing it, and a development tool for creating the on-line interface. "If somebody can do that," Ferguson thought, "why not me?" Ferguson had long harbored an ambition to start his own company, believing that it was a "very good experience to have actually done something as opposed to spending your life advising other people who actually do things." While he had the product idea, Ferguson recognized that he lacked the software expertise to lead its technical implementation. Consequently, he went in search of a partner, someone with the software expertise he lacked.

Finding a Partner

In looking for a co-founder for Vermeer, Ferguson approached his friends in the software industry. A professor at MIT recommended one of his old students, Randy Forgaard. Forgaard was the architect of a wide range of PC and UNIX applications, and was working as a project leader for Banyan, a software development company. After graduating from MIT, Forgaard had, for the next six years, formed a series of small companies with his friends, none of which had been immensely successful. In 1990 he joined Beyond Inc., where he was exposed to shrink-wrapped software development as a key contributor in the development of BeyondMail, an award winning electronic mail software product. The company was later acquired by Banyan.

Ferguson wasted no time in seeking out Forgaard, who recalled the circumstances of the first contact: "I got a call from my wife that someone had telephoned from a car, saying that he wanted to offer me a job. I found this quite intriguing." Having been at Beyond/Banyan now for four years, Forgaard was ready to again do something on his own. He was impressed with Ferguson's credentials and contacts—"Charles seems to know everybody," he said—and with his idea—"It was just astounding." He also saw in Ferguson a personality that complemented his own, and therefore, the makings of an effective business partnership:

> Charles is a go-getter. He is more focused on the business side, fearless. I tend to be more reserved, thinking things through, a little more timid. I find that the balance works out well.

---

[1]A server is any computer that shares files and other services with multiple users.

Ferguson had a similar view of their compatibility:

> Randy is extremely even-keeled. He is very nice and tends to think well of the world and of people. I tend to think the worst of the world and of people. I tend to be quite aggressive. Randy usually thinks before he acts, which is not something I always do. So I think the creative friction works quite well. And then, our skills are complementary. I have spent my life doing strategic and business things. Randy is a deep technologist.

Within four days of the initial contact, Forgaard joined Ferguson as the co-founder and chief technology officer of the new venture.

Early Product Definition

Once allied, Ferguson and Forgaard began to refine Ferguson's initial product concept. About a month into the process, they discovered that a comparable infrastructure and architecture, roughly two-thirds of what Ferguson had conceptualized (the servers and browsers) already existed as the World Wide Web on the Internet.[2] Ferguson had made his earlier diagnosis about the limitations of existing on-line services knowing very little about the Internet, and, by his own admission, even less about the Web. "I had heard of the Web, but never used it or looked at it," he said. Fortunately, no one was yet offering a visual, easy-to-use development tool for creating on-line services, and Ferguson and Forgaard decided to focus on this particular product. They came up with the company name Vermeer, after Ferguson's favorite painter, to capture the visual nature of the product they had in mind. "Anything that ended in '—soft' was out from the start," said Forgaard.

Given a limited initial knowledge about alternative technologies, and the rapid pace of change in the field, ensuring the uniqueness of their idea was a major concern. Ferguson, in particular, was extremely careful about divulging too much information about their plans while gathering competitor intelligence, and the two proceeded cautiously. Forgaard recalled the tension-filled early days:

> We looked very, very hard and used Charles's friends and contacts in the field to try to find what other company might be trying to do exactly what we were doing. What surprised us was that there appeared to be no one. And yet, whenever we talked to people they would say, 'Oh, yes, that's obvious. Somebody will be doing that in two months.' So we were running scared the entire time, constantly worried and concerned that someone was on our tail. We would get reports almost every week about some company that was dead-on, exactly competing with us, that we may as well hang up our coat.

---

[2]The Internet was established in the early 1970s as a way to connect the United States Department of Defense with key researchers and scientists at colleges and universities working on defense-related projects. In 1995, the Internet connected between 5 and 15 million people in nearly 25,000 networks, and was growing at a rate of 10% per month, with a new network being added every 20 minutes. The Web, which was a multimedia system for retrieving and processing the content on the Internet, was started in 1990, and contained tens of thousands of servers, growing at a rate of 20% per month. Its open architecture provided the foundation for the development of standardized, distributed, and universally accessible information services.

During the early days of the partnership, the work atmosphere was as informal as it was intense. Typically, Forgaard would visit Ferguson at his apartment, and they would spend hours exchanging and recording ideas, with Forgaard often challenging Ferguson on their feasibility. Forgaard recalled:

> I'd sit on his couch, and he'd sit in his chair, and we would just trade any conceivable idea that we could possibly come up with that had anything to do with this field, and I would jot them all down dutifully. Ferguson was the idea guy. He would enumerate ideas at the hundred-thousand-foot level. What I tried to do was bring the ideas down to the ten-thousand-foot level by producing a document that enumerated the features we would like to put into the software. But in the process of creating that document, there was this tremendous amount of pressure and urgency, that we had to get this done immediately, and it had to be very high-quality, and had to have a zillion features in it or no one would really buy it.

Building the Organization

As Ferguson and Forgaard continued to focus on defining product specs, they also set about recruiting a strong engineering team. Forgaard described the profile of the people they were hoping to recruit:

> We were looking for bright, high-energy people who hadn't been corrupted by the big company feeling—people who were capable of high level architectural thought, but who would not have ego inhibitions about being individual contributors. In a company this small, the person who architects the system is the person who mops the floor as well.

They approached headhunters, as well as tapped their network of contacts for promising system architects and designers. In recruiting candidates, they looked for experienced people as well as recent graduates, who were comfortable with a small company culture and excited about the technology. Complicating the recruiting process was the need to maintain secrecy about the work, particularly since many of the potential recruits worked for, or were recruiting with, potential competitors.

During the summer of 1994, Ferguson and Forgaard hired two engineers—Andy Schulert and Peter Amstein—who would take on the role of project leaders as the organization grew. Ferguson hoped that these two would lead two development teams, one on each coast, to tap into the wealth of technical talent concentrated in both locations. Fortuitously, Amstein was based in California. Ferguson remarked:

> Both Andy and Peter are amazingly gifted people. Once I described the idea to them, they both knew right away what a big deal it was. To my joy and surprise, they quit their jobs in June and began to devote their full time to working on the project without pay. Now these are not rich people. Andy's wife was about to have a baby. Peter had just bought a house in San Francisco. I was amazed how easily they entrusted their professional lives to two strangers.

Ferguson and Forgaard jointly interviewed each potential hire. Forgaard vetted recruits on their technical capabilities, and the ability to think and communicate well under pressure. He devised a procedure called the "Randy Test" to help make that determination. He said:

> The whole purpose of the test is to understand a person's technical depth and experience in specific skills. I have a series of nine questions that get at a person's computer programming skills, the various algorithmic areas they might be familiar with, areas of the industry, data structures, implementation methods, and so forth. All the questions are multi-part—if they do well on the first part, I dig further and further, and make a note to myself a letter grade that goes from "F" to "A+," on how well they do in each one of those nine areas, and then I throw out the bottom two, and take an average. We have very high standards with respect to intellectual horsepower. If a person ends up with a "B+" or better, then they have done very well on the Randy Test.

No technical person was hired without having taken the Randy Test. Many recruits were unaccustomed to being tested so painstakingly for technical proficiency during an interview. Equally important was the Charles test in which Ferguson assessed the candidate's business judgment, maturity, and psychological and emotional fit with what Vermeer was trying to do. A development engineer recruited by Vermeer remarked:

> After going through the third degree with Randy on technical stuff, I had to go through the wringer with Charles on industry trends. I was thrilled about that. Not only did they expect an engineer to be technically savvy, but they wanted us to have a good sense of the marketplace as well. It was a good sign.

Once they had decided to recruit a particular candidate, Ferguson and Forgaard went to great lengths to woo them into the company. Amstein recalled:

> Charles would take them to the mountain top and show them the view. Randy would have a personal heart to heart conversation with them. Both would impress the recruits with how unusual and huge the opportunity potentially was and how it would not exist indefinitely. Person by person, as the company grew, it became easier to attract high quality people, since really good people like working with other really good people.

By the end of 1994, Vermeer had grown to 9 employees. The team had defined the architecture of the product and developed a working prototype.

Early Operations

Very early on, Ferguson took the responsibility for setting the strategy, drawing up the business plan, and raising capital, while Forgaard took charge of defining the architecture, technology, and functionality of the product. People worked from their homes, without pay, and met once or twice a week in a conference room in Ferguson's consulting offices. They communicated by secure electronic mail because of Ferguson's strong concern about confidentiality, even though the process was time consuming and tedious. As work progressed, Ferguson noted that the key difference between his current position as an entrepreneur and his earlier role as a consultant was that as an entrepreneur "you think a lot more carefully, and you worry a lot more."

By October 1994, Ferguson had assessed the potential of the Internet, and therefore, of his product idea. "The rise of the Internet represents the most fundamental transformation in information technology since the development of personal computers," he wrote in a white paper.

> We are witnessing the emergence of an open, distributed, global information infrastructure, and at the same time, inexpensive servers, fast networks, client-server technology, and visual software tools usable by non-programmers are transforming the strategic use of information by organizations. Taken together, these developments offer an opportunity to revolutionize information services and electronic commerce, generating both an enormous business opportunity and a chance to vastly improve access to information for everyone.

By this point, Ferguson also well understood the Internet's limitations, and particularly, that services on its most accessible part, the World Wide Web, were difficult to create. Establishing data sources (called home pages) still required expensive custom programming. He was convinced more than ever that there was a market opportunity for a powerful, easy-to-use, and inexpensive software package that could enable anyone to develop and operate sophisticated Web services—without any programming whatsoever. "We do not require that everybody learn typesetting and printing in order to write a book," he said, "we should not restrict electronic publishing to those who can write computer programs." Furthermore, the market opportunity was extremely exciting. Expanding 20% per month, the World Wide Web was the fastest growing technology in industrial history. He noted, "To be part of that in a deep way is worth doing." An engineer remarked about Ferguson's input in the product design process:

> It's an asset for Charles that he is not a technical person, but a visionary kind of guy. His ideas know no bounds. The most amazing thoughts pop out of his mouth. Eighty percent of those are not achievable by humans in this century, but the twenty percent that are achievable are things that someone else may not have thought of if they were bound by technical stuff. His pushing us and our pushing back led us to an idea for a software product that is light-years ahead of our potential competitors.

Seeking Venture Capital

Ferguson financed Vermeer's initial operating expenses while the development engineers worked without compensation. However, by the fall of 1994, the company had reached a stage where it needed a significant infusion of capital in order to grow rapidly enough to have a meaningful impact on the Internet market. Ferguson and Forgaard ruled out seeking a corporate sponsor because an exclusive arrangement with one company would run counter to their commitment to open access. Ferguson's extensive industry contacts enabled access to some of the best venture capital firms (VCs) in high technology. To maintain maximum leverage, he dealt with two competing syndicates, the primary of which consisted of Sigma Partners, Matrix Partners, and Atlas Venture. The firms typically concentrated on financing high technology businesses in expanding markets of $100 million or more. Their initial investments ranged from $500,000 to $2 million.

In October 1994, when Ferguson and Forgaard first visited the VCs, they only had the design and specification in hand, and a mockup of what the software would do written in Visual Basic. "We would confidently stride into a VC's office and give our pitch," Forgaard recalled. The VC's were prepared to be choosy: "You get to make two or three new investments per year," said one, "therefore you have to pick your projects fairly carefully." Ferguson recalled these interactions as "perhaps only slightly less unpleasant than being in the middle of a nuclear war."

Initially the VC's were skeptical about Vermeer's idea, not knowing much about the World Wide Web, and thinking that the idea was too big for a small team to be able to put together. However, their receptiveness grew, not only because of enthusiasm about the Internet, but also because of the quality of Vermeer's presentation. Said one VC:

> The presentation showed a tremendous depth of knowledge of the Internet, and a clear vision as to what the product space would be. Probably the most compelling thing was that Randy showed us a demonstration of the product. It was very clear what the benefits were, versus today's methods of solving the problems they are addressing.

Ferguson projected the sales of the first-generation product targeted at professional users and businesses at $50 million per year, with potential revenues from second- and third-generation products at more than $500 million annually. (See **Exhibit 1** for Vermeer's Business Plan.)

Overseeing the Development Work

Despite the fact that they were impressed with the fact that Ferguson had identified a real opportunity and had selected a top-notch development team, the VC team had doubts about backing a company staffed by people who lacked operational experience. "They had a lot of strong individual technical contributors," commented one, "which was actually a plus to the opportunity. But in terms of management structure, they were all warriors with no commander." They began to push Ferguson and Forgaard to appoint a seasoned person as vice president of engineering to oversee the development work.

Ferguson and Forgaard hired Frank Germano to fill the job. (See **Exhibit 2** for bio-data of the key members of Vermeer's management team.) Germano had been Forgaard's boss at Beyond, and the two thought highly of each other. Besides, two of the VC's had also invested in Beyond. They knew Germano personally and respected him. A seasoned veteran of nearly 30 years of software development and management, Germano was excited about the product's potential, and about the prospect of working with Forgaard and Schulert, both of whom he respected highly. With Ferguson, his relationship was less sanguine. "I'm an operations guy. Charles is a thinker. And there is a natural clash there," he said. Germano began working on weekends to get engineering started on the right foot. "If you let bad habits settle in too early, it's very difficult to undo them," he said.

The VCs' Proposal

After considerable give and take about what the appropriate pre-money valuation of the business was, Marcuvitz called Ferguson in mid-January with the Sigma-Matrix-Atlas offer of an initial infusion of $4 million capital in exchange for 51% of company stock and two of the four board seats. See **Exhibit 3** for the proposed equity structure after the first round of financing.

The financing decision would be contingent on Ferguson's addressing the VCs' concerns. The VCs were opposed to the idea of having a second development team in California this early in Vermeer's life. "You can't build a distributed company from day one," one of them said. "You have to have ten people in a room because that's where all the synergy is in building those bonds."

More important, the VCs wanted to recruit an outsider as Vermeer's first CEO. Although everyone felt that Ferguson had done a great job in outlining the core opportunity and assembling a team to get the job done, his lack of operational experience weighed against him. As one VC put it, "Why would you put a lot of money into a company and see whether Charles could potentially learn how to be a CEO?" The VCs offered to vest half of Ferguson's stock immediately upon the hiring of a new CEO.

Ferguson promised to get back to Marcuvitz within the next few days. Ferguson had wanted to be Vermeer's first CEO. He had already hired a vice president of engineering to oversee the operations side of development. As he put the phone down, he wondered whether to proceed further on the deal with the VCs or to pull back and reopen negotiations with the other VC syndicate.

EXHIBIT 1 | Vermeer's Business Plan

Fiscal Year[a]:	1994/95	1995/96	1996/97	1997/98	1998/99	1999/00
(US $000)						
Revenues	0	2,700	7,556	17,153	36,541	74,079
Gross Profit	0	1,930	5,625	13,141	27,731	55,155
Operating Expenses						
Payroll	2,090	3,274	4,446	6,545	9,820	14,740
Contractors Fees	225	35	35	35	35	35
Advertising	450	500	500	500	500	500
Recruiting	267	21	159	298	446	638
Medical	139	210	285	425	635	935
Total opex	3,813	4,859	6,322	8,712	12,451	18,059
Taxes	0	0	0	1,927	6,799	16,508
Net income	(3,813)	(2,929)	(698)	2,502	8,480	20,588
Return on sales (%)	0	0	0	14.6	23.2	27.8
Common shares (000)	5,117	6,935	6,935	6,935	6,935	6,935
EPS ($)	0	0	0	0.36	1.22	2.97

[a] Fiscal year ends October 31.

Source: Vermeer

EXHIBIT 2 | Bio Data of Key Members of Vermeer's Management Team

Charles H. Ferguson, co-founder, Chairman

At 39, Ferguson was a leading authority on comparative corporate strategy, national industrial systems, and global competition in the information technology sectors. Since 1982, he had served as an independent consultant and strategist for leading high-tech companies, including Motorola, Apple, and Intel. Ferguson had authored a prize-winning article in the *Harvard Business Review* on the US semiconductor industry in 1988. In 1993, he co-authored with Charles R. Morris, *Computer Wars: The Fall of IBM and the Future of Global Technology,* named one of the Top 10 business books of the year by *BusinessWeek*. Ferguson held a BA in mathematics from the University of California at Berkeley, and a Ph.D. in political science from the Massachusetts Institute of Technology (MIT). Currently a director of the Alliance Technology Fund, Ferguson had been a postdoctoral research associate at the MIT Center for Technology, Policy, and Industrial Development, and a software technology analyst at IBM's Santa Teresa Laboratory.

Randy Forgaard, co-founder and Chief Technology Officer

Forgaard was a key contributor to the development of BeyondMail, an award-winning electronic mail software product of Beyond Inc. He was also the architect of a wide range of PC and UNIX applications and had managed teams in the development of commercial and customized applications. Prior to joining Beyond, Forgaard had been a development project leader at Addax Inc., where he designed software for airline personnel scheduling systems. He had also been the president of a software development and consulting firm acquired by Addax. Forgaard had also served as a programmer and consultant to Lotus Development Corp., and to MIT's Project Athena. He held SB and SM degrees in Computer Science from MIT.

Frank Germano, Jr., Vice President of Engineering

After nearly 30 years in systems development and development management, Germano joined Vermeer from Banyan, where he was director of messaging development when Banyan acquired Beyond. Prior to Beyond, where he was vice president of Engineering, Germano spent four years at Lotus Development Corporation, where he directed the development of 123/G and other advanced Lotus products. Before Lotus, he held senior software and management positions with Apollo Computer, Digital Equipment Corporation, and several end-user organizations. Germano received his BS in Engineering from Cornell University, an MBA from Stanford University, and a Ph.D. in computer science from the University of Pennsylvania.

Andy Schulert

Schulert had spent 15 years in software engineering, progressing from developer to group leader, to company founder, acquiring technical expertise in distributed and object-oriented systems. He earned a BS in Computer Science from MIT in 1979, and in March 1989, co-founded Alfalfa Software and developed an e-mail package for UNIX that supported the Internet and other standards. When the company dissolved, he consulted with DEC and Siemens Nixdorf. In 1988/1989, he researched, designed, and prototyped the graphics and user-interface components of a software platform for multimedia distributed groupware applications for ON Technology. Prior to that he led the design and implementation of two generations of a user interface management system at Apollo. Prior to that, he had worked in an advanced development group at DEC on software for engineering workstations, specializing in user interfaces, graphics, and networks.

Peter Amstein

Prior to joining Vermeer, Amstein was a staff engineer at Metaphor, in Mountain View, California. He was developing Capsule, a personal productivity tool for Windows that allowed users to automate many routine processes with simple drag and drop visual programming. He was also senior engineer on DIS, a large decision support system that included database query, spreadsheet, word-processing, reporting, charting, and data transformation. Prior to that he was at Pixar and Vicom Systems as software engineer, and prior to that with National Oceanic and Atmospheric Administration, leading a software team in the design and implementation of a prototype advanced weather forecasting workstation. Amstein held a BS in Electrical Engineering and Computer Science from the University of Colorado and the Georgia Institute of Technology.

EXHIBIT 3 | Proposed Equity Structure After First Round of Financing

Owner	% share-holding
Venture Capitalists	51
Charles Ferguson	13
Randy Forgaard	5
Frank Germano	4
Other employees	27

The capital structure would be as above assuming full vesting by all the parties.

Half of Charles Ferguson's stock would vest immediately upon the appointment of a new CEO; the rest would vest after 5 years.

The other individual shareholders would also have a vesting period of 5 years.

None of the other employees would own more than 2% of the stock each.

Source: Vermeer

Endeavor—Determining a Growth Strategy

Everybody thinks we're crazy.

—Linda Rottenberg, Cofounder and CEO, Endeavor (1997)

Endeavor's model is an ideal exit strategy for troubled economies. Our work in Argentina is an example of how Endeavor can help create stable, local private sector infrastructure.

—Peter Kellner, Cofounder, Endeavor (2002)

Endeavor has played an instrumental role in promoting entrepreneurship as a tool for development. It is a model that should be replicated around the world.

—James D. Wolfensohn, President, The World Bank (2001)

On May 21, 2002, Linda Rottenberg surveyed the map of the world hanging on the wall behind her desk. Rottenberg was the CEO of Endeavor, a nonprofit organization dedicated to stimulating and supporting entrepreneurship in emerging markets. In five years, Endeavor had succeeded in building largely self-sustaining local operations in five Latin American countries: Chile, Argentina, Brazil, Uruguay, and, most recently, Mexico. During this time, Endeavor had screened over 4,000 entrepreneur candidates from these countries and elected 119 outstanding entrepreneurs from 64 companies into the Endeavor Entrepreneur Network. These entrepreneurs, in turn, were responsible for generating over 6,000 new jobs and over $400 million in revenues during a period of general economic decline and increasing unemployment throughout the region. Endeavor was widely praised for identifying outstanding entrepreneurial ventures, helping them succeed, and building a local infrastructure to support entrepreneurship.

Professor William A. Sahlman and Dean's Fellow Taz Pirmohamed wrote the original version of this case, "Endeavor," HBS No. 803-075, which is being replaced by this version prepared by Professor William A. Sahlman and Senior Lecturer Michael J. Roberts. HBS cases are developed solely as the basis for class discussion. Cases are not intended to serve as endorsements, sources of primary data, or illustrations of effective or ineffective management.

In one week, Rottenberg would lead a discussion with members of Endeavor's Global Advisory Board. Key topics for that discussion included a discussion of where Endeavor should next seek to establish operations, as well as how to fund the nonprofit's growth.

After a relatively hand-to-mouth existence in its first few years, Endeavor had succeeded in establishing what it referred to as its "country benefactor" model. In Rottenberg's words: "This approach requires local businesspeople in the host country to sign up and support the local effort not only financially, but with their wealth of knowledge, experience, and contacts."

As the local funding model had become successful, it became more difficult to raise funding for Endeavor Global, the New York-based headquarters of the organization: "The local benefactors really take a lot of ownership of the effort so, of course, they want the funds they have raised to stay in-country."

At the same time as Rottenberg and her team were challenged by the funding climate, they were eager to expand the geographic footprint of Endeavor. In Rottenberg's words:

> We want to expand beyond Latin America, in part because we want to prove that the model works in other parts of the world and, in part, because we believe in the power of our model to truly help people. But it is hard to decide where to go next: Spain, India, Africa, and Turkey are all on the radar screen. I know these places differ dramatically on all sorts of dimensions, and we need to think through this choice very carefully.

Rottenberg stared at the map. She was justifiably proud of Endeavor's accomplishments to date and ready to take it to the next stage. At the same time, she had the all-too-familiar knot in her stomach that always tightened when resources were low. Just then, Robin Pinckert, Endeavor's CFO, came to her office to review preliminary financial projections that would help inform discussions with the Global Advisory Board.

Endeavor—The Early Years

Endeavor grew out of a "coalescing of the minds" of its two founders, Linda Rottenberg and Peter Kellner, in mid-1996. (See **Exhibit 1** for background information on Rottenberg and Kellner.) At 27, Kellner had a track record of successful entrepreneurship, having co-founded Russia's largest Western-managed independent oil company, Khanty Mansisyk Oil Corporation, and Hungary's first interdisciplinary, nongovernmental, environmental organization—the Environmental Management and Law Association. Rottenberg, then 28, had graduated from Yale Law School and was working for Ashoka[1] in Latin America, where she learned first-hand how entrepreneurial nonprofits provided innovative solutions to global social problems.

At the same time, there was a growing awareness of the role that entrepreneurship could play in an economy. In the United States, to illustrate, a steady stream

---

[1] Bill Drayton founded Ashoka in 1980 to promote entrepreneurship in the social services sector. (See http://www.ashoka.org for more information.)

of research revealed the importance of entrepreneurship to that economy. Research indicated that:

- Entrepreneurs were responsible for 67% of inventions and 95% of all radical innovations since World War II.[2]

- Entrepreneurial firms were responsible for a disproportionate share of job creation. During the period from 1980 to 1997, the Fortune 500 companies lost more than 5 million jobs, while 350,000 "fast growth firms" (out of 6,000,000 U.S. businesses) created two-thirds of all new jobs.[3]

- Due in part to these factors, researchers described a strong correlation between entrepreneurial activity and economic growth. In the words of one researcher: "holding all other factors constant, entrepreneurial activity appears to explain half the difference in growth in GDP."[4] (See **Exhibit 2a**.)

While working in Latin America, Rottenberg noticed the lack of an infrastructure for entrepreneurship and concluded that its absence had significantly impeded new enterprise development. In her words: "Job creation is the key to getting traction in most other kinds of improvement in society, and entrepreneurship is the key to job creation." Kellner, then a first-year student at Harvard Business School, met Rottenberg when she was recruiting MBA students for Ashoka. They discussed the role of entrepreneurship in stimulating wealth creation and employment opportunities in Latin America. Kellner recalled:

> Most emerging-market countries,[5] unfortunately, have not benefited from entrepreneurship. An Inter-American Development Bank (IDB) study[6] pointed out that entrepreneurs in emerging markets faced a number of additional hurdles. (See **Exhibit 2b** for some excerpts from the study.) Their countries often lacked a strong tradition of entrepreneurial initiative and risk taking. They had few role models, colleagues, or support networks for mentorship or encouragement. They had limited access to information and case studies on the entrepreneurial process. Finally, they had difficulty raising capital to grow their companies since local capital markets were significantly underdeveloped and venture capital was scarce, if available at all.

Following their initial research, Kellner and Rottenberg concluded that there was a significant gap between the micro-credit programs and larger-scale government finance projects. In Rottenberg's words: "There was nothing that attempted to address

---

[2]"Embracing Innovation," National Commission on Entrepreneurship White Paper, p. 3.

[3]Ibid., pp. 3–4.

[4]Andrew Zacharakis, William Bygrave, and Dean Shepherd, "Global Entrepreneurship Monitor, National Entrepreneurship Assessment, United States of America, 2002," Kauffman Center for Entrepreneurial Leadership, p. 8.

[5]"Emerging market" referred to countries that were making significant progress with their economic development, and were on the cusp of becoming developed economies.

[6]The IDB was the oldest and largest regional multilateral development institution. It was established in 1959 to help accelerate economic and social development in Latin America and the Caribbean. See http://www.iadb.org for more information.

the barriers to entrepreneurship in a holistic way. We decided to create Endeavor to bridge this gap."

Kellner and Rottenberg attracted two key partners as founding board members: Jason Green, a successful venture capitalist at U.S. Venture Partners, a Silicon Valley venture capital firm, and Gary Mueller, a successful entrepreneur whose firm, Internet Securities, focused on companies in emerging markets. (See **Exhibit 1** for biographies.) Rottenberg described people's initial reactions to the Endeavor concept:

> When we launched Endeavor, the finance professionals we talked to thought that Peter and I were out of our minds! We were in the midst of the Asian financial crisis and many emerging markets had just collapsed. In the United States, people were skeptical about Endeavor's ability to find competent entrepreneurs in Latin America and other emerging markets. From their perspective, they simply didn't exist—and even presuming we could find local entrepreneurs, U.S. finance experts were skeptical that we could really cultivate a climate of entrepreneurship. To make matters worse, the majority of Latin American business leaders had never heard of venture capital or entrepreneurship. And they weren't willing to trust young entrepreneurs with their money or business savvy.

Rottenberg and Kellner listened carefully to people's objections and concerns—and then set out to develop the Endeavor operating model and to raise seed financing.

By mid-1997, Rottenberg and Kellner had formally established Endeavor as a non-profit organization and set out to test their pioneering global development model in Latin America. They set up the proverbial "garage" in Rottenberg's home in New York and traveled to Chile and Argentina for additional information gathering. Kellner provided $300,000 in seed financing and offered to supply an additional $200,000 if Rottenberg could find a matching investment. Rottenberg—in search of "smart money"—approached Stephan Schmidheiny, a highly regarded Swiss business leader and international philanthropist of the AVINA Group,[7] to match Kellner's contribution. AVINA agreed to give Endeavor $200,000 plus an additional $20,000 for each entrepreneur selected, up to a total of $300,000. Schmidheiny also took a seat on Endeavor's board. (See **Exhibit 1** for bio.)

The First Endeavor—Chile

In 1997, Rottenberg and Kellner developed a framework for evaluating which countries should join the Endeavor network. They determined that an ideal Country Affiliate was characterized by 1) a relatively robust business environment; 2) a strong university system; 3) a viable local market; 4) political stability; and 5) the presence of highly networked private business leaders who shared Endeavor's vision and values. Rottenberg and Kellner selected Chile as the first Country Affiliate. Rottenberg recalled:

> We decided on Chile for two reasons: I had experience and local contacts in Chile from my time with Ashoka, and Chile did not have an overwhelming size or economy. Strictly adhering to our country-selection criteria was less important than finding the right place to

---

[7]AVINA was the nonprofit equivalent of a venture capitalist—a "venture philanthropist" that donates money to nonprofits yet insists on measuring impact. See http://www.avina.net for more information.

pilot our model. Over the next year, we worked hard at building Endeavor Chile and managed to find some really great entrepreneurs, but we didn't have a local board in place. Our original concept was to build a strong local board to help us with fundraising and the contacts we needed to help our entrepreneurs. But because of the somewhat politicized nature of the business landscape, we decided that getting some strong people on our board would alienate others we wanted to work with. So we simply proceeded without a local board.

While the early experience was a struggle, Endeavor nonetheless managed to make progress, selecting nine entrepreneurs from five companies in the January 1998 selection panel in Santiago. (See **Exhibit 3** for the selection criteria used by Endeavor.)

During these early years, Endeavor established and refined several components of its operational model. First, Endeavor developed a multi-step model for transforming its work with a handful of select entrepreneurs into a broader venture-friendly environment and culture of entrepreneurship. (See **Exhibit 4** for details of this approach.)

Early Endeavor Success Stories—OfficeNet and Patagon.com

Although Endeavor struggled in Chile, the organization was successful in identifying some attractive entrepreneurial teams to support. Early on, Endeavor had started to work with two young Argentine entrepreneurs, Andy Freire and Santiago Bilinkis, who aspired to create the "Staples" of Latin America. They were introduced to Endeavor by Martin Bohmer, an Argentine lawyer, whom Rottenberg had met at Yale Law School. In January 1998, at Endeavor's first selection panel, Freire and Bilinkis were selected to be Endeavor Entrepreneurs. Their business plan for OfficeNet resembled the office-supply companies in the U.S. but targeted geographies in the Southern Cone. Within a few years, they had built up a successful business with over $50 million in revenues. Endeavor had helped them negotiate a sensible early-stage deal and later arranged growth capital from a Brazilian private equity firm. In return, Freire and Bilinkis used their success to educate other aspiring entrepreneurs, one of whom became CEO of Patagon.com, which was another Endeavor success story.

Wences Casares, 24, had developed a business plan for a Latin American personal financial management portal named Patagon.com. After his plan was rejected by 33 venture capitalists, he was finally given his first break: he was selected as an Endeavor Entrepreneur in Endeavor's second selection panel in August 1998. Rottenberg accompanied him on his next fundraising trip, which resulted in the receipt of four term sheets. With the coaching of several Endeavor Entrepreneurs and board members, Wences signed an agreement with Chase-Flatiron to fund his operation. Less than two years later, Casares sold approximately 75% of his company to Banco Santander for over $700 million.

Rolling Out the Model

Expanding to Argentina

As the Chilean Affiliate began to gain some traction, Endeavor turned to Argentina to be its next Country Affiliate. Rottenberg explained: "I knew if we had success in one country, people would say it was luck. We needed to prove that the model was replicable.

OfficeNet was a company with strong ties—indeed, headquartered—in Argentina, so when we selected it, we were already looking towards Argentina."

Rottenberg went back to Schmidheiny to seek new funding from AVINA. Schmidheiny agreed to provide $200,000 on the condition that the sum was matched with local funding. In August 1998, Rottenberg convinced Eduardo Elsztain, a successful entrepreneur, to commit seed funding to Endeavor Argentina and to chair that country's board. Elsztain was successful in bringing others aboard as Country Benefactors, and in August 1998 Endeavor ran its first selection panel in Argentina, selecting eight entrepreneurs (including Casares) from an additional five companies.[8]

Rethinking the Funding Model

By 1999, Endeavor had received $75,000 from the World Bank, and the Inter-American Development Bank had pledged between $1.8 and $2.1 million over three years. While the development banks had significant capital resources and offered widespread distribution channels to promote Endeavor's activities, both were perceived as slow and bureaucratic organizations. Still, Endeavor's funding model was not yet sustainable. Rottenberg explained:

> We had a tough time raising money in the U.S.; less than 1.3% of U.S. philanthropy goes to international causes. People have a hard time giving money when they perceive the impact to be distant. And most of the development organizations that exist, like the World Bank, have a "poorest of the poor" mindset. Latin America and the Caribbean receive, in total, about half the official development assistance of sub-Saharan Africa. We talked to the World Bank, and other foundations, and they initially perceived our focus on "emerging markets" as elitist. They said, "go to Africa and work in Malawi" or they said, "work with women-owned businesses or environmental businesses." Every foundation has its own, very specific focus, and we didn't fit into their funding frameworks. In addition, once you do prove that something is effective in the nonprofit sector, no one wants to fund it to take it to scale.
>
> I decided it would be easy to succumb to "mission creep" and to go where the money was, but fundamentally, I really believed in our mission and our model, and had seen enough evidence that it could work. I was resolved to stay the course on our own terms.

In addition to funding issues in the local Country Affiliates, the global office was operating on a very tight budget and shaved costs by making extensive use of volunteers. Moreover, the fact that local offices couldn't raise enough operating capital was draining the global office budget. If Endeavor Global remained on its then-current path, it anticipated accumulating an operating deficit of $850,000 in the short term, and a total budgetary shortfall of $2.8 million by 2001. Endeavor knew the problem would persist until stable sources of long-term financing could be raised.

In April 1999, Rottenberg hired Robin Pinckert (HBS '96) as Endeavor's Chief Operating and Chief Financial Officer to help address the issue of financial sustainability.

---

[8]While the later Endeavor model evolved to independently incorporate and fund each of the Country Affiliates, the first several years of the Chilean and Argentine ventures were simply run as extensions of Endeavor Global.

(See **Exhibit 5a** for management biographies and **Exhibit 5b** for Endeavor board members.) Soon after her arrival, Pinckert helped frame several funding options for Endeavor in preparation for the Global Advisory Board (GAB) meeting in May 1999. These included:

- **Fee for Service**   Under this model, Endeavor start-ups would be required to pay for value-added services. A potential fee structure included annual membership fees ranging from $25,000 to $50,000, plus broker fees paid to Endeavor for introducing entrepreneurs to investors. Several advisory board members liked its market-driven approach, but Rottenberg worried that entrepreneurs would not have the liquidity to pay these fees themselves, and that serving as a broker with financing sources would present a conflict of interest.

- **Endeavor Seed Capital Fund**   Under this model, Endeavor would launch a seed fund managed by professional venture capitalists such that half of the carried interest or "carry" would be given to Endeavor. Rottenberg and many board members were concerned that a fund would divert Endeavor resources away from facilitating entrepreneurship and would alienate stakeholders and the local business community, since Endeavor would lose its transparency as a "neutral party" with entrepreneurs and investors.

- **Launch an Internet Company, Affiliate, or Spin-off**   Under this option, Endeavor would spin off a for-profit Internet company similar to Garage.com. Again, Rottenberg and the board felt that such a model compromised Endeavor's ability to act as a neutral broker on behalf of entrepreneurs and would divert resources away from Endeavor's main role of facilitating entrepreneurship.

Ultimately, Rottenberg and the board settled on the Country Benefactor model. Under this model, Endeavor Global would identify Country Benefactors who would support the first four years of local operating costs, amounting to approximately US$1.8–$2.5 million, depending on country size and currency exchange rate. The funds would be secured up-front through written pledges prior to Endeavor accepting a new Country Affiliate. Over the longer term, however, Endeavor hoped to raise more permanent funding through a local endowment fund; upon selection into Endeavor's network, entrepreneurs would be asked to donate 2% of nondilutable[9] founders' equity into the country endowment fund. Thus, after the first four years of operations, each Country Affiliate was expected to be on the path to self-sustainability.

In terms of helping to fund headquarters operations for Endeavor Global, each Country Affiliate would be required to pay Endeavor Global a management fee of up to 25% of the total initial amount raised through the Country Benefactors. This management fee allocation, paid over the first four years of operations, covered start-up, launch, training, and ongoing services provided to the Country Affiliate. (This amount was included in the $1.8–$2.5 million budget raised through the Country Benefactors.) After the initial four-year Country Benefactor term ended, Affiliates would only be required to pay an annual $15,000 network membership fee.

---

[9]That is, the equity would not be diluted by subsequent rounds of financing, and would thus require the issuance of additional shares to Endeavor in subsequent rounds.

As part of the model, Endeavor selected a managing director for each new Country Affiliate. At the same time, Endeavor developed a franchise-like agreement laying out the roles and responsibilities of the local Country Affiliates as well as Endeavor Global. (See **Exhibit 6** for details on these roles and responsibilities.)

Rottenberg explained Endeavor's decision to select the Country Benefactor funding model:

> Our major goal was to remain aligned with the entrepreneurs' interests. People said we were crazy not to start a fund or a for-profit business. But either option would have undermined our neutral and trustworthy role in the local economy. Furthermore, if we had started a fund, we feared we might deter highly skilled business leaders from volunteering their time and energy to our organization, since they might then view Endeavor as "competition" to their own investment funds or as having a conflict of interest. Moreover, all the evidence we had seen so far suggested that raising local funding really got the local businesspeople committed. Finally, there were other reasons not to start a fund—there are very few exit options in Latin America since only a limited number of trade sales and IPOs occur every year. In sum, the Country Benefactor model was a strong fundraising platform that didn't compromise our neutrality or operating model.

Implementing the New Funding Model

Following the May 1999 meeting, the Global Advisory Board challenged Rottenberg to implement the new funding model in Brazil, a much larger country than either Chile or Argentina. By December 1999, Endeavor Global had succeeded in securing $1.8 million in commitments to fund Endeavor Brazil, including $350,000 of funding that could be used to support Endeavor Global.

In the case of Brazil, Endeavor was able to convince Carlos Sicupira, a successful entrepreneur, to provide all of the required funding for the operation, and then succeeded in attracting Marilia Rocca as managing director. (See **Exhibit 5a** for Rocca's bio.) Endeavor Brazil was formally launched in June 2000. Endeavor Brazil was committed to asking Endeavor Entrepreneurs for 2% of founders' equity or, in the case of more established ventures, 5% of the amount raised in any round that Endeavor helped facilitate (i.e., if a company raised $2 million, Endeavor would get 5% or $100,000 worth of equity—at the price established in that round).

As the Country Benefactor model gathered steam, Endeavor attempted to apply this model to Chile and Argentina. Yet in Chile, Endeavor was still having trouble raising local funds. Rottenberg explained:

> Finally, in May 2001, I decided we should pull out of Chile because we weren't making enough progress. At that point, the IDB and the Chilean government said, "Wait a minute! You can't leave!" They offered us $850,000 to finance the model. We turned down the money. We had nothing against government funding, but felt we couldn't lead with it. We still believed that government involvement must follow private sector involvement. Every newspaper reported how a "crazy woman" turned down funding from a government largely devoid of corruption. At that point, it wasn't clear how to proceed in Chile.
>
> But, after we turned down this government money, the phone started ringing off the hook—members of the Chilean private sector were calling. Using the Country Benefactor

model to guide the negotiations, the local office raised $1.5 million by early 2002. We also created a board comprised of 12 leaders from the Chilean private sector. Recently, the Chilean president called us to express his interest in speaking at an Endeavor workshop. In sum, the Country Benefactor model helped us turn Endeavor Chile into a success story.

In contrast, Endeavor Argentina didn't have any trouble raising local operating funds but wanted entrepreneurs to contribute cash, not equity, as there was almost no liquidity in the market. The Argentina office approached existing Endeavor Entrepreneurs and asked for cash contributions for a local endowment fund. Rottenberg explained:

> We launched our first Country Endowment in Argentina based on a matching system: local board members and businesspeople matched every donation from an entrepreneur. A local entrepreneur pledged $1 million to the local endowment (pending the sale of some of his assets) and a board member offered to match this pledge, on a cash basis, upon liquidation. While this was all great, it did highlight a continuing issue. Going back to successful entrepreneurs and asking them for cash contributions—as Endeavor "alumni"—put us in a precarious situation. We remained hopeful that getting the 2% equity pledge up front (i.e., the Brazilian model) would allow us to remain more in control of our destiny. But if we could not apply this system in Argentina, where "the ship had already sailed," then we would be certain to condition any future expansion to new countries upon adoption of the Brazilian model.

Further Expansion

In July of 2000, Francisco Ravecca (see **Exhibit 5a**), who had been helping with Endeavor's Argentina Affiliate, expressed an interest in bringing Endeavor to Uruguay. He developed backing for the idea within the Uruguayan government, including the president of the country. He succeeded in raising $350,000 in financing under the Country Benefactor model. On the basis of this commitment, Rottenberg was now comfortable going back to the IDB and accepted $1.8 million in backing from them, to be used in Chile, Uruguay, and Argentina. In March 2001, the first entrepreneur selection panel was run in Uruguay.

Finally, in 2001, several of the leading industrialists from Mexico approached Endeavor with the request that they open a Country Affiliate there. After being convinced that the support was real, Endeavor agreed to establish operations in Mexico, and by June 2002 Endeavor had succeeded in raising $2.5 million from some key Mexican business leaders to finance the first four years of local operations. The board hired Cesar Perez Barnes as that country's managing director. (See **Exhibit 5a** for Barnes's bio.)

Thus, by mid-2002, every Endeavor Country Affiliate had adopted the Country Benefactor funding model. While not every office had amassed a large local endowment, several Country Affiliates were closer to the goal of self-sustainability.

Snapshot: Brazil

As an example of the full range of activities undertaken by both Endeavor Global and a local Country Affiliate, consider Endeavor's operation in Brazil during 2001 and early 2002. This local affiliate began its activities in mid-2000, and by mid-2002, it had:

- Recruited a staff of six employees.
- Screened 1,811 companies and selected 30 Endeavor Entrepreneurs from 17 companies in eight industries.
- Fielded a "Venture Corps" of approximately 111 CEOs and senior advisors who helped mentor Endeavor's 30 entrepreneurs.
- Hosted 125 educational events attracting 10,330 attendees.
- Generated 462 press articles and 21 TV programs that featured Endeavor Entrepreneurs.
- Matched 44 U.S. MBAs with Endeavor companies for internships.

During 2001, Endeavor's 17 Brazilian companies generated $56 million in revenues, employed nearly 3,330 people, and had raised a total of $33 million in venture capital financing.

The Brazilian affiliate had also made great strides in developing educational content accessible to all of Brazil's entrepreneurs. Endeavor had licensed materials from several sources, including Harvard Business School, which it made available to the public. Endeavor transcribed the weekly workshops it hosted and made these available via the Web.

Meanwhile, Endeavor Global supported the Brazilian office through initial training on Endeavor's proprietary programs; ongoing eMBA recruitment; final-round interviews of Endeavor Entrepreneur candidates; consulting, editing, and coordination of entrepreneur profile documentation for Endeavor's semi-annual international selection panels; coordination and management of Endeavor's semi-annual international selection panels; global entrepreneur services programs; international networking; professional impact assessment; and sharing of best practices among the Endeavor Affiliate network.

Moving Forward

By May 2002 Endeavor had evolved into a well-functioning team, with a model for promoting entrepreneurship that could be rolled out in new countries. Endeavor could point to 6,000 jobs, $400 million in revenues, and a wide variety of other data that supported the impact it was having in Latin America. (See **Exhibit 7** for Endeavor's financial statements, and **Exhibit 8a** for an overview of Endeavor's accomplishments.) Endeavor believed it had learned what worked, and what did not.

Scores of individual ventures had received help from Endeavor, and it was clear that the entrepreneurs were prepared to re-invest in the network. (See **Exhibit 8b** for a representative list of entrepreneurs helped by Endeavor.) Already, entrepreneurs like Wences Casares of Patagon.com and Andy Freire and Santiago Bilinkis of OfficeNet were playing leadership roles at Endeavor. (See **Exhibit 9** for an assessment of the role played by Endeavor at Sepia, an Argentine cosmetics company.)

Global Expansion

Endeavor's successes in Latin America presented a new challenge for Rottenberg: how to expand the Endeavor model into new regions. The Endeavor model, largely driven by a sustained investment of human capital, was difficult to scale. In general, Endeavor Global maintained a close relationship with each new Country Affiliate during the first four years in order to support their growth and fundraising activities. As such, Endeavor insisted on carefully selecting the locale for each new Country Affiliate. Rottenberg explained:

> We have always believed that Endeavor should be a "pull" rather than a "push" organization. So many nonprofits try to push their answers on the local populations because they have the know-how. We have tried to avoid that kind of operating model. We believe that countries should pull us in. So, in selecting new Country Affiliates, we want a group of private sector leaders who have raised $2 million for local office operations and are willing to join the board. We also want local leaders to demonstrate commitment and passion for the Endeavor model.
>
> So far, groups in India, Turkey, Colombia, Venezuela, Spain, South Africa, Egypt, Jordan, and Bulgaria have attempted to pull us in. They have told us they want to build a thriving venture community "The Endeavor Way." Suddenly, it's like we're entertaining Requests for Proposals. Their enthusiasm has created a new problem: how should we decide between interested countries? And how should we select our next region?
>
> Different places are appealing for different reasons. (See **Exhibit 10a** for World Bank data on various countries, and **Exhibit 10b** for results of international entrepreneurship survey.) With Spain, the prospect of having a language in common with our Latin American organization is appealing. With Africa, the World Bank seems to be getting very interested in supporting our work there, and we do believe we could have a tremendous impact. In India, there is a tremendous base of entrepreneurial activity, and talent, to build upon. Turkey also has a thriving entrepreneurial sector, and we have immense support from members of Turkey's private sector.

Turkey also represented a chance to have a positive impact on a country with a large Muslim population. Kellner explained:

> After the September 11, 2001 terrorist attacks occurred, a lot of attention has been focused on the Muslim world. So far, the public has heard the government and the media call attention to a "good vs. evil" and "us vs. them" strategy. Endeavor has a unique opportunity to collaborate with a Muslim nation such as Turkey, to create a positive dialogue between Muslims and Americans. While Turkey meets all of Endeavor's selection criteria, it also represents a chance to have a strong social and political impact on the country. Although Endeavor is not driven by politics, it is an important secondary consideration. You can't have worked in international development without recognizing the political ramifications of your efforts. (See **Exhibit 10b** for data on entrepreneurial activity by country.)

Raising a Global Endowment Fund

Of course, growth came at a cost. While the Country Benefactor model was a means of ensuring funding for each local affiliate, it was only partially successful in providing the

TABLE A | Unit Level Incremental Country Expansion Expense Summary

Average Incremental Costs per Year to Support a New Country	
	$ per year
Search and Selection Support	$40,307
Educational Programs Support	53,720
Entrepreneur Services Support	60,639
Marketing/Education/Training Support	24,237
Information Technology Systems / Training Support	43,270
Management Support / Financial Controls	5,500
	$227,673

Source: Company.

funding for Endeavor Global's headquarters operations. In May 2002, Endeavor Global had a cash balance of $182,000 and an additional $700,000 in pledges connected with the organization's fundraising "gala" held in November each year. Still, the expense level for the headquarters operation was $1.6 to $1.7 million annually. (See **Exhibit 7** for Endeavor's historical financial statements.) Moreover, Rottenberg estimated that at least $250,000 per year was required to finance Endeavor Global's initial investment and management of each new Country Affiliate on an ongoing basis. (See **Table A,** above.)

In previous years, Endeavor Global had raised most of its revenues from the annual Endeavor gala event, an amount that was expected to approach $600,000 (net to Endeavor) in 2002. Still, Rottenberg felt that Endeavor Global needed to secure stable sources of revenue. After adoption of the new local funding model, the Global budget was no longer used to fund local country operations. However, the new funding model also hurt Global's fundraising capabilities because very few philanthropists or foundations from Endeavor's host countries wanted to fund overhead expenses for the New York headquarters. Rottenberg explained:

> The irony is that we have created a virtuous circle of philanthropy in Latin America—a continent that lacked a culture of philanthropy. By insisting that entrepreneurs give back to their local organizations, we have enlarged the philanthropic pie. Yet it is hard to raise money in New York for an international effort. While our Global board has been fabulous, they don't have the personal wealth to support us at this level. And in general, most philanthropists won't fund our Global headquarters for a couple of reasons. First, only 1% of the U.S. philanthropy goes to international organizations, even if the nonprofit is based in the U.S. Therefore, as a global, economic-development-focused nonprofit we have access to only 1% of total U.S. philanthropic dollars (over $200 billion in 2000). Second, we've been turned down by major U.S.-based foundations because we're not helping the "poorest of the poor." Foundations don't fund organizations that help the middle tiers of society, even if we are creating downstream jobs for women or poor people. Third, it is relatively easy to get seed capital to start a new nonprofit, but mezzanine and public financing are scarce.

Nobody is interested in taking a successful organization to scale. We learned that while the philanthropic sector has a tradition of funding proof of concept, it lacks a tradition of funding growth to help nonprofits scale.

In early 2002, Endeavor Global developed a base case financial scenario which limited its growth to that which could be funded from its existing funding model. Based on the assumption that Endeavor would add one new Country Affiliate in 2002—but no new countries thereafter—the scenario showed that Endeavor Global could break even with its existing funding model and fundraising effort. (See **Exhibit 11a** for this financial scenario.) Pinckert and Rottenberg also developed a growth scenario, which assumed that Endeavor Global would add one new country every year between 2003 and 2007. (See **Exhibit 11b** for this scenario.) This analysis showed that Endeavor Global would incur incremental expenses of nearly $250,000 in 2003, a sum that grew to $1.3 million in 2007 as more countries were added. Without additional funding sources, these expenses would drive a $600,000 annual deficit by 2007.

To fund this growth, Rottenberg and Pinckert decided to attempt to raise a Global endowment fund of $25 million by 2007. Any incremental new country expansion would be conditioned on raising sufficient funding for Endeavor Global to grow from a position of strength. In addition, Rottenberg and Pinckert contemplated whether Endeavor would need to reconfigure Endeavor Global's board to enable this next stage of growth.

* * * * *

Despite having accomplished so much in five years, Rottenberg couldn't stop worrying about the future of Endeavor. She and Kellner had created a very powerful model but did not want to stop there—they wanted to build a self-sustainable, global organization.

EXHIBIT 1 | Founding Board Biographies

Linda Rottenberg is CEO and Cofounder of Endeavor. Selected as one of the 100 "Innovators for the 21st Century" by *Time* magazine, as one of 100 "Global Leaders for Tomorrow" by the World Economic Forum in 2001, and as one of 40 leading social entrepreneurs by the Schwab Foundation, Linda has spent the past decade promoting entrepreneurship, philanthropy, and economic development in emerging markets. From 1994 to 96, she directed the Southern Cone expansion of *Ashoka: Innovators for the Public*, a global organization that pioneered the field of "venture philanthropy" by financing high-potential social entrepreneurs in over 30 developing countries. Previously, she designed and launched the first interdisciplinary Masters of Law program in Argentina with the Universidad de Palermo in Buenos Aires and managed the Yale Law School-U.S. A.I.D. Linkage Programs in Latin America. Linda is an active Term Member of the Council on Foreign Relations, a member of the World Economic Forum's steering committee on the Digital Divide, and a consortium member of a new Global Exchange for Social Investment (GEXSI). Linda received her J.D. from Yale Law School and B.A. magna cum laude in Social Studies from Harvard University.

Peter Kellner is Cofounder of Endeavor. Kellner cofounded Russia's Ural Petroleum Corporation, whose successor is Khanty Mansisyk Oil Corporation (KMOC); TheScience, a science and technology media company; the Environmental Management and Law Association (EMLA), Hungary's leading environmental management and law association; and Vectis Group, an investment consortium that restructured Critical Path, Inc. Peter is a Term Member, Council on Foreign Relations; a member of CFR's National Committee; and a North America Council member of Ashoka, an organization developing social entrepreneurship. Peter graduated from Princeton University with a degree from the Woodrow Wilson School, and he attended Harvard Business School and Yale Law School.

Gary Mueller is Director of Euromoney Institutional Investor, and Chairman and Chief Executive Officer of Internet Securities Incorporated (ISI), an online provider of financial and business information on the emerging markets. Gary founded ISI in 1994 and has led the company ever since. ISI currently has 220 employees in 19 countries and its subscription-based service covers 40 emerging markets, including Turkey, Brazil, Mexico, Russia, China, and India. The company has $16 million in annual revenues and is profitable. In 1999 Euromoney Institutional Investor, a FTSE 250 company, purchased ISI. Gary serves on the Board of Directors of Endeavor, The Fund for Civil Society in Russia, and Shackleton Schools. Gary is a graduate of Harvard College (1988) and Harvard Business School (1994). Gary was a Fulbright Scholar in Frankfurt, Germany, from 1988 to 1990.

Jason Green has been a Partner with U.S. Venture Partners since 1997, a leading Silicon Valley venture capital firm with over $2.5 billion under management. He currently serves on the Board of Directors of AvenueA (AVEA), Abilizer Solutions, Megapath Networks, and Nightfire Software, and was responsible for USVP's investment in Ask Jeeves (ASKJ). Prior to USVP, Jason completed a two-year program as a Ewing Marion Kauffman Fellow with Venrock Associates, the venture capital arm of the Rockefeller family. Before joining Venrock, Jason was awarded the Charles Williams Fellowship at Harvard's Graduate School of Business for post-graduate research in Entrepreneurship and Finance. Jason graduated cum laude with a B.A. in Economics from Dartmouth College and an MBA from Harvard where he graduated with distinction. Jason is the Chairman of the Kauffman Fellows Program, the leading educational fellowship focused on the venture capital process globally.

Stephan Schmidheiny was born in 1947. He received a Doctor of Law degree from Zurich University in 1976. During the 1980s, after successful restructuring of a fourth-generation family group, he built up a multinational conglomerate of broadly diversified business holdings. In 1995 he decided to focus business interests on Latin American forestry, building materials, and the pipe industry and to build up the AVINA foundation for the promotion of sustainable development in Latin America. In 1990, he was principal business advisor to the secretary general of the UN conference on Environment and Development in Rio. He established the Business Council for Sustainable Development (BCSD), published the best-selling book *Changing Course: A Global Business Perspective on Development*, and was named Honorary Chairman of the World Business Council for Sustainable Development. Honors include doctorate degrees from Rollins College, Universidad Católica Andres Bello, INCAE, and Yale University.

Source: Company.

EXHIBIT 2a

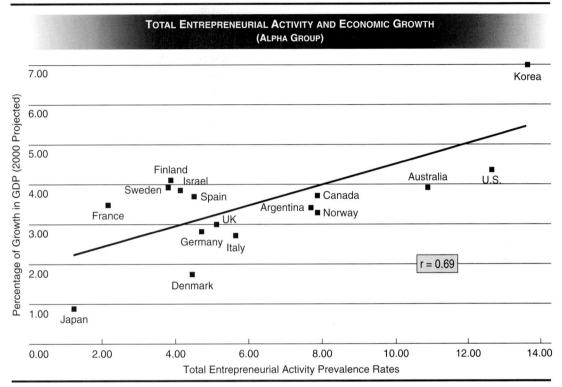

Source: Global Entrepreneurship Monitor, National Entrepreneurship Assessment, United States of America, 2000 Executive Report, p. 8. By Andrew L. Zacharakis, William D. Bygrave, and Dean A. Shepherd. © 2000 Ewing Marion Kauffman Foundation. Used with permission. All rights reserved.

EXHIBIT 2b | Excerpts from IDB Study

Main Motivations to Be an Entrepreneur	% of Firms
For self-realization	90
To improve income (flow)	75
To contribute to society	58
To be your own boss	55
To become wealthy (stock)	30
To become like an entrepreneur you admired in the media	10

Sources for Identifying Business Opportunities	% of Firms
Previous job/ task	78
Discussing with others	74
Trade fair	44
Magazine article	40
Academic papers	25
Newspaper article	24
Internet	13
TV Radio	8

Where Entrepreneurs Get Financing at the Start-up Stage	% of Firms
Savings of partners	64
Trade credits	44
Buying secondhand equipment	27
Bank loans	24
Relatives/ friends	21
Advances from clients	20
Bank overdraft	18
Public national institutions	14
Postponement of tax payments	13
Business angels	6
Local governments	2
Venture capital	2

Main Problems in the First Three Years	% of Firms
To get clients	74.5
To hire skilled workers	74
To finance and manage cash flow	74
To hire managers	35
To adapt products to the client	52
To get suitable suppliers	58
To have suitable equipment	58.5

Source: Adapted from "Entrepreneurship in Emerging Economies: The Creation and Growth of New Firms in Latin America and East Asia," Inter-American Development Bank, http://www.iadb.org/sds/sme, accessed December 13, 2002.

EXHIBIT 3 | Endeavor Selection Criteria

ENDEAVOR EVALUATION CRITERIA

1. Entrepreneurial Initiative

Candidates must possess the energy, passion, drive, and persistence to grow their businesses into successful companies. Candidates should have a track record of entrepreneurship and demonstrated execution abilities needed to mobilize the resources necessary to grow the business

2. Innovation and Creativity

Candidates should be change-makers with the ability to adapt to shifting and uncertain circumstances. Candidates should be building businesses with innovative products and services that establish new paradigms or transform industries within their countries or regions.

3. Role Model Potential

Candidates should have the potential to become dominant players in their markets or niches. In addition, candidates must demonstrate commitment to mentoring and knowledge sharing. Candidates also should possess the strong personal presence and leadership qualities to inspire others.

4. Development Impact

Candidates' businesses must have high growth potential within the countries or regions and should be likely to create substantial economic value through job creation, increased revenues, large-scale change, or, in relevant cases, IPO or other financial exit. Typically, Endeavor looks at entrepreneurs with companies in the range of U.S. $1MM–$15MM in sales at point of selection. With any "concept company," the business must show a clear revenue model for the future, but this will be the exception rather than the rule.

5. Ethical Fiber

Candidates must inspire instinctive trust. Reference checks must confirm the candidates' unquestionable integrity and respect for rule of law.

6. Mutual Value-Added

Endeavor must see a clear opportunity to increase candidates' chances for success through targeted advice on strategy, organization, or resource development. Candidates must be willing to listen, learn, and accept support from Endeavor. Candidates also must demonstrate a willingness to contribute to the sustainability of the local Endeavor entity through personal donations of time and equity/cash.

Source: Company.

EXHIBIT 4 | Endeavor Operating Model

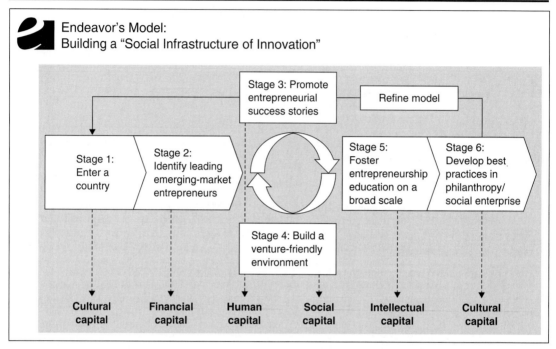

Endeavor's Model:
Building a "Social Infrastructure of Innovation"

The Endeavor model was built upon two core values: local ownership and global accountability. As such, the Endeavor operating model was designed to build sustainable local organizations within four years of entering a country.

Stage 1   Prior to launching a new country office, Endeavor recruited prominent members of the local business community to form a board and to help raise funds. The local board, in turn, selected a qualified Managing Director to lead the day-to-day operations under its supervision. Endeavor Global then trained the local management and licensed its proprietary methodology to the new Country Affiliate.

Stage 2   Endeavor engaged in a rigorous, multi-step 'Search & Selection' process to find the most promising entrepreneurs in each country. Each year, a group of Endeavor staff and volunteers reviewed hundreds of business plans submitted by entrepreneurs. The best candidates—entrepreneurs with the ability to take risks, create jobs, spread wealth, and inspire others with their passion—were selected as finalists. Then, an international jury selected several finalists per country. An international jury ensured that Endeavor Entrepreneurs met the same high standards across the globe.

Stage 3   Endeavor then deployed its professional network of seasoned business experts and MBAs to deliver targeted, demand-driven services to the selected entrepreneurs. Endeavor helped entrepreneurs sharpen their professional skills, develop their business strategies, locate strategic partners and raise capital. In this stage, Endeavor also used its entrepreneurs' success stories to inspire future entrepreneurs.

Stage 4   By leveraging its network of business professionals, angel investors, venture capitalists, and educators, Endeavor built a venture-friendly community. As a 'neutral intermediary,' Endeavor facilitated communication between entrepreneurs and investors. For example, Endeavor organized a conference in Argentina—attended by over 1,400 members of the local business community—in order to create a dialogue about entrepreneurship.

Stage 5   Endeavor collaborated closely with local universities to host public conferences and develop entrepreneurship curricula.

Stage 6   Finally, Endeavor encouraged its entrepreneurs to focus on their roles as community leaders, exposing them to best practices and hands-on training in philanthropy.

Source: Company.

EXHIBIT 5a | Management Biographies

Headquarters Management Team (in addition to Rottenberg)

Robin Pinckert is Endeavor Global's Chief Operating Officer and Chief Financial Officer. Prior to joining Endeavor she served as Director of Strategic and Financial Planning for the Medical Affairs Department of Oxford Health Plans, where she worked with the Chief Medical Officer to help design and implement Oxford's financial and operational turnaround plan. Before this, she was responsible for Medical Management operations in Oxford's largest membership region. Previously, she worked in early stage venture capital at Fidelity Capital, in a turnaround at RAX Restaurants, and in investment banking at Alex Brown & Sons. She holds an MBA from Harvard Business School, a B.A. with distinction in History and Economics from University of North Carolina, and is a member of Phi Beta Kappa.

Kimberly Braswell is a member of Endeavor's Global Advisory Board, Chair of Endeavor's Gala, and serves as senior advisor on strategy and fund development. Formerly an investment banker, first with Morgan Stanley and more recently with GH Venture Partners (the New York subsidiary of Schroeders), Ms. Braswell rejoins Endeavor after completing a World Bank Fellowship at the World Bank Executive Development Program at Harvard Business School and graduating from the Kennedy School of Government at Harvard University.

Blair Pillsbury is Endeavor Global's Vice President of Educational Programs. Most recently, Blair served as a senior associate at the Council of the Americas. Before this, Blair worked for two years in Latin American Loan Syndication and Credit Research at JP Morgan & Co. From 1993–1995, she worked for Equipo Pueblo, a nonprofit development organization based in Mexico City. Blair has a Masters in Public Affairs from the Woodrow Wilson School at Princeton University and a B.A. from Yale University.

Dan Cook is Endeavor's Vice President of Corporate Development. As a Fulbright Fellow to Santiago, Chile, Dan authored the leading investment publication for foreign investment in the Chilean entrepreneurial sector. Dan has worked as a Research Associate for development consultancy Abt Associates and as an analyst for the software developer, Sagemaker. He graduated cum laude from Fairfield University.

Country Affiliate Managing Directors

Patricio Campiani is Managing Director of Endeavor Argentina. Prior to joining Endeavor, Patricio cofounded and served as CEO of Advertium.com, a browser-based e-commerce solution for the buying and selling of media in Latin America. Before founding Advertium, Patricio cofounded and served as VP of Operations and Marketing for U.S.-based Argentine Natural Beef LLC. He also served as CEO of Brickell Key Foods, Corp., a thermo-processed beef trading operation based in Miami, Florida. Before that, he worked as senior manager for Citibank Argentina. Patricio holds a Bachelor of Science in Industrial Engineering from Argentina's Catholic University and was selected Endeavor Entrepreneur in the spring of 2000.

Gonzalo Miranda is Managing Director of Endeavor Chile, based in Santiago. Before joining Endeavor, Gonzalo founded Aflora, a well-recognized gift retailing brand in Chile. Prior to this entrepreneurial venture, Gonzalo served as VP of Business Development at Canal 13 Television, the leading broadcasting corporation in Chile. From that position he developed Señal Internet, the first multicasting service that brought news and entertainment to the Chilean audience through a mix of TV, Cable and Internet services. Gonzalo also cofounded in 1998 The Pet Network and worked for three years as real estate and financial consultant for the Abalos Group, a major Real Estate Holding company based in Chile. Gonzalo holds an MBA from the Haas School of Business at University of California, Berkeley, and a Masters and Bachelor of Science in Mechanical Engineering, both from Pontificia Universidad Católica de Chile.

(continued)

EXHIBIT 5a | Management Biographies (*continued*)

Cesar Perez Barnes is Managing Director of Endeavor Mexico, based in D.F. Prior to joining Endeavor, Mr. Perez Barnes was Director of Investments at Netjuice Capital. From 1997
to 1999, Mr. Perez Barnes worked for McKinsey & Company. Cesar Perez Barnes holds an
MBA from the MIT Sloan School of Management, and an M.S. in the Technology and Policy
Program (TPP) from the MIT School of Engineering.

Francisco Ravecca is Managing Director of Endeavor Uruguay. Before joining Endeavor,
Francisco founded Ravecca, Solari & Associates in 1999, a professional services firm that
supports entrepreneurs. In 1999 he launched DeRemate.com in Uruguay, holding the position of Managing Director. Between 1997 and 1999 he worked for BankBoston Argentina as
an Assistant Manager in the Specialized Industries Division. Previously, he worked for
Advent International at the company's headquarters in Boston, Massachusetts, performing
due diligence and deal sourcing for Private Equity deals both in the U.S. and Latin America.
Francisco holds a Juris Doctor Degree from the University of Uruguay and an MBA from
Harvard Business School.

Marilia Artimonte Rocca is Managing Director for Endeavor Brazil. Previously Expansion
Coordinator at Wal-Mart Brazil, she devised and implemented plans for the Buying, Operations, and Finance divisions during four new store openings. Earlier, as Director of Food-Co,
she opened/operated the Food Division of a super center. She holds a BA in Business from
Fundação Getulio Vargas College and MBA from Columbia Business School.

Source: Company.

EXHIBIT 5b | Endeavor Directors and Global Advisory Board Members, May 2002

ENDEAVOR GLOBAL BOARD OF DIRECTORS
Linda Rottenberg, Endeavor, Cofounder, Chairman and CEO
Peter Kellner, Vectis Group LLC, President; Endeavor, Cofounder
Wences Casares, Patagon.com, Chairman and CEO; Endeavor Entrepreneur
Ric Fulop, Into Networks, Founder; CFR Systems, Founder
Jason Green, US Venture Partners, General Partner
Gary Mueller, Internet Securities, Inc., President and CEO
Stephan Schmidheiny, AVINA and Business Council for Sustainable Development, Founder

ENDEAVOR ARGENTINA BOARD OF DIRECTORS
Eduardo Elsztain, IRSA, Chairman; Endeavor Argentina, President
Santiago Bilinkis, Officenet, Cofounder and CFO
Lisandro Bril, KORNFERRY, Senior Vice President
Wences Casares, Patagon, Chairman and CEO
Francisco de Narvaez, Fundación Creer y Crecer, Director
Maria Eugenia Estenssoro, Fundación Social Equidad, Managing Director
Linda Rottenberg, Endeavor Global, Inc., Cofounder, Chairman and CEO
Woods Staton, McDonald's Argentina, President
Oscar Toppelberg, Dolphin Interventures, President and CEO
Martin Varsavsky, Jazztel Comunicaciones, Founder and President

EXHIBIT 5b | *(continued)*

ENDEAVOR BRAZIL BOARD OF DIRECTORS

Carlos Alberto Sicupira, GP Investimentos, Partner; Endeavor Brazil, President

Paulo Cezar Aragão, Barbosa, Müssnich and Aragão, Partner; Fundação Estudar, Chairman

Peter Graber, Graber Sistemas de Seguranca, Founder and CEO

André Jakurski, JGP S.A, Executive Director and Founding Partner

Jorge Paulo Lemann, GP Investimentos, Partner

Linda Rottenberg, Endeavor Global, Inc., Cofounder, Chairman and CEO

Pedro Moreira Salles, Unibanco, Chairman

ENDEAVOR CHILE BOARD OF DIRECTORS

Alvaro Saieh B., Corp Group, Chairman; Endeavor Chile, President

Kathleen C. Barclay, Inversiones KCB Ltda, CEO

Carlos F. Cáceres, Chiletabacos, S.A., Chairman

Juan Claro G, Chairman, Emel

José Luis del Río G., Empresas Dersa, Chairman

Alfonso Gómez M., Virtualia, Chairman; Endeavor Entrepreneur

Cristian Larroulet V., Director, Instituto Libertad y Desarrollo

Juan Obach G., Inversiones Pathfinder, Chairman

Linda Rottenberg, Endeavor Global, Inc., Cofounder, Chairman and CEO

Salvador Said, Grupo Said, CEO

ENDEAVOR MEXICO BOARD OF DIRECTORS

Pedro Aspe, Protego Administradores S.A., Chairman and CEO; Endeavor Mexico, President

Emilio Azcárraga, Televisa S.A. de C.V., Chairman and CEO

Elías Cababie, GICSA, Chairman

Carlos Fernández, Grupo Modelo, CEO and Vice Chairman

Guillermo González, Protoma S.A. de C.V.

Linda Rottenberg, Endeavor Global, Inc., Cofounder, Chairman and CEO

Alexis Rovzar, White & Case, S.C., Executive Partner

Carlos Sales, Protego Administradores S.A., Director

Juan Pablo San Agustin, CX Ventures, CEO

Mauricio Santillán, Microsoft, Vice President, Intercontinental Region Microsoft Corporation

Marco Antonio Slim, Grupo Financiero Inbursa , Chairman

Lorenzo Zambrano, Cemex S.A. de C.V., Chairman and CEO

ENDEAVOR URUGUAY BOARD OF DIRECTORS

Alberto Brause Berreta, Partner, Jiménez de Aréchaga, Viana & Brause; Senator of the Republic

Leonardo Costa Franco, Under-Secretary of the Presidency of Uruguay

Michael Chu, Pegasus Venture Capital, Managing Director and Founding Partner

Francisco M. Ravecca Arana, Ravecca, Solari & Asociados, Senior Partner

Linda Rottenberg, Endeavor Global, Inc., Cofounder, Chairman and CEO

Source: Company.

EXHIBIT 6 | Role of Endeavor Global and Country Affiliates

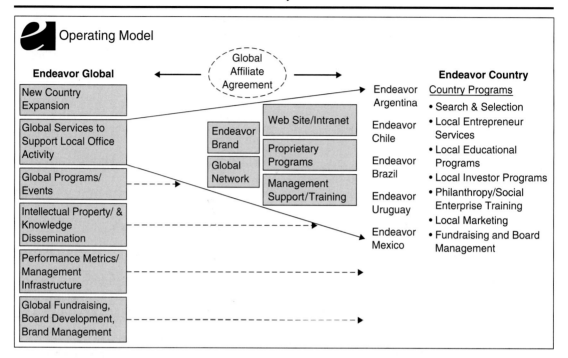

Endeavor operated a decentralized, hub-and-spoke system comprised of a Global Headquarters in New York City that coordinated the overall system and local offices responsible for managing the day-to-day operations of each Country Affiliate (e.g., Endeavor Argentina). The goal of the Endeavor organization was to encourage local innovation without sacrificing global standards.

In 2001, Endeavor Global drafted a "Global Affiliate Agreement" to govern the formal relationship between Endeavor Global and each Country Affiliate. This agreement laid out the rights and responsibilities of both parties, much like a franchise agreement. It also provided general guidelines for safeguarding the global Endeavor brand and intellectual property while ensuring that day-to-day operations were under the purview of local management and boards.

Endeavor Global

New Country Expansion   Endeavor Global played a leading role in researching new region expansion opportunities, identifying local country board members and funders, recruiting the local Managing Director, developing initial VentureCorps[a] teams, and supplying communication tools and training to local staff and board.

Servicing Endeavor Countries   Endeavor Global performed final reviews, identified global panelists for regional selection panels, organized entrepreneur workshops and road shows, recruited MBAs from top business schools to work with Endeavor Entrepreneurs, and managed the global MIS system.

Global Programs and Events   Endeavor Global coordinated global programs including the semi-annual international Selection Panels, Speaker Series, leadership conferences, and roundtable forums. In addition, Endeavor Global also hosted an annual Gala Awards Dinner highlighting the accomplishments of Endeavor venture philanthropists and entrepreneurs.

Intellectual Property and Knowledge Dissemination   Endeavor Global transferred best practices and program innovations to the global network through research, publications, and the Endeavor Web site.

EXHIBIT 6 | *(continued)*

Nonprofit Management and Performance Measurement   Endeavor Global created performance metrics and an IT infrastructure to measure Endeavor's "Social Return on Investment" (SROI) and produced "ROI" ("Return on Involvement") reports for Corporate Partners. Endeavor Global also produced educational videos and CD-ROM training tools.

Global Fundraising, Board Development, and Brand Management   Endeavor Global played a strong role managing all global fundraising initiatives (including local country fundraising). The parent organization was also responsible for managing the Global Board of Directors, the Global Advisory Board, and the Global Policy Committee. Finally, Endeavor Global was responsible for enforcing the Global Affiliate Agreements.

Endeavor Country Affiliates

Endeavor Country Affiliates were established as legally independent, nonprofit entities with their own board and local responsibilities including:

Search & Selection   Responsibilities included identifying and screening entrepreneur nominees, interfacing with local Nominator networks, and hosting semi-annual regional Selection Panels.

Local Entrepreneur Services   Each Country Affiliate managed a local VentureCorps network, hosted peer networking workshops, and organized local road shows.

Local Educational Programs   Country Affiliates also established partnerships with local universities to introduce entrepreneurship case studies to the curricula. In addition, local offices hosted public conferences and speaker series, and developed and maintained local Web sites.

Philanthropy and Social Enterprise Training   Country Affiliates also hosted roundtable discussions to introduce social responsibility and philanthropy to the local community. Local offices also linked Endeavor Entrepreneurs with Ashoka Fellows and AVINA leaders from the nonprofit sector.

Local Marketing   Local offices also helped build brand awareness by highlighting Endeavor Entrepreneur contributions to community improvement and by disseminating Endeavor information through local networks.

Source: Company.

[a]VentureCorps referred to a collection of individuals who volunteered time and resources to help Endeavor Entrepreneurs.

EXHIBIT 7 | Endeavor Global Historical Financial Statements (1997–2001)[a]

INCOME STATEMENT	1997	1998	1999	2000	2001
Revenue					
Entrepreneur fees		30,024	61,945	165,964	38,967
Country Benefactor Grants			117,000	107,486	271,368
Contributions & Donations	360,561	313,800	547,900	1,532,886	971,909
Grants	—	299,965	275,425	542,588	394,808
Interest and other income	1,404	1,799	6,574	(40,487)	(143,506)
In-kind donations	—	33,509	30,484	940,722	290,468
Total income	**361,965**	**679,097**	**1,039,328**	**3,249,159**	**1,824,014**
Expenses					
Search & Selection	46,200	105,337	74,259	106,225	96,411
eMBA	31,046	122,576	148,894	319,675	241,327
Entrepreneur Services	—	58,539	66,425	555,702	405,121
Venture Forum	—	89,145	72,242	163,066	103,096
Endeavor Network	43,651	95,413	108,245	383,732	160,845
Philanthropy & Social Enterprise				235,009	241,387
New Country Expansion	46,200	103,975	182,441	367,842	608,454
Total program expenses	**167,098**	**574,985**	**652,506**	**2,131,251**	**1,856,641**
Management and general	27,124	65,402	95,591	71,042	76,481
Fundraising and development	39,227	80,495	159,636	246,961	241,462
Total expenses	**233,448**	**720,882**	**907,733**	**2,449,254**	**2,174,584**
Net Income	**128,517**	**(41,785)**	**131,595**	**799,905**	**(350,570)**

BALANCE SHEET	1997	1998	1999	2000	2001
Assets					
Cash and cash equivalents	105,553	58,368	185,108	390,569	154,196
Contributions receivable				155,175	254,503
Investments, at fair value	0	0	0	155,803	1,100
Prepaid expenses	6,770	5,109	7,014	8,617	21,155
Fixed assets, net	46,035	46,335	36,011	359,366	310,575
TOTAL ASSETS	**158,358**	**109,812**	**228,133**	**1,069,530**	**741,529**
Liabilities and Net Assets					
Accounts payable, other accrued	0	7,738	8,283	34,831	61,432
Capital lease obligations	29,841	15,342	1,523	16,467	12,435
Unrestricted (or temp rest.) net assets	128,517	86,732	218,327	1,018,232	657,662
Permanently restricted net assets					10,000
TOTAL LIABILITIES	**158,358**	**109,812**	**228,133**	**1,069,530**	**741,529**

Source: Company.

[a]These data are for Endeavor Global (headquarters), which included Chilean operations through 2001. Each country, with the exception of Chile prior to 2001, was operated as a legally independent organization. The headquarters cash operating expenses averaged $1.6 to $1.7 million in 2000 and 2001 (excluding Endeavor Chile expenses, in-kind expenses, and depreciation).

EXHIBIT 7 | *(continued)*

1997–2001 Donors[a]
1997–2001 Cumulative Global Donations by Donor Type

Country Benefactor Grants	$ 6,957,991
In-Kind Donations and Services	2,043,951
Multilateral Organization Grants	1,874,500
U.S. Individual Donations	1,762,314
Corporate Sponsorships & Donations	1,370,465
Foundation Grants	1,363,050
Latin American Individual Donations (excluding Country Benefactors)	806,949
Total Cumulative Donations	$16,179,220
% U.S. Sources	41%

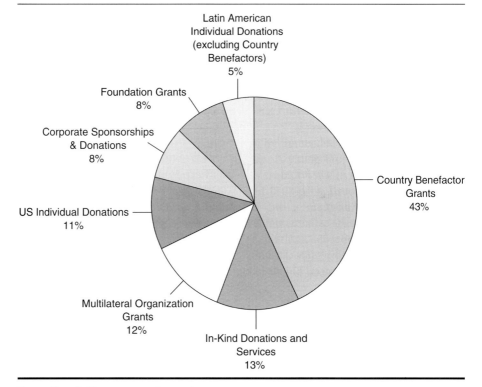

Source: Compiled from company documents.

[a]Includes cash and in-kind donations received to date, as well as multi-year grants and pledges received by Endeavor Global and Endeavor Countries (Argentina, Brazil, Chile, Mexico, and Uruguay).

EXHIBIT 8a | Endeavor Accomplishments: 1998 to 2001

Objective	Value	Impact
	Wealth Creation	
Identify & support leading emerging-market entrepreneurs →	6,000 jobs created, an 18% increase over 2000 $300 million capital raised by 21 Endeavor companies $400 million revenues generated, a 46% increase over 2000	→ **Financial Capital**
	Role Models	
Promote entrepreneurial role models →	100 entrepreneurs from 64 companies selected 4,750 entrepreneurs from 2,700 companies screened for 8 Endeavor International Selection Panels →	**Human Capital**
	Trust & Networks	
Build a venture-friendly environment →	11,100 Professionals, academics and business leaders in the Endeavor Global network	→ **Social Capital**
	Education	
Foster entrepreneurship education on a broad scale →	16,500 Attended Endeavor-sponsored educational events in Argentina, Brazil, Chile, Uruguay, and the U.S. 967 MBAs from Harvard, Wharton, Stanford, MIT, Columbia, screened for eMBA program	→ **Intellectual Capital**
	Philanthropy	
Develop best practices in philanthropy & social enterprise →	$9.5 million raised for Endeavor countries $6.7 million raised for Endeavor Global	→ **Cultural Capital**

Source: Compiled from company documents and data from Endeavor Entrepreneur companies.

EXHIBIT 8b | Selected Endeavor Entrepreneurs by Country

Endeavor Entrepreneurs in ARGENTINA

Agropool: b-to-b marketplace for agricultural supplies (Axel Grippo & Fernando Gonzales Botana)

ASATEJ: travel services (Eduardo Biraben)

BA Clean: institutional hygiene products and services (Gabriel Hornstein)

Ceicom: airline accounting & management software (Guillermo Marchionni)

Core: information technology security systems (Jonathan Altzul)

De la Guarda: alternative theatre group (Diqui James & Pichon Baldinu)

DPS Automation: automation software (Gian Muraglia)

Finca Pilar: gourmet agribusiness (Alejandro Belaga and Diego Radicella)

Lavandas de las Sierras: organic herbs and medicines (Leony Staudt & Bertrand Laxague)

Metrovision: post-production for film (Guillermo Otero)

Patagon.com: online financial services (Wences Casares and Constancio Larguia)

Sepia: cosmetics & beauty consumer products (Fatima Rizzo)

Service Bureau Intetel (SBI): employee productivity monitoring software and services provider (Claudio Lopez Silva)

Southern Winds: regional airline (Juan Maggio)

Trosman Churba: fashion goods (Jessica Trosman & Martin Churba)

Ultracongelados Rosario: frozen bakery products (Miguel Angel Lagrutta)

Endeavor Entrepreneurs in BRAZIL

Automatos/Solvo: information technology and services provider (Agostinho Villela, Andre Fonseca, Marcelo Salim)

Grudy: Fashionable summer and beach wear (Ana Luiza de Almeida)

Infnet: information technology education (Andre Antunes, Andre Kischinevsky, Eduardo Ramos)

MV Sistemas: healthcare technology solutions (Paulo Magnus & Luciano Magnus)

Nano Endoluminal: biotech research & development (Guido Dellagnelo, Pierre Galvagni Silveira, Ricardo Peres)

Poit Energia: power generator leasing (Wilson Martins Poit)

Pollux: machine vision technology (Jose Rizzo Hahn Filho)

S&V Consultoria: smart-card technology provider (Penido Stahlberg & Fredy Valente)

Tecsis: wind blade and industrial fan manufacturing (Bento Massahiko Koike)

Endeavor Entrepreneurs in CHILE

Actigen: biotech research & development (Jaime Villanueva) Chocolates Brunatto: fine fresh chocolate
  (Felix Brunatto, Cristobal Camino)

Geomar: seafood (Javier Donoso)

Micrologica: logistics information services (Mariano Pola)

MICSA Enterprises: a vertically integrated real estate firm (Rene and Rodrigo Silva & Jose Izquierdo)

Prospect: high-tech imaging and security services (Frank & Luis Vera)

Pub-Licity: restaurant franchise (Gabriel & Ricardo Delano)

Storbox: document storage (José & Gonzalo Prieto)

Vertical: outdoor education & leadership for schools and corporations (Rodrigo Jordan)

Endeavor Entrepreneurs in MEXICO

Bbmundo: consumer retail (Martha Debayle)

Endeavor Entrepreneurs in URUGUAY

Assist: mobile software solutions (Julio Cantera)

ISAI: building automation technology (Ruben Rodriguez)

Memory Computacion: accounting and management software provider (Roni Lieberman)

Scanntech: point-of-sale technology provider (Raul Polakof)

Source: Company.

EXHIBIT 9 | Example of Endeavor Role and Assessment by CEO

SEPIA

Company Summary:

Sepia is Argentina's trendiest cosmetics brand—marketed with a "Latin twist"—which has successfully reached the U.S. shelves of LVMH's top beauty chain Sephora

Initial Needs Assessment:

- Raise capital
- Professionalize management

Participation in Endeavor Programs/Activities:

- Participated in 5 Monthly Workshops (April–November)
- Matched with Federico Weil, Venture Corps, as mentor (May–February '02)
- Hosted 2 MBAs from Berkeley and NYU/ Stern (June–August)

Participation in Endeavor Programs/Activities:

Financing

- Top-of-the-line financial model and projections
- Close accompaniment in every stage of financing process (study of alternative forms of financing, meetings with investors, term sheet drafting and negotiation, and closing of transaction)
- Contacts with Investors (Angels and Institutional; Argentina/ U.S.)

Milestones Achieved:

- Closed US$1 million financing round from group of local Angel Investors
- Hired Chief Operating Officer

Give Back:

- Sent items for gift bags for Endeavor Gala 2000
- Participated in lunch with potential corporate donors
- Mentioned Endeavor in several Sepia articles
- Coached entrepreneurs on panel preparation/ Endeavor experience

Next Steps:

- Assist entrepreneur in second round of financing

Key Lesson Learned:

- When there is a good relationship between the mentor and the entrepreneur, the value-added can be enormous. It is important to "institutionalize" this relationship as an Endeavor service.

"Through Endeavor I met many people who believe in Entrepreneurship, and who are ready to help without asking for anything in return. This help is both very necessary and very rewarding. Generally, the entrepreneur is very lonely and needs assistance, words of wisdom and experience to move forward. It is wonderful that a group of people with such ideals actually exists."

—Fatima Rizzo, CEO, Sepia

"The challenge is to create a structure that allows Fatima and her team to exploit their creativity, while projecting the company internationally. I worked with Fatima to successfully close her first round of financing. The second round finds me on the other side of the table: as investor and no longer as mentor. Notwithstanding, the mutual trust between the founders and me persists thanks to the long trajectory that we have undergone together."

—Federico Weil, Endeavor Venture Corps

Source: Company documents.

EXHIBIT 10a | World Bank Economic Data

Country	Population (Millions)	Land Area (1000 of sq. km)	GNI per Capita[a] Dollars	GNI per Capita[a] Dollars at PPP	Real GDP Growth (Avg. Annual%)	Life Expectancy (Avg. Male and Female)	Adult Literacy % of Women	Adult Literacy % of Men	GINI Index[b] (0 = Equality)	% Share of Income[c] Lowest 10%	% Share of Income[c] Highest 10%
Albania	3	27	1,120	3,600	3.3	74	23	8			
Algeria	30	2,382	1,580	5,040	1.9	71	43	24	35	2.8	26.8
Angola	13	1,247	290	1,180	1.3	47					
Argentina	37	2,737	7,460	12,050	4.3	74	3	3	44	2.3	35.2
Armenia	4	28	520	2,580	-1.9	74	2	1	35	2	25.4
Australia	19	7,682	20,240	24,970	4.1	79			31	2.5	22.5
Austria	8	83	25,220	26,330	2.1	78			36	2.8	27.8
Azerbaijan	8	87	600	2,740	-6.3	72			34	3.9	28.6
Bangladesh	131	130	370	1,590	4.8	61	70	48			
Belarus	10	207	2,870	7,550	-1.6	68	1	0	22	5.1	20
Belgium	10	33	24,540	27,470	2	78			29	3.2	23
Benin	6	111	370	980	4.7	53	76	48			
Bolivia	8	1,084	990	2,360	4	63	21	8	45	1.3	32
Botswana	2	567	3,300	7,170	4.7	39	20	25			
Brazil	170	8,457	3,580	7,300	2.9	68	15	15	61	0.7	48
Bulgaria	8	111	1,520	5,560	-2.1	72	2	1	26	4.5	22.8
Burkina Faso	11	274	210	970	4.9	44	86	66	55	2	46.8
Burundi	7	26	110	580	-2.6	42	60	44	43	1.8	32.9
Cambodia	12	177	260	1,440	4.8	54	43	20	40	2.9	33.8
Cameroon	15	465	580	1,590	1.7	50	31	18	48	1.9	36.6
Canada	31	9,221	21,130	27,170	2.9	79			32	2.8	23.8
Cape Verde	0	4	1,330	4,760		69	34	15			
Central African Republic	4	623	280	1,160	2	43	65	40	61	0.7	47.7
Chad	8	1,259	200	870	2.2	48	66	48			
Chile	15	749	4,590	9,100	6.8	76	4	4	57	1.3	45.6
China	1,262	9,327	840	3,920	10.3	70	24	8	40	2.4	30.4
Colombia	42	1,039	2,020	6,060	3	72	8	8	57	1.1	46.1
Comoros	1	2	380	1,590		61	51	37			
Congo, Dem. Rep.	51	2,267	100	680	-5.1	46	50	27			
Congo, Rep.	3	342	570	570	-0.4	51	26	13			

(continued)

EXHIBIT 10a | World Bank Economic Data (continued)

Country	Population (Millions)	Land Area (1000 of sq. km)	GNI per Capita[a] Dollars	Dollars at PPP	Real GDP Growth (Avg. Annual%)	Life Expectancy (Avg. Male and Female)	Adult Literacy % of Women	% of Men	GINI Index[b] (0 = Equality)	% Share of Income[c] Lowest 10%	Highest 10%
Costa Rica	4	51	3,810	7,980	5.3	77	4	4	46	1.7	34.6
Cote d'Ivoire	16	318	600	1,500	3.5	46	61	46	37	3.1	28.8
Croatia	4	56	4,620	7,960	0.6	73	3	1	29	3.7	23.3
Czech Republic	10	77	5,250	13,780	0.9	75			25	4.3	22.4
Denmark	5	42	32,280	27,250	2.5	76			25	3.6	20.5
Dominican Republic	8	48	2,130	5,710	6	67	16	16	47	2.1	37.9
Ecuador	13	277	1,210	2,910	1.8	70	10	7	44	2.2	33.8
Egypt, Arab Rep.	64	995	1,490	3,670	4.6	67	56	33	29	4.4	25
El Salvador	6	21	2,000	4,410	4.7	70	24	18	52	1.2	39.5
Estonia	1	42	3,580	9,340	-0.5	71			38	3	29.8
Ethiopia	64	1,000	100	660	4.7	42	69	53	40	3	33.7
Fiji	1	18	1,820	4,480		69	9	5		3	
Finland	5	305	25,130	24,570	2.8	77			26	4.2	21.6
France	59	550	24,090	24,420	1.7	79			33	2.8	25.1
Gabon	1	258	3,190	5,360	2.8	53					
Gambia, The	1	10	340	1,620	3.1	53	71	56	50	1.6	38.2
Georgia	5	70	630	2,680	-13	73			37	2.3	27.9
Germany	82	357	25,120	24,920	1.5	77			30	3.3	23.7
Ghana	19	228	340	1,910	4.3	57	37	20	41	2.2	30.1
Greece	11	129	11,960	16,860	2.1	78	4	1	33	3	25.3
Guatemala	11	108	1,680	3,770	4.1	65	39	24	56	1.6	46
Guinea	7	246	450	1,930	4.3	46			40	2.6	32
Guinea-Bissau	1	28	180	710	1.2	45	77	46	56	0.5	42.3
Guyana	1	197	860	3,670		63	2	1	40	2.4	32
Haiti	8	28	510	1,470	-0.6	53	52	48			
Honduras	6	112	860	2,400	3.2	66	25	25	56	0.6	42.7
Hong Kong, China	7	1	25,920	25,590	4	80	10	3	52	1.8	43.5
Hungary	10	92	4,710	11,990	1.5	71	1	1	24	4.1	20.5
India	1,016	2,973	450	2,340	6	63	55	32	38	3.5	33.5
Indonesia	210	1,812	570	2,830	4.2	66	18	8	32	4	26.7
Iran, Islamic Rep.	64	1,622	1,680	5,910	3.5	69	31	17			

Ireland	4	69	22,660	25,520	7.3	76	8	3	36	2.5	27.4
Israel	6	21	16,710	19,330	5.1	78	2	1	38	2.4	28.3
Italy	58	294	20,160	23,470	1.6	79	9	17	27	3.5	21.8
Jamaica	3	11	2,610	3,440	0.5	75			38	2.7	30.3
Japan	127	365	35,620	27,080	1.3	81	16	5	25	4.8	21.7
Jordan	5	89	1,710	3,950	5	72			36	3.3	29.8
Kazakhstan	15	2,700	1,260	5,490	−4.1	65	24	11	35	2.7	26.3
Kenya	30	569	350	1,010	2.1	47	4	1	45	2.4	36.1
Korea, Rep.	47	99	8,910	17,300	5.7	73	20	16	32	2.9	24.3
Kuwait	2	18	18,030	18,690	3.2	77					
Kyrgyz Republic	5	192	270	2,540	−4.1	67	67	36	35	3.2	27.2
Lao PDR	5	231	290	1,540	6.5	54	0	0	37	3.2	30.6
Latvia	2	62	2,920	7,070	−3.4	70		8	32	2.9	25.9
Lebanon	4	10	4,010	4,550	6	70	20	28			
Lesotho	2	30	580	2,590	4.1	44	6		56	0.9	43.4
Lithuania	4	65	2,930	6,980	−3.1	73	1	0	32	3.1	25.6
Macedonia, FYR	2	25	1,820	5,020	−0.8	73					
Madagascar	16	582	250	820	2	55	40	26	38	2.6	28.6
Malawi	10	94	170	600	3.8	39	53	26			
Malaysia	23	329	3,380	8,330	7	73	17	9	49	1.7	38.4
Maldives	0	0	1,960	4,240		68	3	3			
Mali	11	1,220	240	780	3.8	42	66	51	51	1.8	40.4
Mauritania	3	1,025	370	1,630	4.2	52	70	49	37	2.5	28.4
Mauritius	1	2	3,750	9,940	5.3	72	19	12			
Mexico	98	1,909	5,070	8,790	3.1	73	10	7	53	1.3	41.7
Moldova	4	33	400	2,230	−9.7	68	2	0	41	2.2	30.7
Mongolia	2	1,567	390	1,760	1	67	1	1	33	2.9	24.5
Morocco	29	446	1,180	3,450	2.3	67	64	38	40	2.6	30.9
Mozambique	18	784	210	800	6.4	42	71	40	40	2.5	31.7
Namibia	2	823	2,030	6,410	4.1	47	19	17			
Nepal	23	143	240	1,370	4.9	59	76	40	37	3.2	29.8
Netherlands	16	34	24,970	25,850	2.8	78			33	2.8	25.1
New Zealand	4	268	12,990	18,530	3	78					
Nicaragua	5	121	400	2,080	3.5	69	33	34	60	0.7	48.8
Niger	11	1,267	180	740	2.4	46	92	76	51	0.8	35.4
Nigeria	127	911	260	800	2.4	47	44	28	51	1.6	40.8
Norway	4	307	34,530	29,630	3.6	79			26	4.1	21.8

(continued)

EXHIBIT 10a | World Bank Economic Data (*continued*)

Country	Population (Millions)	Land Area (1000 of sq. km)	GNI per Capita[a] Dollars	GNI per Capita[a] Dollars at PPP	Real GDP Growth (Avg. Annual%)	Life Expectancy (Avg. Male and Female)	Adult Literacy % of Women	Adult Literacy % of Men	GINI Index[b] (0 = Equality)	% Share of Income[c] Lowest 10%	% Share of Income[c] Highest 10%
Oman	2	212	5,050		5.9	74	38	20			
Pakistan	138	771	440	1,860	3.7	63	72	43	31	4.1	27.6
Panama	3	74	3,260	5,680	4.1	75	9	7	49	1.2	35.7
Papua New Guinea	5	453	700	2,180	4	59	43	29	51	1.7	40.5
Paraguay	5	397	1,440	4,450	2.2	70	8	6	58	0.5	43.8
Peru	26	1,280	2,080	4,660	4.7	69	15	5	46	1.6	35.4
Philippines	76	298	1,040	4,220	3.3	69	5	5	46	2.3	36.6
Poland	39	304	4,190	9,000	4.6	73	0	0	32	3.2	24.7
Portugal	10	92	11,120	16,990	2.7	76	10	5	36	3.1	28.4
Romania	22	230	1,670	6,360	-0.7	70	3	1	31	3.2	25
Russian Federation	146	16,889	1,660	8,010	-4.8	65	1	0	49	1.7	38.7
Rwanda	9	25	230	930	-0.2	40	40	26	29	4.2	24.2
Saudi Arabia	21	2,150	7,230	11,390	1.5	73	33	17			
Senegal	10	193	490	1,480	3.6	52	72	53	41	2.6	33.5
Sierra Leone	5	72	130	480	-4.3	39			63	0.5	43.6
Singapore	4	1	24,740	24,910	7.8	78	12	4			
Slovak Republic	5	48	3,700	11,040	2.1	73	0	0	19	5.1	18.2
Slovenia	2	20	10,050	17,310	2.7	75	0	0	28	3.9	23
South Africa	43	1,221	3,020	9,160	2	48	15	14	59	1.1	45.9
Spain	39	499	15,080	19,260	2.5	78	3	1	33	2.8	25.2
Sri Lanka	19	65	850	3,460	5.3	73	11	6	34	3.5	28
Sudan	31	2,376	310	1,520	8.1	56	54	31			
Suriname	0	156	1,890	3,480		70					
Swaziland	1	17	1,390	4,600	3.3	46	21	19	61	1	50.2
Sweden	9	412	27,140	23,970	1.9	80			25	3.7	20.1
Switzerland	7	40	38,140	30,450	0.8	80			33	2.6	25.2
Syrian Arab Republic	16	184	940	3,340	5.8	70	40	12			
Tajikistan	6	141	180	1,090	-10.4	69	1	0	35	3.2	25.2
Tanzania	34	884	270	520	2.9	44	33	16	38	2.8	30.1
Thailand	61	511	2,000	6,320	4.2	69	6	3	41	2.8	32.4
Togo	5	54	290	1,410	2.3	49	58	28			

Trinidad and Tobago	1	5	4,930	8,220	3	73	8	4	40	2.1	29.9
Tunisia	10	155	2,100	6,070	4.7	72	39	19	42	2.3	31.8
Turkey	65	770	3,100	7,030	3.7	70	23	7	42	2.3	32.3
Turkmenistan	5	470	750	3,800	−4.8	66			41	2.6	31.7
Uganda	22	197	300	1,210	7	42	43	22	37	3	29.8
Ukraine	50	579	700	3,700	−9.3	68	1	0	29	3.7	23.2
United Arab Emirates	3	84	18,060	19,410	2.9	75	21	25			
United Kingdom	60	241	24,430	23,550	2.5	77			37	2.3	27.7
United States	282	9,159	34,100	34,100	3.5	77			41	1.8	30.5
Uruguay	3	175	6,000	8,880	3.4	74	2	3	42	2.1	32.7
Uzbekistan	25	414	360	2,360	−0.5	70	1	0	45	1.2	32.8
Venezuela, RB	24	882	4,310	5,740	1.6	73	8	7	50	0.8	36.5
Vietnam	79	325	390	2,000	7.9	69	9	4	36	3.6	29.9
Yemen, Rep.	18	528	370	770	5.8	56	75	32	33	3	25.9
Zambia	10	743	300	750	0.5	38	29	15	53	1.1	41
Zimbabwe	13	387	460	2,550	2.5	40	15	7	50	2	40.4

Source: Adapted from David Moss and Sarah Brennan, "Basic Statistics from the World Bank's World Development Indicators, 2002," HBS No. 703-030 (Boston, MA: Harvard Business School Publishing, 2002).

[a]GNI per capita is calculated by converting GNI in national currency to U.S. dollars, using the average exchange rate over a three-year period. The Purchasing Power Parity (PPP) method tries to use U.S. prices to value the goods in other countries.

[b]The GINI Index attempts to show a country's level of income (or in some cases, consumption) inequality. Perfect equality is 0; perfect inequality is 100.

[c]Percent share of total income going to people in the lowest and highest decile income brackets. When income statistics were not available, the columns contain the % share of consumption going to people in the lowest and highest consumption brackets.

EXHIBIT 10b | Global Entrepreneurship Monitor Study (GEM) (excerpts)

Entrepreneurship in the United States has become mainstream. At any given time, 11.7 percent of the adult working population (18–64 years old) is either involved in the start-up process or is the owner/manager of an active young business (less than 42 months old). This percentage is what GEM 2001 refers to as America's total entrepreneurship activity (TEA) rate. In comparison to the TEA rates for each of the 29 countries involved in the 2001 Global Entrepreneurship Monitor, the United States ranks as the seventh highest (**Figure 1.1**).

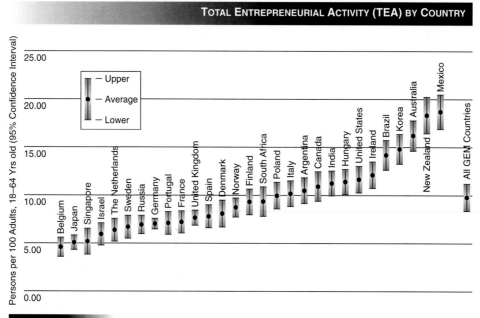

FIGURE 1.1

The 2001 study further segments TEA into two categories: "opportunity entrepreneurship" and "necessity entrepreneurship." This was accomplished by asking survey respondents whether they were starting a business opportunity (i.e., opportunity entrepreneurship) or because they had no better choices for work (i.e., necessity entrepreneurship). It is clear from **Figures 1.2** and **1.3** that the United States is predominantly opportunity-driven with 10.3 percent of adults involved in opportunity-oriented entrepreneurial activity and only 1.2 percent of adults involved in necessity-oriented entrepreneurial activity.

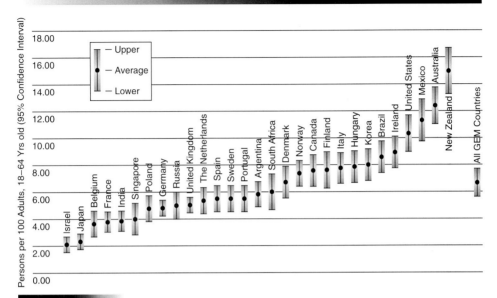

FIGURE 1.2

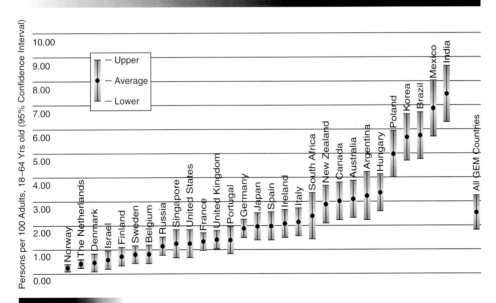

FIGURE 1.3

EXHIBIT 11a | Endeavor Budget—Base Case: One New Country in 2002 Only (US$ in thousands)

	Endeavor Global (Headquarters)					
	2002	2003	2004	2005	2006	2007
SELECTED ENDEAVOR IMPACT DATA:						
New (per year):						
Endeavor Countries	—	—	—	—	—	—
Endeavor Companies Selected	—	—	—	—	—	—
Cumulative:						
Endeavor Countries	—	—	—	—	—	—
Companies Screened	—	—	—	—	—	—
Endeavor Companies Selected	—	—	—	—	—	—
Endeavor Entrepreneurs	—	—	—	—	—	—
Total Participants in Endeavor Events	2,510	2,610	2,710	2,810	2,910	3,010
Endeavor Employees	5	6	6	6	6	6
REVENUES:						
Interest income (1)	8	11	18	19	23	24
Donations (2)	804	1,190	1,290	1,390	1,390	1,390
Entrepreneur Service Fees (3)	122	163	136	136	136	136
Country Benefactor grants (4)	377	250	125	124	60	60
Grants (5)	332	86	39	—	—	—
Sponsorships (6)	77	150	175	175	200	200
TOTAL REVENUES	1,721	1,851	1,783	1,843	1,809	1,810
EXPENSES:						
Variable Costs:						
Education	43	43	43	43	43	43
Marketing	8	6	5	5	5	5
Printing/Publications/Shipping	60	57	57	71	57	57
eMBA program expenses	—	—	—	—	—	—
Events and Activities (7)	358	413	386	386	386	386
Travel	40	44	40	40	40	40
Total Variable Costs	508	564	532	546	532	532
Fixed Costs:						
Salary & Benefits	585	777	872	883	885	886
Annual Grants to Endeavor Global	—	—	—	—	—	—
Professional Fees	334	210	210	210	210	210
IT & Communications	128	99	39	39	39	39
Marketing	—	—	—	—	—	—
Other Administrative	56	59	59	117	117	117
Total Fixed Costs	1,103	1,144	1,179	1,249	1,250	1,252
TOTAL EXPENSES	1,611	1,708	1,711	1,795	1,782	1,783
OPERATING INCOME/LOSS	110	143	72	49	27	27
Total Headquarters Cost Per Entrepreneur (8)	12	10	8	7	6	6

Source: Company.

Note: Endeavor Global's financials are unconsolidated (excluding Endeavor Chile's expenses) and are reflected on a cash basis.

(1) Interest income reflects interest earned on operating cash balance. Base budget does not reflect incremental interest income from an endowment.

(2) Donations include the Gala, but do not include value of stock donations and/or 1%–2% entrepreneur equity donations that accrue to country and/or U.S. endowments.

(3) Service Fees are payments from entrepreneurs for eMBA program stipends.

(4) These grants include the funding raised by the local affiliates as well as the 25th of the initial funding paid to Endeavor Global.

(5) Grants include funding from foundations, governments, NGOs, and organizations like the World Bank and IDB.

(6) Funding raised by Endeavor as sponsorship fees from companies to sponsor Endeavor events.

(7) Includes expenses of programs such as forum events, selection panels, the Gala.

(8) Total cost per entrepreneur is calculated as Endeavor Global's total expense figure divided by the total number of Endeavor Entrepreneurs supported by the local affiliates.

Total Endeavor Countries (Local)						Consolidated					
2002	2003	2004	2005	2006	2007	2002	2003	2004	2005	2006	2007
1	0	0	0	0	0	1	—	—	—	—	—
30	26	26	26	26	26	30	26	26	26	26	26
5	5	5	5	5	5	5	5	5	5	5	5
3,128	4,437	5,746	7,055	8,364	9,673	3,128	4,437	5,746	7,055	8,364	9,673
94	120	146	172	198	224	94	120	146	172	198	224
140	174	208	242	276	310	140	174	208	242	276	310
24,661	32,569	40,458	48,347	56,236	64,321	27,171	35,179	43,168	51,157	59,146	67,331
30	33	35	35	35	40	35	39	41	41	41	46
—	—	—	—	—	—	8	11	18	19	23	24
58	58	58	58	58	58	862	1,248	1,348	1,448	1,448	1,448
—	—	—		—	—	122	163	136	136	136	136
1,882	1,939	1,359	560	—	—	2,258	2,189	1,484	683	60	60
239	232	216	91	91	91	571	319	255	91	91	91
625	671	1,219	2,256	2,872	2,999	702	821	1,394	2,431	3,072	3,199
2,803	2,900	2,852	2,965	3,021	3,148	4,524	4,751	4,635	4,808	4,830	4,958
22	23	24	25	26	27	65	66	67	68	69	70
—	—	—	—	—	—	8	6	5	5	5	5
63	66	67	69	71	73	122	123	124	140	128	130
122	163	136	136	136	136	122	163	136	136	136	136
608	677	703	731	761	793	966	1,090	1,089	1,117	1,147	1,179
84	85	87	90	93	96	123	130	128	131	133	136
898	1,014	1,017	1,051	1,087	1,125	1,406	1,578	1,548	1,597	1,619	1,657
1,198	1,304	1,369	1,437	1,509	1,585	1,784	2,081	2,241	2,321	2,394	2,471
377	250	125	124	60	60	377	250	125	124	60	60
59	55	58	61	63	66	393	265	268	270	273	276
48	50	51	52	54	56	177	148	89	91	92	94
51	53	54	56	58	60	51	53	54	56	58	60
170	174	178	184	190	196	226	233	237	301	307	313
1,905	1,886	1,835	1,913	1,934	2,023	3,008	3,030	3,014	3,162	3,184	3,274
2,803	2,900	2,852	2,965	3,021	3,148	4,414	4,608	4,563	4,759	4,803	4,931
—	—	—	—	—	—	110	143	72	49	27	27
20	17	14	12	11	10	32	26	22	20	17	16

EXHIBIT 11b | Endeavor Budget—Growth Scenario: Base Case + Incremental Revenues Associated with Endowment and Costs Associated with Additional One Country per Year (US$ in thousands)

	Endeavor Global (Headquarters)				
	2003	2004	2005	2006	2007
SELECTED ENDEAVOR IMPACT DATA:					
New (per year):					
Endeavor Countries	—	—	—	—	—
Endeavor Companies Selected	—	—	—	—	—
Cumulative:	—	—	—	—	—
Endeavor Countries	—	—	—	—	—
Companies Screened	—	—	—	—	—
Endeavor Companies Selected	—	—	—	—	—
Endeavor Entrepreneurs	—	—	—	—	—
Total Participants in Endeavor Events	5,520	5,920	6,320	6,720	7,120
Endeavor Employees	7	8	9	11	12
Endowment Raised	5,000	10,000	15,000	20,000	25,000
REVENUES:					
Interest income (1)	162	424	704	981	1,263
Donations (2)	804	1,190	1,290	1,390	1,390
Entrepreneur Service Fees (3)	122	190	218	272	326
Country Benefactor grants (4)	590	600	490	504	455
Grants (5)	332	86	39	—	—
Sponsorships (6)	102	249	274	274	299
TOTAL REVENUES	2,113	2,740	3,014	3,420	3,733
EXPENSES:					
Variable Costs:					
Education	43	58	58	98	123
Marketing	8	8	9	11	12
Printing/Publications/Shipping	65	77	81	117	106
eMBA program expenses	—	—	—	—	—
Events and Activities (7)	466	606	666	721	808
Travel	51	72	75	83	90
Total Variable Costs	633	821	890	1,029	1,140
Fixed Costs:					
Salary & Benefits	708	925	1,135	1,336	1,406
Annual Grants to Endeavor Global	—	—	—	—	—
Professional Fees	334	225	240	240	275
IT & Communications	128	168	113	116	134
Marketing	—	—	—	—	—
Other Administrative	56	61	62	126	128
Total Fixed Costs	1,226	1,378	1,550	1,818	1,943
TOTAL EXPENSES	1,859	2,199	2,440	2,847	3,083
OPERATING INCOME/LOSS	225	541	575	574	650
Total Headquarters Cost Per Entrepreneur (8)	13	11	10	9	8
Incremental expenses per new country supported	248	246	243	263	260

Source: Company.
Note: Endeavor Global's financials are unconsolidated (excluding Endeavor Chile's expenses) and are reflected on a cash basis.
(1) Interest income reflects interest earned on operating cash balance and interest income from endowment. Assumes 5% interest income on endowment.
(2) Donations include the Gala, but do not include value of stock donations and/or 1%–2% entrepreneur equity donations that accrue to country and/or .S. endowments.
(3) Service Fees are payments from entrepreneurs for eMBA program stipends.
(4) These grants include the funding raised by the local affiliates as well as the 25th of the initial funding paid to Endeavor Global.
(5) Grants include funding from foundations, governments, NGOs, and organizations like the World Bank and IDB.
(6) Funding raised by Endeavor as sponsorship fees from companies to sponsor Endeavor events.
(7) Includes expenses of programs such as forum events, selection panels, the Gala.
(8) Total cost per entrepreneur is calculated as Endeavor Global's total expense figure divided by the total number of Endeavor Entrepreneurs supported by the local affiliates.

Total Endeavor Countries (Local Affiliates)					Consolidated				
2003	2004	2005	2006	2007	2003	2004	2005	2006	2007
2	1	1	1	1	2	1	1	1	1
34	38	46	54	62	34	38	46	54	62
—	—	—	—	—	—	—	—	—	—
6	7	8	9	10	6	7	8	9	10
3,253	4,812	6,496	8,305	10,239	3,253	4,812	6,496	8,305	10,239
98	136	182	236	298	98	136	182	236	298
145	195	256	328	411	145	195	256	328	411
25,452	34,771	44,695	55,243	66,415	30,972	40,691	51,015	61,963	73,535
33	40	46	50	54	40	48	55	61	66
—	—	—	—	—	—	—	—	—	—
—	—	—	—	—	162	424	704	981	1,263
58	58	58	58	58	862	1,248	1,348	1,448	1,448
—	—	—	—	—	122	190	218	272	326
2,481	3,076	3,032	2,749	2,189	3,071	3,676	3,523	3,253	2,644
239	304	266	141	141	571	390	305	141	141
590	632	1,181	2,217	3,350	727	920	1,493	2,530	3,688
3,402	4,108	4,575	5,204	5,777	5,516	6,848	7,590	8,624	9,510
22	23	24	25	26	65	81	82	123	149
—	—	—	—	—	8	8	9	11	12
90	123	153	184	215	155	200	235	301	322
122	190	218	272	326	122	190	218	272	326
682	825	925	1,027	1,131	1,148	1,431	1,591	1,748	1,940
102	123	144	165	187	154	195	219	248	277
1,019	1,284	1,463	1,674	1,886	1,652	2,105	2,353	2,702	3,026
1,400	1,764	2,087	2,414	2,744	2,108	2,688	3,223	3,750	4,150
590	600	490	504	455	590	600	490	504	455
73	84	103	122	142	407	309	342	362	417
60	74	87	100	113	189	242	199	215	248
60	70	80	90	101	60	70	80	90	101
200	233	266	301	336	255	293	328	427	464
2,383	2,824	3,112	3,530	3,891	3,609	4,203	4,662	5,348	5,834
3,402	4,108	4,575	5,204	5,777	5,261	6,307	7,015	8,050	8,860
—	—	—	—	—	255	541	575	574	650

PART 2

Recognizing and
Analyzing Opportunity

The entrepreneurial process begins with an idea: a belief about an unmet need, an underserved market, a better way to do something. This idea is the cornerstone of the venture—it animates the entrepreneur's attempts to gather resources and build an organization to deliver the product or service. But we know that many ideas—while they may contain the germ of an insight—need considerable refinement before they can become the basis of a profitable and enduring business. It is the very nature of doing something new that both creates the opportunity *and* the risk. The key to maximizing the potential of the venture is careful analysis of the opportunity. The chapters in this section offer some guideposts for thinking about the factors that create a favorable business idea, as well as some tools and techniques for articulating the business model that will allow the idea to be profitable. It is not that profits per se are the sole objective of the entrepreneurial process; there are many non-financial rewards that drive entrepreneurs and are sources of great satisfaction. It is simply the case that almost all high-potential ventures require capital from external parties, and that acquiring that capital, on reasonable terms, requires demonstrating how the business can be profitable and return those funds to investors.

CHAPTER 2

Some Thoughts on Business Plans

Internet Wicked Ale

Bill Sahlman, Dimitri V. D'Arbeloff Professor of Business Administration, smiled as he was handed the business plan for Internet Wicked Ale, Inc. (IWA), an interactive, on-line marketing company being formed to sell premium beers made by microbreweries over the Internet. According to the president of the company—a soon-to-graduate MBA candidate at a well known eastern business school—a prototype web site had already been developed using the now ubiquitous Java programming language. Literally thousands were visiting the site each day: an early review had described the web site as "way cool." Participating in the meeting were two other MBA candidates. Prior to jointly founding IWA, the three had worked in management consulting and investment banking: each, however, did have substantial experience with beer.

Sahlman glanced over the shoulder of the IWA team—he took note of his ever growing stack of Internet based business plans, each proposing to "revolutionize" an industry, each "conservatively" projecting at least $50 million in revenues within five years based on a modest market share of under 10%, and each containing a projection of likely investor returns of over 100% per annum. He quickly averted his stare from the business plans in the corner of his less than tidy office so as not to offend his eager audience. They looked so young—they were so enthusiastic—their business plan was so meticulously printed on the new color laser printers in the technology lab . . . Sahlman wondered what to say next.

• • • • •

Introduction

This note is about entrepreneurial ventures and the role of business plans. Few areas of new venture creation receive as much attention. There are MBA and undergraduate courses on business plan writing. There are countless books describing how to write a business plan. There is even software that will help create a business plan, complete with integrated financial projections. All across the U.S., and increasingly in other countries, there are contests designed to pick the "best business plan."

Judging by the amount of attention paid to business plans in graduate business schools and the popular press, you would think that the only thing standing between a would-be entrepreneur and spectacular success is a well-crafted and highly regarded business plan. Yet, in my experience, nothing could be further from the truth: on a scale from 1 to 10, business plans rank no higher than 2 as a predictor of likely success. There are many other factors that dominate the business plan, per se.

The disparity between my view and that implicit in the business plan feeding frenzy is rooted in over fifteen years of field research and personal experience in the world of entrepreneurship. The rest of this note develops a conceptual framework for understanding entrepreneurial venture creation and management, which is based on studying hundreds of successful and unsuccessful companies. The goal is to give the reader insights into sensible entrepreneurial management, and, by implication, into the business plan used to describe a venture.

In my framework, there are four dynamic components of any entrepreneurial process or venture:

- the **people;**
- the **opportunity;**
- the **external context;** and,
- the **deal.**

By people, I mean those individuals or groups who perform services or provide resources for the venture, whether or not they are directly employed by the venture. This category encompasses managers, employees, lawyers, accountants, capital providers, and parts suppliers, among others. By opportunity, I mean any activity requiring the investment of scarce resources in hopes of future return. By context, I mean all those factors that affect the outcome of the opportunity but that are generally outside the direct control of management. Examples of contextual factors include the level of interest rates, regulations (rules of the game), macroeconomic activity, and some industry variables like threat of substitutes. Finally, by deal, I mean the complete set of implicit and explicit contractual relationships between the entity and all resource providers. Examples of deals range from contracts with capital suppliers to the terms of employment for managers.

The fundamental insight gained from studying hundreds of successful and unsuccessful ventures is the concept of integration, referred to as "**fit,**" which is defined as the degree to which the people, the opportunity, the deal, and the context together influence the potential for success. Phrased differently, the degree of fit is the answer to the following questions:

- To what degree do the people have the right experience, skills and attitudes, given the nature of the opportunity, the context and the deals struck?
- To what degree does the opportunity make sense, given the people involved, the context and the deals struck?

- To what degree is the context favorable for the venture, given the people involved, the nature of the opportunity and the deals struck?
- To what degree do the deals involved in the venture make sense, given the people involved, the nature of the opportunity, and the context?

These questions focus attention on the fact that excellence in any single dimension is not sufficient: the proper perspective from which to make an evaluation takes into account all of the elements simultaneously. An appropriate analogy might be that of a sports team. It is not sufficient to have the best individual players at each position; rather, success will be a function of how they play together, how the team is managed, what deals have been struck inside and outside the team, and what else goes on in the league. A diagram of the basic framework is provided in **Appendix 1.**

Nor is it sufficient to focus on these elements and their relationship from a static perspective. The people, opportunity, context and deal (and the relationship among them) are all likely to change over time as a company goes from identification of opportunity to harvest. To focus attention on the dynamic aspects of the entrepreneurial process, three related questions can be asked to guide the analysis of any business venture:

- What can go wrong?
- What can go right?
- What decisions can management make today and in the future to ensure that "what can go right" does go right, and "what can go wrong" is avoided, or failing that, is prevented from critically damaging the enterprise? Phrased another way, what decisions can be made to tilt the reward to risk ratio in favor of the venture?

This framework and set of questions are extremely powerful in understanding how ventures evolve over time and how managers can affect outcomes. The balanced emphasis on anticipating (as opposed to predicting) good and bad news is a distinctive feature of the framework. Most students (and practitioners) are adept at identifying risks, far fewer are practiced at foretelling the good news, and even fewer have thought systematically about how they can manage the reward to risk ratio. Yet, there are some recurrent themes in the world of venturing. That projects often take more time and money than originally estimated should not surprise people. Indeed, part of the goal in a course like the one I teach on Entrepreneurial Finance is to provide people with a rich sense of the patterns that underlie real-world entrepreneurship.

These questions described above concerning potential good and bad news also shed light on the fact that current decisions affect future decisions: some decisions open up or preserve options for future action while others destroy options. Managers must be cognizant of this relationship between current and future decisions.

According to this framework, great businesses have some easily identifiable (but hard to assemble) attributes. They have a world class managerial team in all dimensions, from the top to the bottom, and across all relevant functions. The teams have directly relevant skills and experiences for the opportunity they are pursuing. Ideally, the team has worked successfully together in the past. The opportunity has an attractive, sustainable business model: it is possible to create a competitive edge and to defend it. There are multiple options for expanding the scale and scope of the business and these options are unique to the enterprise and its team. There are a number of ways to extract value from the business either in a positive harvest event or in a scale down or liquidation mode. The context is favorable both with respect to the regulatory environment and the macroeconomic situation. The deals binding the people to the opportunity are sensible and robust: they provide the right incentives under a wide range of scenarios. The venture is financed by individuals or firms who add value in addition to their capital, thereby increasing the likelihood of success. The financing terms provide the right incentives for the provider and the recipient. There is access to additional capital on an as-warranted basis. In short, the venture is characterized by a high degree of dynamic **fit** (see **Appendix 2** for a diagram of the expanded fit management framework).

A great business may or may not have currently, or have ever had for that matter, a great business plan. In the beginning, moreover, a great business may not even have demonstrated a high degree of **fit:** the important issue is whether the deficiencies are recognized and fixable. Phrased differently, the role of management is to continuously adapt a business to improve the degree of **fit:** doing so does not guarantee success, but it does increase the odds.

This assessment raises the obvious issue of what role a business plan plays in entrepreneurship. I believe that a useful business plan is one that addresses the elements of the venture—people, opportunity, context, and deal—in the proper dynamic context. In the end, the business plan must provide reasonable answers to the following questions:

- Who are the people involved? What have they done in the past that would lead one to believe that they will be successful in the future? Who is missing from the team and how will they be attracted?

- What is the nature of the opportunity? How will the company make money? How is the opportunity likely to evolve? Can entry barriers be built and maintained?

- What contextual factors will affect the venture? What contextual changes are likely to occur, and how can management respond to those changes?

- What deals have been or are likely to be struck inside and outside the venture? Do the deals struck increase the likelihood of success? How will those deals and the implicit incentives evolve over time?

- What decisions have been made (or can be made) to increase the ratio of reward to risk?

Each of these areas will be addressed in the sections that follow.

People

When reading any business plan, or assessing any business, for that matter, I start with the resume section, not with the description of the business. I ask a series of structured questions, some of which are listed below:

- Who are the founders?
- What have they accomplished in the past?

- What directly relevant experience do they have for the opportunity they are pursuing?
- What skills do they have?
- Whom do they know and who knows them?
- What is their reputation?
- How realistic are they?
- Can they adapt as circumstances warrant?
- Who else needs to be on the team? Are the founders prepared to recruit high quality people?
- How will the team respond to adversity?
- Can they make the inevitable hard choices that have to be made?
- What are their motivations?
- How committed are they to this venture?
- How can I gain objective information about each member of the team including how they will work together?
- What are the possible consequences if one or more of the team members leaves?

We can now come full circle and begin to evaluate the Internet Wicked Ale proposal and the team of MBA founders. Starting first with the people lens, I am not sanguine about IWA's prospects. The founding team has experience drinking, not starting an on-line business or a beer distribution business. Typically, the business plan for such a team talks about the need to recruit experienced people, but it's rather like trying to draw 4 cards to complete a 5-card straight in poker: a low probability event. Moreover, having a founding team without tremendous experience but large equity ownership often makes it extremely difficult to attract high quality people on "acceptable" terms.

I should note that the framework described above and the pessimistic assessment of the prospects for IWA are not foolproof. Lots of inexperienced teams succeed, occasionally because they are not weighted down by conventional wisdom. This is particularly true in new markets, the Internet representing a very important current illustration. In such markets, commercial innovation is often driven by relatively inexperienced entrants, teams that are repeatedly told they are unlikely to succeed. At the same time, starting a new enterprise with little or no management experience is a little like crossing the Mass Turnpike blindfolded: yes, you can make it to the other side, but having done so, you shouldn't assume the trip was riskless.

Reading a business plan from the resume section first also illustrates a truism of professional venture capital investing. A typical venture capital firm receives approximately 2,000 business plans per year. A non-scientific survey of several prominent firms reveals that they only invest in plans that come in with a specific letter of referral from someone well known by the partners of the firm. That is, they do not invest in, nor do they even investigate fully, plans that are unsolicited.

My colleague Myra Hart has a useful way of describing the process of attracting financial and other resources to a venture. Her research suggests that successful venture founders have two characteristics: they are "known" and they "know." Tackling the latter first, the founders know the industry for which they propose to raise capital and launch a venture—they know the key suppliers, the customers, and the competitors. They also know who the talented individuals are who can contribute to the team. At the same time, they are known in the industry: people can comment on their capabilities and can provide objective referrals to resource suppliers like professional venture capitalists. Suppliers, customers, and employees are willing to work with them in spite of the obvious risks of dealing with a new company.

Thus, the model in venture capital is to back teams with great (directly relevant) track records who are pursuing attractive opportunities. The old adage in venture capital circles is: "I'd rather back an 'A' team with a 'B' idea than a 'B' team with an 'A' idea." Of course, the goal is to only back high quality teams with high quality opportunities, but that is not always feasible.

In sum, the IWA business plan doesn't pass the threshold for consideration by professional investors even if the idea is a pretty good one. Again, a truism from the world of venture capital is that ideas are a dime-a-dozen: only execution skills count. Arthur Rock, a venture capital legend associated with the formation of such companies as Intel, Apple, and Teledyne, stated bluntly, "I invest in people, not ideas."[1]

Opportunity

Rather than rejecting the IWA plan out of hand, however, let's assume that the team is acceptable or that there are indications that an appropriate team can be built. What is the next step? What other questions do investors or entrepreneurs ask to evaluate prospective ventures?

In my experience, the next major issue is the nature of the opportunity, starting first with an assessment of the overall market potential and its characteristics. Two key initial questions are:

- Is the total market for the venture's product or service large and/or rapidly growing?
- Is the industry one that is now or can become structurally attractive?

Entrepreneurs and investors look for large or rapidly growing markets for a variety of reasons. First, it is often easier to obtain a share of a growing market than to fight with entrenched competitors for a share of a mature or stagnant market. Professional investors like venture capitalists try to identify high growth potential markets early in their evolution: examples range from integrated circuits to biotechnology. Indeed, they will not invest in a company that cannot reach a significant scale (e.g., $50 million in annual revenues) within five years.

Obviously, all markets are not created equal: some are more attractive than others. Consider, to illustrate, the independent computer disk drive business as it has evolved over the past twenty years. Disk drives were first developed by IBM in the late 1960s

---

[1]Michael W. Miller, "How One Man Helps High-Tech Prospects Get to the Big Leagues," *Wall Street Journal,* December 31, 1985, page 1.

and early 1970s. Some of the original engineering team members ultimately left IBM to form independent companies to develop products based on the same technology. Indeed, over the next two decades, scores of new companies were formed to exploit the rapidly growing market for data storage. Examples include Memorex, Seagate, Priam, Quantum, Conner Peripherals, and EMC.

The problem with disk storage, however, is that the industry is not structurally attractive, nor is it ever likely to be. Disk drive manufacturers must design their products to meet the perceived needs of OEMs (original equipment manufacturers) and end-users. Selling a product to OEMs is complicated and often has low margins. The customers are large relative to the supplier. There are lots of competitors, each with high quality offerings in the same market segment. Because there are so many competitors, product life cycles are short and ongoing technology investments high. The industry is subject to major shifts in technology and customer base (e.g., the shift in form factors or storage medium and the shift from minicomputers to microcomputers). Rivalry also leads to lower prices and hence, lower margins. In the end, it is extremely difficult to build and sustain a profitable business.

In this regard, the disk drive business looks suspiciously like the tire industry. When the tire industry developed, there were many competitors, each trying to sell their tires to the automobile manufacturers and to end-users. Rivalry was intense. The customers got larger and larger, squeezing the profitability of the tire suppliers. Ultimately, the industry evolved to the point where there were a handful of competitors, each with modest margins and highly cyclical results.

Compare the situation described for disk drives to that confronting biotechnology companies. If a biotech company creates a new product, intellectual property laws grant a certain amount of protection from competitive forces. Competitors must invent new approaches to the same underlying problem or they must license the product from the inventor. The extended duration of patent protection makes it possible as well to build a brand image that provides a certain amount of economic protection even after patent coverage expires. In the end, a model for a successful biotechnology company is a pharmaceutical company. On average, the latter companies are far more profitable than most precisely because of the structural attractiveness of their industry.

This extended discussion of growth and industry illustrates another important factor in venture formation and investing. What are the appropriate analogies? If a venture is successful, what will it look like? Identifying opportunities is a complex game of pattern recognition which is aided by experience and by honest assessment of business history. Knowing that the disk drive business is like the tire industry and that biotech is like the pharmaceutical industry is helpful in determining where to invest capital or human resources. Tom Stemberg once described what he was trying to accomplish in founding Staples, "I said I wanted to build the Toys 'R' Us of office supplies." He picked a successful model, one that spoke volumes about what he intended to do and the consequences if he were successful.[2]

To reiterate, the goal is to pick industries that have lots of potential to create and protect value. Growth in sales is not equivalent to growth in value. Also, marrying great

---

[2]For information on the launch of Staples, see Thomas G. Stemberg, *Staples for Success,* KEX Press, 1996.

management to such markets is the primary tool for increasing the likelihood of success. Consider, to illustrate, the story of the formation of Compaq Computer. The founders were senior executives at Texas Instruments. Their original business plan described a plan to enter the disk drive business. They sent the plan to L. J. Sevin and Ben Rosen, venture capitalists with extensive experience in the electronics industry. Sevin and Rosen rejected the plan but liked the team. Ultimately, on a place mat in a local diner in Texas, a plan was sketched out to design, manufacture and market a portable personal computer. The rest, as they say, is history.[3]

I am also reminded of what the immensely successful venture capitalist, Don Valentine, says about venture investing. Most in the venture industry focus on the three determinants of venture success—people, people, and people. Valentine insists that the real trick is to find markets with explosive potential, to back great technology, and to put management in place as needed. He wants to invest in industries where growth can overcome the shortcomings of management. Valentine cites as Exhibit A his $2.0 million investment in Cisco, a networking company, that seven years later was worth over $6 billion.[4] In like vein, Peter Lynch, the famous manager of Fidelity's Magellan Fund, tried to invest in companies whose fundamental industry factors were so favorable that even incompetent management couldn't cause the stock to go down.

What is most important in new venture formation—the market being served, the specific product or service, or the quality of the people involved? I suspect that the correct answer is "yes." In the final analysis, the issues are not unrelated. Great people are those who can identify attractive markets and build compelling strategies. As General Doriot, one of the early pioneers in the venture capital industry once stated, "The problem is to judge ideas and men and the value of the possible combination—a very difficult task."[5]

The next major issue in evaluating a venture is the specific plan for building and launching a product or service. I will not dwell on this topic in spite of its obvious importance but will instead focus on some very simple questions that can help sort out good ideas from potential disasters. I can also quote Arthur Rock to remind the reader of the proper perspective for evaluating business proposals, "If you can find good people, if they're wrong about the product they'll make a switch, so what good is it to understand the product that they're talking about in the first place?"[6] Rock's admonition notwithstanding, there are a few issues that a business plan must address, including the following:

- Who is the customer?

- How does the customer make decisions?

- To what degree is the product or service a compelling purchase for the customer?

---

[3]Benjamin Rosen, "Rosen's Ten Rules," in *Raising Money,* Amacom Press, 1990, pp. ix–xxv.

[4]Valentine's perspective is described in "Rise of the Silicon Patriots," *Worth Magazine,* December/January, 1996, pp. 86–92, 137–146.

[5]Georges F. Doriot: Manufacturing Class Notes, Harvard Business School, 1927–1966, The French Library, 1993, page 85.

[6]*Op. cit.,* page 1.

- How will the product or service be priced?
- How will the venture reach the identified customer segments?
- How much does it cost (time and resources) to acquire a customer?
- How much does it cost to produce and deliver the product or service?
- How much does it cost to support a customer?
- How easy is it to retain a customer?

Often, asking and answering these kinds of questions will reveal a fatal flaw in a plan. For example, it may be too costly to find the customers and convince them to buy the product. Economically viable access to customers is the key to business, yet many entrepreneurs take the Hollywood approach to this area—"Build it and they will come." That strategy is great in the movies but not very sensible in the real world.

I should note that it is not always easy to answer questions about possible customer response to new products or services. One entrepreneur I know proposed to introduce an electronic news clipping service. He made his pitch to a prospective venture capital investor who rejected the plan, stating, "I just don't think the dogs will eat the dogfood." Later, when the entrepreneur's company went public, he sent the venture capitalist an anonymous package comprised of an empty can of dogfood and a copy of his prospectus. If it were easy, there wouldn't be any opportunities.

The issue of pricing is particularly important in analyzing a business proposal. Sometimes the "dogs will eat the dogfood," but only at a price less than cost. Investors always look for opportunities that entail value pricing in which the price the customer is willing to pay is high. A good example is Sandra Kurtzig's description of how she set prices in the early days of ASK Computer Systems. ASK developed programs to help users monitor and evaluate their manufacturing process (scheduling, cost analysis, etc.). The software was extremely valuable to a user and there were few competitors or alternatives: Kurtzig called her pricing model the "flinch method." When asked how much the software was, she would respond, "$50,000." If the buyer didn't flinch, she would add, "per module." Again, if there were no visible choking, she would add, "per year." And so on, and so on. Kurtzig was ultimately able to build a very profitable multi-hundred million dollar business using this kind of "street smart" pricing.

The list of questions above focuses on the top and bottom line of a business—the direct revenues and the costs of producing and marketing a product. That's fine, as far as it goes. Sensible analysis of a proposal, however, involves also assessing the business model from a different perspective that takes into account the investment required (i.e., the balance sheet side of the equation). Consider the following questions that I use to assess the cash flow implications of pursuing an opportunity:

- When do you have to buy resources (supplies, people, etc.)?
- When do you have to pay for them?
- How long does it take to acquire a customer?
- How long before the customer sends you a check?
- How much capital equipment is required to support a dollar of sales?

Underlying these questions on the balance sheet is a simple yet powerful maxim in business:

> **Buy low, sell high, collect early, and pay late.[7]**

The best businesses are those in which you have large profit margins, you get paid by your customers before you have to deliver the product, and the fixed asset requirements are modest. It goes without saying, in addition, that such a business should also be characterized by insuperable entry barriers.

Consider, to illustrate, the magazine publishing business. Once up and running, a successful magazine has remarkably attractive cash flow characteristics. Subscribers pay in advance of receiving the magazine. Often, magazines can even get subscribers to pay for several years in advance. I once discovered that I had nine years worth of service coming on a magazine because I diligently paid the bill each time they sent it to me, taking advantage of multi-year discounts. If the magazine can maintain compelling content, then current subscribers tend to re-subscribe on a regular basis with low incremental marketing cost. It is always easier to retain a customer than to acquire a new one. If the demographic profile of the readers is attractive, then advertisers use the magazine to reach a target audience, a successful example of "if you build it, they will come." It takes very little plant and equipment to run a magazine: printing and fulfillment are often farmed out to vendors who specialize and deliver high quality service at low cost. The editorial costs of a magazine are typically low. In essence, magazine publishing has all the attractive characteristics listed above.

Of course, the fact that a magazine property is valuable once it is up and running has not escaped people's attention. Each year, hundreds of new magazines are launched: most, to quote test pilot Chuck Yeager, "auger in." The Achilles heal in publishing is the cost of acquiring a customer in a world where most niches have already been recognized and served.

There are some other attractive business models that warrant mention. When I assess a business, I look for ways in which a company can expand the range of products or services being offered to the same customer base. Often, companies are able to create virtual "pipelines" which support the economically viable creation of new revenue streams. In the magazine business, for example, it is possible to create other lines of products or services that are attractive to subscribers. *Inc.* magazine, to illustrate, has expanded beyond the basic magazine business to offer seminars, books, and videos for the *Inc.* subscriber (and others). In this example, a virtuous cycle is established in which success in the basic magazine leads to new related business opportunities that might not exist in the absence of the magazine.

A similarly attractive business model is illustrated by Intuit, which is best known for its personal financial program Quicken. The latter program helps users organize their checkbook. After the initial success of Quicken, Intuit was able to offer a wide range of additional services, including electronic banking, personal printing supplies, tax preparation

---

[7]This is the title of a useful book—Richard Levin, *Buy Low, Sell High, Collect Early and Pay Late: The Manager's Guide to Financial Survival,* Prentice-Hall, 1983.

software, and on-line information services. Because some of these ancillary services are so profitable, Intuit is able to give away the software program in hopes of creating a life-long customer who buys additional services and products from the company. Intuit also discovered that many users of its personal finance program Quicken were small businesses: they soon introduced a variant of the program, called QuickBooks, that is designed to meet the specific accounting needs of small businesses. The QuickBooks division is now more profitable than the original consumer focused one, demonstrating how success in one business can lead to success in another that is closely related.[8]

Not all businesses are created equal in terms of the kind of growth opportunities described above. In some businesses, success in one product or service does not necessarily create additional opportunities with the same customer base. Again, the disk drive business is informative because competitors have historically been unable to replicate success in one part of the industry in another. For example those firms that were successful in producing 5.25" drives) were not, for the most part, successful in producing 3.5" drives. Catching one technology wave does not always imply an ability to catch the next one. As colleagues Clayton Christensen and Joseph Bower have observed, the old axiom about staying close to the customer works if and only if you choose the right customer.[9]

An obvious extension of the pipeline model relates to geographic expansion possibilities. Some businesses are attractive because a successful model in one region can be rolled out to other regions. Such is the case in the theme restaurant business. If Hard Rock Cafe works in Paris and London, then it will probably work in New York and Chicago. This kind of business is rich in growth options that result from success.

There are many other successful business models that entrepreneurs and investors look for when making resource commitments to opportunities. I try, for example, to find companies that "sell ammunition to all sides of the war without end" rather than engage in direct combat. An illustration is A. C. Nielsen, which measures marketing response for companies selling products or services but does not have to try to compete in the actual markets (e.g., Coke versus Pepsi, or ABC versus NBC). A similar company called Internet Profiles exists in the Internet world: it measures activity at web sites rather than trying to compete with other web site purveyors.

Another illustration of the "ammunition" strategy is a company called Abacus Direct. This company was founded to help catalog merchants improve the effectiveness of their customer acquisition strategies. Briefly, the co-founders convinced a large number of catalog companies (e.g., Lands' End and Orvis) to give them a data file comprised of the purchasing histories of each catalog's customers. The data on customers of many different catalogs was then pooled and analyzed. Using proprietary software, Abacus Direct was able to help the catalog companies identify high potential customers to whom new catalogs could be mailed and eliminate low potential customers from their lists.

---

[8]Interestingly, the original Intuit business plan was sent to quite a few venture capitalists, including two members of Scott Cook's HBS class. The plan was rejected by one and all. Only later did the two classmates get an opportunity to invest in Intuit while it was still private. The potential small business accounting opportunity was specifically mentioned in the original Intuit plan.

[9]Clayton Christensen and Joseph Bower, "Disruptive Technologies: Catching the Wave," *Harvard Business Review* (January/February, 1995), pp. 43–53.

Six years after starting, Abacus Direct was able to achieve an 75% share of the domestic catalog business. The company was extremely profitable early in its development, with net margins in the 30% range. Three contextual factors helped Abacus Direct enormously. First, competition among catalog companies was fierce and Abacus Direct benefited by helping competitors be more effective. Second, postage cost increases changed the business model for catalog merchants, making it imperative that direct mail effectiveness be improved. Finally, the cost of managing and analyzing a massive database, one containing purchase histories on almost 90 million people, fell dramatically. What used to take a mainframe computer many hours to analyze now takes minutes on a powerful workstation. The founders of Abacus Direct had previously founded a company that handled warranty card registrations for major appliance manufacturers. Again, that company had sold mailing lists based on purchase histories: the company was successful and was sold to a larger company some five years after it was founded. To use the terminology introduced in the section on "people," the founders "knew" the industry and they were "known," dramatically increasing the likelihood of their success.

Another simple example of an oft-repeated successful business model involves the old "razors and razor blades" strategy made famous by Gillette. The razors are sold at cost, and all the money is made on the blades. There are many companies pursuing a variation of this strategy, Gillette being the best known. The recently introduced data storage device called the Zip Drive by Iomega illustrates a policy of giving away the device at cost or a small profit and making all of the money on the proprietary disks that go with the drive. Nintendo makes most of its money on software, not on the game players it sells.

There are some opportunity traps that warrant mention. Some businesses have distinctly unattractive economic prospects, defined as high capital costs (front-loaded), low margins, and high risk. The disk drive business probably fits this description well. So too does the airline business. In such industries, however, the business plans that are written do not really address the problems. They describe instead the opportunity in glowing terms. They state that the market is large and growing, and that all the new entrant needs to do is to attain a 10% market share to achieve great success. Unfortunately, if hundreds of capable teams all enter a market looking for a 10% share, I don't think the math quite works out. In some industries, even great teams can't overcome poor industry business models, as the great investor Warren Buffett discovered when he bought part of US Air.

I have also come to believe that the world of "invention" is fraught with danger. Over the past fifteen years, I have seen scores of individuals who have invented a "better mousetrap." They have developed tools or systems in areas that range from bicycle pumps to inflatable pillows for use on airlines to automated car parking systems. Their technology is patented and seems on the surface to be a "no-brainer" to potential adopters. In spite of the seeming attractiveness of the innovation, however, I have seen very few examples of successful commercialization. It turns out that idea-driven companies typically undervalue commercialization capabilities. The inventor frequently refuses to spend the money required or refuses to share the rewards with the business side of the company, the inevitable consequence of which is that the technology never gets implemented regardless of how compelling it seems to be.

My views of the importance of commercialization skills were influenced by one of the first technology based companies I ever visited. In the early 1980s, a group of Harvard undergraduates acquired the rights to a technology that would help improve the combustion characteristics of certain grades of fuel oil. Essentially, the process would enable fuel burners to use much cheaper oil to accomplish a given task. I was intrigued by the process and admired the dogged determination of the young entrepreneurs.

Ultimately, this company, Fuel Tech, raised $75 million from private investors around the globe. The technology I described never proved to be commercially viable. The company founders scrambled to find an alternative path to business success for Fuel Tech. To my utter amazement, they were able to acquire some operating companies at attractive prices. The company was eventually sold at a price that netted handsome returns for the investors and the founders. Later, the lead entrepreneur, William Haney, acquired the rights to some environmental technology developed at MIT. He founded, and currently is chairman of, a company called Molten Metals, which has a current market capitalization of almost $500 million. During his Fuel Tech days, he learned how to make money, a far more valuable skill, I submit, than the ability to invent.[10]

One final comment on opportunities involves what I call "arbitrage" businesses. Basically, these businesses exist to take advantage of some pricing disparity in the marketplace. The classic entrepreneurial example was MCI Telecommunications which was formed to offer long distance service at a lower price than AT&T. Similar current examples of arbitrage exist in the health care business in which entrepreneurs are finding ways to offer comparable services to hospitals at much lower costs. Or, some of the industry consolidations going on today reflect a different kind of arbitrage—the ability to buy small businesses at a "wholesale" price, roll them up into a larger package, and take them public at a "retail" price, all without necessarily adding true value in the process.

Taking advantage of arbitrage opportunities is a viable and potentially profitable way to enter a business. In the final analysis, however, all arbitrage opportunities go away. It is not a question of whether, only when. The trick in these businesses is to use the arbitrage profits to build a more enduring business model.

Competition

The notion that all arbitrage opportunities go away reflects a more general belief that all opportunities go away. For any given opportunity, there are a myriad of potential competitors. In 1995, to illustrate, almost $30 billion was invested in private equity funds, of which perhaps 20% was in traditional venture capital. In 1995, over 1 million new businesses were incorporated in the U.S. The situation outside the U.S. is similar in the sense that many investors are seeking to back competent entrepreneurial ventures around the world. Moreover, all large companies have become more attuned to opportunity, suggesting a more rapid and competent attempt to identify and exploit them.

---

[10]Actually, Molten Metals is not yet profitable, and, given the inevitable difficulties confronting any company scaling up a new technology, success is certainly not guaranteed.

A business plan must address the current competitors and the potential competitors in a sensible way. Among the specific issues a plan should cover are the following:

- Who are the current competitors?
- What resources do they control? What are their strengths and weaknesses?
- How will they respond to our decision to enter the business?
- How can we respond to their response?
- Who else might be able to observe and exploit the same opportunity?
- Are there ways to co-opt potential or actual competitors by forming alliances?

Business is like chess: to be successful, you must anticipate several moves in advance in order to have any chance. A business plan that describes an insuperable lead or a proprietary position is by definition written by naive people.

Graphical Analysis Tools for Assessing Opportunities (or, Harold and the Purple Crayon Meets Entrepreneurial Finance)

I like to think of business opportunities in terms of their risk/reward profiles. I have two graphical tools that I apply to understand a business model. The first entails drawing a simple cash flow diagram for the business and the second entails assigning probabilities to certain outcomes. Starting first with the cash flow diagram, consider, to illustrate, a proposal to start a new airline. The cash flow pattern depicted in the business plan looks something like the following:

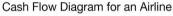

Cash Flow Diagram for an Airline

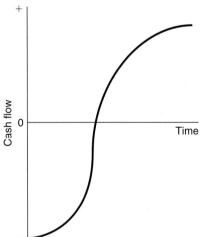

Essentially, starting an airline involves a very large capital commitment up front followed by some unknown returns in the future. When I look at this pattern, I focus first and foremost on the likelihood of achieving positive cash flow, when that event might occur, and the potential payoff structure if I am successful. In my view, the airline business is a bad business because the payoffs are too low and risky and too far in the future, given the upfront capital required. The business has high fixed costs of operation, which is often associated with vicious pricing cycles in which prices are driven down to the level of marginal costs. It's rather like the Harvard freshmen football coach said when describing his team, "They're not big, but they're slow." Airlines aren't very profitable, but they require a huge amount of capital.[11]

Compare an airline with an electronically delivered newsletter for which subscribers pay in advance. As noted earlier, the capital requirements in publishing are modest and the potential margins high. If such a plan had a compelling editorial position and could attract subscribers at acceptable costs, then the cash flow pattern might be as depicted below:

Cash Flow Diagram for a Newsletter

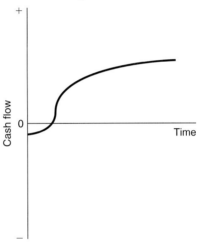

Returning to the discussion earlier of business models, it turns out that successful companies typically have more than one relevant cash flow S-curve. In such companies, there are growth opportunities, defined as opportunities to profitably invest additional funds because of success in the first project. For example, a magazine that is launched and attracts an audience might be able to introduce a related product or service (e.g., seminars or conferences, additional magazines targeted at a segment of the overall leadership). Similarly, a single successful restaurant may form the foundation for a chain of restaurants in different areas. Or, a successful software company might have international expansion possibilities that are as attractive (or more so) than the domestic one. The goal in investing or in identifying opportunities from the perspective of the entrepreneur is to identify businesses that have many such growth options and to preserve the right to exploit them. The following graph depicts a favorable growth option pattern, one like a magazine or a restaurant.

---

[11]Far better than entering the airline business itself is starting a service for all of the companies in the airline business. Prominent successful examples include Flight Safety, which builds flight simulators, and Sabre Corporation, which was originally started by American Airlines to automate flight scheduling and reservations.

Cash Flow Diagram for a Magazine or a Restaurant

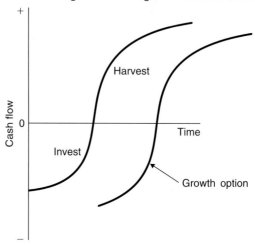

Finding opportunities with ample growth options is a goal: many industries, however, have a pattern that looks attractive but is not. In the disk drive business, for example, success in one investment category does not necessarily lead to success in another: indeed, there is some evidence that success leads to disaster. In such industries, which might be called "wave" industries, it is very hard if not impossible to catch successive waves without crashing and burning. The disk drive industry is portrayed below:

Cash Flow Diagram for the Disk Drive Business

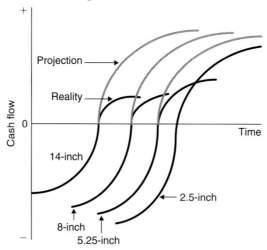

A question that leaps out of the cash flow diagrams depicted above is: how do I make decisions that involve tradeoffs between the present and the future? How do I decide whether the potential future cash is big enough to justify the initial investment? To answer these questions, it is clear that you have to assess the riskiness of the bet you are making.

There are two ways to portray the riskiness of a project such as a new airline or an on-line publication. One is to draw the same diagrams as above but to depict reasonable scenarios as well as the expected values. The graph below shows three scenarios: the original business plan model, a success scenario in which the company achieved its goals but only after investing more time and money (a frequent event for companies that succeed), and a third scenario in which the company failed after a considerable investment and time period.

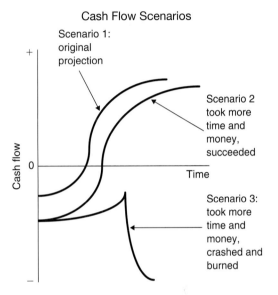

The other way to shed light on the riskiness of a project is to assign probabilities to different outcomes for returns on investment. The following diagram shows the payoff structure for an investment in a new software company:

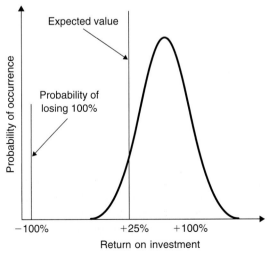

If I make an investment in a new software company, there is some considerable risk that I will lose all of my money. At the same time, I might well invest in the next Microsoft or Netscape, in which case I will have very high returns, perhaps in excess of 100% per year. The picture above suggests that there is a small, perhaps even negligible probability of earning a small rate of return on an investment in a software company. The rationale is that most small software companies are not very profitable and are therefore not worth much very much. Unless the venture reaches escape velocity, it probably won't succeed.

There is a broad class of investments whose payoff structures look like that for the hypothetical software company. There are other investments where the risk reward pattern looks quite different. Consider an investment in a franchise of a well-established fast food company. In such an investment, there is an extended history of profitable operations. The company has a solid business plan and reasonably predictable results. In this case, the payoff structure might be as depicted below:

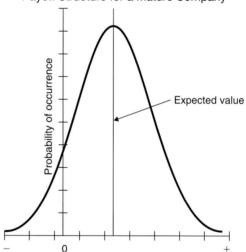

In this example, the likelihood of losing all of your money is modest but so too is the upside potential. Of course, return on investment depends on who is asking the question and on the price paid to invest. If you have to pay a high franchise fee, then you lower your potential return and increase the likelihood of a loss. Or, if you are a venture capital investor who strikes a deal with the entrepreneur that is generous to the entrepreneur (e.g., if you pay a high valuation), then the risk/reward pattern looks different.

In general, these graphical tools can be used to describe investment opportunities. Investments involve different combinations of capital requirements and payoffs. They involve differing degrees of uncertainty. To reiterate the obvious, you want opportunities that offer the prospect of high, safe returns on modest investment, with lots of attractive and proprietary growth options—a simple rule to describe, but one that is almost impossible to follow in the real world.

Context

Opportunities exist in a context. At one level, there is the macroeconomic environment, including the level of economic activity, inflation, exchange rates, and interest rates. There are also a wide range of rules and regulations that affect opportunity and how resources are marshaled to exploit it. Examples range from tax policy to the rules concerning raising capital for a private or public company. Then, there are factors like technology, which affect what a business or its competitors can accomplish.

I will not dwell on context here except to remark that context often has a tremendous impact on every aspect of the entrepreneurial process, from identification of opportunity to harvest. In some cases, changes in some contextual factor create opportunity. For example, when the airline industry was deregulated in the late 1970s, over one hundred new airlines were formed. The context for financing was also favorable, enabling new entrants like People Express to go to the public market for capital even before starting operations.

Conversely, there are periods when the context makes it hard to start new enterprises. In the early 1990s, to illustrate, there was a difficult recession, combined with a difficult financing environment for new companies: venture capital disbursements were low as was the amount of capital raised in the public markets. Paradoxically, these relatively tight conditions, which made it harder for new entrants to get going, were associated with very high investment returns later in the 1990s as the capital market environment heated up.

Sometimes, a shift in context turns an unattractive business into an attractive one, and vice versa. A colleague was on the board of a struggling packaging company some years ago. The board had decided to sell the business. Within weeks of that decision, however, there was an incident in which bottles of Tylenol were tampered with, resulting in multiple deaths. The particular company happened to have an efficient mechanism for putting tamper-proof seals on Tylenol bottles. What had been a poorly performing business quickly turned into a spectacular one, all in a matter of weeks. Conversely, for companies in the real estate business, the tax reforms enacted in 1986 in the U.S. created havoc: almost every positive incentive to invest in real estate was reversed. Many previously successful firms in the real estate industry went out of business soon after the new rules were put in place.

When I read a business plan, I look for two pieces of evidence related to context. First, I want to see that the entrepreneurial team is aware of the context and how it helps or hinders their specific proposal. Second, and more importantly, I look for sensitivity to the fact that the context will inevitably change. If so, how might the changes affect the business? And, what can management do in the event the context worsens? Finally, are there ways in which management can affect context in a positive way? For example, can management have an impact on regulation or on setting industry standards? We will address the issue of dealing with contextual factors in more detail shortly.

Deals

Most people think of valuation and terms when considering deals. What share of the company will they have to give to the investors to raise capital? What are the terms of the financing? These are the prominent questions. In this section, I will address these issues, but only after considering the sources of capital and the amount raised. The rationale for this sequencing will become apparent shortly.

When I talk to young (and old) entrepreneurs looking to finance their ventures, they obsess about valuation. Their explicit goal seems to be to minimize the dilution they will suffer in raising capital. Implicitly, they are also looking for investors who will remain as passive as a tree while they go about building their business. On the food chain of investors, it seems, doctors and dentists are best and venture capitalists worst because of the degree to which the latter group demands a large share of the returns and demands control rights.

I confess to a bias on the subject of financing ventures. My rule is the following:

> **From whom you raise capital is often more important than the terms.**

Let me explain. Ventures are inherently risky. Murphy often is a member of the management team—what can go wrong will. Most ventures end up taking more time and more money than the entrepreneur ever imagined. The name of the game, then, is not to minimize dilution at each stage of a company's existence but rather to maximize the value of your share at the end of the process.

I have seen quite a few examples of entrepreneurs raising money from unsophisticated investors at high prices. When the inevitable bad news arrives, the investors panic and get angry. They refuse to advance the company more money. They are surprised that results are disappointing. In such situations, it is often difficult to recruit new investors. The new investor has to worry about the old investor group—if they're not putting up more money, what's wrong? The old investors are also reticent to accept the valuation proposed by the new investor.

I view the financing decision as having two fundamental elements: a capital raising decision and a hiring decision. Consider, to illustrate, raising capital from a professional venture capitalist. The investor typically seeks to earn high returns, perhaps 50% per year or greater. This seems on the surface like very high cost money, almost loan-shark-like. Suppose, however, that the venture capitalist is the leading expert in the world in the business being financed. Suppose as well that the venture capitalist can increase the potential reward and decrease the potential risk by being involved in the business. In this case, the value of the entrepreneur's share of the company assuming the venture capitalist invests may be higher than it would have been if the company had raised money from less competent investors. Phrased differently, the total pie is increased in size so much that the value of the entrepreneur's smaller slice of the pie is larger.

There are many examples of venture capitalists whose presence in a deal helps enormously. John Doerr, for example, is a partner of the highly successful firm Kleiner, Perkins. Mr. Doerr was a top-ranked salesman at semiconductor powerhouse Intel in the mid 1970s. Doerr has invested in such companies as Sun Microsystems, Intuit and Netscape. He knows the process of building large and successful companies. He has a world-class rolodex, which helps his portfolio companies form valuable connections. I would want John Doerr on my team and I would be prepared to pay a high price to get him. The same is true of other similarly skilled and experienced investors like Arthur

Rock or L. J. Sevin. I should also note that if these individuals work with my company, they won't work with my competitor.

I believe that every high potential venture needs an investor who is "process literate." By this, I mean that they have been through the game many times. They are very good at helping companies grow. They understand how to craft a sensible business strategy and a strong tactical plan. They help recruit, compensate, and motivate great team members. They are coaches and cheerleaders, and they understand the distinction between being an investor and being the entrepreneur. I believe as well that good investors do not panic when bad news arrives. They roll up their sleeves and help the company solve its problems.

There are many decisions in a venture that entrepreneurs will have to face only once or twice in their careers. An example is the decision to go public. The entrepreneur is pitted against highly experienced but not necessarily disinterested service providers like investment bankers, lawyers, and accountants. It is extremely useful in such a situation to have advisors who have "been there and done that." The same is true about other process decisions, such as introducing a new product, dealing with a lawsuit, recruiting a VP of Marketing, or selling a business.

There are other areas in which the choice of a financial partner can help a company. For example, sometimes it is advantageous to raise money from customers. Those customers can help sell the product or service. The best form of customer money is a pre-paid order, but it might also make sense to have the customer own equity. The same might be true of suppliers. Even potential competitors are on the list of possible investors, if by investing they forgo the option of entering the business directly. Raising money from these non-traditional sources might seem to create conflicts of interest. As Howard Stevenson says, however, "without conflict, there is no interest."

Though I have started this discussion of "deals" by focusing on who invests, an issue of great importance is how much money to raise and in what stages. Most ventures need more money than they are initially able to raise. Investors are loath to hand over large sums of capital up front to an eager team of business founders. If a company believes it ultimately will need $10 million to develop and introduce a software product, they are likely to find that no investor will invest the full $10 million. Rather, the investor will stage the commitment of capital over time, preserving the right to invest more money and preserving the right to abandon the project in the event the team or the business idea doesn't work out. The investor might offer to invest $1 million while the software is finished. If the software looks attractive, the investor will put in $4 million for the launch of the product. If the launch is promising, then the investor will put up more money, perhaps the remaining $5 million or more, to support expansion of the company.

The issue of how much money to invest in a company is exceedingly difficult and the perspective of the players often differs. Entrepreneurs want all the money up front, while investors want to stage the capital over time in order to "buy" more information. There is no right answer in this ancient debate. There are, however, some useful ways to think about the issues inherent in financing new ventures.

An old saying is "time is money." In entrepreneurial finance, the expression gets turned around: "money is time." By this I mean that money buys time for a venture to find the right combination of people, strategy, and tactics to succeed. Each chunk of money buys an additional chunk of time.

I think of ventures as complicated options such as one finds in financial markets. In this regard, raising money is like extending the expiration date of the option. If the company runs out of money, investors will have to decide whether or not it makes sense to buy more time and, if so, on what terms.

There is also another way in which money is time. Often, a company is pursuing an opportunity for which time to market is critical: the first mover gets the largest share, and the second place finisher is far less attractive. Money can help a company accelerate its entry plan. Some aspects of the business can be done in parallel rather than in sequence. From one perspective, the decision to accelerate spending would seem risky: just the opposite may be true. To go slow is to risk everything. Consider, to illustrate, the famous case on Science Technology used at Harvard Business School. The case mentions that the company invented the oscilloscope after World War II. The case also mentions a sign on the factory floor that stated, "We don't want to grow too large." Unfortunately, they succeeded beyond their wildest dreams: another company pursued the oscilloscope opportunity faster and captured the market, leaving Science Technology as small as it apparently aspired to be.

There are other paradoxes in the world of raising money. Sometimes having too much money dooms a company. The founders (and employees) don't view money as a scarce resource: this often occurs in large companies, which have managers who rely on the deep pockets of the parent organization. At other times, a company starves an opportunity.

There are some useful questions that speak to the issue of how time and money should relate to each other in a specific venture, including the following:

- What new information would dramatically change your perception of the likelihood of success for a given venture?
- How much time and money are required to "buy" that information?
- To what degree does the company have control over the rate at which it exploits an opportunity?
- Who else might be pursuing the same opportunity and what are the consequences of losing the race?

The final issue to be covered in this section on deals relates specifically to their structure. There are two important aspects of deal structure that preoccupy entrepreneurs, judging by the number of phone calls I get asking for advice: valuation and terms (i.e., other aspects of the deal, such as employment contracts, etc.).

Unfortunately, there are very few definitive rules when it comes to structuring deals. On the one hand, I believe in the golden rule: "He who has the gold rules." On the other hand, I believe that deals that are too tough on either side generally don't work.

Over the years, I have developed a set of principles to guide deal making. First, deals fundamentally allocate risk and reward and therefore value. Whenever risk and reward are allocated, the deal maker has to be concerned with the three issues:

- What are the incentive effects of the allocation?
- Who will be attracted by the terms offered?
- What are the logical implications if the parties to a deal behave in their own perceived best interest?

Consider, to illustrate, a typical deal between a venture capital firm and a venture. During the past twenty years, the structure of such deals has evolved to a recognizable standard. First, venture capitalists invest in stages: they do not give all the money to the entrepreneurial team that will be required to exploit the opportunity. They almost always invest in the form of a convertible preferred. The preferred has liquidation preference: if the company is liquidated, the principal of the preferred must be paid back before the equityholders receive any of the liquidation proceeds. The preferred has a dividend that is payable at the discretion of the board of directors but adds to the liquidation principle if not paid before liquidation. The preferred is convertible into common stock at some stated price: conversion is typically mandatory if the company goes public. The investors preserve the right to invest additional money by having preemptive rights or rights of first refusal on subsequent financing. The investors have some protection against dilution such as might occur if the company raises additional capital at a lower price. Often, the investors have the right to force the company to repurchase the preferred at some point in the future on some prearranged terms. The investors have certain information rights, enabling them to receive timely (and credible) financial reports and to be notified before major events at the company. The investors also have certain governance rights such as the right to appoint directors or the right to replace the founder or founders. The management team, including the founders typically receive common stock (or stock options) and are subject to vesting requirements: if they leave the company, they lose the unvested portion of their options or stock.

Implicit in each element of the standard venture capital deal is a notion of how the incentives ought to be set. Any time an investor gives money to someone else, they have to concern themselves with possible conflicts of interest. The entrepreneur might, for example, pay him/herself a large salary, depleting the funds of the venture. The entrepreneur might decide to keep the company private, never enabling the investor to get a return on investment.

The deal structure described above is designed to protect the investor and provide appropriate incentives to the entrepreneurial venture. Consider, to illustrate, the rationale for staging the commitment of capital—investing less than might ultimately be needed to exploit an opportunity. Suppose a venture needs $20 million to go from concept to commercialization. Why don't investors just give the full $20 million up front? Well, it's not hard to figure out, when you think about it. I have previously noted that there is often a discrepancy between outcomes and plans. In this hypothetical $20 million venture, it is highly likely that there will be some bad news early in its evolution.

Suppose that, six months after the team receives the $20 million, they discover a fatal flaw in their engineering. Will they call the investors, admit to their discovery, and send back the unspent funds? Not on this planet, they won't. Never in the history of entrepreneurship has an entrepreneur announced defeat. They always believe that the problem can be fixed—all they need is a little more time and a little more money. By the way, sometimes they are right. Federal Express approached bankruptcy three times before it gained escape velocity.

The point here is that investors need to have the right to decide whether or not to continue to back the team and the project: they should not cede decision rights to the team because the team will almost always make a self-interested choice. Indeed, if the entrepreneurial team were to insist that the entire $20 million be invested up-front, they would likely find no (rational) investors willing to make the bet, regardless of the share of the company they would acquire. Also, because the entrepreneurs are likely to have to agree to a staged infusion of capital—with each additional investment based on new information and a price reflecting that information—the entrepreneurs signal their belief in their ability to bring the project to fruition.

The incentive effects of deal structuring could occupy a book and I will not attempt to describe this topic in detail in this note.[12] Rather, the important lesson for entrepreneurs writing business plans is that they have to structure deals that reflect their incentives and those of investors. There is an implicit balancing act. The specific deal will be tailored to the characteristics of the individuals involved, the nature of the opportunity, and the contextual setting.

One caution is appropriate about deal structuring: there is an old expression—"too clever by half"—which is directly relevant. Often, deal makers get creative in structuring deals. For example, they design complex valuation schemes that involve conditional pricing of a deal. If the company does as well as management thinks, then management gets some extra options. If the venture only does as well as the venture capitalist thinks, then the terms are more onerously tilted in favor of the investors. Through painful experience, I have come to believe that simple is better than complex. Trying to structure such complex deals often ends up turning partners into adversaries. In the deal described above, perhaps the venture capitalist will be better off if the company does poorly (but not too poorly) for some period and then takes off. Does the venture capitalist really want to be conflicted in this way? I think not.

In my experience, sensible deals have the following characteristics:

- They are simple
- They are fair
- They reflect trust rather than legalese
- They are robust—they do not blow apart if actual differs slightly from plan
- They do not provide perverse incentives that will cause one or both parties to behave in destructive ways
- They do not foreclose valuable options
- The papers used to describe the deal are no greater than one-quarter inch

No discussion of deals would be complete without a section on valuation. How are ventures valued, particularly ones for which there is massive uncertainty? The short (and flip) answer is: "aerial extraction." A less curt answer is that venture valuation is an art, not a science. Every entrepreneur I have met says something like the following: "Based on my projections, you (the investor) should be willing to value my company at $10 million. If you do, you will earn a 78% percent internal rate of return, based on our going public in five years." The response is: "I'll value your company at $3 million—your numbers aren't worth the paper they're written on. . . ."

---

[12]For more information on deals and incentives, see William A. Sahlman, "Note on Financial Contracting: 'Deals,'" Harvard Business School Case # 288-014. See also William A. Sahlman, "The Structure and Governance of Venture Capital Organizations," *Journal of Financial Economics,* October 1990.

Only if you had omniscience would it be easy to value companies early in their life. The venture investor knows from hard-earned experience that few if any ventures come anywhere close to meeting their projections. Only 10% to 20% of the deals in which they invest will do really well. Some 30% will actually result in losses, in some cases complete loss. What seasoned investors do, therefore, is base their valuations on the overall experience they have had. The reasoning goes something like the following: "If I value early stage software companies at $5 million or less, then I will be able—after it is all said and done—to earn a rate of return on my portfolio that is acceptable to me and my limited partners."

My students are always disappointed that there are not formulae for calculating the value of a venture. They do not like the fact that there are a wide range of possible valuations that are OK or "in the ballpark." They do not like the fact that their negotiating skill and assets (i.e., the degree to which the team and the opportunity are outstanding and proprietary) will determine what happens. I too wish it were easier to come up with answers, or at least narrow ranges: it would certainly make my job less stressful![13]

In closing, this section on deals has been implicitly based on a simple set of structured questions, which are listed below:

- From whom should the money be raised?

- How much money is needed and for what purpose?

- What deal terms are fair and provide the appropriate incentives for each side under a wide range of scenarios?

Risk/Reward Management

One fascinating aspect of business is the degree to which the future is hard to predict. It is certainly possible to write down a detailed description of a bright future, but hard to make it happen. The notion above that there is a known probability distribution for outcomes is useful but slightly misleading. There are no immutable distributions of outcomes. It is ultimately the responsibility of management to change the distribution, to increase the likelihood and consequences of success and decrease the likelihood and implications of problems.

One of the great myths about entrepreneurs is that they are risk seekers. My sense is that all sane people want to avoid risk. As colleague Howard Stevenson says, true entrepreneurs want to capture all of the reward and give all of the risk to others. The best business is a post office box to which people send cashiers checks. Yet, risk is unavoidable. So what is a rational person to do?

My answer to this question is that you must assess the risks and find mechanisms to manage them. Consider, to illustrate, a risk inherent in the context, the set of factors outside the control of the entrepreneur. There might be an increase in interest rates: if a venture is highly leveraged, then an increase in interest cost might sink it. To manage this risk, it might make sense to hedge the exposure in the financial futures market so that a

---

[13]For more than you ever wanted to know about valuing venture deals, see Daniel R. Scherlis and William A. Sahlman, "A Method for Valuing High-Risk, Long-Term Investments," Harvard Business School Case # 288-006.

contract is purchased that does well when interest rates go up. This is equivalent to buy-ing insurance: you pay a premium to do so, but you can preserve a company's business model by doing so.

In general, there are a myriad of things that can go wrong or right in a venture. Though it is impossible to predict the future, it is possible to change the odds or manage the consequences of adverse events. For example, suppose you write a great novel. You go to an agent. The agent sells the rights to the book to a publisher. What should you worry about?

Clearly, a successful novel has a number of attractive follow-on possibilities/growth options, including a potential movie based on the book. You can insist that the contract you sign enables you—rather than the publisher—to reap the bulk of the re-wards from a movie. I promise, however, that the initial contract you receive will grant to the publisher all ancillary rights associated with the book, from software to video. I also promise that the contract will be tilted in favor of the publisher in other ways. To illustrate, the contract will spell out possible royalty rates: you must not become so pre-occupied with getting a high royalty rate that you ignore what that rate is applied to. Many naive authors have signed movie deals where they get a share of the net income generated in the movie: lo and behold, the movie grosses $500 million, but the author receives no royalties. She is told the movie was unprofitable . . . .

In this example, you cannot predict the success or failure of the book in the marketplace, but you can preserve the option to benefit if it is a success. You can retain certain rights and you can pay attention to the nature of those rights, including the in-centives of the other party. Or, you can cross the Mass Turnpike blindfolded. The basic model of risk/reward management is depicted below:

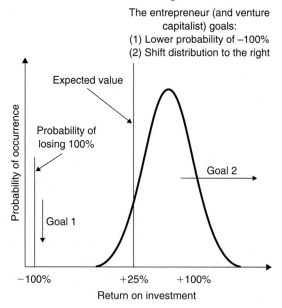

Risk/Reward Management

One specific area of importance in the realm of risk/reward management relates to harvesting. Earlier, I suggested that opportunities differed in terms of the implicit growth options defined as opportunities that companies have by dint of their entering a market (e.g., to sell additional products or services to the same customers). Businesses also differ in terms of their harvest potential by which I mean the ability to reap the rewards of the investment process.

For example, venture capitalists often ask if a company is "IPOable," by which they mean: can the company be taken public at some point in the future? Some businesses are inherently difficult to take public, sometimes because doing so would reveal information that might harm the competitive position of the firm (e.g., reveal profitability, thereby encouraging entry or angering customers or suppliers). Some businesses are not companies, but rather products—they are not sustainable as an independent business.

One important task for entrepreneur and investor alike is to think hard at the beginning about the end of the process. Specifically, how will you get money out of the business, assuming it is successful, or even if it is only marginally successful? Some businesses are rife with harvest potential: they involve products or services that are worth a great deal to many potential buyers. If you are currently in the telecommunications software industry today, for example, you are witnessing one of the great industry consolidations ever. Companies like Cisco, 3Com, and Bay Networks are on acquisition binges. If you have created a successful niche product or service, there is a strong possibility that one of those three companies will try to buy you. Moreover, because each of the three must compete with the other two, the sellers might well get additional (even unwarranted) benefits from playing one firm off against another.

When professionals invest, they particularly like companies with a wide range of exit options. They work hard to preserve and enhance those options along the way. For example, they avoid forming a strategic relationship with a major company early in the process because doing so often forecloses the exit option of having multiple large firms bid against each other for the right to buy the company. There is an old saying: "If you don't know where you are going, any road will get you there." In crafting sensible entrepreneurial strategies, just the opposite is true: you had better know where you might end up and have a plan for getting there.

Financial Projections

No discussion of business plans would be complete without addressing the ubiquitous proformas that populate them. Most business plan writers spend countless hours on detailed financial projections. They imagine that a potential investor will pore over the numbers asking a myriad of questions. They also imagine that the investor will propose a deal based on the numbers in the plan.

When I first started to study entrepreneurial ventures, I too turned first to the numbers. Of late, I have gotten to the point where I hardly even look at them. Indeed, if I receive a plan that has five years of monthly projections, I immediately and enthusiastically throw the plan in the circular file next to my desk.

Every business plan contains the following phrase: "we conservatively project." Only about 1 in 20 plans are conservative in the sense that the company comes even close to meeting its plan. If you observe one hundred companies and only five come close to their original projections, then you begin to pick up a pattern.

I have come to believe that spreadsheets have an innate virus that infects the projections made in business plans. The virus turns what might be sensible people into wildly optimistic, nonsensical maniacs.

There are two or three possible explanations for why the virus is so widespread. First, in every business, there is what I call the "horse race between fear and greed." Entrepreneurs want to preserve the largest possible ownership stake when raising capital. At the same time, they are afraid of running out of capital. Very few if any entrepreneurs correctly anticipate how much capital and time will be required to accomplish their objectives. Venture capitalists automatically discount what is in a plan to reflect the consistency and predictability of the optimism.

Of course, if the entrepreneurs know that the venture capitalist will discount his or her projections, then they pad the projections to offset the likely haircut to be applied. This sounds to me like a vicious cycle in which reality becomes hard to find.

It's rather like the distinction between "buying proformas" and "selling proformas." It all depends on your perspective. Indeed, I always ask a simple question when looking at projections: Who wrote the proforma and why?

When I read a proforma projection, I look first and foremost for evidence of a business model that makes sense and an appreciation of the fact that the specific numbers proffered are almost certain to be wrong. I like to see that the entrepreneurial team has thought through the key drivers that will determine success or failure. In a traditional magazine business, to illustrate, among the key business drivers are: total possible subscribers in the target audience; gross response rate (how many respond to a mailing that they are interested in subscribing?); net response (how many who say they will try the magazine actually pay?); and, renewal rate (how many who subscribe actually renew their subscription when it lapses?). These factors help determine the profitability of a magazine because they affect the cost of acquiring and retaining a subscriber. Also important would be the advertising attractiveness of the audience and the costs of creating (editorial), printing and fulfilling the magazine.

In a software business, the economic drivers differ. Of critical importance are the cost and time schedule for creating the software. Then, the economics of the various distribution channels are at the top of the list. What margins will the retail or OEM channel require? What are the economics of a direct sales force model? How much territory can a salesperson cover? What compensation is required to attract, retain and motivate a talented sales force and a software development team?

Common to all business models is the issue of break-even: at what level does the business begin to make a profit? Even more important, at what level does the company turn cash flow positive?

In addition to a clear appreciation of the factors that will affect the economics of the business, I look for sensible sensitivity analysis. What would happen, for example, if net response rates were 20% lower for the magazine? What would happen if the software project took 20% longer than estimated? These are the kinds of questions that I believe the team should address in presenting their model to prospective resource providers.

Many successful companies find that their basic business model was too optimistic. Though ultimately the business model works, more time and capital are required. I was a director of two companies that started out predicting that they would each need less than $2 million to reach escape velocity. One, Avid Technology, went through $25 million before it reached positive cash flow. Avid sells digital video editing software and went from startup in 1988 to over $400 million in 1995. Another company in the information business went through $10 million as compared to its initial guess of $1.5 million. We had a saying at that company when I was a director: "We never wrote a business plan we couldn't miss." This company now does $160 million in revenue, with $60 million in operating profits. This company also came perilously close to bankruptcy before figuring out its business model.

One final note about proformas in business plans for high potential ventures—they all look the same. Over the past decade, hundreds of books on entrepreneurship and venture capital have been published. Most of these volumes comment that venture capitalists will not consider making an investment in a company that cannot reasonably project $50 million in annual revenues within five years. It is not surprising that almost every plan I receive shows year five sales of $55 million, representing a 10% cushion over the presumed minimum. They also need only a 10% share, and they all show at least a 10% net margin . . . and they are all conservative (see **Appendix 3** for a glossary of terms found in business plans and an explanation of what they really mean).

Due Diligence

A business plan is often used as a blueprint for asking questions. Professional investors conduct due diligence in order to assess the people and the opportunity described in a plan. They will call references including people not suggested by the entrepreneurs. They will call actual or potential customers, suppliers, and other resource providers. They will talk to competitors, both actual and potential. And, they will grill the team based on the questions they believe must be answered before they will invest.

I recently participated in a meeting at which an entrepreneurial team tried to convince a group of individuals to invest. The team leader had a well-practiced pitch, complete with color slides and attractive props. At several points in the meeting, the presenter noted that "the business model was proved," by which he meant that there was substantial evidence that the company knew how the opportunity would play out. Unfortunately, the individuals to whom the presentation was being made had done some homework. One had called a potential advertiser, and another had called someone in the retail channel. Each gave a sharply divergent story about the company, its business model, and the likely evolution of the relationship with the company. If the presenter had only hedged his bets by describing the process by which he intended to convert promises (or hints) to reality, his pitch would have been successful. It was not.

The process of investigating a potential investment is driven by experience. After investing in a few companies, you begin to build up a sense of what can go right and what can go wrong. You learn to ask questions that you wish you had asked in the last unsuccessful deal you did. You develop a repertoire of tools to ferret out what is really going on in a venture. One friend always asks the same question when he visits a company seeking investment: "Why are sales so bad?" In some cases, the entrepreneur launches into a discussion of the failings of the sales force or the manufacturing problems confronted by the company. In other cases, the entrepreneur takes offense and describes why sales are going great. In either case, my friend has the information he needs to assess the business and its management team.

One final comment about due diligence is appropriate: it is not infallible. Before Bain Capital invested in Staples, it commissioned a survey of small businesses on their use of supplies. The results of the survey were not consonant with the assumptions made in the Staples business plan. The founder, Tom Stemberg, insisted that Bain Capital revisit the issue and check how much small businesses actually spent on supplies as compared with what they thought they spent. As it turned out, Stemberg was right, and Staples is now a multi-billion dollar business. Bain Capital did invest, which turned out to be a wise decision.

Summary and Conclusion

In summary, a business plan is neither necessary nor sufficient. Many successful businesses never had a formal plan and many unsuccessful ventures had a beautifully crafted but irrelevant plan.

A business plan must provide reasonable answers to the following questions:

- Who are the people involved? What have they done in the past that would lead one to believe that they will be successful in the future? Who is missing from the team and how will they be attracted?
- What is the nature of the opportunity? How will the company make money? How is the opportunity likely to evolve? Can entry barriers be built and maintained?
- What contextual factors will affect the venture? What contextual changes are likely to occur, and how can management respond to those changes?
- What deals have been or are likely to be struck inside and outside the venture? Do the deals struck increase the likelihood of success? How will those deals and the implicit incentives evolve over time?
- What decisions have been made (or can be made) to increase the ratio of reward to risk?

Among the many sins committed by business plan writers is arrogance—believing they have a completely proprietary idea or an insuperable lead. In today's economy, few ideas are truly proprietary. Moreover, there has never been a time in recorded history when the supply of capital did not outrace the supply of opportunity. The true half-life of opportunity is decreasing with the passage of time.

A plan must not be an albatross, something that is cast and concrete, hangs around the neck of the entrepreneurial team, and drags them into oblivion. As Robert Burns said, "the best laid plans of mice and men . . . :" the world changes, and the team must change accordingly.

A plan must be a dynamic call for action, one that recognizes that the responsibility of management is to fix what is broken prospectively and in real time. Risk is inevitable, avoiding risk impossible. Risk management is the key, always tilting the venture in favor of reward and away from risk.

A plan must demonstrate mastery of the entire entrepreneurial process, from identification of opportunity to harvest. To paraphrase George Bernard Shaw on the subject of love affairs, "Any fool can start a business—it takes a genius to harvest one."

A plan is not a means for separating unsuspecting investors from their money by hiding the fatal flaw. In the final analysis, the only one being fooled is the entrepreneur.

The ultimate tools in business are people, the leaders of the venture, the people who work at the venture, and all of the suppliers, including the financiers. Picking the A-team is the only way to manage reward and risk in the long term.

Personalizing

Writing a business plan can be a terrific educational experience. It is an integrative exercise, requiring the venture team to bring to bear a wide range of skills and experiences. It is human *and* it is analytical. Working on a plan can be a useful tool for gaining commitment and consensus among team members, even if the plan turns out to be impractical.

The real purpose of this note is to get MBAs and others to think about their careers using the entrepreneurship lens. To what degree do they know what an opportunity is and how to marshal the required resources? What is missing, and how can the gaps be addressed?

We live in a golden age, one characterized by tremendous opportunity and a myriad of examples of successful entrepreneurship. A young dropout from college, Bill Gates of Microsoft fame, ends up as the wealthiest individual in America. Three young graduates from Harvard Business School, David Thompson, Bruce Ferguson, and Scott Webster, built Orbital Sciences Corporation into a multi-hundred million dollar, publicly-traded company whose mission is to commercialize space.

Writing a business plan is useful as part of a lifelong educational experience. If and only if the writer has the skills, experience, contacts, and attitude that are required for the business, then, by all means, the Nike model should be invoked—

Just Do It!
If not,
Just Say No!

APPENDIX 1 | The Concept of Fit

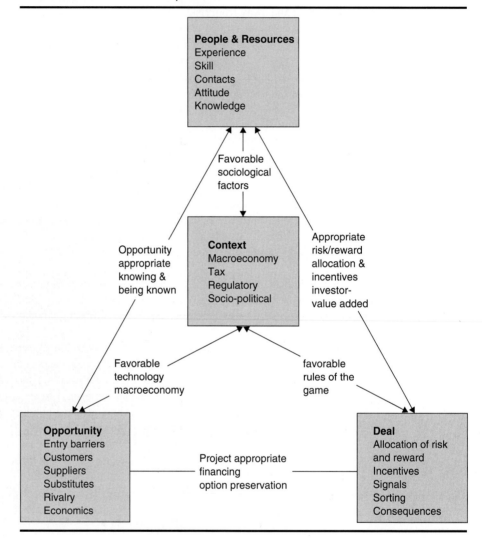

APPENDIX 2 | Dynamic Fit Management

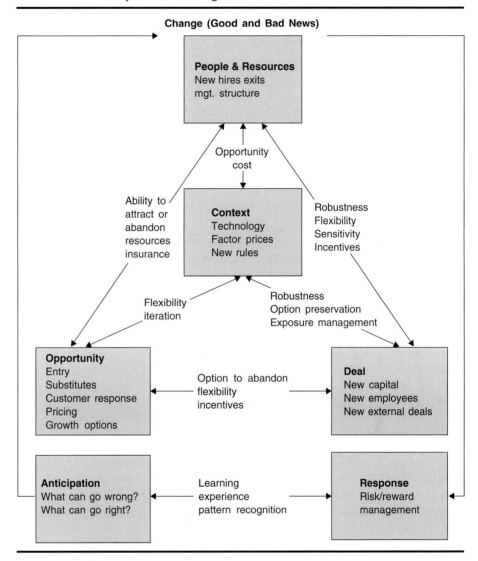

APPENDIX 3 | Translation Glossary for Business Plans

Business Plan Phrase	What It Really Means
We conservatively project . . .	We read a book that said we had to have sales of $50 million in 5 years, and we reverse engineered the numbers . . .
We took our best guess and divided by 2 . . .	We accidentally divided by .5 . . .
We project a 10% margin . . .	We did not modify any of the assumptions in the business plan template we downloaded from the Internet . . .
The project is 98% complete . . .	To complete the remaining 2% will take as long as to create the initial 98%, but will cost twice as much . . .
Our business model is proved . . .	If you take the evidence from the past week for the best of our fifty locations and extrapolate it for all of the others . . .
We have a six month lead . . .	We have not tried to find out how many other people also have a six month lead . . .
We only need a 10% market share . . .	So too do all the other 50 entrants getting funded . . .
Customers are clamoring for our product . . .	We have not yet broached the issue of them paying for it. Also, all of our current customers are relatives . . .
We are the low cost producer . . .	We have not produced anything yet, but we are confident that we will be able to . . .
We have no competition . . .	Only Microsoft, Netscape, IBM, and Sun have announced plans to enter the business . . .
Our management team has a great deal of experience . . .	. . . consuming the product or service . . .
A select group of investors is considering the plan . . .	We mailed a copy of the plan to everyone in Pratt's Guide . . .
We seek a value-added investor . . .	We are looking for a passive, dumb-as-rocks investor . . .
If you invest on our terms, you will earn a 68% IRR . . .	If everything that could conceivably ever go right does go right, you might get your money back . . .

CHAPTER 3

Note on Business Model Analysis for the Entrepreneur

Introduction

Nearly everyone has seen, heard and employed the term 'business model' but how many people really understand what it means? The term is a standard phrase in the lexicon of business managers, and yet the term escapes definition in most books, articles, business plans and annual reports. It is assumed that business managers not only understand the term 'business model' but also that they know how to identify, assess and create them. This note describes the primary elements and defining characteristics of a company's business model from the perspective of an entrepreneur.

In order to assess a potential business model, entrepreneurs must uncover the nature of its 'profit engine' which is often obscured by ambitious financial and market projections. Entrepreneurs must ask themselves whether their business concept can be translated into a viable, profitable business venture and how much cash it will take to achieve that result. Thus, this note introduces several analytic techniques to enable an entrepreneur to answer the following questions: 1) How likely is the business to turn cash flow positive? 2) How much time is required to ramp up the revenue in order to turn cash flow positive? 3) How large an investment is required to pursue the business model? 4) What are the critical success factors and associated risks? In addition to preparing the entrepreneur to answer these questions, this note also provides several illustrative business models to support the analytic frameworks presented.

Business Model Definition

Many businesspeople and academics have offered elaborate definitions for the term business model. This note proposes a more focused definition of the term and is specifically aimed at entrepreneurs who must decide whether a particular business model justifies an

Dean's Fellow Taz Pirmohamed prepared this note under the supervision of Senior Lecturer Richard G. Hamermesh and Professor Paul W. Marshall as the basis for class discussion.

investment of their time and resources. In this context, a business model is defined as *a summation of the core business decisions and trade-offs employed by a company to earn a profit*. As such, every entrepreneur must understand the specific business decisions and accompanying trade-offs that resulted in the creation of a business model. In general, these business decisions and trade-offs fall into four groups: revenue sources, key expenses, investment size and critical success factors.

Revenue Sources

How many different revenue streams will the business model generate? What is the source of each revenue stream (sales, service fees, advertising, subscription)? What is the relative size and importance of each revenue stream? How quickly is each revenue stream likely to grow?

Cost Drivers

What cost drivers have the greatest impact on the cost structure? Are the costs fixed, semi-variable, variable or non-recurring? What is their relative size and importance? Will the cost drivers change over time?

Investment Size

How much cash is required to launch the business model? How much working capital is required to sustain the business? What are the timings of these cash needs? Will the cash expended produce a viable business entity?

Critical Success Factors

Which elements of a company's business model are most important to achieving its profit goals? Which of these elements are the most difficult to execute? Will they change over time?

Framework for Analyzing a Business Model

A framework for analyzing business models must be applicable to the numerous business models in the marketplace. In recent years, the number of business models has increased dramatically for several reasons. First, globalization has facilitated the transfer of business models across geographic boundaries. Second, technological advancements such as the Internet have fostered the development of new business models. Finally, the large infusion of private capital into new ventures has helped to spur the creation of new, innovative business models. As such, business model analysis requires a common starting point that is equally applicable to a manufacturing business or an Internet-based business. To this end, a company's financial statements—the balance sheet, income statement and cash flow statement—all serve as a fundamental starting point for business model analysis.

For early-stage companies, the pro forma or budgeted financial statements are required and for existing companies, a combination of actual financial statements and pro formas are required. Other useful sources of information include the mission statement, business overview, strategic goals and operating principles of a company—all of which may be found in a business plan, annual report, press clippings or media kits. To begin the business model analysis, the following steps should be taken:

- Determine the company's actual and projected revenues and the timing of the cash inflows. Disaggregate revenue data until you have uncovered the revenue drivers or the key factors that influence total revenues.

- Determine the company's actual and projected expenses and the timing of the cash outflows. Disaggregate cost data into discrete cost drivers.

- Determine the total investment required to achieve a positive cash flow position, including working capital.

- Plot cash flow versus time to generate a cash curve. This curve will illustrate the maximum financing needs and the timing of positive cash flows and cash breakeven.

- Perform a systematic sensitivity analysis of the business model to identify the critical success factors or the levers that have the greatest impact on the cash flows of the company.

A preliminary analysis of the company's revenue sources, cost drivers, investment requirements and critical success factors forms the basis of business model analysis. The following sections will facilitate more detailed analysis and provide illustrative case examples for each key element of the business model.

Revenue Sources

Definition

There are four distinct revenue streams that underlie all business models:[1]

Single stream: company relies on one predominant revenue stream stemming from one product or service.

Multiple streams: company collects multiple revenue streams from different products or services. Each revenue stream is sizeable enough to have a meaningful impact on profitability.

Interdependent: company sells one/several products or services in order to stimulate revenues from another set of products or services. Examples of interdependent revenue streams include razors and razor blades or printers and printer cartridges.

Loss leader: company collects multiple revenue streams but not every revenue stream is independently profitable. One or several revenue streams may serve as loss leaders and drive traffic to spur other purchases. Combined, all revenue streams enable the company to achieve profitability. An example of a

---

[1]Mark Mooradian, Nicole Vanderbilt and Heather Dougherty, "Internet Business Model Implications: Real Revenues and Traditional Business Impact," *Forrester Research,* 4th Quarter 1999.

loss leader revenue stream is a grocery store selling laundry detergent below cost in order to stimulate other purchases.

Revenue Models

Business models can incorporate one or several different revenue streams depending on the company's product, industry and customers. The following revenue models are examples of how the four different revenue streams can be manifested in a business model:

Subscription/Membership: Customers pay a fixed amount at regular intervals (week, month, year) in advance of receiving the product or service. Examples include paying an annual subscription fee for a magazine or a fitness club membership.

Volume or Unit-Based: Customers pay a fixed price per unit and receive a product or service in exchange. Examples include retail operations such as a restaurant, clothing shop or beauty parlor.

Advertising-Based: End-user is usually exempt from paying a fee or pays a fee equivalent to only a fraction of the true value of the product or service. Examples include network television stations and content-based web sites.

Licensing & Syndication: Customer pays a one-time licensing or syndication fee to be able to use or resell the product. Alternatively, the buyer may pay a separate licensing or royalty fee in a business-to-business transaction; for example, a pharmaceutical firm may license a drug from a biotechnology firm.

Transaction Fee: Customer pays the company that facilitates the transaction a fixed fee or a percentage of the total value of the transaction. Examples include brokerage firms and auction houses.

Revenue Model Analysis

In answering the following questions, the entrepreneur can gain greater insight into the core business decisions and trade-offs underlying a company's revenue model and the size and relative importance of each revenue stream:

Revenue Streams

- Is the business model based on a single, a multiple or a loss leader revenue stream?
- If the company has a loss leader revenue stream, how likely are the losses to be covered by other revenue streams?

Revenue Model

- Is the business model based on a single or hybrid revenue model?
- In the case of a hybrid model, what are the underlying revenue models (i.e. subscription, transaction, advertising)?

- How quickly will the revenues increase? Are there any barriers to revenue growth?
- How long does it take to collect cash following a sale?

Case Example

The revenue model employed by the legendary sixties rock band *The Grateful Dead* or *The Dead* demonstrates several of the principles of revenue analysis. *The Dead* was one of the highest grossing bands of all time but had only one Top 10 hit and not one of their first 10 albums ever climbed higher than No. 24 on the charts. Instead of creating No. 1 hits to drive record sales, *The Dead*'s revenue model exploited the underlying structure and economics of the music industry.[2]

The high cost music production and distribution system run by the music labels leaves only a small portion of album revenues for the musicians and the revenue is paid out semi-annually—only after the label has paid out all accrued expenses. In contrast, the record companies have no claim on concert revenues—comprised of ticket and merchandise sales. These accrue entirely to the touring band and are paid within thirty days. In response to the favorable economics of touring and selling merchandise, *The Dead* developed a wildly successful revenue model.

The Dead essentially gave away their music. At live shows, *The Dead* invited fans with recording devices to plug them into the engineer's soundboard, allowing them to burn CD quality recordings for free. Moreover, *The Dead* encouraged the copying and trading of concert tapes. Music was the hook or loss leader—the proverbial free toaster for the first 100 people to open a bank account. Instead, the band toured frequently enough to attract loyal fans coined *Deadheads* who followed the band across the country and attended their live shows. *The Dead* routinely achieved over $50 million in annual ticket revenues. Their frequent live concerts stimulated demand for merchandise so the band developed a line of merchandise—etched with their signature monikers—that were sold at each live concert. To discourage bootlegged merchandise, *The Dead* was known to have hired security personnel who scoured the parking lots of concert venues to enforce their trademarks with people illegally selling unlicensed merchandise. On average, *The Dead* generated an additional $70 million in revenue per year in merchandise sales.[3]

While most bands struggled to generate enough album sales to cover their label's marketing and distribution costs, *The Dead*'s revenue model was focused on the larger and unencumbered sources of profit in the music industry. A fishbone diagram (See **Exhibit 1**) illustrates the revenue model employed by *The Grateful Dead* by disaggregating total revenues into three key revenue streams and each component's revenue drivers.

---

[2]Andrew Razeghi, "Commentary Lesson from the Dead," *Los Angeles Times;* August 27, 2001.

[3]Elana Ashanti Jefferson, "Truckin' in Style: Jam-band Vendors Sell Fans Wares to (tie) Dye for"; *Denver Post,* July 19, 2001.

Cost Drivers

Definition

A cost driver is any factor that affects total costs.[4] In general, costs vary with either time or volume of output. More specifically, there are four primary types of cost drivers that comprise a firm's cost structure:[5]

Fixed: Items of cost that do not vary at all with volume. Examples include annual rent, property taxes and management salaries.

Semi-Variable: Items of cost that include a combination of variable costs and fixed costs. Therefore, a semi-variable cost varies in the direction of, but less than proportionately with, changes in volume of output. An example is the payroll expenses of a supermarket. A supermarket must employ a minimum number of staff to operate the store regardless of sales volume. However, as sales volume increases, more staff may be required to handle the increased business.

Variable: Items of cost that vary, in total, directly and proportionately with volume. Examples include materials cost (vary with total number of units produced) and sales commissions (vary with total number of items sold).

Non-Recurring: Items of cost that appear irregularly or infrequently in the company's cost structure. Examples include investments such as purchasing a building or equipment.

Cost Structures

The dominant cost driver of a business model usually characterizes the overall cost structure. The following list is a subset of the most common cost structures:

Payroll-Centered (Direct): Semi-variable costs driven by employees directly involved in the output of the firm. Examples include professional services firms such as consulting firms and investment banks or manufacturing firms with assembly line production.

Payroll-Centered (Support): Fixed costs driven by employees indirectly involved in the output of the firm. Examples include Haute Couture fashion houses or insurance companies.

Inventory: Primary cost center related to maintenance of raw materials and/or finished goods inventory. Examples include manufacturing firms such as automobile manufacturers or retailers such as car dealerships or jewelry retailers.

Space/Rent: Costs driven by the high cost per square foot of office or retail space. Examples include a restaurant located in an affluent neighborhood or a service company such as copy centers located in downtown office buildings.

---

[4] Rakesh Niraj, Mahendra Gupta and Chakravarthi Narasimhan, "Customer Profitability in a Supply Chain," *Journal of Marketing;* July 2001.

[5] Robert Anthony, David Hawkins and Kenneth Merchant, *Accounting: Text & Cases* (New York: McGraw Hill Companies, 1999).

Marketing/Advertising: Costs driven by total marketing or advertising expenditures required to attract and retain customers. Examples include Internet content or commerce web sites.

Cost Driver Analysis

In answering the following questions, the entrepreneur can gain greater insight into the core business decisions and trade-offs underlying a company's cost model and the size and relative importance of each cost driver:

Cost Driver:

- Is the business model's cost based on primarily fixed, semi-variable, variable or non-recurring costs?

- How much volume can be supported with the fixed cost base? How likely is a reduction in the fixed cost base of the company?

- Are the primary cost drivers expected to change over time?

Cost Center:

- What are the largest cost centers for the business model?

- What are the relative size and importance of each cost center?

- Do any of the cost centers deliver a strategic cost advantage?

Case Example

Seven-Eleven Japan—a chain of franchised convenience stores located throughout Japan—changed its cost structure in order to become one of the fastest growing and most profitable retail operations in Japan.[6] From the outset, Seven-Eleven Japan identified two critical cost drivers of the convenience store business and sought to convert them into a competitive advantage.

The first key cost driver was the Cost of Goods Sold (COGS) or the price at which the company acquired its products. Under the traditional system, individual stores had access to manufacturers only through multiple layers of distribution. Seven-Eleven Japan set out to rationalize the cumbersome and costly distribution structure in order to avoid capital expenditures and to lower the supply costs for the entire chain. To do this, Seven-Eleven Japan created the 'combined distribution' system that grouped products by the temperature at which they were stored and then delivered each product group to a different Combined Distribution Center (CDC). There, the products were sorted by store and then loaded onto trucks for delivery. The system eliminated the need for a multi-tiered distribution system and lowered the delivered cost of their products at the store level. Notably, Seven-Eleven Japan owned none of the CDCs or the trucks that shuttled goods between them. Instead, its suppliers and a few specialized distribution companies owned and operated the CDCs while Seven-Eleven Japan's role was limited to coordinating, assisting and supporting. Seven-Eleven Japan's distribution reforms converted fixed and non-recurring costs to variable costs.

---

[6]Thomas K. McCraw, *Creating Modern Capitalism* (Cambridge: Harvard University Press, 1995), pp. 500–519.

The second key cost driver identified by Seven-Eleven Japan was the cost of managing information transfer amongst stores, suppliers and corporate head office. Although the initial foray into information technology (IT) was aimed at improving the ordering process for individual stores, it later had a profound impact on the company's ordering, merchandising and product development functions. Seven-Eleven Japan was the first convenience store chain to incorporate Point-of-Sales (POS) cash registers, an electronic order-booking system and hand-held scanners that store owners used to manage store deliveries. Instead of purchasing the hardware and software for its system, Seven-Eleven Japan worked in conjunction with Nomura Research Institute who helped to develop the software and administered the network, Nippon Electric Company which created the store computer, Tokyo Electric Company who built the register and Nippondenso who produced the scanner terminal. Seven-Eleven Japan insisted that any products developed with its collaboration could not be sold to any competitors for two years. Seven-Eleven Japan's IT partnerships also reduced the need for a large staff of computer experts—the company's IT department accounted for only 50 of its 2,500 employees in the mid-nineties. In sum, Seven-Eleven Japan drastically reduced the cost and risk of developing and implementing a superior IT system by creating partnerships with software and hardware suppliers instead of building the capability in-house.

By the mid-nineties, Seven-Eleven Japan's innovative approach to cost reduction helped it to become the fastest growing and most profitable convenience store chain in Japan. It also played an important role in the Japanese economy by helping to introduce IT into small stores and as a persistent force for rationalizing Japan's distribution channels.

A fishbone diagram (See **Exhibit 2**) illustrates the cost structure of Seven-Eleven Japan and the drivers influencing each major cost.

Investment Size

Definition

Maximum investment is the amount of cash required before a company achieves positive cash flow. The total investment size of a business model depends on several factors including the company's revenue model, cost drivers and critical success factors. A cash flow diagram provides the means for capturing and summarizing information relating to the cash requirements of a business model (See **Exhibit 3** for a cash flow diagram for a hypothetical venture):

A cash flow diagram can be evaluated based on following characteristics:

- *Maximum Financing Needs:* What is the maximum financing need of the business model (i.e. how deep is the cash trough)? Over what period of time is the investment required?

- *Positive Cash Flow:* At what point does cash flow of the company turn positive? How long does it take to arrive at this point?

- *Cash Breakeven:* When does the company achieve cash breakeven (i.e. what does time equal when the curve crosses the x-axis)? How does the slope of the cash curve change after breakeven?

Examples of Total Investment Size

The following examples describe types of business models with markedly different investment requirements:

- *Software:* Large upfront investment is required to build an initial software product. If the product is successful, only relatively small follow-on investments in sales, distribution and customer service are required to capture a large software revenue stream.

- *Retail:* Capital requirements during start-up phase associated with lease or rent costs, inventory and payroll. Financing needs remain relatively consistent over time.

- *Small Consulting Firm:* Very small upfront investment for space, computer, and phone line are necessary to begin serving clients. If the firm is successful, larger follow-on investments may be required to hire additional staff, lease large office space and build IT infrastructure.

Case Example

Medical device start-ups can be used to illustrate how various business model choices—including pricing, manufacturing and distribution—can affect the total investment size required to achieve positive cash flow. Many medical devices companies sell two interdependent products: 1) equipment or instruments required to perform a procedure on an ongoing basis with a price often ranging from $50,000 to $100,000 and, 2) disposable products that are consumed during each individual procedure with a price ranging from $500 to $2,000. For a medical device company, sales of the disposable product are dependent on the total number of instruments installed in hospitals. And, since the price of each instrument or equipment is significantly higher than the cost of each disposable, the pricing, manufacturing and distribution of the instrument or equipment has a significant impact on the total cash requirements of the business.

The instrument or equipment can be sold at a profit, sold at cost or given away for free while the disposables are nearly always sold at a profit. A medical devices company that sells the instrument or equipment at a profit—assuming the market is willing to pay—will have a significantly shallower cash trough than one that gives it away. In addition, a medical devices company that sells the instrument or equipment at a profit—assuming fewer users are willing to pay for it than receive it for free—will have a more gently upwards-sloping cash curve than a company that gives the instrument away and generates a higher volume of disposables sales from its larger installed base of users (See **Exhibit 4** for cash flow diagram of two hypothetical medical device ventures).

Another factor affecting total investment size is the decision about whether to outsource manufacturing of the instrument or equipment. A company that outsources production will have a significantly shallower cash trough than one that builds and manages its own manufacturing facility. Similarly, a company that outsources the sales and distribution of its products to an independent distributor will avoid investments related to building, training and managing a sales force and will therefore have a shallower cash trough than a company with its own sales force. However, outsourcing production and sales—two critical functions within a medical devices company—can result in difficult management problems of controlling outsiders that may offset the advantage of lower total investment size.

The medical device case example illustrates how business model choices related to pricing, manufacturing and distribution can have a major impact on the total investment required to achieve positive cash flow. And, while business model choices should be assessed in the context of investment size, the entrepreneur should also consider how much cash is available to the venture and whether the business model choices confer a long-term competitive advantage to the firm.

Critical Success Factors

Definition

A critical success factor is an operational function or competency that a company must possess in order for it to be sustainable and profitable. Therefore, the success of a business model depends on both the creation of a viable business model and the successful execution of multiple operational functions.

Critical Success Factor Analysis

While a business model provides insight into underlying revenue and cost drivers, some of these factors are more important than others. By performing a sensitivity analysis, the entrepreneur can uncover the parameters or success factors that have the greatest impact on the amount and timing of the cash flows. The parameters with the greatest impact become the critical success factors for the business model. The following steps enable the entrepreneur to perform a sensitivity analysis:

- Construct a business model that illustrates the timing and size of the cash inflows and outflows.
- Select three or four parameters (e.g., sales growth, new customer acquisition rate, inventory turns) with the greatest perceived impact on total cash flows of the business model.
- Select a reasonable range for each parameter and then measure the impact of changing the parameter (across the entire range).
- Repeat this process for each parameter and note which variables have the most significant impact.

While a company's critical success factors may change over time, performing a sensitivity analysis enables the entrepreneur to measure the impact of a critical success factor at any given point in time. In addition, the sensitivity analysis can also help managers decide where to focus their efforts in order for their actions to have the greatest impact on the business model.

Examples of Critical Success Factors by Revenue Model

Critical success factors vary by business model, industry and stage of development. For example, a growing company's success may rest upon its ability to rapidly acquire new customers or to ramp up production fast enough to meet demand. A mature company's success may rest upon its ability to achieve high capacity utilization or reduce unit costs faster than its competitors. The following examples illustrate the critical success factors for three different business models:

*   *Subscription/Membership:* The ability to retain customers for a long period of time; the ability to acquire new customers at a low cost; the ability to consistently increase share of wallet with customers.

*   *Transaction-Based:* The ability to command a price premium for a product/ service without a commensurate increase in costs; the ability to exploit economies of scale to lower fixed/variable costs as sales volume increases.

*   *Advertising-Based:* The ability to maintain advertising revenues during counter-cyclical economic period; the ability to increase advertising spending/ customer.

EXHIBIT 1 | Fishbone Diagram for The Grateful Dead Revenue Model

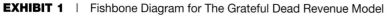

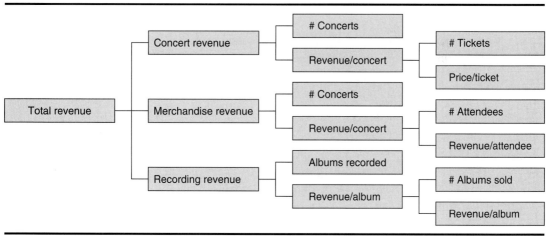

EXHIBIT 2 | Fishbone Diagram for Seven-Eleven Japan Cost Structure

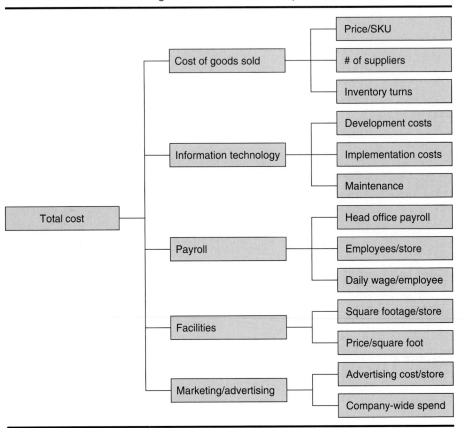

EXHIBIT 3 | Cumulative Cash Flow Diagram for a New Venture

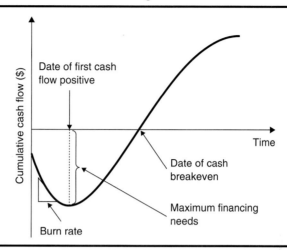

EXHIBIT 4 | Cumulative Cash Flow Diagrams for Two Hypothetical Medical Device Ventures

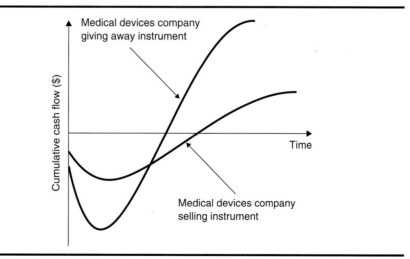

CHAPTER 4

Valuation, Financing and Capitalization Tables in the New Venture Context

Funding a new venture in a private financing raises all sorts of issues. Assuming investors can be found, a key issue is often related to valuation i.e., what percentage of the company will a given amount of money buy? This is called the "valuation" question because of the mathematical fact that a valuation can be imputed from such a financing event: if I buy 10% of your company for $1 million, then I have implicitly valued the business at $10 million.

Entrepreneurs care about this because the lower the percentage of the company they have to give up to raise a given sum (called "dilution" because their proportional equity stake is diluted) the more equity they can keep for themselves and the management team. In addition to the pure economics of this, there may well be certain elements of control that go along with having a higher equity stake (i.e., holding onto a majority of the ownership). Thus, entrepreneurs care a lot about valuation.

Understanding the Fundamental Role of Inherent Rate of Return

One key point that needs to be understood is the vital role that the basic economic attractiveness of the business plays in driving the implicit valuation in financings. To describe a simple example: if you are starting a business that will earn a 25% return on equity, what percentage of that business do you have to give up if your investors want a 25% (Internal Rate of Return IRR) on their investment? The answer is 100%. It is simply true that the proportion of the business the founding team gets to keep is related to the ratio of the inherent return in the business to the investor's required IRR. Of course, the inherent return is impossible to predict prior to the actual operation of the business.

Senior Lecturer Michael J. Roberts and prepared this note as the basis for class discussion.

Nonetheless, investors are making tacit assumptions about this when they negotiate for the slice of the business ownership they want. The best thing you can do to keep a high proportion of equity for yourself and your team is to develop a business with outstanding economic returns, i.e., return on equity.

The principal ways of achieving this are as follows:

- Start a business which requires low amounts of equity capital, either because it is not capital intensive or because it can generate the capital required to grow with its own cash flow;

- Start a business which requires large amounts of capital, but little equity, because it is capable of being financed with debt (e.g., real estate); or,

- Start a business which may require significant amounts of equity, but which simply earns extraordinary rates of return on that equity by dint of its durable competitive advantage in the marketplace.

Implied vs. "Bottom-up" Valuation

As described above, when venture capitalists (or other providers of financing) invest, they may or may not do so based upon a view of what the firm is worth. For example, they may simply feel that getting 40% of a new venture in exchange for $1 million is "fair" given other deals they have participated in. Nonetheless, it is always possible to impute an "implied" valuation to the business *after* the investment has been made. When people talk about valuation in the context of a new venture financing, they are typically talking about this kind of *implied* valuation, rather than any more fundamental, bottom-up valuation of the business. (e.g., a valuation based on cash flow, earnings or assets).

The math of such implied valuations is fairly simple.

If you divide the amount of money raised in the financing by the slice of ownership purchased, you get the "post-money" valuation of the firm. It is called post-money because it is the value *after* the money has been invested. So for example, if I invest $1 million to buy a 10% share, the post-money valuation is $1,000,000/10% = $10,000,000.

The pre-money value is simply the post-money minus the pre-money. That is, if the firm is worth $10,000,000 after the injection of $1 million, then it must have been worth $9 million prior to that investment. So, the general formulas are:

- Post-money − new money = pre-money; and
- Pre-money + new money invested = post-money.

Where Do Valuations Come From?

Of course, you may ask how VCs—and other investors—come to a point of view on a valuation. Such "bottom-up" valuations may arise from more fundamental analysis of the business and its prospects. For instance, suppose investors believe that the company will hit its business plan, and that in 6 years, it will have profit after tax of $5 million. And further suppose that the investors believe that such companies will be valued by the public markets at a 30 times P/E (price earnings ratio) for a total valuation of $150 million. Now, further suppose that the venture capitalist requires an internal rate of return of 40%. Thus, $1 invested in year 1 will need to be worth $7.53; the general formula is:

Future Value $= (1+r)^n \times I$, *where **r** is the required IRR, **n** is the number of years in the holding period, and **I** is the amount of the investment.*

Thus, if the VC invests $4 million it will need to be worth $30.1 million 6 years later; if the total company is worth $150 million, then the VC will need to own 20% of the business. If everything transpires as hoped, this 20% stake will be worth $30 million, delivering the required IRR. Note that this assumes that no further financing—and the consequent dilution to the VC's stake—will occur.

It should be clear why it is so difficult to do a bottoms-up valuation on this basis. It depends on so many assumptions about events so far in the future that it becomes a very difficult, and potentially meaningless, exercise. Nonetheless, it does offer some insight on the key variables that affect perceived valuation.

Alternatives

Note that you can get to the same answers from a variety of different paths. Suppose there are 900,000 shares outstanding before the investment, and the new investors want to own 10% of the company for their $1 million investment. Well, if we sell them 100,000 shares at $10 per share, we will have their $1 million and they will have 10% ownership. If we simply take the newly established per share price of $10 and multiply it by the 900,000 shares outstanding before the new investment round, we get the $9,000,000 pre-money, and can get the $10,000,000 post-money by multiplying the 100,000 shares outstanding after the financing by the $10 per share figure. So, we can get to these valuations through either the "proportional ownership" approach or the "per share" approach.

Complications

There are a few complications to this seemingly simple approach.

Stock options: One complication is stock options. Companies create a pool of stock options (or even stock itself) to use as part of their compensation to employees to incent and reward them. The creation of a pool of options naturally dilutes any shareholder who was an owner prior to that pool being created. Imagine that you and I start a company and we each give ourselves 1,000 shares, so we each own 50%. If we decide to create an option pool of 500 shares and reward current and future employees out of that pool, we have just diluted our percentage ownership stakes by 10 percentage points each, to 40% each. (This assumes that the options are issued and exercised—this is called the "fully diluted" ownership because it assumes the impact of events which dilute ownership.) Note that—in theory—the negative consequences of this dilution are more than offset by the positive impact on the firm's performance and thus ultimate valuation that these option grants will promote.

Thus, if a potential investor believes that a company needs more options in its arsenal of resources to attract and maintain employees, then it will request that the company create that pool of options *prior* to its investment in the company. Thus, if an investor offers to invest $4 million at a $20 million post-money valuation, they want to own 4/20th or 20% of the business, and doesn't want to be diluted the following day by the creation of a new option pool.

Investor "preference": Another complication—which we will not compute precisely—is the impact of investor preferences on these calculations. So, for instance, if the security purchased by the investor is a preferred stock, in which the investor gets back her investment, plus a small return, prior to any funds being distributed to management, and then the remainder is distributed "pro-rata," the investor really has a claim on more than x% of the value, even if they only own x% of the stock (counting both common and preferred stock as the stock base). It is important to recall that the math of implied valuation assumes that the investor is putting in a certain amount of money in return for a claim on a certain proportion of the value. The presence of a preference—or other terms that may allocate a higher proportion of value to the investor—distorts this simple math and makes it difficult to determine the true value in any precise mathematical way. And, often, the simpler and less precise valuation numbers are still used. Nonetheless, the impact of stock preferences and other terms should not be overlooked.

Capitalization Tables

Capitalization tables (or "cap" tables) are the tables that are used to keep track of all this data in an understandable way, particularly as financing unfolds over multiple rounds, and as some investors may buy stock in more than one round. **Exhibit 1** is an example of a cap table from the financing of a hypothetical company, Apex Technologies.

At the company's founding, on January 1 of 2004, the founders buy 2 million shares at $0.01 each, for a total investment of $20,000. After making considerable progress, they successful raise a first round of financing from Starburst Ventures: $1 million at $1 per share, for a total number of shares issued of 1,000,000. This dilutes the founders' ownership stake to 66.66%, and Starburst owns 33.33% of the company. Note that the post-money valuation can be figured as either $3,000,000 (the total number of shares outstanding) × $1 (the price paid per share). Or, it can be figured as $1,000,000/33.33% = $3 million. And, the pre-money valuation is simply $3 million − $1 million = $2 million.

Note further that the founders' stake is now worth $2 million (i.e., 2 million shares × $1 per share), or a paper gain of $1.98 million. This is a measure of the value created in the venture by dint of their efforts since the founding.

In the cap table, we see how this data is organized so that these calculations can be easily done.

In the second round of investment, we see that a new firm, Nova Ventures, has invested $3,750,000 for a 33.33% ownership stake. Obviously, this dilutes both the founders and Starburst Ventures. Nonetheless, the increase in the value of their shares more than offsets the negative impact of dilution.

EXHIBIT 1 | Illustrative Capitalization Tables for Apex Technologies

	Initial Founding Capitalization 1/1/2004				First Round Investment 1/1/2005					Second Round Investment 1/1/2006			
	# of shares	$ per share	Total $ Investment	% Ownership	# of shares	$ per share	Total $ Investment	% Ownership	# of shares	$ per share	Total $ Investment	% Ownership
Founders	2,000,000	0.01	20,000	100.00%	2,000,000			66.67%	2,000,000			44.44%
Starburst Ventures					1,000,000	1.00	1,000,000	33.33%	1,000,000			22.22%
Nova Ventures									1,500,000	2.50	3,750,000	33.33%
Eclipse Ventures												
Total	2,000,000		20,000	100.00%	3,000,000		1,000,000	100.00%	4,500,000		3,750,000	100.00%

Source: Case writer example.

CHAPTER 5

How Venture Capitalists Evaluate Potential Venture Opportunities

We interviewed four venture capitalists from leading Silicon Valley firms to learn about the frameworks they use in evaluating potential venture opportunities. (See **Exhibit 1** for background information on these venture capital firms.) All four were interviewed individually and were asked similar questions, such as "How do you evaluate potential venture opportunities?" "How do you evaluate the venture's prospective business model?" "What due diligence do you conduct?" "What is the process through which funding decisions are made?" "What financial analyses do you perform?" "What role does risk play in your evaluation?" and "How do you think about a potential exit route?" The following are excerpts from these interviews.

Russell Siegelman: Partner, Kleiner Perkins Caufield & Byers (KPCB)

Russ Siegelman joined KPCB in 1996 after seven years with Microsoft Corporation, where he helped found and launch Microsoft Network (MSN). Before working at Microsoft, he wrote artificial intelligence software. Siegelman invests in software, electronic commerce, Web services, telecommunications, and media and sits on the boards of Vertical Networks, Lilliputian Systems, Mobilygen, Quorum Systems, Digital Chocolate, and Vividence. He is one of the managing partners of the KPCB XI Fund, which closed in February 2004. Siegelman earned his B.S. from the Massachusetts Institute of Technology in physics in 1984 and an MBA from Harvard Business School in 1989.

How Do You Evaluate Potential Venture Opportunities?

"We have a generally understood set of things we look for when we evaluate an investment opportunity. The most important requirement is a large market opportunity in a fast-growing sector. Explosive growth makes it difficult for somebody to catch up or incumbents to respond. We like a company to have a $100 million to $300 million revenue stream within five years. This means that the market potential has to be at least $500 million—or more, eventually—and the company needs to achieve at least a 25% market share.

"The second factor involves a competitive edge that is long lasting. It could be a network effect like eBay or an operating system lock-in like Microsoft, but those are few and far between. It is usually an engineering challenge that is tough enough to build an edge, resulting in several years lead or longer, if we're lucky. We look for a tough problem that hasn't been solved before. The solution can't be so straightforward that someone can look at the blackboard and say, 'I know how to do it.' We tend to avoid 'scientific breakthroughs'—we're not great at evaluating or managing science projects. We know how to take technology, commercialize it, and turn it into a viable business.

"We are a little schizophrenic on patents. Personally, I don't care much about patents; they are a nice-to-have but not a requirement. Only a couple of our companies hold patents that are worth much. Once a technology is patented, it's out there and people figure out a way to get around it. However, we do conduct patent searches to make sure no one is blocking us. We have several companies that would rather keep their intellectual property a trade secret. Not everyone agrees with that here; we have some partners who are fond of big patent portfolios.

"The third thing is team. There are lots of aspects to the team. We look for a strong technical founder—if it is a tough, technical problem—and a sales-oriented entrepreneur. The founder is the anchor, more than just an idea person, who understands the whole thrust behind the technology and the industry dynamic around it. The entrepreneur drives the other parts of the business and sells the vision to investors and to other early-stage participants such as full-time employees, partners, and potential customers. We look for engineering vision and execution, sales, and entrepreneurship in a team. Typically, it's at least two people; sometimes it's three.

"In the early stages, I tend to invest behind an entrepreneur, not behind a professional manager as the CEO. Often, the person who can professionally manage as a CEO in the later stages of a company is not as effective in the earlier stages. It requires a different skill set. Entrepreneurs have to have a clear sense of the opportunity and how to build the business. That is why we're willing to bet on them and what we're paying them for. But, the best ones are willing to reexamine their assumptions and are willing to veer left or right or pivot all the way around when the data suggests they're headed in the wrong direction. They amble around until they find something good. The bad ones typically get overcommitted or wed to a particular idea. By the way, professional managers, who join the company later on, are the reverse. Once they're in and there's a proven business model, we want them to be committed and not to be exploring other business models.

"So overall it's a funny mix. When we review an investment opportunity, entrepreneurs have to have a pretty good story to tell about what they want to do. I think it helps to be cocky, there's no doubt about it. You can be too cocky, sometimes we're a little bit mindful of that . . . but if you're not cocky enough, you're not going to be successful in selling your idea."

How Do You Evaluate the Venture's Prospective Business Model?

"To oversimplify, I'd say there are two broad kinds of investment opportunities. In the first bucket, the market or product is somewhat understood. The company is doing a better execution or a better version of an existing product or service—with a twist—in a proven market. We are investing behind a business model that we are fairly sure we understand. We expect the business plan to reflect the anticipated business model and that it's credible—it meets the 'smell test.'

"Then, there are completely new markets or business models where we *think* we may know the bets we're making, but in truth we have no clue. Friendster's a good, recent example: explosive growth, potential network effects, and an unclear business model. We invested in it over six months ago. The business model is either advertising based or pay-for-contact, but we haven't tried either yet. We identified the business model as a big risk when we invested. However, we thought Friendster had enough growth potential, and there were enough 'game-changing' aspects to it that we were willing to make the bet. When we invested in Amazon, it was clearly new. However, there was an early proof point because it was already selling books worth a few million dollars per quarter on the Internet. It was too early to tell if it could maintain significant margins or build a billion-dollar revenue company. But we knew something good was happening.

"Here's a case that didn't work. We invested in a company that conducted a barter-type swap meet, online. It seemed like an interesting idea, a twist on eBay with potentially a different approach to the market. It didn't work. To this day, I'm not sure if it was bad execution or a wrongheaded plan. We certainly have invested behind new ideas that didn't work.

"Timing is critical to successful venture capital investing, but it is not well understood. The timing of the investment and the rate the money goes in make the difference in the financial return. There are some companies where we invested too early. A later investor—perhaps one who entered after the first or second investment round—made the high returns. We've also invested too late: companies that were good companies, but they missed the window and competitors beat them to the punch. Our money was not as efficient as the money that was invested earlier in the sector. But it's hard to fine-tune; it's a gut thing."

What Due Diligence Do You Conduct?

"Technical due diligence is a big part of the data we consider when engineering innovation is involved. One of our companies is trying to solve a really difficult engineering problem, one of the hardest engineering problems I've seen in my eight years here. We did a lot of technical due diligence on this opportunity. We had probably six meetings where professors from Berkeley and consultants we hired pored over every aspect of the technology. We invested partly because the smart guys said it couldn't be done; it was really too hard to do. But after they looked at it, they said, 'These guys have made good progress; they're asking all the right questions; they have a reasonable, potential solution; and, if they can do it, it's the only way because all the other avenues we know about are dead ends.'

"Another part of due diligence involves customers. With most of the opportunities we seriously pursue, the market data is unclear because the company has no customers and revenue. Frequently, we brief potential customers about the product concept, but often they haven't met the company. Sometimes, they've met the company, but there's no product. Sometimes, they've met the company but not under nondisclosure agreement, so they don't have the full story. We have to filter all that. We have to ferret out what the customers' real needs are and their willingness to pay. But it's all sketchy and really hard to do. Occasionally, the companies have customers and revenue, so it's easier to evaluate. Then the question becomes do we want to pay up for that in the valuation. It's typically not in our sweet zone if the venture already has customers and a lot of revenue. But sometimes we do these 'speed ups'—like Amazon—and sometimes they are very successful.

"Then there's a third kind of due diligence, the industry due diligence. There, we probe industry experts about the idea, the team, the market, and the market need. They are not the customers per se but either technical or business experts in our network or people we think might have an opinion on a proposed investment.

"The fourth kind of due diligence is on the entrepreneur and team. We call their references and blind references. We spend a lot of time with them. We try to triangulate on how they've executed, are they honest, and are they people we want to work with.

"Some projects speak to a lot of due diligence—like the company with the difficult engineering challenge. With Friendster, what due diligence did we have to do? It was all about the business angle, the model, and the momentum. There was no new engineering problem being solved. The big due diligence we did for Friendster was to identify the competitors with the most momentum and look at usage and membership statistics. There was some concern that Friendster might be too easy to copy. In the end, we had to decide if we wanted to get behind the model, the entrepreneur, and the team. Usually there is not a ton of data. I go with my gut on whether it is a good bet or not. The due diligence will only take you so far, and then you have to use judgment based on experience."

What Is the Process through Which Funding Decisions Are Made?

"We have particular investment hypotheses we lay out in the investment proposal. We typically list three or four key risks we want to mitigate with the money going in. Sometimes, we stage the investment. We've done this with some medical device companies. They had to build the device and show it could be used in an animal study. In one case, it was only a $3 million investment. We put in one million up front, another million to build the prototype, and the third million for the animal study. The whole idea was to mitigate risk. But often that doesn't make sense. In some cases, there are no meaningful milestones that the team can achieve with a million dollars, so you have to invest more money initially. Or sometimes, there is so much competition coming that you don't have the luxury of the 'test and go slow approach.'

"Our smallest investment is $500,000 for an angel, seed, or incubation type of investment. Typically, our first round is $3 million to $5 million with the assumption that over the course of the company our investment will be about $10 million. We have a couple of companies where we've invested $40 million or $50 million over the course of the company's life, but that is the exception.

"The average plan takes six weeks from initial meeting until we invest in it, sometimes even longer. I invested in a chip company in San Diego that took a long time. We first met the team in October and closed in the second week in March. But during the bubble years, deals got done in an hour. Even now, hot opportunities like Friendster don't take more than two to three weeks. We met Jonathan Abrams—Friendster's founder—over a weekend. That next Monday he was at Kleiner. John Doerr and I went to the company on Tuesday and spent more time on it during the week. The following Monday, Jonathan came in for a partner meeting. We closed the following Sunday. That opportunity was going to get taken away by someone; we couldn't wait."

What Financial Analyses Do You Perform?

"We don't focus on value chain or margin analysis typically. If it's a new market or a twist on an existing product, it's not always clear how much competition there will be or how much customers are willing to pay. In some cases, I think we have some well-understood guideposts. Software should be high gross margin, but the question becomes the cost to distribute or sell. If it is an enterprise product, the company needs to sell it for $200,000 at a minimum, or it can't afford a direct sales force. The margin analysis is implicit in that logic. If the price is lower, then the issue is around channel strategy. Usually we won't invest in an opportunity with a lower-price point product unless there's already some proven low-price channel that can efficiently distribute the product. That is not a very sophisticated margin analysis, but that's how we think about it on the software side.

"On the hardware side, we are focused on the BOM [bill of materials] and the selling price. If the BOM looks like we can get a 50% gross margin at reasonable volumes, then it's a gross margin that's reasonable. We look to see if there are well-established channels to sell that product. If it's a consumer retail product, we need to understand how much inventory to build to calculate carrying costs. I would say we do some analysis, but it's not terribly deep; we basically use rules of thumb.

"Some venture capitalists put a lot of faith in the financials that are projected; I usually put very little. Most of the plan doesn't materialize the way the entrepreneur expects. The financials are usually not even close. Sometimes they're way better; sometimes they're way worse. I look at the financials because they are a credibility test for the entrepreneur. Are they reasonable and consistent with the operational needs of the business? If the person is telling a story about low-cost distribution or premium pricing, I want to see that built into the numbers at a fine level of detail.

"Sometimes I'll think an idea is interesting initially, and then I'll get to the financial section. I'll realize the person had a couple of good ideas but no clue about how to build a business because the financials are so disconnected from the reality of the strategy or operations. I wouldn't necessarily reject the person because it could be a fabulous technical entrepreneur with no business experience. But usually, it is a warning sign that I don't have a complete entrepreneur. A good entrepreneur understands both the technical and business opportunities and how to flesh out the numbers behind it."

What Role Does Risk Play in Your Evaluation?

"I think that a risk-to-reward ratio is a good way to think about the rationale for investing in an opportunity. We are doing that calibration in the back of our minds, but no one goes to the blackboard and says this specific upside is worth this risk. It is too hard to quantify.

"I would say close to 100% of the time the original plan does not come to reality, sometimes in a good way and sometimes in a bad way. The founders didn't realize they had something completely wrong and had to overcome it. Or the opposite, we overlooked some great attribute in the original plan. So the point is, we have to view an opportunity as a multichapter novel. The business plan is the prologue or the book jacket summary because there is no real business yet. We write the contents of the book together, and that is how it works.

"We have these off-sites once a year. Three out of four years, we'll look at companies we were sorry we didn't invest in. I'm not sure how constructive it is other than to confirm that we're seeing a large percentage of the good opportunities here in the Valley. On the ones we saw but didn't invest in that were successful, we say, 'Hey, we screwed that one up.'"

How Do You Think about a Potential Exit Route?

"We want to invest in an opportunity if it is big enough to turn into a successful, sustainable, IPO-able company. Companies that are built to be sold in an acquisition do not typically excite us. That is the culture of the firm. I think it's because we have a limited number of investing partners, and our business model is to build substantial IPO-able companies.

"We may overdo it. I've had the view here that it is great to swing for the fences, but it is also okay to get a ground rule double occasionally if it's got lower risk. Or something that looks like a home run but at a minimum turns into a double is not a bad thing. But, fundamentally, the firm's appetite is for very high return and very high-risk projects. One can't argue with that approach too much since it has worked so well in the past."

Sonja Hoel: Managing Director, Menlo Ventures

Sonja Hoel joined Menlo Ventures in 1994 after working for Symantec Corporation in business development and as an analyst for TA Associates. Her focus is early-stage software, communications, and Internet investments. Hoel's recent investments and board seats are Acme Packet, iS3, MailFrontier, nCircle Network Security, and Q1 Labs. Her prior investments and board seats were AssureNet Pathways, Eloquent, F5 Networks, Priority Call, Recourse Technologies, and Vermeer Technologies. She received her B.S. in commerce from the University of Virginia and an MBA from Harvard Business School in 1993.

How Do You Evaluate Potential Venture Opportunities?

"It is all about the market. I always look at the market first. 'Market' is not how to sell a can of Coke or a car on TV. It is more strategic than that: It includes evaluating market growth, market size, competition, and customer adoption rates. If a company has a great market, it doesn't need to have a complete management team or positioning story or sizzle or PR or whatever. The corporate details can be filled in later. Some venture capitalists say they only want to invest in the very best people; they look at the team first. We funded a deal once because we really liked the CEO; he's a really great CEO. Unfortunately, the company wasn't a great company because it didn't have a large enough market.

"My favorite company is the kind of company that is doing well despite itself. It is a lot of work because we have to find the management team; we have to build. I invested in a company that has technology that looks at corporate networks to determine security system holes and vulnerabilities. The company had an interim CEO and a very good VP of engineering and CFO. But, if you asked the company or customers what the company's product did, you would get a different answer every time. However, the company had seven Fortune 100 customers willing to spend over $100,000 each on the product. We brought in a new CEO, VP of sales, and VP of marketing. We worked with the management team to position the product and develop a new user interface. We have this great company now; we've got amazing customers and a great team. We basically defined a new market space. It's a story of a company that is doing incredibly well despite some early missteps because there was a large, untapped, and growing market for its product.

"Sometimes we don't know if the market is big or small, especially in these emerging spaces. I was involved in a company called F5 Networks that did load balancing for Web sites. We invested when it had very little in cumulative sales. We thought it was going to be hot because the number of Web sites was exploding, and performance mattered to consumers. The company took off like a rocket: revenues went from $200,000 to $27 million to over $100 million. The rest is history, and it's still public. But it was an emerging market; there wasn't a market for this product the year before. This also speaks to hitting a market at the right time. We don't want to miss a market window because it takes a long time for a market to develop.

"We have a process here called 'SEMS,' or systematic emerging market selection. We do a SEMS project for every investment we make. Twice a year at our planning meeting, we talk about new markets or problems that need to be solved. We've been looking at e-mail through this process because there are a lot of unsolved problems, like spam. Every single person and every single enterprise in the world has a problem with spam, and they don't have to be educated about it. We spent a year researching every antispam company out there before we invested in one.

"When we look at markets, we ask, 'Is the Fortune 1000 the target for this company?' For the network security company, it absolutely is. Fortune 1000 companies are willing to pay hundreds of thousands of dollars to solve their network security problems, so we get a pretty big market that way. We look for markets to be $500 million to $1 billion in size. When we analyze our past performance, we find that when we miss, we miss on market size. We thought the market was going to be big, but it wasn't.

"Vertical markets can be difficult. We had a company with a product to detect fraud, but it was only sold to the insurance market. Fraud in insurance is a problem, but it just wasn't a big enough market. On the other hand, we had a company called HNC Software that looked for fraud in credit cards. Fraud in the credit card market is huge, and that company went public and is still selling its product today.

"We track four things and relate them to the success of our investments: market size, the team, unique technology, and whether the product is developed at the time we invest. We found proprietary technology is important but doesn't make much of a difference as a unique differentiator for huge returns. Market size and a developed product matter most. We have much better luck if the product is in beta or shipping, although we do invest in start-ups without a developed product. Often someone comes in and says they have a great new technology, but they haven't looked at the market the technology is going to serve. Security is famous for this: we have better encryption, but who cares? It's all about solving a problem.

"In order to create a barrier, the technology has got to be hard to execute. Some companies have patents; some don't. We encourage them to have patents because it's a more litigious environment than it was 10 years ago. Regardless, the company can't have a product that is easily commoditized and that can be knocked off in a week. Enterprise software applications require man-years of building to develop the user interface and back-end connections.

"We also look at the management team. If we've got a founder who's in it for the lifestyle or unwilling to upgrade the team if necessary, we have a conversation about their willingness to hire new team members. Usually they say yes, and we need that flexibility.

"We also look at location. It is very easy to hire good people in Silicon Valley and in the Boston area. In other places, it's a lot more difficult. I invested in a company in North Carolina early in my career. It was acquired, which was a reasonable outcome for the management team, but it was difficult to get noticed because there wasn't a big technology pool there."

How Do You Evaluate the Venture's Prospective Business Model?

"You need to have a strategy for what your business model is. I get really tough on business models. If a company is selling an enterprise product, we can figure out the margins and distribution before we start. For example, if a company has a $15,000 product that is expected to be sold through a direct sales force, it's not going to work because a direct sales force is going to cost a lot more than the revenue it'll bring in. We don't focus too much on the SOHO [small office, home office] market because we think it requires a direct sale, but the price point is too low. Most of our companies either use direct sales or telesales to sell their product or service. If you can sell your product over the phone, that is fantastic. Over time, many of our companies sell through third-party channels as well."

What Due Diligence Do You Conduct?

"Customers are the most important reference. The conversation goes like this: 'If there were a product that would do this, would you buy it? What problem would it solve for you, and how important is that problem? How much would you pay for this product?' That's the big mistake a lot of entrepreneurs make. They don't talk to customers first. Maybe they have a unique technology, but it doesn't count for much if no one will buy it.

"We do the due diligence in-house, but we also use our entrepreneurs from previous investments. We have been investing in information technology for years. If we've got an opportunity that is related to a previous investment, we'll show it to the VP of engineering or CEO. Those checks are very helpful."

What Is the Process through Which Funding Decisions Are Made?

"A deal takes anywhere from a month to many months to get done. Usually from start to finish is a two- to three-month period. We're looking at a company now that was a seed deal a year and a half ago, but we wanted to wait until they had a few more customers or a few beta sites. Now they're back, and they've made a lot of progress, which is good. We can work fast if it's something that is really hot. We find the more analysis we do trying to figure out something, the weaker the deal is. If it's not clear to us, there is probably a good reason.

"We want to have $20 million to $25 million in each company. We will probably have 60 to 75 investments in Menlo IX, which is a $1.5 billion fund, so that is about right. We invest over the life of the company. With a little company, we might start off with $5 million to $8 million and put in more over time. What we've found is that if we think it's a good deal, we should invest as much money as possible."

What Financial Analyses Do You Perform?

"I look at the financials to see if they make sense. I actually look at them more for mistakes. If someone thinks they will have a 40% after-tax margin after five years, they clearly do not understand the costs of running a business. We do some forecasts and projections for our investment summaries in a really brief way. Detailed projections are usually not accurate and not that meaningful. We can guess all we want, but if we have a big, growing market and some people who can implement well, we should have significant revenues over time.

"Every August, we do this analysis about deals we turned down either because of market, management, technology, or the product wasn't developed. We almost always get it right if we turned down a deal because there wasn't a market. Where we don't always get it right is valuation. If we turn it down because of valuation, we had a 10% error rate. Of all the decisions we made because of valuation, 90% were good but 10% were bad. With market as a reason, 99% were good and only 1% were bad decisions."

What Role Does Risk Play in Your Evaluation?

"We try to reduce our risk by investing in companies that are the market share leader or are going to be the market share leader in their space. We talk to analysts, customers, or other experts in the space to identify and evaluate those companies. Companies that are market leaders typically have greater margin and a larger cushion to make mistakes, and they are usually the first ones to go public. They can also hire the best people. We've looked at thousands and thousands of companies and have evaluated what they've done right and wrong; we've developed a nose for which companies are going to be number one. Our investment processes also help us reduce risk. We've talked about our SEMS process. When we do our valuation analysis, we do comparables, and if the opportunity looks like it will return less than five times our investment, we won't do it. Our returns have to be seven to 10 times because venture capital investments are high risk."

How Do You Think about a Potential Exit Route?

"We have to think IPO [initial public offering] all the time; this company could go public. However, it has become harder for small companies to go public because of new regulations that make an acquisition a more attractive outcome. We've had a couple of liquidity events recently. Big companies didn't do their R&D [research and development] in the last four or five years because of profit pressures. I think there will be a lot of acquisitions coming because there are holes in product lines, and existing companies have access to distribution so they can take a product, insert it in their product line, and sell it."

Fred Wang: General Partner, Trinity Ventures

Fred Wang joined Trinity Ventures as a general partner in 1999 from Spectrum Equity Investors. Wang has spent over 15 years in the communications industry, working at The Boston Consulting Group with clients such as AT&T, Lucent, and Siemens as well as in operating positions in the new technologies groups at Pacific Bell and Intuit. Wang's focus at Trinity is on communications and networked systems, services, and semiconductors. He sits on seven boards of Trinity's portfolio companies. Wang received his B.S. in electrical engineering and M.S. in industrial engineering from Stanford University and an MBA from Harvard Business School in 1992.

How Do You Evaluate Potential Venture Opportunities?

"There is not a formal template, per se. There are some pretty obvious things—in no particular order for us, they are team, market opportunity, and the product/value proposition for the solution. Technology differentiation or business model differentiation is also important to sustain a competitive advantage.

"One potential point of differentiation between us and some other firms relates to how we think about the CEO. A couple of years ago, we analyzed our successful companies across multiple dimensions. The one trait of all our successful companies was that the CEO we backed at funding was still the CEO at the sale of the company or IPO. We'll switch out CEOs; we've done that and had decent outcomes, but our best outcomes are the ones where the CEO takes it to glory. Historically, we have not been as good at bringing in a CEO when a company goes sideways.

"I think our focus on the CEO has helped us eliminate one set of mistakes we might have been making. During the bubble years, we funded companies when we knew that the CEO was the wrong CEO or there wasn't a true CEO in place. We thought we'd find the right CEO down the road. We'd have the conversation with the company about getting a new CEO in place, but it was never the right time. So now, to fund a company, we need to believe that the existing CEO could bring the company to a successful outcome.

"As a result, we spend a lot of time focused on the CEO and the members of the management team: the quality of people they attract, their biases, their strong points, and their overall depth. Part of that is more experiential, and much of it's in the due diligence. We spend a lot of time in a room with the management team going through problems. What's the channel? What happens if the customer comes back and says this? What happens in product development? Hearing how they think and react is very helpful. We pick up a lot of insight on how they would operate the business day to day.

"We've also done some analysis that suggests another big determinant of success is the sector; it's a sector bet. If we're investing in the right sector, even if the team is more mediocre, or the execution isn't as good, the rising market lifted all the companies in the sector. Some did better than the others, but overall everyone made money.

"We are very thesis driven here. We see a ton of deals from our network, through referrals, or that come in over the transom. However, once a quarter we do a strategic off-site where we'll say, 'Let's pick out some interesting subsectors.' We come up with a thesis that says these are specific pain points; this is how we address them. We outline what we think is the right answer and look for a company in that market. More than half our deals, three or four a year, come out of this process.

"Let's say we were hearing more frequently about managing applications at a data center—that this is a really big problem. We'd have a couple of partners investigate it. They'd call CIOs, go to conferences, and have junior people on our team dig up companies in the market and have them come in. We'd either conclude the market is not interesting or it is interesting, but let's revisit it because it's too early. Or it's interesting, and we've found the right company. Occasionally, we'll conclude it's interesting, but let's go start our own company because we can't find the right investment.

"Our rule of thumb is we'd like the company to get to $100 million in revenue. Realistically, if we can see the company get to $50 million in revenue and the valuation is right, it could still be a good venture deal. In a decent IT market, a $50 million revenue company should be worth at least a $100 million to $200 million outcome. At that point, we're making a good venture multiple, potentially a five to 10 times type of return.

"In today's corporate IT environment, CIOs or VPs of IT have two or three priorities. They're usually willing to pay millions of dollars for those, but beyond that, a $20,000 piece of software might not hit their radar. So, how much a customer is willing to dish out for the solution is a combination of willingness to pay and how high up the pain ladder it is.

"It's a little harder to say what the rule of thumb is on total market size. We've funded some companies that have gone after a $500 million market. But it's a sleepy enough market that we're confident the company can take a big market share. If it's a large entrenched market, we want to see a $1 billion to $2 billion market size so that we can see an opportunity to carve out a slice with a differentiated strategy. There's no easy answer because it gets driven a lot by what the competitive dynamic is. There isn't a table that says if there are 10 competitors, the market size has got to be this much. We're often funding companies in unproven markets, and we just don't know how large the market will be. Frankly, we don't put a lot of weight in market size projections. Usually when someone shows us one, it's 'next slide.' Because everything looks like it's going to be a multibillion-dollar market.

"We don't put much emphasis on legal or patent protection even though we do encourage our companies to try to protect themselves. If a big company comes to steal our company's idea, it might not have the resources to protect itself anyway, so from a market standpoint it may be toast. In the e-commerce days, size and branding were protection from competition. That was unnatural for us and still is unnatural. We think a technology secret sauce is important; it's a bet that people aren't going to solve the problem in a cheap and easy way.

"Again, we go back to the personal aspects of it. Often, the technology isn't there yet, so we're betting that this team can develop it and deliver on it. Coming back to the team issue, we want to make sure they're capable. To the extent there is something to kick the tires on, it's a pretty broad swath. We'll look at the architecture, algorithms, or any kind of secret sauce related to how they approach a particular problem. We'll look at internal processes for development, tools they use, code review, and the philosophy around software development or hardware development because there are different schools out there.

"Here's one that we typically won't do: It looks like a great technology, really groundbreaking, could be a huge market, but it's a technologist—sometimes a wild-eyed technologist—who's driving it. The businessperson is either weak or not there at all. We don't historically play in that situation. We've missed some good things because of it. The hit rate and the time it takes to constantly arm wrestle with the technologist are issues we try to avoid."

How Do You Evaluate the Venture's Prospective Business Model?

"In evaluating a business model, we almost always start on the revenue side to understand the price point and the customer acquisition strategy. As we can see in enterprise software today—and has almost always been the case with systems—a direct sales force is too difficult and expensive to maintain. The days of paying the sales guy a couple hundred thousand bucks a year to go sell a million bucks worth of software are over. Many companies we look at are selling software somewhere between $50,000 to $250,000 a shot. So, it is important to understand whether it is a $20,000 or a $200,000 piece of software.

"How does the company increase the value it gets from a customer? Is it additional modules or more users, and how does that affect pricing? This is really important because that drives the go-to-market strategy—what the sales force and channels look like, and whether the company goes after a small or broad set of customers, and who it sells to in the customer department. These revolve around the pricing strategy. So that's one set of issues.

"The other revolves around the technology side of the business model. What's it going to cost to build this thing—the number of engineers the company needs after it breaks down its various development efforts—and how long will it take to get the product out the door?

"We don't spend too much time initially on the marketing. From a financial standpoint, we look to see if it is a technical sale and how much the ROI [return on investment] calculation comes into play. If it's a hardware business, we need a clear understanding of what working capital looks like. Working capital, especially if the company's doing well, can really be a cash drain.

"We weave this into higher-level issues about how much time we are buying and how much money needs to be raised. We're looking at a company that follows the Salesforce.com model. It is a subscription, hosted software model that looks like it's going to take $7 million to $8 million to get to a decent level of revenue. Right now, it's three guys and a business plan. So the math goes: We'll put in $8 million, probably $10 million to be on the safe side, behind this management team that hasn't really proven much so it's hard to ascribe a value to it. This deal doesn't work financially because we give these guys $3 million to $4 million pre-money value, their ownership would be so small, and they'd have to raise more money down the road and get diluted. That business model is just not fundable. They're trying to recraft it.

"We have always been cautious, and even more so recently, about business models that require a lot of capital to be successful. There are these 'big bang' opportunities where the company is going to build the next server to put Sun out of business. Usually that takes $40 million to $50 million of capital before the investors really know if the company is successful. But the outcome could really be gigantic, right? We typically like the other model of going after a slightly smaller opportunity, a more bite-sized and tactical one. But we'll know early on after $5 million to $7 million of investment if we're on the right track. Then, we hope to get into adjacent markets and grow the company from there."

What Due Diligence Do You Conduct?

"From a due-diligence standpoint, we always have at least two general partners who are sponsors of the company. We also try to have a devil's advocate who is somewhat skeptical to raise objective questions and ensure we've gone through the process. A good example is a company we funded called Clarus up in San Francisco. It's a company that had been around a couple of years before we funded it, and Keith Giarman became CEO. Keith is a classmate from HBS. Clarus is building a software solution to help companies put VoIP [voice-over-Internet protocol] into their businesses. Today, you buy one of Cisco's VoIP phones because they promise savings, but there are problems around voice quality and performance if you change out your switch for your data network.

"We met the founder a couple of times when he was trying to raise his first round of capital. He got some angel funding but wasn't able to raise a venture round. He had a very scrappy team that hadn't made a salary in virtually two years, and the technology was good. The team had moved the product along with some first customers, but the company wasn't fundable in its current state. This is a situation where the founder thought he was going to be the CEO. Two years earlier when we talked, he said he was going to be the CEO. It was apparent after not being able to raise money that he wasn't going to be the CEO.

"The founder came to me six months ago—before we introduced him to Keith—and said he was looking for a CEO, which opened the door. We had an open discussion around Keith as a potential CEO and someone who could help him raise money. Keith had just left a start-up in a related space. I asked him to look at Clarus to see if he was interested. Keith spent four or five weeks at the company digging in and looking at it. He got his arms around it and revamped the story. At that point, we got excited about it and kicked off the formal due-diligence process.

"The product wasn't thrown together, but it wasn't a full enterprise-class-ready product because they didn't have the resources. Specifically, we did a technology drill-down with the team to look at the architecture and the processes. I introduced the Clarus team to the person who runs the telecom network at JP Morgan Chase; he's implementing VoIP there. I also asked him to take a look at the product and give me feedback about big holes, etc.

"Keith had to clean up the management team. We did all our reference calls on the management team, background checks, and criminal tests. That is one thing we never want to get burned on. Funding a felon is a bad bet. Even though we knew Keith, we did make a few more calls. From a legal standpoint, Clarus had signed up a small law firm in the city that did them all kinds of disservice around setting up some poor agreements. So, we had to clean that up as well.

"We also spent a lot of time on the financial model. The key question was how much money should they raise, especially given a new CEO who didn't own the financial plan. Also, it was a situation where it had been a very scrappy team that hadn't been taking full salaries. So all kinds of things could have emerged—oh, this person loaned the company $100,000, or we didn't pay these bills. We find liabilities crop up in situations where the company has been living hand-to-mouth. We spend a lot of time flushing that out.

"From a market standpoint, there were some customer things, but it was more of a bet that this problem was going to continue to emerge. We didn't spend a ton of time talking to Cisco to get its view; we had a pretty good handle on that. I had one of our analysts look for other start-ups. We identified two: one that was a component technology and the second a competitor that some other VCs had funded. There were some bigger guys that had product offerings, but customers and resellers didn't seem to think their products were there yet. We went through the whole process and funded the company with Keith.

"We're trying to find more deals like this where we create the situation ourselves. We know the CEO; we don't have to reference that person. We have also spent time with the technology and the product, and so we put them all together. We have ball control of the deal rather than it being a jump ball with 10 other VCs going after it. The last deal we closed, a video deal, was the same thing.

"In situations where we're betting on momentum, we'll spend a lot of time with the sales team. We'll do account reviews. We'll ask them about the status of their top 20 accounts: where are you, what have you talked about, who are the other guys? We go through the pipeline like we are the VP of sales."

What Is the Process through Which Funding Decisions Are Made?

"I would position Trinity as a moderately sized firm that is fairly traditional in how it approaches the business. We're investing Trinity VIII, a $300 million fund. We call ourselves multistage, but it's all within the realm of early stage. We will do seed investing. Our sweet spot tends to be Series A, the first venture round. But we'll also do follow-on rounds if we think there is a venture multiple involved.

"We try not to do tranched investments, although we have. The danger with tranches is it's very hard not to do that next tranche of capital. There are always reasons something didn't work. We find ourselves in board meetings saying you're right, you're right, okay; let's throw in the next tranche. If we don't fund the tranche then there could be legal repercussions, so we try to avoid it.

"We do try to make each round of financing have enough cushion for the company to hit a major milestone or set of milestones. We don't overfund the first round, and we don't underfund because in this environment it takes between three to six months to fund-raise. We rarely fund a company for less than a year because they're out fund-raising again in six months, perhaps without much to show for it. We're usually looking for an 18-month window."

What Financial Analyses Do You Perform?

"The financial model discussion is more often a good insight into how smart a team is. We don't worry as much about whether their first quarter of revenue is $2 million or $4 million; it's the thinking behind it. When a company says this other company spent X% on sales and marketing so we're going to project that, we don't get a lot of confidence that they know what they're doing. The flip side is when management can give it to us at the line-item level. The team can say, 'When we did our last start-up, we spent $20,000 on this trade show that was worthwhile. We hired these three salespeople, and we paid them this much.' They've got this bottom-up model with every piece falling into place, so we have a lot of confidence they know what they're doing.

"We also try to build a bottom-up projection using empirical data about an analogous problem and solution and what the customer was willing to pay. We estimate how many customers there are to determine how big an opportunity it might be. Since we invest in a relatively focused area of IT, we know that if it's a $200,000 or $300,000 enterprise software solution and a broad enough problem, it's a big enough market. If it's a vertical, then we've got to believe the company's selling a $1 million-plus type solution. So, there are some rules of thumb we adhere to."

What Role Does Risk Play in Your Evaluation?

"There's got to be a clear strategy of managing risk. When we fund a plan, we try to get an internal agreement around the positive thesis and key risks. We outline the action plan to review risk as we go through it. Actually, we also try to make sure the management team is on board because they will execute against it. And that is very explicit. After we've funded, we track our milestones around product, first beta customer, first revenue customer.

"There is a concept of a particular financial return, but it differs from stage to stage. If we look at the three Series As we did last year, the valuations were all in the same ballpark. I don't think we thought this one is a little more risky, this one is a little less risky, and therefore the valuations should reflect it. Within a certain stage of an investment, I think the valuations get driven much more by competitive dynamics than anything else. Ideally, we could be more systematic about the analysis, but in reality, it doesn't play out.

"Last year we did two investments that were second rounds of financing. In both cases, they were companies that were in revenue and starting to ramp. We're willing to pay a higher value for that. They should be lower risk: the dogs were starting to eat the dog food. It was a question of how quickly they'd eat and how well the company would scale from an execution standpoint. In those cases, if we made five times our money we'd probably be happy, but we'd also expect the success rate to be much higher."

How Do You Think about a Potential Exit Route?

"The bulk of companies get acquired, so I think we're pretty realistic about that. On several occasions, we've funded companies we knew were going to be acquired. The odds of going public were pretty slim, but at least they had large, addressable markets so they could get big enough. We need to believe the company is sustainable on its own, rather than timing it so someone acquires it before the company needs more cash.

"An IPO is always the best outcome. It means the company's going to be much bigger. But some of these acquisitions are pretty darn large. We look at what valuation we invest in, and a big part of the equation is how much capital the company needs. I've got a company where the investors invested $110 million, and thus with a $150 million outcome, that's not much of a return. Then we've got other companies where we put in $3 million and own half the company, and if it gets bought at $150 million—that's a huge outcome.

"Part of the reason we have a more moderately sized fund is that our outcomes can have an impact on the fund size. If we had a $1 billion fund, finding an outcome that could have an impact would be really hard; it is still hard with a $300 million fund."

Robert Simon: Director, Alta Partners

Robert Simon joined Alta Partners as a director in 2000 from Sierra Ventures, where he was a venture partner. Simon has 17 years of experience in the software development and Internet sectors including starting three companies: DotBank.com, Navitel Communications, and Virgil Corporation. Simon's focus is on information technology, primarily enterprise software. He received a B.S. and M.S. in industrial engineering from Stanford University in 1982 and 1983, respectively.

How Do You Evaluate Potential Venture Opportunities?

"There are two schools of thought. In the first, the venture capitalist says, 'I invest in people first and foremost. Smart people will find great opportunities, and I will never know the sectors or technologies as well as smart people. I back people.' In the other, the venture capitalist says, 'I don't care about people; I care about markets. I look for big opportunities, big painful problems that customers have. If management doesn't work out, I can always fix management.' The truth is obviously somewhere in between, but I'm leaning more on the market side. I think markets trump people and trump technology. We can build something. If no one wants it, we've got a big problem. I've seen that on the entrepreneur side, and now I've seen it on the venture side.

"Under the heading of market, we have customer pain. How much pain does the customer feel, and how much will the customer pay to solve it? We get to market size by estimating how many customers feel the pain. We met with a company here in San Francisco that was developing software for analyzing large log files. Pretty tough stuff, pretty complicated. We asked them about their potential customers. Their solution was best suited to companies that generate a gigabyte a day in log files. How many are there out there? There are two: Yahoo! and eBay. That's a problem.

"On the market side, there are two ways to look at it. The replacement for an existing product is one market: the better, cheaper, faster model. The other is the brave-new-world model where we're introducing a new piece of functionality and don't really know where the markets are. Those tend to fall more on the consumer side. Everybody has an opinion on them because we can relate to them; that's both good and bad. The brave-new-world model certainly has a greater market risk but not necessarily more technical risk. Historically, the venture community has avoided consumer-facing deals for several reasons. The gross margins have typically been pretty slim, the marketing costs are high, and it's a 'hit-driven' business, and we're not good at predicting consumer behavior. Now, on the plus side, we can find consumer-facing deals that are capital efficient. Those are the Internet deals, and some of them have worked out well.

"Everyone wants the $1 billion market. If we're honest, we don't know what and where the $1 billion markets are until we get there. We have to see our way to a $200 million market with the right attributes and a lot of growth potential. We don't target market share for our companies; we target revenue. We expect north of $60 million to $80 million in revenue in three to five years.

"We also look at the technology to see how proprietary and difficult the solution to the problem is. We gauge if we can build defensible barriers. If it's an easy problem that everyone can solve, it's less attractive. The ideal case is four Ph.D.s trying to solve a problem they've been working on for a year or two, and somehow they've struck upon the magic solution. And, it's two orders of magnitude better than whatever else is out there.

"We invested in a company called Aegis that makes an optical component, a tunable filter. The current cost of competitive components is between $2,000 and $5,000. Aegis has developed an almost plug-compatible replacement using a silicon process that puts their cost between $50 and $100. It's a perfect example. The only problem there is the telecom market has fallen off the cliff, so now they have to find new markets.

"Then we look at the people. We want to keep the existing team if possible. They're the ones with the passion and some understanding of the problem. We get a little concerned when the entrepreneur comes in and says, 'I'm in this to flip it in a year.' It rarely works out that way. So if we get the impression they're not in it for the tough times, then it's definitely a problem.

"We have this conversation right up front on their personal motivations, their definition of success, and whether they're wedded to a particular role in the company. We like to avoid a situation where the guy says, 'It's very important for me to be the CEO. It's going to be a big company, and you're either with me or not. You're going to pull me kicking and screaming out of the chair.' So, we say, 'Okay, maybe not a good fit.' Sixty percent of the time or more we're facing a change in management. We want it to be a positive as opposed to a divisive situation for the company.

"Getting back to market versus people and technology, we can have a market where the only issue is the timing. We have an investment in a semiconductor company that's doing a 40-gig network processor. Networking starts out at one megabit, goes to two megabit, 10 megabit, 100 megabit. So all laptops, servers, and switches have 100 megabit connections. The next progression is one gigabit, two gigabit, and we can see our way to 40. Great; we fund it. The only issue is timing: If we're too early, there's no market demand, and we have to survive until the demand reaches us. In that period of time, we have two problems: we have to keep the doors open and feed everybody, and we may be susceptible to being leapfrogged by technology. So we don't want to be too early, but we don't want to be too late."

How Do You Evaluate the Venture's Prospective Business Model?

"I think more of the deals now have clearer business models than the ones from the 1999, 2000, and 2001 period. I think of Hotmail. I know the investors there; they were investors in my previous company. Hotmail never made money; it was acquired for its subscribers rather than its business potential. Microsoft acquired it for $350 million or $450 million; it was one of the first big acquisitions. If you look at that from a classic valuation standpoint, you wouldn't have made the investment. In fact, I had the opportunity and didn't make the investment. Nonetheless, it was a great outcome for the investors. I don't think we want to play that game today because acquisitions are being made for fundamental business reasons rather than other asset reasons. Companies in the Internet space don't feel the need to make those customer acquisition purchases anymore.

"There's a company called Skype that just raised $20 million from Draper Fisher, Tim Draper specifically. I can say this because he's an old college mate. Skype provides the ability to do phone calls over the Net. If both parties have an Internet connection and Skype, they can talk anywhere in the world for the cost of the Internet connection. It's potentially disruptive for international calling, so it potentially has a big market. How Skype makes money is not clear because they don't make money on the calls. Tim Draper is bolder than we are. He's betting that 10 million, at least north of 5 million, people can't be wrong because they're using it, and the company will find a way to monetize that."

What Due Diligence Do You Conduct?

"If I look at a company and like it, I'll do some preliminary due diligence. I'll speak with the entrepreneur by telephone or have them come in. We'll research the company by talking to customers or potential customers to corroborate the customer pain or product utility. We'll ask whether they have experience with the product or service, have they deployed it, and how they would feel if we took it away. If they say they wouldn't care or no way, we can't take it away, that would give us an indication.

"We don't require the company to have paying customers. They can have a pilot or a couple of betas, but we want them to have engaged the customer. We also might introduce them to a portfolio company with the same requirement or CIOs in our network or other potential customers. They'll serve as an off-sheet reference, and we see two things: does the customer confirm and/or have the pain, and how effective is the team at delivering its message.

"We'll also talk to folks who have worked with this particular team and do reference checks on the people. If I really like the company, I'll get another partner engaged. Then, I'll talk up the deal a little bit here and bring it in to the IT partners, which are a smaller set. Finally, as we get more serious, the company will give a presentation to the full partnership in one of our regular Monday meetings. If there are any open issues from that, I'll run them down and bring it back for a decision."

What Is the Process through Which Funding Decisions Are Made?

"Brave-new-world companies are a smaller percentage of our portfolio, although not necessarily a smaller percentage of the deals we see. It's probably worthwhile to put one or two brave-new-world opportunities in a portfolio to see how they end up. The bet can be on the marketing or the technology side. In the brave-new-world case, we start out with a seed investment to see if the company gets any traction. If they can get it deployed, we layer in additional investment once we get some idea about adoption. So we'll seed them with $500,000 or so to get them through product launch, then they'll have to raise money again. Next time, we might go in with $2 million to $4 million.

"There is no set parameter on the amount of capital we invest. Some of it varies by industry. We have to remind ourselves we don't need to invest a ton of money for a software company. I think someone told me PeopleSoft took only $12 million of investment. Adobe only needed $1 million. Adobe got a $1 million advance royalty payment from Apple, but all the equity it needed was $1 million. So I think it's pretty reasonable to do a software company for $15 million to $20 million or less. Telecom systems take more. We may be learning again that they may not be good investments for venture folks because we need 100 to 200 people for 18 to 24 months. That adds up to $200 million and not a happy story—we had one of those.

"We go through a bit of the math with entrepreneurs to show what opportunities are good venture opportunities and what ones are not necessarily good venture opportunities but may still be very good businesses. We can have entrepreneurs who have a $10 million a year business where they own 90%. If it's growing 40% a year, they don't need much capital. So why would they give up half or more of their company to an outside investor? They would have to work at least twice as hard to realize the same personal outcome. Once they take outside investment, they get on this treadmill. Unless they're making progress up that hill, it just becomes a grumpy situation for everybody.

"Across the board, investors are taking anywhere between a month to even six months to make decisions. I had lunch with a guy today who finally did the deal after looking at it for a year. It is more common now to have some time to see the progress a team makes on its own. We meet with the company, and time will pass as we do our research on the opportunity, technology, and customers. Then, we can compare what they actually did with the milestones they set, like signing up a new customer or meeting their quarterly revenue targets."

What Financial Analyses Do You Perform?

"The business presentations usually have both the revenue model and expense model. We first look at the expense model. How much money does the opportunity take to get to cash flow break-even? We construct our own model on revenues because usually they're wildly optimistic: first year $1 million, second year $20 million, third year $100 million—it's a little unrealistic. Often they've also taken a top-down approach on market share. Well, that's all fine and dandy and gives us some idea of market size, but that's really not going to be the revenue ramp. We do a bottom-up analysis for the revenue ramp, and we end up with a fraction of what the top-down is."

What Role Does Risk Play in Your Evaluation?

"Before a decision is made to fund a company, we do a two- to five-page investment memo. There is a section on what we believe the risks are: technical risks, competitive risks, market risks. The financials are not that detailed. They might include revenue over the next four or five years, expenses, etc."

How Do You Think about a Potential Exit Route?

"We'll look at a market size north of $200 million and a company revenue rate north of $60 million to $80 million. We think that will yield a large enough market for an exit. If we can't see the company growing to that size in revenue, then it's probably not an appealing venture investment. And before we go into an investment, we'll definitely have a conversation about who would be likely acquirers, who would be good partners.

"Timing an exit is a bit of a dicey thing. Building lasting companies that continue to grow consistently over time is a more reliable way to make money than getting out just in time."

EXHIBIT 1 | Venture Capital Firm Background Information

Kleiner Perkins Caufield & Byers (KPCB)—Founded in 1972, KPCB has helped entrepreneurs build over 400 companies including America Online, Sun Microsystems, Amazon, Juniper, and Genentech. It closed its $400 million Kleiner Perkins Caufield & Byers XI fund in February 2004. The partners expect to fund emerging growth companies in information technology, life sciences, and other fast-growing industries over a three-year period. KPCB's current portfolio includes companies in the following sectors: broadband equipment and services, consumer devices and services, enterprise software and services, financial services, Internet infrastructure software and services, medical devices, heath-care services, and biotech. In its office on Sand Hill Road in Menlo Park, KPCB has six partners emeritus and 17 investment professionals: 12 partners, one principal, and four associate partners.

Menlo Ventures—Menlo Ventures has seven funds with $2.7 billion under management invested in over 270 companies. Founded in 1976, Menlo Ventures invests in communications, Internet infrastructure, software, semiconductor, data storage, and computer hardware companies. Menlo Ventures typically invests $5 million to $10 million at the start-up phase of a company and $10 million to $25 million at later stages. It is willing to invest in all stages of a U.S.-headquartered private company's growth. Portfolio successes include LSI Logic, UUNET Technologies, Hotmail Corporation, and Clarify. Located on Sand Hill Road in Menlo Park, California, Menlo Ventures has 14 investment professionals: seven managing directors, four associates, and three investment analysts.

Trinity Ventures—Founded in 1986, Trinity Ventures primarily invests in early-stage and emerging growth technology companies. Trinity Fund VIII has approximately $300 million of committed capital to fund opportunities in the following sectors: software, services, communications and networked systems, and semiconductors. Portfolio company successes include Blue Nile (IPO), Crescendo (acquired by Cisco), Network Alchemy (acquired by Nokia), P.F. Chang's (IPO), Starbucks (IPO), and Wall Data (IPO). Located on Sand Hill Road in Menlo Park, California, Trinity's team consists of six general partners, one venture partner, one principal, and one analyst.

Alta Partners—Since its inception in 1996, Alta Partners has funded approximately 120 early- and later-stage life sciences and early-stage information technology companies. Alta manages seven venture funds approximating $1.5 billion in committed capital including $475 million in two life sciences funds that closed in March 2004. Alta's geographic focus is U.S. companies, although it has made selective investments in Europe. Alta's IPOs in 2004 include Corgentech, Eyetech Pharmaceuticals, and Renovis. Prior investments in the information technology sector include Be, Inc. (acquired by Palm Computing), Coloma Wireless (acquired by AT&T), and Fibex Systems (acquired by Cisco Systems). Located in San Francisco, Alta Partners has 10 professionals devoted to life sciences (eight directors and two principals) and four directors in information technology.

Source: Adapted from venture capital firm bios at www.kpcb.com, www.menloventures.com, www.trinityventures.com, www.altapartners.com.

Beta Golf

Bob Zider, founder and managing partner of The Beta Group, placed his handmade golf club prototypes into the back of his Chevrolet Suburban and drove out of the parking lot of San Francisco International Airport. It was June 6, 1997, and he and his partner, John Krumme, had just returned from visiting Callaway Golf in San Diego, where they had introduced executives at the industry leading golf club maker to their proprietary HXL golf club technology. They were tired—they had arrived at Callaway's test facility at 6 a.m. to witness "Iron Byron," Callaway's mechanical golf swing simulator, test Beta's golf clubs. Later that morning, Zider and Krumme had watched as five of Callaway's in-house professionals tested their prototypes. As they prepared to leave for the airport, Callaway's chief engineer had indicated that the company was not interested in Beta's technology because "it did not offer a significant improvement over their existing technology." The engineer was unwilling to disclose "Iron Byron's" test results, but Zider and Krumme had learned that two of the five in-house professionals had rated Beta's club excellent, two had rated it average, and one had rated it below average. Zider considered the feedback:

> I have often been told that Beta's inventions have been insignificant. I have learned to listen carefully to the naysayers. We went to Callaway because we expected the industry leader to kill the technology through data or engineering logic, but they couldn't. Actually, if all the pros had said it was average or below average, I'd know that we didn't have anything. But, two of the them really liked it. I don't consider 1 of 5 'below average' ratings to be a fatal strike. We're not done with HXL until someone presents a logical reason not to pursue it.

In 1983, Zider had founded The Beta Group (Beta) as an "incubator" for technology-based businesses. Over the past fourteen years, Beta had successfully built a portfolio of businesses in the medical, consumer products, and industrial technology sectors by systematically matching proprietary technologies to unmet market needs.

Professors William A. Sahlman and Michael J. Roberts and Senior Researcher Laurence E. Katz prepared this case. HBS cases are developed solely as the basis for class discussion. Cases are not intended to serve as endorsements, sources of primary data, or illustrations of effective or ineffective management.

In January 1996, Krumme, Beta's chief engineer, had designed a golf club prototype using a new metal "pixel" club face which offered an enlarged "sweet spot." Initial test data sponsored by Beta indicated that the club face reduced shaft vibration and the dispersion of miss-hit balls. At first, Zider had been skeptical about Beta's ability to commercialize this technology. Eight years earlier, Beta had declined an investment in the golf club industry because the market was growing slowly, dominated by entrenched brands, and resistant to technological innovation. Since 1990, however, growth in the golf club market had increased significantly, sparked by enhancements in technology, improved marketing from new club makers such as Callaway, and the emergence of Tiger Woods as a leader on the Men's PGA Tour. Encouraged by the industry trends, Zider and Krumme had focused on refining the technology, developing alternate business models, and addressing key risks. After eighteen months, they were confident that the technology was sound and that they could manufacture a quality product within specified tolerances.

However, Zider and Krumme had not resolved one remaining question: how would they commercialize the technology? They had identified four options. First, they could license it to leading club makers, on either an exclusive or non-exclusive basis. This strategy could play off the intense competition in the golf equipment industry for the latest generation of technology. Second, they could manufacture and distribute club inserts which would be inserted into a machined cavity in the club face during assembly. Aldila and True Temper, both club shaft makers, had been successful with this OEM model, supplying shafts to multiple club makers. Several leading club makers recently had adopted inserts because they enabled club makers to market new materials while minimizing design and obsolescence costs. Third, they could buy a former leading club maker which had lost share and revive its brand by promoting HXL. One former industry leader was reportedly for sale, and Beta could leverage its existing brand and distribution infrastructure. Fourth, they could start a new club company from scratch and develop a new line of equipment around Beta's new technology. Cobra, Callaway and Odyssey each had successfully pursued this strategy and sold for a multiple of three times sales within 5 years.

As Zider and Krumme reviewed each of these options, they needed to consider the associated capital requirements, risk profiles, and exit options. At the same time, they needed to evaluate which, if any, of these options was feasible, given investor skepticism of the industry and the industry's reluctance to invest in outside technologies.

The Beta Group

The Beta Group[1] was founded by Zider in 1983 to develop and apply a systematic, multidisciplinary approach to innovation. Zider, a 35-year-old partner at the Boston Consulting Group (BCG), had been an engineer at Pratt & Whitney Aircraft prior to attending Harvard Business School. (See **Exhibit 1** for profiles of Beta's principals.) Through several of his engagements at BCG, Zider had determined that large corporations did not have the internal systems to successfully exploit most innovations from their research departments. He also observed that venture capitalists rarely funded

---

[1]Beta was an acronym for Business Engineering and Technology Applications.

research and development projects and avoided many industries which required significant investment in R&D. He reflected on what he termed "the innovation gap":

> I believe there are structural reasons that systematic innovation has not fully evolved in corporations or venture capital firms. Most successful corporations focus on managing vast numbers of people and resources efficiently, not innovation. To the extent that an explicit R&D process exists in these companies, it is often functionally oriented and usually narrowly tied to an existing strategic product area. The typical corporate compensation structure also makes it very difficult to reward innovation, which discourages groundbreaking R&D and drives the best talent out of companies.
>
> VCs do invest capital in others who innovate, but over 90% of their capital goes to fund working capital requirements and operating losses. In the early 1980s, VCs allocated about one fourth of their investment dollars to seed and startups; today it's less than 6%. In fact, many companies themselves invest more in R&D than the entire VC community. Today, VCs focus on investments with low technology risk and high market growth potential. Typically, technology development occurs before the VCs enter the picture.

Zider founded Beta to foster a systematic approach to innovation through a process that he called Business Engineering.[2] Business Engineering referred to the development of a concept and business strategy through rigorous analysis of markets and technologies by a multi-disciplinary team. Through Business Engineering, Beta matched an identified market opportunity with a proprietary technology, such as a patented technology or innovative process. Zider compared Business Engineering to the aircraft engine development process he had participated in at Pratt & Whitney Aircraft: "Just as engineers 'flight test' new engine designs on paper before they build them, we want to 'flight test' new businesses through the Business Engineering process before we invest significant capital. Like jet engines which work the first time they fly, we believe our businesses should 'fly' the first time out." Zider believed that Business Engineering would increase the probability of an investment's success while limiting the cost of its failure. (See **Exhibit 2** for a description of Beta's mission.)

Zider reflected on his vision for Beta's strategy:

> I wanted to create an investment process that could not only develop ideas and concepts but also could test and implement them. My idea was not to start another venture capital fund, but to originate ideas, develop business plans around them, identify key operating officers, assemble financing, and actually bring small companies to the point of operation. To that end, I wanted to pull together the functional expertise of the corporation, the judgment of the venture capitalist, the creativity and fire of the entrepreneur, and the analytic rigor of the strategic consultant.

Zider recruited one of his BCG partners and incorporated the Beta Group, Inc. with a $300,000 investment from BCG and an in-kind donation of $1.5 million of consulting services. In return, BCG received an equity position in Beta's projects. BCG viewed its investment in Beta not only as an opportunity to achieve attractive returns on its partners' capital, but also as an opportunity to attract and retain talented consultants by promoting its affiliation with Beta.

---

[2]Business Engineering is unrelated to Business Re-engineering, which was popularized in the early 1990s.

Investment Strategy

From the beginning, Beta adopted several operating principles which distinguished its investment strategy. First, Beta funded investments on a deal-by-deal basis with corporate and financial partners:

> We believe that the discipline of having to ask for money lowers our probability of failure. We believe that by forcing ourselves to pass each idea through two external screens—the funding search and the management search—we help to validate the concept. If we fail to complete either, we don't start the business.

Second, Beta created and sponsored its own investment opportunities, usually in sectors such as metallurgy and optometrics in which it had little or no investment competition. (See **Exhibit 3** for description of Beta's investments.) Specifically, they targeted opportunities in which a "trailing edge" technology could be applied to a market need. They believed that this strategy allowed them to avoid overpaying for ideas in "hot" sectors, such as multimedia, genetic engineering, or Internet commerce, while also allowing them to maximize control of their investments.

Third, Beta only pursued opportunities for which it had a superior technology, process, or other significant competitive advantage. Zider commented on this strategy:

> Since we fund each deal on its own merits, we have learned that good ideas alone are not fundable. We can not convince investors that we have a competitive advantage in restaurants, for example. But we have found that if we can patent a technology to insulate ourselves from competition and build a business around that technology, we can fund it and attract a management team.

By 1997, Beta had registered over forty patents and had successfully defended against patent infringements in the United States and Europe.

Fourth, Beta customized its approach to developing a business to meet the needs of the specific market. Beta was prepared to build a business as a start-up, as a joint venture, under license, or via acquisitions. Zider discussed this approach: "We want to fund a business in a way that will give it the best chance of long term success. There isn't one cookie cutter way to commercialize a technology." Of Beta's 12 investments since 1983, 30% had been start-ups, 40% joint ventures, 20% licenses, and 10% acquisitions.

Fifth, Beta was rigorous in conducting a feasibility study of the concept and market opportunity prior to investing significant capital. Typically, Beta outlined the steps and timeline that needed to be met for commercial success and then prioritized key risks. Beta preferred situations in which the risks were highly focused, so that they could be analyzed and assessed with limited investment. Zider explained Beta's approach to capital allocation:

> We believe that capital efficiency can be accomplished by staging investments and minimizing investment during high risk phases. We avoid investing in infrastructure, overhead, and outside management until we feel the primary risks have been adequately addressed. We usually invest less than $250,000 of our own money over a 12–18 month period while we identify and explore key risks.

Finally, Beta adopted a hands-on management relationship with the company throughout its life. Typically, at least one of Beta's partners initially served as a key member of the company's management team. Later in the company's lifecycle, Beta would replace themselves with outside managers but would continue to work closely with the company to implement the strategic plan.

Sourcing New Technologies

Zider commented on Beta's approach to identifying new technologies:

> Lots of people believe that inventions happen only in a moment of brilliance. We don't believe that innovation is simply a spark of naïve creativity. We believe that idea generation is the convergence of several linked but independent events, which include rigorous analysis of market needs, an open mind, and awareness of technical feasibility. We live by Louis Pasteur's quote, "Chance favors only a prepared mind."[3]

At times, Beta identified a market need through analysis and then hunted for a technology to meet that need. For example, Beta uncovered a market need for continuous arterial blood gas monitoring for intensive care patients through a consulting engagement that BCG had completed at a medical device company. At that time, no medical device existed to immediately notify medical professionals when a patient's blood-oxygen, carbon dioxide, or ph level was dangerously low. Through a concentrated technology search, Beta identified and acquired a fiber-optic sensor technology which it believed could be applied to the blood gas market to provide a procedure that was lower cost and less invasive than other competitive technologies. Beta founded FOxS Labs (Fiber-optic Oxygen Sensors) in 1985 with a $50,000 investment and later found a joint venture partner who invested $2.2 million to test the device in human clinicals. Beta sold its interest to their joint venture partner at a $30 million valuation in 1989.

At other times, Beta identified a technology and then looked for an appropriate market need. For example, Krumme previously had worked with a titanium-based alloy called "nitinol" which could bend but then return to its original shape when heated. As nitinol had been refined, a version had been developed that would "spring" back to its original shape at room temperature. On the basis of Zider's market analysis of the eyeglass and contact lens businesses while at BCG, Beta identified an opportunity to apply this memory alloy to eyeglass frames. Beta commercialized the technology in the U.S. through a joint venture with Marchon, a U.S. eyeglass frame distributor, and internationally through license agreements with Japanese and European eyeware manufacturers. When Beta sold its patents to Marchon in 1995, the frames, known domestically by the trade name Flexon, had retail sales worldwide of about $200 million.

Not all of Beta's innovations were ready to be commercialized when developed. At any given time, Beta was actively developing only two to three businesses. Beta kept a file, internally called the "Refrigerator," which contained nearly 50 ideas of lower priority. Each year at its annual retreat, Beta would review its "refrigerator" to identify ideas that might be ready to be commercialized:

> The "refrigerator" is distinct from the "dumpster," where we throw away bad ideas. The 'fridge preserves the ideas that we don't have time for or that don't seem fundable at the time. There are lots of reasons a concept may go into the 'fridge—the market may not

---

[3]Louis Pasteur, Inaugural Address, University of Lille, December 7, 1854.

be big enough, the technology may not be ready, the industry may not be in favor, or there may not be an identifiable exit strategy. We have never rescued an idea from the dumpster, but several of our successful ideas have come from the refrigerator.

Over the past 13 years, Beta had achieved strong investment returns for its investors. See **Exhibit 4** for a analysis of investment returns.[4]

Beta's HXL Golf Technology

In the late 1980s, Beta identified golf equipment as a potential application of nitinol. The initial idea had been generated by one of Zider's BCG partners who had remarked that golf club shafts would be a good application of this alloy, "It would be great joke if I could bend a club over my knee or wrap it around a tree when I'm frustrated with my game, but then could heat it up at home to return it to its original shape." Zider dismissed this idea as only a gag, but did briefly consider making nitinol inserts which could be placed into a machined cavity in the club face during assembly. After making a prototype in 1989, Zider put the idea in the "refrigerator." Zider commented on the decision, "We couldn't make nitinol work in clubs because the price/value relationship was out of line. At that time, our prototype didn't show any discernible performance differences and a nitinol insert would have cost $100, raising the consumer price way beyond then-current price points."

Beta's technological breakthrough occurred in 1996 when Krumme designed a club face with a thin cross section of a bundle of metal wires. While a traditional club face used a cast or forged slab of monolithic metal, Krumme's design used a series of small metal rods aligned together and attached to the back plate of the club like pixels on a television screen. (See **Exhibit 5** for a computer diagram of the club face with insert.) Krumme described how his previous inventions had led him to this design: "Several years earlier, I had invented and patented a connector for circuit boards which used a bunch of tiny nitinol threads, each the width of piece of human hair, to connect a microprocessor to a circuit board. While the application and performance needs are very different in circuit boards, this batch of threads provided the seed for the golf idea."

By decoupling the metal "pixels," Krumme's design altered the club's vibration response pattern so that the "sweet spot"—the ideal impact position—was enlarged and vibration feedback was reduced. This resulted in a better feel for the golfer, better ball speed after impact for off-center hits, and reduced dispersion of golf balls.[5] Beta expected that the characteristics would be more apparent to mid-to-low handicap golfers.[6]

---

[4]In 1989, Beta and BCG agreed to a buyout of BCG's equity position by the Beta principals. Between 1983 and 1989, Beta's realized returns were 55%, while the average venture capital returns of funds raised in 1983 was 11%.

[5]Tests showed that ball speed lost 8% to 10% on miss-hits (i.e. toe or heel hits) with traditional clubs, but only 3% to 5% on similar miss-hits with HXL inserts.

[6]A golfer's handicap referred to the number of strokes above par that the golfer, on average, recorded in a round of 18 holes of golf. Lower handicaps indicated greater proficiency.

Zider described Beta's new technology by analogy:

The club face on a standard club is analogous to a metal trampoline: when the ball impacts the center of the club, energy is transferred from the club to the ball with little feedback. As in a trampoline, however, if the impact is off-center, the ball does not travel the same distance because the energy transfer is imperfect and the response is asymmetrical. Beta's technology makes the club face act more like a mattress, which uses a decoupled support system, so that motion on one part of the mattress is isolated from other parts.

Zider also compared HXL to recent innovations in tennis equipment:

In the last ten years, golf has moved much the way tennis rackets did earlier: from wood to metal to composites and over-sized racquets. But, tennis has moved back to newly designed mid-sized rackets which provide bigger sweet spots on a smaller face while improving control and feel. Golf has not yet moved back to the middle. In golf, larger is not necessarily better. The continually increasing size of the club face means that the club will encounter more grass and dirt resistance, often catching the ground before the shot and completely ruining it. Therefore, a mid-sized club, like a mid-sized tennis racket, with the larger sweet spot might be very marketable. Our technology allows that to happen.

Beta commissioned Golf Laboratories, an independent testing center, to evaluate Beta's HXL prototypes. Initial test results showed that HXL designs produced slightly longer shots with less dispersion than the standard club. However, Beta believed that a finished prototype which had been balanced, sanded, and grooved might reduce the flight distance of a well-hit drive 2 to 3 yards. Beta had also conducted a computer simulation of the HXL technology which demonstrated the increased size of the sweet spot of the HXL insert over monolithic club faces. These test results and simulations confirmed Beta's engineering theory.

In addition to improved performance, HXL offered a distinctive new look to the club face. HXL looked like a honeycomb, which reinforced its unique technology and allowed design innovation unavailable with existing mono-faced clubs. Club makers could vary the pixel numbers, size, design, and material, all using their existing molds and designs which could extend product life cycles and reduce tooling, inventory and obsolescence costs. HXL allowed the face to be dimpled or grooved, like existing club faces, as well as processed for different surface friction characteristics within USGA rules.

The Golf Industry

In 1997, the wholesale golf club industry had $1.5 billion in sales, having grown 15% over the previous 10 years. There were 24.7 million golfers in the United States who spent, on average, $1,000 for a complete new set of clubs (8 iron clubs and 3 wood clubs). In 1996, nearly 2.0 million sets of woods and 1.3 million sets of irons were sold, an increase of 4% and 7%, respectively, over 1995. Wholesale prices had risen rapidly in recent years, as technological innovation allowed wood and iron prices to rise 16% and 6%, respectively, in 1996. Analysts forecasted that the market would grow 12% to 15% over the next five years.

Radical market share changes had accompanied this rapid market growth. Historically, five companies—Wilson, Spalding, Hogan, Dunlop and MacGregor—had dominated the new golf club market. After decades of little innovation, however, the industry had been shaken by four waves of design and technology improvements. In the early 1970's, Karsten Manufacturing introduced perimeter weighted Ping irons which allowed more forgiveness for beginner and intermediate players. In the mid 1970's, Aldila, a shaft manufacturer, began marketing a graphite club shaft that had a higher strength to weight ratio, allowing the golfer to increase club speed through a swing without compromising strength. In the 1980s, Taylor Made introduced metal woods which were 70% stronger than traditional woods. In the 1990s, Callaway Golf introduced the Big Bertha clubs which dramatically increased the size of the club's "sweet spot." As a result of these innovations Hogan, Dunlop and MacGregor together captured less than 5% of the market in 1997.

In their place, new brands such as Callaway, Taylor Made, Cobra, and Odyssey emerged. With the introduction of its Big Bertha clubs, Callaway's sales had increased from $55 million in 1991 to $683 mil in 1996, resulting in a market value of over $2 billion. Similarly, Cobra, which had gained the endorsement of Australian-born Men's PGA leader Greg Norman, had achieved great success through the design innovation of its oversized irons. In 1995, Cobra had been acquired by American Brands for $700 million, or four times sales. In 1996, Taylor Made had introduced the Bubble Shaft, a graphite composite design in which the shaft swelled dramatically beneath the grip and tapered to a reinforced lip just above the club head. Lastly, Odyssey Sports had entered the putter business in the late 1980's by offering an unmistakable metal headed club with a "stronomic" black insert that was marketed to put "more feel into the putt." In 1997, Callaway acquired Odyssey for $130 million, or approximately 3x sales.

In 1996, no one company led all market segments. Callaway, for example, led the woods segment, while it captured virtually no share of specialty clubs (i.e. wedges and putters). Similarly, Ping, Cobra, and Tommy Armour led the irons market, but Ping had almost no share of the woods market and Cobra and Tommy Armour had only a small share of the putter market. **Exhibit 6** presents Beta's analysis of leaders by market segment.

Accompanying the rapid innovation, marketing budgets for golf clubs had skyrocketed. While technology appeared critical to success, Callaway, Taylor Made, and Odyssey had proven that adopting a strong consumer marketing focus was necessary as well. Industry analysts estimated that Callaway would spend over $100 million on sales and marketing in 1997.

The industry was known for rapid "knock offs" of popular club designs, as most patents in the golf industry were on "design" or "method" which offered very little protection from imitators. Nearly every club sold under a brand name was available through mail order catalogs and at discount retailers under a private label brand at less than half price.

Golf club makers generally performed research and development internally but outsourced production of components to both American and Asian companies. Club makers assembled the three sub-components—grip, shaft, and club head—and spent heavily to market both to retailers and consumers. Wholesale gross margins for club makers were attractive, approaching 60% for clubs made from standard materials and 50% for more specialized materials, such as titanium.

Since 1894, the United States Golf Association (USGA) had served as the oversight body which had monitored and enforced equipment standards to protect the rules of the game. Rules for equipment, particularly clubs and balls, were strict and specific. The USGA received submissions for approval for nearly 400 club designs per year, about 40% of which were for putters. The USGA approved about half of these submissions each year. Rarely would a manufacturer try to commercially market a club not approved by the USGA. **Exhibit 7** presents excerpts from the USGA rules book on club faces.

Business Engineering HXL

In January 1996, Zider turned his attention to address the risks that Beta considered hurdles to HXL's success: USGA approval, patent approval, manufacturing economics, and pricing. While Beta had dedicated only minimal financial resources to explore HXL, Zider began spending nearly half his time evaluating HXL's potential.

Beta initially submitted the pixel design to the USGA for approval. The USGA replied within several weeks that their design, which used round pixels, did not meet specifications because the round pixels and epoxy filler constituted two materials on the impact surface, which was prohibited by their rules. At the same time, they commented that they had never seen a submission analogous to Beta's proposal. Beta resubmitted a revised proposal using hexagonal pixels which fit tightly together. This time, the USGA responded within several weeks that the prototypes "Conformed with USGA Rules." (See **Exhibit 8.**)

After finding no related patents, Beta applied for product patents for HXL covering several materials, including plastics, elastomers, traditional metals and shape memory alloys, and several pixel shapes, including hexagonal, rectangular, and triangular patterns. Product patents provided significantly more protection than the process or design patents typical to club manufacturers. Beta received a notice of allowance by the U.S. Patent and Trademarks Office within six months, which was significantly expedited over the usual twelve to eighteen month process. From prior experience, though, Beta was aware that patents were continually subject to review and reversal.

From the beginning, Krumme believed that the manufacturing process would not be a barrier to success, but that product costs needed to be determined. The manufacturing process for the pixel technology was different from the traditional monolithic casting or forging process, requiring precision tolerances (plus or minus one thousandth of an inch) and additional assembly operations. However, it employed standard electronics industry manufacturing techniques which did not pose major technical hurdles and allowed the use of existing club designs. Individual hexagonal wires first would be cut and machined, using standard screw machine technology, to create the pixels. They would then be aligned in a close-packed pattern and inserted into the club head cavity[7] for bonding to the back plate. Finally, they would be machined for grooves as well as

---

[7]Club head makers had routinely made cavities in the club face for other monolithic inserts.

surface treatment. Beta estimated that HXL inserts would initially cost $5 to $40, depending on volumes, material selection, and pixel density.

Finally, Zider attacked the pricing model. Initially, he was concerned that there might not be enough room in the industry pricing structure for a technology which was higher cost. Through industry analysis and interviews, Beta pieced together the cost structure of club manufacturers. On average, assemblers spent $20 to make a club that sold at wholesale for $40. The same club would be sold at retail for $60. Based upon manufacturing cost analysis, Beta expected that a $10 to $20 price per insert would require a $20 to $40 premium at wholesale, and a $30 to $60 premium at retail. Zider's analysis of the retail market indicated that, at the higher end of the market which Beta would target, a $30 to $60 incremental price per club for eight irons was acceptable. Zider concluded, "When golfers spend $100,000 to join a country club, spending an extra $250 to $500 on clubs is not extraordinary, if they think the technology is worthwhile."

The Decision

After successfully addressing the key initial risks of patentability, performance, USGA approval, and market potential, Beta turned its attention to evaluate alternative business models for commercializing its HXL technology. Among its options, Beta evaluated licensing its technology to an existing company, supplying a component insert, acquiring an existing company, starting a new equipment company, or entering into a joint venture. Beta had employed each of these strategies in at least one previous investment.

License

Beta considered trying to license its patented technology, on either an exclusive or non-exclusive basis, to a leading club maker. An exclusive license might command an 8% to 10% royalty on wholesale sales and a $10 million marketing commitment, while a non-exclusive license might command a 6% to 8% royalty. Licensees would have control over all aspects of production and marketing, including pricing and quality standards. Beta would retain responsibility for research and development and patent defense. In the past, Beta had spent over $3 million defending patents against infringement. Beta expected that any licensee would be able to command a 20% to 50% price premium for the technology.

OEM Supplier

Beta also considered manufacturing pixel inserts and selling them to several leading club makers, who would insert them into the club heads during assembly. Club makers were accustomed to purchasing monolithic club inserts, made of different materials, and placing them into a pre-machined cavity in the club head during assembly. Aldila and True Temper, both leading club shaft manufacturers, had been successful with the OEM supplier model, building companies with a market value of approximately one times sales.

Based upon detailed costing studies, Beta believed that it would be able to manufacture club inserts for $5 to $40 per insert and sell them at a 30% to 60% gross margin. Beta could acquire machines with 1,200 to 2,000 pixels per hour capacity (depending upon materials) for $70,000 each. Beta expected that it would need to charge club makers an

80% to 100% markup on direct cost and a 8% to 10% "technology license" on the wholesale value of the club. But would club makers buy the product?

Beta referred to this strategy as the "Gore-Tex approach." Like Gore-Tex, the waterproof fabric sold to garment makers, Beta would sell branded inserts to several golf club makers who would compete on their own pixel designs and materials as well as on the features of their own clubs.

Acquisition

Beta considered bidding for a former leading golf club brand ("Acorn") which recorded a loss of $2 million in 1996 on sales of $20 million. At its peak in the 1970s and 1980s, Acorn had consistently recorded sales of $90 million and profits of $10 million. Since 1990, the company continually had been losing money on declining sales volumes.

Zider had identified a financial investor, The Parkside Group, who was prepared to join Beta in bidding for Acorn. Together, they would form a newly capitalized company ("Newco") which would hold the assets of both Acorn and Beta's HXL technology. Terms of the proposed agreement specified that Parkside would acquire Acorn's brand and tangible assets for 50% of 1997 projected sales, or $10 million, and contribute them to Newco along with $15 million to fund working capital requirements. Beta would contribute to Newco its technology, which would be valued at $5 million. The investor would assume operating responsibilities for the merged company while Beta would continue to manage research and development as well as defend against patent infringement.

Beta was interested in this opportunity because it would provide a "platform" to enter the business with an existing distribution organization and brand franchise. Together, Beta and Parkside planned to try to revitalize the brand by introducing a new product line which incorporated Beta's HXL technology. Re-launching the brand would require $35 million in marketing expenses over the next three years. **Exhibits 9** and **10** present the details of the proposed transaction and associated financial projections. Beta was aware that other strategic buyers also were considering bidding for the company.

Start-up

Following the model of Callaway, Cobra, and Odyssey, all of which had introduced new golf brands within the past 10 years, Beta explored starting a new club company. Beta considered Odyssey to be a model of a successful start-up golf equipment business. Odyssey, which had started in 1990 with $5 million of capital from financial partners, had grown to $35 million in sales in 1996 when it was bought by Callaway for $130 million.

To launch a start-up, Beta would need to find a financial partner willing to commit $10 million in start-up capital and would need to recruit a management team with significant experience in the golf industry. The new company would outsource manufacturing but would manage R&D and marketing internally. Beta needed to address several strategic questions which would impact the start-up's economics, including how they would market their brand. Would they try to market clubs through professionals, who had expensive golf contracts, or through infomercials, which cost nearly $1 million each to run? How would they secure distribution through the retail channel? How would they price their clubs?

Conclusion

As Zider pulled out of San Francisco International Airport's parking lot and headed toward Beta's offices in Menlo Park, he considered which launch strategy he would recommend to his partners:

> We hate businesses like golf. Investing in sporting goods goes against every principle we have at Beta. It's a hobby industry which attracts many people with deep pockets who are in it to stroke their ego—just like boats and wineries. It's a trendy consumer business based on image and perception, and many smart people have lost a lot of money in it. We also are violating the single most basic tenet of business—know something about the industry. We don't know a damn thing about golf.
>
> However, we've seen the combination of technology and good marketing lead to significant market share changes very rapidly at the expense of old line brands. Our technology is new. As Callaway and Cobra have proven, there seems to be little loyalty in the retail channel or at the consumer level, and people seem to be willing to pay for the "next thing." The price points and margins are high, and the few companies who have been successful have been extremely well rewarded. To date, we've taken some of the risk out and limited our downside. But we're outsiders to the industry so we're unlikely to find friendly investors. The VCs are into the Internet and medical devices. Even if we do have a preferred model, who can we find to invest?

EXHIBIT 1 | Profiles of Beta Group Principals

John Krumme

John Krumme initially joined The Beta Group in 1986. John served as President and later Chairman of Beta Phase from 1986 to 1993. In 1993, John formally returned to The Beta Group to participate in the firm's new investment activities. Prior to joining The Beta Group, John was a founding general partner of two start-up companies: Metcal (1981–1986), a self-regulating heating technology company; and Alchemia (1981–1986), a shape memory alloy product development company which became Beta Phase in 1986. Prior to his start-up of Metcal and Alchemia, John was a development engineer at Raychem (1973–1979), Hewlett-Packard (1969–1973), and General Electric Medical (1967–1969). John graduated from Stanford in 1967 with a MS/MSE degree in mechanical engineering. John holds more than 20 issued patents.

Bob Newell

Bob Newell joined The Beta Group in 1997. From 1992 to 1997, Bob was CFO of Cardiometrics, a medical device company. In 1985, Bob assisted Bob Zider and John Krumme in the formation of Beta Phase and was CFO of Beta Phase from 1985 to 1992. Bob has held financial management positions with WordStar International Corporation, Donaldson, Lufkin, & Jenrette and Bank of America. He has helped start several medical companies. Bob was also an Air Force pilot. He received a Bachelor of Arts degree in mathematics from the College of William and Mary in 1970 and a Master in Business Administration from Harvard Business School in 1976.

Dave Plough

Dave Plough joined The Beta Group in 1986. Dave has led the firm's investments in CollOptics and Altair Eyewear. He served as initial President of two portfolio companies, CollOptics and Reflex Sunglasses, and as General Manager of another portfolio company, FOxS Labs. From 1982 to 1984, Dave was an associate with The Boston Consulting Group where, among other activities, he had The Beta Group as a client. Dave received a Bachelor of Arts degree in 1981 from Dartmouth College where he graduated cum laude and a Master of Business Administration degree in 1986 from the Stanford Graduate School of Business.

Bob Zider

Bob Zider founded The Beta Group in 1983 with backing from The Boston Consulting Group. Bob initiated and led the firm's investments in Beta Phase, FOxS Labs, CVI/Beta Ventures, Beta Optical, Marchon, Eschenbach, CVIBeta Japan, Nitinol Devices and Components, and Reflex Sunglasses. Bob served as initial President of CVI/Beta Ventures and initial Chairman of Nitinol Development, Reflex Sunglasses, and the Business Engineering, Inc. consulting firm. Bob spent seven years from 1976 to 1983 at The Boston Consulting Group, where he developed the Business Engineering investment approach. Bob began his career from 1969 to 1971 as an analytical engineer with Pratt & Whitney in the Advanced Engines Group. From 1971 to 1973, and on a part-time basis from 1974 to 1976 while attending school, Bob was a Lieutenant with the National Oceanic and Atmospheric Administration. Bob received a Bachelor of Science degree in civil engineering in 1969 from the University of Virginia and a Master of Business Administration degree with Distinction in 1976 from the Harvard Business School, where he was class president.

Source: The Beta Group.

EXHIBIT 2 | Beta Group Mission

The Beta Group

The Beta Mission

Exploring for gold was exciting 140 years ago. Upon learning of a random discovery, thousands of men with little or no experience would pick up and "rush" to the gold fields in the hopes of finding gold. A few became fabulously rich. The majority ended up flat broke.

Mineral exploration today is far less exciting. Pattern recognition, pathfinders, air and satellite reconnaissance have replaced the mule and pick. Information and analysis have replaced random exploration. The simple task of mining has evolved into a systematic, highly engineered process designed to increase the odds of success and reduce the probability of failure.

Business innovation today is exciting. Billions of dollars are standing by to be invested in engineers, scientists, and marketers who have an innovative new idea. Most of these "business explorers" lack a comprehensive knowledge of the market, finances, the competition and the multitude of other key factors required to build a business and grow it to long term success. A few will become fabulously rich. The majority will not.

Just like yesterday's gold miners, today's "business explorers" face long odds in the attempt to create wealth as they strive to find a new product, provide a new service, or restructure an obsolete means of doing business. Despite seemingly endless enthusiasm, many fail to achieve their objectives. Successful businesses, like yesterday's gold fields, are not easy to find.

The Beta Mission is to develop and apply a systematic, multi-disciplinary approach to innovation which we refer to as Business Engineering. The Business Engineering process utilizes analytic systems to assist business development. It relies less heavily on chance. As in exploration, it relies on the art of pathfinders and pattern recognition to provide clues. As in engineering, it relies on data and analysis of competitors, market and product characteristics to develop options and simulate their success or failure on paper or in a highly focused test before committing major resources. Business Engineering is the natural extension of disciplined approaches applied elsewhere. Business Engineering coupled with creativity and drive is a powerful approach to innovation.

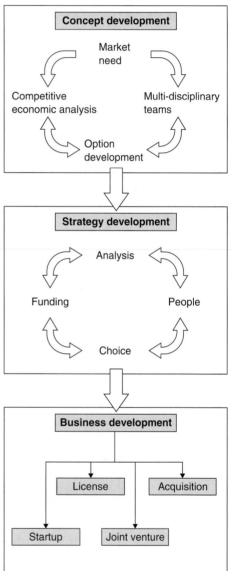

Business engineering

Robert B. Zider

EXHIBIT 3 | Description of Beta Group Investments

Medical Sector

The Beta Group believes that the ongoing structural changes that are taking place in the health care industry will create significant investment opportunities. In particular, the historical focus on *quality of care*, irrespective of cost, has been replaced by a focus on the *cost of care*, as long as the care provided is consistent with or superior to the existing quality of care. The Beta Group believes this new *cost of care* focus will be the dominant theme in medical care throughout this decade. The Beta Group believes that technologies, proprietary processes or other competitive advantages that lower the total cost of care, while maintaining or increasing the quality of care, will create attractive investment opportunities. Examples of medical sector investments that The Beta Group has made include:

Medical sensors   The Beta Group successfully developed a fiber optic blood gas sensor technology, achieving a 132% internal rate of return on a staged investment of $3.8 million in a start-up company it founded called *FOxS Labs*. The *FOxS Labs* investment was the result of a methodological exploration of medical sensors opportunities. The Beta Group, working in conjunction with The Boston Consulting Group, conducted an in-depth assessment of the opportunities within blood gas continuous sensing. Interviews and field research were conducted in cardiology, intensive care medicine, surgery and other specialties. The work team assessed the four most promising technology options and evaluated a fiber optic technology as the superior option. After an in-depth patent review and a rigorous assessment of the technology by outside technical consultants, The Beta Group acquired a fiber optic technology patent from Richard G. Buckles. After successful development to the point of human clinical trials, *FOxS Labs* was sold to Puritan-Bennett Corporation, a corporate strategic partner that The Beta Group had brought in to aid in the development and marketing of the Buckles fiber optic sensor technology.

Medical devices   The Beta Group has made several investments in shape memory metal alloy applications, including an intravenous flow controller, surgical tools, and incontinence devices.

The Beta Group extended its experience and expertise in shape memory alloys with its 1991 start-up of Nitinol Devices and Components ("NDC"). NDC is a manufacturing company dedicated to the engineering, design, and fabrication of shape memory alloy components. Products include guidewires, catheters, and coronary stents. Beta's $2.0 million investment in NDC achieved a 125% compound annual return with its sale to Johnson and Johnson's Cordis division in 1997.

In January 1992, Beta started up *CollOptics, Inc*. *CollOptics*, which is jointly owned by The Beta Group, Collagen Corporation, and GE Medical, acquired the GE Medical Systems Laser Adjustable Synthetic Epikeratoplasty (LASE) technology in January 1992. *CollOptics'* mission is to provide a semi-permanent contact lens to the consumer on a minimally invasive, reversible, and adjustable basis. The semi-permanent contact lens would be placed under the epithelium of the eye in a simple, outpatient procedure. Unlike other refractive surgery approaches, the LASE approach is only minimally invasive and is reversible. It is too early to tell whether The Beta Group's $800,000 investment in the company will prove successful.

Consumer Products Sector

The Beta Group believes the diverse and constantly evolving consumer marketplace offers significant investment opportunities. The principals of The Beta Group believe that the development of new consumer product concepts which address underlying consumer cultural, demographic, and behavioral trends will create attractive investment opportunities. The Beta Group believes this is particularly true where a proprietary technology or process or other

(continued)

EXHIBIT 3 | Description of Beta Group Investments (*continued*)

competitive advantage is brought to the consumer marketplace. Examples of consumer sector investments that The Beta Group has made follow:

Eyewear   The Beta Group has acquired significant experience and expertise in the development of shape memory alloy applications. Beta applied this expertise to the consumer products arena by developing and commercializing shape memory eyeglass frames in the *CVI/Beta Ventures* start-up company. Beta Group developed and patented the use of nitinol metals in ophthalmic frames. The shape memory properties of nitinol eyeglass frames (primarily known by the "Flexon" trade name) allow the frames to maintain a consistent, comfortable fit despite wear and handling. Beta Group achieved a *134%* compound annual return on a staged investment of $500,000 in *CVI/Beta Ventures*.

Electronic music distribution   The Beta Group funded the start-up of *Personics* in 1984. *Personics* permits the music retail consumer to make in-store custom mixes of artists and songs. The consumer samples songs at a listening booth located in the music retail store and has hundreds of songs and artists to choose from. Once the consumer has made his selections, he or she submits the choices to a sales clerk. In approximately 10 minutes the consumer receives an audio cassette tape with the mix of songs he or she selected. The Beta Group achieved a 73% compound annual return on *Personics*, on a staged investment of $3.3 million.

Industrial Technology Sector

The Beta Group believes that the industrial technology sector presents significant investment opportunities, particularly where a new technology, proprietary process or other competitive advantage is transplanted from an existing application into either a new application or an entirely new market. Examples of industrial technology sector investments that The Beta Group has made follow:

Electronic connectors   One of Beta's first start-ups, Beta Phase (1984) developed a high density (up to 500 lines per inch) zero insertion force connector system using a flex print and shape memory actuator combination. Though technically successful (it is still used in Cray's supercomputers), Beta suffered two dilutive financings prior to the sale of the company to Molex.

Other industrial products   As part of its continuing development efforts, Beta has obtained rights to FOxS' fiber optic sensor technology for use in industrial applications such as hazardous waste and hydrocarbon monitoring. Beta also developed under contract a PC based communications test system for Motorola, launched commercially in 1997. Beta continues development of shape memory applications including pipe couplings, electrical cable connectors, sporting goods and resettable fuses.

Source: The Beta Group.

EXHIBIT 4 | Beta Group Financial Performance Summary (only investments exceeding $250,000)

Investment	Description	Investment Date	Internal Rate of Return
Beta Phase	Electronic connectors	1984–89	Loss
FOxS	Blood gas sensors	1985–89	132%
Personics	In-store custom music	1984–89	73%
Beta Optical	U.S. eyeglass frame manufacturing LBO	1986–88	<u>Loss</u>
Total (1983–1989)			55%
CVI/Beta[8]	Shape memory eyeglass frames	1990–97	86%
Nitinol Devices and Components	Coronary stents	1992–97	125%
Reflex Sunglasses	Shape memory sunglasses	1992–94	Loss
CollOptics	Reversible refractive eye surgery	1992–97	Loss
Altair Eyewear	Ophthalmic products marketing	1992–97	<u>34%</u>
Total (1990–1997)			86%

Source: The Beta Group.

[8]Includes the Marchon Joint Venture, Eschenbach Joint Venture, and Japanese Manufacturing Consortium.

EXHIBIT 5 | Computer Diagram of HXL Club Insert

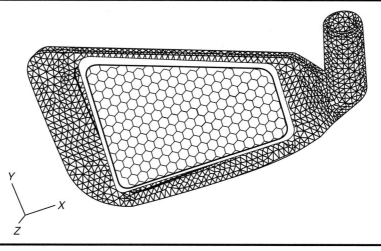

Source: The Beta Group.

EXHIBIT 6 | Market Segmentation

	Woods	Irons	Wedges	Putters
Super Premium	>$400	>$1,000	>$120	>$120
	Callaway	Armour Titanium	Armour Titanium	Snake Eyes
	Lynx	Callaway	Callaway	Taylor Made
	Taylor Made	Daiwa	Ping	
		Ping	Taylor Made	
High	$300	$800	$100	$100
	Cleveland	Armour	Cleveland	Callaway
	Cobra	Hogan	Hogan	Cobra
	Nicklaus	Cobra	Cobra	Ping
		Mizuno	Ram	Odyssey
		Nicklaus	Wilson	Alien
		Taylor Made		
Medium	$200	$600	$80	$50
	Golfsmith	MacGregor	Golfsmith	Dunlop
	Ping	Powerbilt	Dunlop	Powerbilt
	Wilson	Ram	Ram	Golfsmith
		Wilson		
Low	$80–120	<$500	$40	$30
	Dunlop	Dunlop	Golfworks	Golfworks
	Golfsmith	Golfsmith	Magique	Magique
	Mitsushiba	Rawlings		

Source: The Beta Group.

EXHIBIT 7 | The Rule of Golf 1997–1998

b) transparent material added for other than decorative or structural purposes,

c) appendages to the main body of the head such as knobs, plates, rods or fins, for the purpose of meeting dimensional specifications, for aiming or for any other purpose. Exceptions may be made for putters.

Any furrows in or runners on the sole shall not extend into the face.

4-1e. Club Face

GENERAL

The material and construction of the face shall not have the effect at impact of a spring, or impart significantly more spin to the ball than a standard steel face, or have any other effect which would unduly influence the movement of the ball.

IMPACT AREA ROUGHNESS AND MATERIAL

Except for markings specified in the following paragraphs, the surface roughness within the area where impact is intended (the "impact area") must not exceed that of decorative sandblasting, or of fine milling.

The impact area must be of a single material. Exceptions may be made for wooden clubs (see Fig. VIII, illustrative impact area).

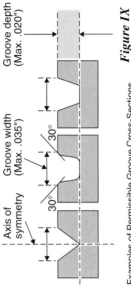

Illustrative impact area

Figure VIII

IMPACT AREA MARKINGS

Markings in the impact area must not have sharp edges or raised lips, as determined by a finger test. Grooves or punch marks in the impact area must meet the following specifications:

(i) Grooves. A series of straight grooves with diverging sides and a symmetrical cross-section may be used (see Fig. IX). The width and cross-section must be consistent across the face of the club and along the length of the grooves. Any rounding of groove edges shall be in the form of a radius which does not exceed 0.020 inches (0.5 mm). The width of the grooves shall not exceed 0.035 inches (0.9 mm), using the 30 degree method of measurement on file with the United States Golf Association. The distance between edges of adjacent grooves must not be less than three times the width of a groove, and not less than 0.075 inches (1.9 mm). The depth of a groove must not exceed 0.020 inches (0.5 mm).

Note: Exception - see US Decision 4-1/100.

(ii) *Punch Marks.* Punch marks may be used. The area of any such mark must not exceed 0.0044 square inches (2.8 sq. mm). A mark must not be closer to an adjacent mark than 0.168 inches (4.3 mm) measured from center to center. The depth of a punch mark must not exceed 0.040 inches (1.0 mm). If punch marks are used in combination with grooves, a punch mark must not be closer to a groove than 0.168 inches (4.3 mm), measured from center to center.

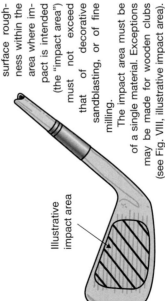

Axis of symmetry · Groove width (Max. .035") · Groove depth (Max. .020")

30° 30° 30°

Examples of Permissible Groove Cross-Sections

Figure IX

EXHIBIT 8 | USGA Letter to Beta Group

United States Golf Association

Golf House   PO Box 708   Far Hills, NJ 07931-0708

908 234-2300   Fax 908 234-9687

http://www.usga.org

　Technical Department Fax: 908 234-0138

September 25, 1997

Mr. John Krumme

President

Beta Development

2454 Embarcadero Way

Palo Alto, CA 94303

Dear Mr. Krumme:　　　　　　　　　　　　　　　Decision: 97-291 & 97-306

This is in reference to your letter dated July 24, 1997 and the iron (97-291) and putter (97-306) which you submitted for an official ruling. The cavity back iron has an insert in the face made of a copper alloy material, that is formed from hexagonal steel columns which join together creating a smooth surface. The toe-heel weighted putter has a similar face insert made of stainless steel.

I am pleased to advise you that the clubs, as submitted, have been inspected and it has been determined that they conform with the Rules of Golf.

In advertisements of this iron (97-291) and putter (97-306), you are authorized to make the statement: "Conforms with USGA Rules." Use of such statements as "USGA Approved" or "USGA Tested" are prohibited. Use of the USGA seal or logo, without specific permission, is prohibited.

We are retaining the samples as a record of this decision.

The USGA reserves the right to change the Rules and interpretations regulating equipment at any time.

Yours sincerely,

Frank Thomas

Frank W. Thomas

Technical Director

FWT: wp

cc:　Reed K. Mackenzie, Chairman, I&B Committee

　　O. Gordon Brewer, Jr.

　　David B. Fay

　　Michael Butz

　　John Matheny

EXHIBIT 9 | Proposed Acquisition Structure and Financials

THE PARKSIDE GROUP
Strategic Equity Investors

September 1, 1997

Barry L. Schneider

Managing Partner

Mr. Bob Zider
Beta Group

Via Fax

Dear Bob:

I was not able to fax you the financials tonight because Cory and I finished them after midnight. The plan is for Cory to get you this letter and our latest pro forma financials so that you and I can talk at some point Monday.

Our understanding has always been that we would create a Newco by merging a newly capitalized "Acorn" with HXL. You can refer to the handwritten schematic that I faxed to you several months ago, indicating such a structure. We specifically asked you the value you placed on HXL, so we would be able to value it as a "contributed asset" in the business combination. Your response was clear; you wanted somewhere near a $5 million valuation.

Attached are our sources and uses, and forecasted financial statements. Please feel free to call Cory to inquire about any part of the financials, and I will try and call you either from the plane or from the hotel Monday night.

The bottom line is that Beta is getting its $5 million valuation, both in terms of a preferred return of $5 million, and in a 16.6% carried ownership interest ($5M/$30M post $). It is likely that the Seller will also want a carried interest, and coincidentally, he will swap $5 million in assets that would otherwise have been purchased for cash. If he does so, we will require $5 million less cash to close, but the seller will maintain a 16.67% carried interest (no dilution; the IRRs would essentially stay the same).

It is contemplated that The Parkside Group (TPG) will be the managing general partner, and in exchange for our work, we will receive a $300,000/year management fee and 20% of the distributions in excess of the preferred distributions (invested capital). Thus, Beta would receive $5 million before the general partner received any of the 20%. Finally, TPG will receive all of the tax loss allocations.

The ironic part of this structure is that we are planning to fund 100% of the LP share as well. However, given the interest in this industry, it would not surprise me if ultimately, there were LPs other than just TPG. Hopefully, after reviewing this financial structuring information, you will agree it is responsive to the issues we have been discussing. Obviously, this information is extremely confidential.

We expect that the operating responsibilities will reside with TPG, and that The Beta Group would continue with research, development and commercialization of the technology, and use their experience to help protect any patent infringements. Certainly, in addition to equity in Newco, we could discuss a technology consulting agreement. I guess it depends a bit on how many generations of technology you have, and ultimately, how well the market accepts HXL.

One point of interest, you will note that we are planning on spending $15 million to support brand in '98 (leading to a pro forma $40 million in sales for the year). In 1996, for the year, Callaway spent $37 million in marketing on its way to $650 million in sales for the year.

Talk to you soon.

Barry Schneider

Barry L. Schneider

EXHIBIT 10 | Proposed Acorn Financial Projections and Acquisition Structure

Income Statement ($000)

	Post-Closing	1997 (4 mos)	1998	1999	2000
Revenues	—	$4,000	$25,000	$40,000	$60,000
Cost of goods sold	—	2,400	14,000	20,500	30,000
Gross profit	—	$1,600	$11,000	$19,500	$30,000
Gross Profit %	—	40.0%	44.40%	48.8%	50.0%
Operating Expenses					
Management fees	—	$ 75	$ 300	$ 300	$ 300
Selling, general and administrative	—	750	5,000	8,500	14,000
Marketing	—	2,200	15,000	10,000	10,000
R&D/innovation	—	150	500	500	500
Depreciation	—	17	21	88	186
Amortization of goodwill	—	—	—	—	—
Total operating expenses	—	$3,192	$20,821	$19,388	$24,986
EBIT	—	$(1,592)	$(9,821)	$113	$5,014
EBIT %	—	(39.8%)	(39.3%)	0.2%	8.4%
Nonrecurring asset liquidation	$2,000				
Interest income	—				
Interest expense	—	$820	$97	349	859
Pretax income	$(2,000)	$(772)	$(9,724)	$(237)	$4,155
Income taxes	—				1,620
Net income	$(2,000)	$(772)	$(9,724)	$(237)	$2,534
Net income %	—	(19.3%)	(38.9%)	(4.6%)	4.2%
Preferred dividends	—				—
Convertible preferred dividends	—				—
Net income to common	$(2,000)	$(772)	$(9,724)	$(237)	$2,534

Sources and Uses of Funds

Sources	
Contributed cash	$20,000
Seller contributed assets	5,000
Contributed HXL	5,000
Total Sources	$30,000

Uses	
Cash reserves	$ 2,950
Accounts receivable	6,000
Inventory	10,200
Other assets	5,500
Intangible assets	5,000
Net PP&E	150
Long-term assets	200
Total Uses	$30,000

Zipcar: Refining the Business Model

It was October 14, 2000, and Robin Chase was leaving yet another meeting with potential providers of capital for her fledgling venture, Zipcar. Chase was CEO and cofounder of the company, which she and Antje Danielson had started some 10 months before. The idea behind Zipcar—a sophisticated form of car sharing—was simple, yet potentially revolutionary. Chase and Danielson had conducted some initial research during late 1999, and by the end of that year, the two had developed a business plan. They had incorporated in January 2000 and raised their first $50,000 from one angel investor.

By June of 2000, the two entrepreneurs had leased 12 cars and were ready to open for business in Boston. By October, the fledgling company had 19 vehicles, nearly 250 members, and the founders had raised—and spent—an additional $325,000 to fund the early stages of operations. Yet, even with this demonstration of viability, Chase and Danielson had not succeeded in raising the equity capital they needed to really grow Zipcar.

Beginning in early 2000, Chase had made a series of presentations to potential investors in which she sought $1 million in capital to prove the business model in Boston and, eventually, to set the stage for expanding the business to other U.S. cities. Potential investors seemed intrigued and enthusiastic about the Zipcar idea. While Chase hoped to close on this first round of financing in the fall of 2000, she continued to look for funding alternatives because the money was not yet in the bank. At the end of October 2000, she and Danielson would have the opportunity to make their pitch at Springboard 2000 New England, a venture forum for women-led enterprises. Chase commented: "I am anxious to raise this funding and focus my energies on really trying to grow Zipcar. I want to put our best foot forward with the VCs who will be at Springboard. I need to

Professor of Management Practice Myra Hart, Senior Lecturer Michael J. Roberts, and Research Associate Julia D. Stevens prepared this case. This case draws upon portions of an earlier case, "Zipcar," HBS No. 802-085 (Boston: Harvard Business School Publishing, 2002), written by Professor Myra Hart and Research Associate Wendy Carter. HBS cases are developed solely as the basis for class discussion. Cases are not intended to serve as endorsements, sources of primary data, or illustrations of effective or ineffective management.

review our presentation and make sure we're making the strongest argument we can on why this business deserves funding."

Background

In September 1999, Chase's friend, Danielson, returned from a trip to Germany with an idea for a new start-up. While in Berlin, Danielson had been impressed with a car-sharing concept that seemed to be catching on across Europe. Under this new concept, car-sharing companies provided short-term, on-demand use of private cars conveniently located and easily accessible to service subscribers. She believed that such a business could be equally successful in urban areas in the United States.

Danielson, a Ph.D. geochemist who supervised undergraduate energy policy research at Harvard, saw both the environmental and convenience implications of the service. She turned to Chase, who had an MBA from MIT and substantial business experience, to partner with her in the start-up.

Chase agreed that car sharing provided an exciting opportunity, and she was confident that they could build the technology infrastructure to make it work. She committed to the project and began developing the business plan. When she met with Glenn Urban, the former dean and a mentor from MIT's Sloan School of Management, in December 1999, he not only encouraged her to go ahead but also urged her to move quickly. He noted, "This idea is much bigger than you are imagining. You have to do this at twice the speed and think twice as big."

The Founders

Chase majored in English, French, and philosophy at Wellesley College. While a student, she also held several positions at the college newspaper and was president of the philosophy club. After graduating cum laude in 1980, she joined the Boston-based health care consulting firm John Snow Inc.

In 1986, she received her MBA in applied economics and finance from MIT's Sloan School of Management. She then joined a private school as director of finance and operations. Over the next 13 years, Chase continued her professional career, taking some time off after the birth of each of her three children and structuring her work schedule to accommodate her desire to raise a family. Chase returned to work for John Snow during some of this time, ultimately serving as interim director of the international division. In 1995, Chase left to become managing editor of the 110-year old scientific journal *Public Health Reports*. Throughout that time, she often thought about the possibility of starting her own business.

In 1998, Chase and her husband came to the conclusion that the pressure of maintaining two high-powered careers and caring for three children under age 10 was increasingly difficult to manage. She retired from her position at *Public Health Reports* to spend more time with the children. During the next 12 months, Chase devoted herself to organizing her household and becoming more involved with her children's school activities. As a result, she made many new friends—most of them the parents of her children's playmates. Danielson was among these.

Danielson worked for the University Committee on the Environment at Harvard University, directing interdisciplinary research on energy consumption and greenhouse gases. Prior to receiving her Ph.D. from the Freie Universitat Berlin, she had held several jobs, including two years in car sales and three years as a research assistant at the Hahn-Meitner Institute working with semiconductors. When she completed her Ph.D., she went to Rand Afrikaans University in Johannesburg, then on to Harvard in 1991 on a NATO research fellowship. Danielson's husband was finishing his Ph.D. at MIT, and their five-year-old son was enrolled in the same kindergarten that Chase's daughter attended.

Chase did not hesitate when Danielson proposed the venture. She had wanted to become an entrepreneur for years. The opportunity was exciting, and she and her husband believed that the time was right to take on such a venture, given that they had made enormous strides in getting their family life working well over the past year and all three of their children were now school age. In the fall of 1999, she committed to the venture full time. Danielson, on the other hand, continued working at Harvard, spending evenings and weekends on the new venture.

The two founders divided the tasks along the lines of their respective areas of expertise. During the fall of 1999, Chase refined the concept, researched the market, wrote the business plan, and built the assumptions necessary to create a budget. She created the list of critical business and financing contacts. As she began to build the organization in the spring of 2000, she designed and wrote the Web site and, with the help of contract engineers, started work on the online reservation system.

Danielson's car experience and her connections with Ford, one of the major funders of her research group at Harvard, made her the natural choice to focus on building car industry relationships. She also took responsibility for specifying the necessary in-car technology and negotiating the first car purchases. In addition, Danielson worked on any environmental issues related to the business and served as editor for the documents that Chase created.

Pursuing the Idea

The business of organized car sharing originated in Switzerland in 1987 when two separate cooperatives (subsequently merged in 1997) were founded. Within a year, similar operations came into existence independently in Germany, Austria, and the Netherlands. The cooperatives were created to provide both convenience and cost savings to the users.

Organized car sharing was the coordinated use of vehicles by various subscribers in succession and independently of one another. The concept was not unlike condominium time sharing, except that the "real estate" had wheels and the prescribed usage time was not fixed. Additionally, any member could reserve any vehicle in the network. Typically, members of the service paid a large up-front deposit, an annual fee, and a per usage fee that was determined by time and mileage.

Members could reserve car time regularly or *ad hoc*. Though most subscribers used a car for a few hours, it was possible to reserve longer blocks of time. Members made reservations for the closest available car. Because cars were not housed at a central location but were parked in designated spaces in neighborhoods convenient to the users, the subscriber rarely had more than a five-minute walk to a parking location.

Car sharing was best suited to urban locations where there was a dense base of potential users, parking was expensive, and the need to drive was limited. Research indicated that, among urban dwellers, college-educated individuals were the most receptive to the proposition.

Chase believed that there was a strong demand for this "niche" product in the United States. It could provide a new, low-cost, convenient alternative to owning an automobile for drivers who logged less than 6,000 miles per year (see **Exhibit 1** for car ownership economics). She observed, "For those who don't own a car, taxis can fill the need for short trips. Rental cars are available for daily or weekly usage, but the hassle factor keeps people from using them as often as they might like. So there is a big hole in the market: short-term, on-demand private car access."

Sizing the Market

Chase's early market research indicated that penetration in Western Europe was relatively small (0.01% of all drivers) but growing rapidly. In 1999, approximately 200 car-sharing organizations operated in 450 cities in Switzerland, Germany, Austria, the Netherlands, Denmark, Sweden, Norway, the United Kingdom, France, and Italy.[1] Although car-sharing organizations had invested very little in marketing, usage was growing at 30% annually. In 1999, there were more than 130,000 members[2] in what was estimated to be a $200 million industry.[3]

Volkswagen, one supplier of the shared vehicles, projected that 2.45 million shared vehicles would be in use throughout Europe by the year 2007 and that they would serve approximately 0.04% of the general population.[4]

Chase's research indicated that the U.S. market was large and virtually untouched. In 1999, 66 million Americans lived in the top 20 metropolitan areas, and 20 million Americans used public transportation to get to work.[5] (See **Exhibit 2** for data.)

Competition

In 1999, the two largest car-sharing organizations in Europe were Swiss Mobility CarSharing, with 1,400 cars, and Drive Stadtauto (formerly StattAuto Berlin), with approximately 300 cars. Swiss Mobility CarSharing, the product of a 1997 merger of two independent cooperatives, operated in 700 locations and had more than 30,000 members. It had concentrated its expansion efforts on building its network in Switzerland. Drive Stadtauto was launched in 1988 and operated in 110 locations with approximately 7,500 members.[6]

---

[1]Daniel Sperling, Susan Shaheen, Conrad Wagner, "CarSharing and Mobility Services, An Updated Overview," *CalStart,* February 2000.

[2]Ibid.

[3]Rachel Geise, "Wheels When You Want 'Em," *The Toronto Globe and Mail,* February 2001.

[4]"At The Wheel, Volkswagen Pioneers Car Sharing Programs," *Fastlane,* October 1997.

[5]1990 U.S. Census data.

[6]Sperling, et al.

Chase's research turned up three potential competitors already operating in North America. There was a start-up operation in Canada, CommunAuto, which was launched in Quebec City in 1994 and in Montreal in 1995. Like Chase, the founder had developed the business after studying 15 different car-sharing organizations operating in Europe. U.S. competition consisted of two West Coast companies: Portland-based Car-Sharing Inc., founded in 1998, and Seattle-based Flexcar, launched in January 2000. Though both were for-profit companies, they focused on the environmental impact of car sharing rather than on its convenience and cost effectiveness.

Chase also anticipated that traditional car rental agencies, such as Hertz or Avis, might enter the market if they saw it as a substantial new business opportunity. Chase believed that they generated an average of $10,000 to $12,000 per vehicle per year in revenue. Car manufacturers were also potential competitors. Volkswagen had already conducted its own studies of the market potential. It could participate as a supplier or could consider entering the market directly.

Developing the Business Plan

By late 1999, Chase's research had convinced her that the car-sharing idea was viable, especially in the relatively uncontested North American marketplace. Chase completed the first draft of a business plan for a U.S.-based car-sharing venture in December 1999. The service she envisioned would deliver convenience, ease of use, freedom to travel, and hassle-free "ownership" for urbanites. The cars would provide a solution for people who did not need a car to get to work but wanted the convenience of a private vehicle to run occasional errands, go to appointments, visit friends, or get out of the city for a few days.

Though the primary emphasis was on convenience and cost savings, the concept could also be marketed as environmentally friendly. According to European studies Chase uncovered, every car shared would eliminate the need for approximately 7.5 individually owned cars in the marketplace.

Chase's plan anticipated that most paid subscribers would log on to the company Web site to reserve specific cars in specific locations, but she understood the need to provide telephone support as well. Reservations would be taken up to two months in advance but could also be made without notice—subject to availability. One of the challenges that Chase faced was developing technology that would admit only the confirmed driver to the car and that would also capture usage data (to serve as the basis for billing) when the car was returned.

Pricing was a critical component of business development. To develop a price structure, Chase looked at variables and variations found in existing models elsewhere in the world. She described her conclusions:

> It was clear that there are several components to an overall price structure: security deposit, initiation fee, annual fee, monthly fee, per mile fee, and hourly or daily rates. When I looked at how most car-sharing organizations in Europe managed their pricing, they had significant up-front initiation fees—$300, $400, even $500. I later learned that this was because many of these organizations are cooperatives, and they needed that money to go out and buy cars.

My thinking on pricing was that I needed to cover my COGS [cost of goods sold] and then cover overhead at some target volume and utilization level. And, I had talked to enough people to know that many of our target users—people who don't own cars—compare our prices to the price of renting a car—say $45 per day. So, I needed to stay under that umbrella.

Chase spent almost two months modeling different pricing structures and cost assumptions. Her first business plan made the following assumptions: potential users would be required to become members and pay a $25 nonrefundable application fee, a $300 fully refundable security deposit, and a $300 annual subscription fee. Additionally, members would be charged for driving time at $1.50 per hour and $0.40 per mile. (See **Exhibit 3** for a summary of financials from this original plan.) Members had to be at least 21 years old, have a valid driver's license, and have no major traffic violations (see **Exhibit 4** for Zipcar driver requirements).

The users were expected to handle simple maintenance themselves. For example, drivers were asked to refuel and submit receipts for reimbursement whenever the gas level reached one-quarter full. They were also required to keep the car clean and to take responsibility for any traffic or parking tickets incurred. The car had to be returned to its original location before the reservation time expired. There was a $20 fine for late return. Chase assumed a renewal rate for members of 95%, which translated into a 5% attrition rate each year.

Chase's research had indicated that mature European companies had found that 50% utilization of each vehicle (i.e., 360 hours per month) was the most that could be achieved if customer satisfaction was to be maintained. Because of uncertainty regarding actual usage patterns, Chase had planned to initially target a maximum of 40% utilization. Chase assumed the average member would take four trips per month at an average of four hours and 22 miles per trip. (See **Exhibit 3** for this initial financial model.)

Chase planned to launch the business in a single market. Once the basic operations were running smoothly and the business model was proven, she believed that there were at least 14 cities in the United States that would be excellent long-term growth targets. Boston was a logical choice for launching the concept because it met all the key criteria for developing a robust user base. Like most European cities, Boston had insufficient and expensive off-street parking but a good public transportation system. Chase believed that Boston lent itself well to a network of cars positioned close to transit stations. Furthermore, Boston had a large population of college-educated and Web-connected individuals.

Chase believed that a well-designed wireless technology platform would be crucial to Zipcar's ability to deliver good service to its members. She and Danielson planned to use a large portion of their capital to fund the development of this technology platform.

Financing the Venture

When Chase completed the plan in late 1999, she tested its viability with a group of trusted advisors, then began the fund-raising process. Chase had been advised to seek the "smartest" money first and use family and friends only as a last resort. Her list of prospects included professionals, classmates, friends, and family members. In December 1999, Chase contacted Dan Holland, a venture partner at One Liberty Ventures whom she had met socially several years earlier. He took her call and, when she explained the concept to him over the phone, he agreed to meet with her. Holland was intrigued by the idea, and he asked several hard questions that Chase had not yet addressed. She did not walk away from the meeting with any money, but she felt his coaching had been invaluable: "He asked me a lot of questions about the business model: what utilization rate was required to cover COGS? How many cars would require an increase in staff?"

Zipcar was incorporated in January 2000. Chase and Danielson split the equity ownership of the business equally, understanding that their respective 50% ownership stakes would be diluted by subsequent financings.

Chase was devoting her full attention to funding the business. Besides forgoing salary, she and Danielson funded initial expenses out of their own resources. Chase succeeded in obtaining a $50,000 "convertible loan" from a former Sloan classmate who had founded and sold her own company. It was agreed that the loan would convert to equity when a valuation had been established by a Series A funding round. The principal amount would accrete at 1% per month and would convert into equity at the price per share established in the contemplated Series A financing.

Building the Technology Platform

With this money, Chase and Danielson were able to begin building the technology platform.

Chase envisioned a system that enabled the user to make a reservation online, arrive at the parked car, access it easily, and drive off. Because members were charged a usage fee based on the hours used and the mileage driven, she also wanted the system to capture information about when the car was returned and the number of miles the member had driven and send this information back to a central location for billing. The solution to these requirements was wireless transmission of data between the car and the server in order to authorize users and to log in odometer readings, mileage, and time stamps. Finding the right engineer for the job was not easy. After several false starts, Danielson found a promising young MIT engineer, Paul Covell, who wrote the software for a proximity card reader. A card reader was installed inside the windshield of each Zipcar. Members would be issued unique proximity cards known as Zipcards.

Chase explained how the technology would work, once implemented:

> Members make their reservations online. The server wirelessly sends the reservation to the black box in the car, telling the car when and for whom to unlock the door. When the member presents the right card at the right car at the right time, the car unlocks, enables the starter, and starts a billing record noting time and odometer reading. The member always uses the card to lock and unlock the doors. The billing data is sent wirelessly back to the server, and it is billed in real time. We have a patent filed on this technology.

Continuing the Search for Funding

As the technology platform was being developed, Chase and Danielson continued to seek more funding for actually starting the business based on the projections they had made in their December 1999 business plan.

Chase's first formal presentation came in late February 2000, when she was invited to present the plan to an angel investor group called the Investor's Circle. She worked tirelessly to put together Zipcar's first presentation pack. She was the final presenter of the four teams selected that day, and when she finished, she thought there would be a deal. She recalled, "We were the pick of the bunch. However, no money was forthcoming. Throughout the period from January through August, I kept thinking that money was just around the corner, constantly, just around the corner."

While the $50,000 loan had provided much-needed capital, Chase recalled that she "was often behind and occasionally quite desperate." The founders continued to invest and stretched payables as long as possible. They also found ways to enlist other people who worked or advised without charge, including Chase's husband, who spent many hours working on the technology side.

While she was raising money, Chase was also building the infrastructure necessary to launch the operation. She negotiated and signed contracts for Zipcar parking with large institutions and began to bring on the management team.

Naming the Business

Chase and Danielson were convinced that it was important to choose the right name for their business. They wanted something that would communicate the concept and its value clearly and simply. They were also interested in developing a simple tag line that was catchy and informative. It was very important to them that whatever name they selected have the associated domain name available. They wanted the name to convey friendliness, convenience, ease of use, affordability, and social value. They particularly wanted to appeal to users who considered themselves smart, forward thinking, and environmentally responsible.

Starting Zipcar

By late May, Chase had decided to change Zipcar's pricing model. Discussions had revealed that some potential customers found the $300 annual fee too high a hurdle, so Chase decided to lower the membership fee to $75 per year and implement a tiered pricing structure, raising the hourly charge from $1.50 per hour to between $4.50 and $7.00 per hour, depending on the parking costs associated with the area. Chase had also decided to establish a $44 per day "maximum daily rate" as a means of appealing to daily renters, while staying within the price umbrella established by traditional rental car companies. Taking these different pricing plans into account, Chase assumed the company would earn an average of $5.50 per hour per customer. Other changes to the financial model (see **Exhibit 5** for this new financial model) that had transpired as Chase got closer to actually starting the business included:

- Parking: It had not been as easy to secure free parking as had been originally hoped; Chase now assumed it would cost an average of $600 per car per year for parking.
- Attrition: On the basis of more analysis of trends in the turnover of Boston residents, Chase increased the assumed attrition rate to 15% per year.

- Lease cost: increased to $4,400 per vehicle per year.
- Access equipment: increased to $500 per vehicle per year.

In early June, with $68 left of the original $50,000 loan, Chase needed to order the first 12 cars. She told a new prospective investor of this need, and he agreed to a loan of $25,000 that, like the original loan, would eventually convert to equity. Chase was able to lease the cars and meet Zipcar's launch schedule. On June 22, 2000, Zipcar put its first three cars on the street, with the remainder to be deployed over the coming months. Now, the challenge was to attract members.

Marketing

Zipcar's marketing plan relied on several low-budget tactics. Chase and Danielson expected that approximately 30% to 40% of their marketing impact would be driven by word of mouth, another 25% by free media coverage generated through public relations, and the rest through their own grass-roots guerilla marketing efforts.

Chase chose what she called an "urban hip" look for Zipcar. She consulted a designer to create the logo, specifying that it should convey simplicity, cleanliness, a professional (but not corporate) look with a hint of "green." The logo they selected incorporated a "Z" tracked through a green field (see **Exhibit 6** for Zipcar logo). The logo was used on the Web site, stationery, promotional materials, and the cars themselves. Chase deliberately omitted the logo from the driver's side door so members would not think of themselves as mobile advertisements every time they used the car. However, she did place the logo on the passenger door and the trunk of each car. Bumper stickers featuring the Zipcar logo were designed for placement on other cars; one, for example, read "My Other Car is a Zipcar."

Chase was consistent in her efforts to present the same image in all her marketing materials. She rejected traditional 8½-inch × 11-inch trifold collateral pieces, instead choosing to develop simple but humorous postcard advertisements for seven cents each. Zipcar distributed these postcards, which Chase believed would stand out from the crowd. Though other members of the team pressured Chase to print a brochure that would describe the service in detail, she recalled: "I kept pushing back. I said that the goal was to direct potential customers to the Zipcar Web site. If they couldn't handle the Web, they wouldn't be our type of members." This strategy also kept costs down; while the postcards remained the same, new features and new pictures could be incorporated into the Web site.

Plexiglas mailboxes filled with the postcards were installed at each Zipcar parking location. Both Chase and Danielson began speaking to community groups, where they also distributed the cards. They handed them out at subway stops and placed advertisements in local papers.

The first Zipcar was a green Volkswagen Beetle, chosen to convey the "urban hip" green image the company desired. Chase felt it was clearly distinguished from traditional rental cars and would serve as a moving billboard. The first fleet of 12 cars consisted of six of the green Beetles, as well as six white vehicles: four Volkswagen Golfs and two Volkswagen Passat station wagons. Chase planned to add Volkswagen Jettas in December 2000 and Honda Civics in April 2001.

Chase believed that the Web site would be the primary interface for information and the point of purchase for the majority of subscribers. She was willing to invest the time and money necessary to get the Web site right. She wrote the text, organized it into categories, and developed a logical flow.

In June 2000, Zipcar got its first major press coverage. Chase commented, "It all happened very fast and furiously. An *AP* reporter had seen one of our cars (it was the first beta car) and wanted to do a story on the company. The story went national exactly at the time of the formal launch of the company. Zipcar attracted extensive press coverage both nationally and internationally." (See **Exhibit 7** for *Associated Press* article.)

Continuing the Search for Financing and Building the Management Team

Between January and September 2000, Chase had used the same convertible loan terms with several different investors, raising an incremental $300,000 and bringing the total raised to $375,000. Neither Chase nor Danielson had taken any salary. The major expenditures had been related to the development of the technology platform for member services and car access. For most of those early months, the personnel expenses were limited to a few consultants at $15 and $20 per hour and software developers at $90 to $150 per hour. "Everything else was 'nickeled and dimed,'" Chase recalled.

While Chase raised money, she listened to what people were saying about the team. Chase had never run a successful start-up before but quickly learned that "a solid team is a number one requirement if you want to get capital." Investors seemed to be anxious about Chase and Danielson's qualifications, particularly their lack of car expertise and their perceived inexperience at running complex operations.

On the advice of a former professor, Chase began to look for someone who could bring that expertise and credibility to the team. Following up on a strong referral from a prospective board member, Chase and her advisors interviewed a man whose experience and age they hoped would bring more industry credibility. He was named president, Chase became CEO, and Danielson was named vice president of environmental affairs and strategy.

The new president would draw no salary until the financing came through, then he would receive a bonus roughly equivalent to back pay. The honeymoon period was brief. Chase recalled the many problems:

> Our mistake: hiring a big-company guy for a start-up. He spent a lot of money in lunches and parking, created huge lists and detailed tasks and procedures that were 25% out of date by the time they hit my desk and 50% out of date by the following day. He was used to working at a much later-stage company where the goal was to put procedures in place and follow them strictly.

Chase decided to act swiftly. She called on all of her advisors and legal counsel then took the necessary steps to sever the relationship in July 2000. She noted, "Letting him go was absolutely one of the hardest things I have ever had to do in my life. But he was truly the wrong guy for the job, and we had to cut our losses as quickly as possible."

The relationship between Chase and Danielson was also continuing to evolve. Chase was now CEO and Danielson remained vice president of environmental affairs and strategy. Chase was full time, while Danielson had not yet committed to the business full time. Indeed, she worked part time at Zipcar while continuing to hold her full-time job at Harvard and take care of her son after school. Danielson was due to give birth to her second child in late November, and Chase wondered how likely it was that Danielson would be able to commit full time to Zipcar soon.

Progress

By mid-October of 2000, Zipcar had spent the approximately $375,000 that Chase had raised from angel investors, family, and friends. Chase had further developed Zipcar's technology platform, filed a patent on the technology, deployed vehicles at parking locations throughout the city, and enlisted nearly 250 members. Demand for the service had led Chase to increase the number of vehicles, from the planned dozen to 19 by month's end (see **Exhibit 8a** for Zipcar membership acquisition data). This was several more cars than Chase believed she truly needed to service the existing level of membership, but she believed it was important to get cars widely distributed to the target locations.

When Zipcar was launched in June, the complete technology platform had not been ready, but Chase and Danielson had decided to launch anyway, deploying a more primitive solution. Chase said, "We didn't have the wireless access ready, and we decided to deploy a system that allowed any Zipcard to open any Zipcar, and the keys were then left in the glove compartment." Records were kept on paper driving logs by the members, and Chase and her colleagues visited each vehicle once a month to retrieve and record this data for billing purposes.

Chase recalled the difficulty of deciding exactly when to open the doors for business:

> We never felt we were quite ready to open. The technology wasn't perfect; we didn't have all the parking deals negotiated. And, we certainly did not have the funding we wanted. People said, "So, put it off a month, no one will care." I just kept thinking about all the people I had talked to and told we were going to open in May, and I knew that investors would perceive us differently once we were in business and had revenue. So, I just kept pushing to get off the ground as soon as we had the bare minimum in place.

Growth Prospects and the Continued Search for Funding

While the $375,000 had allowed Chase to start the business, she believed that it would take an additional $1.3 million or so to really prove the Boston market's viability. This funding would be used to finish development of the technology, prove the business model, and better understand demand.

Moreover, she believed that Boston not only provided an ideal location to prove the business model but also offered an attractive opportunity for growth. As she further analyzed the Boston market, she determined that there were approximately 15,000 people who fit the Zipcar user profile. She believed it might be possible to reach at least 10,000 of them by year five. Finally, Chase believed that Zipcar's success in Boston could be replicated in at least 14 other cities nationwide.

Assuming Zipcar would be able to raise $1.3 million quickly, Chase believed she would be back on the street in six to nine months raising expansion funds. She knew she could create strong network effects by increasing usage within a single market, but

Chase was anxious to begin claiming other major markets on the East Coast and possibly in the Midwest.

In the few days following the end of September, Chase worked hard to collect the month's operating and financial data. She was eager to better understand the operating and financial parameters of the business as well as customers' actual usage patterns. (See **Exhibit 8b** for details of September usage and revenue.)

Chase was also beginning to get a handle on operating and overhead costs. She explained:

> At the variable cost level, lease costs were actually coming in a bit higher than anticipated—$4,800 per vehicle per year. As we got bigger, the car companies thought we were a bigger risk. They look at one person leasing one car, and they can manage that risk pretty well. But, when we started leasing 10 or a dozen cars, all of a sudden we are a big credit risk, and they needed to price the lease at a premium. Parking was coming in more expensive also—about $750 per car per year. And, our fuel bills are running about 10% higher than expected. The other expenses are coming in about where expected, on a per-car basis.
>
> Overhead is more difficult to think about. We invested about $200,000 in what I would call pure start-up costs—the technology, legally incorporating, naming the business. And, I would estimate that our overhead is now running about $44,000 per month. As I analyze that figure, I am allocating $30,000 per month of that figure to corporate overhead, meaning activities that we would be funding whether we were in one or many cities: legal, Web site design, overall design, and development of technology and marketing materials. And, $14,000 per month is the Boston-specific overhead.
>
> On the marketing side, we have succeeded in keeping pretty close to budget, spending between $1,000 and $1,500 per month, or about $7,300 so far. People have been amazed that we have kept marketing this low. The key has been incredible, free publicity; advertising generated by the cars; brochures, which we put wherever we park a car; and just great word of mouth. Basically, we had no money, so this forced us to be incredibly disciplined. I knew we had to prove the business model, and showing we could acquire customers at a reasonable cost was a very important part of that.

Meanwhile, the Springboard 2000 New England venture forum was approaching quickly. By the end of October, Chase needed to have developed as effective a presentation to the Springboard conference as possible.

EXHIBIT 1 | Economics of Individual Car Ownership

Monthly Expenditures	Monthly Costs
Vehicle depreciation/Lease	$270
Insurance	99
Parking	125
Gas	45
Maintenance	36
Total	$575

Source: Casewriter analysis based upon company data.

EXHIBIT 2 | Population of Top 20 U.S. Markets

City	Population (millions)	Households (millions)	Density per sq. mile
1 Los Angeles–Long Beach	8.9	3.42	2,183
2 New York	8.5	3.27	7,447
3 Chicago	6.0	2.31	3,221
4 Philadelphia	4.9	1.88	1,380
5 Detroit	4.4	1.69	981
6 Washington, D.C.	3.9	1.50	989
7 Miami–Ft. Lauderdale	3.2	1.23	1,012
8 Boston	2.9	1.12	1,631
9 Minneapolis–St. Paul	2.5	0.96	487
10 St. Louis	2.5	0.96	458
11 Baltimore	2.4	0.92	913
12 Anaheim–Santa Ana	2.4	0.92	3,052
13 Pittsburgh	2.0	0.77	604
14 Seattle	2.0	0.77	468
15 Cleveland	1.8	0.69	1,211
16 Newark	1.8	0.69	1,495
17 San Francisco	1.6	0.62	1,579
18 San Jose	1.5	0.58	1,159
19 Milwaukee	1.4	0.54	996
20 Bergen–Passaic Counties, N.J.	1.3	0.50	3,049
TOTAL	65.9	25.35	

Source: U.S. Census, <http://census.gov/population/censusdata/90den_ma.txt>, accessed December 9, 2002.

EXHIBIT 3 | Original Financial Plan for Boston, December 1999

	Assumption (per unit)	YEAR 1	YEAR 2	YEAR 3	YEAR 4	YEAR 5
Revenues						
Trips/member/month	4					
miles/trip	22					
hours/trip	4					
Beginning Members		0	440	856	908	1180
Attrition	0.05	0	22	42.8	45.4	59
Ending Members		440	856	908	1180	1196
New Members		440	438	94.8	317.4	75
Avg # of Members		220	648	882	1,044	1,188
Application fee (per new member)	25	11,000	10,950	2,370	7,935	1,875
Annual fees (per avg member)	300	66,000	194,400	264,600	313,200	356,400
Per mile charge	0.4	92,928	273,715	372,557	440,986	501,811
Per hour charge	1.5	63,360	186,624	254,016	300,672	342,144
Security Deposits (avg. balance)	300	66,000	194,400	264,600	313,200	356,400
Interest income (on avg. sec. dep. balance)	4%	2,640	7,776	10,584	12,528	14,256
Total Revenue		235,928	673,465	904,127	1,075,321	1,216,486

(continued)

EXHIBIT 3 | Original Financial Plan for Boston, December 1999 (*continued*)

	Assumption (per unit)	YEAR 1	YEAR 2	YEAR 3	YEAR 4	YEAR 5
Costs						
Variable Costs/Car						
Beginning Cars		0	24	48	50	66
Ending Cars		24	48	50	66	66
Avg # of Cars		12	36	49	58	66
Lease Cost (car/year)	4,000	48,000	144,000	196,000	232,000	264,000
Access equip. (car/year)	400	4,800	14,400	19,600	23,200	26,400
Fuel (car/year)	1,080	12,960	38,880	52,920	62,640	71,280
Insurance (car/year)	1,700	20,400	61,200	83,300	98,600	112,200
Maintenance (car/year)	400	4,800	14,400	19,600	23,200	26,400
Parking (car/year)	0	0	0	0	0	0
Total Variable Costs		90,960	272,880	371,420	439,640	500,280
Fixed costs—Corp. level						
Corporate insurance		800	800	800	800	800
Reservation system		2,895	3,160	12,000	6,000	7,000
Administration—Corp.		100,000	100,000	100,000	100,000	100,000
Benefits	20%	20,000	20,000	20,000	20,000	20,000
Office Space		0	0	5,000	5,000	5,000
Office equip. & supplies		1,000	1,000	1,000	1,000	1,000
Phone		1,200	1,800	1,800	1,800	2,500
Total Corp. Overhead		125,895	126,760	140,600	134,600	136,300
Fixed costs—Boston Office						
Billing (member/year)	24	5,280	15,552	21,168	25,056	28,512
Administration—local		24,000	24,000	24,000	24,000	24,000
Benefits	20%	4,800	24,780	24,780	24,780	24,780
Office space		0	0	5,000	5,000	5,000
Office equip. & supply		1000	1000	1000	1000	1000
Telephone and Datalines		1,200	1,800	1,800	1,800	2,500
Marketing		10,000	12,000	12,000	12,000	12,000
Background checks (per new member)	20	8,800	8,760	1,896	6,348	1,500
Total Boston Overhead		55,080	87,892	91,644	99,984	99,292
Total Overhead Costs		180,975	214,652	232,244	234,584	235,592
Net Income Before Tax		−36,007	185,933	300,463	401,097	480,614

Source: Company.

EXHIBIT 4 | Zipcar Driver Requirements

1. No more than two incidents (moving violations plus accidents) in the past three years and no more than one in the past 18 months.
2. No major moving violations:
   - Excessive speed (20+ MPH over speed limit)
   - Operating to endanger, reckless driving, etc.
   - Driving under the influence of alcohol or drugs
   - Leaving the scene of an accident involving property damage
   - Operating a motor vehicle with a suspended or revoked license
   - School bus stopping-flag violations (or similar) in the past three years

Source: Company.

EXHIBIT 5 | Revised Financial Plan for Boston, May 2000

	Assumption (per unit)	YEAR 1	YEAR 2	YEAR 3	YEAR 4	YEAR 5
Revenues						
Trips/member/month	4					
miles/trip	22					
hours/trip	4					
Beginning Members		0	440	856	908	1180
Attrition	0.15	0	66	128.4	136.2	177
Ending Members		440	856	908	1180	1196
New Members		440	482	180.4	408.2	193
Avg # of Members		220	648	882	1,044	1,188
Application fee (per new member)	25	11,000	12,050	4,510	10,205	4,825
Annual fees (per avg member)	75	16,500	48,600	66,150	78,300	89,100
Per mile charge	0.4	92,928	273,715	372,557	440,986	501,811
Per hour charge	5.5	232,320	684,288	931,392	1,102,464	1,254,528
Security Deposits (avg. balance)	300	66,000	194,400	264,600	313,200	356,400
Interest income (on avg. sec. dep. balance)	4%	2,640	7,776	10,584	12,528	14,256
Total Revenue		355,388	1,026,429	1,385,193	1,644,483	1,864,520
Costs						
Variable Costs/Car						
Beginning Cars		0	24	48	50	66
Ending Cars		24	48	50	66	66
Avg # of Cars		12	36	49	58	66
Lease Cost (car/year)	4,400	52,800	158,400	215,600	255,200	290,400
Access equip. (car/year)	500	6,000	18,000	24,500	29,000	33,000
Fuel (car/year)	1,080	12,960	38,880	52,920	62,640	71,280
Insurance (car/year)	1,700	20,400	61,200	83,300	98,600	112,200
Maintenance (car/year)	400	4,800	14,400	19,600	23,200	26,400
Parking (car/year)	600	7,200	21,600	29,400	34,800	39,600
Total Variable Costs		104,160	312,480	425,320	503,440	572,880
Fixed costs—Corp. level						
Corporate insurance		800	800	800	800	800
Reservation system		2,895	3,160	12,000	6,000	7,000
Administration—Corp.		100,000	100,000	100,000	100,000	100,000
Benefits	20%	20,000	20,000	20,000	20,000	20,000
Office Space		0	0	5,000	5,000	5,000
Office equip. & supplies		1,000	1,000	1,000	1,000	1,000
Phone		1,200	1,800	1,800	1,800	2,500
Total Corp. Overhead		125,895	126,760	140,600	134,600	136,300
Fixed costs—Boston Office						
Billing (member/year)	24	5,280	15,552	21,168	25,056	28,512
Administration—local		24,000	24,000	24,000	24,000	24,000
Benefits	20%	4,800	24,780	24,780	24,780	24,780
Office space		0	0	5,000	5,000	5,000
Office equip. & supply		1000	1000	1000	1000	1000
Telephone and Datalines		1,200	1,800	1,800	1,800	2,500
Marketing		10,000	12,000	12,000	12,000	12,000
Background checks (per new member)	20	8,800	9,640	3,608	8,164	3,860
Total Boston Overhead		55,080	88,772	93,356	101,800	101,652
Total Overhead Costs		180,975	215,532	233,956	236,400	237,952
Net Income Before Tax		70,253	498,417	725,917	904,643	1,053,688

Source: Company.

EXHIBIT 6 | Zipcar Logo

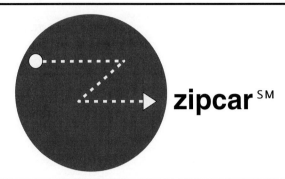

Source: Company.

EXHIBIT 7 | Associated Press Article

Car Sharing on Rise
By Heidi B. Perlman—*The Associated Press*

Sunday, June 25, 2000

BOSTON — It took only a month for the traffic jams, insurance costs and parking woes of Cambridge to convince Katherine Watkins to sell her car when she moved from Kentucky.

But after two years riding the bus and taking cabs, she finally broke down and got a car again. Sort of.

Watkins is a new member of Zipcar, a service that allows her to share a car with more than a dozen other people for $4.50 an hour.

"My cat was sick and I had to bring her to the vet, and it was just too much to do in a cab," she said. "I finally decided I really do need a car, just not all the time."

Zipcar, based in the Boston suburb of Cambridge, caters to drivers such as Watkins, who like the convenience of having a car but don't like what it costs to maintain one in the city.

"Some people don't need a car about 85 percent of the time," said co-founder Robin Chase. "But they have to buy a whole car just to fill that tiny need. Those are the people we want to come to us."

Zipcar, which opened this spring, is the first car-sharing service in Massachusetts. Here's how it works:

The company owns and insures all the cars. Members get cards or keys to get into the cars, which are parked at a designated spot. Reservations can be made online or over the phone, and the only rule is to get the car back on time. If the car is already booked, members either have to take an alternate car, or wait until the car they usually drive is available. Members can fill the gas tank with a company credit card.

Zipcar charges a $20 late fee, and drivers who are consistently late lose their membership.

The annual membership is $75 a year, plus a $300 deposit. Each use costs $4.50 an hour and 40 cents a mile. Fees at other companies range from less than $2 an hour to up to $9.

That can get pricey for people who drive long distances, or take the car for an overnight trip, Chase said. But for people who just need to go to the grocery store, a doctor's appointment or visit a friend out of town, car sharing may be cheaper than renting a car.

EXHIBIT 7 | *(continued)*

At Budget Rent-A-Car, which pledges "low daily and weekly rates," a rental car in Boston costs about $45 a day. Other companies charge between $40 and $50 a day, plus additional charges for mileage and insurance.

The idea of car sharing was spawned in Switzerland in 1987, when Mobility CarSharing put its first car on the road in the traffic-congested city of Lucerne. The company now has 1,300 cars at 800 locations around Switzerland, and serves more than 33,000 customers, according to the company's Web site.

The Swiss company's success was duplicated in big cities in Austria, France, Sweden and Germany, and the idea spread overseas to Canada in 1995.

The first American car-sharing company opened in Portland, Ore., in 1998. Others are in Seattle, San Francisco and Washington, D.C.

"People come to us who don't need to drive to work every day," said Maren Souders, spokeswoman for Carsharing Portland Inc. "They all work from home or ride their bikes, but every now and then need a car to get somewhere fast."

Right now the company has just one lime green Volkswagen Beetle, which is parked in a garage in Cambridge. A second Bug will soon be available in Boston's posh Beacon Hill neighborhood.

"You might get in each time and find the preset radio stations have been changed," he said. "But otherwise, people will find it's just like having your own car."

Chase said she is optimistic her company will see the same kind of success in Boston and Cambridge as other car-sharing companies have around the country.

In Seattle, for example, Flexcar opened in January with just four cars. It now has 12 cars and 350 members, said spokesman Ref Lindmark.

"I hear people talking all the time about how they couldn't get somewhere by subway, or how long they spent on the bus, or that parking was awful in the city," she said. "I think this fills a need that hasn't been met in Boston yet."

Watkins agreed.

"It's a relief not to have a car anymore," she said. "But it's also a relief to know if we need one, it's there."

EXHIBIT 8a | Zipcar Membership Data, 2000

	New Members	Attrition	Ending Members
Beta	14	0	14
June	20	0	34
July	49	3	80
August	64	3	141
September	101	3	239

Source: Company.

EXHIBIT 8b | September Operating Data

Note: Zipcar offered a daily rate of $44 for 24 hours, which included 125 free miles. In the table below, these uses, as well as the hours and miles associated with them, are broken out and described as "daily" uses. The other uses—and their miles, hours and revenues—are described as "hourly" uses.

Overhead Expenses

Boston	14,000.00
Corporate	30,000.00

Applications & Membership

Beginning members	141.00
Applications	112.00
Applications Approved	105.00
New members	101.00
Attrition	3.00
Ending Members	239.00
Total "member days"[a]	5,088.00
Application Fees	2,800.00
Annual Member Fees received	7,575.00
Annual Member Fees "booked"[b]	1,512.00

Deposits

Deposits received in September	42,300.00
Total deposit balance month end	71,700.00
Average deposit balance	42,090.00
Interest earned on total deposits	155.00

Usage

Available "car days"[a]	439.00
Total trips taken (uses)	335.00
hourly uses	218.00
daily uses	117.00
Total miles driven	16,339.00
miles driven—hourly uses	5,341.00
miles driven—daily uses	10,998.00
Total hours used	3,223.00
hours used—hourly uses	1,351.00
hours used—daily uses	1,872.00
Trips—night & weekend %[c]	60.00%
Hours of use—night and weekend %[c]	53.00%

(continued)

EXHIBIT 8b | *(continued)*

Revenues	
Total miles billed	5,765.00
miles billed—hourly uses	5,341.00
miles billed—daily uses	424.00
Total hours billed	2,287.00
hours billed—hourly uses	1,351.00
hours billed—daily uses	936.00
Total mileage revenue	2,276.00
mileage revenue—hourly uses	2,106.40
mileage revenue—daily uses	169.60
Total hourly revenue	12,368.50
hourly revenue—hourly uses	7,220.50
hourly revenue—daily uses	5,148.00
Total usage revenue	14,644.50
revenue from daily uses	5,317.60
revenue from hourly uses	9,326.90

Source: Company.

[a]Member days = the total number of members on any given day for each of the 30 days of the month, e.g., a member for a full month generates 30 member days. Similarly, a car day is one day of one car being in service.

[b]While Zipcar members paid a $75 annual membership fee upon joining, only 1/12 of that fee was "booked" to revenue each month.

[c]Night and weekend = 6 p.m. to 8 a.m. and all day Saturday and Sunday.

Keurig

Nick Lazaris waited patiently at the stoplight, knowing he had plenty of time to make the early meeting at his Wakefield, MA office. This morning, Lazaris—President and CEO of Keurig, Inc.—would bring his top management team (**Exhibit 1**) up to date on problems developing in the company's relationships with two critical vendors. The problems had already caused delays in the full roll-out of Keurig's revolutionary coffee brewing system.

Whenever he wondered if the term "revolutionary" was a bit too strong to describe his company's products (**Exhibits 2 and 3**), he usually found quick re-affirmation of the potential impact the new system—which according to the company's slogan could produce "coffee house taste by the cup." Lazaris grinned when he saw the driver of the car next to his fumbling with a biscotti and a large cup of coffee from Starbucks while talking on a cellular phone. He liked to bring up anecdotes such as this to illustrate the vast potential he foresaw for his company. "Ten years ago, that guy would have had one cup from his Mr. Coffee at home and then another from the office coffee pot when he got to work," said Lazaris. "Now, he goes out of his way to spend a couple of bucks each morning—on something that he used to get for just a few cents, mind you." Keurig sought to ride the wave created by Starbucks and capitalize on America's growing love for premium coffee.

It was Spring of 1998, just over a year since Lazaris had assumed the role of President and CEO at the now six-year-old company. When he was hired in early 1997 by the venture capitalist who headed Keurig's board, he inherited a company that had missed several internally generated deadlines for completing key aspects of its strategic plan. Keurig had segmented America's $15 billion market for coffee and associated products into three main segments. The firm was already behind schedule in launching its two-pronged campaign into the commercial segments: office coffee services and food-service establishments. Eventually Keurig hoped to launch a version of its product to cater to the third market segment, the consumer market. Since most coffee was consumed at home, the market was very tempting, but the company wanted to make sure it

Professor Paul W. Marshall and Research Associate Jeremy B. Dann prepared this case. HBS cases are developed solely as the basis for class discussion. Cases are not intended to serve as endorsements, sources of primary data, or illustrations of effective or ineffective management.

established a strong brand and product reputation before tackling the complex consumer market. The home version of the Keurig brewing system was still probably three years away.

Lazaris and his management team knew they had only a limited number of chances to win over office coffee system distributors, major food retailing establishments, top-tier coffee roasting companies and other industry collaborators whose "buy-in" would be essential in rolling out Keurig's unique product. As he pulled into the parking lot at his office, Lazaris' mind was swimming with all of the issues he would be dealing with that day and in coming weeks. "It's too early in the morning to think about this stuff," he mused. "I need a cup of coffee."

The Founding of Keurig, Inc.

In 1992, Ian Greenwood, an engineer in the electronics industry, approached Peter Dragone, his friend and former college roommate, about a new technique for brewing coffee that he was developing. Dragone, who received his MBA from Harvard Business School in 1985, was at the time working for the Chiquita banana company. Greenwood thought Dragone's formal business training and food industry experience would complement his own product engineering abilities. The concept Greenwood wished to turn into a business was centered on creating portion packs of premium coffee. The coffee inside would stay fresh because nearly all the oxygen would be removed through special packaging techniques (not yet developed at the time). Each pack held its own filter and was enclosed by a foil lid. The portion pack concept held the promise of creating a way to brew coffee much more precisely and consistently than any method available at the time. "He came to me with a mock-up made out of a used yogurt cup. So, I started to create a business plan," said Dragone. Greenwood, perusing a Dutch-English dictionary, spotted the word "Keurig"—Dutch for "excellence"—and chose it as the name of the new company. The modified yogurt cup (and its more refined later versions) was dubbed the "K-Cup."

Greenwood would serve as President and CEO of the nascent venture, while Dragone would be the Chief Financial Officer. The partners started presenting their ideas to coffee-maker manufacturers such as Westbend and Grindmaster in late 1992. They sought to find an experienced manufacturer with strong distribution channels who might be interested in collaborating with them. "We got absolutely nowhere because, 1) they did not believe that we could create a coffee-maker, and 2) they thought we were crackpots," recalled Dragone, tongue-in-cheek.

Greenwood had soon created a makeshift coffee-maker to prove that the portion pack concept actually worked. Dragone continued to fine-tune the business plan, gaining critical input from experienced entrepreneurs and venture capitalists after he presented the concept to the MIT Enterprise Forum. He also discussed the plan with representatives of the Northeast Office Coffee Association, a trade organization composed of distributors, equipment manufacturers and other companies involved in marketing coffee and services to businesses. The partners needed to determine whether they would work with existing distributors servicing the office market or create their own channel employing a direct mail fulfillment program.

In late 1993, Greenwood and Dragone began to seek financial backing from venture capitalists. They met with Larry Kernan, a 1979 HBS graduate. Kernan was with MDT Advisers, a financial management company responsible for the Memorial Drive Trust, the $1 billion pension fund of Arthur D. Little, a consultancy based in Cambridge, MA. As a part of its holdings, MDT Advisers managed a $100 million venture capital fund focusing on high technology, communications and consumer products. "These guys were not ready for prime time," recalled Kernan. "Their machine leaked all over the conference table; it could barely make coffee." The Keurig partners planned on producing their own branded line—True North Coffee—and showed Kernan an example of a K-Cup with a True North logo emblazoned on its foil seal. Not convinced of the technical feasibility or the economics of the business model, Kernan told Greenwood and Dragone that his firm would pass on the deal.

Rebuffed in their first attempt to get VC funding, the duo again sought out industry partners to help them realize their plans. They scheduled another round of meetings with manufacturers of consumer coffee-makers. Greenwood and Dragone also met with several premium roasters who they thought might appreciate the quantum leap in product freshness and consistent brewing the K-Cup would represent. "Both the appliance manufacturers and the roasters were extremely positive about the quality of the coffee the K-Cup produced," said Dragone. "But the appliance guys were convinced we could never produce large quantities of K-Cups economically and the roasters were convinced we would never get the coffee-maker to work flawlessly."

By early 1994, Keurig had received a small investment from the Food Fund, a VC firm specializing in food-related products. The company used the money to create a handful of higher quality brewer prototypes. In late 1994, Dunkin' Donuts, an international chain selling donuts, bagels and other breakfast pastries, agreed to purchase two prototype brewers for $15,000. The chain had been trying to grow its sales of premium coffees, but was finding it difficult to do so because the distinct flavors of specialty blends were degraded when brewed in the same machine. Because of the K-Cup brewing technique, Keurig's system would allow Dunkin' Donuts to offer a variety of fresh coffee choices without any mixing of flavors. In addition, the chain was seeking a coffee brewing system appropriate for non-store settings such as kiosks, often staffed by only one person at a time. Dunkin' Donuts thought that Keurig's system—which featured short set-up times and quick brewing—was promising for this sort of retail outlet.

Keurig had also developed a promising relationship with Green Mountain Coffee Roasters, a premium coffee producer (**Exhibit 4**). Greenwood met Stephen Sabol, Green Mountain's Vice President of Sales, at a food products trade show in late 1992. "When I met Ian, he had no drawings or samples, really. But my gut feeling told me that there could be a lot of rewards for my company if we could be a partner with Keurig as it developed its system," said Sabol. As Keurig upgraded its plans and prototypes, Sabol's interest in working with the fledgling venture increased. By 1994, Keurig and Green Mountain were working on a research and development partnership. Although Greenwood pushed the roaster to produce the "True North" brand for Keurig, Sabol insisted that his company's participation hinged on employing the Green Mountain brand. "We were not at all interested in a private label arrangement," said Sabol. "We only wanted to work with them if we were producing a high-end product using our own name."

New Funding, New Management

In late 1994, Keurig reopened a dialogue with MDT Advisers about obtaining funding for their company. The venture capitalist from the Food Fund who had placed the earlier investment asked Larry Kernan if he would like to participate in the next round of funding. "With the Dunkin' Donuts project, the Green Mountain arrangement, more reliable prototypes and a patent application in the pipeline (**Exhibit 5**), this was starting to look like a real company," said Kernan. "From what we heard, it seemed most of the kinks had been worked out and these guys could be in production in three to four months if they received funding."

In April 1995, MDT and the Food Fund were the major investors in a $1 million equity round of financing that gave them a combined 45% stake in Keurig. However, at the closing meeting, some complications arose. "It was unlike anything I had dealt with during all of my time in venture capital," said MDT's Kernan. "Peter Dragone pulled me aside and said that he and Dick Sweeney [a product development consultant who was slated to join Keurig full-time when funding was finalized] were having doubts about Ian's abilities to run the company going forward."

"It wasn't a power play," recalled Dragone. "Ian was a *fantastic* idea guy, but he wasn't a businessman. Dick and I just didn't believe he could be a good manager for a $1 million investment." The deal went forward with the management structure intact, although the discussion with Dragone put Kernan—Keurig's new chairman—on guard for potential problems. Greenwood chafed under the new arrangement and often disagreed with Kernan on what the firm's priorities should be. After several months of being stonewalled on information requests and seeing little in terms of tangible achievements toward a product launch, Kernan began to investigate making a change at CEO. While hearing a great deal from Keurig employees about how Greenwood's product ideas were key to the company's future, he heard little in support of Greenwood's management skills. In the late summer of 1995, Larry Kernan asked Ian Greenwood to step aside as CEO in favor of Peter Dragone. Greenwood became Keurig's chief engineer, assigned to devote all of his time to the development of a reliable brewer and a packaging line capable of mass producing K-Cups.

"MDT was very afraid of Ian bolting, because he was still key to recovering their investment. We really tried to go out of our way to keep him happy," said Dragone. Greenwood immersed himself even more in refining the technical aspects of the brewer and K-Cup packaging line. However, he still wanted to pursue certain "pet" development projects in spite of resistance from the growing group of Keurig engineers and product design consultants working on the effort. "Ian was a really clever guy and his concept was great," said Sweeney, who was collaborating with Greenwood on key design projects. "However, he wanted to try all kinds of things which would have been really difficult to execute, just because of basic physics. I mean, gravity isn't just a good idea, it's the law."

At the beginning of 1996 an additional $1 million was raised from MDT and the Food Fund, bringing their ownership share to 58%. At the time it was obvious that Keurig was going to miss its projected window for bringing its system into operation. Greenwood's adaptations to the products were not panning out. Keurig management,

MDT and Green Mountain had been targeting a summer 1996 launch date, but neither the brewer nor the packaging line were going to be ready. In January 1996 the Board decided to make Sweeney head of engineering, charged with the task of getting the brewer and K-Cup line ready for market. At the same time Greenwood was moved into an R&D role. However, Sweeney and his new engineering team found Greenwood difficult to work with. In June of 1996, after conferring with MDT, Dragone made the decision to fire Greenwood.

More New Management

In the late summer of 1996 Peter Dragone approached Larry Kernan to discuss the possibility of his stepping aside as CEO. "Peter was a high energy guy . . . a straight shooter . . . great for the company," said Kernan. "I think he had lost some of the confidence in his ability to lead Keurig, given the missteps and delays to date. We agreed that it might be good if he move on and we bring in another person to head the company." Kernan initially asked Dragone to take the position of CFO when a new Keurig CEO was tapped, but Dragone wanted the new leader to feel he had free rein, without one of the founders looking over his shoulder.

Kernan led Keurig's search for a new CEO. He knew it would be a critical decision, in that Keurig probably only had one more shot to bring its system to market. The board of directors decided the new CEO should have experience in the consumer products industry, preferably with a marketing background. "We talked to nine candidates. We saw some really talented folks. There were quite a few out-of-work executives from the consumer small appliance industry thanks to 'Chainsaw' Al Dunlap's work at Sunbeam," recalled Kernan.

Keurig had retained the Onstott Group, an executive search firm, to manage the search for a new CEO. Trying to think "out of the box" about additional candidates, the head of the firm, Joe Onstott, remembered an executive for whom he had performed searches in the past. Feeling there might be a good fit, Onstott gave Nick Lazaris a call. Lazaris was then a division vice president for Office Specialists, responsible for the company's $12 million technical staffing operation. From 1989 to 1995, he served as President and CEO of M.W. Carr, $20 million manufacturer and importer of high-end picture frames. "He was not at all a natural candidate," commented Kernan. "Nick was definitely not as *externally* focused as we thought we might have liked. He didn't have the sales and marketing background we were looking for. But he did a lot of research . . . he assessed possible strategies. His interviews were very impressive." Lazaris came on board as Keurig's CEO and President in February of 1997. Dragone remained for three months to help ensure a smooth transition.

One More Shot at the Market

Missteps and missed deadlines caused some to doubt if Keurig's system would ever be rolled out in a major way. In December of 1996, MDT and the Food Fund put an additional $1.7 million into Keurig, making them owners of 75% of the company's equity. "I thought we had one more chance to get this thing off the ground, so we stopped, retrenched and invested even more," said Kernan. "You never like to 'throw good money after bad,' but there was one thing that kept giving us confidence: *everyone* who took part in our prototype pilot programs *loved* the coffee."

As Lazaris took the reins as CEO, he and the board of directors spent a great deal of time refining Keurig's overall business model and reassessing what the company should concentrate on going forward. In early 1997, Keurig decided to outsource more of the development work on both the brewer and the packaging line. The company would still have their own engineers devoted full-time to each product, but they would serve as liaisons with the outside design firms. Lazaris also cemented the plan to license the firm's technologies on a non-exclusive basis to coffee roasters who would market K-Cups under their own brands. Keurig had considered launching its own line of branded coffee under the True North label, but management decided to forge alliances with premium roasters because of their prestige, channels, manpower and marketing experience. The company made Green Mountain its first partner, structuring an agreement by the end of 1997 whereby Keurig would own the K-Cup packaging lines and earn back a licensing fee for each K-Cup produced. "We were excited about the business model we were developing. Licensing would give us four to five cents per K-Cup of almost pure profit and very little downside risk," said Lazaris. However, the decision to follow the licensing rather than private label model led to some unforeseen problems when Keurig tried to raise additional equity capital. "Some of the other V.C. firms we talked to said they value early stage companies at multiples of *sales*. Our licensing plan gave us good profits and cash flow, but lower sales."

Customers, Channels and Distribution

Chris Stevens had been brought on as Keurig's Vice President for Sales and Marketing in February 1996. Stevens had been hired in anticipation of a rapid product roll-out. However, since neither the brewer nor the packaging line was ready for widespread usage, he conducted a number of customer studies at Boston-area businesses. Ian Greenwood had ordered several hundred prototypes of a flawed brewer design some months before; the company's engineers under Dick Sweeney's direction corrected the defects in a few dozen so that they could be used in the study. K-Cups were "mass-produced" by a labor-intensive, makeshift assembly line also created by Sweeney. "We were making K-Cups in the back of our office, using a clothes iron to adhere the foil seal onto the top. It wasn't pretty," said Sweeney.

Stevens used all of the K-Cups and functional brewers he could get to gain more information on how end customers would receive the product. Keurig grouped its potential customer base into three main categories: office users, food service establishments and households (**Exhibits 6 and 7**). The company decided to focus its early efforts on offices and food service establishments for two reasons. First, the brewer Keurig was developing would be priced above $1000, much more than consumers were used to spending on even prestige kitchen appliances such as espresso machines and bread-makers. As it stood, Keurig's development staff and contractors were already scrambling to bring a high quality commercial version to market and developing a consumer model in parallel would tax the firm's limited resources. Secondly, Keurig thought establishing the system in the commercial marketplace would greatly aid a later launch in the consumer segment. People used to having a number of choices of high quality coffees at their workplace or in restaurants would be more likely to purchase a less expensive household version when it was finally rolled out.

Office Coffee Systems (OCS)

Stevens placed units in office environments around the city of Boston and would frequently discuss the system's performance with the office/facility manager in charge of coffee service. Test locations included Thomas H. Lee, Goldman Sachs' Boston office, a Toshiba manufacturing facility and the Executive Education building at the Harvard Business School. According to Stevens:

> We had so many questions about the way people would react to the units in an office setting. Would they want to wait 30 seconds for the cup of coffee instead of pouring it immediately from a pre-brewed pot? Would they figure out how to use the machine? Would people see the benefit of the flavor variety? Also, would office managers be willing to pay a premium for the coffee? According to my findings, the answer to all of these questions was a resounding "Yes."

Office managers viewed the Keurig system as a tangible benefit they could provide to enhance the workplace. "Usually, it's difficult for office managers to please anyone. The copier's broken . . . you're out of paper clips . . . the computer network's down. This was a chance for the office manager to be a hero," commented Stevens. Anecdotal information from office managers supported Keurig's assertion that if premium coffees were offered, even the most coffee-conscious employees would use the brewer in the break room rather than running out for a cup at Starbucks or another retail establishment. Stevens also gathered data concerning the importance of one of the unique characteristics of his company's system: flavor variety. Each of the eight flavors offered in Keurig's merchandising display represented between 11 and 15% of the total demand at any site on average.

Stevens maintained that low wastage, portion-pack brewing and easy clean-up/maintenance would help OCS customers earn back much of the premium they would pay for coffee brewed in Keurig's machines. After distributors took their 80–100% mark-up on the sale of K-Cups, they would be sold to offices for 40–50 cents per serving. This compares to a price of about 12.5 cents per brewed cup for the regular packaged coffees offices currently used. However, approximately one-third of coffee brewed in an office environment wound up "down the drain" because it was brewed incorrectly, became stale or was simply jettisoned in favor of a different blend. In addition, support employees—usually making around $15 per hour—often spent as much as 30 minutes per day making coffee and cleaning the brewer. Finally, because the coffee and filters used in traditional OCS units were interchangeable with products used in consumer brewing systems (Mr. Coffee, etc.), employees sometimes took packaged coffee and brewing supplies home.

Keurig's products—both the brewers and supplies of K-Cups—would be sold to offices by one of an assortment of regional distributors. This segment of the U.S. coffee market was serviced by approximately 1,700 OCS distributors with sales of at least $1.4 million each. One-third of those distributors enjoyed sales over $2.5 million. OCS distributors would usually purchase brewers from a manufacturer and then provide them free of charge to clients if they committed to an office coffee service contract. Sometimes other arrangements—such as rental or lease programs for the machines instead of free placement—might be brokered depending on the customer's coffee consumption patterns. Typically, distributors spent approximately $400 on the brewers. Keurig foresaw marketing its brewer at a price point around $1000. Distributors would also offer an array of supporting products such as displays and vending machines, which allowed offices to charge 25 or 50 cents for a K-Cup.

"We're going to be working closely with the distributors on how they should position the Keurig system with OCS customers," said Stevens. "The sales process isn't going to be a quick hand-off. It will be more like a 'Fuller Brush' sale [a reference to a company which sold its products door-to-door, relying heavily on demonstrations]." Stevens likened the demonstration to a "keg party," where distributors of Keurig's coffee system would bring pastries, biscotti and other food and drinks. The demo would be designed to appeal not just to the office manager, but also to the employees who would be utilizing the system. Keurig would urge distributors to leave a machine in the office for a few days so that the office manager could judge the potential impact of the new brewing system.

Food Service

Concurrent with its effort to penetrate the OCS market, Keurig was also making a strong push to get its brewing system into restaurants, convenience stores and other establishments. In 1995 Keurig received negative feedback from Dunkin' Donuts—a chain which sells more coffee per store than Starbucks—about the prototypes it purchased. They had commented that they could not reach the "taste profile" they were looking for, and they were concerned that the brewing process took too long given the volume of coffee sold between 7 and 9 a.m.

Despite this early setback, some within the company felt that Keurig had underestimated the potential of this market and should invest even more resources in pursuing it. Keurig was investigating the type of food service establishments that would be most likely to purchase its brewing system. "The more we thought about it, it seemed that restaurants with fairly low coffee sales could be a strong market for us," said Lazaris. "An International House of Pancakes—with its 'never empty cup of coffee'—has next-to-no wastage and always has fresh coffee brewing because of the extraordinary volumes they do at their peak hours." Keurig's technology featured single-serve brewing on demand, allowing restaurant concepts with lower volumes to brew coffee *after* they had received an order, saving time and decreasing wastage. In addition, food service establishments might be able to charge a premium because of the higher quality and the flavor assortment. By early 1998 Keurig and Green Mountain were demonstrating the Keurig system to a number of food service chains with high coffee sales but peak demand profiles different than Dunkin' Donuts'. Companies like Ben & Jerry's Ice Cream and The Great American Cookie Company committed to test-programs.

In this market segment, brewers and coffee were usually sold to foodservice distribution companies and then placed in restaurants under a variety of financial arrangements: purchase, lease, long-term service contract, etc. Some of the distributors that served this segment were multibillion dollar giants; examples included Sysco and

Alliant (a Kraft spin-off). They operated in markets all over the country and offered broad product lines of food, drinks, equipment and consumables/disposables. Roasters like Green Mountain sometimes sold their products directly to restaurant accounts. Smaller regional players were not as prevalent as they were in the OCS market.

Another critical segment of the foodservice market included accounts such as grocery chains and convenience stores, which could either be free-standing or associated with gas stations. Such establishments had long sold brewed coffee to customers, but with the increasing popularity of premium coffees, they had started offering greater variety in recent years. Currently most convenience stores employed a process where an employee would brew one or two flavors of coffee at a time on a commercial brewer costing $400-500. Instead of leaving the brewed coffee on the heating element, the employee would place it in a specially designed carafe that helped retain heat and flavor. The store required at least one carafe—each priced between $60 and 90—for every flavor variety it wished to offer.

Consumer Segment

While the company had begun to formulate some preliminary plans for entering the consumer market, even the most optimistic projections had them launching a line several years down the road. MDT Advisers originally figured a consumer version of the K-Cup and brewer would be ready two to three years after the initial investment. "We all saw the potential of the consumer market from the beginning. It was a key to the deal," said Larry Kernan. "But we also feel we have an incredible business model on the commercial side, and we want to make sure *that* is executed well. I think we're looking at 2001 at the earliest for the household version."

The vast majority of coffee consumed in the U.S. is drunk at home. Folgers, Maxwell House and Hills Brothers were among the most popular brands; all were owned by multibillion-dollar international packaged goods companies. Most coffee marketed by the American megabrands was sold pre-ground in metal coffee cans, but some of the brands had produced individual portion packs similar to tea bags. These microwavable portion packs cost consumers approximately 25 cents each. Premium roasters such as Starbucks controlled a small, but growing, segment of the market for coffee consumed in the home. To gain more market share in the supermarket channel, Starbucks had recently formed an alliance with Kraft Foods. Many specialty coffee roasters were planning to sell some version of their premium coffees in supermarkets and other retail outlets.

By the late 1990s, over 80% of the coffee made at home was brewed in automatic electric drip coffee-makers, with a much smaller percentage made in percolators, espresso machines and other machines. Nearly 16 million coffee-makers were sold in the United States each year. Electric drip coffee-makers usually cost between $25 and $70. However, certain low-end models would sell for as little as $10 and high-end manufacturers such as Krupps offered units for as much as $150. Keurig management knew that developing a brewer in the $100–150 range would be a huge engineering challenge. Selling large numbers of such brewers might be an even higher hurdle. "The expensive espresso machines, bread-makers, waffle irons and juicers people have collecting dust at the back of millions of kitchen cabinets work against us," quipped Lazaris.

Marketing channels for a consumer version of the brewer and K-Cup also presented new puzzles for the company. In the OCS and foodservice markets, customers signed contracts for complete systems, which include the provision of both equipment and coffee. In the consumer markets, the choice of which brewer to purchase was totally disconnected from the choice of which coffee to buy and where to buy it. Keurig had thought of a number of options for selling brewers and K-Cups, including department stores, gourmet clubs, specialty coffee stores, direct sales events and the Internet.

Coffee Competitors

Although Keurig's management felt its coffee packaging and brewing concept was unique enough to distinguish it in the marketplace, they faced competition from several larger companies. Each was already selling brewing systems that also represented significant upgrades over the $400–500 electric drip brewers currently in millions of office break rooms and restaurants. Among the stronger competitors offering advanced product and service offerings were:

Filterfresh: Headquartered in Westwood, MA, Filterfresh was the $60 million American subsidiary of a Canadian food and drink manufacturer. Filterfresh's system kept fresh ground coffee in covered chambers inside of its brewing machine. When a user wished to brew an individual cup of coffee, a few grams of the coffee grounds would be injected along with hot water into a brewing cell. While this was a significant taste upgrade over traditional drip systems, some in the industry maintained although the cup of coffee was "freshly brewed," it was often made from ground coffee that had grown stale in the hopper due to exposure to oxygen and humidity. Each of Filterfresh's brewing units was sold to franchisees for $2000–2500. Since the brewer's introduction in the late 1980s, the company had placed 40,000 units in the U.S. and Canada (90,000 worldwide). Keurig estimated the cost of a brewed cup of Filterfresh coffee to be 29 cents.

Café System 7:   This line of brewing systems was marketed by Crane National Vendors, based in St. Louis, MO. The machine contained three hoppers that could be filled with different types of coffees or hot chocolate mix. The unit was also capable of making cappuccino, espresso and mochaccino. Like the Filterfresh system, the machine's brewing and storage chambers needed to be cleaned frequently to avoid odors and mold. In the previous five years, Crane had sold over 17,000 of its $2500 machines. It was estimated that the full brewed cost of a cup of coffee was 22 cents.

Flavia: The pioneer of portion-pack brewing technology in the late 1980's, Flavia was a division of American food giant M&M/Mars. Although it was a very successful brewing system in Europe, it had only been introduced in the U.S. in 1996. Since that time, the company had sold 2,000 of its $1200 brewers in a limited marketing campaign focused on the eastern seaboard. Flavia sold a wide variety of coffee blends and flavors in foil packs that included the coffee filter. According to Keurig management, Flavia's portion packs held 6–6.8 grams of coffee and were originally designed to produce a six-ounce serving, the size popular in Europe. Several varieties of tea and a chocolate drink were also available for the system. Flavia's machine took 23 seconds to brew a cup of coffee and then deposited used packets in an internal waste chamber. Including the lease price of the machine, the full cost of an eight ounce cup of Flavia coffee was around 39 cents (the machines sold in the U.S. were adjusted to pump two more ounces of water through the portion pack). Keurig management was impressed by the reliability of Flavia's brewer. However, Keurig did not see Flavia as the fiercest of competitors. "We've met a lot of their people at trade shows," said Lazaris. "While they're very talented, most of them are just rotating through various Mars divisions. They don't necessarily have the entrepreneurial passion for the coffee business . . . and certainly not the sense of desperation we have. This product is *everything* for us."

Trouble Brewing: Keurig's Suppliers Disappoint

Development of the K-Cup Packaging Line

In late February of 1998, Lazaris journeyed to Minneapolis to meet with a consortium of investors interested in investing up to $4.5 million in Keurig's next round of equity financing. The capital from this round of investment would be split almost equally among three main areas: equipment/tooling for the commercial market, developmental programs for the consumer market and working capital. Lazaris was very pleased with the progress as the series of meetings were coming to a close. He was almost certain Keurig's story had impressed the investor group, most of whom had experience in the food industry (several large packaged food companies were headquartered in Minnesota, and this investor group included a number of top executives).

After two days of meetings, Lazaris was preparing to fly home to Boston on Friday when he received a phone call from Mike Moore, CEO of Manufacturing Technology Systems (MTS), the Boston, MA-based company which was developing the packaging line for the mass production of K-Cups. Moore asked to meet with Lazaris on Saturday morning to discuss some urgent matters. At the Saturday meeting Moore informed Lazaris that his company would not ship the first completed packaging line—finished just days earlier—until it received an additional $180,000 payment on top of the $700,000 fixed price development and production contract for the first unit. Moore explained that the machine had cost MTS far in excess of what had been planned and that the increased costs were caused by Keurig's design modifications during development. "I told Mike he was making absolutely *the* wrong decision. I told him that I would have to inform my board about this and that it would be hard to do business together in the future," said Keurig's CEO. Lazaris offered to go to arbitration as provided for in the MTS-Keurig contract, but Moore refused. According to Lazaris, Moore felt that control over the machine gave him considerable leverage. Lazaris knew he could not let MTS delay the delivery of the first unit, which was already supposed to be on-site at Green Mountain.

During the next week, Kernan and Lazaris were able to broker an agreement where MTS would ship the packaging line with the proviso that it would be disabled after one month if no understanding was reached on the additional payment. While their goals were the same, this was a stressful time for the relationship between Kernan and Lazaris because of their different approaches to the problem. "Larry spent a great deal of time working with me on this . . . it was a high pressure situation. He was really upset. Larry saw it as an ethical issue and was not about to submit to extortion to solve a short term problem," said Lazaris. "But as management for the company, we had a different perspective because our futures were invested in Keurig, and we were more willing to negotiate a middle ground so we could move forward with the product launch." Moore sensed the divide between Kernan and Lazaris, taking advantage of it in order to drag out the negotiations. Kernan took the lead in the final discussions and agreed to make a payment to MTS in exchange for immediate control over the machine.

After the packaging line was delivered to Green Mountain and installed in March, Keurig needed to quickly order two more packaging lines to support the installed base of brewers they projected for the next eight months. Without additional K-Cup manufacturing capacity, Keurig's distributors would not be able to satisfy customer demand, leaving the system's roll-out in jeopardy. As soon as Moore had held back delivery of the first packaging line, Sweeney started a search to identify alternative vendors. Because the packaging line was still in a working prototype stage, there was no assurance that another vendor could complete the next two lines on-time and on-budget.

Despite the rocky relationship with MTS, Keurig left open the possibility of contracting with them for the next two lines before making the switch to another vendor. Moore expressed to Lazaris a strong interest in building more packaging lines. While the first machine was initially quoted at $550,000, MTS proposed to build future machines for $900,000 each. Lazaris knew that price was not even close to the other quotes that Sweeney had obtained. After being informed that they were too high to even be considered, MTS later revised its bid down to around $700,000. In its amended bid, MTS asserted that it was the only company which could deliver the machines in the time frame required by Keurig. The original Keurig-MTS contract made all intellectual property associated with the development of the packaging line the property of Keurig. Although Lazaris' firm controlled the plans, any new vendor would still have to conduct a great deal of reverse engineering of the first packaging line in order to successfully execute the project. Lazaris knew that if he changed suppliers, a great deal of time would be lost as the new company came up the learning curve. In April Keurig management assessed their sourcing options going forward if they did not stay with MTS.

Pilgrim: Located in Boston, Pilgrim was a well-respected and relatively large producer of specialized industrial machinery, including packaging lines. While Pilgrim's references were excellent and their interest level was high, some Keurig managers were hesitant to award the contract to them because they lacked an internal machine shop. If non-standard parts had to be ordered from an outside machine shop, the production process could be delayed. Pilgrim bid $575,000 for each machine. Lazaris estimated that delivery timetables for new packaging units would be pushed back two months because Pilgrim would need to develop engineering schematics and purchase some new production equipment.

Quantum Industries: Though experienced in developing packaging solutions for the food industry (they developed the packaging line for Act One microwave popcorn among other products), Minnesota-based Quantum had lost a great deal of business recently. The lost accounts had negatively impacted the company's financial stability and forced layoffs. Quantum did, however, possess a large production facility and operated its own machine shop. Its Owner/President had taken a personal interest in the packaging line and had traveled to Green Mountain with two engineers to assess the scope of the project. In its proposal, Quantum stressed that it had the engineering talent to not only reverse engineer the first packaging line, but also the space to build several machines simultaneously. Quantum bid $500,000 for each machine, but would take three months longer than MTS to deliver the next automated production line. Some Keurig managers were reluctant to award the contract to them because of their financial instability and the fact that they were located 1500 miles away.

Amalgamated Technologies: Another Minnesota company with experience in the food industry, Amalgamated's factory usually buzzed with activity. Their capabilities, reputation and cutting edge equipment garnered them a great deal of business. In initial conversations, however, Keurig management did not feel that their modest potential first order—two units over the next six months—generated a great deal of excitement at Amalgamated. They bid $525,000 for each machine and would take four months longer than MTS to produce and deliver the next packaging lines.

Kernan and Lazaris also needed to assess how the MTS issues would impact the new round of funding they were trying to complete by June. Several months of work had been spent attracting the Minnesota investors, and Keurig could not afford another delay in either its fundraising or the roll-out of its packaging system.

Brewer Brouhahas

As the first K-Cups rolled off of Green Mountain's new packaging line, Lazaris and Sweeney became very concerned about the quality of the brewers its supplier—Vandelay Industries—was producing. Keurig had estimated that each packaging line could support around 1500 brewer placements, assuming an average of 43 cups per brewer per day. The roll-out schedules for brewing units and packaging lines were totally linked to each other. In addition, Keurig needed to maintain its timetable if it wished to continue to develop its network of distributors and premium roasters.

Vandelay, based near Wellesley, MA, was a designer and manufacturer of precision oceanographic instrumentation. The company was searching for new types of projects because of cutbacks in the defense industry. On the initial order of 1000 units, brewers were passing through Vandelay's final quality checks with loose screws and parts literally falling out. Sweeney was concerned about the defect rate since repairing brewers in the field would cost $50-100 per service call. In addition, Keurig management felt their supplier was trying to squeeze additional money out of the project beyond its initial low bid. Vandelay consistently approached Sweeney about getting additional money per unit any time there was any alteration in the product or manufacturing process. When the supplier submitted its bid for the next order of 1000 units—needed by the fall—its price per unit increased significantly. "They went from $789 per machine to a bid of $825. This wasn't exactly the 'learning curve effect' we'd been hoping for," said Sweeney.

As soon as Sweeney had finished identifying alternative packaging line vendors, he was on the road searching for a new contract brewer manufacturer. During this process Keurig was approached by another possible manufacturer, one which had heard about the brewer project from a member of the Minnesota investment group. Lakeland Instruments, located in Rochester, MN, was a manufacturing operation started by former IBM employees to take on outsourced projects for their former company. Most of the company's work emphasized technology products such as disk drives, cellular telephones and medical instruments. Lakeland Instruments also owned a *maquiladora* plant in Mexico. Lakeland bid $680 per brewer and stated that it had the capabilities to easily support over 10,000 brewers per year. But even with that volume, Keurig would only be 3% of Lakeland's volume. Some of Keurig's management was concerned that Keurig would not get Lakeland's attention if there were problems in the roll-out.

As alternatives to Vandelay and Lakeland, Sweeney had identified a contract manufacturer in Poughkeepsie, NY that had similar capabilities to Lakeland, but also possessed its own sheet metal fabrication shop. The company, Pilla Manufacturing, had experienced financial difficulty recently. As a highly leveraged and thinly traded public company, Pilla was in desperate need of sales to cover the fixed expenses of its facilities and machinery. Pilla quoted $700 per unit but made it clear they would lower the bid if that was what it would take to get the business.

Lazaris and Sweeney were extremely disappointed in Keurig's relationships with its main suppliers. "We either needed to get our current suppliers to approach us like we were partners for the long-haul, or make a change," said Lazaris. "We felt like these guys just didn't get it. Didn't they see that this could all turn into something huge eventually?"

EXHIBIT 1 | Keurig Senior Management Team (as of Summer 1998)

Nicholas Lazaris: President/CEO and Board Member

Nicholas Lazaris, age 47, has been President/CEO and Board Member since February 1997. From 1996 to 1997 he was Division Vice President of Office Specialists, responsible for the Tech Specialists division, a $12 million contract technical staffing company. From 1989 to 1995 Mr. Lazaris was President/CEO and Board Member for MW Carr, a $20 million upscale picture frame manufacturer and importer. From 1985 to 1989 Mr. Lazaris worked in a variety of positions for Barry Wright Corporation. ($200 million NYSE diversified manufacturer) including Division VP Marketing, Division VP Finance and Corporate Director of Business Development. From 1977 to 1985 Mr. Lazaris served in a variety of positions for the State of West Virginia including Chief of Staff for Governor John D. Rockefeller IV for four years. From 1975 to 1977 he worked as a CPA for Ernst & Young. He received his BS from MIT in 1972 and his MBA from Harvard Business School in 1975.

Christopher Stevens: Vice President, Sales and Marketing

Christopher Stevens, age 45, has been Vice President Sales and Marketing since February 1996. From 1995 to 1996 Mr. Stevens was Executive Director of The Sports Museum of New England, a nonprofit institution, and from 1994 to 1995 he was Vice President of Sales for the Consolidated Group, a third-party insurance administrator. From 1991 to 1994 he worked as Executive Vice President and General Manager for United Liquors, Ltd. From 1982 to 1991 Mr. Stevens worked for Anheuser-Busch, Inc. as Division Manager of the New England Division. From 1975 to 1982 he worked for Procter & Gamble. Mr. Stevens played for the Belgian Professional Basketball Club from 1974 to 1975. He received his BA from Notre Dame in 1974 and completed the Executive Education Program at Columbia Business School in 1994.

Richard Sweeney: Vice President, Operations and Engineering

Richard Sweeney, age 50, is co-founder of Keurig and, after being involved at Keurig on a part-time consulting basis from 1993 to 1996, he became Vice President Operations and Engineering in January 1996. From 1991 to 1996, Mr. Sweeney operated Liberty Resources, Inc., a manufacturing management consulting firm. From 1986 to 1990, he was Vice President Manufacturing for Canrad-Hanovia Inc., a manufacturer of scientific and UV lighting. From 1981 to 1986, Mr. Sweeney worked as Vice President Manufacturing for V-M Industries, a manufacturer and importer of upscale consumer appliances including espresso machines. From 1970 to 1980, Mr. Sweeney worked in various manufacturing management positions for White Machine Company. He received his BS from NJIT 1982 and his MBA from Fairleigh Dickinson University in 1986.

Source: Keurig Business Plan.

EXHIBIT 2 | Keurig Products

K-Cup being inserted into brewing chamber (above)

Keurig Brewer (left)

Keurig's eight varieties of coffee with plastic K-Cup display (right).

EXHIBIT 3 | Description of Keurig Products and Technology

Keurig K-Cups

The K-Cup is a pre-measured coffee portion pack containing on average 9.5 grams of freshly roasted and ground coffee and a conical shaped filter paper that holds the coffee. The current K-Cup container is a nonproprietary plastic cup comprised of three layers of co-extruded-thermoformed plastic. The inner layer of plastic is FDA certified polyethylene, the middle layer is oxygen impermeable EVOL plastic, and the outer layer is polystyrene for structural stability. The filter is welded to the upper rim of the cup, filled with the appropriate amount of coffee based on bean type, purged with nitrogen to reduce oxygen content to below 3% to preserve freshness and extend shelf life, and then sealed with a metal foil and plastic lid.

The K-Cup seals in the freshness of freshly roasted and ground specialty coffee by preventing oxygen and moisture contamination via the impermeable EVOL layer of plastic. The quantity of coffee and the grind vary with each type of offered coffee to maximize flavor as determined by quality control specialists ("cuppers"). The expected shelf life for K-Cups is six months. An individual K-Cup is used to produce a 10-ounce cup of coffee.

Keurig contracted with Manufacturing Technology Systems, Inc. (MTS) of Boston, Massachusetts in February 1997 for the design, development and production of a K-Cup production line capable of producing 100 K-Cups per minute. The unit has passed acceptance testing in Boston and was installed at Green Mountain Coffee Roasters in Vermont in March 1998.

The roaster's K-Cup cost structure is currently estimated at 13 cents for coffee, packaging materials and direct labor.

Keurig Brewers

The Keurig commercial market brewer is a compact, counter-top unit measuring 10 inches wide, 16 inches tall and 19 inches deep. Its four key subassemblies insure that the 30-second brewing process maximizes the taste profile of each K-Cup variety. The subassemblies include the following: (1) water heating and storage in preparation for brewing; (2) hot water pumping to generate Keurig's unique pressurized brewing process; (3) the brew head servosystem which engages, punctures, injects hot water and extracts brewed coffee from the K-Cup and then disposes of the K-Cup automatically; and, (4) the printed circuit board which provides the machine intelligence to operate and monitor the performance of the Keurig brewer.

EXHIBIT 4 | Profile of Green Mountain Coffee Roasters, 1998

Revenues:	$55.8 million
Assets:	$24.6 million
Employees:	321
Market Value:	$25.8 million

Publicly traded on NASD since 1993, symbol GMCR.

Green Mountain produces over 60 varieties of coffees. It distributes its products (coffees and accessories) through both wholesalers and direct mail programs. The company has over 5,000 wholesale customers such as supermarkets, convenience stores, restaurants, hotels and specialty food shops. Mobil convenience stores account for 16% of Green Mountain sales. Other large customers have included Hannaford Brothers supermarket, Delta Airlines and Business Express Airlines. Green Mountain operated several retail establishments until they were closed in 1998.

Green Mountain employs roasting software to ensure product quality, with a specific program for each flavor and type.

Green Mountain Income Statement
$ Millions

Fiscal year ending September	1997	1996
Sales	42.9	33.4
COGS	27.2	20.6
SG&A	13.7	10.6
Other	0.2	0
Total Expenses	41.1	31.2
Interest Expense	−0.5	−0.4
Income Taxes	−0.3	0.3
Income After Taxes	1.5	1.4

Source: OneSource.

EXHIBIT 5 | Patent for Keurig Brewing Technology

United States Patent   [19]

[11]	**Patent Number:**
[45]	**Date of Patent:**

[54] BEVERAGE FILTER CARTRIDGE

[75] Inventors:

[73] Assignee: Keurig, Inc., Waltham, Mass.

[21] Appl. No.:

[22] Filed:

[51] Int. CL^5 . . . . A47J 31/24; A47J 31/14

[52] U.S. CL . . . . 99/295; 99/302 R;
99/317; 426/77; 426/433; 426/435

[58] Field of Search 426/77, 82, 473, 477,
426/479, 482, 435, 112, 433; 99/279, 295, 300,
302 R, 302 P, 304, 306, 307, 316, 317, 321

[56]   **References Cited**

U.S. PATENT DOCUMENTS

240,402	4/1881	Gee
346,278	7/1886	Halstead
370,141	9/1887	Hobbs
845,968	3/1907	Murray
1,168,544	1/1916	Newlin
1,302,483	4/1919	Vierling
2,997,940	8/1961	Pecoraro et al.
3,199,682	8/1965	Scholtz
3,260,190	7/1966	Levinson 99/295
3,403,617	10/1968	Lampe 99/295
3,579,351	5/1971	Wege et al. 426/82
3,615,708	10/1971	Abile-Gal

3,754,463	8/1973	Vernooy 99/302
3,971,305	7/1976	Daswick 426/77
4,204,966	5/1980	Morgan, Jr.
4,321,139	3/1982	Auclair
4,417,504	11/1983	Yamamoto
4,584,101	4/1986	Kataoka 426/82
4,859,337	8/1989	Woltermann
4,981,588	1/1991	Poulallion 426/77

Primary Examiner—Robert W. Jenkins
Attorney, Agent, or Firm—Samuels, Gauthier & Stevens

[57]   **ABSTRACT**

A beverage filter cartridge includes an impermeable pierce-able base having a predetermined shape and an opening at one end; a self-supporting wettable filter element disposed in the base sealingly engages with the opening in the base and has a form different and smaller than the predetermined shape of the base so that the filter element diverges from the base and divides the base into two sealed chambers, a first chamber for storing an extract of the beverage to be made, and a second empty chamber for accessing the beverage after the beverage outflow from the filter has been made by combining a liquid with the extract; and an impermeable pierceable cover sealingly engaged with the opening in the base to form an impermeable cartridge.

16 Claims, 4 Drawing Sheets

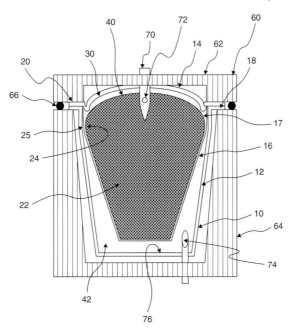

(continued)

EXHIBIT 5 | Patent for Keurig Brewing Technology (*continued*)

3

a combination of polystyrene, ethylene vinyl alcohol and poly-ethylene. There is a self-supporting wettable filter element disposed in the base and sealingly engaged with the lip or rim of the base. The filter element may be made of a lightweight, two-phase heat sealable paper of cellulosic and synthetic fibers. The synthetic fibers may be PVC or polypropylene so that they are compatible with the material of the base and are therefore easily sealed to the base using heat, ultrasonic energy or microwave energy. In addition, the material of the filter is such that the filter is totally self-supporting. Even when it is wetted, it will not collapse or sag against the inner walls of the base. The filter can have the shape of a cone, a truncated cone, or a triangular prism which fans out and blends into a circular base. The filter is smaller than and non-congruent with the base so that it diverges and divides the base into two sealed chambers. In the first chamber there is stored the extract of the beverage such as coffee that is to be made, and the second chamber has a substantial empty volume for accessing the beverage outflow from the filter after the beverage has been made by combining liquid with the extract. This enlarged volume of the second chamber enhances the filter flow since the filter is not in contact or in any way blocked by the walls of the base, and water can flow through the entire filter surface. In addition it provides ample room so that a penetrator which perforates the base will not injure or sacrifice the integrity of the filter itself. There is an impermeable pierceable cover which is sealingly engaged with the opening in the base to form a complete impermeable cartridge. The cover, which is made of the same material, also has a flange or rim or lip which extends radially outwardly and engages the mating rim on the base. The cover is typically domed convexly outwardly, so that for example when coffee is piled in the cartridge in the form of a typically rounded mound, the placement of the cover does not displace the coffee powder so that it leaks or sprays outwardly and degrades the quality of the seal along the flanges. In addition, the convex shape provides an increased rigidity for the cover so that it provides resistance to produce a clean penetration when a needle or other penetrator is inserted through it into the first chamber. It is through this penetration that the hot water is delivered to the coffee. The penetration in the base provides the exit for the liquid coffee to be dispensed.

There is shown in FIG. 1 a cartridge 10 according to this invention which includes base 12, cover 14, and filter 16. Base 12 includes opening 17 and outwardly facing flange rim or lip 18 similar to the rim 20 on cover 14. Base 12 has the shape of an inverted truncated cone, as does filter 16, which contains coffee powder 22.

Filter 16 can be drawn or formed as a monolithic structure or may be made in a pattern and then rolled and sealed such as at seam 26. Filter 16 is sealingly engaged at its edge 24 with the adjacent surface 25 of base 12. Cover 14 may have a domed portion 30, as seen more clearly in FIG. 2, which extends outwardly beyond opening 17 and rims 18 and 20. This domed shape 30 not only nicely accommodates the rounded top 32 of the coffee 22 in filter 16, but it also provides an extra measure of rigidity for cover 14 so that it can present

4

a firm opposition resulting in a clean penetration from a needle or other penetrator in an automatic brewing machine or other type of machine. The seal formed between filter 16 and base 12 creates two chambers, chamber 40 in which coffee 22 is stored, and chamber 42 which receives the outflow from filter 16. Chamber 42 is produced by the fact that filter 16 is smaller and divergent, although often similar in shape to base 12. This larger chamber 42 enhances the outflow from filter 16 and also provides ample room for a penetrator to penetrate base 12 without puncturing filter 16. Although filter 16 is shown as a truncated conical structure, this is not a necessary limitation of the invention, as it might as well be what might be generally called a triangular prism, filter 16*a*, FIG. 3A, having sloping sides 50, 52, a reduced apex 54, and a generally circular base 56. In an alternative form, filter 16*b*, FIG. 3B, may take the form of a cone whose reduced apex 54*b* is simply the tip of the cone. In either case the apices 54, 54*b* would be spaced from the bottom of base 12.

Cartridge 10 is well adapted for use in an automatic machine such as a coffee brewing machine where it will be delivered to and gripped in a housing 60, FIG. 4, which has an upper part 62 and a lower part 64 sealingly engaged at seal 66 by a portion of the machine not shown. Part 62 includes a penetrator or needle 70 which penetrates domed cover 14 to provide pressurized hot water through hole 72 to coffee 22 in filter 16. A second penetrator or needle 74 is pushed through the bottom 76 of base 12 to receive the outflow of the coffee beverage and dispense it to a cup or container.

Although specific features of the invention are shown in some drawings and not others, this is for convenience only as some feature may be combined with any or all of the other features in accordance with the invention.

Other embodiments will occur to those skilled in the art and are within the following claims:

What is claimed is:

1. A beverage brewing apparatus comprising:

a housing having a first component defining a brewing chamber with an access opening, and a second component which may be opened to afford access to said brewing chamber via said access opening, and which may be closed to coact in sealing engagement with said first component to close said access opening;

an impermeable pierceable cartridge removably received in said brewing chamber via said access opening, said cartridge being internally subdivided by a filter element into first and second cartridge chambers;

a beverage extract contained in said first cartridge chamber;

liquid inlet and outlet means extending through said housing into said brewing chamber to penetrate through said cartridge into communication respectively with said first and second cartridge chambers; and

means for injecting liquid into said first cartridge chamber via said inlet means for combination with said beverage extract to produce a liquid beverage, said filter element being adapted to accommodate passage therethrough of said beverage into said second cartridge chamber for outflow through said outlet means.

EXHIBIT 5 | (continued)

5

2. The beverage brewing apparatus of claim 1 wherein said cartridge comprises a base having a predetermined shape and an open end, said filter element being disposed in said base, sealingly engaged with said open end and having a form different and smaller than said predetermined shape of said base so that said filter element diverges with respect to said base to divide said base into first and second cartridge chambers; and a cover sealingly engaged with said open end.

3. The beverage brewing apparatus of claim 2 wherein said cover is domed convexly outwardly.

4. The beverage brewing apparatus of claim 2 wherein said base and cover include mating flanges coacting in sealing engagement to define an exterior rim surrounding said cartridge.

5. The beverage brewing apparatus of claim 4 wherein said rim is held between the first and second housing components when said second housing component is closed.

6. The beverage brewing apparatus of claim 2 wherein said inlet and said outlet means penetrate said cartridge when said second component is closed.

7. The beverage brewing apparatus of claim 2 wherein said filter element and said base are both generally truncated non-congruent cones.

8. The beverage brewing apparatus of claim 2 wherein said filter element is generally a cone shape and said base is generally a truncated cone shape.

6

9. The beverage brewing apparatus of claim 2 wherein said filter element is a triangular prism with a circular base and said base is a truncated cone shape.

10. The beverage brewing apparatus of claim 2 wherein said base is made of polystyrene, ethylene vinyl alcohol and polyethylene.

11. The beverage brewing apparatus of claim 2 wherein said cover is made of polystyrene, ethylene vinyl alcohol and polyethylene.

12. The beverage brewing apparatus of claim 2 wherein said filter element is made of lightweight two phase heat sealable paper of cellulosic and synthetic fibers.

13. The beverage brewing apparatus of claim 12 wherein said synthetic fibers are PVC or polypropylene.

14. The beverage brewing apparatus of claim 2 wherein filter element terminates in a reduced apex portion spaced from the bottom of said base to accommodate penetration of said outlet means into the lower portion of said base without subjecting said filter element to penetration.

15. The beverage brewing apparatus of claim 1 wherein said liquid inlet means protrudes through said second housing component, and said liquid outlet means protrudes through said first housing component.

16. The beverage brewing apparatus of claim 1 wherein said filter element is arranged within said cartridge to avoid penetration by said inlet and outlet means.

• • • • •

EXHIBIT 6 | U.S. Market Sizes for Coffee and Brewer Sales

All figures are in billions of dollars per year unless otherwise noted.

| | Coffee Type | | Brewing Equipment |
	Commodity	Specialty	
Consumer Channels*			
Supermarket	$3.50 B	$0.64 B	$ 0.45 B
			90,000 K installed base
			15,000 K units/year
Gourmet food stores	*	$1.56 B	
Commercial Channels**			
Food service	$3.86 B	$1.50 B	$0.09 B
			1,700 K installed base
			170 K units/year
Office coffee	$2.33 B	$0.26 B	$0.07 B
			1,937 K installed base
			138 K units/year
Vending	$ 1.35 B	*	$0.11 B
			377 K installed base
			38 K units/year
TOTAL	**$11.04 B**	**$3.96 B**	**$0.72** B

* Connotes insignificant amount.

** Retail prices. In form of packaged coffee grind or beans.

***Retail prices. In form of brewed coffee.

Source: Keurig Business Plan.

EXHIBIT 7 | U.S. Coffee Purchase and Consumption Statistics

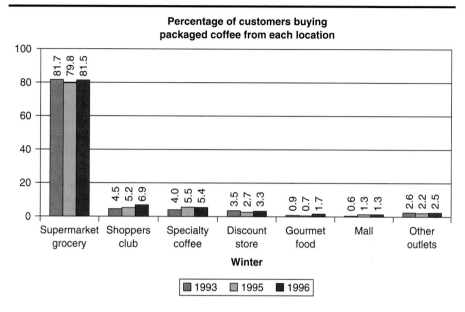

Percentage of customers buying packaged coffee from each location

Winter

■ 1993   ▨ 1995   ■ 1996

Source of Coffee by Geographic Region—1996 Winter

	Total U.S.	Northeast	North Central	South	West
Supermarket/grocery	81.5%	80.7%	84.2%	85.1%	73.9%
Specialty coffee store	5.4	5.6	3.7	3.0	10.5
Shoppers club	5.9	3.7	2.7	4.6	13.4
Discount store	3.3	2.1	3.9	3.4	3.6
Gourmet food store	1.7	1.1	1.2	1.8	2.6
Mail	1.3	1.1	2.6	0.7	1.0
Other outlets	2.5	2.5	1.5	2.5	3.4

(continued)

EXHIBIT 7 | U.S. Coffee Purchase and Consumption Statistics (*continued*)

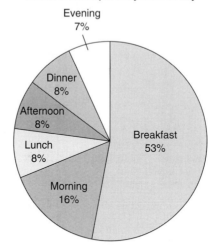

Coffee consumption by time of day

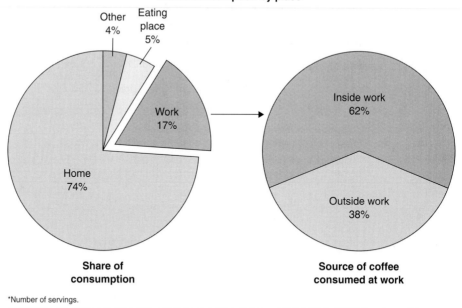

Coffee consumption by place*

*Number of servings.

Source: Keurig Business Plan.

Crunch

Doug Levine, founder and Chief Executive Officer of Crunch Fitness, hustled along New York's 5th Avenue, trying to get back to his office before the ominous clouds above him opened up into a full-blown rainstorm. It was an unusually warm day for February, so he neglected to take a jacket when he walked to the Crunch gym on Lafayette Street, just nine blocks away from the company's small but bustling corporate headquarters. The main office had just received an order of new brochures and Levine had decided to deliver them to the gym himself so he could catch up with the staff. Knowing that New York street vendors jacked up their umbrella prices just before a storm, he decided to pick up the pace instead of getting ripped off.

As he speed-walked down the street, he thought about the decision he would soon have to make about a very large acquisition in Atlanta, one which could add six clubs to his company's current base of nine. How could the company—which had always pursued a "bootstrap" financial strategy—pay for the proposed acquisition? Was it a problem that the clubs were a totally different format from those his company had experience operating? Perhaps most importantly, how would the members of the largely suburban chain react to Crunch's hip, irreverent brand and fitness concept? Deep in thought, he did not even notice that he was drenched when he arrived back at his office for a meeting with his lawyers to discuss the possible deal.

Creating Crunch

In 1988, 29 year old Doug Levine left his job as a securities trader in San Francisco. Over the next two years, he moved to New York, engaged in a series of odd jobs, studied acting and attended aerobics classes regularly. "Aerobics was really a craze at the time," he remembered. "I got an idea that *guys* would really get into aerobics in a big way very soon. I was going to be out in front of that wave. We would attract a base of female participants, who would in turn attract a large number of male clients. That was the big play."

Jeremy B. Dann, Research Associate and MBA '98, prepared this case under the supervision of Professor Paul Marshall as the basis for class discussion rather than to illustrate either effective or ineffective handling of an administrative situation.

Levine found a 1288 square foot aerobics studio in the East Village and set about establishing his new fitness concept. He christened the aerobics studio "In-Shape," but was soon getting threatening letters from another fitness facility which was already employing that name. Levine was forced to change the name of his business and decided to go with his second choice: "Crunch." Since Manhattan was already flooded with aerobics studios, he tried to create a concept which would set his club apart from his competitors. Levine asked the aerobics instructors working in the studio to develop routines which were unlike anything else people were doing at the time. "Our differentiated programming was key," he said. "The total goal was to make it a very theatrical experience." Crunch's early programs were an eclectic mix, indeed. "Hip Hop Aerobics" featured a live rap performance in each class. The company introduced "Cyked," a unique blend of yoga and cycling. Finally, Crunch's "Co-Ed Action Wrestling" let aspiring Hulk Hogans body slam their way to fitness. Several local journalists—many of them East Village residents and Crunch regulars—wrote articles about the innovative programming at Levine's aerobics studio. After flattering pieces in the *New York Times*, *New York Magazine* and other media outlets, Crunch was beginning to attract attention throughout Manhattan and in other parts of the country as well.

Levine wanted to move out of Crunch's tiny basement studio because of the tremendous crowds his top aerobics classes were drawing. "Even though we were doing well, we pleaded poverty and held up the rent. It was a common practice in New York," recalled Levine. He helped the landlord find a tenant for the space and then moved his operation to a 5000 square foot facility on Charles Street in 1991. Crunch had already opened another location in 1990, a 3500 square foot space on St. Marks Place which also included a small weight room.

If You Build It . . .

The 1990s saw America's aerobics craze fade, but fitness remained an important part of people's lives and the number of people with health club memberships continued to increase (see **Exhibit 1** for statistics on the health club industry). In spite of Crunch's growing notoriety, male customers did not flock to the studio in the numbers Levine predicted. With the ebbing of aerobics' popularity, Levine knew he would never be able to attract that demographic with his current fitness concept. Additionally, other aerobics studios in Manhattan had refined their offerings, becoming stronger competitors in a market which many believed had topped out.

Crunch charged customers on a per visit basis, so revenues were more variable than Levine would have liked. Scheduling both clients and instructors became a nightmare as he tried to eke out more revenue from his studios. His company had built its reputation by employing the top aerobics instructors in the city, but they came at a high price, around $50–80 per hour. "I was beginning to see real problems with both my overall strategy and the economics of my business model," said Levine. "Labor costs were out of control. We needed a concept which utilized more exercise equipment, but I had this irrational fear of treadmills. I couldn't bring myself to spend $5000 on a machine for a long time, but I paid aerobics instructors $750 a week without even thinking twice."

Levine realized that he needed to transform Crunch's underlying business concept. He believed that while the fitness industry would remain dynamic, his company had placed too much emphasis on the group exercise model. "Aerobics had given us our start and developed the personality of the clubs, but we were going to have to get into the gym business, putting more investment into weights and cardiovascular exercise equipment," he stated. "The original concept was to create an aerobics studio which would attract men. Now we were going to develop a gym that would also be a good place for women to work out." Crunch's first major foray into the "gym" business came via acquisition. In 1994, it paid $900,000 to acquire a struggling operation on Lafayette Street which was a part of the World Gym franchising system (see **Exhibit 2** for a breakdown of industry competitors). In the first year it owned the gym, Crunch added over $350,000 of new equipment and other enhancements to a club which already had an installed base of $500,000 worth of equipment. Next, while the facility originally had four phone lines, Levine increased the number to 20 in order to provide a higher level of service. Finally, with three facilities in Manhattan, Levine could finally justify television advertising, a move which helped all of his gyms, but particularly the Lafayette Street location. "We were seeing our heavy investment really pay off. Revenues grew from $1.6 million per year before we bought the club to $3.2 million the first year we ran it. Over 70% of the new revenues came from women."

Crunch also saw positive results when it changed from a pay per use system to a membership-based system. The company had always operated as a "bootstrap" operation, meaning growth efforts were financed from internally generated cash rather than equity or debt investments from outside sources. "Membership dollars were just a huge windfall. I couldn't believe I hadn't figured out the economics before. We could invest in expansion and new machines by pre-selling memberships," he said.

By the beginning of 1999, Crunch owned and operated facilities in Los Angeles, San Francisco and Miami in addition to the five clubs (and one under construction) in New York. In addition, it had partnered with a giant Japanese real estate developer to build a club in Tokyo. Crunch was in the process of building new locations in Chicago, Las Vegas and Mission Viejo, CA (**Exhibit 3**).

The Crunch Brand

"This company was built on the foundation of a strong brand. It's been *the* key to our success and growth," commented Levine. "When I was in banking, I didn't learn a thing about how to manage people or how to run a facility. But I did learn about what investors pay for . . . what creates lasting value . . . and that's a strong brand."

In creating the Crunch brand, Levine tried to tie in a philosophy which he thought would set his company apart from the other players in the fitness market. "I saw the market being dominated by two types of operations. First you had the companies like Gold's Gym, which were all about huge muscles, chalk dust and body building trophies everywhere. Then there were the clubs where everyone looked like Ken and Barbie. The message was: 'If you want to look like us, get in here soon'," he said. Crunch differentiated itself with its "No Judgements" philosophy (**Exhibit 4**), which supported an environment where people could stay in shape and be entertained without the intimidation factor Levine saw in other types of clubs. "Our core demographic is in America's urban centers. Today's young people—twenty somethings—have *real* jobs with high stress. The main thing they need in a workout center is a welcoming environment where they can improve their fitness and their state of mind," commented Levine.

Small Company, National Brand

"Even as a very small company, we always tried to project a big image. We knew how to create a buzz and take advantage of it," asserted Levine. Part of this strategy included licensing the Crunch logo to fitness apparel manufacturers, who were interested in putting the innovative emblem on clothing because of the "buzz" the company had received in the national press. In the early 90s, while the company still had only two Manhattan locations, Crunch gained national brand exposure when large chains like Footlocker and Sports Authority picked up the line of licensed apparel. "It was strange. We had barely thought about setting up facilities outside of New York, and then I see kids in Phoenix, Arizona wearing our clothes," recalled Levine.

Crunch made sure it stayed in the spotlight after it garnered its first headlines by constantly introducing innovative offerings. While aerobics was no longer at the heart of the company's economics, Crunch continued to gain attention by creating unusual group exercise concepts available nowhere else. Lisa Mortman became Crunch's Director of Public Relations in 1996, after a career in political consulting. Cross-dressing aerobics instructors and Gospel Aerobics had allowed the company to ride waves of free publicity, but Mortman wanted to take it to the next level. In 1996, Crunch's innovative rollerblading aerobics class attracted coverage from model Cindy Crawford of MTV's "House of Style." A year later, when the United States Bobsled team asked if they could put fliers about an event into one of Crunch's gyms, Mortman convinced them to enter into an entirely different level of partnership. USA Bobsled and Crunch created "Bobsled Training," a fitness course taught by Olympic aspirants. Crunch members who completed the course were guaranteed a chance to try out for the Olympic team. In another instance, Mortman heard that one of Crunch's aerobics instructors was a New York City firefighter. She collaborated with that individual to create "Firefighter Training," a class where participants dressed in firefighting gear, carried heavy hoses and "rescued" weighted mannequins. "We subscribe to the 'Big Bang' theory of brand-building—as in 'Big Bang for the buck,'" she said. "Firefighting costs us $60 per week, but we got millions of dollars worth of free publicity from it. We are absolute pigs about P.R."

Crunch's advertising campaigns were unique in the industry. While most fitness chains featured models showing off their perfect biceps and toned abs, Levine's company chose irreverent, humorous themes for both TV and print ads (see **Exhibit 5** for examples of print advertisements). Crunch also fielded dozens of inquiries per week from organizations which wanted to work with the company on joint promotional efforts. This allowed Mortman to be very selective in the types of companies or events she would work with. "We like *owning* events. Unless we're going to be the title sponsor or the event is going to be televised, I say, 'So what?' Also, we never really pay for anything. You'd be amazed at what can be bought with gym memberships," said Mortman.

Projecting the Image

In 1993, a producer of exercise tapes approached Crunch about creating a set of videos featuring its aerobics instructors showcasing their unique programs. After Levine agreed, the producer presented the idea to three video distribution companies. Crunch received offers from two of the companies, but one—Anchor Bay—also wanted to produce a daily exercise program on the popular cable sports network ESPN. Anchor Bay's offer was accepted.

The Crunch-branded exercise program went on the air in 1994. Anchor Bay and ESPN shared in the advertising revenue from the half hour broadcast, seen each weekday at 9 a.m. EST on ESPN2. By 1999, the show was watched by nearly 800,000 viewers per week in the U.S. and was distributed internationally via satellite.

Pumping Up Operations

"Here we were, with a brand that looked larger than life. We had a TV show. We had licensed products selling like you would not believe all over the country. But we had essentially no corporate organization, everything was at the club level," said Levine. In early 1996, Crunch's corporate staff consisted of Levine, his assistant and a bookkeeper. All other Crunch employees resided in the company's four Manhattan clubs. The company was heavily supported by an external accounting firm, P.R. consultants and advertising agencies. But as Crunch prepared to open its fifth New York location and started the construction of its Los Angeles club, Levine felt it was time to set the stage for further growth by augmenting and professionalizing the corporate operation.

Levine leased office space just south of Manhattan's Union Square, and then set about filling it. With five years of experience in the fitness industry, Roger Harvey had been the "roaming manager" of all locations. As the new Chief Operating Officer, he would be responsible for overseeing Crunch's facilities, payroll and construction projects. Howard Brodsky became Crunch's Vice President for Sales and Marketing. He had been managing the membership sales process for a year by travelling between the four Manhattan locations. Previously, he had served as the Advertising Director for Time-Warner's cable television system in Connecticut. In the fall of 1997, Levine tapped Michael Staisil to become Vice President and Chief Strategy Officer. A 1995 Harvard MBA, Staisil's prior experiences included work with Montgomery Securities, Deloitte & Touche's consulting group and Michigan State University's offensive line (see **Exhibit 6** for selected management biographies). By early 1999, Crunch had packed 45 corporate employees in an office designed for around 25. They supported the efforts of over 1000 club employees, representing nearly 500 full-time equivalents.

Club Management

In 1999, COO Roger Harvey was "in the loop" for more decisions than he cared to be. "I've just been here so long and had such a wide range of responsibilities, I'm on contact lists for just about everything. I spend a lot of time just channeling stuff to the people here who need to deal with it," he said. Harvey's main responsibility was managing and refining Crunch's core "product": its gyms. "I spend almost 75% of my time at the clubs. It's really important to view the product as the customer does," he said.

All club general managers—generally in their mid-30s with five or more years in club management—reported to Harvey. Nearly all gym management employees at Crunch came to the company after already gaining experience elsewhere in the fitness industry. "We really should have more facilities management personnel from other industries—retail, hotels and restaurants, for example. But we have literally invested *zero* in training and development," he commented. "Any documentation we have on procedures is scattered in various places. We need to have a manual on our computer network which could be easily referenced by management and club employees. I think if we just fine-tuned our operations a little more, we would blow the other guys out of the water." Harvey felt the company's first-ever national general managers' meeting—scheduled for later in 1999—would be a big step in sharing best practices and refining procedures.

Crunch had recently upgraded and standardized the software it used to manage its health club facilities. The company worked with a fitness management software vendor to customize an information system to meet its needs. The software supported front counter check-in operations, membership sales/contract processing and billing, either via credit card or electronic funds transfer (EFT) from bank accounts. The system cost $15,000 for the corporate office and $5000 for each fitness facility. It provided a flexible, scalable solution which could accommodate Crunch's growth plans. Crunch installed another information system of sorts in all of its location. At a cost of around $20,000 per club, video cameras were placed in strategic locations to monitor desk coverage, check staff interaction with customers and support theft prevention efforts in gym retail areas. Full motion video was transmitted real-time to the corporate headquarters via the Internet.

Revenue Generation

As the company prepared to open new clubs in Las Vegas, Chicago and southern California, Howard Brodsky saw less and less of his family. It was his job to fly out in advance of these club openings and recruit a sales force who would pre-sell memberships for the clubs under construction. "It's a huge challenge. We built this company with an aggressive East Coast mentality," he said. "It's tough to go out to California and get a sales force with the same kind of attitude and approach that we have in New York." Brodksy likened sales in the fitness industry to running on a treadmill—constant turnover led the sales force to always have ambitious goals for new memberships. Crunch sales people were paid with a base salary plus commission, while other club employees received just a flat salary. "I really think there should be incentive pay club wide. It would really help in both sales and retention of existing members," said Brodsky.

Crunch positioned itself as a mid-priced, high quality fitness facility. "We want to stay in the price range of a youthful demographic, to try to keep an edge and sense of excitement in the clubs" commented Levine. "I'd like to attract the aspiring actress in New York who bounces three checks, but finally stretches and makes her membership payment." New members could either choose to pay the $800 yearly fee up-front, or go month-to-month and pay $75 by EFT (members choosing this option were also required to pay a $150 initiation fee). Presales of yearly memberships were the method of choice among many in the industry for financing new clubs and, historically, Crunch had been no exception. However, Brodsky's analysis showed that the company not only made more money from month-to-month memberships, but that people who paid via EFT were actually more likely to maintain their club membership through their first anniversary. Brodsky prioritized raising the number of members paying via EFT in 1998; the work paid off as the percentage rose from 18 to 32% by the end of the year. "But now we're building all of these new clubs, so the decision has been made to now emphasize pre-paid memberships in order to get the cash flow," he said. "I don't think it's an ideal situation for our sales and retention goals, but when your financial strategy is bootstrapping, you have to resort to measures like this."

Brodksy had enacted another major program aimed at raising the company's membership retention levels. Crunch—like the rest of the fitness industry—experienced a great deal of member turnover. In 1997, only 35% of Crunch's clients continued with the club after a period of one year. To alleviate this problem, Brodsky created a system whereby Crunch would keep in constant contact with members through "light touches"—club events, mailings and phone calls. "It continues the dialogue with the members about the benefits Crunch provides them," said Brosdky. "I distribute the retention numbers among all of the club general managers so that people can learn from the clubs who are having the most success retaining members." By the beginning of 1999, renewal levels across the Crunch system had risen to nearly 50%.

Not only did Crunch want to retain its members from year to year, it wanted them to visit the clubs as much as possible. "The model most companies in the industry espouse is: sell a lot of memberships and hope they never show up. Other clubs want to have a lot of membership revenue, but maintain low staffing and equipment costs," commented Levine. "We're introducing a whole new model. We *want* people to come because we'll sell them all sorts of ancillary services." In 1995, Crunch's non-membership revenue levels were around the industry average of 5–10%. By 1998, sales had increased dramatically. Crunch aimed to further augment these revenue streams in the future. The company wanted them to account for 50% of total revenue within two years (see **Exhibit 7** for Crunch income statement).

Personal training was Crunch's largest source of revenues outside of memberships. The company also had plans to roll out a full juice/smoothie bar concept in all of its new locations and retrofit many of the existing locations within the next few years. In addition, Crunch had been reorganizing its licensed and branded product programs. Celeste Chung, a young manager hired in 1997, spearheaded Crunch's efforts to revamp its licensing and retail operations. While early licensing efforts had increased Crunch's brand exposure, some of the products were of dubious quality. Levine had terminated the contracts of all of the company's first licensees in early 1998. Management hoped to sign up top licensees and drive sales primarily through Crunch gyms so that quality and marketing techniques could be controlled. Chung forged agreements with Canadian clothing manufacturer Roots and fashion designer Todd Oldham in order to increase garment quality and bolster the image of the Crunch line. "History proves we know how to make a product hot," she said. "Our fashion forward instructors can be our test market and models."

Setting a Strategy, Planning for Expansion

"I was hired to be the outside voice at Crunch, to try to bring a different perspective to everything," said Michael Staisil, V.P. and Chief Strategy Officer. Staisil was responsible for competitive analysis, business development, project planning and expansion/ acquisition efforts. Crunch had always been a company which emphasized "learning by doing," but Staisil and Levine agreed they would try to interject some sort of planning process into the mix. "Doug is a classic entrepreneur. Since we have very little outside funding, there's not a lot that 'controls' the CEO," said Staisil. "But now, if someone has an idea, we at least put it on paper and probably have around two days of discussion on it. That probably gets you 75% of the way there in terms of figuring out what the issues are. Then it's go or no-go."

In heading up the company's expansion and acquisition endeavors, Staisil sorted through a flood of potential deals. Because of Crunch's high profile, dozens of inquiries were made each week through real estate brokers, investment banks and even Levine's friends. "For every twenty deals we see, maybe two have the chance of becoming real. Because of the flow of offers and opportunities that come through here, we can afford to just concentrate on the best ones," he stated.

The agreement which Crunch was able to strike for its Los Angeles location was still held up by the company as its definition of a "sweet deal." Crunch was approached by Hazama, a Japanese real estate developer, in early 1996 about creating a gym in a retail project it had built on Sunset Boulevard, one of the top locales in the city. The development already included a multiplex cinema, a Virgin Record Store and a Wolfgang Puck restaurant. Hazama offered Crunch the 28,000 square foot space rent-free for two years. In addition, Crunch received a $1.8 million tenant improvement allowance, which it could use to build out the space. "The L.A location really proved our brand and our gym concept. And the best part was, we were able to build our dream gym with someone else's money," said Levine. Where Crunch's average expenditure for its existing gyms was approximately $30 per square foot, it was able to spend $110 per square foot to outfit the Los Angeles club. "With the extra resources, we could put in the highest levels of amenities and really customize the club for L.A. One of my favorite features is the peek-a-boo showers, which are back-lit and show a silhouette of people while they're bathing. Those people out in L.A. can be very uninhibited," chuckled Levine. Other Crunch clubs were being planned for such "destination" retail and entertainment venues. In Chicago, Crunch would be located in a development with the House of Blues Hotel, Michael Jordan's AMF Bowling Alley and other premiere attractions.

While fitness clubs had not traditionally been viewed as good tenants for real estate developments, new gym concepts like Crunch were beginning to change that notion. "A big part of my job is educating developers about how many synergies we bring to a project. The top builders are beginning to see that Crunch drives a ton of traffic to a retail site," said Staisil. Levine elaborated, "I think premiere leisure destinations are *the* anchor of the future. Nordstrom's, Macy's and other traditional retailing anchors are going to lose their pre-eminence because the Internet and other things will lower their ability to pull in customers. We will be among the top tier of the new anchors because of our strong brand and the centrality of fitness in people's lives."

On the basis of its experience in developing clubs—especially the newer sites outside of Manhattan—Crunch had been designing a prototype gym which would help it roll out its unique fitness concept more rapidly. While the company still wanted the flexibility to customize its clubs to the distinct tastes of any market, certain elements would be standardized based on best practices it had learned from its existing facilities and input from architectural and design firms. For instance, Crunch was gathering ideas on the features for a new front counter concept. In its current clubs, check-in, membership sales, retail and vending operations were often spread out in different parts of the facility. This led to either inadequate staff coverage of some operations or increased personnel costs to ensure someone manned each post. Crunch aimed to develop a "Mother Station" which would include all customer service and transaction functions within a confined area. "It's the small details that really enhance the club experience. Here's another example: we're introducing heated floors in the shower areas. We were spending a fortune on expensive marble for the floor and then covering it up with ugly rubber mats because the condensation made it slippery. The heated coils get rid of the condensation," said Levine. "Bringing everyone together to talk about our ideal prototype club has represented a real managerial challenge for us. You really have to integrate a lot of ideas dealing with design, fitness operations, back of house, retail and other issues."

Tinkering at the Top

While Levine felt he had significantly upgraded Crunch's management capabilities throughout 1996 and early 1997, he still wanted to fill some gaps he saw in his team. "We were learning a great deal about how to run a company in the $35–50 million range, but I wanted to set us up for that next level of growth, to get us to $100 million and beyond," he said. "The goal was to find people who already had management experience in companies with at least a couple hundred million dollars in sales." He decided that in the next year, he would recruit two additional managers: a president and a chief financial officer.

In June of 1997, Levine began his search for a president for Crunch, someone with whom he would split top level responsibilities. After five months of meetings with executive search firms and interviews with candidates, Levine and the existing managers decided to hire Norman Storm[1] as Crunch's number two. Storm had been the head of marketing for Ray Ban sunglasses, more than doubling that brand's sales during his tenure. Following his successful stint with Ray Ban, Storm became President of Gucci USA and served in that position for five years. "We got the guy we wanted: someone who knew how to grow the sales of strong consumer brands and could professionalize and institutionalize many aspects of our business," said Levine.

---

[1]Name and past companies have been disguised.

Levine and Storm next sought to find a chief financial officer. Most of the company's financial work up until this point had been handled by the outside accounting firm or by Levine himself (calling on his training as an investment banker). The only significant external source of financing for the company had been an equity purchase by Westchester, NY–based Marlin Capital. Marlin had paid $3 million for a 10% ownership stake in the company in mid-1997. Levine had declined all other offers from other venture capital firms—all of whom wanted to place at least $10 million in the company. He had also resisted the advances of large numbers of investment bankers who wanted to handle an IPO for Crunch. By early 1998, however, Levine and Storm knew that the company would soon need to tap into the equity or debt markets to finance its ambitious growth agenda.

Storm had retained an executive search firm to find a CFO for Crunch. Storm, Levine and other Crunch managers met with many candidates suggested by the headhunter. But one candidate had both the financial experience and the fitness industry background that made him a strong fit. Wally Brooks worked for Authentic Fitness for 10 years, the last 18 months as Chief Financial Officer. Authentic Fitness manufactured and marketed swimwear and other athletic apparel under the Speedo brand name. "I was really excited about this opportunity from the get-go. The people I met from the management team were great—really enthusiastic. Plus, I thought this would be an opportunity to do something totally different from what I had been involved with before," said Brooks. "There was the potential for real upside if you were willing to dig in and work hard." Brooks joined Crunch in June of 1998.

By the Fall, some friction had started to develop at the top of the company. Storm's style was not fitting in well in the entrepreneurial environment at Crunch. "Norm was used to working in companies where you had a receptionist and a secretary. At Crunch, top managers really have to get their hands dirty and do a lot of stuff for themselves," commented Harvey. "Being a 'President' at this company was not at all like the position at his previous companies." Top managers and other Crunch employees had been used to dealing directly with Levine on almost every issue the company faced. Even after Storm joined the firm, many Crunch veterans would short-circuit the new reporting structure and go to Levine for advice or sign-off on key projects. Brodsky recalled that Storm was even taken out of the loop on issues that should have been his strong suit. "It even got to the point where licensing deals weren't going through him anymore even though he had *years* of experience in that area," said Brodsky.

Eventually, Crunch's managers came to the conclusion that the selection of Storm as President of the company had not been the right choice, in part because the job's requirements and list of responsibilities had not been developed correctly. "Basically, Norm did not have any specific expertise that Doug did not have, so people kept going to Doug," said Brooks. "Doug's a guy who was used to doing everything at the company—signing checks, running errands for the gyms, whatever it took—so he just naturally dove in again. Things got pretty muddled." In November of 1998, Levine and Storm met to discuss the situation. "We both acknowledged things were not working out. He and I had negotiated a severance package prior to his joining, so we could quickly deal with his departure," said Levine. "I think all in all it was a pretty amicable parting."

A Bunch of Choices for Crunch

Creating the Organization of the Future

Storm's departure highlighted the fact that Crunch was still not organized to handle the growth spurt it was expecting in 1999 and 2000 (see **Exhibit 8** for the company's organization chart as of February 1999). "Pretty much every employee in this company feels that he or she is a direct-report to Doug," said Staisil. "He still has his hands in almost everything and is the center of information flows in the company. As a manager, you *kind of* know what other folks are working on, but we have to improve the communication." Staisil was working on a reorganization plan which would more precisely group the company's key functions under some of Crunch's veteran managers. The new structure would give Levine six direct-reports. Levine would also manage a "brand team" which would be responsible an assortment of public relations, marketing and advertising issues.

Doug Levine planned to hire a new president to help him manage the company. He aimed to fill the position by the third quarter of 1999. As he pondered the search for the new president, he assessed the managerial gaps he saw in the company. "I know what has to be done to promote Crunch *the brand,* but I have zero experience as a manager. We need someone with operations and systems experience to help develop Crunch *the company,*" he said. Levine planned to meet with an executive search firm in the next few days to discuss the position and possible sources for candidates.

The March on Atlanta

Crunch had been in discussions for several months with SportsLife, an Atlanta-based company, about acquiring its chain of six fitness facilities. The clubs pulled in approximately $17 million worth of revenue each year; if Crunch purchased them, it would represent an immediate 60% increase in the size of the company.

Atlanta had been at the top of the list of cities Crunch was targeting for its next round of expansion. Some within the company felt this would be the perfect acquisition because the company would immediately have a critical mass of clubs in a very desirable market. The company's expansion plans called for it to build a "flagship" facility in several markets and then fill in to get greater coverage within those cities later. Then, advertising and other city-specific costs could be spread over more clubs and a larger potential membership base. The Atlanta deal would give Crunch a set-up in this market that it might otherwise take years to develop through either new construction or piecemeal acquisitions. The SportsLife clubs—which currently boasted around 70,000 members—had lower renewal rates than the average within the Crunch system. There was an opportunity to increase the Atlanta clubs' profitability significantly if they could just be upgraded to Crunch's standard. Management felt it could raise the clubs' retention rates from their current level of 30% and drive non-membership revenue streams up to the level of other Crunch locations within a year.

While there was a great deal of excitement within Crunch about the potential of increasing the company's size dramatically with one fell swoop, there were a number of aspects of this potential acquisition that made it far from a sure thing. First, although two of the locations fit the "urban profile" Crunch sought for its clubs—proximity to restaurants, shopping and entertainment venues—most of them were suburban gyms. Additionally, the clubs were an entirely different format from those Crunch was used to operating. The prototype gym Crunch had been developing for several months called for a 30,000–40,000 square foot facility. SportsLife's clubs were mostly around 60,000 square feet in size and one of them was over 100,000 square feet. These "megaclubs" featured amenities such as Olympic-sized swimming pools and several courts for basketball, squash and racquetball. None of Crunch's current clubs had any of these facilities. Next, the demographic profile of the members in Atlanta was about five to seven years older than the core customer for Crunch's other gyms. Some managers wondered whether the company's unique, irreverent style would appeal to this membership base. Finally, SportsLife's current billing structure was very different than the one Crunch used. The Atlanta clubs had traditionally charged $1200 for a three-year membership contract which included a guaranteed renewal rate of $25 per month after the contract expired. SportsLife members sometimes set up installment plans for their memberships, but the contract required them to pay the full amount unless they proved they were moving 30 miles outside of Atlanta. In that case, they could terminate their memberships for a $300 fee.

Crunch and SportsLife had discussed the cost of the possible acquisition. The elements of the deal on the table were as follows:

- $2.5 million cash payment
- $2.0 million in debt assumed by Crunch
- $3.5 million through an "earn-out" agreement whereby the current owners would help manage the clubs for an additional three years.

Levine and Harvey estimated that Crunch would need to spend at least $300,000 in the short term on each club to upgrade key aspects of the facilities and operations (see **Exhibit 9** for SportsLife income statement).

A Plethora of Possibilities

Michael Staisil's "To Do" file veritably overflowed with projects the company was considering. "The Crunch brand is extremely powerful and very versatile, we feel," he said. "We want to take advantage of that to pursue as many avenues of growth as possible."

Crunch.com: The company was investigating leveraging the power of its brands to create "the ultimate fitness portal on the Internet." Whether pursued independently or in partnership with an established Internet player, the site would provide health and fitness information to members and non-members alike. Additionally, the site would market Crunch-branded products and potentially other products and services such as adventure travel packages.

International Expansion: Licensed products and the Crunch workout show had driven a fairly high awareness of the Crunch brand overseas. The company could either choose to develop its own facilities internationally, develop a franchise system or craft a licensing agreement like it did in Tokyo. "This could be a really good opportunity for us, especially Europe. I mean, Europe is the world's ultimate leisure culture," commented Staisil.

Crunch-Plex: Several of the company's gyms were co-located with movie theatres in major retail/entertainment developments. Celeste Chung and other Crunch managers worked with a project team from the Wharton School at the University of Pennsylvania to assess the potential of creating a combined fitness and theatre concept, one which could be rolled out in new markets. "We think there are a lot of synergies between a strong fitness operation and a theatre, prime among them parking," said Levine. "We would never be a major theatre chain in terms of ticket sales, but we have great demographics for ancillary revenue streams such as vending and advertising."

Retail and Restaurant Concepts: Crunch was investing a great deal of time and energy augmenting the retail presence within its fitness centers, both for food/beverage and Crunch-branded products. Some felt that Crunch could take its retail concepts outside of its gyms, allowing for quicker roll-out in more markets. Ideas included a "Crunch Café" which would serve smoothies and dishes geared toward the health conscious crowd.

Guarding "The Brand"

There was no shortage of projects bouncing around the corporate headquarters. Other ideas included developing "Crunch for Kids," franchising the Crunch concept domestically and managing existing fitness facilities for universities and other institutions. The Crunch brand was undeniably hot; potential partners clamored to work with the company on all of these projects. Some managers within the company worried about being stretched too thin in the resource constrained environment which was a part of any bootstrap financing strategy. Others worried about the integrity of Crunch's main asset: its brand. "I just don't want this company to become like a Hard Rock Café or Planet Hollywood, which lost their way as they expanded," said P.R. Director Lisa Mortman. "I look at Starbucks as a model. I admire the depth they've given to their brand even as they've grown."

Levine, too, spent a great deal of time mulling over how growth would affect the public's perception of the Crunch brand. As he sat in the meeting on the pending Atlanta acquisition, he pondered, "Could the brand get lost in suburbia if we do the Atlanta deal? Would an Internet project enhance or water down Crunch's strong image? Do I have any dry T-shirts in my office?"

EXHIBIT 1 | Health Club Industry Statistics

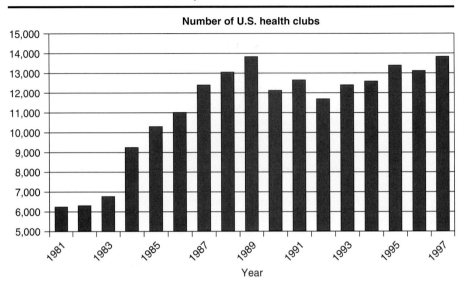

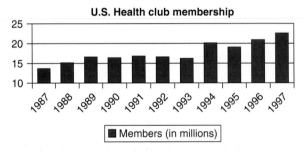

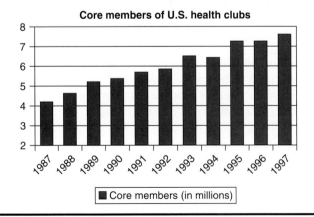

Note: Core members use their club 100+ days per year.

Source: International Health, Racquet and Sportsclub Association; Crunch.

EXHIBIT 2 | Health Club Operators

U.S. Fitness Industry - Competition	CRUNCH 1998 AOP SITUATION ANALYSIS	

National

	High-End	Mid-Priced	Low-End
Owned	Club Corporation of America The Sports Club* *Tennis Corporation of America*	Crunch Fitness International	Bally Total Fitness* YMCA Four Corners - Livingwell Lady *Powerhouse*
Managed	Club Sports International (CSI) *Tennis Corporation of America*		Health Fitness Physical Therapy*
Licensed			World Gym Gold's Gym *Powerhouse*

Regional

	High-End	Mid-Priced	Low-End
Owned	Western Athletic Clubs (west) EBC (mid-west) Lakeshore Athletic Club (midwest) Equinox (east) New York Health and Racquet (east)	Q-Club (south/west) Fitness USA (midwest) F.C.A.-Life Time Fitness (midwest) Sportslife (south) *Town Sports Int.-TSI (east)* *Sport & Health Inc. (east)* *Fitness Company Management (east/south)*	24 Hour Fitness (west) Lucille Roberts-only women (east) World Fitness (south)
Managed	Four Seasons Resort & Club (south)	American Leisure Corp (east/south) *Town Sports Int.-TSI (east)* *Sport & Health Inc. (east)* *Fitness Company Management (east/south)*	

* Public Company

Crunch_aop3.PPT

- 37 -

Note: "Low-End" clubs usually charge $400–500 per year, "Mid-Priced" around $700–900 per year, "High-End" $1000 and above per year.

Source: Crunch Annual Operating Plan.

EXHIBIT 3 | Crunch Locations

Location	Size (In square feet)	Members
New York City		
1109 Second Avenue (at 59th Street)	44,000	6500
162 West 83rd Street (off Amsterdam)	25,000	6100
404 Lafayette Street (between 4th and Astor)	40,000	8500
54 East 13th Street (off Broadway)	18,000	6100
152 Christopher Street (at the Archive)	12,000	3300
144 W.38th Street (at Broadway)	25,000	(Opens summer '99)
Los Angeles		
8000 Sunset Boulevard	27,000	6800
San Francisco		
1000 Van Ness	30,000	2200
South Beach, Miami		
1253 Washington Avenue	15,000	3000
Mission Viejo		
The Kaleidoscope Center	30,000	(Opens summer '99)
27741 Crown Valley Parkway		
Chicago		
House Of Blues Hotel	30,000	(Opens summer '99)
Las Vegas		
Tropicana & Decatur	32,000	(Opens winter '99)
Tokyo		
CRUNCH Omotesando	15,000	2500
4-2-34 Jingumae Sibuya		

Source: Crunch.

EXHIBIT 4 | Crunch "Vision" and "No Judgements" Philosophy

Vision

CRUNCH will emerge as a leading national brand of mid-priced fitness clubs catering to urban, 25–34 year olds. CRUNCH is unique among fitness clubs, because it is more than just a gym. It is an innovative, bold and vibrant expression of fitness, fashion, music, entertainment and style.

Philosophy

We at CRUNCH warmly welcome and accept people from all walks of life, regardless of shape, size, sex or ability. You don't have to be flawless to feel at home in at CRUNCH.

We don't care if you're 18 or 80, fat or thin, short or tall, muscular or mushy, blonde or bald or anywhere in between.

CRUNCH is not competitive, it is non-judgmental, it is not elitist, it does not represent a kind of person.

CRUNCH is a gym; a movement that is growing as we continue to perfect our ability to create an environment where you won't feel self-conscious or worry about what others think.

At the heart of CRUNCH's very core stands a tremendously experienced and energetic staff offering members the finest instructors with personalities and imaginations who make working out fun.

Source: Crunch Annual Operating Plan.

EXHIBIT 5 | Crunch Print Advertisements

Source: Crunch.

EXHIBIT 6 | Management Profiles

Douglas H. Levine has been Chairman and Chief Executive Officer of the Company since its inception in 1989. From 1986 to 1988 Mr. Levine was employed by and was the founding partner in charge of sales and trading of Volpe and Covington, a West Coast investment banking firm (the predecessor of Volpe, Velty, & Company). Prior thereto, Mr. Levine worked in the sales and trading department at the predecessor of Prudential Securities in New York and for the Montgomery Securities in San Francisco. Mr. Levine received a B.A. in economics from Tufts University.

Wallis H. Brooks has been Senior Vice President, Chief Administrative Officer and Chief Financial Officer of the Company since June of 1998. From 1988 to 1998, Mr. Brooks was the Senior Vice President and Chief Financial Officer of the Authentic Fitness Corporation. He also served as Vice President, Controller, and Treasurer of the Warnaco Group Inc.. Prior thereto, Mr. Brooks was employed at Arthur Young & Company (the predecessor to Ernst & Young). Mr. Brooks was also employed at Aetna Life & Casualty, performing internal audits, and Shapiro, Rosenthal, & Co. CPAs, (the predecessor to Blum Shapiro & Co., CPAs), as the staff accountant. Mr. Brooks received a B.S. in accounting at the University of Connecticut. He is a certified public accountant.

Roger Harvey has been Vice President and Chief Operating Officer of the Company since August 1993. Prior thereto Mr. Harvey was employed as a full-time consultant regarding fitness and programming for health clubs in the Northeast for The Fitness Company. Mr. Harvey was also previously employed as a personal trainer and fitness counselor for two local fitness clubs as well as the Executive Fitness Center at the World Trade Center, where he was promoted to Fitness and Programming Director. Prior thereto, Mr. Harvey was working as a physical therapist assistant and as the branch office manager for Metropolitan Physical Therapy. Mr. Harvey received a B.S. in Kinesiology from the University of Michigan.

Howard Brodsky has been Vice President of Marketing and sales for the Company since April 1995. Mr. Brodsky was previously employed at Time Warner Cable as Advertising Sales Manager, responsible for in-house television advertising and production. From 1993 to early 1994, Mr. Brodsky worked for AT&T as International Account Manager. From 1989 to 1993, Mr. Brodsky was the regional marketing/sales director for Nutri System Corporation. From 1987 to 1988, Mr. Brodsky was employed as an account executive at WABC Radio. Mr. Brodsky received a degree in Communications from Pennsylvania State University.

Michael Staisil has been Vice President and Chief Strategy Officer for the Company since 1997. From 1996 to 1997 Mr. Staisil was employed as a consulting manager for Deloitte & Touche LLP. Prior thereto, Mr. Staisil was employed as an investment banker at Montgomery Securities (now NationsBanc Montgomery Securities). From 1990 to 1993, Mr. Staisil worked with purchasing management at Ford Motor Company. Mr. Staisil received both his M.B.A. from Harvard Business School and his B.A. from Michigan State University with honors. At Michigan State University, Staisil was an Academic All-American football player and Rose Bowl champion in 1988.

Celeste V. Chung has been the Director of Business Development for the Company since April 1997. From 1996 to early 1997, Ms. Chung was employed at he Walt Disney Company in the Strategic Planning Group. Prior thereto, Ms. Chung was an investment banker at Morgan Stanley & Co., Incorporated (now Morgan Stanley Dean Witter & Co.) in the Mergers, Acquisitions and Restructuring Department. Ms. Chung received a B.S. in Management Science from the Massachusetts Institute of Technology.

Andrew J. Moger has been the Director of Development for the company since 1998. From 1995 to 1998, Mr. Moger was employed at Morton's Restaurant Group as a Food and Beverage Controller and, later, as the Corporate Project Manager responsible for opening all domestic and international locations. Prior thereto, Mr. Moger was the General Manager of Dish restaurant in NYC and Sfuzzi restaurant in Philadelphia. Mr. Moger received a B.A. in Political Science from Washington University in St. Louis.

Lance Diamond has been Vice President of Accounting and Information for the Company since January 1997. Mr. Diamond began his employment at Crunch as the Accounting Manager/Controller in September 1995. Mr. Diamond was employed at Ernst and Young since October 1991 in the audit department. He worked as a Senior Accountant managing client relationships in the Entertainment and Healthcare industries. Mr. Diamond received a Bachelor of Business Administration (B.B.A.) with a concentration in Accounting from the University of Michigan school of Business Administration.

Source: Crunch.

EXHIBIT 7 | Crunch Financial Statements

INCOME STATEMENT

	1997	1998	Projected 1999
REVENUE			
Membership revenue	14,666,298	17,277,299	24,984,094
Personal training	1,699,275	4,975,460	7,994,774
Other revenue	1,873,614	3,261,165	4,086,027
Net revenue	18,239,187	25,513,924	37,064,895
COST OF REVENUE			
Cost of member services	7,982,386	10,572,481	19,241,236
Cost of training	1,188,171	3,238,381	4,814,253
Cost of goods sold	477,069	707,952	828,299
Cost of revenue	9,647,626	14,518,814	24,883,788
SELLING, GENERAL & ADMINISTRATIVE EXPENSES	5,386,252	6,479,621	8,331,405
EBITDA	3,205,309	4,515,489	3,849,702
OTHER EXPENSE			
Depreciation and amortization	1,812,478	1,273,813	2,649,000
Interest/other income (expense)—net	(236,713)	(227,132)	(790,890)
INCOME BEFORE PROVISION FOR INCOME TAXES	1,156,118	3,014,544	409,812
PROVISION FOR INCOME TAXES	125,610	1,296,254	176,219
NET INCOME	1,030,508	1,718,290	233,593
ADJUSTED EBITDA			
EBITDA	3,205,309	4,515,489	3,849,702
Change in deferred rent	842,923	690,839	2,417,813
Change in deferred revenue	1,055,693	1,768,629	4,286,798
ADJUSTED EBITDA	5,103,925	6,974,957	10,554,313

EXHIBIT 7 | (continued)

CONSOLIDATED BALANCE SHEETS	1997	1998
ASSETS		
Current assets		
Cash	2,538,758	1,644,524
Accounts receivable	299,393	706,822
Inventory	207,323	332,949
Prepaid expenses	146,543	133,546
Deposits w/ vendors	194,213	0
Deferred membership costs	529,656	794,643
Deferred income taxes	236,012	676,185
Total current assets	4,151,898	4,288,669
Property and equipment—beginning	8,398,946	8,398,946
Property and equipment—additions	0	5,948,372
Accumulated depreciation—beginning	(1,918,611)	(1,918,611)
Accumulated depreciation—current	0	(1,460,452)
Goodwill	581,531	1,131,106
Investment in subsidiairies	0	0
Other intangible assets—net	310,350	591,265
Security deposits	236,985	1,005,593
Deferred income taxes	240,426	1,007,839
TOTAL ASSETS	**12,001,525**	**18,992,727**
LIABILITIES AND STOCKHOLDERS' EQUITY (DEFICIT)		
Current Liabilities		
Accounts payable and accrued expenses	1,368,665	2,640,234
Customer deposits	11,100	0
Income taxes payable	251,723	1,429,419
Total current liabilities	1,631,488	4,069,653
Deferred revenue	8,740,031	10,412,832
Deferred rent	1,645,398	2,314,114
Long term debt	0	1,240,670
Stockholders' equity (deficit)		
Preferred stock 7%	3,106,056	3,000,000
Common stock	489,600	525,138
Net income—current	0	2,766,033
Accumulated deficit—beginning	(3,611,050)	(5,335,713)
Stockholders' equity (deficit)	(15,394)	955,458
TOTAL LIABILITIES AND STOCKHOLDERS' EQUITY (DEFICIT)	**12,001,525**	**18,992,727**

Source: Crunch.

EXHIBIT 8 | Crunch Organizational Chart

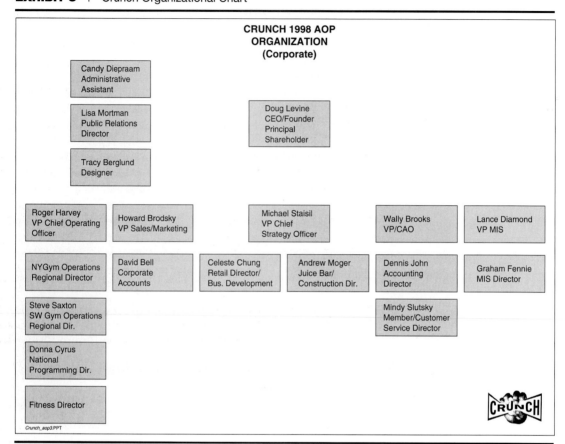

Source: Crunch Annual Operating Plan.

EXHIBIT 9 | SportsLife Financial Statements

INCOME STATEMENT		
	1997	**1998**
REVENUE		
Membership revenue	14,910,745	15,400,365
Personal training	992,237	1,335,019
Other revenue	505,463	425,845
Net revenue	16,408,445	17,161,229
COST OF REVENUE		
Cost of member services	10,882,701	10,516,366
Cost of training	0	1,006,076
Cost of goods sold	0	0
Cost of revenue	10,882,701	11,522,442
SELLING, GENERAL AND ADMINSTRATIVE EXPENSES	4,162,500	4,689,215
EBITDA	1,363,244	949,572
OTHER EXPENSE		
Depreciation and amozrtization	730,151	719,777
Interest/other income (expense)—net	(387,468)	(332,076)
INCOME BEFORE PROVISION FOR INCOME TAXES	245,625	(102,281)
PROVISION FOR INCOME TAXES	245,000	0
NET INCOME	625	(102,281)
Adjusted EBITDA		
EBITDA	1,363,244	949,572
Change in deferred rent	0	0
Change in deferred revenue	693,000	927,072
	2,056,244	1,876,644

(*continued*)

EXHIBIT 9 | SportsLife Financial Statements (*continued*)

CONSOLIDATED BALANCE SHEETS		
	1997	**1998**
ASSETS		
Current assets		
Cash	915,210	868,569
Accounts receivable	6,315,130	6,592,000
Inventory	0	0
Prepaid expenses	24,544	20,419
Deposits w/ vendors	0	0
Deferred membership costs	0	0
Deferred income taxes	0	0
Total current assets	7,254,884	7,480,988
Property and equipment—beginning	7,465,374	7,465,374
Property and equipment—additions	0	641,034
Accumulated depreciation—beginning	(5,167,488)	(4,832,890)
Accumulated depreciation—current	0	(719,777)
Goodwill	0	0
Investment in subsidiairies	0	0
Other intangible assets—net	0	0
Security deposits	149,103	260,841
Deferred income taxes	0	0
TOTAL ASSETS	**9,701,873**	**10,295,570**
LIABILITIES AND STOCKHOLDERS' EQUITY (DEFICIT)		
Current Liabilities		
Accounts payable and accrued expenses	1,668,340	1,496,908
Customer deposits	0	0
Income taxes payable	16,000	247,969
Total current liabilities	1,684,340	1,744,877
Deferred revenue	0	14,728,740
Deferred rent	141,961	129,228
Long term debt	3,274,390	3,303,191
Stockholders' equity (deficit)		
Preferred stock 7%	0	0
Common stock	1,271,500	1,271,500
Net income—current	0	(102,281)
Accumulated deficit—beginning	3,329,682	(10,779,686)
Stockholders' equity (deficit)	4,601,182	(9,610,467)
TOTAL LIABILITIES AND STOCKHOLDERS' EQUITY (DEFICIT)	**9,701,873**	**10,295,570**

Source: Crunch.

PART 3

Assembling Intellectual, Human, and Financial Resources

As suggested in previous sections, most entrepreneurial ventures start with little more than an idea and the accumulated experience and wisdom of the entrepreneur. Turning that idea into a real business requires that the entrepreneur assemble a collection of resources to pursue that opportunity. Thus, a hallmark of the entrepreneurial process is "bridging the resource gap." Certainly, getting money is a part of this, but the intellectual and human resources required are equally important and less fungible. The chapters in this section describe some of the tools and frameworks for thinking about financial and non-financial resources, and the cases offer up an opportunity to apply some of those ideas.

CHAPTER 6

The Legal Protection of Intellectual Property

In recent years, the world's major economies have become considerably more knowledge-based. High value-added, knowledge-intensive industries such as software and information services businesses have grown at the expense of resource-based and commodity businesses. The rationale for this trend is clear: such knowledge-intensive industries offer superior opportunities to create sustainable competitive advantage and superior economic returns.

As the U.S. economy has become more knowledge-intensive, legal minds have grappled with the issue of intellectual property: Who owns an idea? How can valuable knowledge and information be protected?

This note will address the various categories of protection afforded by the law, describe the nature of what can be protected, and discuss how that protection is achieved.

Intellectual Property

The area of intellectual property has challenged the legal system for hundreds of years, and continues to do so. Common law has historically protected property rights of individuals and corporations. But the area of intellectual property presents challenges to the legal system. If someone stole a piece of physical property—like your wedding band—it would be fairly easy to prove: that individual would have the ring, and you would be without it.

Yet, how can you tell when someone has taken an idea or a concept? A copy of a software program does not diminish the physical attributes of the original, only the economic interests of the owner. Intellectual property issues are particularly complex in situations where an individual is working on some state-of-the-art process for his

This note was prepared by Lecturer Michael J. Roberts as the basis for class discussion. It is based upon an earlier note HBS No. 384-188 prepared by Michael J. Roberts under the supervision of Professor Howard H. Stevenson.

employer. During the course of developing the design, the employee has some "inspiration" which was outside the scope of the project's original bounds. Does this idea belong to the employer or the employee? Does it matter whether the inspiration occurred on the company's premises or while the employee was at home in the shower? Could the employee continue to work for the employer, but set up an independent business to exploit the idea?

A special system of patent law and patent court system was developed to deal specifically with these questions. Recently, however, intellectual property issues have arisen outside the bounds of traditional patent and trade secret law. The legal system is currently in the midst of grappling with these problems, and recent (1995) legislation has attempted to clarify certain issues.

Intellectual Property and the Law

Historically, it has been a specific goal of U.S. public policy to create the incentives required for the progress of technology. One of the means to this end has been through the system of patents and copyrights. These classes of intellectual property have arisen out of the statutes of the United States government, which are, quite literally, the laws of the United States as passed by Congress.

They include "titles" such as: Title 11-Bankruptcy; Title 23-Highways; Title 39-Postal Service; and Title 50-War and National Defense.

Each of the "Titles" lays down the law relating to the subject at hand, as well as the administrative systems the U.S. government will put in place to support each of the areas. There are two titles specifically relating to intellectual property: Title 17-Copyrights; and Title 35-Patents.

Patents and copyrights receive protection directly under this statutory framework, but the law in these areas is not governed exclusively by the language of the U.S. Code itself. Through their application and interpretation of the statutes in individual cases, judges define (and, indeed create) relevant legal standards. Such "common law," or judge-made law, adapts the patent and copyright laws to modern circumstances (short of constitutional amendments to the statutes themselves).

Out of common law principles have grown other areas of law which address intellectual property issues. These areas include trademarks, trade secrets, and confidential business information. Each of these topics will be explored in detail.

Patents

Patents are issued by the U.S. Patent and Trademark Office. There are three specific types of patents:

- Utility Patents: for new articles, processes, machines, etc;
- Design Patents: for new and original ornamental designs for articles of manufacture; and
- Plant Patents: for new varieties of plant life.

It is important to understand the concept of a patent. A patent *does not* grant an individual exclusive rights to an invention. The inventor *already* has that exclusive right by dint of having invented the device in the first place; he/she can merely keep the invention a secret and enjoy its exclusive use. Rather, the government grants the inventor the "negative right" to exclude others from making or using the invention. This right is granted in exchange for placing the information in the public domain.[1]

For instance, let's assume that the electronic calculator was a patentable invention, and that Mr. Sharp was issued a patent on the device. Now, let us further assume that the idea of a checkbook holder containing an electronic calculator was also patented, and that Mr. Chex was issued a patent on this invention. Mr. Chex would have the right to prevent others including Mr. Sharp from manufacturing this device. However, Mr. Chex *could not* produce his article without the consent of Mr. Sharp. In the event that patent infringement does occur, the patent holder can sue in civil court for damages. Should the patent holder become aware of potential infringement before the actual infringement occurs, he/she can sue for an injunction to prevent the infringement from actually occurring.

As mentioned, these kinds of legal battles occur in the civil courts. The purpose of the patent court system is to mediate patent claims. For example, when a patent claim is published in the *Patent Gazette,* others could come forward and challenge the patentability of the invention in the patent court system. One basis of challenge is for another inventor to claim that he/she was actually the first inventor. For this reason, it is recommended that inventors keep a daily record of their progress in a notebook. These notes should record the inventor's progress, and be signed and witnessed on a daily basis. In the event of a challenge, such a record will prove invaluable.

The three types of patents each cover different kinds of intellectual property, and are governed by different regulations.

Utility Patents: A utility patent is issued to protect new, useful processes, devices or inventions. Utility patents are issued for a term of 20 years from date of application. First, what constitutes a patentable "invention"? The invention must meet several requirements:[2]

— It must fall within one of the statutory categories of subject matter. There are four brand classes of subject matter: machines, manufacture, composition of matter, and processes.

— Only the actual, original inventor may apply for patent protection. In the case of corporations, for instance, the patent, when issued, is always granted to the individual and then *assigned* to the corporation.

— The invention must be new. That is, it will be considered novel if it is:

  • not known or used by others in the U.S.;

  • not patented or described by others in a printed publication in this or a foreign country;

---

[1]David A. Burge, *Patent and Trademark Tactics and Practice* (New York: John Wiley & Sons, 1980), p. 25.

[2]Illinois Institute for Continuing Legal Education, *Intellectual Property Law for the General Business Counselor* (Springfield, IL: Illinois Bar Center, 1973), pp. 1–16 through 1–24.

- not patented in this country;
- not made in this country by another who had not abandoned, suppressed, or concealed it.

— The invention must be useful, even if only in some minimal way.

— The invention must be nonobvious. If the invention has been obvious to anyone skilled in the art, then it is not patentable.

Finally, even if an invention meets all of these requirements, a patent can be denied if the application was not filed in a timely fashion. Specifically, if you used, sold, described in print, or attempted to secure a foreign patent application *more than one year prior* to your U.S. application, the patent will be denied.

The process of obtaining a patent is quite laborious. Patent attorneys, who specialize in the area, will draft the patent application which includes specific claims for the patentability of the invention. After several iterations of discussions with the patent office, some or all of the claims may be approved. This process frequently takes two years or longer.

Following acceptance of the patent by the Patent Office, a general description of the invention is published in the *Patent Gazette*. Interested parties may request the full patent from the Patent Office for a very nominal fee.

During the time between application for a patent and its issue, the invention has "patent pending" status. In some ways, this offers more protection than the actual patent. The invention will not be revealed by the government during this time, and others may be afraid to copy the invention for fear of infringing on the forthcoming patent.

Design Patents: A design patent protects the nonfunctional features of useful objects. Design patents are issued for 14 years. In order to obtain a design patent, the following requirements must be met:[3]

- Ornamentality—the design must be aesthetically appealing and must not be dictated solely by functional or utilitarian considerations.

- Novelty—the design must be new. The same criteria used for a utility patent will be applied here.

- Nonobvious—the design must not be obvious to anyone skilled in the art. This is a difficult standard to apply to a design, and is quite subjective.

- Embodied in an article of manufacture—the design must be an inseparable part of a manufactured article.

Plant Patents: A plant patent is attainable on any new variety of plant which that individual is able to reproduce asexually. The new plant must be nonobvious. A plant patent is issued for a term of 20 years.

Copyrights

Copyright protection is afforded to artists and authors, giving them the sole right to print, copy, sell, and distribute the work. Books, musical and dramatic compositions, maps, paintings, sculptures, motion pictures and sound recordings can all be copyrighted.

---

[3]Burge, pp. 137, 138.

To obtain copyright protection, the work must simply bear a copyright notice which includes the symbol © or the word "copyright," the date of first publication, and the name of the owner of the copyright.

Copyrighted works are protected for a term of 50 years beyond the death of the author.

Trademarks, Service Marks, and Trade Dress

A trademark is any name, symbol, or configuration which an individual or organization uses to distinguish its products from others. A service mark is such a name which is used to distinguish a service, rather than a tangible product.

Trademark law is *not* derived from statutes of the Constitution, but is an outgrowth of the common law and service dealing with unfair competition. Unfair competition is deemed to exist when the activities of a competitor result in confusion in the mind of the buying public.

There are several regulations which govern the proper use and protection of trade- and service marks.[4] The scope of protection under the law is a function of the nature of the mark itself.

- Coined marks—a newly coined, previously unknown mark is afforded the broadest protection, e.g., Xerox as a brand of copier, Charmin as a brand of toilet tissue.

- Arbitrary marks—a name already in use, and applied to a certain product by a firm, but without suggesting any of the product's attributes, e.g., Apple Computer, Milky Way candy bars.

- Suggestive marks—a name in use, but suggesting some desirable attribute of the product, e.g., Sweet'N Low as a low-calorie sweetener, Wite-Out correction fluid.

- Descriptive marks—a name which describes the purpose or function of the product. Descriptive marks cannot be registered until, over time, they have proven to be distinctive terms, e.g., "sticky" would probably not be approved as a trademarked brand name for glue.

- Unprotectable terms—generic names, which refer to the general class of product. Escalator, for instance, once a trade name, is now a generic term for moving staircases. One could not introduce a new brand of orange juice and call it "O.J."

In order to maintain a trademark, an owner must continue to use it and protect it. In this vein, some consumer product companies routinely produce and sell a few hundred items of several brand names which they have trademarked and wish to protect, but are not in normal production. Similarly, Coca-Cola has a crew of agents who routinely order "a coke" in establishments which do not serve Coca-Cola. If they are served a soda, they prosecute. In this way, they can maintain that they have attempted to keep their brand name from becoming a generic. Aspirin, Cellophane, Zipper and Escalator, are all names which lost their trademark status due to failure of their owners to protect the usage of the term.

---

[4]Burge, p. 114.

Until a trademark is registered with the Patents and Trademark Office, it is desirable to use the ™ symbol after the name of a product, SM for services. After registration, the legend ® should be used.

Trade dress is a term that refers to the look and feel of a retail establishment. Just as the courts have sought to protect the value businesses have built up in a brand name, they have been asked to protect the distinctive "look and feel" of certain retail concepts. In a recent example, for instance, one Mexican restaurant chain successfully sued a "knock-off" of the concept, arguing that the imitator had copied the unique trade dress of the original concept, unfairly trading on the value created by the concept's originator.

Trade Secrets

A trade secret is typically defined as any formula, device, process or information which gives a business an advantage over its competitors. To be classified as a trade secret, the information must not be generally known in the trade.

One cannot, by definition, patent a trade secret, because the patent laws require that the invention be fully disclosed.

One advantage of a trade secret is that the protection will not expire after the 20-year term of the patent. Coke, for instance, maintains its recipe as a trade secret rather than patent it. Yet, should the information become public knowledge, their advantage could disappear quickly, and the inventor would have no claim on the process because it had not been patented.

Finally, should a firm decide to maintain a patentable advantage as a trade secret, and should another firm independently discover and patent that invention, this "second" inventor will have the right to collect royalties or force the "first" inventor to cease patent infringement. For this reason, many corporations routinely "defensively patent" and publish inventions so that others cannot.

In order for a company to maintain trade secret status for advantageous information, the company must keep the information secret and take precautions to keep it secret. These precautions include:

- Having certain policies relating to secret information.
- Making employees sign confidentiality and noncompete agreements.
- Marking documents "confidential" or "secret."

Confidential Business Information

The courts have also seen fit to protect a class of information less "secret" than a trade secret, but which is nonetheless confidential. The key here is that the information is disclosed in confidence, with the clear understanding that the information was confidential. A contractual obligation is established in which the receiver of the information agrees to treat it as confidential, and to use it only in furtherance of the objectives deemed appropriate by the owner. Even if the information is in the public domain, if the recipient derives some value from the confidential disclosure, he/she can be held liable for claims of unjust enrichment. There are several cases, for instance, where an inventor disclosed an idea, the recipient searched out the idea in *existing* U.S. patents, found the idea was already the subject of a patent, and bought that patent from the holder. The courts held that he had to give the patent to the submitter of the disclosure because of the confidential nature of their relationship.[5] One class of information that is commonly treated in this way, for instance, is a company's customer list.

Employees' Rights

Much of the law in this arena has evolved in an attempt to protect the rights of the enterprise. This has always been balanced, however, by the employee's right to earn a livelihood in the *best* potential source of livelihood. For instance, the courts would protect my right as an atomic engineer, to make a living *as an atomic engineer,* not merely earn a wage as a waiter or a bartender.

When a relationship between an employee and employer is severed, it is often the content of the written documents that will govern who has rights to what. Employment contracts, confidentiality, nondisclosure and noncompete agreements all come into play. For this reason, prospective employees are well advised to read these documents carefully, and negotiate, rather than merely signing all of the papers which are typically associated with the first day on the job.

An employee can bargain away some of his/her rights in this area by signing inventions agreements, noncompete contracts or employment agreements. However, the courts will not let an employee bargain away his/her fundamental right to earn a living from the best potential source.

If an employee signed an agreement which the courts found to be overly restrictive, the entire agreement would be thrown out. It is this fact which gives rise to the lawyer's advice that "It is better to sign an unreasonable employment agreement than a reasonable one."

There are three dimensions to the reasonableness test that the courts apply to employment agreements:

- time horizon;
- geographic scope;
- nature of employment.

For instance, an employment contract which required an employee not to compete for 6 months, in the state of New York, as a designer of petroleum process facilities might be viewed as reasonable, while an agreement which specified a time horizon of one year and a geographic area of the United States would probably be viewed as unreasonable.

Summary

In summary, it is clear that the body of legal knowledge in the intellectual property area is evolving rapidly. Yet, the processes which the law prescribes remain vitally important; in this area in particular, dotting the "i's" and crossing the "t's" is key. Whether it

---

[5]Illinois Institute for Continuing Legal Education, pp. 6–9, 10.

be keeping notebooks and records, filing patent claims or reading the fine print on an employment contract, it is hard to overemphasize the importance of understanding the detail.

In order to gain sufficient command of the relevant body of law, specialized legal counsel is called for. In an area which is changing so rapidly, one cannot rely on prior practices and "industry standard policies" for protection.

Bibliography

American Bar Association. *Sorting Out the Ownership Rights in Intellectual Property: A Guide to Practical Counseling and Legal Representation.* American Bar Association, 1980.

Burge, David A. *Patent and Trademark Tactics and Practice.* John Wiley & Sons, 1980.

Gallafent, R.J., N.A. Eastway, and V.A.F. Dauppe. *Intellectual Property Law and Taxation.* Oyez Publishing Ltd., 1981.

Illinois Institute for Continuing Legal Education. *Intellectual Property Law for the General Business Counselor.* Illinois Bar Center, 1973.

Johnston, Donald F. *Copyright Handbook.* R.R. Bowker Company, 1978.

Lietman, Alan. *Howell's Copyright Law.* BNA Incorporated, 1962.

White, Herbert S. *The Copyright Dilemma.* American Library Association, 1977.

CHAPTER 7

New Venture Financing

One of the most common issues which an entrepreneur faces revolves around securing financing for the new venture. The questions of how and when to raise money and from whom are frequent topics of concern. This piece will attempt to describe some common sources of capital, and the conditions under which money is typically lent or invested.

Overview

As in most transactions, the owners of capital expect to get something in return for providing financing for the venture. In evaluating potential opportunities, the providers of funds will typically use some form of a risk/return model. That is, they will demand a higher return when they perceive a higher risk; and they will seek to maximize their return for any given level of risk.

The entrepreneur's objective, of course, is to secure financing at the lowest possible cost. The art of successful financing, therefore, lies in obtaining funds in a manner which those providers of funds view as relatively less risky.

The entrepreneur can do several things to obtain financing so it will be perceived as "less risky":

- pledge personal or corporate assets against a loan.

- promise to pay the money back in a short period of time, when the investors can judge the health of the business, rather than over the long term, when its financial strength is less certain.

- give investors a preferred or priority return (i.e., a disproportionately large share of early financial returns).

- give investors some measure of control over the business, either through loan covenants, deal terms, or participation in management (i.e., a seat on the board).

This note derives from an earlier note, "Alternative Sources of Financing" HBS No. 384-187, by Professors Howard H. Stevenson and Michael J. Roberts. This version was prepared by Professors Howard H. Stevenson and Michael J. Roberts. HBS cases are developed solely as the basis for class discussion. Cases are not intended to serve as endorsements, sources of primary data, or illustrations of effective or ineffective management.

- Seek financing from investors who are knowledgeable about "the space" and, therefore, more comfortable with the uncertainties inherent in that specific sector.

Note that these are only a few of the possible mechanisms.

The liabilities side of the balance sheet itself provides a good overview of the potential sources of financing. Because this side of the balance sheet is arranged in order of increasing risk, it follows that the lowest cost forms of financing will usually be available from the higher balance sheet items.

Equity Financing

New Venture financing provides the entrepreneur with a host of unique challenges. The highest risk capital (and therefore potentially highest return capital to the investor/ highest cost capital to the entrepreneur) is at the bottom of the balance sheet as equity. When a business is in the start-up phase, it is at its riskiest point. Therefore, equity capital is usually an appropriate source of financing during this period. That is not to say that debt capital is unattractive. It may even be available when secured by assets of the business, such as a building or equipment. However, some equity is usually required to get a business "off the ground." There is virtually no getting around the fact that the first investment in the business will be equity capital. This is required to demonstrate commitment on the part of the entrepreneur. Investors perceive, and rightly so, that the individual entrepreneur will be more committed to the venture if s/he has a substantial portion of personal assets invested in the venture. It is this fact which has led some to claim that: "You're better off trying to start a business with $50,000 than with $1 million in personal resources. If you are relatively poor, you can demonstrate your commitment for a smaller sum." This statement presumes that you will be seeking capital from some *outside* source. If you were going to fund the venture all by yourself, you would naturally prefer to have $1 million instead of $50,000.

There is another, more practical reason why this start-up phase will usually be financed with the entrepreneur's own funds. In order to raise money, the entrepreneur typically needs more than an idea. The entrepreneur will have to invest some money in the idea, perhaps to build a prototype or do a market study, in order to convince prospective providers of capital that the idea has potential.

This is not to say that these funds must be equity capital in the purest sense. That is, the money need only be equity from the point of view of potential investors in the business. The entrepreneur can obtain these "equity funds" by mortgaging personal assets like a house or car, borrowing from friends or relatives, even from a personal bank loan or credit card advances. The important fact is that when the money goes into the business, it does so as equity, not as debt to be repaid to the entrepreneur.

Some specialized firms provide "seed capital." Most venture capital firms require that a business move beyond the idea stage before they will consider financing it. Yet, some businesses require a good deal of work, and money, to get from the concept phase to the point where they can obtain venture capital financing. These seed funds can provide this kind of capital, as can "angel" investors (see below) and friends and family.

Bootstrapping

First, it is worth pointing out that many successful ventures receive no outside funding of any kind. Entrepreneurs use their own savings, credit cards, a second mortgage, even personally guaranteed loans, to start their businesses. The appeal of this strategy is clear: 100% ownership of the equity.

Amar Bhidé conducted a study[1] in the late 1980s that found that 80% of the 500 companies on *Inc.* Magazine's list of the 500 fastest growing companies were started—and grown—with no outside equity capital. Indeed, the median start-up capital required was $10,000.

Certainly, one factor that enables a bootstrap approach is the selection of a business without a particularly deep cash flow trough. Thus, inventing a new drug or starting a semiconductor manufacturing enterprise would be difficult to bootstrap, simply because of the huge amounts of capital required. The ideal business for bootstrapping is one which quickly generates positive cash flow.

Certainly, the dramatic increase in the amount of venture capital under management in the 1990s—from approximately $35 billion in 1994 to $260 billion in 2004[2] may have changed this picture. Nonetheless, the significance of formal venture capital in the new venture financing process is clearly overstated in the popular press and media view of the entrepreneurial world. In 2004, for example, approximately 2,400 companies were funded with venture capital—a small fraction of the new ventures created.

Outside Equity Capital

Typically, the entrepreneur will exhaust his/her own funds before the business has made it through its cash flow trough and has turned cash positive. At this point, it is usually still too early to obtain all of the required financing in the form of debt. The entrepreneur must approach outside sources for equity capital.

Private Investors/Angels: One popular source of equity capital is private investors, also known as "angels." These investors may range from family and friends with a few extra dollars to extremely wealthy individuals who manage their own money. Successful entrepreneurs frequently come to mind, and do, in fact, represent a significant source of private equity capital. Angels may be advised by their accountants, lawyers or other professionals, and sometimes the entrepreneur must deal with these people as well. In the late 1990s, a new form of angel financing evolved. Individual angels grouped together and tried to invest more formally: recruiting members with specialized expertise—(typically former or current entrepreneurs, retired venture capitalists) sharing due diligence and contacts, structuring more formal and sophisticated financing terms, and involving themselves more deeply in the enterprise (e.g., via a board seat).

In order to approach individual investors, you will usually need at least a business plan. A formal offering memorandum has the advantage of providing more legal protection for the entrepreneur in the form of disclaimers and legal language. However,

---

[1]Amar Bhidé, "Bootstrap Finance: The Art of Start-ups," *Harvard Business Review,* Nov/Dec 1992, p. 109.

[2]National Venture Capital Association, *2005 Yearbook*, Thomson Venture Economics, p. 9.

it suffers from appearing overly negative, being more costly to prepare (usually requires legal counsel) and also being limited by the SEC laws in terms of its distribution. That is, some of the SEC rules permit only 35 "offerees." With a business plan, you can exceed this number, and then formally "offer" to only those individuals who have a real interest in investing.

One of the best ways to find angel investors is through a network of friends, acquaintances and advisors. For instance, if you have used a local lawyer and accountant to help you prepare a business plan or offering document, these advisors may know of wealthy individuals who invest in ventures like yours.

At this point, it is worth reiterating the importance of following the securities laws and obtaining the advice of counsel. Because many of these wealthy individuals are "unsophisticated," they can (and often do, if the venture is unsuccessful) claim that they were misled by you, the conniving entrepreneur. A carefully drawn offering document is the key to legal protection in this instance.

Angel investors may be well-suited to participation in equity financings that are too small for a venture capital firm to consider (e.g., under $1 million). Angel investors are also typically thought of as being a less expensive source of equity than venture capital firms. This may be true. It is also true that:

- many private investors do not possess the expertise or time to advise the entrepreneur on the operations of the business;

- individual investors are far less likely to come up with additional funds if required, particularly if the venture is successful and requires a significant sum; and,

- these investors are more likely to be a source of "problems" or frustration, particularly if there are a large number of them. Phoning frequently, or complaining when things are not going according to plan, they can create headaches for even the most well-intentioned of entrepreneurs.

Data on the size of the angel financing universe is difficult to obtain. One recent study determined that the average investment per company, per angel was approximately $80,000 and that these individuals invested, on average, $335,000 ("per angel") in 1998.[3]

In 1996—a year in which formal venture capital financing totaled approximately $10 billion, angels were estimated to have invested between $10 and $20 billion in new ventures.[4] By 2000, with the Internet in full bloom, analysts estimated that angels were financing 50,000 start-ups with $40 billion per year.[5]

Venture Capital: Venture capital refers to a pool of equity capital which is professionally managed. Wealthy individuals may invest in these funds as limited partners, although pension funds and endowments make up a larger share of the capital invested

---

[3]Michael J. Roberts, Howard H. Stevenson and Kenneth P. Morse, "Angel Investing," HBS Note No. 800-273, p. 5.

[4]B. Freear, J. Sohl, J.E. and W.E. Wetzel, "Creating New Capital Markets for Emerging Ventures," SBA contract SBAHQ-95-M-1062.

[5]John Helyar, "The Venture Capitalist Next Door," *Fortune,* November 13, 2000, p. 294.

TABLE A | Venture Capital Returns vs. Other Benchmarks (12/31/04)[6]

Investment Horizon Performance for Period Ending 12/31/2004				
Fund Type	**1 YR**	**3 YR**	**5 YR**	**10 YR**	**20 YR**
Seed/Early Focused	38.9	−7.7	−1.5	44.7	19.9
Balanced Focused	14.7	0.0	0.4	18.2	13.3
Later Stage Focused	10.4	0.0	−4.7	15.4	13.7
All Venture	**19.3**	**−2.9**	**−1.3**	**26.0**	**15.7**
Buyout Funds	14.3	6.9	2.3	8.4	12.8
Mezzanine Debt	8.0	3.1	2.9	6.9	9.3
All Private Equity	**16.4**	**3.7**	**1.5**	**12.7**	**13.8**
NASDAQ	8.6	3.7	−11.8	11.2	12.4
S&P500	9.0	1.8	−3.8	10.2	11.7

Source: Adapted from *National Venture Capital Association Yearbook 2005,* Thomson Venture Economics, p. 14.

in venture funds. The general partners manage the pool in exchange for a fee and a percentage of the gain on investments.

In order to compensate for the riskiness of their investments, give their own investors a handsome return, and make a profit for themselves, venture firms seek a high rate of return on their investments. Target returns of 50% or 60% are not uncommon hurdles for firms to apply to prospective venture capital investments (see **Table A** above).

As the table above indicates, venture capital returns can be quite volatile. Indeed, for the year 2000, for example, many funds had returns of over 100%, driven by the wave of internet IPOs.

In exchange for this high return, venture firms will often provide advice to their portfolio companies. Experienced venture capitalists people have been through many times what the entrepreneur is usually experiencing for the first time. They can often provide useful counsel on the problems a company may experience in the start-up phase.

Venture firms can differ along several dimensions. Some prefer investing in certain kinds of companies; "hi-tech" is popular with most, although perceptions of what precisely this is will vary widely. Some firms have a reputation for being very involved with the day-to-day operations of the business; others exhibit a more hands-off policy.

In approaching venture capitalists, the entrepreneur needs a business plan to capture the firm's interest. Here the document serves a far different purpose than it would in the case of private individuals. A venture capital firm will expend a good deal of effort investigating potential investments. Not only is this sound business practice on their part, but they have legal obligations to their own investors. Therefore, a business plan targeted to venture firms should be short, concise and attempt to stimulate further interest, rather than present the business in exhaustive detail.

Most venture capitalists also report that it is only the naive entrepreneur who will propose the actual terms of the investment in the initial document. While the plan should

---

[6]Returns are for the investment horizon noted as of 6/30/01; 3- and 6-month figures are not annualized.

certainly spell out how much financing the entrepreneur is seeking, to detail the terms (i.e., "for 28% of the stock . . .") is viewed as premature for an initial presentation.

One topic which is frequently of concern to entrepreneurs is confidentiality. On the one hand, it seems wise to tell potential investors about your good ideas to get them interested in the company; on the other, what if someone else takes them? In general, venture capitalists are a professional group, and will not disclose confidential information. It is more difficult, however, to make this statement about private sources of capital, like private individuals.

Whatever the target investor audience, it is generally *not* a good idea to put truly proprietary material in a business plan. These plans are frequently copied, and could certainly be left accidentally on a plane or in an office. A business plan might, for example, describe the functions a new product would perform, but should probably not include circuit designs, engineering, drawings, formulas, etc.

Venture firms may not invest via a pure equity security. Some may invest a mix of debt and equity, convertible debt or a preferred security. Each of these has its advantages:

- a debt/equity package provides for the venture firm to get some of its funds back via interest, which is deductible to the company, and hence results in a tax savings to the new enterprise (if it is profitable).

- convertible debt or preferred gives the venture firm a priority return. If the venture should fail, or be liquidated at a relatively low value, the venture capitalist will have a priority claim on the assets of the business.

Venture firms "syndicate" a large investment. That is, they will attempt to interest other firms in taking a piece of the investment. This permits the firm to invest in a larger number of companies, and thus spread its risk. This is particularly important on subsequent "rounds" or stages of financing. Other venture firms will want to see that the original firm(s) will continue their investment in the company. If existing, more knowledgeable investors aren't interested in the company, why should a new venture firm be interested?

The amount of venture capital financing rose dramatically in the 1990s, from approximately $7.8 billion invested in 1995 to $106 billion in 2000, back down to $22 billion in 2005.[7] (See **Exhibit 1** for investment patterns 1990–2004).

As the amount of venture capital invested grew in the late 1990s, the number of companies funded with VC grew as well, but at a much slower pace. The result was a dramatic increase in the amount of financing per company (see **Table B** on page 297).

Public Equity Markets: Of course, the largest source of equity capital remains the public equity markets: The New York, American and over-the-counter stock exchanges. Typically, however, a firm must have a history of successful operation before it can raise money in this way. In "hot" markets, some smaller, start-up companies have been able to raise public equity. The process is lengthy, detailed and expensive.

Whether the investment is made by wealthy individuals or a venture capital firm, terms will have to be negotiated. In exchange for their investment, the investor will

---

[7]PriceWaterhouseCoopers, Moneytree, http://www.pwcmoneytree.com/nav.jsp?page=historical.

TABLE B | Venture Capital Investment 1990–2004 ($million)

Year	No. of Companies Funded	Investment Total	Average Per Company
1990	1,050	2,781	2.64
1992	1,017	3,580	3.52
1994	961	4,169	4.34
1996	2,087	11,510	5.51
1998	2,990	21,270	7.11
2000	6,406	105,832	16.52
2002	2,574	21,615	8.40
2004	2,399	20,993	8.75

Source: PriceWaterhouseCoopers, Moneytree, http://www.pwmoneytree.com/nav.jsp?page=historical.

receive a "security" which represents the terms of his/her investment in the company. In the case of a public offering, the investment bank negotiates the terms on behalf of its clients. Venture capital firms, and investment banks, of course, tend to be more sophisticated than the average private investor.

Corporate Partners

Corporate Partners—or strategic investors—are an increasingly popular source of growth capital for entrepreneurial firms. Corporations will rarely fund raw start-ups; the risk is still too great at this stage. But, in a later round, when the technology appears viable and the firm seems to have potential, corporations may play a role. They are typically willing to pay a higher price (i.e., place a higher value on the firm), because they want something more that just dollars back for their investment.

In some cases, the corporate investor wants an up-close window on a new and evolving technology. In other cases, the larger partner seeks a relationship that may lead to acquisition down the road.

Debt Capital

The other large category of capital is debt. Debt is presumed to be lower risk capital because it is repaid according to a set schedule of principal and interest. Moreover, the use of covenants and the pledging of specific assets as collateral give the bank an opportunity to step in and claim assets which will protect their capital.

Nonetheless, banks vastly prefer to be repaid out of the normal operation of the business. In order to have a reasonable expectation of being paid according to this schedule, creditors lend against:

- Assets: Firms can obtain asset-based financing for most hard assets which have a market value. A building, equipment, or soluble inventory are all assets which a company could borrow against.

- Cash flow: Lenders will allow firms to borrow against their expected ability to generate the cash to repay the loan. Creditors attempt to check this ability through such measures as interest coverage (EBIT ÷ interest payments) or debt/equity ratio. And, creditors build these same kinds of ratios into the covenants that the borrower must agree to as a condition of the loan. Thus, if cash flow falls below a certain level, the bank has certain "control rights" that kick in. Obviously, a healthy business with little debt and high cash flow will have an easier time borrowing money than a new venture.

Cash Flow Financing

Cash flow financing is of several types, and can come from several different sources. Even though it is called cash flow financing, the bank will still attempt to secure its debt with specific assets.

- Short-term debt: Short-term financing is frequently available to cover seasonal working capital needs for periods of less than one year, usually 30 to 40 days.

- Line-of-credit financing: A company can arrange for a line of credit, to be drawn upon as needed. Interest is paid on the outstanding principal, and a "commitment fee" is paid up front. Generally, a line of credit must be "paid down" to an agreed-upon level at some point during the year.

- Long-term debt: Generally available to solid "creditworthy" companies, long-term debt may be available for up to 10 years. Long-term debt is usually repaid according to a fixed schedule of interest and principal.

Cash flow financing is most commonly available from commercial banks, but can also be obtained from savings and loan institutions, finance companies and other institutional lenders (i.e., insurance companies, pension funds). Because cash-flow financing is generally riskier than asset-based financing, banks will frequently attempt to reduce their risk through the use of covenants. These covenants place certain restrictions on a business if it wishes to maintain its credit with the bank. Typical loan covenants concern:

- limits on the company's debt/equity ratio;
- minimum standards on interest coverage;
- lower limits on working capital;
- minimum cash balance; and,
- restrictions on the company's ability to issue senior debt.

These, and other covenants, attempt to protect the lender from actions which would increase the likelihood of the bank's not getting its money back.

Asset-Based Financing

Most assets in a business can be financed. Because cash-flow financing usually requires an earnings history, far more new ventures are able to obtain asset-based financing. In an asset-based financing, the company pledges or gives the financier a first lien on the asset. In the event of a default on the financing payments, the lender can repossess the asset. The following types of financing are generally available:

- Accounts receivable: Up to 85% or 90% of the accounts receivable from credit-worthy customers can usually be financed. The bank will conduct a thorough investigation to determine which accounts are eligible for this kind of financing. In some industries, such as the fashion business, accounts receivable are often "factored." A factor buys approved receivables for a discount from their face value, but collects from the accounts.

- Inventory: Inventory is often financed if it consists of merchandise which could be easily sold. Typically, 50% or so of finished goods inventory can be financed.

- Equipment: Equipment can usually be financed for a period of 3 to 10 years. One-half to 80% of the value of the equipment can be financed, depending on the saleability or "liquidity" of the assets. Leasing is also a form of equipment financing, where the company never takes ownership of the equipment, but rents it.

- Real estate: Mortgage financing is usually readily available to finance a company's plant or buildings; 75% to 85% of the value of the building is a typical figure.

- Personally secured loans: A business can obtain large amounts of financing if one of its principals (or someone else) is willing to pledge a sufficient amount of assets to guarantee the loan.

- Letter-of-credit financing: A letter of credit is a bank guarantee which a company can obtain to enable it to purchase goods. A letter of credit functions almost like a credit card, allowing businesses to make commitments and purchases in other parts of the world where the company does not have relationships with local banks.

- Government secured loans: Certain government agencies will guarantee loans to allow businesses to obtain financing when they could not obtain it on their own. The Small Business Administration, the Farmers Home Administration, and other government agencies will guarantee bank loans.

Asset-based financing is available from commercial banks and other financial institutions. Insurance companies, pension funds, and commercial finance companies provide mortgages and other forms of asset-backed financing.

Hybrid Financing

While debt and equity constitute relatively "pure" forms of financing, in reality, the spectrum of financing alternatives is more finely articulated. There are several hybrid forms of financing that combine the key attributes of each. These are:

- for equity: an unlimited participation in the venture's upside; and,
- for debt: an (on average) lower, but more certain return.

A few common examples of these hybrid financing tools will now be described, but the alternatives are almost infinite.

Venture Leasing

A typical lease involves the "rental" of a piece of equipment for a fixed term of 3 to 5 years. Because the equipment may drop in attainable market value very quickly, the lessor is taking a credit risk on the lessee: if the new venture should fail, the lessor will be left with equipment worth less than the remaining payments on the lease. For those reasons, it may be difficult for the new venture to lease much equipment on reasonable terms.

Venture leasing involves the leasing of such equipment to a new venture, on relatively favorable terms. In exchange for the higher risk it is taking, the venture leasing firm receives warrants to purchase equity in the venture at a fixed price—typically the price of the shares in the most recent venture capital financing. The venture leasing firms in essence "piggy-back" on the due diligence and investment decisions of the VCs. And, the VCs don't mind because venture leasing is a less expensive source of capital than the pure equity venture capital financing it is replacing. This enhances the overall rate of return to the VCs (assuming things go well).

While there is little reliable data on the amount of capital raised each year via venture leasing, some industry observers place the figure at roughly 10% of the amount of capital invested via traditional venture capital.

Equity/Subordinated Debt

In some cases venture capital firms may also invest subordinated debt (sub debt) in the venture, rather than in one "pure equity" security that is more typical. This almost always occurs when the VC invests both equity and sub debt. In this instance, the cash flow profile of the venture may be such that—if successful—it will generate cash relatively quickly (3 years or so) and be in a position to repay the debt. The debt, because it is subordinated to all other forms of debt on the balance sheet, is more risky, and thus pays a higher rate of interest—often in the 15% to 18% range. It may well be the case that even this interest rate is lower than would be called for by a "market" assessment of the risk involved. But, in return, the VCs get a "higher than market" return on their equity, bringing the blended rate to a market level.

Internally Generated Financing

A final category of financing is internally generated. This term describes:

- Retained earnings: Profits are one of the last sources for financing. Unfortunately, it is also a source new ventures are unlikely to have at their disposal.
- Credit from suppliers: Paying bills in a less timely fashion is one way to increase working capital. Sometimes, suppliers will charge you interest for this practice. In other instances, the costs may be more severe if a key supplier resource decides to stop serving you.
- Accounts receivable: Collecting bills more quickly will also generate financing.
- Reducing working capital: A business can generate internal financing by reducing other working capital items: inventory, cash, etc.
- Sale of assets: Perhaps a more drastic move, selling assets will also generate capital.

Each of these techniques represents an approach to generating funds internally, without the help of a financial partner. Although the purely financial costs are low, the entrepreneur must be wary of attempting to run the business "too lean."

Implications of Financing Choices

When an entrepreneur takes other people's money, she assumes certain legal, contractual and moral obligations. Of course, investors seek not merely to be paid back, but to earn a return—a profit. The magnitude depends not only on the perceived risk, but on the "type" of money. Venture Capitalists need to cover their expenses, keep a slice for themselves (typically 20%) and still generate quite high returns for their limited partners. Thus, the sense on the part of some entrepreneurs that some VCs encourage "swinging for the fences."

Because they are investors in many different businesses, they can afford to play the averages, taking low probability—but high pay-off—bets. The entrepreneur, with all her eggs in one basket, may not be so willing to play such a pure "expected value" game.

Angels include individuals with a wide variety of motivations. Some are investing purely for the financial pay-off. Others believe—sometimes rightly so—that they have considerable value to add, and wish to be involved in the decisions that affect the business.

Corporate partners—strategic investors—clearly are in the game for more than money. They have typically paid a higher price to get in the game than would a purely financial investor. In order to get a return on their investment, the entrepreneur and the firm usually have to behave differently than they otherwise would—producing a particular component to a particular specification, using a particular distribution channel. Sometimes this "synergy" can benefit both parties. Other times, it is a distraction—or source—to the entrepreneurial firm trying to make its way forward.

Finally, bankers want to get paid back. Their view is that they are not paid enough to assume the risk that equity providers have signed up for. Indeed, their returns are far lower—that's the reason the equity holders have sought debt financing in the first place: to lever up their own returns. At the moment when risk appears, the bankers will do what they can to assume that they are repaid. This includes threatening to call collateral, or call the loan itself.

Summary

This note describes the spectrum of financial sources which an entrepreneur can tap both during the start-up phase and as a going concern. **Exhibit 2** is an attempt to summarize these sources. Along the horizontal axis, we've tried to note whether the provider of capital tries to manage the risk/reward ratio by 1) increasing reward by raising the cost of funds, or 2) decreasing risk by asserting some measure of control over the business. This is not an exhaustive list, but an overview of the most popular sources. In every case, there is a high premium on understanding both your own needs and the specific needs of the financier.

EXHIBIT 1 | Venture Capital Funding Flows ($Millions)

Venture Capital Investments 1992 to 2004 by Industry ($ Millions)							
Industry	1992	1994	1996	1998	2000	2002	2004
Computer Software	615.5	675.4	2,310.9	4,544.9	23,345.3	5,101.1	5,058.9
Biotechnology	561.0	583.6	1,204.7	1,554.6	4,210.4	3,098.3	3,877.3
Communications	433.4	695.6	1,919.7	4,406.4	28,956.1	4,923.3	336.2
Healthcare Related	727.4	648.9	1,350.5	2,145.3	4,249.6	2,307.5	2,238.5
Semiconductor and Electronics	208.1	214.2	498.3	837.0	4,271.1	1,649.9	2,181.8
Retailing and Media	372.7	607.1	2,107.9	3,131.0	18,172.2	1,187.8	1,375.9
Computer Hardware	218.1	293.7	879.0	1,475.4	10,506.7	1,543.9	1,341.2
Business/Financial	128.3	168.5	705.4	1,656.0	9,442.0	1,015.0	899.7
Industry/Energy	315.8	281.8	534.5	1,519.6	2,678.9	788.2	683.9
Total	5,572.3	6,162.8	13,506.9	23,268.2	107,832.3	23,617.0	19,997.4

Venture Capital Investments 1992 to 2004 by Stage ($ Millions)							
Stage	1992	1994	1996	1998	2000	2002	2004
Startup-Seed	555.9	767.8	1,516.3	1,818.1	3,012.0	274.3	347.7
Early	579.1	863.5	2,851.5	5,580.0	25,873.9	4,058.6	3,889.5
Expansion	1,847.6	1,602.7	5,395.9	10,592.5	60,474.1	12,743.8	9,577.2
Later	597.7	934.9	1,747.2	3,279.5	16,472.3	4,538.4	7,179.0
Total	3,580.3	4,168.9	11,510.9	21,270.1	105,832.3	21,615.1	20,993.4

Source: Adapted from *National Venture Capital Association Yearbook 2005*, Thomson Venture Economics, p. 30.

EXHIBIT 2 | Alternative Sources of Financing

	Cost				Control	
	Zero	Interest	Equity	Covenants	Voting Rights	Guarantee of Debt
SOURCE OF FINANCING						
Self		X	X		X	X
Family and Friends		X	X		X	X
Suppliers and Trade Credit	X	X				
Commercial Banks		X		X		X
Asset-based Lenders/Lessors		X		X		
Specialized Finance Cos.		X		X		
Venture Leasing		X	X			
Institutions and Insurance Companies		X		X		
Pension Funds		X		X		
Subordinated Debt/Warrants		X	X	X		
Venture Capital			X		X	
Private Equity Placements			X			
Public Equity Offerings			X			

CHAPTER 8

Deal Structure and Deal Terms

A critical aspect of the entrepreneur's attempt to obtain resources is the development of an actual "deal" with the owner of the resources. Typically, the entrepreneur needs a variety of resources, including dollars, people, and outside expertise. As in any situation, the individual who desires to own, or use, these resources must give up something. Because the entrepreneur typically has so little to start with, she will usually give up a claim on some future value in exchange for the ability to use these resources now.

Entrepreneurs can obtain funds in the form of trade credit, short- and long-term debt, and equity or risk capital. This note will focus on the structure and terms of the deal which may be used to obtain the required financial resources from investors. The note will center on financial resources because raising capital is a common problem which virtually all entrepreneurs face.

What Is a Deal?

In general, a deal represents the terms of a transaction between two (or more) groups or individuals. Entrepreneurs want money to use in a (hopefully) productive venture, and individuals and institutions wish to earn a return on the cash that they have at risk.

The entrepreneur's key task is to make the whole equal to more than the sum of the parts. That is, to carve up the economic benefits of the venture into pieces which meet the needs of particular financial backers. The entrepreneur can maximize his/her own return by selling these pieces at the highest possible price, that is, to individuals who demand the lowest return. And the individuals who demand the lowest return will typically be those that perceive the lowest risk.

Sr. Lecturer Michael J. Roberts and Professor Howard H. Stevenson prepared the original version of this note, "Deal Structure," HBS No. 384-186, which is being replaced by this version prepared by the same authors.

Factors That Drive a Deal

In order to craft a deal which maximizes his/her own economic return, the entrepreneur must

- understand the fundamental economic nature of the business;
- understand financiers' needs, and perceptions of risk and reward; and,
- understand his/her own needs and requirements.

Understanding the Business

The first thing the entrepreneur must do is assess the fundamental economic nature of the business itself. Most business plans project a set of economics which determine

- the amount of funds required:
  — the absolute amount; and,
  — the timing of these requirements.
- the riskiness of the venture:
  — the absolute level of risk; and,
  — the underlying factors which determine risk.
- the timing and potential magnitude of returns.

It is important to remember that the venture itself does not necessarily have an *inherent* set of economics. The entrepreneur determines the fundamental economics when he makes critical decisions about the business. Still, there may be certain economic characteristics which are a function of the industry and environment, and which the entrepreneur will generally be guided by.

For instance, a venture such as a biotech start-up has a much different set of characteristics than a real estate deal. The biotech start-up may require large investments over the first several years, followed by years with zero cash flow, followed by a huge potential return many years out. The real estate project, on the other hand, may require a one-time investment, generate immediate cash flow, and provide a means of exit only several years down the road.

One technique for understanding a venture's economic nature is to analyze the potential source of return. Let's take this example: a manufacturing business with the following projected cash flows, including a sale in year 5.

Year	0	1	2	3	4	5
Cash flow ($000)	(1,000)	400	400	400	400	5,600

Now, we can break this cash flow down into its components.

- investment: money required to fund the venture;
- tax consequences: not precisely a cash flow, but nonetheless a cash benefit which may accrue if an investment has operating losses in the early years;
- free cash flow: cash which the business throws off as a result of its operations before financing and distributions to providers of capital; and,

- terminal value: the after-tax cash which the business returns as a result of its sale. Here, this is assumed to occur at the end of year 5.

Let's assume that these flows are as follows (where figures in parentheses are negative cash flows):

Cash Flows ($000)	Year					
	0	1	2	3	4	5
Original investment	(1,000)					
Tax consequences		300	300	0	(100)	(200)
Free cash flows		100	100	400	500	800
Terminal value (after tax)						5,000
Total	(1,000)	400	400	400	400	5,600

Now, we can take the internal rate of return (IRR) of these cash flows—i.e., the IRR for the total investment = 64.5%.

Next, we calculate the present value of each of the individual elements of the return *at that IRR,* and then, the percent which each element contributes to the total return. Of course, the present value of the total return will be equal to the original investment.

Element	Present Value @ 64.5% ($000)	% of Total
Tax consequences	263	26.3
Free cash flows	322	32.2
+ Terminal value	415	41.5
Total	$1,000	100.0%

This analysis illuminates the potential sources of return inherent in the business, as projected.

Now, the task of the entrepreneur is to carve up the cash flows and returns and "sell" them to the individuals/institutions that are willing to accept the lowest return. That is, the parties that are willing to take the smallest share of these cash flows in exchange for a given amount of capital. This will leave the biggest piece of the economic pie for the entrepreneur. To do so requires an understanding of the financiers' needs and perceptions.

Understanding Financiers Needs and Objectives

Providers of capital clearly desire a "good" return on their money, but their needs and priorities are far more complex. Differences do exist among different financial sources, and they vary along a number of dimensions, including:

- magnitude of return desired;
- magnitude and nature of risk which is acceptable;

- perception of risk and reward;
- magnitude of investment;
- timing of return;
- form of return;
- degree of control; and,
- mechanisms for control.

And, the priorities attached to these various elements may differ widely. For instance, certain institutions (e.g., insurance companies, pension funds) have legal standards which determine the type of investment which they can undertake. For others, the time horizon for their return may be influenced by organizational or legal constraints.

Certain investors may want a high rate of return and be willing to wait a long period, and bear a large amount of risk to get it. Still other investors may consider any type of investment, as long as there exists some mechanism for them to exert their own control over the venture. To the extent that the entrepreneur is able to break down the basic value of the business into components which vary along each of these dimensions, and then find investors who want this specific package, the entrepreneur will be able to structure a better transaction: a deal which creates more value for her.

If we return to our example of the manufacturing business which requires a $1 million investment, we can see how the entrepreneur can take advantage of these differences in investor characteristics.

- The tax benefits, for example, are well-suited for sale to a risk-averse wealthy individual in a high marginal tax bracket. Because the benefits accrue as a result of operating losses, if the business does poorly, the tax benefits may be even greater. But let's assume that a wealthy individual believes that these forecasts are realistic, and requires a 25% return. If we discount the tax benefits at this 25% required return, we arrive at a present value of $325,500. Therefore, this individual should be willing to invest $325,500 in order to purchase this portion of the cash flows.

- The operating cash flows would, in total, be perceived as fairly risky. However, some portion of them should be viewed as a "safe bet" by a bank. Let's assume that the entrepreneur could convince a banker that no less than $60,000 would be available in any given year for interest expenses. Further, if the banker were willing to accept 12.0% interest and take all of the principal repayment at the end of year 5 (when the business is sold), then he should be willing to provide $60,000 ÷ .12 = $500,000 in the form of a loan.

- Now, the entrepreneur has raised $825,500 and needs only $174,500 to get into business.

- The terminal value, and the riskier portion of the operating cash flows, remain to be sold. Let's assume that a venture investor would be willing to provide funds at a 50% rate of return.

First, we need to see precisely what cash flows remain:

Year		1	2	3	4	5
	Total	400	400	400	400	5,600
−	Wealthy investor	300	300	0	(100)	(200)
−	Bank	60	60	60	60	560
=	Remaining	40	40	340	440	5,240

Now, the remaining cash flows in years 1 through 5 have a present value, at the venture firm's 50% rate, of $922,140. If we need $174,500, we need to give up $174,500 ÷ $922,140 = 18.9% of these flows in order to entice the venture investor to provide risk capital.

This leaves the entrepreneur with a significant portion of the above "remaining" flows. One can see how these differences in needs and perceived risk allow the entrepreneur to create value for her.

In an attempt to highlight the logic and underlying principles, this example is both simplistic and overly precise. In the real world, all of these assumptions would be the subject of negotiation. But, the principles at work remain the same.

Understanding the Entrepreneur's Own Needs

The example we have just worked through was based on the assumption that the entrepreneur wants to obtain funds at the lowest possible cost. While this is generally true, there are often other mitigating factors.

The entrepreneur's needs and priorities do vary across a number of aspects including the time horizon for involvement in the venture, nature of that involvement, degree of business risk, etc. All of these variables will affect the entrepreneur's choice of a venture to pursue. However, once the entrepreneur has decided to embark on a particular business, his needs and priorities with respect to the financing of the venture will vary with respect to:

- degree of control desired;
- mechanisms of control desired;
- amount of financing required;
- magnitude of financial return desired; and,
- degree of risk which is acceptable.

For instance, in the above example, the entrepreneur could have decided to obtain an additional $100,000 or $200,000 as a cushion to make the venture less risky. This would certainly have lowered the economic return, but might have made the entrepreneur more comfortable with the venture.

Similarly, the bank which offered funds at 12%, or the venture investor, might have imposed a series of very restrictive covenants. Rather than accept this loss of control, the entrepreneur might rather have given up more of the economic potential.

In addition, the entrepreneur may need more than just money. There are times when some investor's money is better than others. This occurs in situations where once an individual is tied into a venture financially, she has an incentive to help the entrepreneur in nonfinancial ways. For instance, an entrepreneur starting a business which depended on securing good retail locations would prefer to obtain financing from an individual with good real estate contacts than from someone without those contacts. Venture capital firms are frequently cited for providing advice and support in addition to financing.

Alternative Structures

Once the fundamental economics of a deal have been worked out, the entrepreneur must still structure the deal. This requires the use of a certain legal form of organization, and a certain set of securities.

The vehicles through which the entrepreneur can raise capital include the general partnership, the limited partnership, an LLC, and a "regular" (or "C") corporation. While these forms of organization differ with respect to their tax consequences, they also differ substantially in regard to the precision with which cash flows may be carved up and returned to various investors. In a limited partnership, for instance, virtually any distribution of profits and cash flow is feasible so long as it is spelled out clearly, and in advance in the limited partnership agreement. (Losses, however, are usually distributed in proportion to capital provided.)

Securities can involve debt, warrants, straight or preferred equity, and a host of other legal arrangements. The structuring of securities requires the assistance of good legal counsel, with an eye towards securities and corporate law, as well as an intimate knowledge of the tax code.

An Example: A Venture Capital Term Sheet

The specifics of a deal are set out in writing in the form of a term sheet, which are the business terms of the deal. These terms, if agreed to by the involved parties, will ultimately be memorialized in a much longer set of legal documents which will be signed by all parties at the closing, where the entrepreneur will get a check to finance the venture, and the investors will legally acquire the securities they have purchased.

The most common form of term sheet is one which is obtained from venture capitalists (VCs)—or other sophisticated equity investors—related to an investment in the venture. Such term sheets are designed to address the important dimensions of the deal. They usually have a few standard sections and components.

Representations, Warranties and Due Diligence: First, the firm vouches for some of the information it has provided to the investors during their due diligence, including a list of the existing shareholders and the number and type of shares of stock outstanding. The firm also agrees to let investors perform additional due diligence prior to the closing, including the inspection of the company's minutes of board meetings, financial statements, employment contracts, budget, status of R&D projects, lease agreements, and any other details which the investors believe will give them comfort on the assumptions they have made about the business.

The Security: The second major aspect of the term sheet is the description of the security being sold by the firm/bought by investors. Common stock is the classic equity security, and one share of stock is treated like others in terms of participation in the rewards such as dividends and payments upon liquidation. Preferred stock has a preference, which means that it will be paid "first" when there is a liquidation event (i.e., a sale of the company). That preference may be simply the amount of money invested, or it may increase at some rate, by using accrued dividends. That is, the preferred stock may have an imputed dividend that accrues until such a liquidation event, where the amount of the accrual is added on to the original purchase price and this total is the amount of the preference. A convertible security has the right to convert into common stock at an agreed upon conversion price. So, the holders of a convertible security would choose to convert if the company did well and the price of the common stock was higher than the conversion price. If the company did less well, they might choose not to convert, and instead, have the right to "redeem" the security for the price they originally paid, plus some accrued dividend (in the case of a convertible preferred) or accrued interest (in the case of a convertible debt security). All of these terms that differ from straight common are designed to give the investor a *more-than-pro rata share* of the value of the company (i.e., higher than in proportion to the value they would have received if they owned straight common stock) in a scenario where the company does not perform sufficiently well to earn them their desired return.

The term sheet will be very specific about the number of shares, price per share, and other terms, the most common of which include:

- *Voting:* The voting rights attached to the security. Where only common stock is issued and outstanding, it is easy to treat all securities equally. When convertible and preferred shares are issued, the voting rights of those securities must be detailed (i.e., "The holders of the preferred stock will be entitled to vote their shares as though they had been converted to common").

- *Dividends:* Whether dividends are paid, how much (in absolute dollars or percent on the price of each share), and whether dividends must be paid annually or whether they can accrue over time.

- *Participation rights:* Participation refers to the right to "participate" in the upside of the company. That is, a preferred security may get its preferred return and no other return, or it may get the amount of preferred return stated, and then also have the right to participate in the upside (i.e., a share of what is left after the preferred return has been paid). Thus a participating preferred stock gets both its preferred return and a share of the upside, and participates in that upside as though it were common stock.

- *Conversion rights:* A convertible security has the right to convert to common stock. The conversion price is the price at which that conversion will occur. So, if the original price of a share of convertible preferred stock is $100 per share, and if the conversion price is also set at $100, then the shares would convert on a 1:1 basis. If the conversion price was set at $10 per share, then a share of convertible preferred could convert into 10 shares of common stock.

- *Redemption rights:* Redemption is the "calling" back of the preferred stock and "paying it off" by the company to eliminate it from the balance sheet. An optional redemption right gives the company the ability to decide whether or not it wishes to call the stock in. A mandatory redemption right gives the investor the right to decide if they want to "put" the stock back to the company. The price may be the original purchase price, or it may be a greater amount if dividends have been allowed to accrue.

- *Anti-dilution provisions:* Investors may also receive anti-dilution protection. That is, if an offering of shares is subsequently done at a lower price, the investors' desire to protect themselves from the excess dilution that this offering would impose upon their ownership. Without getting into the very complicated specifics of "full ratchet" or "weighted average" anti-dilution provisions, suffice to say that the ratchet provision simply lowers the effective price of shares to the previous investors by forcing the company to issue new shares to these existing investors sufficient to lower their effective cost to the new lower price being paid by the new investors. A weighted average formula lowers the price less, in proportion to the amount of new investment relative to the amount invested by the existing investors.

Control: Finally, the document will spell out the rights which the holders have to control, or at least have a voice in, the company. This includes the right to attend board meetings or, perhaps, to name a board member. It spells out the overall composition of the board, and in general, who gets the right to appoint directors. Certain actions will be specified as requiring the consent of a majority of the investors (or a majority of the security they hold, or of a majority of the investor-appointed board members). These rights might include the issuance of new stock or the payment of dividends, as well as a sale of the company. This section will also spell out the rights of the investors to receive timely information, including financial statements, annual audits, etc.

Other Terms and Conditions: The term sheet also spells out certain actions that the company must take either prior to closing, or within 30 or 60 or 90 days. For instance, it could be a condition of closing that the company gets a new employment contract with a senior researcher that lasts for at least 2 years; that the company receives a lease extension from its landlord for at least an additional 5 years. Investors may require that within 90 days, the company hire an executive recruiter and begin a formal search for a new CEO or another member of the executive team, or that it hire to fill a new position (i.e., get a CFO instead of having only a controller).

Summary

Of course, there are a variety of non-financial aspects to any deal, including the kind of working relationship the entrepreneur has with her new partners and the value they can add to the venture. Indeed, as our colleague Bill Sahlman likes to say, "From whom you raise money is more important than the terms upon which that money is raised."

It is also worth pointing out the asymmetrical nature of the "bets" that are being made by the entrepreneur and the typical venture capitalist (or other investor who invests in many deals). The investor is playing a portfolio game, and, in such a situation, it can make a lot of sense to take higher and higher levels of risk as long as the possible increase in return is more than commensurate. For the entrepreneur, this is not the case. VCs are often characterized as "swinging for the fences" and this may make a lot of sense for them, but not for the entrepreneur.

Finally, the entrepreneur typically has a great deal of confidence in the venture and the business plan, and has usually done a lot of "selling" during the money raising process, projecting a great deal of faith in the market and the company's ability to generate revenues and value. A venture capitalist—or any investor—can use that confidence to their advantage. For instance, the terms of a VC investment often include a preferred return up until a certain point. For instance, if a VC invests $10 million, they might do it in the form of a convertible security that earns imputed interest. Upon a liquidity event, they get their money back, plus the imputed interest, and then participate in what's left on a "pro rata" basis, i.e., as though they had owned their equity share all along. The implication of this is that they may get 100% of the value created unless that number hits a certain point. They can make a forceful argument about doing this by pointing to the entrepreneur's confidence: "If you are so sure your company will be a success and achieve the results you suggest, then there will be plenty of value for you." Entrepreneurs need to be aware that deal structures and deal terms do have the effect of carving up value differentially under different outcomes. The natural optimism of the entrepreneur can be used against him in such circumstances.

Sheila Mason & Craig Shepherd

It was October 17, 2002, and Sheila Mason was driving home from her job as vice president of sales and marketing at American Telecommunications Software, Inc. (ATS). It would be yet another late evening, as Mason would have a quick dinner with her husband and children, and then head over to Craig Shepherd's house to continue work on their plan to start a new company in the software industry. This potential new venture—tentatively named Intelisoft—would develop and sell a software "translation engine" that would convert software programs written for one operating system into programs suitable for use in other operating environments. In particular, the engine was capable of converting programs written for older operating systems into programs that could run on a variety of UNIX-based operating systems. As these UNIX-based systems were becoming popular platforms in corporate settings, and as many corporations had old software—"legacy systems"—that they were rewriting to run on UNIX-based systems, the translation engine could save these companies considerable time and expense. Mason and Shepherd had been working together since Labor Day, and their meeting this evening was scheduled to resolve several important issues that had come up regarding their decisions to leave their existing employers and actually start the business. In Mason's words:

> The prospect of leaving a good job is pretty scary, especially when this still seems so risky. But it is already feeling uncomfortable to be at ATS while I am working on this, and making progress is going to require us to be much more public about our ideas—with VCs, potential partners, and customers. I don't want my colleagues here to learn I am leaving from anyone but me.

Senior Lecturer Michael J. Roberts and Research Associate Todd Thedinga prepared this case with the kind assistance of Karen Copenhaver Esq. of the firm of Testa, Hurwitz and Thibeault. HBS cases are developed solely as the basis for class discussion. Cases are not intended to serve as endorsements, sources of primary data, or illustrations of effective or ineffective management. The identities of firms and individuals mentioned in this case, as well as certain facts, have been disguised.

Background: Craig Shepherd

Mason's prospective cofounder and business partner, Craig Shepherd, 42, was manager of documentation and support at Nova Software Company. He had a master's degree in computer science from Cal Tech, and had spent his career in the software business. Early on Shepherd had been a programmer, and had ultimately become a manager at a large software company—Riverhead Systems—running complex software development efforts. Riverhead sold software that helped other programmers write application programs. In 1990, Shepherd felt that he had "burned out" and requested a transfer to the documentation and support area: "I always liked thinking about software from the end user's perspective, and I felt that my technical background would allow me to see all the functionality available in a product. I liked the challenge of capturing that information and explaining it so other developers could utilize it. And, the hours seemed more manageable." Shepherd enjoyed the work, was good at it, and progressed at Riverhead. During this time, he also had an idea that would form the basis of the translation engine:

> As I worked more closely with customers, I saw that they were using Riverhead's products to basically port applications from one operating system to another. I realized that programmers had old applications on their desks, and were essentially rewriting them from scratch. I thought—why not write a piece of software that could perform this translation task?

In 1992, Shepherd and his wife decided to move to Virginia to be closer to their families. Shepherd found a job with Nova as manager of documentation and support. He directed the nine-person department that provided technical descriptions of how Nova's software worked and also supported customers' post-purchase technical questions. Nova's products were similar to Riverhead's in that they were used by other software developers—at both software firms as well as the IT department of non-software companies—as development tools to create end-user software applications. Nova's products supplied an entire programming development environment that facilitated both development and support of applications utilizing a UNIX operating system. The documentation developed by Shepherd's department was published in the firm's manuals and product bulletins, and was provided to developers who purchased and used Nova software in their application development efforts.

In the ten years that Shepherd had been at Nova he had done well, receiving a promotion and solid raises. However, he began to feel like his career was stagnating, and he had periodically continued to work on his idea for a translation engine:

> For several years, I would just kind of noodle in my head—you know, waiting for a bus or driving somewhere—and just think about how to do this. In 2001, I finally had one of those "eureka" moments when my wife and I were on vacation at the shore. It came to me how I could write a piece of code that would actually do this translation. It took me about nine months of playing with it on nights and weekends, but I finally wrote a little prototype of the software on my home computer that basically worked. I knew that a real product would take a lot more work—and money—but I felt that this prototype pretty well proved the concept.

Because Shepherd did not work in product development, and because Nova did no research on translation engines and sold no similar products, Shepherd felt confident that Nova held no claim on his idea. He began to think about starting a company to develop and sell the product, and as a result of his networking efforts, met Sheila Mason through a mutual acquaintance:

> I went to a few of these "venture fairs" that the local business and engineering schools run, and would talk to people who were starting companies—and also to the people who were financing them—just to get a feel for how this process worked. I never said much about my idea, and basically tried to make some contacts so that when I felt ready, I would have more of a clue what I was doing.

Background: Sheila Mason

Sheila Mason had worked at ATS for five years, having graduated from Harvard Business School in 1994. She spent the first three years of her post-MBA career at a large consulting firm, working primarily in the high-tech practice. Frustrated by the more analytical nature of her job, Mason sought an operating role with a company in the software space, preferably a start-up. Through a former client she was introduced to several software veterans who were developing "killer apps" for UNIX in mission-critical operations, and who were starting a company that intended to develop software applications for telecommunications firms: "Telecom was a really hot space, and it is a business that requires lots of specialized software—billing and customer support systems, for instance." ATS had developed a successful suite of products that served telecom customers, as well as a significant "services" business that included helping customers implement software solutions. Mason signed on as director of business development, drawing on her analytical skills and contacts in the industry to develop relationships with partners and customers of ATS. The company had been a great success, had gone public in late 1999, and Mason's early equity stake and subsequent option grants had left her with approximately $2 million in equity in the company. At the time of the IPO, Mason had exercised a tranche of options and gained $1 million in cash from the sale. The remaining $1 million in options was scheduled to vest over the succeeding three years, on an annual basis. Moreover, she had risen to VP of sales and marketing in the company, reporting to the company's chief operating officer, Dave Hatfield.

But the CEO of ATS was only 44, and Mason knew she was unlikely to rise much higher in the company. So, for the past year or so, Mason had been considering her options and likely next career steps: "I thought if I could come up with an idea of my own, I'd start a company, but I was having trouble coming up with anything that I thought really had a lot of potential." Mason had several HBS classmates who were venture capitalists and with whom she had kept in contact since her graduation eight years earlier. As she began to think seriously about leaving ATS, she contacted several of her friends, saying she was interested in joining a start-up. One venture capitalist, Fred Thysen, put her in touch with Craig Shepherd, who Thysen had met at a "venture fair." Thysen said Shephard had an interesting idea and could use some help. Mason commented:

> I met Craig for coffee one morning at Fred's suggestion. He had developed what I thought was a great idea, and had a prototype of the translation engine that he could demo on his laptop. I knew from my role at ATS that customers would value this product, if it was for real, and that my contacts would give us great entrée into potential customers and partners.

It was clear that this would be a product that would be sold to CIOs (chief information officers), and my Palm is chock full of these people.

Pursuing the Translation Engine Concept

Mason and Shepherd had pursued the idea for the previous six weeks, working nights and weekends to flesh out some likely applications of the technology, potential markets, and the scale of the opportunity, as well as to sort through the capabilities of potential competitors.

By the end of the six weeks, Mason thought the idea had the potential she needed to make her leave what was an attractive position at a solid company. And she felt that she could work well with Shepherd. Still, Mason knew that leaving ATS to start a new venture posed significant risks.

One issue that she knew was important, but didn't know how to get her hands around, was the technology. When Shepherd first described the key concepts behind the engine, Mason thought it was too simple to work. As she became convinced that it was, in fact, the simplicity of the concepts that made the idea so attractive, she began to worry about how they would prevent competitors from copying the concepts. She knew the first thing the venture capitalists (VCs) would want to know is why the big companies wouldn't simply take a free ride after Mason and Shepherd did all the hard work to prove the market.

Mason talked about leaving ATS and other issues that were keeping her awake at night, including her concern about competing with her current employer:

> First, I was concerned with competing with ATS—it just didn't seem right. So one of the first things I tried to sort out with Craig was what products we were likely to develop, and whether they would compete with ATS. I concluded that ATS created applications software, and that the "translation engine" was such a generic product that it would not compete at all with ATS's product. Moreover, ATS had never sold a product remotely like a translation engine and, as far as I know, had never even considered developing such a thing. Although the translator might be used by customers to create products that could compete with ATS offerings, the translator itself was not something that would ever be marketed in direct competition with any ATS product. In fact, the availability of the translator could be a great boost to ATS's efforts to enhance the reputation of UNIX-based systems as the preferred platform for mission-critical software. The more applications that are available for these systems, the more robust the service and support offerings would become. We always assumed that anything that furthered UNIX-based systems was a good thing for ATS no matter where it came from.
>
> Once I convinced myself of this, I felt a lot better. I began really spending a lot of time on nights and weekends working with Craig, and believing that it was going to happen. Craig and I finished a business plan around October 1, and we wanted to show it around town to a few VCs we knew. We left out my name and the exact description of ATS, but I knew that the VCs I planned to contact would know it was me. I planned on asking them to agree to keep my involvement confidential until I officially gave notice to ATS. Basically, I wanted to get a round of feedback from some VCs I trusted that this was a good idea, and that money could be raised before I left my job. And I have my last tranche of options vesting in six weeks and don't want to leave this on the table if I can help it.

Planning to Start a Business

During the first week of October, Shepherd and Mason agreed it was time "to put a toe in the water," and that Mason would send a draft business plan for Intelisoft to two or three of her close friends in the VC business:

First, I decided to talk to some of my former classmates who were entrepreneurs, and they advised us to get the VCs to sign a non-disclosure agreement (NDA). A friend gave us a copy of the one that he had used, and we changed a few words but basically copied it (see **Exhibit 1** for NDA). But when I talked to my VC friends about signing a confidentiality agreement before sending the plan, they all refused. They said that they meet with people all the time, and that they couldn't guarantee that whatever my idea was, it wasn't something that was already cooking in one of their portfolio companies. They couldn't subject themselves to the risk of a lawsuit with every entrepreneur they met.

So I figured that these were friends, and that we could revisit the issue once we were circulating a final plan more broadly. So, I sent the plan to the three VCs I knew who I would also describe as good friends. Now they had more questions. One of the VCs asked about my relationship with ATS: Would the company come after me and sue me? So I dug out a copy of my employment contract (see **Exhibit 2** for copy of employment agreement signed by Sheila Mason), and I also talked to Paul Bagatell, ATS's former VP of business development who was a friend, and who had left the company to join a competitor 18 months ago. He told me that I should not assume that ATS would see things the way I did, that they had been burned before by people who left. He said they would tend to assume the worst and act accordingly. He faxed me a copy of a letter that ATS's lawyers sent to him soon after his resignation. (See **Exhibit 3** for copy of letter from ATS's law firm to Bagatell.)

The VCs also asked about the protectability of the idea: Was it patentable? Had we sought a patent? I confessed that we hadn't really gone down this road yet—that we had hoped to get a better read on whether the deal was really fundable and to what extent our product would rely on the patent—before we spent that kind of money. But I suppose if the VCs wanted this buttoned up, then we were going to have to do it.

Finally, the VCs also mentioned that they would want to talk to potential customers to evaluate the business opportunity, so Shepherd and I discussed which ATS customers I should "warm up" in the event that the VCs might call. I figured we might as well talk to a potential customer ourselves to see what they would say, so I scheduled a meeting with a potential customer—someone I knew well from my time at ATS who was also an HBS section-mate. Again, I wanted to test our idea and learn a bit more about the process. We sent them basically the same NDA we had prepared for the VCs, and I got a fax yesterday where they refused to sign it without some changes. (See **Exhibit 4** for letter, requesting inclusion of a "residuals clause.")

As Mason drove towards Shepherd's home, she began to think harder about some of the concerns that she had put off thinking about all day:

I know that we are right on the verge of taking a big step here—talking to VCs and potential partners—and that it is a small world. And it is hard for me at work; these are people I have been with for seven years, whom I consider to be friends, yet I can't be forthright about my plans. We are in the annual planning cycle, and we sit around the table saying "we should do this" and I commit to my pieces of the plan, and I am beginning to feel disingenuous. So for the first time, I am really starting to think about walking into my boss (COO Dave Hatfield) and letting him know what is going on. But then I wonder, is this the right way to do it? Should I make it formal, like a letter of resignation? That seems so stiff. I could just be up front with him about what I am doing and seek his advice.

The longer Mason waited to announce her departure, however, the more she ran into potentially awkward situations at work. For example, during a recent round of golf with a subordinate—ATS's director of business development—he mentioned that if Mason ever saw an interesting opportunity for a new venture, to include him in it. Knowing that she had signed an employment agreement with a non-solicitation clause, Mason was unsure whether she could mention her potential new venture with Shepherd to her colleague. (See **Exhibit 2** for Mason's employment agreement.)

As the prospect of leaving became more of a reality, Mason became increasingly concerned about all of the potential legal issues surrounding her prospective departure from ATS. She was worried about the fact that she frequently used her personal laptop for business so she could travel efficiently. As a result, she "synched" her desktop computer at ATS with her personal computer, thus moving many of her work files, including her entire contact database, onto her home computer and Palm. Was this a problem, she wondered?

Finally, there was the issue of hiring an attorney. It did seem like it was getting to be that time. ATS worked with attorneys at a large, prestigious, "downtown" law firm, some of whom Mason had worked with on various negotiations over the past few years; she could certainly call one of these attorneys. On the other hand, she knew that there were smaller firms that were generally less expensive that worked with smaller start-ups. Mason was sure that her VC friends could provide her with the names of the law firms they liked to worked with, but this seemed to her to be a potential conflict—wouldn't she be sitting across the table negotiating with the VCs? Did she want to use lawyers who depended on the VCs for business—i.e., where would their loyalties lie? Finally, Shepherd had a programmer friend who occasionally consulted with an intellectual property "boutique" firm and who had offered to introduce them to an attorney there.

As Mason pulled into Shepherd's driveway, Shepherd walked out the front door and met Mason near her car:

> Sheila, I didn't want to talk about this over the phone from work today, but we have a problem. My boss came into the office today and told me that I was being considered for a promotion, and he wanted to make sure I wanted it before he went to bat for me. I felt I had to tell him that I was thinking about leaving and why, and when I did so, he just said, "I think this could be a problem" and left my office. An hour later, the company's general counsel walked into my office and handed me this letter.

He handed Mason a copy of the letter, in which Nova claimed all rights to Shepherd's invention. (See **Exhibit 5** for a copy.)

EXHIBIT 1 | Draft Non-Disclosure Agreement

CONFIDENTIALITY AGREEMENT

THIS CONFIDENTIALITY AGREEMENT (the "Agreement") is made this _____ day of October, 2002, by and between Intelisoft Software Systems, Inc. (INTELISOFT) and _____ ("Venture Capitalist").

Background

Venture Capitalist proposes to evaluate a potential business that INTELISOFT is currently discussing with certain other parties. In order to facilitate same, INTELISOFT proposes to share certain proprietary and confidential information with Venture Capitalist relating to the Venture. The parties are entering into this Agreement in order to restrict Venture Capitalist's use and disclosure of such information.

Terms

In consideration of the premises and mutual covenants contained herein and intending to be legally bound, the parties hereto agree as follows:

1. Information. "Information" means all data or information, whether oral or written, about the Venture (including without limitation the fact of its potential existence, the occurrence of negotiations and the identities of the potential parties thereto) furnished or available to, or otherwise obtained by, Venture Capitalist or its Associates (defined below) which is not otherwise generally available to the public. Information includes, without limitation, all specifications, drawings, sketches, models, samples, reports, plans, forecasts, current or historical data, computer programs or documentation, and all other technical, financial or business data. Unless INTELISOFT acknowledges in writing to the contrary, all Information obtained by Venture Capitalist and its Associates shall be presumed to be confidential and proprietary and shall be so treated by Venture Capitalist and its Associates.

2. Non-Disclosure. Venture Capitalist shall not directly or indirectly disclose Information to any third party (including without limitation to its officers, employees, representatives, investors, portfolio companies, advisors, agents, subcontractors and the like [collectively, its "Associates"]) without the prior written consent of INTELISOFT, and shall provide INTELISOFT with a written list of all persons to whom such information is disclosed.

3. Non-Use. Neither Venture Capitalist nor any of its Associates shall directly or indirectly use any Information for any purpose other than in connection with evaluation of the proposed Venture and only for purposes directly related to the purpose for which such Information was provided or obtained. Venture Capitalist shall retain full responsibility and shall be fully accountable to INTELISOFT for any use of Information by Venture Capitalist's Associates which is not in accordance with the terms hereof (regardless of whether such Associate is a party hereto).

4. No License. Nothing contained in this Agreement shall be construed as granting or conferring any rights by license or otherwise to Venture Capitalist or its Associates in or to any Information.

5. Return of Information. All Information shall remain the property of INTELISOFT and shall be returned by Venture Capitalist to INTELISOFT upon request. Any abstracts, notes, memoranda, or other documents containing any Information or any description, summary, or analysis of any Information shall be destroyed by Venture Capitalist upon such request, which destruction shall be certified in writing by Venture Capitalist.

6. Limitation of Agreement. This Agreement is entered into in contemplation of the negotiation of the possible investment by the Venture Capitalist in the Venture. Nothing contained herein shall obligate or be deemed to obligate INTELISOFT (including, without limitation, the Venture entity) to accept any investment from Venture Capitalist.

7. Entire Agreement. This Agreement constitutes the entire agreement between the parties and supersedes any prior or contemporaneous oral or written representations with regard to the subject matter hereof.

(continued)

EXHIBIT 1 | Draft Non-Disclosure Agreement (*continued*)

---

8. <u>Amendment and Waiver.</u>   This Agreement may not be amended, modified or waived except by a specific writing signed by both parties. No waiver hereunder shall constitute an ongoing waiver, or a waiver in any other context, unless such waiver specifically so states.

9. <u>Governing Law.</u>   This Agreement shall be governed by and construed under and in accordance with the laws of the State of Delaware, without regard to principles of conflicts of laws.

10. <u>Execution and Delivery.</u>   This Agreement may be executed and delivered either originally or by facsimile and in counterparts, each of which shall constitute an original but taken together shall constitute one and the same instrument.

IN WITNESS WHEREOF and intending to be legally bound hereby, the parties have duly executed this Agreement on the date first above written.

By: _____
Title: _____ [VENTURE CAPITALIST]

By: _____
Title:_____ [INTELISOFT]

EXHIBIT 2 | ATS Employment Agreement Signed By Sheila Mason

**EMPLOYEE NONCOMPETITION, NONSOLICITATION,
NONDISCLOSURE AND DEVELOPMENTS AGREEMENT**

In consideration and as a condition of my employment and/or continued employment by AMERICAN TELECOM-MUNICATIONS SOFTWARE, INC. and/or any of its subsidiaries, subdivisions, affiliates, successors, assigns and/or duly authorized representatives (collectively the "Company"), I hereby agree with the Company as follows:

1. <u>Non-competition.</u>   During the period of my employment by the Company and for one year thereafter (the "Non-competition Term"), regardless of the reasons for my termination, I shall not, directly or indirectly, alone or as a consultant, partner, officer, director, employee, joint venturer, lender or stockholder of any entity, (a) accept employment with any business that is in competition with the products or services being created, developed, manufactured, marketed, distributed or sold by the Company, or (b) engage in any business or activity that is in competition with the products or services being created, developed, manufactured, marketed, distributed or sold by the Company.

2. <u>Non-solicitation of Customers.</u>   During the Non-competition Term, regardless of the reasons for my termination, I will not (except on the Company's behalf), directly or indirectly, alone or as a consultant, partner, officer, director, employee, joint venturer, lender or stockholder of any entity, solicit or do business with any customer of the Company or any potential customer of the Company (i) with whom I have had contact or (ii) about whom I obtained, or became familiar with through, Confidential Information (as defined herein) during the course of my employment with the Company.

3. <u>Non-solicitation of Employees.</u>   During the Non-competition Term, regardless of the reasons for my termination, I will not (except on the Company's behalf), directly or indirectly, alone or as a consultant, partner, officer, director, employee, joint venturer, lender or stockholder of any entity, employ, attempt to employ or knowingly permit any company or business organization by which I am employed or which is directly or indirectly controlled by me to employ, any Company employee, agent, representative or consultant, or any such person whose employment with the Company has terminated within six months of my departure from the Company, or in any manner seek to solicit or induce any such person to leave his or her employment with the Company, or assist in the recruitment or hiring of any such person.

EXHIBIT 2 | (*continued*)

4. <u>Nondisclosure.</u>   I shall not at any time, whether during or after the termination of my employment, reveal to any person or entity any Confidential Information except to employees of the Company who need to know such Confidential Information for the purposes of their employment, or as otherwise authorized by the Company in writing. The term "Confidential Information" shall include, without limitation, any information concerning the organization, business or finances of the Company or of any third party which the Company is under an obligation to keep confidential or that is maintained by the Company as confidential. Such Confidential Information shall include, but is not limited to, trade secrets or confidential information respecting inventions, products, designs, methods, know-how, techniques, systems, processes, engineering data, software programs, software code, works of authorship, customer lists, customer information, supplier lists, supplier information, marketing or sales information, financial information, financial projections, pricing information, business plans, projects, plans and proposals. I shall keep confidential all matters entrusted to me and shall not use or attempt to use any Confidential Information except as may be required in the ordinary course of performing my duties as an employee of the Company, nor shall I use any Confidential Information in any manner which may injure or cause loss or may be calculated to injure or cause loss to the Company, whether directly or indirectly.

5. <u>Company Property.</u>   I agree that during my employment I shall not make, use or permit to be used any Company Property otherwise than for the benefit of the Company. The term "Company Property" shall include all notes, memoranda, reports, lists, records, files, drawings, sketches, specifications, designs, software programs, software code, data, computers, cellular telephones, pagers, credit and/or calling cards, keys, access cards, documentation or other materials of any nature and in any form, whether written, printed, electronic or in digital format or otherwise, relating to any matter within the scope of the business of the Company or concerning any of its dealings or affairs and any other Company property in my possession, custody or control. I further agree that I shall not, after the termination of my employment, use or permit others to use any such Company Property. I acknowledge and agree that all Company Property shall be and remain the sole and exclusive property of the Company. Immediately upon the termination of my employment I shall deliver all Company Property in my possession, and all copies thereof, to the Company.

6. <u>Assignment of Developments.</u>

(a) If at any time or times during my employment, I shall (either alone or with others) make, conceive, create, discover, invent or reduce to practice any Development that (i) relates to the business of the Company or any customer of or supplier to the Company or any of the products or services being developed, manufactured or sold by the Company or which may be used in relation therewith; or (ii) results from tasks assigned to me by the Company; or (iii) results from the use of premises or personal property (whether tangible or intangible) owned, leased or contracted for by the Company, then all such Developments and the benefits thereof are and shall immediately become the sole and absolute property of the Company and its assigns, as works made for hire or otherwise. The term "Development" shall mean any invention, modification, discovery, design, development, improvement, process, software program, work of authorship, documentation, formula, data, technique, know-how, trade secret or intellectual property right whatsoever or any interest therein (whether or not patentable or registrable under copyright, trademark or similar statutes (including, but not limited to, the Semiconductor Chip Protection Act) or subject to analogous protection). I shall promptly disclose to the Company (or any persons designated by it) each such Development. I hereby assign all rights (including, but not limited to, rights to inventions, patentable subject matter, copyrights and trademarks) I may have or may acquire in the Developments and all benefits and/or rights resulting therefrom to the Company and its assigns without further compensation and shall communicate, without cost or delay, and without disclosing to others the same, all available information relating thereto (with all necessary plans and models) to the Company.

(b) Excluded Developments. I represent that the Developments identified in the Appendix, if any, attached hereto comprise all the Developments that I have made or conceived prior to my employment by the Company, which Developments are excluded from this Agreement. I understand that it is only necessary to list the title of such Developments and the purpose thereof but not details of the Development itself. If there are any such developments to be excluded, the undersigned should initial here _____; otherwise it will be deemed that there are no such exclusions.

(*continued*)

EXHIBIT 2 | ATS Employment Agreement Signed By Sheila Mason (*continued*)

7. <u>Further Assurances</u>.   I shall, during my employment and at any time thereafter, at the request and cost of the Company, promptly sign, execute, make and do all such deeds, documents, acts and things as the Company and its duly authorized officers may reasonably require:

(a) to apply for, obtain, register and vest in the name of the Company alone (unless the Company otherwise directs) patents, copyrights, trademarks or other analogous protection in any country throughout the world relating to a Development of the Company and when so obtained or vested to renew and restore the same;

(b) to assist in the defense of any judicial, opposition or other proceedings in respect of such applications and any judicial, opposition or other proceeding, petition or application for revocation of any such patent, copyright, trademark or other analogous protection; and

If the Company is unable, after reasonable effort, to secure my signature as required by this paragraph on any application for patent, copyright, trademark or other analogous registration or other documents regarding any legal protection relating to a Development, whether because of my physical or mental incapacity or for any other reason whatsoever, I hereby irrevocably designate and appoint the Company and its duly authorized officers and agents as my agent and attorney-in-fact, to act for and in my behalf and stead to execute and file any such application or applications or other documents and to do all other lawfully permitted acts to further the prosecution and issuance of patent, copyright or trademark registrations or any other legal protection thereon with the same legal force and effect as if executed by me.

8. <u>Consent to Use Name/Likeness.</u>   I hereby consent to the use of my name, picture, signature, voice, image, and/or likeness by the Company during the term of this Agreement and at any time thereafter. Further, I waive all claims I may now have or may ever have against the Company and its officers, employees, and agents arising out of the Company's use, adaptation, reproduction, modification, distribution, exhibition or other commercial exploitation of my name, picture, signature, voice, image and/or likeness, including, but not limited to, right of privacy, right of publicity and celebrity, use of voice, name or likeness, defamation and copyright infringement. I represent and warrant that I have not made any contract or commitment in conflict with this consent and waiver.

9. <u>Representations</u>.

(a) I represent that my employment with the Company and my performance of all of the terms of this Agreement do not and will not breach any agreement to keep in confidence proprietary information acquired by me in confidence or in trust prior to my employment by the Company, nor will it violate any nonsolicitation and/or noncompetition agreements entered into prior to my employment with the Company. I have not entered into, and I shall not enter into, any agreement either written or oral in conflict herewith.

(b) I further agree that any breach of this Agreement by me will cause irreparable damage to the Company and that in the event of such breach the Company shall have, in addition to any and all remedies of law, the right to an injunction, specific performance or other equitable relief to prevent the violation of my obligations hereunder.

10. <u>Waiver; Amendments</u>.   Any waiver by the Company of a breach of any provision of this Agreement shall not operate or be construed as a waiver of any subsequent breach of such provision or any other provision hereof. In addition, any amendment to or modification of this Agreement or any waiver of any provision hereof must be in writing and signed by the Company's Chief Executive Officer.

11. <u>Severability</u>.   I agree that each provision and the subparts of each provision herein shall be treated as separate and independent clauses, and the unenforceability of any one clause shall in no way impair the enforceability of any of the other clauses of the Agreement. Moreover, if one or more of the provisions contained in this Agreement shall for any reason be held to be excessively broad as to scope, activity, subject or otherwise so as to be unenforceable at law, such provision or provisions shall be construed by the appropriate judicial body by limiting or reducing it or them, so as to be enforceable to the maximum extent compatible with the applicable law as it shall then appear. I hereby further agree that the language of all parts of this Agreement shall in all cases be construed as a whole according to its fair meaning and not strictly for or against either of the parties.

12. <u>Survival</u>.   This Agreement shall be effective as of the date entered below. My obligations under this Agreement shall survive the termination of my employment regardless of the manner of such termination and shall be binding upon my heirs, executors, administrators and legal representatives.

EXHIBIT 2 | *(continued)*

13. <u>Assignment</u>.   The Company shall have the right to assign this Agreement to its successors and assigns, and all covenants and agreements hereunder shall inure to the benefit of and be enforceable by said successors or assigns. I will not assign this Agreement.

14. <u>Governing Law</u>.   This Agreement shall be governed by and construed in accordance with the laws of Delaware and shall in all respects be interpreted, enforced and governed under the internal and domestic laws of Delaware, without giving effect to the principles of conflicts of laws of such state. Any claims or legal actions by one party against the other arising out of the relationship between the parties contemplated herein (whether or not arising under this Agreement) shall be governed by the laws of Delaware. I further agree that any claims or legal actions by one party against the other arising out of the relationship between the parties contemplated herein (whether or not arising under this Agreement) shall be governed by the laws of Delaware and shall be commenced and maintained in any state or federal court located in such state, and I hereby submit to the jurisdiction and venue of any such court.

15. <u>Entire Agreement</u>.   This Agreement sets forth the complete, sole and entire agreement between the parties with respect to the subject matter herein and supersedes any and all other agreements, negotiations, discussions, proposals, or understandings, whether oral or written, previously entered into, discussed or considered by the parties.

IN WITNESS HEREOF, I have executed this Agreement as of the date first written below.

Signature: <u>(signed) Sheila Mason</u>

Date: <u>November 12, 1994</u>

Appendix: List of Developments and Purpose:

— NONE —

EXHIBIT 3 | Letter from ATS's Counsel to Paul Bagatell, Former Director of Business Development and Friend of Sheila Mason

March 22, 2001

<u>**Via Federal Express and First Class Mail**</u>

Mr. Paul Bagatell

RE: ATS, Inc.

Dear Mr. Bagatell:

This firm represents American Telecommunications Software, Inc. ("ATS" or the "Company"). I write regarding your obligations under your Employee Noncompetition, Nonsolicitation, Nondisclosure and Developments Agreement (the "Agreement") which you executed as a condition of your ATS employment. ATS has serious concerns that you may be violating this Agreement, as well as certain common law and statutory obligations.

It is our understanding that effective Friday, March 17, 2001 you resigned as ATS's Vice-President of Business Development, and that on the very next business day—Monday, March 20, 2001—you began employment with Jaguar Systems, a company in direct competition with ATS. It further is our understanding that when asked by the Company where you were going to work, you refused to provide the name of your new employer but repeatedly represented to ATS that you were not going to work for one of ATS's competitors.

ATS has significant concerns that you are breaching two key contractual obligations that you owe to ATS by virtue of your Jaguar employment. First, you agreed in paragraph 1 of the Agreement that you would not, for one year from the termination of your ATS employment, directly or indirectly "engage in any business activity that is in competition with the products or services being created, developed, manufactured, marketed, distributed or sold by the Company." Your Jaguar Systems employment appears to breach this provision.

Second, you expressly agreed in paragraph 2 of the Agreement that you would not, for one year from the termination of your ATS employment, "solicit or do business with any customer of the Company, or any potential customer of the Company (i) with whom I have had contact or (ii) about whom I obtained, or became familiar with through, Confidential Information (as defined herein) during the course of my employment with the Company." To the extent that you are conducting such prohibited business with ATS's clients or prospective clients, you are violating this provision. And without limiting the generality of the foregoing, please be advised that ATS will consider you to have violated this provision (and possibly other provisions) to the extent that you make any statements to Jaguar Systems with respect to ATS's business dealings with its clients, whether actual or prospective.

Irrespective of whether you are violating your noncompete and nonsolicit obligations to ATS, our client nonetheless has serious concerns that, during your employment with Jaguar Systems, you may reveal, use or inevitably disclose ATS's confidential, proprietary and/or trade secret information. As you know, during your ATS employment you were exposed to and entrusted with a considerable amount of the Company's confidential, proprietary, and trade secret information, including, but not limited to, the Company's proprietary sales database, customer contact list, pricing plans, pricing methodologies, customer demand, order and pipeline information, product architecture, development and roadmaps, and marketing strategies. In your capacity as the Company's Vice President of Business Development, you had frequent contact with and intimate knowledge of ATS's customers. The Agreement expressly forbids you from improperly using or disclosing such Company Confidential Information and goodwill. In addition, you have common law and statutory obligations (including such obligations pursuant to the Federal Economic Espionage Act of 1996) that prohibit such conduct.

Similarly, paragraph 5 of the Agreement prohibits you from using or retaining any Company Property. You are violating that Agreement to the extent that you have retained any Company Property, including, but not limited to, any Company Property that may reside on any home computer. Please return all Company Property immediately.

EXHIBIT 3 | (*continued*)

The Company takes its contractual, common law, and statutory rights very seriously and will not tolerate any conduct on your part that would violate such rights. In order to avoid escalating this matter, please describe (in writing) your current position with Jaguar Systems, including the exact nature and extent of your duties (both present and contemplated), the customers and/or accounts to whom you have been assigned, and the products or services that you are marketing, selling and/or distributing. In addition, please provide a written representation to the undersigned that you are abiding by your obligations in the Agreement. The requested information and representations should be submitted to this office no later than Friday, March 24, 2001. If you fail to submit this information, the Company will have no alternative but to take all actions necessary to safeguard its rights.

ATS expects you to scrupulously abide by your obligations. I suggest that you carefully review the Noncompetition, Nonsolicitation, Nondisclosure and Developments Agreement to reacquaint yourself with your contractual obligations and ATS's rights when faced with your violation or threatened violation of the Agreement. ATS will continue to monitor this situation closely and will not tolerate any unfair and deceptive trade practices. If such conduct occurs, ATS may initiate appropriate legal proceedings including, but not limited to, seeking injunctive relief. At this point, ATS is reserving all rights pending receipt of your assurances as outlined above.

I look forward to your prompt response.

Very truly yours,

EXHIBIT 4 | Customer Letter Requesting "Residuals" Clause Language in NDA

Sheila:

Got your proposed NDA. We are comfortable signing as long as you insert the following language:

Residuals. Notwithstanding anything herein to the contrary, either party may use Residuals for any purpose, including without limitation use in development, manufacture, promotion, sale and maintenance of its products and services; provided that this right to Residuals does not represent a license under any patents, copyrights or other intellectual property rights of the disclosing party. The term "Residuals" means any information retained in the unaided memories of the receiving party's employees who have had access to the disclosing party's Confidential Information pursuant to the terms of this Agreement. An employee's memory is unaided if the employee has not intentionally memorized the Confidential Information for the purpose of retaining and subsequently using or disclosing it.

Let me know.

Thanks,

John Hammersmith

EXHIBIT 5 | Nova Letter to Craig Shepherd (including copy of his employment agreement)

Dear Craig:

On July 14, 1992, Nova hired you to work for our firm as Manager of documentation and support and you and Nova entered into an Agreement Regarding Assignment of Inventions and Non-Disclosure (see Exhibit A, hereinafter, "the Agreement") at the onset of this employment relationship. The terms of the Agreement speak to two types of inventions: (1) those conceived prior to your employment by Nova and (2) those conceived during your employment with Nova. With respect to the first, you declared you had none. With respect to the second, the Agreement clearly obligates you to ". . . communicate to an officer of the Company promptly and fully all inventions (including but not limited to all matters subject to patent, i.e., processes, machines, computer programs, etc.) made or conceived by me (whether made solely by me or jointly with others) from the time of entering the Company's employ until I leave (1) which are along the lines of the business, work or investigations of the Company or of companies which it owns or controls at the time of such inventions, or (2) which result from or are suggested by any work which I may do for or on behalf of the Company."

Nova is a corporation engaged in the business of developing software that solves its customers technology problems. Over your ten years with the company you were employed in various positions, each providing you with insight into the company's products and customers. As you know from your own experience, Nova's customer's are often engaged in the frustrating and time-consuming task of porting legacy software applications to the UNIX operating environment. As such, there would be great commercial advantage to Nova to be able to provide to its customers a more cost-efficient method of performing porting tasks or to offer a cost-effective legacy application porting service to its customers. Such a product offering would not only generate direct revenue, but would also result in follow-on revenue from support services or utilities to maintain and upgrade the ported applications.

To state our position succinctly, during and as a result of your employment at Nova, you became aware of the enormous resources currently invested in legacy applications, as well as the difficulties that currently exist in porting and updating this code. Having learned these facts, during and as a result of your employment at Nova, you realized how valuable an automated translation process would be and you conceived and developed this invention, to which Nova holds the "sole and exclusive" right.

The field of software is highly competitive. Inventions, new concepts, ideas, and trade secrets are among the most valuable assets of companies like Nova. By this letter, we are notifying you of our claim on this invention, and request that you sign below and return to Nova, indicating your agreement with this letter, and that you deliver, in writing, to Nova your notes, drawings, and prototypes of this product, along with whatever other explanation is required to reduce this invention to practice.

Craig, it is our sincere hope that we can resolve this situation amicably.

Sincerely,

Catherine Klein
Nova Software Company, General Counsel

EXHIBIT 5 | *(continued)*

Nova Software Company

AGREEMENT REGARDING ASSIGNMENT OF INVENTIONS AND NON-DISCLOSURE

Name: **CRAIG SHEPHERD**

In consideration of my employment (or continued employment in the event I am already in the employ of the Company at the time of execution hereof) with Nova Software Company or any subsidiary or affiliate thereof (the "Company") and of the salary or wages paid for my services in such employment, the Company and I agree as follows:

(A) I will communicate to an officer of the Company promptly and fully all inventions (including but not limited to all matters subject to patent, i.e., processes, machines, computer programs, etc.) made or conceived by me (whether made solely by me or jointly with others) from the time of entering the Company's employ until I leave, (1) which are along the lines of the business, work or investigations of the Company or of companies which it owns or controls at the time of such inventions, or (2) which result from or are suggested by any work which I may do for or on behalf of the Company.

(B) I will assist the Company and its nominees during or subsequent to such employment in every proper way (entirely at its or their expense) to obtain for its or their own benefit patents for such inventions in any and all countries (including the assignment of any inventions to the Company), and said inventions will remain the sole and exclusive property of the Company or its nominees whether patented or not.

(C) In accordance with Company policy as in effect from time to time, I will make and maintain adequate records of all such inventions, in the form of notes, sketches, drawings, or reports relating thereto, which records shall be and remain the property of, and available to, the Company at all times.

(D) Except as the Company may otherwise consent in writing, I will not disclose at any time (except as my Company duties may require) either during or within a period of (2) years subsequent to the term of employment, any information, knowledge, or data of the Company I may receive or develop during the course of my employment, relating to trade secrets, formulas, business processes, methods, machines, inventions, discoveries, computer programs, customer records, lists, accounts or other matters which are of a private, secret or confidential nature.

(E) I will notify the Company in writing before I make any disclosure or perform or cause to be performed any work for or on behalf of the Company, which might conflict with (1) the rights I claim in any invention or idea (a) conceived by me or others prior to my employment or (b) otherwise outside the scope of this Agreement, or (2) rights of others arising out of obligations incurred by me (a) prior to this Agreement or (b) otherwise outside the scope of this Agreement. In the event of my failure to give notice under the circumstances specified in (1) the foregoing, the Company may assume that no such conflicting invention or idea exists, and I agree that I will make no claim against the Company with respect to the use of any such invention or idea in any work or the product of any work which I perform or cause to be performed for or on behalf of the Company. All discoveries owned or controlled by me, in whole or in part, as of the date of this Agreement are listed below.

Discoveries owned or controlled: (If none, so state. Attach separate sheet if necessary.)

——————————————————————————————————

————————————————NONE————————————————

——————————————————————————————————

EXHIBIT 5 | Nova Letter to Craig Shepherd (including copy of his employment agreement) (*continued*)

(F) I will allow the Company, without charge, fee, license or other arrangement and free from any allegation of infringement whatsoever to make full use of any matter developed by me (whether developed or written solely by me or jointly with others) during the course of my employment along the lines of the business, work or investigations of the Company or of companies which it owns or controls at the time of such development and/or which result from or are suggested by any work which I may do for or on behalf of the Company.

This Agreement may not be changed, modified, released, discharged, abandoned or otherwise terminated, in whole or in part, except by an instrument in writing signed by me and by an officer or other authorized executive of the Company.

This Agreement shall be binding upon my heirs, executors, administrators or other legal representatives or assigns. Any reference to the Company shall include the Company's subsidiaries, successors and assigns.

Except as stated below, I have no agreements with or obligations to others in conflict with the foregoing. (If "none," so state.)

Arrangements with or obligations to others: (If none, so state. Attach separate sheet if necessary.)

————————————————————————

——————————NONE—————————————

————————————————————————

The Company and I acknowledge that this Agreement does not constitute a contract of employment and that either the Company or I can terminate the employment relationship at any time subject to any applicable employment policies of the Company then in effect. However, my agreement not to use or disclose the Company's proprietary data or information and to protect the Company's interest in any inventions shall survive termination of my employment.

Employee

Name: (signed) **CRAIG SHEPHERD**

Date: **JULY 14, 1992**

Nova Software Company

By: (signed) **STEVEN JOBSON**

Title: VP, Human Resources

NanoGene Technologies, Inc.

It was Friday, November 9, 2002, and Will Tompkins was both excited and concerned. The 41-year-old Biochemistry Ph.D. had quit his job at Eastern Institute of Technology's Advanced Materials Sciences Lab (AMSL) six months earlier to become CEO of NanoGene Technologies, a life sciences start-up based on nanotechnology. Over the previous six months, he and his four co-founders from AMSL had made tremendous progress in developing the underlying science that would enable the company to attract venture capital funding. Within the past 24 hours, Tompkins had participated in three meetings about issues that might have a dramatic impact on the future success of the business. The first meeting had taken place the day before with Paige Miller, a 1995 Harvard Business School (HBS) graduate who had been doing some consulting for NanoGene, and whom Tompkins was trying to recruit to join the management team. The second had taken place that morning between Tompkins and his four co-founders. He had just finished the third with Susan Stone, a venture capitalist (VC) who Tompkins hoped would become a lead investor for NanoGene's Series A funding.

Tompkins's co-founders included Don Rupert, the head of AMSL, as well as three fellow scientists from the lab: Mark Masterson, Ravi Rhoota, and Gary Garfield. The five had met that morning to discuss negotiating a compensation package that would entice Miller to join NanoGene as its VP of Operations. Miller had considerable experience in the life sciences industry as VP of Operations at a successful biotech company. (See **Exhibit 1** for resume.) Tompkins and his team were eager to have her on board. However, as Tompkins and Miller began to negotiate her compensation package, they soon realized that they were very far apart in terms of their expectations. Tompkins summarized the situation:

> Everyone likes Paige, and we have grown to respect her abilities a great deal. But she said she needed to make $175,000 in salary and have 3% of the equity (post-Series A financing). This basically means she will be making almost twice as much in compensation as the

Senior Lecturer Michael J. Roberts and Professor Linda A. Cyr and prepared this case. HBS cases are developed solely as the basis for class discussion. Cases are not intended to serve as endorsements, sources of primary data, or illustrations of effective or ineffective management. The identities of individuals and institutions in this case have been disguised.

founders and have nearly the same amount of equity. All of the founders have worked very hard to build a culture of equality—it is important to us—but it is hard to imagine that a non-founder should make so much more than the rest of us.

Miller explained her view:

I have been consulting in the biotech industry since I left my job two years ago, and I have gotten four job offers from post-Series A companies that have all been between $160,000 and $180,000 in salary and 2.75% to 3% of the equity. I feel like I know what my market value is, and as much as I like Will, the whole team, and the prospects for the business, I don't see why I should settle for less than I am worth.

Tompkins's co-founders were disappointed and angered when they heard about the negotiations, and they raised several questions:

Does this mean that Paige is not buying into our vision for the company? Do we even need someone of this caliber yet? Why hire a VP of Operations when we have no operations? I understand why we need an office manager and a bookkeeper, but what exactly are we buying for this big price tag?

The discussion was at times quite heated, and Tompkins knew that the issue was far from resolved when he had to excuse himself to go meet with Susan Stone, a local venture capitalist. His meeting with Stone got off to a much better start; Tompkins was encouraged when Stone told him that she was nearly ready to put together a preliminary term sheet and run it by her partners. The emotional boost was short-lived as Stone began to voice several concerns. Tompkins recalled:

She said she liked the team and the technology that we were developing, but that we had made some very unconventional choices that she was going to have a hard time selling to her partners. First, was the large founding team. She said they see very few teams with more than three founders. Second, was the fact that we decided to split the equity equally among ourselves. She walked me through the numbers on the assumption that we raise $10 million for roughly 60% of the equity, which translates into each of us being left with only 3%, which she thought was quite a low figure at this stage of financing.

Moreover, the fact that I would have the same percentage ownership, as CEO, also troubled her. And she felt the same way about my salary. I told her that each of the founders planned to draw $120,000 in salary. She thought that was above market for the co-founders who would be senior scientists—she thought $95,000 was market for them. And for me, she thought $120,000 was too low.

When Stone left his office, Tompkins sat for a moment with his head spinning. While he wanted time to think about the issues Stone had raised, he felt he had to turn his attention back to several business issues that would not wait: "In anticipation of funding, we had begun to interview candidates, and Paige had been stressing to me the importance of defining a set of hiring practices and a compensation plan for employees. Similarly, we needed to discuss our company culture. As we began to hire people, it seemed like it was time to formalize our thinking on this topic."

As Friday came to a close, it was clear that each of the three parties—Tompkins, Miller, and Stone—had a lot to think through in the coming days.

Developing an Idea and Building a Team

The AMSL was one of the top material science labs in the world, and was associated with Eastern Institute of Technology (EIT). The lab was an eclectic mix of 50 or so scientists, including faculty from the ranks of EIT, post-doctoral students, and staff scientists, all of whom pursued a broad array of material science projects. The lab was well known for having made important discoveries that underpinned advances in semiconductor technologies in the 1980s and early 1990s, and had turned its attention to nanotechnology and its applications in the mid 1990s. Nanotechnology refers to a set of technologies that allow the fabrication of materials at the scale of 10 to 100 nanometers (a nanometer is a billionth of a meter). The first commercial applications of the technology were on the horizon, and the area had become a reasonably "hot" area for venture investing. Between 2001 and late 2002, six start-ups had spun out of AMSL in the Boston area.

All of the NanoGene founders had worked at AMSL, although their work was in different sections of the lab. The scientists were working on a set of technologies that they knew linked some potentially exciting commercial applications of nanotechnology with advances in genomics. Specifically, work on the human genome project had identified specific genes that were the underlying cause of several diseases, such as certain forms of cancer. Moreover, it was widely believed that continuing advances in genomics would soon unlock the biological underpinnings of many more diseases. While scientists expected that it would be many years before such technology could be used for *treating* diseases, the prospect of using the technology to *diagnose* diseases before they became active in the body was widely believed to offer great, and earlier, promise.

One technique that had been developed to accomplish this relied upon isolating the specific genes responsible for a disease, and then testing individual patients to see if they carried those genes. Scientists were developing approaches to this testing that required depositing genes on a sophisticated substrate material and "slicing and dicing" the genes to permit this identification.

The founders of NanoGene had developed techniques and compounds that—when used as the substrate material—caused the genes to "stretch out and straighten up," making it much easier to do the cutting and manipulation that was required. The company's business plan was to first perfect, and then begin to sell, the patented substrate chips already "lined" with the particular genetic code in question (e.g., the two genes responsible to colon cancer) so that diagnostic testing labs around the world could simply wash patient samples over a chip and read the results.

By the summer of 2001, the founders decided that the technology indeed had promise, and were nearly ready to file the provisional patents—on behalf of AMSL—that underpinned this technology. As they continued to "gel" as a team, and as they felt more confident in the technology's promise, the scientists felt that they needed to talk to Rupert, AMSL's Director. Tompkins recalled the situation:

> By the summer of 2001, we knew what we wanted to do. We began to talk to Don because we genuinely wanted his advice. Don was an expert in substrate surface tension at the molecular level, and we knew his knowledge could really help us.

Don was excited about what we were doing and said he was interested in becoming a co-founder. We were thrilled; Don had served on many companies' scientific advisory boards in the past, but had never agreed to be a co-founder before. Don said that he wanted to stay at the lab, and the terms of his employment limited his working with us to only one day a week, but we were sure that his endorsement would help us get funded and that his contacts would also be pivotal to our success.

Actually Starting the Company

In November 2001, the team met for dinner at Rupert's house to discuss formally incorporating the company. They discussed a number of important issues including equity splits, salaries, funding strategies, and naming Tompkins CEO. One of the co-founders, Mark Masterson, explained:

> Each of us kicked in $1,000 to incorporate the company and get things going. We decided to split the equity equally. We also decided that we would begin seeking $600,000 or so in angel financing.
>
> The money-raising discussion led us to start talking about what kinds of salaries we would take upon leaving the lab. We thought $120,000 in salary was reasonable even though there was variance in what each of us was making at the lab. Our salaries ranged from $55,000 to $90,000 depending on discipline (e.g., physicists were paid more than biologists) and whether you were a post-doc or on staff or an academic senior scientist, but it was well known that industry salaries were 50% higher than the academic salaries. I think it would have been disruptive to try to slice and dice the equity and compensation according to a more complicated set of principles; it would have upset the team.
>
> We determined that Will would take the CEO role by universal acclamation. He just exuded natural leadership and he already had contacts with VCs and with a law firm and had already learned much more than any of us about what it took to start a company.

At the time of the company's founding:

- Tompkins was a scientist in the biophysics group earning $80,000.
- Mark Masterson was a senior scientist in biophysics group earning $90,000.
- Ravi Rhoota was a scientist in the biology group earning $65,000.
- Gary Garfield was a post-doctoral fellow in biology earning $55,000.

Through early 2002, the team continued to work on their plans for starting a business, and sought funding to get the enterprise off the ground. The first 12 to 18 months of the company's life would involve perfecting the technology and proving that it would work at a commercial scale. In Tompkins' words:

> The basic principles have been worked out and demonstrated in the lab. But, we need to put several different pieces of technology together, and then prove that they will all work at commercial scale. The angel round will really just scratch the surface—we need about $10 million to get through this 18-month phase. But the angel round will buy us a little time and let us get organized to raise some serious money.

Raising the Angel Round

One of Tompkins's contacts was a former CEO of a biotech company who was an active angel investor. After hearing the team's plan, and with Rupert's strong backing, he agreed to pull a group together to invest $600,000 at a $2.25 million post-money valuation. The deal closed in June 2002. At the time the financing was negotiated, the founders decided they would make their own stock vest according to the following schedule: 20% immediately, 20% at the end of the first year, and then the remaining 60% at the rate of 2% per month. Tompkins and the team began the process of looking for lab space and buying some of the equipment they would need.

When Tompkins resigned from the lab in May 2002, the angel round was pretty well negotiated, and he began working seriously on raising a more substantial venture round, and on recruiting a "business person" to the team. It was shortly after this point that one of the VCs whom Tompkins had met referred him to Miller.

Recruiting Paige Miller

Paige Miller had six years of operational experience in biotech. After graduating from UCLA with a B.S. in Business, she spent the next few years working at a tennis club in the San Francisco Bay area before attending Harvard Business School to focus on manufacturing. Miller described her path:

> I played tennis competitively in college and wanted to continue playing, but court time was expensive in San Francisco, so I made a deal with this club that I would trade an hour of court time for an hour of my working around the club. Before long, I was spending more and more time around the club and was working full-time doing a lot of their back-office operations. But it didn't seem like this was destined to lead anywhere that I wanted to go—I felt like I wanted to make more of a difference in the world.
>
> At the time, there was a fear that the United States was falling behind as a world-class manufacturer, and some people suggested that this was an arena that needed bright young people. I spent a year working for Intel in their Washington, D.C., office doing research on U.S. manufacturing competitiveness. A friend suggested I apply to HBS, and I got in. I spent the next two years taking as many manufacturing and operations courses as I could.

Miller graduated from HBS in 1995. When she began looking for a job, she soon realized that she wasn't going to get a job through traditional recruiting channels. She set off on her own search:

> I decided that only three things mattered to me: I wanted to be in manufacturing, in biotech, or in medical instruments, and in Boston. I got a list of all the biotech and medical devices firms in Boston and wrote cold-call letters to the CEOs describing my background and telling them that I wanted to work in manufacturing. The CEO of BioMolecular Technologies followed up with me and we created a job where I would be the sidekick to the VP of Manufacturing. BioMolecular was a pre-IPO life sciences instrumentation company with about 120 people, and over the next couple of years it had gone public, and I had the opportunity to work in every kind of job in manufacturing as well as doing stints in finance and marketing.

In 1997, Miller took over as director of manufacturing and was in that role when Bio-Molecular was acquired by International Biotech. Miller was the youngest senior executive in this international company and was responsible for integrating global operations into the current site. After having seen BioMolecular go public and seeing it through its acquisition, Miller decided that she was ready to move on to new challenges. In late 2001, a business-school friend encouraged Miller to leave her current position without having another job. In early 2002, she began working through her VC network to look for another job, and took on some consulting work as well. She recalled meeting Tompkins:

> By summer, Will was trying to raise VC money in earnest and he was getting feedback about not having any business experience on the team. I was introduced to Will by some of the VCs I was networking with. I recall his asking me in one of our interviews what I would expect to make if I joined the team. I had received a handful of offers over the past twelve months to be VP of Operations at post-Series A companies. The typical offer was in the $175,000 salary range with 2.5% to 3% of the equity, and I told them I would look for something consistent with that. The initial reaction from Will and the team was, "oh, that doesn't seem too bad."

Tompkins recalled his thinking:

> I knew my strength was the science, not operations. I wanted a generalist—someone who was very much a team player and who was willing to do whatever it took to get the job done. Initially, it was clear what she would do and the areas in which she would contribute. I expected that she would set HR policies, work on getting access to appropriate facilities, manage vendor relationships, deal with the landlords, and do the bookkeeping. She would do all the little things that would let us focus on the science.

Miller offered to do some consulting projects for NanoGene until it had raised its Series A round.

Acquiring the Intellectual Property

By late July 2002, NanoGene seemed well on its way, but before it could attract serious investors, it had to lock up the required intellectual property (IP). The key patents included four patents in Mark Masterson's name (but owned by EIT) which covered most of the key technology. One additional patent was in Ravi Rhoota's name (also owned by EIT) but was, in Tompkins' words, "critical to making all the technology work." In August, after a few months of negotiations, EIT agreed to license the required patents to NanoGene in exchange for 400,000 shares (15%) of the company's equity as well as a 3% royalty on sales.

Raising Venture Capital

Tompkins had been working on raising VC financing in an informal way since early summer 2002, and once the IP was firmed up, he began more serious meetings: "For the first few meetings, all five of us would pile into Gary's van and head over to meet with the VCs. After a few of these sessions, I got the feedback that this was sending a bad signal to the VCs, so just Ravi and I started going to the meetings."

NanoGene was seeking $10 million in Series A financing. The team had decided this was sufficient to fund them for 18 months, and to get them to technical proof-of-concept and pilot production. For the first year or so, all of the work would be on the "science" side of the project—perfecting the technology. Then, it would shift to commercializing that technology. It was anticipated that the team would be at roughly 30 people by that point, including the founders.

In September 2002, Tompkins was meeting frequently with VCs, trying to interest them in investing in the company. By October, several VCs were performing serious due diligence on the company. And most of the VCs had issues with some aspects of the team and the decisions they had made. Tompkins explained what he heard from the VCs:

> The first thing that raised a red flag was the very large founding team. The VCs said that about two-thirds of the teams they fund are pure scientists, but there are generally only two or three of them and usually one of them has had experience as a Chief Scientific Officer of an established firm, so they have experience driving the commercialization of technology. Here were five guys, none of whom had ever worked in a company. Both the number of founders and the collective business inexperience was very rare, in their view.
>
> Another big cause for concern was the way we had decided to split the equity. Their view was that a market exists for the way equity should be divided, and equally is *not* it. According to the VCs, biotech CEOs usually have 7 to 10% equity post-Series A and founder-CEOs have upwards of 15%. Typically, CEOs will retain about 2.5 times as much equity as VP-level founders.
>
> Their concerns were similar with regard to our decision to take equal salaries. They thought $120,000 was low for a CEO and too high for everyone else. A typical early-stage biotech CEO makes about $250,000 and "market" for a senior scientist is $95,000. They didn't expect that I would make anywhere near that much because the $250,000 figure is for a much more seasoned executive, but they thought I should certainly make more than the other founders.

Tompkins had analyzed the likely distribution of equity ownership, assuming the company was successful in raising $10 million for roughly 60% of the equity, as the VCs had indicated. The VCs had also conveyed the sense that the company would have to create an option pool of roughly 13% of the shares, which Tompkins also modeled. (See **Exhibit 2** for Tompkins's pro-forma analysis of the company following the Series A financing.) Still, he was not convinced that there was a problem; he described his reactions to the VCs' concerns:

> I thought the equal distribution of equity was important for a number of reasons. First, I didn't really view myself as more important than the rest of these guys—we all started this together and success would depend upon all of us, and I was CEO because my skills most closely fit those requirements. There was no argument among us with the notion of equality.

Building an Organization

In anticipation of the funding coming together by the year's end, Masterson quit his job at the lab in June 2002, shortly after Tompkins resigned. Rhoota quit his job at the lab in October 2002. Thus, three of the founders were drawing a salary from the money raised in the angle round, although they had decided to take the relatively low amount of $750 per week. In Tompkin's words, "We figured we could get by on a small amount for living expenses until the funding closed." Garfield was planning on quitting as soon as the Series A round closed. In Masterson's words, "Gary had a bigger family to support and mortgage payments to make. We didn't think it was fair for him to squeak by while we were waiting to raise the money."

Tompkins had kept in touch with Miller. In September, he asked Miller to begin doing some consulting work and at the same time enter into more serious discussions about coming on board in the Vice President of Operations role.

Defining the Hiring Process

By early November, the funding seemed imminent, and the founders decided to begin the process of hiring the next layer of scientists. The planned organization was that each of the other three full-time founders (i.e., the ones other than Tompkins and Rupert) would comprise the company's senior scientists, and that each would report to Tompkins, as would Miller. Each senior scientist would have reporting to him a scientist and two research assistants (RAs). This team of 12 scientists was anticipated to be in place through the first six months or so, and would expand to 25 or so by the end of the year. Although it was not yet clear exactly how many of each type of scientist would be hired, Tompkins's best guess was, "By year end, we'll have to hire 16 RAs, eight scientists, and one more senior scientist."

As the company got closer to funding, Tompkins encouraged his co-founders to begin to recruit some of the scientists and RAs they would need as they began to build the company. Miller—who was continuing to do consulting work for the company—described the discussion:

> People talked about how they should go about hiring someone—I realized they hadn't done much hiring. So, the issue for me was, how do I help these guys develop a better sense of how the hiring process should work, what principles should drive it. Should everyone at the company interview each candidate? Will has already said he is not sure he adds much value to the process. He, and some of the others, voiced the view that the decision should be up to whomever the candidate would report to. I feel that we should all interview everyone, and that any one of us should be able to veto a candidate. In a small company at a critical stage, one bad apple can really have a huge negative impact. I stressed to Will the importance of our meeting with the team to lay out a vision of a more formal set of hiring processes and policies.

Designing a Compensation Policy

Another issue that needed to be addressed concerned the policies around compensation for the new hires. Miller had done some work developing a sense of the market compensation for RAs and scientists, and she had defined a standard salary and option grant for each position level. RAs would be paid $45,000 and would receive 40,000 options, and scientists would be paid $72,000 and would receive 60,000 options. As the company had begun to interview to make its first hires, several founders had begun to push back, arguing that they needed more flexibility to attract the right talent to the business. Miller shared her thoughts:

> I believed that you should use as many objective measures as possible to figure out what kind of offer to make in terms of salary and equity and then put forth your best offer. Philosophically, I didn't believe in negotiating over these things—you clearly defined the job, asked yourself whether the person could do the job, and then just paid for the job. I just didn't believe that the potential ill-will created by side deals was worth the trouble. I told Will that I felt the same way about my offer. Make the best offer and if the person accepts, great; if not, so be it.
>
> We did some work on a compensation grid, deciding that the scientists we hired would all be paid $72,000 and all get the same number of options. But after interviewing a few people, one scientist said he is a serious triathlete and he knows that this will mean he needs some extra time away from work, and he would like to take 90% of the "standard" in exchange for an extra 20 vacation days. Another potential hire said his wife makes a lot of money and he would rather have less salary and more options. I really feel that we need to stick to our policies, but some of the co-founders say that we will never get the most creative scientists out of the academic labs if we are not more flexible. I can tell they kind of bristle at what they perceive to be my "bureaucratic" leanings.
>
> It is also clear to me that we cannot give this level of options to each employee we hire. Basically, the VCs have signaled that they will give us an option pool of 13% or so of the shares (i.e., 1,400,000 shares assuming 10,565,000 shares outstanding post the Series A round). If my 3% comes out of that, this leaves 10%, or a little over 1 million shares for everyone else. I think it is fair to basically reduce the size of option grants associated with each position for every month we are in business—each step of progress we make reduces the risk in the company. The plan is to give a new hire an option grant on day one, and then for the options to vest 25% at the end of year one, and then 25% each year thereafter, but on a monthly basis. We don't anticipate making a second, follow-on grant to anyone until the option pool is refreshed in the Series B round. The VCs have told us that—since they are getting preferred stock and the options are for common stock—the strike price on the options can be 10% of their share price, or $0.15 per share in the model Will has run.

Company Culture

Finally, both Tompkins and Miller had agreed that it was important to spend some time up-front talking about what they wanted the culture of the company to be, and how they could make this a reality. Tompkins recalled: "A couple of the VCs I met with seemed to make a point of saying that they thought the academic lab culture was not the right one for a start-up company, and they wanted to be sure we had a more performance-oriented model in mind."

Miller amplified:

> I felt pretty strongly on a couple of issues; one was instilling a sense of frugality in the company and the other was building a culture based on setting very concrete goals and objectives. One of the huge negatives of the dot-com era is the sense that a big round of venture capital makes you rich, and you should spend lots of money on office space and fancy furniture and a cappuccino machine.

On the issue of goal setting, my experience with academic scientists is that the concept of goals is an abstract one for them. They are often distracted by a notion of discovery; they pursue interesting findings even when it takes them off track. In business, it is important to be focused on meeting specific, measurable goals and objectives. I think it is important to weave that into the fabric of the culture.

What to Do?

Early that evening as Tompkins prepared to leave the office, he realized that he, Miller and the VCs would have a lot to think about over the weekend. As he gathered a briefcase full of material from his desk, he thought to himself:

On one hand, I think Paige could help us a lot. And, I do believe her sense of the market value of her services. But, I also feel as though we've arrived at an equity distribution for ourselves that is fair and reasonable, and based on some solid principles. So, I'm not sure how two seemingly reasonable points of view can be in such conflict. I guess it's my job as CEO to figure it out . . . . Maybe I should be getting more money for this job after all.

EXHIBIT 1 | Paige Miller Resume

PAIGE MILLER

EXPERIENCE

December 2001–present   Consulting

Clients include BioMolecular Technologies (former employer) and several biotech start-ups.

1995–November 2001   Biomolecular Technologies   Cambridge, MA

Director, Manufacturing 1997–November 2000

- Senior Executive responsible for all manufacturing operations including production, procurement, asset management, sustaining engineering, and distribution for this $150 million a year site
- Directed the activities of 85 people through 5 managers
- Responsible for $8.5 million annual expense budget
- Managed Corporate Information Systems for two years
- Point person for this site for all global operations integration since acquisition
- Took company from pre-IPO to acquisition
- Received every award and form of merit compensation given
- Youngest senior executive in the company

Manufacturing Analyst/Internal Consultant 1995–1996

- Projects included: Manufacturing, Marketing, Finance, Corporate/Engineering, Customer Service, Facilities
- Highlights: Led Company-wide team in the creation and implementation of New Product Development process; Top Grossing Sales Person for 1996; Performed "turnaround" of stockroom operations

1993   Intel Corporation   Washington, DC

Research Project Consultant

1989–1992   Bayside Tennis Center   Sausalito, CA

Operations Manager: Grew company into one of the premier tennis centers on the West Coast.

EDUCATION

1993–1995   Harvard Business School   Boston, MA

- Masters, Business Administration

1983–1989   University of California, Los Angeles   Los Angeles, CA

- Bachelor of Science, Business Administration

EXHIBIT 2 | NanoGene Capitalization Table, Assuming Venture Capital Financing

	Founding / Incorporation 12/01		Angel Round 6/02		IP Deal 8/02		Assumed Series A	
	# shares	%	# shares	%	# shares	%	# shares	%
Tompkins	333,000	20.00%	333,000	14.70%	333,000	12.50%	333,000	3.15%
Rupert	333,000	20.00%	333,000	14.70%	333,000	12.50%	333,000	3.15%
Masterson	333,000	20.00%	333,000	14.70%	333,000	12.50%	333,000	3.15%
Rhoota	333,000	20.00%	333,000	14.70%	333,000	12.50%	333,000	3.15%
Garfield	333,000	20.00%	333,000	14.70%	333,000	12.50%	333,000	3.15%
Total	**1,665,000**	**100.00%**						
Angel Investors			600,000	26.49%	600,000	22.51%	600,000	5.68%
Total			**2,265,000**	**100.00%**				
EIT					400,000	15.01%	400,000	3.79%
Total					**2,665,000**	**100.00%**		
Option Pool							1,400,000	13.25%
Total VC investors							6,500,000	61.52%
Total							**10,565,000**	**100.00%**

Note: Assumed financing is $10 million in Series A Preferred Stock at approximately $1.54 per share.

Business Plan
for
Room For Dessert™

Adding Unique Ingredients
to Life's Balancing Act

The following document is the complete business plan submitted by Paul Conforti, Kristen Krzyzewski, and Kim Moore to the HBS Business Plan Contest.

Professor Joseph B. Lassiter, III and Lecturer Michael J. Roberts prepared this case from a field study report prepared by Paul Conforti, MBA '97, Kristen Krzyzewski, MBA '97 and Kim Moore, MBA '97 under the supervision of Professor Ray A. Goldberg as the basis for class discussion rather than to illustrate either effective or ineffective handling of an administrative situation.

A Day in the Life of Room For Dessert

It's 11:00 a.m. on a Thursday in January, and the doors open for business at the Room For Dessert™ (RFD™) restaurant on Newbury Street. The bakery phone rings, and an administrative assistant who works in the Hancock Tower places an order for a pastry tray for an afternoon meeting. As the lunch hour approaches, people working in the surrounding office buildings walk to the store to pick up cakes and desserts they have previously ordered, to place orders, or to purchase some baking ingredients or liqueurs (for an upcoming weekend party) at the retail shop. Some of the shoppers, tourists, and locals come in from the cold for a light lunch and a small indulgence.

In the early afternoon, a business meeting is held in the special function room at the rear of the restaurant, where pastries and coffee are served. In the main dining room, shoppers and tourists stop in for a treat and a warm drink after being on their feet for hours. For some, RFD™ offers the opportunity to indulge in "afternoon tea" without the attitude that usually accompanies it.

Around 4:30, the after work traffic begins to pick up. Once again, office workers stop by on their way to the T to bring some delightful desserts home. Business people fill some of the tables as they sip a cognac or scotch and talk shop—RFD™ provides a great alternative to a noisy bar. With the Boylston Street Green T stop only a few minutes from Copley or Arlington, some theatre-goers stop in for a quick sandwich before the show.

In the early evening, "dessert-desire" really kicks-in for many. After eating dinner at home, or at the Friday's or Joe's American Cafe up the street, people come to RFD™ for a change of scenery or a decadent dessert. John, a regular RFD™ customer, has called ahead for a reservation. His favorite table is prepared, and his personal bottle of port is readied. John has invited an old friend to meet him at RFD™ so they can catch up. To him, the restaurant provides a time and monetarily cost effective alternative to meeting for a fine-dining meal at Morton's, L'Espalier, or Sonsie, but has better atmosphere and service than Starbucks.

During the late evening, people come to RFD™ for dessert after a movie or the theatre. They watch the pastry artist put the finishing touches on each plate at the dining-room-exposed dessert station. As the store closes at midnight, the manager mentally prepares for the usual weekend rush that begins the following day . . .

Executive Summary

Room For Dessert™ (RFD™) is a full service, fine dining restaurant serving desserts and beverages (coffee, tea, wine and spirits). The concept also includes a retail store featuring take-out desserts, wine, spirits, and signature ingredients. Units will be located in high foot-traffic areas in metropolitan markets and surrounding upscale communities. The management team has the following objectives:

- Secure $600,000 funding to open a start-up unit in Boston during the third quarter of 1997
- Prove the business model generates $1,000,000 in unit sales and 35% cash-on-cash returns
- Establish 10 units in the Northeast by the end of 1999
- Grow into a national chain, with over 40 units and $50 million in sales by the end of 2002

RFD will offer Ritz-Carlton quality service by emphasizing a highly trained staff and information technology. This will be complemented by an unpretentiously elegant ambiance and premium quality products that are made on premise. Desserts will be available in sample sizes and individual portions, and will be prepared at a dessert station in the main dining room. This experience will be priced at $10 per person—at the high end for desserts, but value-priced when compared to fine dining alternatives.

Dessert, coffee, wine and spirits consumption in full-service restaurants is a $7.2 billion industry. Within this market, RFD's concept targets upscale urban singles and couples without children. Target customers are 24–54 year old college graduates and professionals, earning upwards of $52,000 in household income. These consumers lead generally healthy lives, but also enjoy small indulgences. They seek eating experiences that are pampering and entertaining, and they search for new avenues of social interaction. A dessert-focused restaurant is uniquely suited to meeting these needs.

The business model RFD™ will use to compete in this niche emphasizes four elements: (1) multiple revenue streams, (2) high margins, (3) low investment cost, and (4) geographic expansion. Once a beach-head unit is established in a given market, the business model is further enhanced by increased economies of scale and capacity utilization in the initial unit.

The RFD founders are passionate about the food industry; experienced with service operations, public relations, and execution under pressure; and educated by Harvard Business School. They are also in the process of building a management team and board of directors with unparalleled restaurant industry experience. The resulting combination of professional management and restaurant savvy creates a team well-positioned to pursue this opportunity.

The Concept

Room For Dessert (RFD) is a full-service, fine dining restaurant serving desserts and beverages such as coffee, tea, wine and spirits. (See **Appendix A.**) The concept also includes a retail store featuring take-out desserts, wine, spirits, and signature ingredients. The restaurant will have a 70 seat dining room, a private function room, and a small bar (See **Appendix B.**) This chart describes the essential components of the business:

	Restaurant / Bar	**Retail**
Primary Product Offering	• desserts • coffees & teas • wines & spirits • lighter fare—soups, salads, sandwiches	• desserts • coffees & teas • wines & spirits • cigars • signature ingredients & supplies
Services	• offer on-site educational classes and tastings (e.g., wines, desserts, baking) • host special events (e.g., baby showers, corporate events, holiday parties)	• sell made-to-order desserts and pastries (e.g., birthday cakes, wedding cakes) • provide recommendations for wine/dessert/food pairing & gifts

Like other restaurants, RFD's business will be concentrated on weekends and evenings. RFD is also likely to see a robust late night business after most traditional eating establishments close their kitchens. RFD's product offerings create an opportunity, however, to utilize the restaurant throughout the day, rather than only at the usual restaurant core business hours:

Daypart	RFD Weekday Activity	RFD Weekend Activity	Avg. Restaurant
11am–2pm	lunch, retail	lunch, retail	lunch
2pm–5pm	afternoon tea, business meetings, classes, retail	afternoon tea, bridal showers, private parties	no activity
5pm–7pm*	happy hour, after-work mtg, pre-movie dinner	pre-theater dinner, desserts	early dinner
7pm–9pm	classes, special events, dinner, desserts	pre-event dinner, desserts, private parties	core business
9pm–2am	core business, after theater dessert/drinks, bar alternative, lite dinner, occasions, private parties	core business, after theater dessert/drinks, bar alternative, lite dinner, occasions, private parties	typically close kitchen at 11:00 p.m.

*Retail operations will close at 7pm

Value Proposition

The RFD mission is to add unique ingredients to life's balancing act. RFD will use fine desserts and beverages to deliver frequent fine dining, unpretentious elegance, and a social alternative to consumers.

Frequent Fine-Dining: A fine dining experience is an exercise of indulgence and reward. It is sometimes difficult, however, to justify spending the time and money associated with this special treat. RFD will offer the same quality food, service, and atmosphere as the nation's best restaurants, but with a time commitment and cost that makes it easy to justify more frequent indulgence.

Unpretentious Elegance: While many fine dining restaurants offer an almost "snobbish" experience, it is harder for a dessert focused restaurant to do so. Why? Because desserts are fun! This helps RFD ensure the customer has a relaxing yet refined dining experience—a true escape from life's demands. Moreover, RFD can become a place to experience new things and satisfy curiosities. By hosting on-site educational classes and encouraging aspiring musicians/artists to share their work in the restaurant, RFD will make the so-called "finer things in life" accessible in an unpretentious environment.

A Social Alternative: As a result of the individualistic "cocooning" trends of the 1990s (e.g. home videos, internet, grocery home delivery), consumer homes will no longer be a sanctuary from the pressures of the outside world. Instead, people will begin to search for an oasis outside of the home at which they can enjoy social interaction.

RFD will be positioned as the target customers' own Cheers, where "everybody knows their name." By creating a restaurant that emphasizes service but requires a relatively low personal investment (time, money, etc.), RFD fills the gap in social options that exist between bars/cafes and full service restaurants.

Differentiation & Sustainability

RFD will deliver these ingredients as a complete experience that will be difficult to replicate. Significant elements of this experience include:

People: All RFD servers will complete a comprehensive training program, and will be encouraged to pursue relevant professional designations (e.g. barista; sommelier; associate/bachelors degree in baking & pastry arts or restaurant & hospitality management). Pastry chefs, rather than playing the supporting role as they do in most restaurants, will be provided the space, equipment, and tools necessary to successfully showcase their artistic and baking skills. RFD's emphasis on employee development will create a competitive advantage by allowing the company to attract and retain the highest caliber people.

Customized Service: Guest specific information, such as previous orders, favorite drinks , or dietary needs will be compiled and stored in company databases. In addition, through the use of state-of-the-art Information Technology, or through voluntary means (such as sign-up forms for the monthly RFD newsletter), RFD will develop the capability to use direct mail marketing with the follow-up telephone contact to build customer loyalty. For example, RFD will be able to notify chocolate loving guests when a new chocolate dessert is introduced. In addition RFD will seek to personalize the guests's experience to the point of allowing individuals to establish declining balance accounts or leave a bottle of liqueur at the restaurant for their future personal consumption.

Quality: While technological advances in dessert baking have greatly improved the quality of frozen desserts, there is still nothing like the smell, presentation, and taste of a dessert baked on premise. Even if the difference is only perceived by the consumer, perception is reality. All of RFD's desserts will be "baked fresh daily." The restaurant will offer a 100% satisfaction guarantee on guests' overall experience, reinforcing RFD's quality positioning. This also allows each unit to track the sources of customer dissatisfaction and to take steps to eliminating these problems.

Portioning: RFD will offer desserts in two portion sizes—individually plated and sample size. Sample size desserts allow the consumer to taste several desserts, and allow the RFD to manage food cost. RFD's individually plated desserts will be portioned to maximize impact while minimizing the likelihood of customers splitting a single dessert between them.

Ambiance: Although RFD will be upscale, the interior will create a comfortable and welcoming ambiance. Guests will enter the restaurant through an elegant store-front.

Furniture and place settings will be sturdy and high quality. A combination of class and casual will attract customers wearing anything from jeans to dinner jackets. This environment is critical to delivering an unpretentiously elegant RFD experience.

Additional Products & Services

The management team envisions establishing RFD as the entertaining headquarters for our customers. Future opportunities for enhancing corporate revenues and same-store-sales include: catering, catalogue orders, kiosk sales, and supplying other local restaurants. For example, during an informal meeting with a group of potential investors, one women commented, "I would be willing to pay $20 per person for the convenience of someone coming into my house to cater the dessert portion of a dinner. It would allow me to enjoy the end of an evening with my guests, and would be much more cost effective than having the whole thing catered." In addition supplying other restaurants with RFD's fresh-baked product would increase capacity utilization for RFD and give local restaurants the ability to differentiate themselves from competitors who serve frozen desserts. Opportunities such as these will be weighed against RFD's ability to control quality and limit over-exposure of the brand.

The Market

The RFD founders conducted a comprehensive four-month study of the dessert restaurant niche in the fall of 1996. The following is a summary of the relevant food industry trends and market factors.

Context

There are a variety of trends in consumer tastes and behavior that create a favorable environment for the launch of a dessert-focused restaurant, including:

Moderation: The "health craze" has subsided, as consumers lean toward more moderate eating habits. The Prevention Index, published by Prevention Magazine, shows the continuation of a downward trend over the last three years (from its peak in 1993) in 21 major health-promoting behaviors. A second study, conducted by Progressive Grocer magazine, reported a 4.4% increase in dessert and toppings sales, and a 5.0% increase in candy and gum sales, while total edible groceries grew only 2.9% in 1995. Third, Grocery Marketing magazine reported in September of 1996 in "21 Food Trends for the 21st Century" that, "People are realizing that no food is bad if consumed in moderation." The first trend they identified in their list was "Expect A Backlash Against 'Healthy' Foods." Finally, the National Restaurant Association (NRA) presents data categorizing consumers into three distinct groups:

- *Unconcerned consumers* are not concerned with health and nutrition.
- *Vacillating consumers* are concerned about health and nutrition, but are driven primarily by taste when dining out.

- *Committed consumers* exhibit behaviors and attitudes consistent with their commitment to good nutrition.

As summarized below, the number of consumers in the unconcerned category has grown significantly:

Segment	1992	1994
Unconcerned	32%	37%
Vacillating	31%	32%
Committed	37%	31%

All this evidence clearly shows consumers have brought moderation back to their food consumption.

Personal Gratification: The appearance of premium whiskeys, cognacs, and ports on menus; the proliferation of specialty coffee, cigar, martini and microbrew concepts; the expansion of high-end steakhouses; and the increase in sales of prepared gourmet foods all show that time-starved consumers are willing to "take a time out" and pay to indulge in the best. As one noted researcher of consumer trends observed, "There's a resurgence in people wanting to enjoy their lives. Customers are saying, 'I want a new experience, I want a pleasant experience, and I want to be king for a little while.'"

Convenience: Customers are willing to pay for convenience, too. Nearly two-thirds of women are in the work force. Families don't have time to prepare meals as they once did. The success of Home Meal Replacement (HMR) concepts (e.g., EatZi's, Boston Market) and home delivery (e.g. Streamline, HomeRuns, Peapod) is clear evidence of this fact. Commercial foodservice and the prepared food segment are expected to account for virtually all growth in U.S. food sales until the year 2005.

Segment	1995	2005	Annual Growth
Non-commercial foodservice	9%	8%	.2%
Commercial foodservice	35%	41%	3.4%
Prepared foods/meals	1%	3%	11.8%
Other retail	15%	12%	−1.1%
Grocery stores	40%	36%	.4%
Total market	**$635 billion**	**$785 billion**	**1.4%**

Relaxation & Comfort: Forty-one percent of people surveyed in 1995 went out to eat as a way to relax, up from thirty-five percent in 1992. A study conducted by McKinsey & Company for the International Foodservice Distributors Association states, "Food-related activities are becoming more important sources of relaxation and comfort." The report concludes that consumers are seeking more pleasure and fun from everyday life and will demand form and function from restaurants.

Eat-tertainment: People want an entertaining eating experience. The growth of concepts such as Planet Hollywood and Hard Rock Cafe are two prime examples. One renowned Boston chef commented, "Now we have to entertain and stimulate in other ways. Unfortunately, restaurants that don't entertain are going to have a harder time. People are looking for more open kitchens, more visuals."

Target Customers

The management team believes two segments of the dessert-consuming population are the most likely to demand the eating experience offered by RFD.

Primary Segment: The RFD target segment consists of upscale urban singles and couples without children, most of whom are college graduates with professional, managerial, or other white-collar occupations. They earn a median household income of $52,100 and live in multi-unit housing in urban uptown areas. Their predominant age ranges are 25–34 and 35–54. They are most densely concentrated in Northern and Southern California, Minnesota, Texas and the greater metropolitan areas surrounding New York, Philadelphia, Chicago, and Boston.

There are a number of variables that provide RFD with a deeper understanding of the target customer and his/her habits. A leading targeted marketing research firm, Claritas, Inc. (www.claritas.com) has found that these target customers are more likely to go scuba diving, attend the live theater, have a gold/premium credit card, read *Metropolitan Home* and watch The Simpsons. This psychographic data, as well as media consumption and product/service preference data, will allow RFD to market directly to the primary segment.

Management expects these customers will come to Room For Dessert after the theater, a movie, another social event, or eating at home. They will also identify RFD as a place to catch up with an old acquaintance, or to hold a business discussion. The concept provides a cost-effective, upscale alternative to going to a bar, full-service restaurant, or other meeting place. The consumer can also take advantage of RFD's personalized services. For example, the service team can help the consumer develop the perfect match between a dessert and a dessert wine for a special occasion in the home. More frequent customers may have a personal bottle of liqueur held in a private locker at the restaurant.

Secondary Target Segment: The secondary segment will be in the same age ranges as the primary, but will have less disposable income. These customers will view RFD as an affordable, approachable opportunity to get a taste of life's finer things. For instance, a couple can leave their children with a baby-sitter for an hour and escape to RFD. A group of friends can choose to dine at a reasonably priced, casual dining restaurant (e.g. Chili's, Applebee's, T.G.I. Friday's), and then upgrade to RFD for dessert. These customers will also think of RFD as a place to host a special event like a birthday party or a wedding shower. The members of this secondary segment generally can not afford to spend $50 to $100 per person for a four-star dining experience with any regularity, but will be able to justify spending $10 per person for an experience that is almost as good. This customer's decision process is more deliberate—RFD will be visited relatively infrequently vis-à-vis the primary target segment.

Boston Demographics.   Boston's demographic make-up is good for RFD's initial launch

RFD™ Target Segment	Boston (vs. US Avg. Index of 100)
Single w/o Kids*	114
Couples w/o Kids*	104
Education (College +)	141
Household Income (50,000 +)	128
Occupation (Professionals)	116

*measures 18–44 instead of 25–54

Source: Lifestyle Market Analyst 1995

Other lifestyle and demographic variables show Boston to have a higher than average levels of disposable income, interest in fine foods, and spending on food away from home. The first RFD store will be located in Boston's upscale retail and restaurant area on Newbury Street. Three additional units will be added in the Boston area by the end of 1998. Site considerations are shown below:

Target Market Characteristics	Average HH Inc.	HH w/o Children (% of Trade Area)	White Collar Workers (% Trade Area)
Newbury Street Location	$40,000	80.9%	85.4%
Lexington, MA	$76,775	66.6%	83.2%
Newton, MA	$71,117	76.2%	81.7%
Chestnut Hill, MA	$55,600	81.0%	79.7%
Cambridge, MA	$42,173	81.7%	74.3%

Market Potential

Dessert, coffee, wine and spirits consumption nationally in full-service restaurants is a $7.2 billion industry, with annual growth projected at 4.2%. However, it is more meaningful to analyze a restaurant opportunity by looking for a percentage of market share in an individual city rather than a national market. For instance, RFD expects to capture a 2.6% share of the Boston market by the end of 1998:

Boston, Projected Market Share	Share	Sales MM
Dessert Sales in Full-Service Restaurants	100%	$91
RFD™ Market Share - End of 1998 (4 locations)	2.6%	$2.4

		Market Rank & Size		Demographics		
Region	Market	US Rank Dessert Sales	Full Service Dessert Sales ($MM)	50,000+	% Professional	Aged 25–54 Years
New England	Boston	7	91	39.6%	28.6%	60.9%
	Hartford/New Haven	n/a	22	42.2%	28.9%	60.3%
	Fairfield County, CT	n/a	17	54.2%	26.1%	59.9%
	Providence, RI	n/a	16	29.9%	22.8%	57.3%
	New England	n/a	267	n/a	n/a	n/a
Northern CA	San Francisco	15	59	47.8%	30.5%	64.7%
Southern CA	Los Angeles	2	169	37.9%	27.4%	64.9%
	Orange County	14	62	47.5%	28.5%	66.3%
Midwest	Chicago	1	187	33.0%	24.8%	62.4%
	Detroit	5	105	38.3%	23.3%	61.8%
	Minneapolis - St. Paul	13	67	39.6%	25.1%	63.4%
Southwest	Houston	9	85	38.0%	30.2%	68.6%
	Dallas	11	67	33.5%	27.4%	66.7%
Southeast	Atlanta	6	93	33.5%	26.5%	67.3%
Northwest	Seattle	18	57	38.7%	28.2%	63.8%
Mid-Atlantic	Philadelphia	8	90	38.0%	26.2%	58.7%
	Washington	4	113	48.0%	35.5%	67.6%

With individual unit sales of approximately $1 million, RFD will seek to capture between 5% and 10% of the market in smaller cities. Larger cities will support multiple units to achieve a similar share.

Industry Analysis

The dessert restaurant industry presents ample opportunity for an upscale dessert restaurant to carve out an attractive niche. First, switching costs for buyers are relatively low, so a successful competitor must differentiate their product/service offering and build customer loyalty. Second, barriers to entry in the restaurant business are relatively low. As a result, first mover advantage in core markets is critical to success. Third, substitutes (e.g., bars, coffee-shops, full-service restaurants, other social venues/events, staying at home) do not offer any price/performance advantage. Fourth, suppliers are generally providing commodity goods, and generally position themselves as partners with the restaurants they serve. However, some companies are able to obtain exclusive arrangements with high quality branded ingredients (e.g. Godiva) to set apart their offerings from others. Finally, as discussed in greater detail in the following section, while existing rivals are intensifying competition in the quick-service and casual segments, the upscale segment is characterized by fragmented and unfocused players.

The Competition

The analysis of dessert-niche competitors will be organized according to the three prominent service-segments of the industry: Fine Dining, Casual, and Quick-Serve. Tables following this discussion summarize our research of specific competitive concepts.

Fine Dining

This segment consists of three types of competitors: (1) upscale national chains (e.g., Morton's, Capital Grille, Ruth's Chris, The Palm), (2) full-menu independents with outstanding pastry chefs, and (3) dessert-focused independent operators. However, none of the national competitors place significant emphasis on the dessert portion of their business. In fact, these competitors increasingly offer desserts that are baked in dessert "factories," frozen, and shipped to their location for decoration. In addition, most full-menu independent operators fail to allocate sufficient resources (space, equipment, etc.) to attract and retain high quality pastry chefs. Restaurants that successfully do so, such as Boston's Sonsie (pastry chef Art Welch) and Olives (Paige Retus), lack economies of scale in purchasing, production, real estate, and advertising that a dessert-focused chain competitor would possess. Finally, none of the current dessert-focused independents have any geographic expansion plans. Examples include L'Elizabeth in Providence, RI, serving six dessert selections and a variety of wine and spirits, and Side Berns in Tampa, FL (affiliated with Berns Steakhouse) offering 30 dessert selections, wine and spirits, cigars, and a retail wine shop. These operators provide proof that an RFD-type concept is viable, and minimize the risk associated with consumer acceptance of the concept. As mentioned above, however, a dessert chain would achieve economies of scale and provide a new addition to this underexploited niche.

Casual Dining

The casual segment of the dessert niche is also fragmented, but poised for increased competition. Nationally, casual chain restaurants place varying degrees of emphasis on desserts. Cheesecake Factory has established themselves as a formidable player in the upscale end of the casual segment with their dessert-theme and wide selection of name-sake products. Other national, full-menu chains are placing increased emphasis on desserts as a means of increasing average check. However, most of these operators, including Cheesecake Factory, serve desserts that were produced in national dessert "factories," frozen, and shipped to the restaurant. Local, dessert-focused operators are also playing an increasingly important role in the niche. Jeff's Desserts of Tampa, Florida has seven units in that area, and corporate parent Just Desserts (Toronto, Canada) is looking for partners to expand into other U.S. regions. Another operator, Cafe Intermezzo in Atlanta, has two locations and a strong local reputation. Casual European cafes, like Cafe Lalo and Cafe Edgar in New York City, or Dolce Vita and Caffe Vittoria in Boston's North End, are the classic examples of competitors in this segment—independently-owned, individual units with no plans for expansion. Many of these competitors obtain their desserts from local bakeries, and provide poor ambiance and service. For example, during an examination of eight dessert cafes in New York City, only one baked their desserts on premise, and most offered only counter service.

Quick-Service

Finally, the quick service segment is the one with the greatest amount of competition. Most current quick-serve operators are bakeries. They place varying degrees of emphasis on take-out sales, restaurant supply, and on-premise consumption (but usually in that order). Local operators with growth plans include Just Desserts in San Francisco

Room For Dessert

(10 units) and William Greenburg Jr. Desserts & Cafes in New York (with 3 retail locations and seven kiosk units in Macy's stores). In Boston, examples would include Rosie's Bakery (3 locations), Mike's Pastry (North End), and Sweet Endings (Watertown). In this segment, though product quality is usually quite abundant, service is not.

Potential Entrants & Encroaching Concepts

In the recent past, the restaurant business has seen a proliferation of casual cafe concepts. Many of these stores follow the traditional bakery model, focusing on homemade breads. (See table of restaurant/eatery alternatives on page 355.) Au Bon Pain, St. Louis Bread, La Madeleine and Corner Bakery are a few of the successful models that compete in this segment. While they offer cafeteria style service with a flair, none of these concepts focuses on desserts. However, they could view desserts as complementary products to be used to bolster same store sales.

In addition, it is worth noting the increase in niched, beverage-focused concepts. The market has seen growth in the number of night-time venues including bars focused on martinis, champagne, scotches, ports and cigars. Arguably, these bar concepts, however, are burdened with a short life—few faddish concepts last beyond two years. Microbrew pubs have also seen a great deal of growth over the past few years. These competitors steal share in the late night hours when RFD will be doing its core business.

Operators	Niche	Full Svc	Dessert Focus	Growth Plans	# of Unit	Bake on Site	Sq Ft	Invest MM	Yr Sale MM	Margin	# of Seats	Covers/day	Avg Chk	Other Comments
Corner Bakery Chicago, IL	Bistro/Cafe	No	No	Yes	13	Commisary	500 to 4,500	0.96	1.5	4.8% op. inc.	65–100		<$10	holidays best for sweets
Au Bon Pain Chain	Bistro/Cafe	No	No	Yes										
Starbucks Chain	Coffee	No	No	Yes	1,100	No	varies		0.84	7 to 10% op. inc.			$3	Bakery = 12% of sales
Mortons, etc. Chain	Fine Dining	Yes	No	Yes									$53 Dinner $14 Lunch	
Armani Cafe Boston, MA	Fine Dining	Yes	No		1	Yes					112			fill 60 seats dessert only; $16-6 dessert
Cheesecake Factory Chain	Casual Upscale	Yes	Yes	Yes	17	No	12,000 total	6.25*	8.5	19.5%	250–650	2000	$13.70	275 employees per store
Side Berns Tampa, FL	Dessert Cafe	Yes	Yes	No	1	Yes	5,000 total				100	150–700	$7	
Kaminsky's Charleston, SC	Dessert Cafe	Yes	Yes	Yes	2	Yes	1000 total				50	500	$6	
Just Desserts San Francisco, CA	Dessert Cafe	No	Yes	Yes	10	No			0.70				$5	
Just Desserts Toronto, CAN	Dessert Cafe	Yes	Yes	Yes	30	No							$5	
Jeff's Desserts Tampa, FL	Dessert Cafe	Yes	Yes	Yes	5	No			0.5 to 1.0					5,000–10,000 customers/mo.
Cafe Lalo New York, NY	Dessert Cafe	Yes	Yes	No	1	No	750 total		0.45		75	400–1500	$5–10	open 9 a.m.–4 a.m.
Cafe Intermezzo Atlanta, GA	Dessert Cafe	Yes	Yes	No	2	No			$1.5	20% COGS	150	300–650	$5–10	events & catering, too
Brazil Detroit, MI	Dessert Cafe	Yes	Yes		1	No	3000 total				100	600+ Sat.	$5–10	est. 30% come after dinner elsewhere
William Greenberg Desserts & Cafes	Dessert Cafe	No	Yes	Yes	7	No	700 to 1,000	0.16 to .30	0.80	losing $			$5	kiosk startup cost $50–65k
Pastiche Providence, RI	Dessert/Cafe/Bake	Yes	Yes	No	1	Yes	1200			10–15% COGS	30	150–250 @ night	$6	30+, upper middle income customers
Rosie's Bakery Boston, MA	Bakery	No	Yes	No	3	Commisary	4000 total		<$1.0		18–20	200–300	$8	covers include takeout orders

*Cheesecake Factory can get up to $1.5 million back from landlords.

Source: Industry & Corporate publications and interviews conducted by RFD management.

They could also consider adding desserts to their menus to satisfy customers' "late night munchies."

The most successful of the new beverage concepts are the premium coffee and espresso bars like Starbucks, Second Cup, and Coffee Beanery. Although most players in this category are not focused on desserts as a competitive advantage, we anticipate increasing interest in this area given the intense competitive pressures. As these competitors saturate desirable markets, growth opportunities through geographic expansion (especially in the U.S.) will decline. Once this happens, much more pressure will be placed on increasing same store sales through new product introductions and brand extensions.

Finally, restaurant chain companies like Brinker International (national) or Back Bay Restaurant Group (Northeast), who currently do not have dessert-focused concepts, could decide it was time to create one. These types of competitors have the resources (people, capital, infrastructure, alliances) and track records (management & industry experience, operational expertise) to attempt entry into a niche like desserts. They also compete with niche players by offering desserts on their current restaurant menus. These players could in fact be valuable sources of capital, or could provide RFD with an exit strategy.

All the added focus on the casual and quick-service segments described above reinforces management's assessment of them as unattractive for entry. In the underexploited dessert-focused fine dining segment, however, companies that achieve first-mover advantage in a given market will capitalize on the opportunity described in this plan.

Marketing Strategy

The following strategic marketing tools will allow RFD to create consumer awareness of its value proposition and encourage trial:

Location   Each RFD unit will act as a billboard for the business. Locations will have a high degree of pedestrian traffic, and a high concentration of the target customer (demographic & psychographic). The flexibility of the RFD concept allows the Company to develop successful restaurants near a variety of locations, including: (1) theatre, movie, or music venues; (2) high-end hotels; (3) high foot-traffic residential areas; (4) large universities; (5) upscale shopping centers; and (6) busy downtown areas.

Pricing   RFD's prices are positioned at the high end of the dessert niche. Consumers in the target market are willing to pay for quality, and will therefore be tempted to try the "best dessert" in town. This pricing strategy builds on Starbucks' positioning of charging a premium for relatively low cost "feel-good" items. See the sample menu in **Appendix A** for proposed prices.

Advertising/Promotion   The management team will work to obtain positive reviews in local papers, publications, and web sites (e.g. The Boston Phoenix, The Boston Globe, Boston.com, Zagat's Restaurant Review). In addition, influential word-of-mouth advocates (e.g. Four Seasons' concierge, executive assistants) will be reached via telephone or personally. Nationally, features in magazines read by target customers and frequent diners out (e.g. Bon Appetit, Martha Stewart Living, Conde Nast Traveler, major airline magazines) will build prestige in early markets and pull for the concept in potential markets.

Grand Opening Events   The week prior to a location's opening RFD will host private parties for groups with a high concentration of target customers, including: graduate schools, professional services companies (consulting, banking, trading), charities, etc. These events will introduce our restaurant to opinion leaders and jump start influential word-of-mouth referrals.

Restaurant & Hotel Alliances   Full menu restaurants might choose to refer customers to RFD for dessert to increase their table turns (as frequently occurs in Boston's North End). Hotels can use RFD's space to augment their conference facilities. As influential word-of-mouth advocates, hotel concierges will be given free trial of RFD so they can give unqualified recommendations of the restaurant to guests.

Community Involvement   RFD will encourage local artists and musicians to display their work at the restaurant. In addition, the company will donate facilities and product to worthy charities to defray costs of fund-raising dinners, etc. These activities also increase consumer awareness of the concept.

Special Events & Meeting Space   Administrative assistants will be provided incentives (e.g. free product, free classes) to consider RFD for company "offsite" meetings. Guests will be unobtrusivly informed that RFD will host wedding showers, birthday parties, and other private functions.

These strategic marketing tools are low risk and low cost, but provide significant benefits to the consumer and to RFD.

Operations & Facilities

Though a restaurant concept may be sound and its competitive positioning may be clear, all is for naught if service is slow, food quality is poor, presentation is sloppy, and "the little things" are ignored.

Interior Design   RFD is not about linen tablecloths or trendy fixtures, but instead is represented by timeless and classic design. Furniture will be cherry-colored wood with a matte-gloss finish. The seating arrangement, combined with a well-lit dining room, will allow customers to have a clear view of the pastry station. A prototype layout is included in **Appendix B.**

Restaurant Operations   Before being seated, customers will be able to browse a pastry display of the chef's featured selections. Once seated, guests will also be able to review a menu and obtain recommendations about their order. Servers will have process time goals for making initial contact with a table, and for checking to ensure the customer's experience is satisfactory.

Baking Operations   RFD's kitchen requires only 25% of the unit's space, versus an industry norm of 40%. Baking inputs will be purchased in bulk when appropriate. In some instances, RFD will negotiate exclusive arrangements with ingredient suppliers to create signature items. Initial preparation of ingredients, batters, etc. will occur prior to rush periods to facilitate short lead times. Recipes and processes will be highly standardized, which is facilitated by a dessert-focused menu. The pastry station, which is adjacent to the kitchen, will be a functional facility used to dazzle patrons with a "dessert decorating show" Pastry artists will have process time goals measured from order receipt to completion.

Retail Store Operations   One wall of the unit (and some adjacent floor space) will be dedicated to retail sales. Restaurant servers or dedicated retail staff will assist the customer in making selections. The counter at which check-out occurs is also where customers will place orders for and pick up baked-to-order cakes and other baked goods that are purchased for take-out.

Commissary   Since desserts are conducive to being partially produced in one location and finished in another, RFD may build regional commissaries as the concept expands. This will allow units in a region to eliminate most of their baking equipment investment, and free up or reduce space. Since the baking industry is characterized by excess capacity, RFD could avoid equipment investment entirely by purchasing capacity from other producers (e.g. Boston Beer's Sam Adams production strategy). In no circumstance, however, will RFD jeopardize the fresh-baked, high quality positioning of the concept.

Process Management   The operational elements outlined above will be integrated with a comprehensive information management system (including Efficient Food Replenishment links with suppliers). The end result will create an operation that can be standardized, measured, and managed as a single process. Even so, the creativity that is injected into the Final Decoration phase of the process will give the customer the perception that they are receiving a work of art instead of a product of science.

Management

Two RFD founders and a store-level management team will launch the business. The board of directors will be composed of a group of accomplished industry experts. The resulting combination of professional management and restaurant savvy creates a team well-positioned to pursue this opportunity.

Paul Conforti, President Paul is the originator of the RFD Concept. His interest in foodservice began in 1985, when he was an ice-cream cone maker and dishwasher at Celebration! Ice Cream in Warwick, RI. Paul has over ten years of experience leading organizations, including three years of people-intensive service management in insurance claim/call centers. In June, 1997 Paul earned his MBA at Harvard Business School, where he focused his studies on entrepreneurship. He also completed a year-long research project on the restaurant industry, resulting in this business plan. He has an undergraduate degree in Management (Finance and Operations) from Rensselaer Polytechnic Institute.

   Kim Moore, Vice-President Kim is a founding member of the RFD team. She started pursuing her lifelong interest in food at H.E. Butt Grocery of San Antonio, Texas, the nation's tenth largest grocery chain. There, Kim led an internal consulting project developing strategy, operations, and marketing for ten underperforming Houston stores. Prior to that, as an Associate Producer (journalist) at ABC News, she developed skills core to operating a successful restaurant: attention to detail, execution under pressure, and working with people to accomplish goals. Kim earned a B.A. in Journalism from the University of Texas, Austin, and an HBS MBA focused on entrepreneurship and service management.

Unit Management Team   The individual unit management team will include a General Manager, an Assistant Manager, and two Pastry Chefs/Kitchen Managers. These employees will all have significant restaurant and baking experience. The founders have already begun using an extensive industry network developed over the last year to identify and interview potential candidates for these roles.

Additional Corporate Management   RFD will eventually recruit additional industry experience into the management team. If necessary, the founders will hire a CEO to lead geographic expansion. A CFO/CIO will be hired to manage supplier relations, financial reporting & control, and IT. A Corporate Chef with a degree from a culinary institution and significant pastry/baking experience will be hired to develop innovative menu items that balance artistry with ease of replication. Other positions to be filled include Regional VPs, a Human Resource Manager, a Corporate Trainer, and a Purchasing Director.

Board of Directors/Advisors   Realizing that the founders need to augment their restaurant industry experience, the board will primarily be composed of strategic members in addition to significant equity holders. Potential members of the board include:

- Jim Kern, Retired Chairman, Creative Food Management
- Mike Nardozza, General Manager - Restaurant Operations, Windy City International LTD
- Michael Roberts, CFO, Baldini's Restaurants (former HBS professor)
- Leonard A. Schlesinger, Service Management Professor, HBS (former EVP of Au Bon Pain Cafes)

Financials

RFD's corporate financial projections are based on the strength of the individual restaurant unit's cash-on-cash return (EBITDA/Initial Investment). Industry analysts expect chain concepts to produce returns in the 30–40% range. The following table shows RFD's unit economics compare favorably to some of the country's most successful national chains.

	Room For Dessert	Cheesecake Factory	Starbucks
Seats	70	400	60
Square Feet	2,450	12,000	1,500
Investment Cost	$480,452	$4,750,000	$250,000
Sales	$1,091,052	$8,650,000	$840,000
Sales/Investment	2.27	1.82	3.36
Average Check	$10.31	$13.75	$3.00
Customers Per Day	210	1,724	767
Customers Per Seat	3	4	13
EBITDA	$178,487	$1,660,000	$90,000
% of Sales	16.4%	19.2%	10.7%
% of Investment	37.1%	34.9%	36.0%

As the following graphs illustrate, an individual RFD unit will have "paid back" its investment within two years of beginning operations, as positive cash flow is achieved almost immediately. These projections are supported by the comments of the COO of a successful dessert-themed restaurant, "Within a few months after we opened we were able to get each store [five in the Tampa area] into the black."

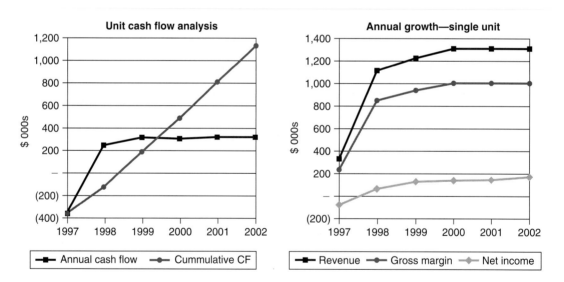

Business Model

There are four important elements driving the economics of the RFD concept:

Multiple Revenue Streams: RFD has three revenue streams (restaurant sales, retail sales, and special events). As the concept builds brand equity, a second tier of additional revenue streams, including catering, kiosks, restaurant supply, and catalogue sales, could be pursued. To ensure conservative projections, the management team has excluded these second tier revenue streams from our unit analysis. Revenue is distributed between the restaurant, retail, and special functions as follows:

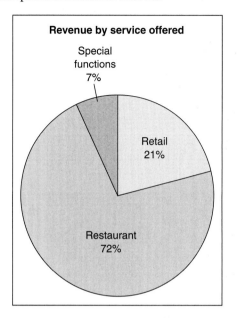

Restaurant	Retail	Special Function	Total
$779,323	$233,797	$77,932	$1,091,052

Proforma projections assume a unit will be able to add six percent additional sales on this total sales number after 18 months of operation. This increase is attributed to increased traffic and average check.

High Gross Margins: Desserts and beverages are the two highest gross margin items on any restaurant menu. Most desserts require relatively low cost, commodity ingredients, and are not very labor intensive to cook or serve. Though these advantages will be somewhat offset by the concept's high quality, margins will still be more attractive than the "average" full-service restaurant:

Margin Analysis	Restaurant Sales			Retail Sales	Special Functions
	Desserts/Food	Soft Bev.	Hard Bev.		
Gross Margin	74.5%	85.0%	80.0%	65.0%	75.0%
% of Sales	50.0%	14.3%	7.1%	21.4%	7.1%
Margin Contribution	37.3%	12.1%	5.7%	13.9%	5.4%
Wt'd Avg. RFD Margin	74.4%	Nat'l Restaurant Assoc. Full Service Avg.			66.9%

Dollar margins will also be preserved with a premium pricing strategy. Relative to four-star, fine dining establishments, the RFD experience is value-priced. However, compared to other desserts offered in restaurants, the concept is positioned in the upper quartile of prices. Use of a prix fixe menu focused on sampler portions and a minimum per guest charge will ensure margin goals are achieved. The attached proformas assume production efficiencies facilitate an additional 10% reduction in COGS, spread across years 3–5.

Low Per Unit Investment Costs: RFD's lite entree menu (salads, soups, sandwiches, etc.) eliminates the need for traditional kitchen equipment and preparation space, lowering the investment required in each unit. Additionally, much of the required baking equipment can be leased, further lowering capital requirements and up-front cash investment. Working capital needs are also low given the cash nature of the business. These factors combine to produce per unit investment costs below $500,000.

Property, Plant, & Equip.	
Furnishings	$42,000
Baking Equipment	$70,000
Leasehold Improvements	$245,000
Information Systems	$10,000
Deposits & Prepaids	
Rent	$20,417
Utilities	$2,455
Insurance	$5,000
Other Capitalized Costs	
Professional Services	$25,000
Grand Opening Promotions	$11,031
Licenses & Permits	$50,000
Total Investment	**$480,902**
Working Capital	$58,558
Training	$18,388
Opening Inventory	$4,686
Contingency	$50,000
Total Start-Up Cost	**$612,534**

The attached proformas assume all units require purchase of brand new baking equipment. To the extent used equipment is acquired, equipment is lease-financed, or commissary production is used, financial projections will appear more favorable.

Geographic Expansion: Once the economics presented above are substantiated by the performance of the first location, the company will seek to expand regionally. By the end of 1999, ten units will be opened throughout New England. Thereafter, expansion of corporate owned stores will continue in other regions of the country. By the end of year five (2002), RFD will have built national brand recognition as a fine-dining chain with 44 units and $48 million in sales.

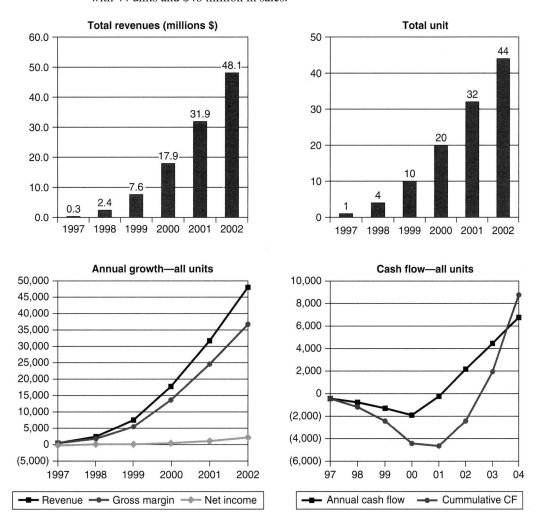

Although the individual unit economics are compelling, the company as a whole will not achieve significant profitability or cash flow until year five. RFD has elected to incur the expenses associated with opening locations in new geographic areas as soon as possible. Management believes the benefits that can be obtained by early market penetration and economies of scale will create critical long-term competitive advantages, such as:

- obtaining better real-state
- building brand recognition and customer loyalty before competition arrives
- reducing COGS through corporate purchasing and commissary production
- facilitating an exit strategy of an IPO or a sale to a large chain restaurant company

Following the growth strategy proposed here, by the end of 2002 the value of the company could be in the range established by previous industry transactions:

Valuation Criteria	.4x Sales	14 P/E	15x EBIT	25 P/E	10x EBITDA	1.5x Sales
Enterprise Value ($mm)	19.2	21.3	35.2	38.1	59.5	72.1

The proformas that are attached represent only the financial performance of an individual unit, as RFD's first financial stage is for the purpose of launching this unit. (See **Appendix C.**) The revenue and cash flow projections shown above assume unit growth according to the accompanying chart. Each new unit added exhibits the same characteristics as the initial unit (though RFD management will move down a learning curve for efficiency and effectiveness in opening new stores). Corporate overhead as a percent of sales is assumed to be the following (spike in 1999 is due to launch of national expansion plan):

1997	1998	1999	2000	2001	2002
12.7%	3.5%	5.4%	3.6%	2.5%	1.8%

Revenue Assumptions

The following assumptions were used to develop the attached proforma financial statements, and reflect management's conservative estimation of each variable.

Restaurant Sales: Restaurant sales are driven by the following formula:

Average Check Per Person ($10) × Number of Seats (70)

× Number of Turns per Seat per Day (3) × Days Open (360)

The $10 average check is based on the use of a prix fixe menu options with a check minimum per person requirement. Meeting this check goal is not an unreasonable assumption. A survey of 25 individuals in the RFD target market, using the sample menu presented in **Appendix A,** yielded an average check transaction of $10.37 per person. Eighty-five percent of respondents envisioned being on a date. Some saw the experience as a special occasion and were more willing to pay for quality products and services. Even when participants chose to share a single dessert, the average check goal was met. Below are the results:

Items Ordered	Drinks Ordered	Total Sales	Customer Count	Average Check/ Person
21	25	$259.20	25	$10.37

Considering retail, restaurant and back-room operations, 70 seats yields space requirements below 2,500 square feet—an upper boundary given the high cost of real estate in high traffic locations. These high traffic locations, however, are one of the drivers of the turns/seats assumption of three times per day. The other driver is the ability to rapidly turn over tables with short production lead times and fast table service. The seats and turns assumptions result in customer traffic expectations of 210 per day, or approximately 1500 per week. This compares favorably with the following benchmarks:

	Side Berns	Jeff's Desserts	Pastiche
Customers/Week	1400	1700	1500

Retail Sales: RFD will sell cakes and pies, bottled liqueurs and spirits, and the special ingredients we use in our recipes. Our proforma financial statements assume the concept sells only 12 cakes per day at $40 per cake (versus 25 cakes per day sold at each Rosie's Bakery in the Boston area), and five bottles of wine and spirits per day at $15 per bottle (versus 12 bottles per day of cognac sold at Martinetti's liquor store in Brighton). Any additional sales of cakes, wine and spirits, or any other signature ingredients would augment RFD's unit revenues.

Special Events: RFD will have a special function room for meetings, showers, parties, etc. In addition, the pastry preparation station located in the main dining room will facilitate hosting special classes about baking, selecting wines, and other topics that interest our target market. We expect to offer eight classes per year of six sessions each, at $20 per session (yielding $120 per person per class). We assume a subscription rate of 40 people per class. These assumptions are consistent with the experience of Side Berns in offering a similar program.

Cyclicality & Seasonality

Many restaurant analysts believe the cyclicality of the industry will dissipate as the proportion of food dollars spent on meals eaten outside of the home exceeds 50% of the total food budget (which occurred in 1996). Management believes this concept can be positioned as even more "recession-proof" than the average restaurant, because of our emphasis on "affordable indulgences." During the great depression, movie ticket sales boomed. Historians hypothesize this occurred because people needed to find an affordable indulgence—a way to escape the hardship that surrounded them. Though this is an extreme example, it illustrates our point. If and when a full-menu fine dining experience becomes too great a luxury, a trip to RFD can be an affordable alternative.

Seasonality will also affect RFD's business to some extent, and is reflected in the Unit Proformas. Aggregate NRA data shows most retailers see a dip in sales after the traditional holiday season. After February, eating and drinking establishments have typically seen sales increase steadily throughout the warmer months. At the onset of the school year in September, sales take another dip. At year end (December and the holiday season) there is a slight jump up in restaurant activity. Understanding these chronic industry swings, we will be able to plan accordingly for labor, purchasing, inventory and other operational concerns.

Other Major Assumptions

Labor: Having a focused menu limits the need for professional chefs in each unit. In addition, though our service will be fine-dining quality, our emphasis on "one-course" will allow us to increase the utilization of our servers because they will have to make less trips to each table for which they are responsible. The following table summarizes our anticipated staff for each unit:

Position	Salary	# Req'd
General Manager	$ 40,000	1
Assistant Manager	$ 30,000	1
Servers (40hrs, excl. tips)	$ 5,200	8
Bartender	$ 16,640	1.5
Maitre D'	$ 14,560	1.5
Pastry Artists	$ 20,000	4
Busboys	$ 10,400	2
Chef/Kitchen Manager	$ 35,000	1

Rent: RFD's concept relies upon locations that have high foot traffic and/or a high concentration of high disposable income people. This translates into relatively expensive real estate costs. Our projections assume an average cost per square foot of $50. Super-premium areas, like Newbury Street in Boston, will cost $60/sq. ft. or more.

Balance Sheet Items: Required cash is assumed at 2% of sales, a relatively low number due to the cash nature of the business. Receivables are at 3 days' sales, representing sales made on credit cards. Inventory turns 4 times per month, showing an average between higher perishable food turns and lower turns of merchandise for sale in the retail portion of the store. Accounts payable are estimated at 30 days' COGS, an industry average. Other assumptions are stated on the proformas.

Break-Even & Sensitivity Analysis

At the bottom of the cash flow statement for the prototype unit, a break-even analysis is presented for the first 5+ years of operation. The results are summarized here:

	1997	1998	1999	2000	2001	2002
B-E Sales Level	$661,669	$940,243	$929,249	$925,422	$912,617	$847,141
% of Expected Sales	208%	87%	82%	77%	76%	71%

After the initial year's ramp-up period, the unit's break-even point versus expected level of sales becomes increasingly favorable. The break-even is sensitive to numerous variables, the two most important of which are average check and table turns/traffic. RFD's break/even average check, holding all other variables constant, is approximately $8. RFD's break-even table turns, holding all other variable constant, is approximately 2.25. The management team is confident that these numbers are attainable.

Financing

The unit-level proformas that are attached assume the start-up capital of $600,000 (see use of proceeds in investment section above) is financed by private placed convertible debt (70%) and equity (30%). RFD management seeks accredited investors who either (1) have restaurant experience, understand the nature of the industry, and seek an opportunity to add value to management team as advisors or (2) view this investment as an addition to their diversified portfolio of angel capital investments. Investors in the initial round will receive common stock and debt convertible into common stock based on certain investor or management triggers (described in a separate document). The initial round of financing buys the management team the ability to launch and prove the concepts viability with an initial unit. Once this is accomplished, an additional $4,000,000 will need to be raised in two separate financing rounds that occur in 1998 and 2000. The first of these rounds will most likely be privately placed debt and equity. The second round will be presented to venture capitalists, who generally refuse to examine restaurant deals until the restaurant concept and economics are fine tuned.

Scenario Analysis

If the first unit performs below expectations, management will forgo expansion plans and focus all energies on this unit. In this case, the concept and marketing mix will be modified to maximize cash flow. This could result in either (1) a simple delay in regional/national roll-out as fine-tuning occurs, (2) a decision to operate a single unit only, using cash-flow to payback investors, or (3) a decision to discontinue operations, in which case investors will receive the proceeds from liquidation of the firm's assets. If, on the other hand, performance far exceeds management's estimation, expansion capital will be sought sooner and a national roll-out will be pursued aggressively.

Risks

Certain negative events can cause RFD's performance to fall below expectations. These include:

- **Economic model doesn't work:** RFD's assumptions about average check and table turns fall far below management estimates.
- **Competition intensifies:** Other competitors seek to enter the Dessert-Focused Fine Dining segment, either in RFD's immediate market, or in other markets (limiting opportunities for expansion).
- **Consumer trends shift:** If eating in moderation is actually only a "fad," and the health craze becomes a health norm, a dessert-focused concept will have limited appeal.
- **Real estate is difficult to obtain:** RFD's economic model assumes $50/sq. ft. annual rent. To the extent that quality locations cost significantly more that this, RFD's economic model deteriorates.

The management team and board of directors will promptly respond to these risks should they occur.

APPENDIX A | Sample Menu

Dessert Prix Fixe Menu

Chef's Dessert & Beverage Selections

Chocolate Carnival	$16/$11

White chocolate mousse in a cookie silo, fudge torte and chocolate tea cake filled with ganache. Plus '94 Cockburn Port or Espresso.

The Classic	$17/$11

RFD's Classic Cheesecake, Espresso Truffles & Seasonal Berries in a Chocolate Bag, with a tall flute of Perrier Jouet or a Cappuccino.

Loads of Lemon	$15/$10

Lemon filled pound cake, cheesecake, pudding and assortment of cookies. Herbal Tea or a glass of Chardonnay.

Beverage substitutions available

A la Mode

RFD Signatures

Special Chocolate Fondue (for 2)	$ 14.00
House Chocolate Mousse with Seasonal Berries	$ 9.00
Tuxedo Truffle Torte	$ 9.00
Chocolate Hazelnut Torte (low-fat)	$ 8.00
Peanut Butter Cheesecake	$ 7.00
Maple Bread Pudding	$ 6.50

Chocolate Delights

Chocolate Brownie Tart	$ 7.50
Chocolate Almond Torte	$ 7.50
Chocolate Terrine	$ 7.50
White Chocolate Tartlet with Strawberry Coulis	$ 7.00

Specialty Desserts

Classic Cheesecake	$ 7.50
Apple Crisp with Homemade Vanilla Ice Cream	$ 7.00
Strawberry Tart	$ 7.00
Baked Pear with Crumbled Amaretti Cookies	$ 6.50
Rice Pudding Cake with Cherry-Apricot Compote	$ 6.50

Ices & Cremes

Raspberry Sorbet in Champagne	$ 6.50
Gelati du Jour	$ 6.00
Homemade Ice Cream	$ 5.50

Potpourri

Petit Four Assortment or Hand-Dipped Chocolates	$ 7.00
Decorated Cookies or Assorted Biscotti	$ 5.00

Lite Entrees

Fruit & Cheese Plate	$ 7.00
Soups, Salads, Quiche, Sandwiches	n/a

Ask for daily specials

Wines & Spirits

Dessert Wines (3 oz pour)

Marques de Caceres Saninella (5 oz pour)	$	4.00
Muscat de Revesaltes, Domaine de la Casenove	$	4.00
1983er Trittenheimer Apotheke Auslese Riesling	$	5.50

Champagne

Napa Rhine Reserve	$	8.50
Veuve Clicquote Brut N.V.	$	12.00
Perrier Jouet	$	13.00

Ports

Quinta do Noval Tawny	$	4.00
Taylor-Fladgate Special Ruby	$	7.00
1963 Sandeman Vintage	$	14.00

Sherries

Harvey's Bristol Cream	$	3.00
Emilio Lustau Pedro Ximenez, Solara Reserva "San Emilio"	$	3.00

Cognacs & Brandies

Remy Martin Cognac VSOP	$	6.50
Metaxa 5 Star Brandy	$	5.50
Cardenal Mendoza Brandy	$	5.50
Courvoisier Grande Fine Cognac	$	21.00
Hennessy Paradis Cognac	$	30.00

Armagnacs

Baron de Sigognac XO	$	7.00
1970 Domaine de St. Aubin Bas	$	15.50

White Wine

	$	6.50

Bourgogne Blanc, Bernard Morey, Vichon Chardonnay, Napa, Flora Springs Barrel Fermented Chardonnay, Lagaria Pino Grigio, Italy; Guntrum Riesling, Germany

Red Wine

	$	7.50

Los Vascos Cabernet Sauvignon, Chile; Mezzacorona Merlot, Italy; Gluhwein, Switzerland; Morgon 1992 Pinot Noir, Reserve

Scotches

12 Year Old Singleton	$	5.00
10 Year Old Abelour	$	5.50
18 Year Old Glenlivet	$	10.00
25 Year Old Macallan	$	25.00

Bourbons & Whiskies

Makers Mark	$	5.00
Knob Creek 9 Year Old Small Batch	$	6.00

International & Craft Brews

	$	5.00

Allagash, Maine; Ybor Gold; Shiner Bock, Nut Brown Ale, Belhaven Scottish Ale, Efes, Cider and Others

Ask for Full and Half-Bottle prices

APPENDIX A | (continued)

Coffees

Espresso

Espresso	$	2.75
La Creme de Cafe		
Expresso Doppio	$	2.75
Double Espresso		
Espresso Extra	$	5.00
Add any liquer. Espresso & Sambuca is a traditional combination .		
Caffe Nocciola	$	4.50
Espresso creme de cafe with steamed Hazelnut milk		

Cappuccino

Cappuccino	$	2.75
Espresso, the Essense of Coffee, steamed cream, sugar, cocoa, toped with schlag.		
Cappuccino Minus	$	2.75
Traditional Cappuccino made with skim milk.		
Olympia		
Traditional European Cappuccino.		
Cappuccino L'Amore	$	2.95
With extracts of brandy and rum plus fresh schlag and shaved chocolate		
Mocha	$	2.95
Espresso, steamed milk, Swiss Chocolate and schlag, crowned with chocolate.		

Coffee

RFD House-Roasted Blend	$	1.60
Cafe Con Leche	$	2.60
Just like they drink it in Havana.		
Turkish Coffee	$	2.65
As served throughout the Arab and Greek nations.		
Cafe Au Lait		
With steamed milk		

Special requests available

Teas & Herbal Beverages

Teas

Orange Pekoe, Earl Grey, Irish Times, English Breakfast Russian, Oolong, Darjeeling	$	2.00

Herbals

Chamomile, Lavender, Jasmine, Lemon Grass, Ceylon Decaf Apricot, Mango, Decaf Pekoe	$	2.00

Specialty Drinks

Coffees With Spirit

Godiva Cappuccino RFD	$	5.50
With Godiva Liquer		
Beantown Mint	$	5.50
Coffee, mint and chocolate liquers topped with chocolate shavings and whipped cream.		
Frozen Praline Coffee	$	5.50
Blend of coffee and vanila ice cream with cappuccino and Texas praline liquers.		
Hot Nutty Irishman	$	5.50
With Bailey's and Frangelico, cream and chocolate		
Irish Coffee	$	5.25
With Bushmills and Schlag		
Haute Chocolate	$	3.00
Traditional Dutch chocolate and shaved Swiss chocolate		
Make Your Own Drink		$ 6/7.00
Any Coffee & Liquer plus extras		

Chilled Delights

Very Berrie Smoothie (low-fat)	$	4.50
Seasonal berries		
Paul's Iced Cappuccino	$	5.00
Paul's recipe with secret ingredient		
The Ultimate Milkshake		$4.5/6.5
Thickest shake this side of the Mississippi, 3 flavors		
Cafe Verdi	$	4.25
Espresso over ice with milk and brandy		

Water, Juice and Other Beverages

Sparkling Water	$	2.50
San Pelligrino		
Perrier		
Spring Water	$	2.00
Evian		
Fresh Juices, Aguas Frescas	$	3.50
Orange, Strawberry, Kiwi, Lemon-Ade, Cranberry Grapefruit, Tomato, Carrot		
Carbonated Beverages	$	1.75
Feel free to ask for special requests		

Entry

25 Seats

Dining room

22 Seats

10 Seats

Retail display

6 Seats

Retail area

Retail display

Dessert prep
station

Wait
station

Bar area

Wine/liqueurs
display

70'-0"

Private function
room
9'-8" x 14'-0"
8–12 seats

Womens
lav.

Mens lav.

Kitchen

Walk-in
cooler

Service
entry

35'-0"

Table

Stove

Table

oven

Connector

Room For Dessert

Concept plan
2,500 sq.ft. • 70 seats

Graphic scale

0   5   10 FT

APPENDIX C | Unit Proformas

	Assumptions	97Q2	97Q3	97Q4	98Q1	98Q2	98Q3	98Q4	99Q1	99Q2	99Q3	99Q4
Ramp up—restaurant	8 mos. to reach target sales	0%	37%	78%	95%	100%	100%	100%	101%	103%	104%	106%
Seasonality	Taken from NRA averages	25.5%	26.0%	25.2%	23.2%	25.5%	26.0%	25.2%	23.2%	25.5%	26.0%	25.2%
COGS/labor efficiency	6 mos. to reach target levels	0%	145%	120%	100%	100%	100%	100%	100%	100%	100%	100%
Income Statement												
Revenues	See business plan	—	103,116	215,657	240,836	278,587	283,988	275,465	256,447	286,043	296,252	291,056
–COGS	26.6% of sales	—	38,217	65,922	61,671	71,338	72,721	70,539	65,669	73,247	75,862	74,531
Gross margin	74.4%	—	**64,899**	**149,735**	**179,165**	**207,249**	**211,266**	**204,926**	**190,779**	**212,795**	**220,391**	**216,525**
Salary, wages, & benefits	See business plan	—	92,038	89,151	68,224	75,121	76,577	74,278	68,224	75,121	76,577	74,278
OpEx and G&A	17.4% of sales	—	31,640	47,461	47,461	47,461	47,461	47,461	47,461	47,461	47,461	47,461
Occupancy	$50/sq. ft * 2,500 ft.	—	20,417	30,625	30,625	30,625	30,625	30,625	30,625	30,625	30,625	30,625
Depreciation & amortization	5 depreciation life	—	13,434	20,152	20,152	20,152	20,152	20,152	20,152	20,152	20,152	20,152
Operating income		—	**(92,630)**	**(37,653)**	**12,703**	**33,891**	**36,452**	**32,410**	**24,317**	**39,438**	**45,577**	**44,009**
Interest income	4.0% of market sec.	—	2,027	424	528	879	1,361	1,862	2,331	2,771	3,312	3,895
Interest on bank debt	10.0% on balance	—	—	—	—	—	—	—	—	—	—	—
Interest on sub. debt	12.0% on balance	—	10,638	13,115	13,514	13,926	14,350	14,787	15,237	15,702	16,180	16,672
Income B4 taxes		—	**(101,241)**	**(50,344)**	**(283)**	**20,844**	**23,463**	**19,485**	**11,411**	**26,507**	**32,709**	**31,231**
Tax provision (benefit)	35.0% tax rate	—	(35,434)	(17,621)	(99)	7,296	212	6,820	3,994	9,277	11,448	10,931
Net income		—	**(65,807)**	**(32,724)**	**(184)**	**13,549**	**15,251**	**12,665**	**7,417**	**17,229**	**21,261**	**20,300**
Balance Sheet												
Current Assets												
Cash		—	119,127	134,169	174,030	223,729	217,417	320,774	363,071	418,916	475,634	536,113
Req'd	10.0% of sales	—	65,181	94,923	108,619	112,214	108,634	111,674	110,791	115,580	114,066	118,375
Marketable securities		—	53,946	39,245	65,411	111,515	62,783	209,100	252,280	303,335	361,568	417,739
Receivables	3 days sales	—	5,432	7,910	9,052	9,351	9,053	9,306	9,233	9,632	9,506	9,865
Inventories	4 turns/mo.	—	4,868	5,570	5,795	5,986	5,795	5,958	5,911	6,166	6,085	6,315
Other current assets	Deposits & prepaids	—	27,872	27,872	27,872	27,872	27,872	27,872	27,872	27,872	27,872	27,872
Total current assets		—	**157,298**	**175,521**	**216,747**	**266,938**	**314,137**	**363,910**	**406,086**	**462,585**	**519,096**	**580,165**
Gross PPE	See business plan	—	403,031	403,031	403,031	403,031	403,031	403,031	403,031	403,031	403,031	403,031
Accumulated depreciated		—	13,434	33,586	53,737	73,889	94,040	114,192	134,344	154,495	174,647	194,798
Net PPE		—	389,596	369,445	349,293	329,142	308,990	288,839	268,687	248,535	228,384	208,232
Other assets	Licenses & permits	—	50,000	50,000	50,000	50,000	50,000	50,000	50,000	50,000	50,000	50,000
Total assets		—	**596,894**	**594,965**	**616,040**	**646,080**	**673,127**	**702,748**	**724,773**	**761,120**	**797,480**	**838,397**

(continued)

APPENDIX C | Unit Proformas (continued)

	Assumptions	97Q2	97Q3	97Q4	98Q1	98Q2	98Q3	98Q4	99Q1	99Q2	99Q3	99Q4
Current Liabilities												
Accounts payable	30 days sales	—	19,473	22,282	23,179	23,946	23,182	23,830	23,642	24,664	24,341	25,260
Other current liabilities	50.0% of sales	—	32,590	46,462	54,309	56,107	54,317	55,837	55,396	57,790	57,033	59,187
Income taxes payable	NOL carried	—	—	—	—	—	—	—	—	—	—	870
Total current liabilities		—	**52,063**	**69,743**	**77,488**	**80,053**	**77,499**	**79,668**	**79,038**	**82,454**	**81,374**	**85,318**
Bank debt		—	—	—	—	—	—	—	—	—	—	—
Subordinated debt		—	430,638	443,753	457,267	471,193	485,543	500,330	515,568	531,269	547,449	564,122
Total liabilities		—	**482,701**	**513,496**	**534,755**	**551,246**	**563,042**	**579,998**	**594,606**	**613,724**	**628,823**	**649,439**
Paid-in capital		—	180,000	180,000	180,000	180,000	180,000	180,000	180,000	180,000	180,000	180,000
Retained earnings		—	(65,807)	(98,530)	(98,715)	(85,166)	(69,915)	(57,250)	(49,833)	(32,603)	(11,343)	8,958
Total equity		—	**114,193**	**81,470**	**81,285**	**94,834**	**110,085**	**122,750**	**130,167**	**147,397**	**168,657**	**188,958**
Total liabilities & equity		—	**596,894**	**594,965**	**616,040**	**646,080**	**673,127**	**702,748**	**724,773**	**761,120**	**797,480**	**838,397**
Statement of Cash Flows												
Cash Flow From Operating Activities												
Net income		—	(65,807)	(32,724)	(184)	13,549	15,251	12,665	7,417	17,229	21,261	20,300
+ Depreciation		—	13,434	20,152	20,152	20,152	20,152	20,152	20,152	20,152	20,152	20,152
+ Decrease in accounts receivable		—	(5,432)	(2,479)	(1,141)	(300)	298	(253)	74	(399)	126	(359)
+ Decrease in inventory		—	(4,868)	(702)	(224)	(192)	191	(162)	47	(255)	81	(230)
+ Decrease in other current assets		—	(27,872)	—	—	—	—	—	—	—	—	—
+ Increase in accounts payable		—	19,473	2,809	897	767	(764)	649	(188)	(1,022)	(323)	919
+ Increase in other current liabilities		—	32,590	14,871	6,484	1,798	(1,790)	1,520	(441)	2,395	(757)	2,154
+ Increase in income tax payable		—	—	—	—	—	—	—	—	—	—	870
+ Change in NWC		—	13,892	14,499	6,379	2,073	(2,064)	1,753	(509)	2,762	(873)	3,355
+ Accrued bank interest		—	—	—	—	—	—	—	—	—	—	—
+ Accrued sub interest		—	10,638	13,115	13,514	13,926	14,350	14,787	15,237	15,702	16,180	16,672
Cash Flow from Operating Activities		**—**	**(27,843)**	**15,042**	**39,861**	**49,700**	**47,688**	**49,357**	**42,297**	**55,844**	**56,719**	**60,479**
Cash Flow from Investing Activities												
– Capital expenditures		(403,031)	—	—	—	—	—	—	—	—	—	—
– Other assets		950,000	—	—	—	—	—	—	—	—	—	—
Cash Flow from Investing Activities		**(453,031)**	—	—	—	—	—	—	—	—	—	—
Cash Flow from Financing Activities												
+ Additional borrowing—bank debt		—	—	—	—	—	—	—	—	—	—	—
– Principal payments—bank debt		—	—	—	—	—	—	—	—	—	—	—
+ Additional borrowing—sub debt		420,000	—	—	—	—	—	—	—	—	—	—
– Principal payments—sub debt		—	—	—	—	—	—	—	—	—	—	—
+ Proceeds from equity issues		180,000	—	—	—	—	—	—	—	—	—	—

Cash Flow from Financing Activities	—	600,000	—	—	—	—	—	—	—	—	—
Cash & equivalent @ beg. period	—	—	19,127	134,169	174,030	,729	271,417	302,774	363,071	418,916	475,634
Cash flow	—	119,127	15,042	39,861	49,700	47,688	49,357	42,297	55,844	56,719	60,479
Cash & equivalent @ end period	—	119,127	134,169	174,030	223,729	217,417	320,774	363,071	418,916	475,634	536,113
Free Cash Flow											
Net income	—	(65,807)	(32,724)	(184)	13,549	15,251	12,665	7,417	17,229	21,261	20,300
+ Depreciation	—	13,434	20,152	20,152	20,152	20,152	20,152	20,152	20,152	20,152	20,152
+ Accrued interest	—	10,638	13,115	13,514	13,926	14,350	14,787	15,237	15,702	16,180	16,672
+ Change in NWC	—	13,892	14,499	6,379	2,073	(2,064)	1,753	(509)	2,762	(873)	3,355
− Capex	—	(453,031)	—	—	—	—	—	—	—	—	—
Free cash flow	—	**(480,873)**	**15,042**	**39,861**	**49,700**	**47,688**	**49,357**	**42,297**	**55,844**	**56,719**	**60,479**
Accumulated surplus (deficit)	—	(480,873)	(465,831)	(425,970)	(376,271)	(328,583)	(279,226)	(236,929)	(181,084)	(124,366)	(63,887)
Break-even											
Fixed costs											
Gross margin (%)											
B-E sales level											
% Of expected sales											

	Assumptions	1997	1998	1999	2000	2001	2002	
Ramp up—restaurant	8 mos. to reach target sales	38%	99%	104%	110%	110%	110%	⇐ Sales enhanced via traffic increase, price increase, etc.
Seasonality	Taken from NRA averages							
COGS/labor efficiency	6 mos. to reach target levels	133%	100%	100%	97%	94%	90%	⇐ Efficiencies achieved in production techniques
Income Statement								
Revenues	See business plan	318,772	1,078,875	1,129,798	1,200,157	1,200,157	1,200,157	
−COGS	25.6% of sales	104,138	276,269	289,309	298,106	288,886	276,593	
Gross margin	74.4%	**214,634**	**802,606**	**840,489**	**902,051**	**911,270**	**923,564**	
Salary, wages, & benefits	See business plan	181,189	294,200	294,200	308,910	308,910	308,910	⇐ Labor increase by 5% to compensate for sales increase
OpEx and G&A	17.4% of sales	79,101	189,843	189,843	189,843	189,843	189,843	
Occupancy	$ 50/sq.ft.*2,500 ft.	51,042	122,500	122,500	122,500	122,500	122,500	⇐ 5 year lease
Depreciation & amortization	5 depreciation life	33,586	80,606	80,606	80,606	80,606	47,020	
Operating income		**(130,284)**	**115,457**	**153,340**	**200,192**	**209,411**	**255,290**	

(continued)

APPENDIX C | Unit Proformas (continued)

	Assumptions	1997	1998	1999	2000	2001	2002	
Interest income	4.0% of marketable securities	2,451	4,629	12,309	21,756	32,117	42,901	
Interest on bank debt	10.0% on balance	—	—	—	—	—	—	⇐ No conversion of debt until end of 2002
Interest on sub. debt	12.0% on balance	23,753	56,578	63,791	72,016	81,209	91,576	
Income B4 Taxes		**(151,585)**	**63,509**	**101,857**	**149,932**	**160,319**	**206,616**	
Tax provision (benefit)	35.0% tax rate	(53,055)	22,228	35,650	52,476	56,112	72,315	
Net income		**(98,530)**	**41,281**	**66,207**	**97,456**	**104,208**	**134,300**	
Balance Sheet								
Current Assets								
Cash		134,169	320,774	356,113	790,064	1,055,813	1,329,292	
Rec'd	10.0% of sales	94,923	111,674	118,375	120,016	120,016	120,016	
Marketable securities		39,245	209,100	417,739	670,048	935,979	1,209,276	
Receivables	3 days sales	7,910	9,306	9,865	10,001	10,001	10,001	
Inventories	4 turns/mo.	5,570	5,958	6,315	6,211	6,018	5,762	
Other current assets	Deposits & prepaids	27,872	27,872	27,872	27,872	27,872	27,872	⇐ Rent, utilities, insurance
Total current assets		**175,521**	**363,910**	**580,165**	**834,147**	**1,099,704**	**1,372,927**	
Gross PPE	See business plan	403,031	403,031	403,031	403,031	403,031	403,031	
Accumulated depreciation		33,586	114,192	194,798	275,404	356,010	403,031	
Net PPE		369,445	288,839	208,232	127,626	47,020	—	
Other assets	Licenses & permits	50,000	50,000	50,000	50,000	50,000	50,000	⇐ MA liquor license
Total assets		**594,965**	**702,748**	**838,397**	**1,011,773**	**1,196,725**	**1,422,927**	
Current Liabilities								
Accounts payable	30 days COGS	22,282	23,830	25,260	24,842	24,074	23,049	
Other current liabilities	5.0% of sales	47,462	55,837	59,187	60,008	60,008	60,008	⇐ Deposits from employees & customers
Income taxes payable	NOL carried	—	—	870	4,373	4,676	6,026	⇐ Estimated taxes paid quarterly
Total current liabilities		**69,743**	**79,668**	**85,318**	**89,223**	**88,758**	**89,084**	
Bank debt		—	—	—	—	—	—	
Subordinated debt		443,753	500,330	564,122	636,137	717,346	808,922	
Total liabilities		**513,496**	**579,998**	**649,439**	**725,360**	**806,104**	**898,006**	
Paid-in capital		180,000	180,000	180,000	180,000	180,000	180,000	
Retained earnings		(98,530)	(57,250)	8,958	106,413	310,621	344,921	
Total equity		**81,470**	**122,750**	**188,958**	**286,413**	**390,621**	**524,921**	
Total liabilities & equity		**594,965**	**702,748**	**838,397**	**1,011,773**	**1,196,725**	**1,422,927**	
Statement of Cash Flows								
Cash Flow From Operating Activities								

Net income	(98,530)	41,281	66,207	96,456	104,208	134,300
+ Depreciation	33,586	80,606	80,606	80,606	80,606	47,020
+ Decrease in accounts receivable	(7,910)	(1,396)	(558)	(137)	192	—
+ Decrease in inventory	(5,570)	(387)	(357)	105	—	256
+ Decrease in other current assets	(27,872)	—	—	—	—	—
+ Increase in accounts payable	22,282	1,549	1,430	(418)	(768)	(1,024)
+ Increase in other current liabilities	47,462	8,376	3,350	820	303	1,350
+ Increase in income tax payable	—	—	—	3,503	—	—
+ Change in NWC	28,391	8,141	4,734	3,873	(273)	582
+ Accrued bank interest	—	—	—	—	—	—
+ Accrued sub interest	23,753	56,578	63,791	72,016	81,209	91,576
Cash Flow from Operating Activities	**(12,801)**	**186,606**	**215,339**	**253,950**	**265,749**	**273,479**
Cash Flow from Investing Activities						
− Capital expenditures	(403,031)	—	—	—	—	—
− Other assets	(50,000)	—	—	—	—	—
Cash Flow from Investing Activities	**(453,031)**	**—**	**—**	**—**	**—**	**—**
Cash Flow from Financing Activities						
+ Additional borrowing—bank debt	—	—	—	—	—	—
− Principal payments—bank debt	—	—	—	—	—	—
+ Additional borrowing—sub debt	420,000	—	—	—	—	—
− Principal payments—sub debt	—	—	—	—	—	—
+ Proceeds from equity issues	180,000	—	—	—	—	—
Cash Flow from Financing Activities	**600,000**	**—**	**—**	**—**	**—**	**—**
Cash & equivalent @ beg. period	—	134,169	320,774	536,113	790,064	1,055,813
Cash flow	134,169	186,606	215,339	253,950	265,749	273,479
Cash & equivalent @ end period	134,169	320,774	536,113	790,064	1,055,813	1,329,292
Free Cash Flow						
Net income	(98,530)	41,281	66,207	97,456	104,208	134,300
+ Depreciation	33,586	80,606	80,606	80,606	80,606	47,020
+ Accrued interest	23,753	56,578	63,791	72,016	81,209	91,576
+ Change in NWC	28,391	8,141	4,734	3,873	(273)	582
− Capex	(453,031)	—	—	—	—	—
Free cash flow	**(465,831)**	**186,606**	**215,339**	**253,950**	**265,749**	**273,479**
Accumulated surplus (deficit)	(465,831)	(279,226)	(63,887)	190,064	455,813	729,292
Break-even						
Fixed costs	$275,625	$591,997	$591,532	$597,664	$596,496	$562,493
Gross margin (%)	38.9%	60.8%	61.4%	62.3%	63.1%	64.1%
B-E sales level	$708,335	$974,348	$963,833	$959,463	$945,923	$877,743
% Of expected sales	222.2%	90.3%	85.3%	79.9%	78.8%	73.1%

APPENDIX D | Team Member Resumes

PAUL D. CONFORTI
50 Adamson Street
Allston, MA 02134
(617) 787-7814
pconforti@mba97.hbs.edu

education

1995–1997   **HARVARD UNIVERSITY GRADUATE SCHOOL**
OF BUSINESS ADMINISTRATION   **BOSTON, MA**

Candidate for Master in Business Administration degree, June 1997. Entrepreneurial Management Emphasis. Awarded First Year Honors. Elected Section President. Appointed Co-Chair of HBS Ventures' Board of Directors (overseeing Student Association campus businesses). Member of the Small Business & New Enterprise Club, Venture Capital Club, and Food Industry Club.

Organized and led a year-long field study analyzing the dessert niche of the restaurant industry. Completed a feasibility study, and writing a business plan for a concept focused on this niche.

1988–1992   **RENSSELAER POLYTECHNIC INSTITUTE**   **TROY, NY**

Bachelor of Science Degree, summa cum laude, in Management, Concentrations in Finance and Operations. Awarded the Willie Stanton Award as the senior who "contributed the most in the service of the student body."

Elected Student Union President, responsible for overseeing $6.5 million annual budget, chairing a 12 member Executive Board, and representing the student body to the Administration, Faculty, Staff, and outside community.

experience

1996   **THE TOPOL GROUP, INC.**   **BOSTON, MA**
Assistant to the President, **Summer Internship**

Coordinated the summer activities of this growing, privately-held consulting and investment management company.

- Investigated angel capital investment opportunities. Performed strategic and financial analyses of five business plans. Worked with entrepreneurs and principal to structure initial investment deals.
- Developed allocation strategy for $8 million investment portfolio. Integrated investor preferences, market forecasts, and investment vehicle research into executable recommendations. Identified opportunities to reduce management fees by 25% and increase expected returns from 8% to 10% annually.
- Facilitated continued growth of the firm. Identified additional consulting and speaking engagement opportunities for the principal. Acquired space, furniture, equipment, etc., in order to relocate business offices.

1995   **METROPOLITAN LIFE INSURANCE COMPANY**   **UTICA, NY**
Manager, **Dental Insurance Claim Customer Service Center**

Reorganized this $12 million, 250 employee business to improve operating performance and prepare for significant growth due to consolidations. Created office mission and vision, and focused the organization on three critical areas:

- Customers: Conceived and established MS Excel based customer-specific performance summary reports. Obtained customer feedback and implemented appropriate changes in service delivery.
- Processes and Goals: Improved ten business day claim turnaround time from 70% to 90% processed. Improved customer service response time from 60% to 90% of calls answered within 30 seconds.
- People: Created and delivered supervisor performance appraisals. Initiated management development workshops. Developed employee appreciation and motivation programs tied to performance. Designed and introduced MS Excel based individual performance feedback report.

1992–1994   **THE TRAVELERS INSURANCE COMPANY, Managed Care & Employee Benefits Organization**
1994   *Business Manager,* **Dental Insurance Claim Customer Service Center**   **ALBANY, NY**

Managed $2 million, 40 person production and customer service team. Led transition to cross-functional, customer-focused units. Developed and implemented initiatives resulting in 10% customer approval rating increase, 50% improvement in operating performance, and 25% reduction in operating costs.

1992–1993   *Project Manager,* **Office Consolidations and Process Improvements**   **HARTFORD, CT**

Managed national projects to consolidate claim service centers. Developed strategies with senior management, and coordinated efforts of 20 member cross-functional team. Project resulted in 20% reduction in annual operating costs.

personal   Keynote speaker at the Rensselaer Class of 1998 convocation. Enjoy listening to music, running, and traveling.

APPENDIX D | *(continued)*

KRISTEN E. KRZYZEWSKI
205 Mount Auburn Street, 4B
Cambridge, MA 02138
kristenk@mba97.hbs.edu
(617)864-2763

education
1995–1997   **HARVARD UNIVERSITY GRADUATE SCHOOL
OF BUSINESS ADMINISTRATION**   **BOSTON, MA**

Candidate for Master in Business Administration degree, June 1997. Appointed Director of Finance, Project Out-reach Volunteer Program. Co-Chairperson of Health Care Panel, Women's Student Association Annual Confer-ence. Member of Small Business & Entrepreneurship and Health Industry Clubs.

1989–1991   **CORNELL UNIVERSITY**   **ITHACA, NY**

Bachelor of Arts degree in Economics, with distinction in all subjects. Elected *Phi Beta Kappa.* Awarded IBM Watson Memorial Scholarship. Selected by faculty as Teaching Assistant for Insurance & Risk Management course at Cornell's School of Hotel Administration. Resident Advisor. Dean's List.

1987–1989   **BOSTON COLLEGE**   **CHESTNUT HILL, MA**

Honors Program, School of Arts and Sciences. Campus tour guide. Minority recruitment volunteer. Dean's List.

experience
1991–1995   **CROWN STERLING SUITES**   **SAN FRANCISCO, CA**
1993–1995   *Director of Employee Benefits and Risk Management Systems*

Structured and managed employee benefit plans, worker's compensation, risk management programs, payroll, personnel policy, and $10 million budget for hotel management company with 24 hotels and 3,500 employees.

General Management & Administration

- Assessed organizational needs regarding risk exposure and focused management attention and resources on highest priorities. Researched loss prevention and financing options. Accountable to senior management.
- Designed strategy to minimize risk and manage costs. Implemented policy, procedure, and training which reduced insurance losses by 67% and annual insurance premiums by $2.5 million.
- Created systems resulting in proprietary claims management process, standardized performance measure-ments, and billing review procedure.
- Negotiated insurance contracts and costs.
- Managed external relationships with 12 insurance carriers, 5 brokers, and hotel customers.

Employee Benefits and Personnel

- Hired and supervised corporate administrative employees. Directed activities of 24 benefit administrators.
- Evaluated medical, dental, and 401(k) benefit plans, researched viable alternatives, and implemented pro-grams which resulted in annual savings of $1 million and increased coverage for employees.
- Developed first corporate safety policy and revised employee handbook for operations in 6 states.

1991–1993   *Insurance Administrator*   **DALLAS, TX**

Developed corporate procedure to report and handle guest related incidents at hotels. Analyzed claim experi-ence to identify trends. Monitored reserves and developed strategies to minimize losses.

summer 1996   **THE CITIBANK PRIVATE BANK**   **NEW YORK, NY**
Summer Management Associate
Assumed project management responsibilities as member of internal consulting team on portfolio of global per-formance improvement initiatives.

- Designed analytical model to prioritize re-engineering projects. Directed creation of user-friendly database and documentation used by global staff. Submitted by bank for patent protection.
- Led project to rationalize global deployment of bank resources in 33 countries. Framed analysis, researched global wealth market, collected and analyzed internal data.

personal   Rotary International Exchange Student to West Germany from 1986–1987. Proficient in German. Enjoy skiing, ballroom dancing, and travel.

(continued)

APPENDIX D | Team Member Resumes (*continued*)

KIM MOORE
One Soldiers Field Park, Apt. 602
Boston, MA 02163
(617) 661-1558

education

1995–1997

**HARVARD UNIVERSITY GRADUATE SCHOOL
OF BUSINESS ADMINISTRATION**   **BOSTON, MA**

Candidate for Master in Business Administration degree, June 1997. Elected to *Harbus News* Board of Directors. Active in Marketing Club, Women's Student Association and Texas Club.

1985–1989

THE UNIVERSITY OF TEXAS   **AUSTIN, TX**

Awarded Bachelor of Journalism degree. Received Texas Achievement Award (scholarship). Appointed Director of 30-member news staff at student radio station, responsible for hourly newscasts. Active member of Student Issues Committee, La Amistad (mentor program), Women in Communications.

experience

summer 1996

H.E.BUTT GROCERY COMPANY   **HOUSTON, TX**

Summer Associate, Special Projects. Structured and led comprehensive examination of stores for nation's 10th largest grocery chain with goals of improving profitability and increasing sales. Presented findings and store-specific recommendations, projected to result in a 12% increase above expected growth in a no-growth industry.

- *Strategy.* Performed industry analysis to determine market position. Conducted competitive study. Created metrics for continually monitoring level of competitive intensity. Devised advertising strategy to combat entrenched competition and to foster long-term growth.
- *Marketing.* Examined trade area demographics. Identified key variables having impact on sales and profitability. Produced communication strategy to reach large ethnic population. Recommended innovative shuttle service to address concerns created by high percentage of pedestrian shoppers.
- *Operations.* Developed objective measures to quantify store director performance. Recommended creative methods to attract and retain quality employees. Suggested information sharing program designed to promote store-level efficiencies and continuous improvement.

1992–1995

CAPITAL CITIES/ABC, INC.   **NEW YORK, NY**

Associate Producer, ABC News *Day One.* Project coordinator for start-up, network television program.

- Initiated, structured and co-supervised development and execution of story projects, from proposal to broadcast, budgets up to $100,000. Supervised 5-15 member teams on location.
- Researched, analyzed and presented relevant data and background information. Developed ideas on project content and framework, resulting in more effective story presentation. Assembled and coordinated teams of experts to evaluate ethical and legal concerns on individual projects.
- Developed strategic plans for optimal news coverage. Responsible for coverage of breaking news events (David Koresh, State vs. OJ Simpson, Oklahoma City Bombing).
- Awarded Emmy for story on Ross Perot and his relationship with EDS and GM. Received Casey Medal for Meritorious Journalism for story on HCA and fraudulent insurance practices.

1990–1992

Senior Production Associate, ABC News *This Week With David Brinkley.*
Managed production-area team of 15 producers and editors for Washington-based weekly program. Coordinated union schedules, identified newsworthy clips to seniors and trained junior staff members.

1990

Desk Assistant, ABC News *World News Tonight with Peter Jennings.*
Identified and relayed news stories to international bureaus. Assisted editors in coordinating schedules of producers and news correspondents. Led team in delivery of broadcast materials.

summer 1988

CNN (CABLE NEWS NETWORK)   **WASHINGTON, DC**

Intern, CNN Political Unit. Covered 1988 Presidential campaign. Selected to work on Republican and Democratic conventions.

personal

Created, published and edited alumni newsletter for University of Texas (New York Chapter). Self-described cook of obscure Texas cuisine. Enjoy traditional Mexican, American, ballroom and Latin dance.

Walnut Venture Associates (D): RBS Deal Terms

It was Friday, June 5, 1998, and Bob O'Connor was headed home for the weekend. He knew it would be a busy one, for he had many decisions to make. He had been trying to raise capital for his company—the RBS Group, a software firm—for almost a year. He felt like he was finally nearing the end of this process, but now more issues had arisen.

First, his prospective investors wanted to *increase* the amount of their investment. While he would be happy to have the extra money, he felt that the valuation on RBS was already lower than he had hoped, and he was reluctant to take more money at this price.

Second, he had received a draft term sheet the day before. He'd only had a few minutes to scan it, but it seemed a long way from the simple deal they'd discussed weeks before. O'Connor knew he would be spending a lot of time with this document over the coming weekend.

Background

Wagner and other "angels" from the Walnut group had successfully gotten over several of the issues that had arisen during their due diligence process. (See Walnut Ventures Associates (A), (B) and (C) Nos.899-062, 063 and 064) Wagner described those issues and the due diligence process:

> The customer feedback was all quite good. O'Connor was a great salesman. The issue was: Is he a one man band? And we decided—yes, he was a one man band, but more by necessity than by choice. After watching him in action with his organization, we were comfortable that he could grow the organization and remain an effective leader.
>
> On the market size issue, we fundamentally decided that it was not a market with "home run" potential, but that—at the right valuation—we could still make an investment that offered attractive returns.

By late January, Wagner felt that he had a "soft" commitment from the group for $600,000 or so. O'Connor was attempting to raise $2 million, so this left a $1.4 million shortfall. Given this level of support from his group, Wagner felt it was up to Walnut to try to help O'Connor raise the remaining funds:

> We wanted to do this deal, and that meant doing more than sitting on our hands waiting for Bob to pull together the rest of the money. We held ourselves up as "value-added investors" and this was our opportunity to show that we meant it.

Wagner and other "Walnuters" contacted several New England area VC firms who they believed might have an appetite for an investment in RBS. On the basis of the appeal of RBS's business and the Walnut recommendation, 3 or 4 firms initiated serious due diligence efforts. But, these efforts came to naught. Wagner explained:

> Each of the venture firms decided that the market was small and therefore, that they could not put enough money to work. Finally, one firm—Mid-Atlantic Ventures—got to the same point but rather than deciding that they couldn't put enough money to work, seemed to come to the conclusion that—at the right price—it was a good deal. Mid-Atlantic had talked to us, and we had shared our due diligence efforts and perspective with them. Bob had a meeting scheduled with them, and we knew they were going to get to the issue of price.

At this point in time, Walnut had not yet had a discussion with O'Connor related to the valuation on which they intended to invest. Wagner knew that RBS's prior round had been an investment of $400,000 for 10% of the company. The remaining 90% was owned by O'Connor (25%) and two other founders, one of whom was still active in the business (20% each); the remaining 25% was held by a variety of other past and current employees.

RBS had made substantial progress since the UST financing and, indeed, had just had a strong quarter ending 3/31/98. Wagner offered his view of the valuation discussion:

> Everything we had learned about Bob during the process of pulling together the $2 million was positive. Bob was looking for an $8 to $10 million pre-money valuation, and we were at a figure more like $6.0 million. We felt we needed to talk to Bob prior to his meeting with Mid-Atlantic just so he knew where he stood. I explained to Bob our take on the valuation issue, and also that there would be some sort of preferred stock involved. This was not an easy conversation, and I think Bob was both surprised and disappointed with the valuation range we were in, but in the end, I believe he understood where we were coming from.
>
> By early April, we were talking to both Steve Smith at Mid-Atlantic and Bob about deal terms. It turned out that Mid-Atlantic thought that $6.0 was too high—Smith focused on the hurdles the company had yet to get over—it had no controller, no VP sales, and little marketing staff.
>
> As Mid-Atlantic began to pull a formal offer together they needed to know how much Walnut intended to invest. I told Steve $600,000, and he said he could handle the other $1.4 million.

A few weeks went by as the documents got pulled together and I got a call from Jim Sloane at EVC—one of the venture firms who had looked at the deal several months before. They said they hadn't heard from O'Connor and wanted to know what was going on. I told him that we had the $2 million pretty well pulled together.

Jim said he was disappointed and that EVC wanted to be involved, and that—while they did not want an active role—he thought they could be quite helpful. EVC did have quite a few software companies in its portfolio, and it would be helpful to have a relationship with them and these portfolio companies.

Jim said they'd like to do $750,000 and I said it was doubtful, but I would see what we could do. I called Mid-Atlantic and they agreed EVC would be a good addition, but they did not want to cut back their $1.4 million. Thus, we went to Bob and asked him how he felt about taking $2.5 million. He was not happy about the prospect of taking another $500,000 at what he believed was a low valuation.

*   *   *

Thus, as the first weekend in June approached, the ball was in O'Connor's court. Walnut and Mid-Atlantic had worked out the term sheet for their prospective investment, which they had just sent to O'Connor, and which he was studying. (see **Exhibit 1**) And now, the proposed investment had increased from $2.0 to 2.5 million at the same valuation.

EXHIBIT 1 | Proposed Term Sheet

JUNE 2, 1998

THE TERMS SET FORTH BELOW ARE SOLELY FOR THE PURPOSE OF OUTLINING THOSE TERMS PURSUANT TO WHICH A DEFINITIVE AGREEMENT OR AGREEMENTS MAY BE ENTERED INTO AND DO NOT AT THIS TIME CONSTITUTE A BINDING CONTRACT, EXCEPT THAT BY ACCEPTING THESE TERMS, RBS GROUP, INC. (THE COMPANY) AGREES THAT FOR A PERIOD OF 45 DAYS FOLLOWING THE DATE OF SIGNATURE, PROVIDED THAT THE PARTIES CONTINUE TO NEGOTIATE IN GOOD FAITH TO CONCLUDE AN INVESTMENT, THEY WILL NOT NEGOTIATE OR ENTER INTO DISCUSSIONS WITH ANY OTHER INVESTORS OR GROUP OF INVESTORS. AN INVESTMENT IN THE COMPANY IS CONTINGENT UPON, AMONG OTHER THINGS, SATISFACTORY COMPLETION OF DUE DILIGENCE AND THE NEGOTIATION AND EXECUTION OF A SATISFACTORY STOCK PURCHASE AGREEMENT.

TERM SHEET

Issuer   **RBS Group, Inc**. (a Massachusetts "C" Corporation, hereinafter referred to as the "Company").

Investors   **Mid-Atlantic Venture Fund III, L.P. ("MAVF")**

                Walnut Venture Associates ("WVA") (hereinafter, collectively referred to as the "Investors")

(continued)

EXHIBIT 1 | Proposed Term Sheet (*continued*)

Current Outstanding Securities	15,456 shares of Class A Voting Common Stock ("Class A Common", or "Common") 94,244 shares of Class B Non-Voting Common Stock ("Class B Common") and Options to purchase 10,000 shares of Class B Common
Securities to be Issued	
Security 1	Series A Redeemable Preferred Stock ("Series A Preferred")
	Price per Share: $1,000 ("Series A Original Purchase Price")
	Number of Shares: 1,800
Security 2	Series B Convertible Preferred Stock ("Series B Preferred")
	Price per Share: $3.60 ("Series B Original Purchase Price")
	Number of Shares: 55,556
	(Series A Preferred and Series B Preferred together, the "Preferred")
Amount of Investment	A total of $2.0 Million, of which $1.8 Million will purchase Series A Preferred and $0.2 Million will purchase Series B Preferred, from the Investors as follows:
	MAVF $1.4 Million
	WVA $0.6 Million
Post-Investment Ownership	The Company will be capitalized such that post investment common share equivalents will be held as follows:

	Shares/Equivalents	% of Total Post-Inv.
New Investors	55,556	27.9%
UST Capital Corp.	12,600	6.3%
Other SHs/Founders	35,395	17.8%
Management:		
Founders	61,705	31.0%
Reserved Shares-Granted	6,000	3.0%
Reserved Shares-Available	27,778	14.0%
Total Management	95,483	48.0%
Total Share equivalent ownership	199,034	100%

Reserved Shares	The Company currently has 10,000 shares of Series B Common reserved for issuance to directors, officers, employees and consultants upon exercise of outstanding options (6,000 of which have been granted or "promised"). The Company shall reserve 23,778 additional shares of Series B Common for issuance to such persons (Such total of 33,778 shares, is referred to as the "Reserved Shares".)
	The Reserved Shares will be issued from time to time to directors, officers, employees and consultants of the Company under such arrangements, contracts or plans as are recommended by management and approved by the Board, provided that, without unanimous consent of the Compensation Committee, the vesting of any such shares (or options therefor) issued to any such person shall not be at a rate in excess of 20% per annum from date of issuance. Unless agreed to the contrary by the holders of 66 2/3% of the Preferred voting as a single class, any issuance of shares in excess of the Reserved Shares will be a dilutive event requiring adjustment of the conversion price as provided

EXHIBIT 1 | (continued)

below under Antidilution Provisions, and will be subject to the Investors' first refusal right as described below. Holders of Reserved Shares who are officers or employees of the Company will be required to execute Stock Restriction Agreements generally as described below.

Closing Date

Closing for the investment is targeted for June 30, 1998, provided that all requirements for the closing (the "Closing") have been met or expressly waived in writing by the Investors and that sufficient investment capital is available to complete the financing from investors acceptable to MAVF.

Board Representation And Meetings

The Charter will provide that the authorized number of directors is five (5). Holders of Preferred will be entitled to elect two (2) directors ("Investor Directors"), one of which shall be elected by MAVF (initially, the MAVF director shall be Tom Smith) and one of which shall be elected by WVA (initially, the WVA director shall be Ralph Wagner). Holders of Common will elect two (2) directors, one of which shall be designated by UST Capital Corp. (initially, the UST Capital director shall be Art Snyder). The fifth director shall be the CEO, who shall be selected by a majority of Directors other than the CEO. The CEO shall be the only director who is an officer of the Company.

Board of Directors meetings shall be scheduled on a bi-monthly basis until such time as the Board of Directors unanimously votes to schedule them less frequently. The bylaws will provide, in addition to any provisions required by law, that any two directors or holders of at least 51% of the Preferred, may call a meeting of the Board.

Board Committees

The Board will create an Audit Committee and a Compensation Committee. Each of these committees will consist of not more than three outside directors and will include at least one director elected by MAVF. Salary increases for any officer of the Company earning over $100,000 per year in base salary shall not exceed 10% unless approved unanimously by the compensation committee.

The Company shall reimburse each Director's reasonable out of pocket expenses incurred in attending all Board of Directors' meetings and Board Committee meetings or any other activities (e.g., meetings, trade shows) which are required and/or requested on the Company's behalf.

RIGHTS, PREFERENCES, PRIVILEGES
AND RESTRICTIONS OF PREFERRED

General

Unless otherwise specified, the Preferred shall have rights, preferences and privileges senior to the Common.

Dividends

A cumulative dividend will accrue on the Preferred at the rate of 8% per annum compounded annually ("Accruing Dividends"). Accruing Dividends will be payable only (a) if, as and when declared by the Company's Board of Directors, (b) upon the liquidation or winding up of the Company, or (c) upon redemption of the Preferred. No dividends may be declared or paid on the Common until all Accruing Dividends have been paid in full on the Preferred. The Preferred will also participate pari passu in any dividends declared on Common. Dividends will cease to accrue in the event that the Investors convert their holdings to Common Stock.

Liquidation Preference

In the event of a liquidation or winding up of the Company, a) holders of Series A Preferred shall be entitled to receive, in preference to the holders of Common, an amount ("Series A Liquidation Amount") equal to the Series A Original Purchase Price plus any Accruing Dividends which have not been paid and b) holders of series B Preferred shall be entitled to receive, in preference to the holders of the common, the amount (Series B Liquidation Amount") equal to the greater of (1) the Series B original Purchase Price

(continued)

EXHIBIT 1 | Proposed Term Sheet (*continued*)

	plus any Accruing Dividends which have not been paid or (2) such amount that holders of Series B Preferred would have received had their shares been converted to Common immediately before the Liquidation Event.
	A consolidation or merger of the Company or sale of all or substantially all of its assets or the sale of all or substantially all of the Company's outstanding equity securities will be deemed to be a liquidation or winding up ("Liquidation Event") for purposes of the Liquidation Preference.
Conversion	Series A Preferred shall not be convertible.
	A holder of Series B Preferred will have the right to convert the Series B Preferred, at the option of the holder, at any time, into shares of Common. The total number of shares of Common into which the Series B Preferred may be converted initially will be determined by dividing the Series B Original Purchase Price by the conversion price. The initial conversion price will be the Series B Original Purchase Price, and will be subject to adjustment as provided below (see "antidilution provisions"). In the event of conversion, all Accruing Dividends that have not been paid (or declared) shall be waived. The number of shares of Class A and Class B Common issues upon conversion of the Preferred shall be proportionate to the then outstanding shares of Class A Common and Class B Common calculated on a fully diluted basis (currently 14.09% Class A Common and 85.91% Class B Common)
Automatic Conversion	The Series B Preferred shall be automatically converted into Common, at the then applicable conversion price, in the event of an underwritten public offering of shares of Common at a public offering price per share that is not less than $108 in an offering of not less than $15 million dollars.
Antidilution Provisions	In the event of stock splits, stock dividends, reorganizations, mergers, consolidations or sale of assets, there shall be a proportional adjustment in the conversion price of the Series B Preferred.
	In the event that the Company issues or sells any shares, including warrants, options, convertible securities or other rights to purchase Common ("Common Stock Equivalents"), other than Reserved Shares described above, at a price per share less than ten times (10X) the then-effective conversion price of the Series B Preferred, the conversion price of the Series B Preferred shall be reduced on a weighted average formula basis to diminish the effect of such dilutive issuance.
Voting Rights	Except with respect to election of directors and certain protective provisions, the holders of Series B Preferred will have the right to that number of votes equal to the number of shares Common issuable upon conversion of the Series B Preferred. Election of directors and the protective provisions are described under "Board Representation and Meetings" and "Protective Provisions", respectively.
Protective Provisions	Consent of the holders of at least 66 2/3% of the Preferred, voting together as a separate class, will be required for any actions which:

i) alter or change the rights, powers, preferences or privileges of the Series A or B Preferred;

ii) increase the authorized number of shares of Series A or B Preferred;

iii) increase the authorized number of shares of any other class of Preferred Stock;

iv) create any new class or series of stock which has preference over or is on parity with the Preferred;

v) involve a merger, consolidation or reorganization, winding up or sale of all or substantially all of the assets or sale of more than 50% of the Company's voting stock;

EXHIBIT 1 | (*continued*)

<table>
<tr><td></td><td>vi) involve a repurchase or other acquisition of shares of the Company's stock other than pursuant to redemption provisions described below under "Redemption";</td></tr>
<tr><td></td><td>vii) amend the Company's charter or bylaws; or</td></tr>
<tr><td></td><td>viii) certain other events that may adversely affect the rights of the Preferred stock</td></tr>
<tr><td>*Redemption*</td><td>At any time following the fifth anniversary of the sale of Series A Preferred, the Company, upon the request of the holders of at least 66 2/3 % of the Series A Preferred, shall redeem any portion or up to 100% of the Series A Preferred shares, by paying in cash 110% of the Original Purchase Price per share plus all accrued but unpaid dividends.</td></tr>
</table>

OTHER MATTERS

Conditions precedent to
Investors' obligation to invest

(i) Legal documentation satisfactory to Investors and Investors counsel.

(ii) Satisfactory completion of due diligence (A schedule of due diligence information items still outstanding from the company is attached hereto as Exhibit A)

(iii) Approval by MAVF and the Boards of Directors of the other investors participating in the contemplated financing.

(iv) Before closing, all key employees shall be required to sign non-compete and non-disclosure agreements, which such agreements shall include assignment of invention provisions, in a form satisfactory to the Investors. In addition, the Company may be required to obtain employment agreements with key employees.

Addition(s) to
Management

No later than 45 days after the close, the Company shall retain an executive search firm to assist in filling at least two and possibly three key senior level management positions to oversee sales, operations and finance. The first search initiated shall be for a VP Finance/Controller. The search firm selected must be approved by MAVF, which such approval shall not be unreasonably withheld.

Audit

No later than 90 days following the retention of a VP Finance/Controller, but in no event later than 150 days after the close, the Company shall retain a Big Six accounting firm (or an equivalent acceptable to the Investors) to complete an audit of the Company's financial statements for the fiscal year ended March 31, 1998.

Key Person Insurance

The Company will obtain and maintain life insurance on Mr. Bob O'Connor in an amount equal to $2.0 Million, with proceeds payable for the benefit of the Company.

Founder's Shares

Shares held at the closing date by key founders of the Company ("Founders Shares") including Robert O'Connor and Dave Milligan shall vest at the rate of 25% per year. The unvested portion of these shares may be repurchased by the Company at the sole discretion of the Board of Directors upon employee's death, disability or dismissal for cause, or if employee voluntarily resigns. Under any of the foregoing circumstances, the price paid for the unvested shares will be determined as follows: (1) Shares repurchased upon death or disability will be at a price equal to the fair market value as determined by an independent appraiser, (2) Shares repurchased following dismissal for cause or voluntary resignation will be at employee's average cost per share.

Cause shall be defined as:

a) conviction in a court of law of any felony crime;

b) willful violation of specific and lawful directions from the Board of Directors or excessive absenteeism which persists for a period of thirty days after a written notice is given of such absenteeism or violation;

(continued)

EXHIBIT 1 | Proposed Term Sheet (*continued*)

c) fraud as determined in a court of law;

d) a material failure of the founder to perform or observe provisions of his employment agreement which persists for a period of thirty days after a written notice is given of such failure to perform or observe;

e) breach of any of the covenants or obligations contained in the final agreements negotiated as part of this agreement which persists for a period of thirty days after written notice is given of such breach;

In the event that a sale, merger, or IPO of the company is completed with the approval of the majority of the Preferred shareholders, then those shares that are unvested shall be considered as having been fully vested at the time of such sale or merger.

Registration Rights	The holders of Preferred shall be entitled to:

i) Two long-form demand registrations.

ii) Unlimited piggyback rights

iii) Semi-annual short-form registrations (on forms S-2 or S-3) if the Company qualifies for the use of such short-form registration statements.

Right of First Refusal	Each holder of Preferred shall have a right of participation to purchase a share of all offerings of new securities of the Company (other than Reserved Shares) equal to the proportion which the number of shares of Preferred held by such holder (on an as-converted basis) bears to the Company's total issued and outstanding shares of Common. Such right shall terminate immediately prior to closing of a qualified public offering.

In the event that any of the holders of Common or Preferred proposes to sell or otherwise transfer any shares of stock of the Company, or any interest in such shares, holders of Preferred shall have a pro-rata right of first refusal to purchase such shares, at the same price and terms as those offered to the selling shareholders by any third party (excluding distributions or transfers to affiliates of such holder).

Right of Co-Sale	In the event that any employee desires to sell or transfer some or all of their shares to a third party, holders of Preferred shall have the right to participate in such sale at the same price and terms based on proportionate ownership.
Covenants	The following actions shall require approval of a majority of the Board of Directors, which such approval must include at least one affirmative vote from an Investor Director:

(i) Dividends paid on Common.

(ii) Issuance of capital stock or securities convertible into capital stock.

(iii) Any debt which would increase the Company's total indebtedness by more than $100,000 in any fiscal year.

(iv) Establishment of or investment in any subsidiary.

Information Rights	The Company shall furnish to each holder of Preferred the following:

(i) <u>Monthly Reports.</u> Within 20 days following the end of each month, an income statement, statement of cash flows and balance sheet for the prior monthly period. Statements shall include year-to-date figures compared to budgets, with variances delineated. A brief written summary shall be prepared by the CEO and attached to the Monthly Report which summarizes performance highlights, lowlights, variances from budget, and an outlook for the ensuing period.

EXHIBIT 1 | *(continued)*

(ii) <u>Annual Financial Statements.</u> Within 90 days following the end of the fiscal year, an unqualified audit, together with a copy of the auditor's letter to management, from a Big Six accounting firm or equivalent, which firm shall be approved by the Investors.

(iii) In the event the Company fails to provide monthly reports or financial statements in accordance with the foregoing, Investors shall have the authority, at the Company's expense, to request an audit by an accounting firm of its choice, such that statements are produced to the satisfaction of the Investor.

(iv) <u>Annual Budget.</u> At least 60 days before the end of each fiscal year, a budget, including projected income statement, cash flow and balance sheet, on a monthly basis for the ensuing fiscal year, together with underlying assumptions and a brief qualitative description of the company's plan by the Chief Executive Officer in support of that budget.

(v) <u>Non-compliance.</u> Within 10 days after the discovery of any default in the terms of the Preferred Stock Purchase Agreement or any ancillary agreement, or of any other material adverse event, a statement outlining such default or event, and management's proposed response.

Purchase Agreement   The purchase of the Company's Preferred will be made pursuant to a Preferred Stock Purchase Agreement drafted by counsel to the Investors. This agreement shall contain, among other things, appropriate representations and warranties of the Company, covenants of the Company reflecting the provisions set forth herein and other typical covenants, and appropriate conditions of closing, including, among other things, qualification of the shares under applicable Blue Sky laws, the filing of a certificate of amendment to the Company's charter to authorize the Series A Preferred, and an opinion of counsel customary for such transactions. Until the Purchase Agreement is signed by both the Company and the Investors, there will not exist any binding obligation on the part of either party to consummate the transaction.

Use of Proceeds   Working capital and other general corporate purposes.

Other   (i) Legal, consulting and major out of pocket expenses incurred by the Investors will be paid at closing by the Company from the proceeds of the investment. The Investors shall make all reasonable efforts to restrict legal expenses to a maximum of $ 20,000. Once this term sheet is signed the Company shall accept responsibility for legal fees incurred by the Investors if the transaction does not close. The Company will also secure a quote from legal counsel which will reflect a cap for services of $ 10,000.

Finders Fees   Neither the Company nor the Investors have retained any finder or consultant in connection with the transaction envisioned hereunder. The Company and the Investors will each indemnify the other for any finder's fees for which either is responsible.

Exclusivity   (i) Upon the acceptance hereof, RBS Group, its officers and shareholders agree not to discuss the sale of any equity or equity type securities, provide any information to or close any such transaction with any other investor or prospective investor, unless Purchaser is unable to close this transaction under similar terms to those contained herein on or before July 31, 1998 or Purchaser waives its rights under this provision in writing.

(ii) The undersigned agree to proceed in good faith to execute and deliver definitive agreements incorporating the terms outlined above and such additional terms as are customary for transactions of the type described herein. This letter expresses the intent of the parties and is not legally binding on any of them unless and until such mutually satisfactory definitive agreements are executed and delivered by the undersigned. This letter of intent may be signed by the parties in counterparts.

(continued)

EXHIBIT 1 | Proposed Term Sheet (*continued*)

Agreed to and accepted:

Date _____   By: _____

President & Chief Executive Officer

RBS Group, Inc.

Date _____   By: _____

General Partner

Mid-Atlantic Venture Fund III, L.P.

Date _____   By: _____

(Purchaser)

Schedule A

Listed below are the significant due diligence points that must be completed/resolved prior to closing. This is not an exhaustive list, but rather is meant to convey the most important due diligence action steps requiring your attention. We will communicate any and all other necessary information requests, not outlined below, as soon as we become aware of the need for such additional information.

1. Compiled RBS Group, Inc. financial statements (income statement, balance sheet, statement of cash flows, statement of change in stockholder's equity), with corresponding notes, for the three years ending 3/31/96, 3/31/97 and 3/31/98

2. Copies of all RBS Group, Inc. Board of Directors minutes for the prior three years;

3. Detailed 12-month post-funding budget, including a pro-forma income statement, balance sheet and cash flow statement;

4. Personal references for Lane Ford;

5. RBS Group, Inc. bank loan agreements;

6. (If not included in the notes to the compiled financial statements) Written documentation of significant accounting principles (i.e. revenue recognition, bad debt reserves, warranties and other contingent liabilities, etc.);

7. Employee retirement plan agreement(s), if any;

8. Satisfactory completion of a chart of accounts review by MAVF;

9. List of major development projects currently being worked on indicating the state of completion (%) and the targeted completion date;

10. Lease agreements and any other agreements providing off-balance sheet financing.

Jim Sharpe: Extrusion Technology, Inc. (Abridged)

It was November 21, 1987, and Jim Sharpe was staring out at a sea of faces—the employees of the company he had just purchased, Extrusion Technology, Inc. Sharpe was a 38-year old Harvard MBA ('76) who, after 11 years of working for others, had finally become his own boss, and 100% owner of the $3.3 million (revenues) manufacturer of aluminum extrusions. (See **Exhibit 1** for Sharpe's resume.)

Sharpe related the set of experiences that had brought him to this juncture:

Initial Yearnings to Manage

From an early age, I had always wanted to work in business, but owning my own business was never a plan until later in my career. As a youth I had many jobs: at a hardware store, at a camp, at a restaurant, on a newspaper route. By the time I graduated from high school, I already had some good business skills. I enrolled in Babson College and got a job with a small company in Wellesley (Information Services) doing computer work (40–60 hours a week) to pay for my schooling. When I left Babson, influenced by the company's owner, I applied to the Harvard Business School, and was rejected pretty much out of hand. I was about 20 years old, and although I thought I had a terrific work experience (as did my boss), the school thought otherwise. Three years later, after continuing to work for the software firm, I decided to apply again to business schools—this time having a broad list of schools to ensure that I got in somewhere—and HBS accepted me.

Between my first and second years at HBS, I worked for the Heinz Food Company in an intern program. Being in a manufacturing environment was a good experience

Professor H. Kent Bowen and Research Associate Barbara Feinberg prepared the original version of this case, "Jim Sharpe: Extrusion Technology, Inc." (parts A and B), HBS Nos. 697-078 and 697-079. HBS cases are developed solely as the basis for class discussion. Cases are not intended to serve as endorsements, sources of primary data, or illustrations of effective or ineffective management.

since I had wanted to get away from the data processing field. After graduating (in 1976), I looked at a number of career opportunities—some in manufacturing, including Owens-Illinois and General Electric; some in sales, including IBM and Xerox; and some in implementation consulting, including Arthur Andersen. I finally chose GE. For a year I did strategic planning in one of GE's operating units, and found the assignment very interesting.

The General Electric Experience

Getting the job at GE was a story in itself. The job was to work for a group executive in Pittsfield, Massachusetts. Four of us from HBS were selected for the final round of interviews. We flew back and forth on a Lear jet, and none of us knew beforehand that we were all coming to interview on the same day, on the same plane. This was somewhat unusual in my interviewing experience—to be faced with your competition on the plane out and back. The group executive made it very clear to all of us that we should keep our options open for job opportunities, because in two months, it would be very clear to him if we were doing the job or not—and if we weren't, we were out of a job. This executive (who also ended up hiring me) was Jack Welch. His goal was to have a Harvard MBA on his staff to work on special assignments for him, and he was very clear about what the objective was—my getting an operating job after a year, which he came through with. The job was product general manager in GE's super-abrasive business in Ohio (Borazon, CBN Products). I did that for a year, and then had a three-year general management assignment in Virginia (Carboloy Cutting Tools) selling products to coal mines. I was responsible for a plant as well as sales and P&L, and I reported to a division executive. This was one of the smallest operating units in GE. (See resume, **Exhibit 1.**)

I later learned, while looking at both of those assignments and questioning Jack Welch about why I was selected, that this was an unusual program. There weren't many MBAs at GE when I was hired. I imagine Welch's thought was, "Gee, I can put you out someplace where, if you screw up, you won't hurt anything." The business (coal mining products) was sold a year after I left, and it's obvious that my assignment was to clean it up and get it ready for sale. If I failed, they would have sold it, and if I succeeded, they would have just sold it for more, so it was a no-risk situation for GE.

Meanwhile I had met my future wife, who also worked for GE. She had a chemical engineering degree from MIT. After we married, she went on to get her MBA from Harvard while I was in Virginia running the cutting-tool business. When it came time for her to graduate, I searched within the GE organization to find another position where both of us could work in the same location. One of the contacts I approached during this process was Jack Welch. This did not result in a job, but it provided a lesson. A guy like Jack Welch remembers you as the person you were when he first met you—but after that, you're out of sight, out of mind. The Jim Sharpe of five years later, now ready to run a larger operating unit, was not who Welch remembered when he thought about me. Nevertheless, I did get an offer to be a marketing manager in GE's fledgling robotics business, which I turned down, and in retrospect it was a good decision. GE never was successful in that robotics business in Gainesville, Florida, and I don't think my wife could have found a job in that area anyway.

Other Large Company Experience

However, I had a mentor at GE who had left earlier to work for Hoover Universal, an automotive parts/component supplier in Ann Arbor, Michigan. He and I had kept in touch, and I moved on with him to become a general manager of a $40-million plastics operations within Hoover Universal, bringing a significant amount of change to a rust-belt company, again being assigned to turn around a core manufacturing kind of business. However, a year and a half after I joined Hoover, the president of the company, the chief financial officer, and seven other general managers were fired unceremoniously. The political shake-up left me without a job.

For six months I looked for a job that would be a good fit. I looked at businesses to buy, I looked at jobs, and finally decided I needed to go back and get some more work experience. In fact, my old mentor and I had looked at businesses to buy, and we both concluded that we weren't ready. He went off to take a CEO position at a company in Texas, and I went to work for a British company that owned a machinery manufacturing operation in Northern Michigan (Brown Machine Company). I served as president for two years, and then transferred with the company to another machinery business in Providence, Rhode Island, which manufactured machinery for the plastics industry. By this time, I had spent about 10 years turning around manufacturing-oriented businesses for big companies, and I finally decided I wanted to run my own show.

I can clearly say that when I joined GE, my goal was to be the president of a major company that was not my own; that is, I wanted to be a professional manager. But over that 10-year period, I became more and more interested in doing this kind of turnaround for a manufacturing operation without a large corporation looking over my shoulder. I decided I was ready to do so, gave my company six-months' notice, and collected as much bonus money as I could. On January 1, 1987, I embarked on a 10-month, 21-day search for a business to buy.

Lessons Learned from Big Company Experiences

Lesson 1:   The biggest lesson I learned was that working for someone else and making mistakes on their nickel provided invaluable experience in developing my career. I didn't have to answer to a bank, I didn't have to worry about making payroll every week, I didn't have to worry about financing and figuring out where my next funding for capital expenditure would be. I was allowed to make lots of mistakes and I learned from those mistakes, while still being a responsible corporate manager. None of my businesses were about to go out of business. They all had long histories, they were clearly potentially profitable, and they weren't near bankruptcy or foreclosure. Then again, none were tremendously healthy or profitable. But because I didn't have to worry about the issues of true survival, I was able to gain valuable work experience.

Lesson 2:   Another thing I learned was how to manage in both good times and bad. I went through a recession, and running a business in a recession is a lot different than running a business during good times. It changed my perspective about the way you operate—when things aren't always following the "I'm going to grow 10% a year and profits are going to improve 10% a year for my ten-year business plan" approach. Life isn't like that. Having to manage in a large corporation during recessionary times helped me learn what to do when times are tough.

Lesson 3:   I also learned a lot about where to find opportunities for margin and profit improvement. The biggest lesson I learned through a one-year forecasting cycle at GE was, *don't bet on volume.* I predicted in the mining-tool business that it would turn around because we could grow at 15% to 20%—but the numbers just fell through to the bottom line. It had been pretty obvious to me that this could be a profitable business if only the volume could be increased 10% to 20%. However, in reality it was a lot harder to get those volume numbers up, and I learned a good lesson about the drawbacks of predicting improvements in profitability by simply going after volume.

Lesson 4:   I learned, instead, that profit improvements come from good solid cost reduction; attention to details; and margin improvement, especially through pricing changes and modifications. I learned the cost reduction issues at the feet of some masters during a recession, when GE said to me, "You have to cut 20% of your workforce. It's clear to us that the recession is here, and one way to get your costs down is to cut your workforce." I protested: "We can't do that. If we cut 20% of our workforce, we won't have a viable business." So, I went and cut 10% and discovered four months later that we needed to cut more. It was painful to go back to the organization and describe how things were still bad and that we had to cut more people. The morale problems and the issues of walking the floor after the second cutback were very demoralizing to me. The lesson from that was, when it's time to cut, cut deeper than you need to, because you can always add back. When you don't cut deep enough, it really impacts both your credibility within the organization and your effectiveness for a number of months, as you cut and cut and cut instead of making one significant cut.

During this time, I also learned techniques for staying focused on cost. For example, I learned early on to sign every invoice that our vendors gave us, as well as signing every check. That gave me a look, for perhaps a half-hour a week, at every single item that we were spending money on, and consequently gave me a good feel for where our cash was going.

For instance, I could ask why were we spending money on a service contract on equipment that wasn't running and hadn't been running for a year. "Look [someone would say], the sales guy, when he sold us the equipment, said we should buy one of these service contracts and then it got on a renewal program, and we just renewed it every year because the invoice came in." Let's stop that! Or, why are we buying cardboard from six cardboard vendors? "Well, you know, we had a relationship with one guy and then another guy came along, and another guy came along, and another guy came along. . . ." Let's look at why we are doing that! This attention to detail went a level deeper than where the controller would come to me with a report about "this is where we are spending our expense dollars."

Lesson 5:   The experience at large companies also gave me a framework for dealing with a number of personnel issues, particularly with labor union and nonunion situations. The sure-fire way to lose your job at GE (you could lose a lot of money before you would be fired) was to become unionized in a nonunion facility. You—and your human relations manager—immediately lost your jobs. I learned how to run a business in the coal fields of West Virginia, which was heavy union territory. The business unit did not have a union, but I managed it as if there was one, and that experience helped me along the way in dealing with a number of labor issues—having wage levels, an employee handbook, grievance procedures, and clear hiring practices.

Lesson 6:   While working at the large companies, I also learned how to work with big customers: How to deal with them, how to present myself and my products to them, how to remember their names. From the respect people had for the large companies I worked for, I learned the tools to create professional customer relations which I would need in my small company later on.

Lesson 7:   Another important lesson had to do with pricing and margins. In almost all the businesses I was involved in, the biggest profit opportunity came from a review of margins and pricing. Looking at a business for opportunities to gain a higher price required some analysis. For example, all of the businesses I worked for in the machinery area had spare parts businesses, and there was always opportunity, margin opportunity, left on the table. Most pricing was based on cost, not on customer need and value. In the spare parts business, getting a machine back up and running—with customers unable to make the parts on their own—was often an overlooked margin opportunity. In the machinery businesses I ran, we significantly raised prices in the spare parts business to gain profitability, and we were very successful at it.

A second way of analyzing cost was to look at all of the products and try and give the best estimate of what the margin on each product was—not only through the accounting system, but also by assessing the "soft" part of cost accounting: The latter involved determining how much sales time was spent on a particular line, and how much manufacturing time is spent on a particular product—to get a true picture of the product's cost—and then to adjust pricing accordingly.

A third way to optimize margins was to raise prices during recessionary or tough times. At GE, I was incapable of doing that on my own and needed a GE division manager to visit the mining tool business after I had been there for about a year and a half. He asked, "When was the last time you raised prices?" I said, "Gee it's been a while and we are in a recession now—we can't raise prices, we'll lose business." As he walked out the door, he *required* that I raise the prices within the next two weeks and report back in six months. Indeed, six months later, 80% of the raised prices had stuck and we had no customer flight. Without that push, I never would have learned that valuable lesson about pricing, which was—do it frequently, do it often, and don't forget to do it.

Later on, when I asked the division executive how he knew that raising prices would be successful, he said, "Jim, when you are a thousand miles away and a division executive, it's a lot easier to raise prices. When you are right in the middle of the business, I know how hard it is—I've been there." I also learned, at the larger companies, that being the low-price guy on the market is generally not the best strategy. With the overhead at GE and the overhead at John Brown Co., you couldn't be the low-price guy. There are a lot of other things besides price; customers buy, and you develop the confidence that you can have a higher price and still get business.

Lesson 8:   Finally, each one of those companies was managed differently. GE, with its division structure, had a very tightly controlled operating format. As I got further into my career, I found that it was a lot more fun and a lot more challenging to be in operations where the division had a lot of autonomy. I went from GE—with a product plant manufacturing facility that I thought had a lot of autonomy but probably didn't in retrospect—to Hoover Universal, which still had a lot of corporate structure around it, but more autonomy than GE. Then I went to operations at John Brown, which were basically standalone, with a lot of flexibility. At that company, if you made mistakes, it was easy for everyone, including myself, to see them. Eventually, I concluded, "Hey, I'm pretty good at this, and I want to do it on my own."

Looking for a Business to Buy

When my wife and I moved back to New England with the John Brown organization, we strategically downsized our living expenses: We moved into a smaller home, and had fewer commitments in mortgages, car payments, and so on. We also put some money aside; thus, the day I left John Brown, I had about $150,000 of cash and my wife was working. I knew that if I hadn't found a business in 18 months, I was probably going to have to go out and find a job. However, I felt fairly confident in that ability, because I had been tested five years earlier and had found that job opportunities for someone with my skills were pretty good. Most important, I had confidence in my ability to turn around a sick manufacturing business.

So, although I had very little cash from a seller's standpoint, I had lots of enthusiasm and capability. I started to look for manufacturing, low-technology businesses, most of which were in trouble of some kind—because if they weren't in trouble and were profitable, I couldn't afford to buy them. One of my goals was to retain 100% ownership and not have to be a partial owner or bring in significant venture money or a partner to work with me.

I proceeded to draw a 50-mile circle around my home and discovered that there were about 600 companies that fit my criteria. Over 11 months, I contacted, or was able to look at, 60 of these. I made offers on 12, raised financing on three, and successfully completed the transaction on one. From a strategic standpoint, I never imagined I would find myself in the aluminum extrusion business, because that's not the way I did the search. I was searching for a company, not for an industry. (See **Exhibit 2** for Sharpe's search criteria and prospecting process.)

Because my previous 10 years had been involved in mining tools, plastics, high-tech machinery, and low-tech machinery, it was not a daunting prospect to look at a variety of businesses that I was either not familiar with or didn't know much about, and I learned a lot in the process.

One lesson was that looking for a business was a full-time job. I couldn't look for a job and look for a business at the same time. Also, I learned that a lot of small company owners were very anxious to find partners or employees with whom they would be willing to share some profit, but were very reluctant to give up their whole company. These owners viewed me as a kind of golden opportunity: they had generally been running their company for a number of years and had produced significant income for themselves; here was a chance to let someone else run it day-to-day. After talking to a number of people who had tried this route, I learned that generally your life span in one of those companies is one to two years. The owner reluctantly goes along with some changes initially. But if there is real change to be made, the owner really doesn't want that, and ultimately, since they have control of the company, you are out. I had heard many stories of bright, aggressive, arrogant Harvard MBAs coming into companies in high-level positions and kind of being thrown out. I knew I wanted to control my own destiny, but it wasn't easy.

I found that compared with my previous job searches, which I thought at the time were emotional events (standing in the unemployment line, etc.), looking for a company was even worse. The emotional highs were terrific, of course: "Here is an excellent opportunity. A couple of owner issues, but this would be great. Clear opportunities for turnaround." I knew where I would be driving and parking my car. I figured out the distance from my home, how long the commute would be, knew exactly what the strategy would be for the company—and then the deal would fall apart right before my eyes, which was total devastation. So, from a high of projecting where I would be, to a low of not being able to own the company, I had times when I was totally depressed and times when I was totally elated.

Two offers that I made, and raised financing for, fell apart; one thing I learned from that was, it's a problem to have no other deals in the pipeline. With one of the deals, I was on a tremendous high. People would ask me, "Are you there yet?" "Yeah, I have a closing date set, this is going to happen." "What else are you working on?" they'd ask. "Nothing, this is going to happen." Well it turned out *not* to happen. In the middle of March, I had to start my search all over again, and concluded that I would never again have only one deal in the pipeline at a time. In November, when I purchased Press Alloys, I called a plastics injection-molding company that I had negotiated a letter of intent with, and told them that I wasn't interested. Having that deal in the pipeline had certainly given me a much better and healthier perspective in my negotiations for Press Alloys.

I also learned to make offers quickly. Initially, it took me two or three weeks of massaging the numbers to come up with an offer and letter of intent, to work out the details with the owner. Toward the end I was able, with a Lotus spreadsheet, to make a fairly reasonable offer in a couple of days—because I discovered that these owners don't want to do anything until they have an offer in front of them. Making the offer was also an emotionally trying event, and the sooner I got it over with, the better I felt about the direction I was headed in. Many people claim they've looked around at a lot of companies but didn't find anything they liked. "How many offers did you make?" I would ask. When someone would tell me they'd made either no offers or just a few, I knew they hadn't gotten over that psychological hurdle of making a commitment with an offer on paper to actually buy something—acknowledging that "this is going to happen, I'm really going to do this. If the seller accepts my offer, this is it." There's no second-guessing.

Buying Press Alloys, Inc.

For the first couple of months in my search, I lined up insurance companies, bankers, lawyers, venture capitalists, business brokers, and started networking. The banks I ran into—and I probably talked to five or ten banks—all said to me, "What's the deal?" I said I didn't have a deal yet, but would they loan me money if I went out and looked for such and such a business? They would respond, "Well, what's the deal?" It became fairly clear to me that (a) they weren't the source of deals, and (b), they wouldn't really talk to me unless I had the structure of a deal in place—so they knew what they would be financing. Banks were neither good sources of finding prospects nor good to work with early on. Venture capitalists? I learned a good lesson from them: If they had a "dog" that was not running well, they generally preferred to run it into the ground and shut it down than get out and sell to a "bottom feeder," which I was sometimes called because I didn't have any money. Venture capitalists didn't have businesses they were willing to sell. What they *did* have was opportunities for management-ownership. "Oh yeah, you can be 10% owner or a 20% owner"—but that wasn't what I wanted.

Lawyers were lousy prospects, too; they all seemed to have misconceptions of what businesses were worth and what they were about. Accountants always had their favorite clients and inflated ideas of what their businesses were worth, so those were difficult sources too. Brokers had some businesses, but I discovered that if a business was for sale that fit my criteria and a broker was involved, then I had to deal with a broker, even though the broker might be in the way much of the time. Otherwise, you couldn't get in to see the business. Ultimately, most of my sources of good business opportunities and offers that were important came from my contacting companies directly.

I also religiously perused *The Wall Street Journal* to see both what kind of companies were available and whether any were in the New England area. The plastics business that was in the pipeline when I bought Press Alloys came through a Journal ad as well as a broker, and it would probably have worked fine.

Some of the 600 potential companies I originally identified were subsidiaries of major firms. I never wrote to the subsidiary itself, but I found the next level up through research: the name of the group executive responsible for that business, or a strategic planning or divestiture person at headquarters, or the company president. I would write, "I'm aware of this business in Massachusetts and I am interested in it." Those turned out to be the most dispassionate, reasonable situations. Either they were for sale or they weren't, and if they were, all the numbers came forward, and I was kind of a "corporate guy" so they liked dealing with me. One transaction I worked on went very well until the very end, when the board turned down the decision. But I'd had good experience in a big company and the board was confident in my abilities, and I could talk to them well.

But the bulk of the opportunities came from directly contacting company owners— and as a company owner today, I get a couple of letters a month from a variety of sources asking me if I am interested in selling my business. I see this as a kind of prospecting: If you hit the owner at the right time, you might score. Indeed, Press Alloys' owner called me from his car on the way home, after a particularly frustrating couple of months of poor profitability, and was thinking about what he wanted to do with his business. I was at the right place at the right time.

I had found the company in August, and went to see the owner. He had some criteria for selling, however: "You can't talk to the employees, and I don't want you talking to any of my customers. The day you own the business, you can talk to everyone. I will give you, meanwhile, as many plant tours as you want; you can bring other people in, but you cannot talk to the people in the business. Oh, and by the way, we have the Teamsters union here, and you probably should get rid of them. In fact, if you buy the business, you should lock them out." So, with that start, we began to share numbers, and within two weeks, I made him an offer. At the same time, I started work on a plan— a document to help me raise the financing I would need to buy the company. (See **Appendix** for the document in its entirety.)

I was low. He told me more things: "I forgot to mention that my dad is on the payroll. We have some company cars on the payroll, hidden away." I redid the expenses he gave me and made a higher offer. I was still low. He had come down a little bit. After the third or fourth offer and letter of intent, it was clear that we were about $250,000 apart. He wanted $2 million—to tell his dad and his friends that he got $2 million for the business— and I felt on paper that the way I structured the deal, it was only worth $1.7 million. I walked out of his office one day saying, "It looks like we can't come to an agreement on this." I was bluffing. He didn't think I was. I waited three days for him to call but he never did. On the fourth day I called him and he said, "I thought the deal was over."

What I learned from that was, always keep communications open, because (he told me later), the day that I walked out of his office, he went home and was sick. He wanted so badly to sell the company and he thought it was over. I had been a little too hard in my negotiating. When we got back together, I saw that my concept of buying a business was strategically flawed. If the seller set the price and I could negotiate the terms, we could always come to a deal. So the owner got his $2 million. He just got it a different way, over a different period of time, and paid in a way that I was comfortable with.

Corporations, in contrast, had a number in mind but were willing to negotiate about price: In most cases, the subsidiaries in question had been written off years earlier; they had no value, and anything they got would be viewed as a gain; or they had been through a restructuring where reserves were set aside for full losses. For a private owner, it's different.

So, I had a deal with the owner of Press Alloys in early September, with a letter of intent; but he was very concerned about getting his money, and spent the next 2½ months assembling a pile of legal documents to protect himself from losing his business—or more important, from my stealing it. We spent a lot of time and money on legal issues that we never ever touched again after November 21, 1987, when the company became mine. But for his confidence level, he needed and wanted a lot of legal protection in the deal.

This was the LBO (leveraged buyout) period in the late 1980s, and one common, not so savory technique of purchasing in a highly leveraged transaction—and the $2 million I was paying consisted of $1,200,000 that he was taking back in paper—was a flip. In flipping, you buy the business, take over full ownership, and in a couple of years, if you can't pay off the creditors, you wipe out the debt by declaring bankruptcy. The old owner, who has a second position, gets no money, the bank takes a "haircut," and you retain ownership of the business. The owner of Press Alloys was deathly afraid that could happen. He made sure that, in our deal, I couldn't buy another company, that I couldn't take too much out of the company in salary; most important, he put a clause into the transaction saying that if any defaults were triggered within my relationship, either with the bank or with the covenants related to his seller and non-compete notes, that he could regain 99% control of the company, by taking back the stock I'd pledged against the notes. In addition, I had to cover his and his parents' medical insurance for five years, and I had to keep him on as a consultant. I couldn't hire any of my relatives without his approval. In sum, he didn't want me to take money out of the company at a faster rate than he was getting paid.

All this was his guarantee that if anything went wrong, he could get the company back, liquidate it if he had to, to get his money out. I would get it back, of course, with whatever was left; but he would be protected. I can tell you, that former owner stock pledge hung over my head for five years. For five years, I was ready. I anticipated, I worried about him doing it. For five years, he worried that he would have to do it. But when he sold the business, he never wanted to come back. His father had founded the company 40 years earlier. It had gone bankrupt in 1978. The son had pleaded with his father to let him run the company and get it out of bankruptcy. The father agreed, and the son successfully turned the company around, paid off all the debt, and by the early 1980s had a viable business again. At this point the father said, "Now it's time to pay me," and for year after year, the son had to deal with his father and family, which had essentially given up on the business, hadn't participated—so the son wanted out.

Taking Charge at Press Alloys: Day One

As I walked into my new company's building on November 21, 1987, I had a lot on my mind. I had both a lot of information about the company and too little. (See **Appendix.**) So, while I knew the names, ages, and salaries of everyone, and had talked with the previous owner about them (but had never met them), I also knew from background checks that my company had a "poor" reputation for quality, delivery, and general business practices. The building itself had been clearly neglected, surrounded by weeds outside and filmed with carbon and soot inside. It hadn't been painted in years. I wasn't the owner of the building, but the lease included an option to buy.

The Teamsters union had been there for about 25 years, and during the past 15 had struck at each three-year contract period—the longest for six weeks. That strike had been bitter, with nails scattered in the parking lot and the owner under considerable pressure from outside union people. He had also shown me a letter from 20 of the 40 unionized workers that said the union was "weak" and perhaps should be disbanded. But I hadn't met with either unionized people at the firm or outside union representatives. Moreover, when I'd asked about how benefits worked, he said, "Well, we kind of follow union guidelines wherever possible, but for people in the office, I kind of make up the rules as I go along."

My financial data suggested that the amount of raw material being purchased was far greater than what was needed for maintaining production. "It's easier to think about 'that' once a quarter, not regularly," the owner had noted. I also knew the names of various customers and their industries, but I wasn't given any information about margins, pricing structure, profitability—even about the difficulties we were experiencing with some of them. Historical financial projections showed a business moving up and down in sales volume—but the owner had claimed that it was really more profitable than it looked, because he and his father took a lot of money out. He also mentioned a couple of opportunities with some customers he'd been negotiating with. They could be significant in volume, he said, but not in profit. Receivables looked good, however.

But the technology was very old; all the equipment was old. The extruder itself was 20 years old, and although I told the bank it could last another 20 years, I really didn't know. The owner had said he learned about the extruder press by running it himself for two years—and recommended that I do so too, so if there was a problem, I'd know how to fix it. This was just one piece of advice, among many, that he offered, along with a general indication that he'd be available "whenever" to provide additional advice.

My focus, I knew, would be on paying down the bank debt—my signing personally for $2 million put everything at risk for me, including my house. With my wife pregnant with our first child (due at any moment), I felt like the pressure was really on.

So, I entered the cafeteria to be introduced as Press Alloy's new owner. The factory had been shut down for the occasion. The previous owner announced that he had sold the company to me, told the employees that I had changed the company's name to Extrusion Technology, wished them well, and walked out of the room. Every face turned towards me and registered shock. "Is John (the previous owner) really leaving?" everyone said. Were they saying this in dismay or hopefulness?

EXHIBIT 1 | Resume of Jim Sharpe

JAMES M. SHARPE

| 1984–1987 | CUMBERLAND ENGINEERING COMPANY | PROVIDENCE, RHODE ISLAND |

President, Reporting to President—John Brown, INC.

Cumberland Engineering is a subsidiary of JOHN BROWN, INC., owned by TRAFALGAR HOUSE, London, England, with over $3 billion in sales worldwide. Businesses include shipping, real estate, hotels, engineering contracting, plastics machinery, textile machinery, and gas turbines.

P&L responsibility for unit with $20 million in sales of machinery for granulating plastic into small pieces suitable for scrap reprocessing. Producing over 500 machines/year ranging in price from $3,000/unit to over $250,000. Markets include plastic injection molders, extruders, thermoformers, blow molders and compounder. Business employed over 200 in USA and 8 in the UK.

Returned unit to profitability during first year and increased income to over $l million during second and $2 million in third year on sales increases of 8% and 25% respectively. Revitalized small unit product line by developing offshore manufacturing source, changing distribution channels and modifying pricing structure resulting in volume increase of 80%. Restructured UK operation to regain lost market share in Europe. Developed a variety of employee involvement programs to address complacency and morale issues in 50 year old business.

| 1983–1984 | BROWN MACHINE COMPANY | BEAVERTON, MICHIGAN |

President, Reporting to President—John Brown, Inc.

P&L responsibility for unit with $16 million in sales, 25% overseas, of machinery for thermforming plastic items such as drinking cups, refrigerator liners and boats. Markets included packaging, appliance and automotive. Plant employed 200, including 75 salaried with no union.

Increased profitability 27% while reducing capital employed 17% by redirecting product development activities, standardizing pricing for spare parts and resolving a variety of legal and licensing issues. High level of involvement with customers led to improved company image.

| 1981–1983 | HOOVER UNIVERSAL INCORPORATED | ANN ARBOR, MICHIGAN |

General Manager Plastic Components Division, Reporting to Group Vice President

P&L responsibility for operations with $30 million in sales derived from customs, precision injection molded plastic parts and tooling. Markets included automotive, appliance, plumbing and hardware. Unionized plant sites employed over 400 including 100 salaried. Consolidated 2 previously separate units. Achieved sales growth of 28% in 1981 despite recession. During downturn, reduced overhead and operating costs through personnel reductions of 200 and closing a facility.

(continued)

EXHIBIT 1 | Resume of Jim Sharpe (*continued*)

1978–1981	GENERAL ELECTRIC—CARBOLOY MINING PRODUCTS	BRISTOL, VIRGINIA

<u>Product General Manager</u>, Reporting to G.M. Products Department (Houston, TX)

P&L responsibility for unit with $15 million in sales, employing 100. Section produced tungsten carbide cutting tools for sale to underground and construction operations. Product line also included a polyester resin roof support system produced at another GE location. Initiated share gain strategy and cost reduction programs which resulted in first positive net income in 5 years and sales growth of 12% in 1979 and 15% in 1980.

1977–1978	GENERAL ELECTRIC—BORAZON CBN PRODUCTS	WORTHINGTON, OHIO

Product Manager, Reporting to G.M.—Specialty Materials Department

P&L responsibility for $5 million venture producing Cubic Boron Nitride, a superabrasive grinding material similar to industrial diamonds. 60% of sales base in international markets. Responsible for market and product development achieving sales growth of 20% in 1977, 25% in 1978.

1976–1977	GENERAL ELECTRIC—COMPONENTS & MATERIALS GROUP HQ	PITTSFIELD, MASSACHUSETTS

<u>Analyst, Strategic Planning</u>, Reporting to Group Planner

Reviewed strategic plans and issues and presented recommendations to Group Executive. Businesses included engineering plastics, medical systems, chemical and metallurgical businesses, electronic components and appliance motors. Active role in preparing 1 and 5 year business plans for this $2 billion Group.

1968–1974	INFORMATION SERVICES	WELLESLEY, MASSACHUSETTS

<u>Software Systems Manager</u>, Reporting to Vice President of Operations

$2.5MM business specializing in data processing systems for magazine subscriptions and fund raising. Managed 16 professionals. Worked full time while attending college.

EDUCATION

1974–1976	HARVARD GRADUATE SCHOOL OF BUSINESS ADMINISTRATION	BOSTON, MASSACHUSETTS

MBA degree, June 1976. Course work included General Management, Marketing and Finance.

1968–1971	BABSON COLLEGE	WELLESLEY, MASSACHUSETTS

BSBA degree, cum laude, June 1971. Accelerated 3-year program with management concentration.

EXHIBIT 2 | Jim Sharpe's Overview of the Purchase Process

A. Purchasing a Small Company

Business acquisition:
"a numbers game"

Initial Criteria	**Results**
• Sales $7-50mm	• $5mm in sales
• Manufacturing	• Aluminum extrusions
• RI and Mass. Location	• Randolph, MA
• Basic/Low technology	• Old line technology
• Any financial condition	• Marginal financials
• Active involvement	• Young owner retiring

(continued)

EXHIBIT 2 | Jim Sharpe's Overview of the Purchase Process (*continued*)

B. Sources of Prospects

	Description	Analysis
1. Networking		
	• Brokers	+ Few credible, but necessary
	• Bankers	+ Poor sources, legal concerns
	• Accountants	+ Just know clients (biased)
	• Lawyers	+ Poor business acumen
	• Venture capital	+ Have no prospects!!!
	• Business friends	+ Some good ideas

*** Get the Word Out, Ask for More Contracts ***

2. Company Subsidiaries		
	• Public directories	+ Prepare for research
	• Personalize letter	+ Target decision maker
	• Changing status	+ Send mailing 2–3 months
	• Common practice	+ "One of many"
	• Intermediates	+ Stress no broker

*** Good Negotiators, Dispassionate and Professional ***

3. Company Prospects		
	• Public directories	+ Put on computer file
	• Personalize letter	+ Be straightforward
	• Employee vs. sellout	+ Hold your objective
	• Common practice	+ "One of many"
	• Get in the door	+ Never say "no" immediately

*** The Best, Quickest Source of Leads ***

4. Advertising		
	• *Wall Street Journal*	+ Thursday editions
	• Long memories	+ Three months of back issues
	• Intermediaries	+ Stress no brokers
	• Long waiting period	+ Keep track of inquiries

*** Be Prepared for a Lot of Effort and Detail ***

Appendix

Acquisition Financing Proposal and Business Plan

Acquisition Financing Proposal and Business Plan

Press Alloys, Inc.

by

James M. Sharpe

November 1987

Executive Summary

The purpose of this proposal is to secure financing in the form of a term loan secured by Machinery and Equipment (M&E) for $510,000 and a line of credit for $394,000 secured by Receivables and Inventory for a total of $904,000, of which $707,000 will be required to purchase the *assets* of Press Alloys, Inc. under the new name Extrusion Technology, Inc. (Thus, only $197,000 of the $394,000 line of credit—or revolver—will be drawn at closing.)

Press Alloys, Inc. is holding $25,000 in escrow and has signed an Asset Purchase Agreement covering the sale of the business for $2,000,000 plus the assumption of accounts payable, not to exceed $240,000 at Closing, plus an additional $47,000 for prepayment of an equipment lease.[a] This proposal is seeking financing for the purchase as follows:

Financing	Amount ($000)
Working Capital Revolver	$ 197
Asset-based Term Loan	$ 510
Seller Note	$ 700
Seller Non-Compete	$ 540
Equity—Jim Sharpe	$ 100
Total	$2,047

In addition to the requested bank financing, the seller is providing financing in the form of a $700,000 note and a 6-year $540,000 non-compete agreement. The non-compete has the advantage of being a deductible expense to the company.

Founded in 1948, Press Alloys, Inc. provides components fabricated from aluminum extrusions to a variety of markets. Receivables are collected, on the average, in less than 42 days with minimal historical bad debt expense. Inventory, primarily aluminum in various states of processing, has a high scrap value which is about 80% of the current $.90/lb. aluminum price. M&E includes a 2,500 Ton Aluminum extruder and a variety of machine tools used in secondary operations and recently appraised at *forced liquidation* value of approximately $637,000 by T.H.E. Appraisal. The building will be leased from the seller with a fixed rate for the first five years, renewable for two 5-year periods with a right of refusal during the term and an option to purchase after 10 years.

After eliminating owner's salaries and owner financed leases, the business can support the proposed level of debt and obligations. My own personal experience for the last ten years as President or General Manager of manufacturing based businesses, gives me the confidence that operating improvements and business growth can be attained to improve the profitability of this company in the future.

Utilizing existing management, except the current owner, I plan to personally operate the business as President. Although the financial projections presented are relatively

---

[a]The seller owns this equipment personally and leases it to the company. The entire balance remaining on the lease will be paid to the seller at closing.

conservative, the business has the in-place capacity to produce over $10,000,000 in sales if supported by aggressive penetration within and beyond the current geographic range.

Business Overview

Press Alloys, Inc. produces custom components for a variety of industries which are fabricated from aluminum extrusions. The extrusion process yields a highly rigid part in a broad range of profile shapes. These shapes are cut to length and further fabricated with holes, openings and shapes to meet the customer's requirements. As a finishing operation, the parts can be painted, anodized, polished or buffed.

Since its founding by Hamilton Jones in 1945, Press Alloys has always focused on aluminum extrusions. Historically, the company serviced the growing construction industry with window components, railings, signage, etc. During the last 10 years, John R. Jones, the founder's son, has significantly reduced the dependence upon these "commodity" markets and focused primarily on custom, short-run, precision components. This new focus allowed the company to recover successfully from Chapter 11 in 1977.

The total market for aluminum extruded shapes in the USA is approximately 2.4 billion pounds. With consumption of 1,000,000 pounds of aluminum billets/year, Press Alloys, Inc. is obviously a small player. However, Press has avoided the volatile Building, Construction and Transportation markets by focusing on the more stable and growth oriented Consumer Durables, Electrical and Machinery segments. Selected statistics produced by the Aluminum Association of America are:

Extruded Shapes (Millions of Pounds)	1981	1982	1983	1984	1985	1986
Building & Construction	1,163	1,045	1,233	1,334	1,432	1,506
Transportation	325	270	345	479	470	488
Consumer Durables	88	79	103	134	151	183
Electrical	76	71	74	110	119	114
Machinery & Equipment	80	71	75	90	106	106
Containers & Packaging	0	0	3	1	0	0
Other	63	72	75	76	68	57
Total	1,795	1,608	1,908	2,224	2,346	2,454
Change/Year	—	−10.4%	18.7%	16.6%	5.5%	4.6%

Approximately 150 fabricators compete for the business. In northern New England, the 3 other competitors, Northeast in Lawrence, Royce in Taunton and EG&G-Alutech in Fall River are in the process of evaluating their custom operations. Press has developed a market niche for small run, quick delivery, high value added components for its customers. Traditionally this customer base has not been well served by the larger fabricators.

Components sell for as much as $20.00 each to as low as $.14. The average price is $7.39/unit and average order size 378 units. Material costs are 23–27% of sales which indicates a high "value added" content for secondary operations. Each new component requires an extrusion die, which although charged to the customer for approximately $1,000, is owned by Press Alloys, Inc.

Aluminum is highly regarded for its strength, fabrication ease, low cost, and durability. More specifically, aluminum can be easily formed, compared to steel, to provide a variety of shapes from a single piece, whereas a steel fabrication would require bending and welding. Most plastics do not have the tensile strength to compete with aluminum parts. Aluminum's properties of heat dissipation and electrical conductivity also make it desirable for many electronics applications.

The management organization consists of the traditional line functions of Manufacturing, Sales, and Finance. The plant is unionized by the Teamsters and employs 37 direct factory workers and 20 in the other functions. Many of the management employees have been with the company for a number of years and have good familiarity with customers, process and company procedures. None are expected to leave or quit based on the sale of the business. A summary of key management statistics is provided:

Title	Annual Wage	Age	Yrs. Sen.
Vice President	$44,512	40	23
Operations Manager	$39,104	52	35
Controller	$38,376	34	4
Personnel/Purchasing	$30,472	49	11
Field Salesman	$32,500	60	16
Production Manager	$28,600	38	17

The union contract has basically 1½ years to go and expires in June of 1989. The Asset Agreement requires that the Seller secure an Assignment to new ownership with no changes in the existing contract. Provisions for Part Time workers and for flexible job switching are included in the contract.

No increase occurred after the first year as sales volume targets were not achieved. At projected volume for 1988, wages will go up 3.0% next June. As a relatively small Teamster's shop, the unit gets very little attention. Four years ago, shop employees signed a petition to decertify the union and the owner decided not to take any action.

Customer/Market Analysis

Active customers during any given year range between 200 and 300. No customer represents more than 10% of sales. 50% of shipments are within Massachusetts and 80% within Massachusetts and the states that border Massachusetts. A broad range of industry segments is covered through the customer base thus insulating it from historical dependence upon the construction industry.

Sales are covered by one field salesman in New England with 3 manufacturer's representatives across the country. A significant opportunity exists to expand the market

Customers Representing 50% of Sales:		Top 75% Market Segments:	
Company	**Market Segment**	**Market Segment**	**% of Sales**
1. EMHART (Fire Door)	Arch—Hardware	1. Equipment Mfgrs.	18%
2. JAMES RUSSELL ENG.	Equipment Mfg.		
3. HEWLETT PACKARD CO.	Medical	2. Architectural	17%
4. FIRE CONTROL INST.	Arch—Fire Protection		
5. AT&T TECHNOLOGIES	Communications	3. Communications	10%
6. CRAWFORD PRODUCTS	Consumer Products		
7. JET SPRAY CORP.	Construction	4. Medical	8%
8. DOLAN & JENNER	Equipment Mfg.		
9. HARMER SIMMONS POW.	Equipment Mfg.	5. Office Equipment	7%
10. EG&G WAKEFIELD ENG	Electronics		
11. ELECTRO POWERPACS	Arch—Signs	6. Electronics	6%
12. WATERS ASSOCIATES	Electronics		
13. M/A COM MAC, INC.	Consumer Products	7. Consumer Products	6%
14. SCHAEFER MARINE	Marine		
		8. Leisure (Marine)	3%

coverage through aggressive use of telemarketing and customer service appealing to fast delivery and quality. Since orders are generally small in quantity, shipping costs are not a significant factor.

Financial Performance

Historically, Press Alloys, Inc. has had erratic reported financial results due to the closely held ownership position. In order to minimize Corporate taxes, personal salaries were adjusted each year and equipment was leased by the company from the owner. Selected, audited Income Statements appear for 1982–1986. The company elected Sub-Chapter S Status and changed to calendar year December 31, 1986. Results for 1987(u) are unaudited and reflect the 5-month period ending in December plus the first 7 months of 1987.

Income Statement ($000)	1982	1983	1984	1985	1986	1987(U)[a]
Sales	3,118	2,799	4,076	3,909	2,913	3,319
Cost of Sales	2,582	2,360	3,186	2,989	2,401	2,628
Gross Margin	536	439	890	920	512	691
SG&A	576	613	790	938	634	640
EBIT	(40)	(174)	100	(18)	(122)	51
Interest Expense	77	75	83	79	19	19
Profit From Ops.	(117)	(249)	17	(97)	(141)	32

(continued)

Income Statement ($000)	1982	1983	1984	1985	1986	1987(U)[a]
Other (Inc)/Exp	0	(51)	0	(135)	0	0
Profit/(Loss) B.T.	(117)	(198)	17	38	(141)	32
Income Taxes	(44)	(90)	(11)	199	(65)	0
Net Income(Loss)	(73)	(108)	28	(161)	(76)	32
Selected Ratios						
Gross Margin/Sales	17.2%	15.7%	21.8%	23.5%	17.6%	20.8%
SGA/Sales	18.5%	21.9%	19.4%	24.0%	21.8%	19.3%
EBIT/Sales	−1.3%	−6.2%	2.5%	−0.5%	−4.2%	1.5%
Net Income(AT)/Sales	−2.3%	−3.9%	0.7%	−4.1%	−2.6%	1.0%
Cur. Assets/Cur. Liab.	3.5	2.1	1.9	1.9	1.9	2.4
Receivable Days	43	47	43	35	45	38
Inventory Turns (COGS)	21	14	21	23	16	17

Note: SG&A does not match audited statements, as interest expense has been removed from that expense category and shown in a separate line item.
[a]U = unaudited.

Financial Performance—Balance Sheet

(Year End 7/31) ($000)	1982	1983	1984	1985	1986	1987(U)
Balance Sheet						
Cash	226	165	170	464	155	165
Receivables	370	367	486	382	365	351
Inventory	125	165	150	132	149	156
Prepaid Expenses	41	67	78	76	74	71
Income Tax Refund	63	90	11	0	65	0
Other	44	24	39	0	0	0
Total Current Assets	869	878	934	1,054	808	743
Gross Fixed Assets	2,932	2,986	3,208	1,895	1,970	2,004
Less Accumulated Depn.	1,882	1,944	2,047	1,633	1,713	1,796
Net Fixed Assets	1,050	1,042	1,161	262	257	208
Other Assets	112	113	104	44	0	0
Loan Rec.—Off.	79	97	97	97	97	97
Total Assets	2,110	2,130	2,296	1,457	1,162	1,048
Accounts Payable	193	387	255	216	247	210
Accrued Expenses	28	14	153	257	29	25
Note—Mortgage	14	18	22	0	0	0
Note—Vehicle	10	7	10	4	4	3
Lease—Equipment	0	0	39	39	64	50
Note—Other	0	0	19	28	76	26
Total Current Liabilities	245	426	498	544	420	314

(continued)

(Year End 7/31) ($000)	1982	1983	1984	1985	1986	1987(U)
Note—Mortgage	729	683	659	0	0	0
Note—Vehicle	13	6	12	7	3	0
Note—Equipment	0	0	132	93	29	12
Note—Other	18	18	89	67	44	18
Total Long-Term Notes	760	707	892	167	76	30
Stockholders' Equity	832	832	712	712	712	712
Retained Earnings	273	165	194	34	(46)	(8)
Total Liabilities and Equity	2,110	2,130	2,296	1,457	1,162	1,048

Financial Performance—Income Restatement

Cash flow for the business has been positive and a restatement of the financials to reflect the elimination of officer's salaries, lease payments and extraordinary gains/losses:

Adjusted Cash Flow ($000)	1982	1983	1984	1985	1986	1987(u)
Sales	3,118	2,799	4,076	3,909	2,913	3,319
Baseline EBIT	(40)	(174)	100	(18)	(122)	51
Officer's Salaries	139	139	252	322	160	147
Officer's Benefits	14	14	25	32	16	15
Officer's Autos	15	15	15	15	0	0
Bonus/Profit Sharing	0	0	27	20	0	22
Leases Paid to Owner	82	65	65	88	92	72
Restated EBIT	210	59	484	459	146	307
Depreciation	83	86	115	116	92	93
Restated EBITDA (Cash Generated)	293	145	599	575	238	400

Officer's Salaries were paid to John Jones and Hamilton Jones over the years. At year end, salaries were adjusted to reflect profitability levels of the business in an attempt to minimize tax liability. An IRS audit for 1984, 1985, and 1986 was completed with only a $500 adjustment. Company-paid automobiles were provided to the owners in all but the last two years. The owners purchased machine tools and leased them back to the company at a high profitability rate and for periods of time beyond their depreciated life. Since the building was purchased from the Corporation by the owner in 1985, the lease/rental rate has been $2.80/sq.ft. for the 60,000 sq.ft. property.

Although 1986 and 1987 were relatively good years in the industry, the owner, John Jones, diverted his attention from the day-to-day operation to spend time developing computer software systems for small businesses. For a period of 18 months, he devoted only 50% of his time to the company. Margins, Profits and sales suffered as a consequence and have only recently begun to recover.

Hamilton Jones has not been active in the business for a number of years and is now in his 70's. John, age 37, now 100% owner, has been involved in the business all his life and feels incapable of taking the business to a larger size. He also has developed a lucrative sideline in providing data processing systems and wants to pursue that on a full time basis. John will transition for 6 months and has signed a 6-year non-compete.

Financial Projections

Sales growth of 15% in the next year is projected based on orders and backlog for the last 6 months. Annualizing the actual results for the first 9 months of 1987 yields sales of $3,586, already up 8% over 1986. While aluminum prices are at a historically high level, only 25% of the selling price is raw material, so significant fluctuations generally do not impact sales levels with the exception of extrude-and-ship business which represents less that 25% of historical sales.

During September, EG&G made a sourcing decision to bring "Heat Sink" components back from Mexico and gave Press 14 new jobs worth $20,000/month and are prepared to provide $40,000 more in the next 6 months. The potential closing of EG&G Alutech in Fall River is also causing a flurry of quotation activity and should provide additional business for Press.

Inside sales support of a telemarketing program will generate increasing sales levels in the years to come. Sales coverage has been somewhat limited with only one person on the road and an additional salesman will be hired during the 2nd year to correct this. 6% per year over the period is very achievable and conservative, especially given that the extruder is significantly under utilized at 20 hours per week.

Higher margins at 25%–27% are expected to be achieved which will bring them back to levels which were attainable during 1985 when the business was receiving full management attention. First of all, since the "internal" leases will be abandoned, future margins reflect the improvement in lower manufacturing costs. Restating the historical actuals indicates that these levels have been attained in the past:

Margin Analysis	1982	1983	1984	1985	1986	1987(u)	1987(a)
Reported Gross Margins	17.2%	15.7%	21.8%	23.5%	17.6%	20.8%	23.4%
"Internal" Leases—$000	82	65	65	88	92	72	72
Restated Gross Margins	19.8%	18.0%	23.4%	25.8%	20.7%	23.0%	25.4%

Note: 1987(a) is nine months through September 30 annualized.

Aggressive changes in pricing will be made to more closely reflect material and production costs. Only recently has the computerized system become available to accurately track costs for each part. This will allow selective "pruning" of business and judicious price increases to improve margins. Additionally, current management has been slow to raise prices to reflect the recent increases in aluminum billets. An increase was implemented in August and is just beginning to be seen in margins. Fortunately, 75% of the sales volume is non-commodity and consequently less price sensitive.

An immediate change will be made to eliminate one extraneous layer of management by assigning the current Vice President to Sales and Marketing and having the Finance, Purchasing and Operations managers report to the President. This will be coupled with routine weekly operations reviews in an attempt to better utilize the fairly sophisticated management information system's output and more closely monitor production efficiency.

The purchase of aluminum will be reviewed and raised to the level of President. Historically, the Buyer has been releasing orders without much consideration for negotiation of prices, terms or conditions.

Capital investment of $240,000 at $40,000/yr. is projected during the six-year period, primarily in the area of equipment upgrade for efficiency and building/facilities maintenance. The extruder, although over 20 years old, has a projected life of 40 years or more. Recently purchased CNC equipment should be sufficient to handle additional demand with the further possibility of a second production shift to expand even further.

Working capital will be receiving special attention, especially in the area of collections and improved inventory turns. Again, management had not been paying as much attention to these areas in recent years as borrowings were non-existent and attention was focused elsewhere.

In the event of a downturn in the economy, Press' mix is sufficiently broad that it will not see sales volume reductions beyond a general recession. However, in that event, capital spending would be put on hold saving $40,000/year, direct labor reductions would be accommodated by laying off Part Time shop employees. Owner's salary could be reduced and fixed G&A personnel cut back to reflect reduced volume and conserve cash flow.

Financial Projections—Income Statement

Income Statement ($000)	1988	1989	1990	1991	1992	1993
Sales	3,817	4,199	4,534	4,806	5,095	5,401
Cost of Sales	2,855	3,115	3,346	3,538	3,750	3,975
Gross Margin	962	1,083	1,188	1,269	1,345	1,426
SG&A	634	634	680	716	754	794
EBIT	328	449	508	553	591	632
Interest Expense	150	131	110	84	53	16
Profit From Ops.	178	318	398	469	538	616
Other (Inc)/Exp [Non-Compete]	60	90	120	90	90	90
Profit/(Loss) B.T.	118	228	278	379	448	526
Income Taxes	47	91	111	151	179	210
Net Income(Loss)	71	137	167	227	269	316
Selected Statistics						
Sales Growth	15.0%	10.0%	8.0%	6.0%	6.0%	6.0%
Gross Margin/Sales	25.2%	25.8%	26.2%	26.4%	26.4%	26.4%
SGA/Sales	16.6%	15.1%	15.0%	14.9%	14.8%	14.7%
EBIT/Sales	8.6%	10.7%	11.2%	11.5%	11.6%	11.7%

Cost of Sales includes the building lease of $168,000/year, fixed for 5 years. SG&A during the first year includes $50,000 in transactions costs for the purchase. "Other Expense" is the non-compete contract with the owner over the six years. Salary for the new owner is limited to $60,000 for the first year.

A tax rate of 40% was assumed and a 10 year depreciation rate for the assets. In all probability, no taxes will be paid during the early years because of accelerated depreciation, freeing up more cash flow, not accounted for here.

Financial Projections—Balance Sheet

Balance Sheet ($000)	Closing	1988	1989	1990	1991	1992	1993
Cash	0	10	10	10	10	10	10
Receivables	376	424	458	485	514	545	578
Inventory	224	168	174	181	184	187	199
Prepaid Expenses	47	47	47	47	47	47	47
Total Current Assets	647	649	689	723	755	790	834
Gross Fixed Assets	1,100	1,140	1,180	1,220	1,260	1,300	1,340
Less Accumulated Depn.	0	110	220	330	440	550	660
Net Fixed Assets	1,100	1,030	960	890	820	750	680
Total Assets	1,747	1,679	1,649	1,613	1,575	1,540	1,514
Accounts Payable	240	243	265	284	301	319	338
Accrued Expenses	0	30	30	30	30	30	30
Note—Bank Revolver	197	126	97	40	(69)	(215)	(506)
Total Current Liabilities	437	398	391	354	262	134	(138)
Note—Bank Term	510	453	340	227	113	0	0
Note—Owner Term	700	657	610	557	499	435	365
Total Long-Term Notes	1,210	1,110	950	784	612	435	365
Stockholders' Equity	100	100	100	100	100	100	100
Retained Earnings	0	71	208	374	602	871	1,186
Total Liabilities and Equity	1,747	1,679	1,649	1,613	1,575	1,540	1,514

Note: Closing figures based on September 30, 1987 actual balances.

Selected Statistics						
Cur. Assets/Cur. Liab.		1.6	1.8	2.0	2.9	5.9
Receivable Days		40	39	39	39	39
Inventory Turns(COGS)		17	18	19	19	20

Receivables and Inventories show improvements over prior years with more attention on working capital. Gross Assets have been written up for the closing balance sheet to reflect the premium paid over book. Debt structure is further described in the following section.

Financial Projections—Debt Service

Cash Flow-Source/(Use) ($000)	Closing	1988	1989	1990	1991	1992	1993
EBIT		328	449	508	553	591	632
Depreciation		110	110	110	110	110	110
Working Capital (Req.)/Sources		31	(18)	(14)	(16)	(16)	(25)
PPE Expenditures		(40)	(40)	(40)	(40)	(40)	(40)
Avail. for Debt Service		429	501	564	607	645	677
Debt Structure							
Bank Revolver	197	126	97	40	(69)	(215)	(506)
Bank Term Note	510	453	340	227	113	0	0
Owner Term Note	700	657	610	557	499	435	365
Total Debt Outstanding	1,407	1,236	1,047	824	543	220	(141)
Bank Revolver—Interest		22	14	11	4	(8)	(24)
Bank Term Note—Interest		60	53	40	27	13	0
Bank Term Note—Principal		57	113	113	114	113	0
Secured Debt Service		139	180	164	145	119	(24)
Owner Note—Interest		68	64	59	53	47	40
Owner Note—Principal		43	47	53	58	64	70
Owner Non-Compete		60	90	120	90	90	90
Owner Obligation Service		171	201	232	201	201	200
Total Obligation Service		310	381	396	346	320	176
Excess Available		119	120	168	260	325	501

Assumptions:
- Bank Revolver—11.25% interest, revolving, secured by Receivables and Inventory.
- Bank Term 11.75% interest on $510,000, $9,444/mo. after 6 months, secured by M&E.
- Owner Note 10% interest, $111,000/year (monthly), balloon fifth year, subordinated.
- Owner Non-Compete—(payable monthly), $60,000, $90,000, $120,000, then $90,000 for last 3 years.

Financial Structure of the Asset Purchase

A Purchase and Sale Agreement has been signed with Press Alloys, Inc. which is contingent upon securing financing. A commitment for bank financing for a line of credit (revolver) and a term loan is being sought. Cash at closing shall be derived from the following sources:

Financial Category	Lending Basis	Draw Rate	Possible Loan Amount ($000)	Actual Loan Amount ($000)
M&E—Bank Term Loan	$637	80%	$510	$510
Receivables—Revolver	$376	75%	$282	$141[a]
Inventory—Revolver	$224	50%	$112	$ 56[a]
Total Bank Debt Drawn				$707

[a]Plan to draw only 50% of possible loan amount (i.e., $197,000 of $394,000 total) leaving an additional $197,000 available for future draw down.

- M&E was appraised by T.H.E. Appraisal in August, 1987 and evaluated on a forced liquidation basis as $617,000. Since some items were overlooked during the appraisal, its value could rise by another $20,000.

- *Receivables* average under 45 days and have had a history of good collections from financially healthy customers.

- *Inventory* represents approximately 300,000 pounds of aluminum in various states including raw billets, WIP, Finished Goods and Scrap. Current conversion cost is $.17/pound yielding $.73/pound with today's $.90/pound market prices. Scrap conversion value of total inventory would be $219,000. Book carrying value does not include labor and overhead, just metal value.

Sources and Uses of Cash at Closing			
Sources		**Uses**	
• Bank debt (per above)	$707	• Cash to seller	$760
• Equity from Jim Sharpe	100	• Retirement of seller equipment notes	47
Total sources	$807	Total uses	$807

Summary

Press Alloys, Inc. has shown an historically strong cash flow performance and has sufficient assets to support both a Bank Term loan for $510,000 and an initial draw down from the $350,000 Revolver Loan of $197,000 for a total of $707,000 at Closing.

The structure of the Bank Debt and Owner obligations are well within the projected cash flow estimates and demonstrate acceptable principal payments for all parties.

The business has the capacity, range, technical capability and track record to grow substantially during the next 5 years in a manner well beyond the conservative financial projections.

PART 4

Managing the Early-Stage Venture

Entrepreneurial ventures are usually thought of as "risky"; and indeed, this is often the case. It's not that entrepreneurs desire risk; it is simply that the price of doing something new is that it is unproven. We know from experience that many new things do not work out: the technology cannot be made to deliver the desired performance, or the cost is simply higher than people are willing to pay. Perhaps consumers turn out not to be really interested in the new product in sufficient numbers to make a profitable business. Thus, the art of successful entrepreneurship lies not in avoiding risk, but in managing risk. Successful entrepreneurs and investors have developed a series of techniques to do this, including conducting inexpensive experiments to validate (or not) the key premises on which the venture rests, and on doling out capital in a staged fashion so as not to deploy more financial resources than needed to prove—or disprove—any of these premises. The chapters in this section expand on these ideas, and the cases provide an opportunity to see them in action.

Managing Risk and Reward in the Entrepreneurial Venture

Entrepreneurial ventures—by their very nature—pursue opportunity in an environment of scarce resources. As we have seen in the wide variety of cases studied in the course, this twin set of conditions makes risk and uncertainty a fact of life in the entrepreneurial venture. To elaborate:

1. The pursuit of opportunity generally requires that the entrepreneurial venture do something new. Sometimes this involves developing a new technology or distribution channel, other times it involves combining existing elements of a product or service in new ways. This newness is the flip side of the opportunity coin—i.e., if someone were already providing the same product or service, the opportunity would likely not exist. But this newness creates uncertainty. For example, can the same product be made for a reasonable cost? Will the technology work as hoped? Will the market be sufficiently large?

2. The very definition of entrepreneurship—the pursuit of opportunity without regard to resources currently controlled—implies a context of resource scarcity. The entrepreneurial venture typically operates with too few people, not enough money, and too little time. Thus, there is a premium on making decisions quickly. There is usually neither the time nor the money for the large amounts of analysis and study that large companies often do when considering major investments. Moreover, as we have often seen, resource scarcity will often force the firm to rely upon a network of partners, and to beg and borrow resources it cannot afford to own and control. While these practices minimize the amount of money to be lost if the venture fails, these practices can increase uncertainty by giving the firm and its managers less control over their destiny.

The riskiness of entrepreneurial ventures seems borne out by the data, which shows that even in successful venture capital funds, portfolios rarely include more than 50%

"winners." Yet, while the risks are significant in entrepreneurial ventures, so are the potential rewards. And, while venture capitalists can play the portfolio diversification game and the law of averages, individual entrepreneurs cannot. Thus, the art of successful entrepreneurial management lies not in avoiding risk, but in managing it.

In the face of this uncertainty, entrepreneurs and those who finance their ventures have developed certain practices that seek to minimize the negative consequences this uncertainty can generate. Specifically, these practices seek to change the ratio of reward to risk *in favor* of the venture and its owners. That is, successful entrepreneurs do not simply roll the dice and accept the risks inherent in the venture. They manage the risks—as well as the potential rewards—through conscious and deliberate actions. These strategies can be grouped in the following general categories, and each will be explored in more detail:

- Define and understand the business model.
- Start small.
- Conduct conscious experiments.
- Make fixed costs variable costs.
- Manage the nature and timing of commitments.
- Stage financing (a special—but very important—case of the above general principle).
- Stay flexible.

Each of these strategies can help entrepreneurs (and those financing them) spend money and time wisely, thus creating value by reducing risk, as well as maintaining the option to abandon ventures where the prospects for returns grow dimmer as more is learned. Of course, as with all general rules, there are plenty of times when they don't apply. There may be circumstances where an entrepreneur chooses to take steps that actually *increase* risk, but because the steps increase rewards more than commensurately, the ratio of reward to risk is improved. One could imagine a scenario, for instance, where it made sense to roll out a product nationally, at great expense, because—if successful—it would pre-empt a competitor. While this increases the risks of failure (in the sense that something that could have been learned inexpensively in a small test market is learned more expensively), this risk may be more than offset by the increased market share the firm will enjoy if, in fact, the product is successful.

In general, however, entrepreneurs and their fledgling ventures face such significant risks that any strategy that reduces risk is a good one.

Defining Risk and Uncertainty

Many scholars have attempted to define uncertainty and risk. For our purposes, it will suffice to define them in the following way:

First, it makes sense to define risk as some function of "the probability of a bad outcome" times some measure of "how bad that outcome is." So, by any measure, a high probability of losing a large sum represents a greater risk than a low probability of losing a small sum. Similarly, reward is also a probabilistic function that results from the

FIGURE A | Risk and Reward Curve

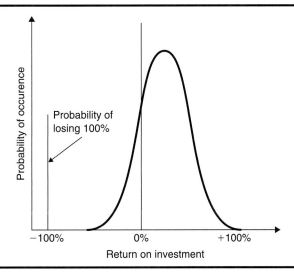

Source: William A. Sahlman et al., *The Entrepreneurial Venture*, 2nd edition (Boston: Harvard Business School Publishing, 1999), p. 157.

"probability of a good outcome" times some measure of "how good it is." Thus, both of these concepts have a probability component (what are the odds something will happen) and a value component (what is the benefit or cost if it does occur).

In this course, we use the notion of risk and reward curves to capture these ideas conceptually (see Sahlman, "Some Thoughts on Business Plans," in *The Entrepreneurial Venture*[1]). These curves attempt to describe the risks (i.e., the probability of losing money, and how much) as well as the rewards (i.e., the probability of earning a positive return, and how large it might be). In the example in **Figure A,** for instance, all of the probability to the left of 0% is a risk, and all of the probability to the right of 0% is reward. Improving the ratio of reward to risk is a matter of both reducing the probability of loss and the potential amount of the loss, as well as increasing the probability of reward and the amount of that potential reward.

Similarly, we use the mental exercise of asking ourselves, "What could go right? What could go wrong?" as a vehicle for identifying the specific risks and rewards. (Again, see Sahlman, "Some Thoughts on Business Plans," in *The Entrepreneurial Venture.*) Obviously, a complementary piece of this exercise is to try to minimize the probabilities and values of the bad outcomes, while maximizing the probabilities and values of the good ones.

For a variety of reasons, this note will focus more on the strategies for managing risk than on those for managing reward. In part, the reward-maximization strategies

---

[1]William A. Sahlman et al., *The Entrepreneurial Venture,* 2nd edition (Boston: Harvard Business School Publishing, 1999).

seem less generic, and have more in common with traditional business practices, while the risk-reduction strategies really come to the fore in entrepreneurial ventures.

At the outset, we defined risk as the probability of a bad outcome times some value that represents how bad that outcome is (usually the dollars we lose). Obviously, if we could predict the future with certainty, there would be no risk—we could look into our crystal ball, see the outcomes that would result from a course of action, and then act (or not) as a function of what we saw. We know, however, that the future is uncertain. We can't predict the results of our own actions—If we invest in developing this drug, will it work? Will it have bad side effects?—let alone how others will act—Will a competitor develop a more effective version? Will the patent office approve it? It is this uncertainty that creates some probability of a bad outcome. If we examine the factors that combine to create uncertainty, they can be imagined as series of concentric circles that capture the various elements of "not knowing the future." The following statements represent the circles:

- What is truly unknowable.
- What is knowable, but which you don't know, and further, don't even know you don't know.
- What is knowable, but which you know you don't know.
- What you do know, but with an imprecise estimate of the probability.
- What you do know, and with a precise estimate of probability.

Thus, buying a lottery ticket is simply uncertain because of the last element—there is a known probability of winning, and it is a lot less than 1. Most businesses are more complicated than a lottery ticket, and involve some mix of all of these elements of uncertainty.

Thus, the probability of some bad outcome is a function of all of these factors acting together, many of which we may not even realize are at work. Risk is this probability "times" the cost of the (bad) outcome. Thus, there is much higher risk associated with the development of a new software program with an estimated cost of $1 million but where the probability of success is 50%, than there is with the development of a new mechanical device, where the probability of success is the same 50%, but the estimated cost is only $5,000.

The strategies that reduce risk can then be thought of as achieving their objective because they reduce the probability of a bad outcome—i.e., they reduce the "badness" (i.e., the cost) of that outcome if it does occur, or both.

The strategies that can effectively reduce risk are described in the remainder of this note.

Define and Analyze the Business Model

Notes besides this one[2] in The Entrepreneurial Manager course have explored in detail the concept of business models and the cost and revenue drivers behind them. Suffice it to say that, before one begins a new venture, it makes sense to have a crystal-clear view

---

[2]See Richard Hamermesh and Paul Marshall, "Note on Business Model Analysis for the Entrepreneur," HBS Case No. 802-048 (Boston: Harvard Business School Publishing, 2002).

of the underlying economics of the business—the basics of how the enterprise will generate profits, cash, and value for its owners. This is the analysis that we have referred to as a "fishbone" in several cases. Once the drivers are understood at the conceptual level (i.e., the response rate to a direct-mail campaign will influence the cost of acquiring subscribers), it makes sense to understand the actual values of those variables—i.e., what is a likely response rate for a direct-mail campaign? What is the renewal rate for existing subscribers? In the Zipcar case, we focused on the number of trips taken by members each month, the hours and miles driven, and the price per mile and per hour actually achieved by the company.

Research that is done before one actually begins operations (and spends money) can often help calibrate the key variables in the business model. This reduces uncertainty in the sense that it narrows the likely range of possible outcomes. Of course one can always be surprised, but there are fewer surprises when one's expectations are well-grounded. Again, in the Zipcar case, we saw how Robin Chase's research helped calibrate the target utilization per vehicle as well as price and cost parameters.

This advance research also helps answer the questions "What can go right" and "What can go wrong?" In Zipcar, for instance, we could see the favorable impact of more rapid growth in the subscriber base or higher utilization. Similarly, the case revealed the negative impact of high attrition and low utilization.

Given scarce financial and management resources, such analysis can help the team in several ways. Not only does this kind of analysis and research help the venture obtain financing and other resources, but it also helps the entrepreneur and the management team understand where to apply their managerial energies and efforts. The latter is accomplished by understanding where the leverage is in the business model (e.g., it is more valuable to raise the response rate by 4% than to decrease the costs of the promotional brochure by $0.10 each). Moreover, by establishing a baseline and a set of expectations, the management team has a well-defined set of standards against which to benchmark actual results. This enables the team to more quickly see where the venture is performing below "par" and be in a position to step in and act more quickly.

Thus, this kind of careful up-front thinking manages risk by reducing uncertainty through advance research, which helps improve the accuracy of estimates and projections. Such thinking can also help reduce the cost of failure, by focusing expenses and investments on those areas that truly can have an impact.

Start Small

One very common approach to managing uncertainty is to start small. First, this approach certainly minimizes the cost of failure. And, assuming "starting small" means starting sooner than would otherwise be the case, then potentially valuable information will be available sooner as well.

Of course, ventures have a minimum efficient scale for each of the activities that underpin them. You may be able to hire one salesperson to sell your software product and see how it goes, and then later expand to cover the whole country. But you can't hire one programmer and only write 10% of the code and try to sell the product for 10% of the price of the whole product. Thus, starting small may not be possible for all ventures.

But where feasible, it limits the potential cost of failure, and jump-starts the process of learning from experience that is so valuable to all entrepreneurs.

Conduct Conscious Experiments

One of the key strategies that entrepreneurs have at their disposal is to conduct conscious experiments. Such experiments, when properly designed and executed, produce valuable information for a lower cost than full-blown implementation. There are several key elements to successful execution of this strategy.

First, the cost of the experiment must be less than the cost of a full-blown rollout. If doing a test-mailing to 1% of the target market will let you assess which price and promotional message achieves the highest response rate, great. But, if you are building a restaurant, you can't experiment with a "minimalist/modern" look versus a "retro" look. It pays to recognize which variables can be nailed down with experimentation and which will need to remain uncertain until full-scale operation begins.

Next, some experiments are pure "research" while others are conducted within the context of an operating business. For instance, a new company with a novel drug-delivery technology found resistance to its idea at the conceptual level. The technology required encapsulating the drug in a powder, and drug companies believed that the chemical qualities of the drug would render the powder unfit for this use. In particular, they were worried about the ability of the powder to work with the fat and water components of drug molecules. So the new venture found two compounds—one that was almost pure "fat" and another that was very watery, and proved that the powder encapsulation technology worked with both of these drugs. Drug companies were quickly convinced that the technology would work with most of their drugs, which were less watery or less fatty than these two extreme examples the company had tested.

In some cases, however, it is possible to experiment at the same time that you actually make some progress with the real business—"on-line" experimentation. For example, in the case of a real estate development project, the environmental tests generate information that helps determine the value of the land, but also produce data that will be required for regulatory and zoning purposes.

The goal of experimentation is maximum "unit" of risk reduction per dollar spent. Thus, two variables come into play—the cost of the experiment and the amount of risk reduction it buys. That is, it pays to do cheap experiments first, but it also pays to experiment early on those business model drivers that have a high probability of failure. In the following example, assume the success of the venture is a function of five variables, each of which is assumed to have a 90% chance of success. Observe the impact on the overall probability of venture success when one of the five key variables falls from a "success rate" of 90% to only 10%:

$$.9 \times .9 \times .9 \times .9 \times .9 = 59\%$$
$$.1 \times .9 \times .9 \times .9 \times .9 = 7\%$$

In this (overly simplified) example, experimenting to learn the "true" value of the last four variables does not buy you nearly as valuable a piece of information as learning the state of the first variable. If the probability of a bad outcome is high, then learning this early can save you a lot of money. This is why the "option to abandon" is so valuable in risky ventures, because there is a substantial probability that the option will be exercised.

Thus, it makes sense to run experiments on the "weak links" and "deal killers" as soon as practical.

Make Fixed Costs Variable Costs

Making fixed costs variable costs is one very effective strategy for reducing the resources required to get into business, run cheap experiments, and, thus, reduce uncertainty. Often, strategies based on variable costs have far less lead time than their fixed-cost alternatives. For example, using sales reps is often a quicker and less expensive means of getting into business, although it has its disadvantages (including less control and higher total costs at a high volume of sales). Using subcontractors to manufacture rather than build a facility is a similar approach. In the MACD case, paying per usable acre of land is an analogous approach to making what could have been a fixed cost—a set price for the entire parcel—a variable cost as a function of the number of usable acres.

Not only do these approaches minimize up-front costs, but they also increase flexibility. It is easier to shift sales strategies if you don't have to fire an entire sales force. And, at low volumes, the accumulated variable costs are likely to be far less than the fixed cost of the higher commitment strategy.

Finally, this strategy also reduces the cost of failure, by minimizing the investment requirements. At some point in the life of a successful venture, volume will begin to build, and it will become appealing to gain some of the economies of scale by reversing course and making some of those variable costs fixed. This may well be the right move and can certainly have a positive effect on profitability and returns, but it should usually be taken only when the significant risks have been wrung out of the venture.

Manage the Nature and Timing of Commitments

Managing commitments is one of the key tools available to the entrepreneur to manager risk. First, contingent commitments offer the entrepreneur more flexibility and are a valuable way to offload some of the risk on the other party. That is, if you can commit to doing something only if some other piece of the puzzle falls into place (i.e., close on a purchase only if financing has materialized), then you can build in the ability to respond to future events.

Managing the timing of the commitments you make is a similar strategy for managing risk. That is, if you can avoid making commitments until after you have secured a particular resource or obtained a valuable piece of information, then that commitment is less risky. In the case of Bob Reiss, for example, the fixed costs of designing the game were $50,000, and the unit contribution margin was $4.27. Dividing $50,000 by $4.27 we arrive at a breakeven of 11,682 units. However, Reiss did not have to *commit* to spending the fixed costs for design until after he had already obtained large orders from stores like Kmart and Sears. This approach renders the concept of breakeven meaningless. If you've already sold more than the breakeven amount before you have to commit to the fixed costs, then the risk of the proposition is vastly reduced. The same is true of real estate developers who can get the results of soil tests before committing to buy land, or who pre-sell or pre-lease property.

These strategies all transfer some of the risk to other parties. However, it should be recognized that this is not always a zero-sum game of simply transferring risk from the entrepreneur to some other party. In some cases, total risk is reduced because the incentives of the parties are changed. In the R&R case, Reiss paid many of his partners on a commission basis. Not only did this have the effect of making what would otherwise be fixed costs variable (in itself a good thing), but it changed the incentives of the parties. Instead of capping their rewards Reiss created a situation with an unlimited upside.

Stage Financing

The staging of financing is another way of managing risk, although, of course, there is a price for this. For the financier, it means that—if the venture is successful in its attempts to wring uncertainty out of the business model, and reaches the next stage of financing, then investors will pay a higher price per share than they would have paid if they put all the money in up front. Investors have learned, however, that in the long run, this is a price worth paying in order to preserve the option to abandon after the early phase of experimentation has proven that the venture is not viable.

In this sense, staged financing benefits the entrepreneur as well. It reduces the level of risk to a bearable level, allowing risky ventures an opportunity to get financed. It also allows founders to hold on to more equity than would be the case if they succeeded in raising all of the required financing up front.

Stay Flexible

Finally, flexibility is a risk-reducing strategy. As we've seen, entrepreneurs make guesses about the future and the ability of their firms to exploit the future. But the future rarely evolves as predicted, and even those factors that are seemingly within the entrepreneur's control can fail to work as hoped. Technology costs more to develop, salespeople don't sell enough to make quota, and manufacturing costs are higher than planned. For all these reasons, entrepreneurs and their firms need to preserve the ability to adapt. In order for them to make use of all of the learning that has taken place, firms need to be able to change the products they produce, the customers they serve, and their business models.

CHAPTER 10

The Legal Forms of Organization

One of the key issues an entrepreneur must resolve at the outset of a new venture concerns the legal form of organization the enterprise should adopt. This decision is driven chiefly by the objectives of the entrepreneur and the firm's investors, in terms of tax status, exposure to legal liabilities, and flexibility in the operation and financing of the business. The choices are made difficult by the inherent tradeoffs in the law. In order to get the most favorable tax treatment, one must often give up some protection from liability exposure, flexibility or both.

This note will describe the various alternative forms of organization, and the advantages and disadvantages of each. These factors are summarized in **Exhibit 1.** This note will cover only the most fundamental elements of the various forms; a competent accountant or attorney should be consulted if such a decision presents itself.

Overview

The most prevalent legal forms of organization include:

— The sole proprietorship
— The partnership
  • general partnership
  • limited partnership
— The corporation
  • the "regular" C corporation
  • the S corporation (formerly Subchapter S)
  • the limited liability company

Senior Lecturer Michael J. Roberts prepared this note as the basis for class discussion rather than to illustrate either effective or ineffective handling of an administrative situation. It replaces a previous note of the same title written by Michael J. Roberts under the supervision of Howard H. Stevenson.

The two most basic differences between these various legal forms of organization are the tax status each is afforded, and the protection from liabilities each form offers to the owners. This can be seen most easily by briefly examining the C corporation and the sole proprietorship as legal forms.

Sole Proprietorship

The sole proprietorship is the oldest and simplest form of organization: a person who undertakes a business without any of the formalities associated with other forms of organization; the individual and the business are one and the same for tax and legal liability purposes.

The proprietorship does not pay taxes as a separate entity. The individual reports all income and deductible expenses for the business on schedule C of the personal income tax return. Note that these earnings of the business are taxed at the individual level whether or not they are actually distributed in cash. There is no vehicle for sheltering income.

For liability purposes, the individual and the business are also one and the same. Thus, legal claimants can pursue the personal property of the proprietor, not simply the assets which are utilized in the business.

The C Corporation

The "C" corporation is the most common form of large business organization for several reasons.

First, in contrast to the point made above regarding the sole proprietorship, the firm's owners are personally protected from liability. Thus, in the case of the Exxon Valdez, for instance, even if the damages against Exxon had bankrupted the company, the courts could not have pursued the individual shareholders for further damages—liability is limited to the extent of investment in the firm. There is a corporate shell or "veil" which can only be "pierced" in the event of fraud.

In exchange for this status, the C corporation is considered a taxpaying entity. Because the firm does not get any deduction for dividends paid, the earnings of a corporation are thus taxed twice: once at the corporate level, and again at the individual level. The maximum rate on corporate income is 35%, so $1.00 of pretax corporate income becomes $0.65 of pre-*personal*-tax income to the individual. Prior to mid-2003, this dividend income was taxed at normal, ordinary income rates, which approximated 40% once federal and state taxes are taken into account. Thus, $0.65 became $0.39 of after-tax personal income [.65−(40%×.65)]. Effective May 8, 2003, the tax law changed to reduce the federal taxation of dividends to individuals to a 15% rate. Thus, the average personal tax rate on dividend income (including federal and an average of state tax rates) is approximately 20%. This raises the amount an individual receives—after-tax—from $1.00 of corporate income from $0.39 to $0.52 [.65−(20%×.65)]. This double taxation creates incentives for those enterprises that anticipate distributing earnings to utilize a tax-advantaged form.

Other forms of organization can best be understood in relation to these two forms. After discussing the tax status and liability protection afforded by each of the other forms, we will return to discuss a series of other factors that distinguish these forms, and which should be considered when selecting a legal form under which to operate a business.

Partnerships

Partnerships are business entities that consist of two or more owners.

The General Partnership

A partnership is defined as "a voluntary association of two or more persons to carry on as co-owners of a business for profit." A partnership is more complicated than merely a collection of individuals. The partners must resolve, and should set down in writing, their agreement on a number of issues:

— The amount and nature of their respective capital contributions. One partner might contribute cash, another a patent and a third property and cash.
— The allocation of the business' profits and losses.
— Salaries and drawings against profits.
— Management responsibilities.
— Consequences of withdrawal retirement, disability, or death of a partner.
— Means of dissolution and liquidation of the partnership.

A partnership is treated like a proprietorship for tax and liability purposes. Earnings are distributed according to the partnership agreement, and taxes paid at the personal level on the partner's share. For liability purposes, each of the partners is jointly and severally liable. Thus, a damaged party may pursue either or both of the partners for any amount—the claim may not be proportional to invested capital or the distribution of earnings.

The Limited Partnership

Limited partnerships are a hybrid form of organization. A limited partnership is a partnership which has *both* limited and general partners.

— The general partner assumes the management responsibility *and* unlimited liability for the business and must have at least a 1% interest in profits and losses.
— The limited partner has no voice in management and is legally liable only for the amount of capital contribution plus any other debt specifically accepted.

In a limited partnership, the general partner may be a corporation (a corporate general partner). In situations where a corporation is the sole general partner, in order to ensure that there are sufficient assets to cover the unlimited liability which the general partner must assume, the corporate general partner must have a net worth of at least $250,000 or 10% of the total capitalization of the partnership, whichever is less.

Note that in a limited partnership, profits and losses may be allocated differently from each other. That is, even if profits are allocated 20% to the general partner and

80% to the limiteds, the limiteds may get 99% of the losses. However, losses are deductible only up to the amount of capital at risk. Note that the distribution of profits is subject to all sorts of creative structuring, such as that which is often observed in certain venture capital and real estate partnerships: the limiteds get 99% of the profits until they have gotten their capital back, and then the general partner gets 20% and the limiteds only 80%. This flexibility is an important advantage of the partnership form.

The S Corporation and the Limited Liability Company

The S corporation is a creature of the law which is afforded the tax status of a partnership, but the protection from legal liability of a corporation. And, a limited liability company is a new creature designed to afford the same benefits. By this point, you will have concluded that there is no free lunch, and that this advantageous treatment must come at some cost—the IRS being unlikely to give up its ability to tax corporate entities out of the goodness of its heart. And, indeed there are such limitations.

In order to qualify for S corporation status, the organization must meet a number of rather restrictive conditions:

— have only one class of stock, although differences in voting rights are allowed.

• be a domestic corporation, owned wholly by U.S. citizens, and derive no more than 80% of its revenues from non-U.S. sources.

— have 75 or fewer stockholders.

• derive no more than 25% of revenues from passive sources, i.e., interest, dividends, rents and royalties.

• have only individuals, estates and certain trusts as shareholders, i.e., no corporations or partnerships.

The election of S corporation tax status requires the unanimous, timely consent of all shareholders. This status may be terminated by unanimous election, or if one of the above mentioned conditions is broken.

The limited liability company (LLC) is similar to an S corporation in that it enjoys the tax advantages of a partnership and the liability protections of a corporation. While state laws differ somewhat, an LLC is like an S corporation, with none of the restrictions on number or type of shareholders. The LLC is similar to a partnership in that the LLC's operating agreement (the equivalent of a partnership agreement) may distribute profits and losses in a variety of ways, not necessarily in proportion to capital contributions.

How to Decide

There are a number of criteria which can be used to help choose a legal form of organization.

Who will the investors and owners be? If the investors and owners will be a small group of individuals, a partnership of some form is clearly a possibility, as is an S corp or LLC. If, however, it is anticipated that the business will require venture capital or other types of professional investors, a corporation may be more suitable. This is because venture capital firms cannot be shareholders in S corps (because the VC firms are usually partnerships, which can not hold shares in an S corp). In addition, the potential tax liability of a flow-through entity makes VCs and their limited partners nervous. For this reason, VCs do not typically invest in LLCs. Finally, a corporation offers the most flexibility in incentive stock option plans, as well as various types of preferred securities, all of which may be important in a venture-backed, high potential venture. Finally, a public offering will most likely require a C corporation.

What are the capital requirements and cash flow characteristics of the business likely to be? If the venture is projected to create large losses in the early years, then there may be some benefit to passing those losses through to investors, if the investors are in a position to use them to offset income and thus reduce taxes. This would favor the partnership or LLC. Similarly, if the business intends to generate substantial cash flow and return it to investors as the primary means of creating value for investors, then a flow through entity is attractive. If, however, the business will require cash investment over the long term, and value is intended to be harvested through a sale or public offering, then a C corp is probably most attractive.

What is the time frame for the life of the business? Partnerships dissolve upon the death or retirement of any one of the partners. Corporations, on the other hand, have a continuity of life that goes beyond that of any of the management or investors.

Other Tax Issues

As you have no doubt gathered, tax implications are an important factor in the choice of an entity. Indeed, the incentives of the tax code gives rise to certain tactics which can be risky. For instance, the fact that distributed earnings of the corporation are doubly taxed gives rise to an incentive for the owners to pay themselves all of those profits as compensation, which is deductible as an expense to the cooperation (unlike dividends) and is thus not taxed twice. The IRS has certain rules on "reasonable" compensation designed to protect against just such behavior.

Note that the tax on individuals in "flow-through entities" like partnerships and LLCs is on the share of income *earned,* not cash *distributed:*

— The income of the partnership is taxed at the personal level of the individual whether or not any cash is actually distributed.

— The distribution of cash out of income or retained earnings is not itself a taxable event. The only time when cash distributions are a taxable event is when the cash distribution exceeds the partners' basis in the partnership.

— The basis in equal to the amount of capital originally contributed, plus the amount of income on which tax is paid, less any cash distributions. (Example: An individual invests $100 in a partnership, and his share of income in 1 year equals $30. He must pay tax on this $30 at the personal rate. His basis is now $130. If he receives a $20 cash distribution, his basis drops to $110.)

Summary

Of course, a business may move through many forms in its lifetime. A sole proprietorship may become a partnership and finally a C corporation. A limited partnership may become an LLC and then a C corporation. Rest assured that each of these changes will require considerable legal work and administrative burden for the current management and owners of the firm. The advantages of the right form of organization at each particular stage certainly may warrant this series of changes. On the other hand, high-potential ventures on a fast-track do not want to lose time and focus by getting tied up jumping through these hoops in the last moments before a financing. Entrepreneurs would do well to consider the likely evolution of their business before selecting a form of organization, and should certainly consult with a qualified tax attorney or accountant before making this important choice.

EXHIBIT 1 | Comparison of the Various Legal Forms

	C Corporation	S Corporation	Limited Partnership	Limited Liability Company
Who pays tax on entity's earnings?	• Double tax: at entity and owner levels • Payouts to owners as compensation (deductible to entity, therefore taxed only to owners) limited by tax rules denying deductions for unreasonable comp. • Asset sales: taxed twice (up to 57.75% combined federal tax at entity and owner levels, unless owners are tax-exempt)	• Federal gov't and most states impose single tax at owner level • A few states (including Mass.) impose some tax at entity level • In a single-level tax regime, tax authorities have much less incentive to focus on unreasonable comp.	• Single tax at owner level • A very few states (and NYC) impose entity-level tax • In a single-level tax regime, tax authorities have much less incentive to focus on unreasonable comp.	• Federal gov't and most states impose single tax at owner level • A few states tax at entity level • In a single-level tax regime, tax authorities have much less incentive to focus on unreasonable comp.
Who is liable for entity's obligations?	• The gold standard: corporate shareholders rarely held liable for entity's obligations absent fraud • No escape from securities-law liability; limited protection from environmental claims	• As shareholders in a corporation, investors get same treatment as owners of C Corporation stock	• Must have at least one general partner with unlimited liability for unsatisfied obligations of entity • General partner can be a shell corporation (effectively yielding limited liability) • Limited partners escape liability (Delaware provides broadest protection), same issues as C Corp. with respect to environmental and securities law liability	• Drafters of statutes intended to give all equity owners the same liability protection as corporate shareholders • Liability limitations not tested in court, however, so cautious investors may be concerned

(continued)

EXHIBIT 1 | Comparison of the Various Legal Forms (*continued*)

	C Corporation	S Corporation	Limited Partnership	Limited Liability Company
What kind of equity interests can be issued?	• Common and preferred stock; warrants • Can issue tax-favored incentive stock options (ISOs) • State corporate statutes and tax rules regarding constructive dividends effectively limit flexibility in structuring equity	• Limited to a single class of stock; all shares must have identical *economic* rights (nonvoting shares OK), so all distributions must be proportional to share holdings (No preferences) • Employee options (including ISOs) are safe, as are plain vanilla warrants if out of the money both when issued and when transferred • Discounted warrants or other arrangements intended to provide a return mimicking preferred stock may constitute a prohibited 2nd class of stock	• Provides enormous flexibility in sharing profits and losses; can have multiple classes of interests • Cost: complexity caused in part by decades of anti-tax shelter rules • No ISOs, and all employee options are problematical; in theory (unlike corporations), exercise of employee options should trigger taxable gain to existing owners	• Treated as partnerships for tax purposes if properly structured • Same flexibility; same complexity • No ISOs, same issues with employee options as limited partnerships
Limitations on who can own equity?	• Effectively, no limitations outside of heavily-regulated industries (*e.g.,* FCC limitations on foreign ownership of media companies) • The only practical vehicle for publicly-traded businesses	• No more than 75 shareholders • All must be individual US citizens or residents, types of certain trusts or certain otherwise tax-exempt entities (charities, pension funds, etc.) willing to pay tax on their shares of the S. Corp income; No other institutional investors (e.g., partnerships or taxable corporations); no non-US persons can be shareholders	• No limits on who can own interests • Not appropriate for **foreign** investors unless they are willing to file US tax returns (or unless the entity's activities are limited to investing in stocks and securities) • Not appropriate for **tax-exempt** investors unless they are willing to file "Unrelated Business Taxable Income" returns and pay taxes (unless the entity foregoes borrowing and limits its activities to investing or trading in securities and/or lending)	• Again, treated as partnerships for tax purposes if properly structured • Same issues with foreigners and tax-exempts

Can entity make tax-free distributions?

- Venture capital funds often have both tax-exempt and foreign partners.

- Generally not possible if entity is profitable
- Distributions of cash usually treated as made out of profits; if so, taxable as dividends (ordinary income, not capital gain)
- Distributions of appreciated property trigger tax at entity level on appreciation and at owner level at dividend rates on value of property received

- Owners taxed on entity's earnings as those earnings accrue can receive distributions of these previously-taxed earnings without incurring additional tax
- Distributions of appreciated property can be made without triggering any tax, subject to complex anti-abuse rules
- Not an appropriate vehicle for pooled investments (owners cannot take their shares of assets in kind without triggering tax.

- Again, treated as partnerships for tax purposes if properly structured

What happens to losses generated by the entity?

- Warehoused and carried forward as net operating losses (NOLs) to be used against future earnings
- NOLs subject to limitation if entity undergoes "ownership change" (NOL limitations have little economic effect if company is growing rapidly in value)
- Venture capitalists generally favor preserving NOLs for benefit of entity

- Owner/managers may be able to use their shares of the entity's losses to offset wages and also other income not attributable to entity
- "Passive loss" and "at risk" rules limit ability of an owner who is an individual to use entity's losses to offset income and gains from other sources if those losses exceed the sum of the owner's paid-in capital (including direct loans to entity) and proportionate share of the entities' undistributed profits

- Owner/managers may be able to use their shares of the entity's losses to offset wages and also other income not attributable to entity
- "Passive loss" and "at risk" rules limit individual owners' ability to use entity losses, but other investors not subject to these rules can shelter income with entity losses

- Again, treated as partnerships for tax purposes if properly structured

(continued)

EXHIBIT 1 | Comparison of the Various Legal Forms (continued)

	C Corporation	S Corporation	Limited Partnership	Limited Liability Company
What are likely exit strategies for investors?	• Asset sales are not tax-efficient unless entity has useable NOLs to offset income and gain it realizes on those sales • Stock sales (IPO or private) are best for investors; sales generally result in capital gains taxed at favorable rates	• Allows flexibility to sell assets without triggering more than one level of tax (buyers often pay more because they get tax basis step-up and additional future depreciation) • Conversion to C Corporation status can be done tax-free, so conversions followed by IPOs are common	• Easy to sell assets without triggering two levels of tax • Roll-up into C Corporation for IPO often can be accomplished tax-free, but can be very complicated to structure	• Same issues as limited partnership
What operational problems are peculiar to the entity?	• None	• Hard to structure investments by venture capitalists and other institutions without risking forfeiture of S status. • No flexibility in allocating economic benefits (all must be per share)	• None, other than complexity	• None, other than complexity

ONSET Ventures

Terry Opdendyk scooped a stack of files off his desk and loaded them into his briefcase. As he did so, he was careful to include materials he would need to think through several significant issues that faced ONSET Ventures, the venture capital firm of which he was a founding partner. It was a Friday afternoon in July 1997, and ONSET was in the midst of raising an $80 million fund—its fourth and largest to date. Terry was proud of what ONSET had achieved over the past 13 years, since its initial $5 million fund. The firm had become known as a top-tier seed investor in the major leagues of Silicon Valley Venture Capital (VC) firms. It had an enviable deal flow, and its limited partners had "re-upped" for the new fund in only nine days. Indeed, they had made commitments for $140 million, significantly more than the partners wanted to raise.

ONSET had been founded on a well-thought-out analysis of the VC industry and operated according to strict principles that its partners had articulated and refined over the years. But, the VC business was changing, and Terry wanted to be sure that ONSET's strategy evolved in an intelligent manner along with the industry. Thus, one of the issues he and his partners had to resolve related to whether the fund should raise more money than they had originally decided upon.

Finally ONSET's partners faced an additional issue related to investing some of the funds that remained in ONSET II, the previous fund. ONSET had been "incubating" an interesting investment opportunity: a team of entrepreneurs had been working to develop a new software product for managing sales force compensation. This company—TallyUp—had been in incubation for about a year, under the sponsorship of ONSET partner Darlene Mann. The team and business model had come together during this time, but the Company had not achieved all of the objectives ONSET had set when the original seed financing of $1 million had been provided. Specifically, TallyUp had not yet developed a "beta" version of the software product. Thus, the partners at ONSET needed to decide whether to invest an additional $1 million round of seed-level financing in

Senior Researcher Nicole Tempest and Lecturer Michael J. Roberts prepared this case at the HBS California Research Center as the basis for class discussion rather than to illustrate either effective or ineffective handling of an administrative situation.

TallyUp or to bring the company—in its current state of development—to more traditional VCs for follow-on first round funding.

Opdendyk waved to Mann as he walked through ONSET's offices and headed home for the weekend. "See you Monday," he said, looking forward to the partners' meeting where they would discuss both how much money they should accept for ONSET's latest fund, and what financing approach they should advocate for TallyUp.

Background

ONSET was founded in 1984 as a seed stage venture fund. The first fund—simply called ONSET—had been raised by Opdendyk and David Kelley in 1984. This was a $5 million "feeder" fund that had been financed by three later-stage venture capital firms and 31 CEOs and entrepreneurs. The purpose of the "feeder" fund was to make seed stage investments that would move up the "food chain" to the three later-stage VC firms for follow-on financing. From 1984 through 1989, Terry, David Kelley and, later, Rob Kuhling honed the seed stage strategies that were to become the basis for later funds.

Following this first fund, a $30 million fund—ONSET I—was raised in 1989. ONSET II, a $67 million fund, was raised in 1994. By mid-1997, two-thirds of that capital had been invested in seed and follow-on investments, and the principals were reserving the remainder of the funds in ONSET II for follow-on investments in businesses already funded. Thus, ONSET was seeking to raise its fourth fund—and its largest fund to date. The partners had decided to seek a minimum of $80 million of capital and a maximum of $95 million.

(See **Exhibit 1** for excerpts from ONSET III offering memorandum that describe the investment history and performance of ONSET I and II, as well as a more detailed description of ONSET III.)

ONSET Ventures: Strategic Foundation

Opdendyk had a masters degree in computer science and had joined Hewlett-Packard as a software engineer in 1970. Three years later he left to join Intel, and after seven years there, he became president of Visicorp, one of the early successes in the personal software industry (e.g., "Visicalc," one of the first spreadsheet programs). Upon leaving Visicorp in 1984, Opdendyk was intrigued with the process of starting and growing a new business. Thus, he decided to undertake a systematic study of how this process worked, at least as practiced by venture capitalists.

> We knew that only 1% of the businesses that sought VC funding actually obtained it. And, of those companies that did get funded, less than 25% succeeded in getting to a future financing event that valued the company above the valuation in the first financing. We wanted to see if we could figure out if there were any principles that explained which companies were successful.

Opdendyk and his partners interested several large and successful VC firms in an investigation of these issues. These firms opened their records for a confidential study of

300 separate investments that were included in their portfolios. Opdendyk explained the principles that were distilled from the analysis:

> First, if you had a full-time mentor who was not part of the company's management team, and who had actually run both a start-up *and* a larger business, the success rate increased from less than 25% to over 80%. Genentech, Compaq, Lotus, all fit this model. Certain venture capitalists had this skill set, and were willing to invest the time to add this level of value. It was clear that if VC partners defined their relationship with a company as a personal commitment rather than simply as a portfolio investment they simply did not let most failures happen.
>
> The second principle related to whether or not the business continued operating on its initial business model. It turned out that this was a good way to fail. The successful companies almost always *changed* their business model as they progressed; a business plan is great, but only the market will tell you if you have a business model that really works. You need to be sensitive to what the market is telling you, and adapt. And you have to do this continuously.
>
> Third, it makes sense to wait until the business model is validated before hiring the CEO. If the CEO is hired before the business model is refined, you will get the business model that the individual used in their last job. If you wait until you have refined the business model through several iterations, you have a much better shot at choosing a person who can really execute that model.
>
> Fourth, you spend money *only* to add value as perceived by those individuals providing the next round of investment capital. Once you get to cash flow positive, you have the luxury of focusing solely on the operating tasks of the business—those activities that generate revenues and profits. But, until you get there, you are dependent upon the next set of investors to survive. So, also you need to focus as well on what will add value in *their* eyes.
>
> Fifth, there has to be a want, not just a need, for the product. The company needs to have a unique reason to succeed. During the early years of a business, it is very difficult to change the way that potential customers think. You need to find an immediate source of pain that people will pay to eliminate. For example, when Lotus 123 came out, it was a more sophisticated product than Visicalc—it integrated database, graphic, and spreadsheet tools. But the reason it was successful was that the product had variable column widths. Financial analysts were screaming for variable column width, and Lotus had it; they made the pain disappear.
>
> Finally, only special people make a special business. You simply cannot compete successfully with larger, established companies if you have ordinary people.

ONSET in 1997

On the basis of these ideas, ONSET was founded in 1984. The firm evolved over the next dozen years, and refined the principles articulated above. As of mid-1997, ONSET had offices in both Silicon Valley and Austin, Texas. It had 4 partners and had invested in 47 companies. Given the importance of experienced mentors in the ONSET model, the firm had no junior-level personnel (see **Exhibit 1, Appendix C** for ONSET partners' resumes). Opdendyk observed: "When you look at what we are doing during the incubation process, we are often serving as the CEO. You need people who have actually run a business to do this effectively and credibly."

The process of refining ONSET's business principles had led to the development of the firm's incubation process. This was a series of steps through which business ideas were developed, refined and ultimately pursued—or, alternatively, rejected. There were two distinct phases to the incubation process: "pre-seed," which referred to the stage prior to a funding commitment, and "seed," after a financing.

The Incubation Process: Pre-Seed Phase

The pre-seed stage referred to the phase during which a partner from ONSET worked with an entrepreneur or team, trying to decide if their business concept could be the basis of an attractive investment. During this phase, ONSET attempted to discern the assumptions that lay behind the business proposition, as well as the analysis that could be done to determine the merit of those assumptions. The issue was whether ONSET could spend a "reasonable" amount of money—approximately $1 million—to substantially reduce the risk. As Rob Kuhling, an ONSET partner, described it:

> The basic principle of what we do is to take as much risk out of the equation for as little money as possible in as short a period of time as we can. This means something different each time, depending on the business model and the industry. In medical devices, the early risk reduction points are proving that the technology works in animals, proving it works in humans, and then demonstrating that it can obtain FDA approval.

Another dimension of the pre-seed analysis concerned the people involved: were the entrepreneur and the team up to the task? Opdendyk described how ONSET addressed this issue:

> We work with the founders, trying to gauge their skills and temperament. One of the key hurdles is the "would you rather be rich, or would you rather be king?" test. When we start working with an entrepreneur, they are in the selling mode. But, usually, after a few meetings, they get more comfortable talking about the problems they see, rather than simply trying to convince us to invest. This is a key step. They have to demonstrate that they are willing to learn and adapt, not just take our money and charge ahead with their original business plan.
>
> We also assume that we may need a new CEO. Fifteen years ago, we took for granted the ability to find the person we wanted. Now, talent is so scarce in the Valley that we need to be more confident of getting the right person. Now, before we are willing to go into the seed stage, we need to have some sense of who the individual is, and also that we will be able to get a headhunter to sign up for the job.
>
> You might ask, "What about the entrepreneur who comes through the door with the business idea—isn't he or she the CEO?" Well, we have learned that they are often not the right person. We are up-front with everyone who comes to us about the process. Most people think that they will be the exception to the rule, and there *are* exceptions. What usually happens is that we ask the founding team to do some piece of analysis to help refine the business model—to pull apart the value chain and see what elements of the business are really crucial. Well, the team comes back a few days later and asks for help; they haven't made much progress. So, we help them do it. And then, there is another assignment, and they ask for more help. And after a few iterations, they ask, "Can you get someone full-time to help us—this is just what we need." And we say, "That person would be a CEO." And they get the idea. Often, we will push them to wait beyond that point, because we want the business model better defined; this helps us articulate exactly the kind of CEO we

need. And this is a luxury we can afford because of the role that we are willing to play in the process. The key to playing this role credibly is to add value in every single meeting we have with the entrepreneurs. Sometimes, we get part way down this path, and it is clear that it is not working. And we have to be willing to walk away.

In addition to the work described above, ONSET also talked to both potential customers and other venture capitalists during this phase. In discussions with customers, ONSET was trying to get a feel for whether "the dogs will eat the dogfood." And, meetings with VCs were aimed at discerning what would be required to add value in the eyes of those who would be providing the next round of financing, assuming ONSET decided to fund the seed stage. The output of a successful pre-seed analysis was an incubation plan that described the analysis that would be undertaken during the seed stage, as well as the milestones the team would meet.

The Incubation Process: Seed Phase

Opdendyk described how the process unfolded once ONSET made a financing commitment:

Once we write the check—usually about $1 million—we are in the seed stage. We start to work on the incubation plan that was the output of the pre-seed process. We attack the issues where the business model seems most vulnerable.

We have developed a process to ensure that we are adding real value during this process called "projection and reflection." We go to the venture funds whom we think would make good first or second round investors and tell them what we plan on accomplishing during incubation. We ask them what the business would be worth in a financing if we actually reach those objectives, and then we do the math. Simply put, we know what kind of step-up in value we need to make our internal hurdle rates. On a classic seed stage investment it is 2.5x. So, if the VCs will value it at $5 million pre-money at our milestone, and if it will take $1 million of capital to get there, then we know how much we can pay in the seed stage. Almost every time we do this with a potential investment, the initial answer is that you can't get there from here. We need to reengineer the model, either make it worth more, or get there with less money.

As an example of what can go wrong when we do not think carefully about this, we had a seed stage company whose plan included spending $500,000 to get an ASIC (chip design) done. Well, all the potential VC investors believed that this was an easily accomplished task—they never saw any risk in it. So the fact that we did it did not raise the value of the company in their eyes.

By going to other VCs early, we quickly validate what the most significant risk is. It's usually one of five issues: the technical risk (will the technology work?); market risk (are there enough customers?); operating risk (can we actually build it for the required cost?); distribution and pricing (is there a distribution channel that will get the product to the customer cost effectively?); and, finally, the team (can they execute?).

Rob Kuhling described the lessons he'd gleaned from years of going through ONSET's incubation process:

Initially, when I started looking at venture investments, I thought that a solid "business strategy" was the most important determinant of success. Maybe this isn't surprising, given my background at BCG. Later, I thought the key was proprietary technology, because it gave you time to make the inevitable mistakes and fix the strategy that was often off the mark. Now, I think it is people. The skills and energy of the entrepreneur can make even a mediocre idea a success, but average people will ruin even a good idea. If a team walks through the door, and it is populated with second-rate people, I have learned that it is just too much work to drag them up the hill. My time has a significant opportunity cost, given the number of deals we can do. Unless the idea is so big and so powerful that it could be an absolutely huge hit, it just isn't worth the sacrifice of committing the time and energy to a mediocre team.

The Venture Capital Industry in 1997

In July 1997, as ONSET was raising the capital for ONSET III, the venture capital industry was in the midst of an extraordinary year. High returns on VC investments had caused limited partners to put more and more money into venture capital and private equity investments. Venture capital firms with reputations for high returns were in the best position to compete for these funds, and the economics of the business provided a significant incentive to create larger and larger funds. Thus, by mid-1997, the size of the average VC fund had increased 40%, from $50 million in 1996 to $71 million (source: *Venture Capital Journal*, February 1997). There were several consequences to this infusion of money. The VC firms were forced to bring new employees into the business to do some of the work. In 1997, for instance, 72 graduating MBAs from HBS—8% of the graduating class—found jobs at VC/private equity firms. For other summary statistics on the venture capital industry, see **Exhibit 2.**

The active state of the IPO market from 1995 to 1997 was a further boost to the VC market, as investments became liquid more quickly and at high multiples, improving returns to investors. Thus, by many measures the timing of ONSET's entry into the market for ONSET III could hardly have been better.

Economics of ONSET's Business

Over time, ONSET refined its incubation process in order to build on practices that were most likely to generate the high returns (generally measured by limited partner investors as internal rate of return, or IRR) that would attract investors for future rounds, as well as reward the ONSET partners themselves. Opdendyk described some of the key economic dimensions of the business:

> Our bare minimum target rate of return—at the fund level—is a 30% IRR over a 12-year cycle. This translates into higher numbers for individual investments, in order to cover fees, expenses, and the General Partners' carried interest. Given standard investment liquidity cycle times, this implies a 2.5x step up in the seed to first round, a 2.0x step up from the first to second round, and a 1.5x step up in the second to third round. We assume about a year between these "steps." If you look at our last fund, we invested in 18 companies. We have four partners, and the "investing" life of a fund is about four years. So, we are basically incubating one company per year per partner. With the kind of intensive work we do with a company, it is hard to do more. On average, we put in about $4.5 million per

company: $1 million in the seed round, $1.5 in the second, $2 million in the third. Even though we are putting in more money per round, valuation is going up by a sufficient amount that we are not staying even with our original ownership position. Interestingly, people have looked hard at the numbers in terms of what you need to do to get the full benefits of "diversification" in a portfolio. It turns out that once you get to 10 companies, you have almost all of the diversification you can get. Any more, and you really have very little benefit to show for it.

When you look at the economics, you will understand a fatal flaw of our first fund. We teamed up with three of the premier VC firms in the Valley. We had a $5 million fund, and we did the seed round, and they had the right to do the future rounds. They had no obligation to let us put any money in on anything but the seed round. At their option, we could invest in follow-on rounds. But we only got this opportunity when they didn't fully subscribe for the company's financing. Well, they did 100% of the A and B level deals, and we only got to do the C & D level deals. This skewed our returns badly, and we gave up on that strategy and went out on our own.

Now, the fact that we control deal flow is a huge plus for us. We usually do 100% of the seed stage for any company we back. This is a hard round to share. We like to say, "It's tough having more than one chef in the kitchen when you don't know what the recipe is yet." Once you know the recipe, you get some leverage from multiple chefs, but before that all you get is confusion.

Yet, because we are so dependent on the seed round—and because of our philosophy—we are vulnerable to local "irrationality" in deal pricing. We believe that each round has to stand on its own. You can't do a bad deal in the seed round and hope to fix the problem in later rounds. If a big venture fund decides that they don't have the deal flow they want, they can decide to pay what we think of as an "uneconomic price" in the seed round, and hope to make it up in later stages. This is one of the reasons why we opened an office in Austin. We decided that having a presence in multiple markets would diversify the risk of pricing abnormalities in a single market.

ONSET had developed some "rules of thumb" which the partners believed would help the firm meet its return targets. Opdendyk explained:

- We will not lead a start-up in an industry where we don't have the ability to reinvent a business model. If we haven't led a deal in a segment before, we won't try to learn that segment by leading a start-up.

- We will only invest in a deal where we have a local presence. We've learned that if we are not in close touch with the company, it is much harder to add value.

- In general, if a company needs more than $30 million of private capital then it is not an opportunity for us. We will simply suffer too much dilution at the back end to make it worth our while.

- We will not invest in a deal that is "under the spotlights." There are certain industry segments that everyone is chasing, where—we believe—other investors are likely to make irrational decisions about valuations and financing size. We'd rather play off to the side a bit, and give ourselves a chance to make a few mistakes.

ONSET's returns were, of course, influenced by its strategy of focusing on seed stage investments. The table below describes private equity returns by type of investment.

Limited Partner Returns by Stage of VC Investment					
Year	Seed	Early	Balanced	Later	All Venture
1981	5.60%	33.70%	16.40%	17.40%	19.00%
1982	−18.70	57.00	27.40	25.50	32.20
1983	20.50	61.40	35.30	37.50	40.00
1984	−9.50	−6.20	−2.70	−3.50	−3.40
1985	−9.10	−5.60	2.50	2.00	1.20
1986	5.10	5.20	8.90	1.70	8.00
1987	4.30	8.80	6.20	15.70	7.20
1988	−1.00	−2.00	3.10	4.10	2.60
1989	7.10	−0.30	6.10	7.80	5.40
1990	6.60	5.90	0.00	5.80	1.20
1991	15.70	29.70	17.10	47.10	22.10
1992	8.10	5.30	12.80	19.40	12.70
1993	17.30	12.20	17.60	43.90	18.90
1994	14.70	13.10	13.50	12.40	14.60
1995	46.30	62.60	43.70	51.00	49.50
1996	46.70	43.60	41.00	33.70	42.10

Note: Returns are calculated on a year-by-year basis using year-end appraisals of investment values. Returns are net of fees, expenses, and carried interest. These are not fund IRRs or "class year" IRRs.

Source: Venture Economics

ONSET: Deciding How Much Money to Raise

As ONSET II entered its third year of existence, approximately $22 million of capital remained in the fund, which the principals anticipated using primarily for later-round investments in companies already in the portfolio. Thus, thoughts turned to raising a new fund—ONSET III. Opdendyk described the thought process:

> As we thought about ONSET III, we naturally did some calculations. We have four partners, and we do one seed stage deal per partner per year. The average number of dollars per deal has increased over the past several years. In ONSET I it was $2.5 million, in ONSET II it was $3.5 to $4 million, and in ONSET III we anticipate $4.5 to $5 million. In part, this is due to the fact that it costs a little more just to get into business, so the seed stage investment is somewhat larger. This has also been a result of our getting more disciplined in our own approach, and doing the seed round increasingly on our own. But, for ONSET I and II, we have gone back and analyzed the data, and found that we under-invest in our winners. Our returns would have increased if we had put more money in the follow-on rounds of all of our deals. So, we anticipate that the average company in ONSET III will take a little more capital than in the past—say $5 million. If you look at the time cycle of the fund, it is 10 to 12 years. Because we are a seed fund, it takes—on average—6 years from initial investment to

liquidity. (Lately, due to the cycle we are in, it has taken only four years to get from seed to liquidity, but it would be unwise to count on this going forward.) Thus, if we want to shoot to close out the fund in 10 years, we can make our last seed investment in Year 4. So, four partners times one deal per partner times $5 million per deal times 4 years is $80 million. If you add $10 [million] to $15 million in expenses and fees, you get to $95 million or so. This was the upper end of the target for the amount of money we set out to raise.

When we bring new VCs in during follow-on financings, we want to add top-tier players to the deal. To do this, we have to be willing to let them invest the amount of money that makes their economics work. So, if we are doing a $5 million round, we might like to split it equally with a large venture fund. But they need to put more money in simply because their funds are so big. Some of these funds, for example, are trying to put out over $400 million per year.

When we called on our limited partners to make our pitch for $80 million for ONSET III (see excerpts, **Exhibit 1**), it only took two weeks before we had commitments for $140 million. So, now we have a decision to make. If you look around, you can certainly conclude that times are unusually good—that we should take the money because you can't be sure it will be there in four years when we go out to raise another fund. But, that raises the question of what we actually do with the money. We have thought hard about the business model we have built, and how it fits into the basic economics of the venture business. We like the niche we have staked out, and we are doing well in it. We don't want to be just another "diversified balanced" venture fund. And, it is clear that our limited partners behave like rational institutions—they all want to put their money in "top quartile" funds.

Rob Kuhling offered his perspective on the decision confronting the partners:

Seed stage is where we want to play. While there are periods during a business cycle where seed stage investments perform less well than other stages, generally, over time, seed stage provides a better return. The other round that historically does very well is the round closest to the liquidity event, and this is driven more by the short time horizon to liquidity as it is by the multiple you are getting on your investment. But, it is very tough to just play in *just* this round—you usually need to be in the deal earlier to have the opportunity to invest in this round.

ONSET II: The TallyUp Decision

In addition to deciding how much capital to raise in ONSET III, the partners at ONSET needed to make a decision about one of the companies that had been seeded in ONSET II—TallyUp. Darlene Mann, a partner at ONSET, had been working closely with TallyUp since August 1996. She described the issues that ONSET and the TallyUp management team faced:

TallyUp is developing a new software product for use in managing complex compensation systems, like those used for a commissioned sales force. Our original incubation plan called for them to hit a number of key milestones, and then go out and raise a first round of traditional VC money. Well, we've spent the seed round capital and hit many of the key milestones, but we still do not have a product in the beta stage yet. The issue we face is whether

ONSET should invest an additional $1,000,000 to enable TallyUp to develop its beta product, and hold off on raising the first round of venture funding from traditional VCs until the product is ready in mid-1998, or go out to the market now to raise $3 [million]-$4 million and use the money for both product development and sales and marketing. And, if we do proceed now with a round of outside financing, what is the appropriate valuation for TallyUp?

TallyUp Company Background

Andy Swett, the co-founder of TallyUp, was introduced to Mann, a partner at ONSET, through a mutual friend in August 1996. Mann reflected on their early meetings:

> When Andy first came to ONSET, he described his business idea as a billing system for service and content providers on the Internet. With the rapid growth of small companies doing business over the Internet, he believed there was a real need for an inexpensive billing system since the existing systems in the market cost on the order of $500,000. Based on my experience in the software industry I didn't think there was a sufficient market for the product, but I was very impressed by Andy's technical background, determined entrepreneurial personality, and his willingness to accept help. I felt that even if this was not a great product, Andy was an entrepreneur who possessed all the traits necessary for success. I suggested that Andy work with a consultant, Scott Kitayama—who later joined Andy as co-founder of TallyUp—to validate his business idea, using a loan from ONSET to pay the consulting fees. This study quickly concluded that there was not yet a sufficient market for an Internet billing system. However, I was still very intrigued by the settlements technology which was at the core of Andy's product and we brainstormed about the various business opportunities which could leverage this technology.

Swett reflected on this period:

> I thought ONSET was going to bail out after the Internet billing system idea didn't work out. That's what I expected from a venture capital firm. But, ONSET was different—they really stuck with us through this period while we came up with the next idea.

Mann continued:

> Based on these brainstorming sessions, Andy came up with the idea for a sales force compensation system. Having previously been a VP of Sales, I knew there was a real need for a product like this. However, to better understand the level of market demand, we interviewed over 25 companies to determine what systems they were currently using and what issues they were facing. We found that these companies were spending $100,000 to $200,000 per year on managing the administration of sales force compensation, and would be willing to pay hundreds of thousands of dollars for a sales force compensation system without blinking. We were very encouraged and decided to move ahead with the idea.
>
> Collectively, Andy, Scott and I sat down to determine what questions needed to be answered and what issues needed to be addressed before ONSET would invest the seed capital required to get started. Two critical issues quickly surfaced.
>
> First, we needed an expert in the compensation field to work with us on product design, to set up and lead discussions with potential users, and to give TallyUp credibility

with customers. However, we were not prepared to bring someone on full time at this stage, so the person had to be willing to serve in a consulting role. We interviewed about 30 people and identified one, Jim Finkelstein, who would be an excellent fit for the company. Jim had been the director of compensation at Pepsi-Cola and a compensation consultant at Towers Perrin before starting his own compensation consulting practice. The fact that he had his own practice worked well for us because he could work with us on a part-time basis and with his own clients the rest of the time. We negotiated a deal with Jim where he would be paid partly in cash and partly with both participation-based and milestone-driven equity. ONSET's role in the interviewing process was critical since we lent credibility to the team and the business model.

The second question we had to answer was whether we could design a sales force compensation system that could be an off-the-shelf product. Many of the potential customers we interviewed expressed the view that compensation plans were too complex and varied too widely between companies to be supported by a standardized product. However, as we dug deeper, we learned that in reality there were only so many different compensation methods, with the real variability revolving around the percentage commission, the number and type of distribution channels used, the complexity of products offered, and overall size of the sales force. So, using the latest rules-based technology, we could capture this in an off-the-shelf product.

Incubating TallyUp

By December 1996, the team had developed an operating plan (see **Exhibit 3** for excerpts from the operating plan) and ONSET invested $750,000 to purchase preferred shares (at $1 each), in return for 31.6% of the company, based on a $2,375,000 post-money valuation. The agreement was structured so that ONSET would later invest an additional $250,000—at the same $1 per share price—to further help the company accomplish its key milestones, if needed. The company elected a Board of Directors, which included Mann, Swett and Terry Opdendyk, with the agreement that Terry would turn over his board seat to the new CEO when he or she was hired. In addition, ONSET also required that they play a role in all substantive decisions, such as hiring senior staff and purchasing capital equipment. However, on a day-to-day basis, ONSET's involvement primarily focused on the team's work plan.

Once ONSET invested, the real incubation process began. Mann acted in a day-to-day CEO role for TallyUp, working to achieve the five goals that she and the management team had established:

- Validate, size and segment the market;
- Bring the product to the beta stage;
- Develop the business plan;
- Hire a top-flight CEO; and,
- Bring in 2–3 development partners who would put in money in return for early access to a sales force compensation system designed with their requirements in mind.

Mann reflected on how the plan helped them minimize risk:

> In every new business there's technical risk and market risk. We did not feel that the technical risk centered on *whether* the product could be built, but rather *what* product was built—what customer needs it addressed. We felt the technical risk was really on the execution side. In terms of market risk, our biggest concern was whether the market was large enough. In order to minimize both of these risks, we invested significant time and resources into market research. As we interviewed companies to gain a better understanding of the market and their specific needs, we also marketed our product idea in hopes of attracting at least two corporate partners with whom we could develop a product. We were successful in attracting two paying development partners. This reduced the risk for us; not only were they putting their own capital at risk, but serious, paying customers helped us attract the attention of the venture capital community.

Kitayama, now serving as vice president of marketing, reflected on ONSET's role in the process:

> ONSET kept putting manageable hurdles in front of us—these took the form of questions we needed to answer before proceeding. It made it tough at times, but it also gave us a clear roadmap for what we needed to focus on. For example, ONSET believed that either you develop a $500 product and sell hundreds of thousands of them through the retail channel or you develop a $100,000 product that you sell through a direct sales force. Anything in the middle is purgatory. So we had to prove that our product could be priced at, or above, $100,000.

The team worked on several of the goals in parallel: Kitayama and Mann focused on developing a detailed understanding of the market, while Swett pushed forward on product design. Early on, it became clear that to tackle both these issues they needed to get access to potential customers to understand their needs in detail. They set up 31 one-on-one interviews with potential customers to determine how the sales force compensation function was currently being handled and what a technical solution could possibly look like. Mann reflected on their findings:

> We talked with CFOs, directors of compensation, and sales managers, and the answer came back the same—the administration of compensation plans is a real headache. It's a highly time-consuming and unproductive process. Most companies have one administrative person per 50 sales people and that person spends most of his or her time poring over spreadsheets trying to understand the discrepancies between what the salespeople had been paid and what they thought they should have been paid. Furthermore, many of these companies would rebuild their system each year as the compensation plans changed. There was clearly a need for a system that streamlined this whole process. We discovered that the early adopters would be companies in the high tech and financial services industries since their distribution capabilities created complicated sales environments.

Mann also sounded out four venture capital firms as part of ONSET's projection and reflection process to determine the risks that they perceived. Mann found that the venture capital firms were most concerned with who the CEO would be and whether the market was large enough to justify an investment. Since the market size issue came up several times during their discussions, the TallyUp team dedicated a significant amount of time to studying the market in order to develop a fact-based estimate of its size. The team estimated the market for replacing existing dedicated sales force compensation systems to be around $400 million. However, when the market was expanded to include all variable-based incentive plans, the team estimated the size of this larger market at $1.5–$2.0 billion.

In 1996, 7.6% of all exempt employees in the United States were paid based on variable compensation plans and the trend was accelerating: incentive compensation was becoming popular at more companies and at lower levels of these organizations.[1] This large and growing market had naturally attracted the attention of several major software firms, including Oracle, SAP, and Peoplesoft. Some of these firms were developing applications targeted toward the same market as TallyUp's product. The TallyUp team believed that its product was superior, and that they had a lead in developing an offering for the market which they needed to protect by moving quickly.

Hiring a CEO

In keeping with ONSET's key principles, Mann and TallyUp held off on hiring a CEO until they had completed their extensive market research to validate the attractiveness of the market and understand the nature of the business opportunity. As was frequently the case with start-ups, it was clear early on that TallyUp would need to bring in a CEO from the outside. Mann described how ONSET dealt with this issue:

> We always have conversations with the founders up front about their positions in the company. We don't invest if the founders don't understand that they may not have their current positions in the future. In fact, the more successful the company is, the less likely it is that they'll keep the role they began with.

Swett reflected on ONSET's role in the recruiting process:

> At the time we were looking for a CEO, there were 300 CEO searches going on in the valley and only 150 of those got the attention of an executive recruiter. ONSET's relationship with an executive recruiter, who they keep on a retainer basis, was a tremendous advantage to us since finding the right CEO was a make-or-break decision for us.

The team's investment in market research and in the development of a compelling business concept enabled them to successfully attract an experienced software executive to be the CEO of TallyUp. Mann considered this to be a major victory given the shortage of senior leadership talent in Silicon Valley. TallyUp's new CEO—Reed Taussig—came to the company after having served as the SVP of Worldwide Operations for Unify Corporation and SVP of Sales and Marketing for Gupta, both database tools companies, and most recently had founded an Internet company, named inquiry.com. Taussig reflected on his decision to join TallyUp:

> I was looking for an opportunity with a company with a very clear value proposition. Software companies were spending 10%–12% of revenue on the administration of

---

[1] *Compensation and Benefits Review,* September/October 1996.

compensation plans, and those dollars were mostly going towards developing and maintaining complex Excel spreadsheets. That was a very compelling value proposition for me.

Once Taussig was hired, ONSET invested the additional $250,000 they had planned to put in, raising TallyUp's (post-money) valuation to $2,625,000.

Decisions Ahead

Conducting market research and hiring a CEO had taken almost nine months. This was longer than the team had planned. It had also cost TallyUp most of the $1,000,000 in capital it had raised from ONSET. Mann reflected on the decision to spend the money on developing a solid understanding of the market versus building the product:

> It's an interesting question: do you spend the initial money on building the product or developing the business model? A lot of venture firms and entrepreneurs will build the product first, then refine the business model. However, at ONSET, if we are fairly confident that a product can be built, which is generally the case for software these days, then we'll focus our efforts on reducing the market and execution risk. The way we like to work is to spend $1,000,000 or less to understand the business and determine *how* to build the product. The question really comes down to whether you prefer market risk or technical risk—is your bias toward how the business model is formulated or how the product is developed? In this case, we were more worried about the market and the business model.

Thus, in July 1997, ONSET and TallyUp needed to decide whether ONSET should invest an additional $1,000,000 into TallyUp to develop a beta version of the product, or whether TallyUp should go out to the venture capital community at the current stage—without a product—to raise $3 [million]-$4 million for product development and product launch.

Mann explained why $1 million was needed to complete the beta product, when this figure was equal to the amount of TallyUp's entire initial funding:

> Given the growth in the organization and the need to support both existing development partners and sales to new customers, the company would require an additional $1 million to get to the beta stage while supporting baseline marketing and sales capabilities.

Mann knew that either option would raise difficult choices:

> A beta product would certainly raise TallyUp's valuation by at least the $1,000,000 it would cost to develop the product. If we go this route, ONSET would likely be the sole investor and we'd get tangled in a discussion with management over the valuation in this interim round. On the other hand, securing first round VC financing would be a lengthy and all-consuming process for the management team, and I worried about the impact this would have on the momentum the team had generated coming out of their intensive market research process. I'd also be concerned that Taussig—with so little experience at the Company—might have a tough time selling the concept, without a product, to the venture capital community.

Mann was optimistic that if TallyUp went to market for $3 million to $4 million of VC now—without a beta product—the venture capital firms would be very interested.

She based this view partly on the sense that the VC market was "hot"—who knew if the money would be available in six months? Finally, there was the issue of time. Given the looming presence of some of the larger software companies in this segment, Mann was eager to get to market as soon as possible. Was she better off recommending the company raise the money now and getting this phase behind them, so that the team could concentrate on getting a product to market without interruption?

Mann knew there were many criteria to consider in determining the valuation for TallyUp if they went forward with the outside financing now. First, TallyUp had decided to set aside a portion of shares to be used as stock options for new employees hired. The value of these options would likely be $750,000 (750,000 shares at $1 per share), which would increase TallyUp's valuation by the same amount. Second, she knew that ONSET's business model called for a 2 to 3 times step up in valuation from the seed stage (from a base which now included the value of the stock option pool). Third, she knew that in a first round financing of this nature, venture firms would want a 15% to 20% ownership stake (post their investment). Finally, she knew that ideally, ONSET wanted to invest 50% of the $3 to $4 million raised.

* * * * *

"Have a good weekend Terry," Mann called out to Opdendyk as he headed out the door. She turned her attention to the stack of files on her own desk. Mann wondered whether she should advocate outside VC financing for TallyUp, and if so, on what terms? How much of this financing should she recommend ONSET itself provide?

EXHIBIT 1 | Excerpts from ONSET III Investment Memorandum

Table of Contents

SUMMARY OF TERMS

OVERVIEW
- Introduction
- *Investment Focus
- *Key Success Factors
- Investment Allocation
- The General Partner
- *Prior Funds
- Summary

OFFERING DESCRIPTION
- *The Offering
- Use of Proceeds
- *Allocation of Income, Gains and Losses
- Distributions
- *Investor Committee
- Service Agreement with ONSET Venture Services Corporation

(*continued*)

EXHIBIT 1 | Excerpts from ONSET III Investment Memorandum (*continued*)

Potential Conflicts of Interest

Risk Factors

Summary of Certain Income Tax Considerations

ERISA Considerations

Questions

Legal Counsel

Accounting and Reporting

Custodian

Availability of Principal Agreements

APPENDICES

Appendix A—ONSET I Portfolio Investments

Appendix B—ONSET II Portfolio Investments

*****Appendix C**—Resumes—Partners of General Partner

*****Appendix D**—Limited Partners

*Included.

OVERVIEW

Investment Focus

Like its predecessor funds, ONSET III will distinguish itself from other venture capital funds by its investment focus. First, ONSET III will focus on initial and follow-on investments in seed stage projects, because excellent returns are possible from such investments. Second, ONSET III will increase seed stage company success rates by investing the partners' time, skills and resources using the Partnership's proven value-added incubation and development methodology. Third, ONSET III will primarily invest in technology-based companies that match the partners' experience and ability to add value. Fourth, ONSET III will locate most of its companies in Northern California and Austin, Texas, to facilitate the ability of the partners to work closely with the companies as they develop.

Seed-Stage Investments

ONSET III will target seed-stage projects because the returns from successful seed-stage investments can be several times higher than later-stage investments. Even though the potential for higher returns is generally recognized, relatively few venture capital funds focus primarily on such investments, mostly because successfully managing the risks of seed-stage investments demands more from the investment management team than the traditional monitoring approach used for later-stage investments. Selecting the targets requires greater care and investment discipline, and implementing the supportive incubation process requires more experience and hands-on, day-to-day involvement. This under-served investment segment creates an opportunity for ONSET II, a venture fund focused on and capable of developing seed-stage companies.

Selecting seed-stage projects requires great skill. All ventures will be evaluated on not only the merits of technology, product, personnel, and marketplace, but also on how well the incubation process can offset the risks. For example, ONSET III will seek projects that it can develop into companies that

- have excellent personnel,
- can be the leaders in their markets,
- are in emerging growth markets,

EXHIBIT 1 | (*continued*)

- have proprietary product technology with compelling competitive advantages,
- have clear return on investment leverage,
- can be financed easily after a successful seed financing,
- require moderate amounts of capital, and
- have the types of risks that can be mitigated during the incubation stage.

However, at the point ONSET III will make its initial investment decision, a project may be little more than an intriguing idea, an exciting technology, or a capable entrepreneur. Such projects generally lack one or more key elements that traditional venture investors look for and that are necessary for eventual success. For example, a seed project will often have one or more of the following characteristics:

- an unproven technology,
- incomplete marketing and distribution plans,
- inadequate business and operational plans, and
- an incomplete or inadequate management team.

ONSET II is structured through its proven incubation process to provide the expertise and attention necessary to assist its seed projects in overcoming these inadequacies.

The Incubation Process

The incubation process to be employed by ONSET III was developed by its predecessor funds and the general partner organization. The ONSET Ventures' incubation process and its importance to ONSET III's investment strategy have already been described briefly. But how does it really operate?

The incubation process will often begin prior to ONSET III making an investment commitment. When an idea, technology, or entrepreneur shows promise, the first step is to explore fully the opportunity. To do so, ONSET III often will locate the entrepreneur in its Menlo Park or Austin facility. The exploration process may last months and will involve the equivalent of one full-time partner. In some cases, small amounts of capital may be used to finance particular exploration goals prior to a formal seed financing, further ensuring the viability of the business and reducing investment risk. ONSET III will make its seed stage financing commitment only after both the entrepreneurial team and ONSET III are convinced of the project's potential and appropriateness for the ONSET ventures' incubation process.

The second step is to articulate clearly and agree on what should be accomplished during the incubation. Once the goals are articulated, ONSET III's partners (generally acting as interim officers of the company), the company's management and other professionals work together as a team to accomplish the goals.

Typically, the incubation process takes 6 to 12 months. The process ends when the company is sound enough to succeed without the support structure provided by ONSET Ventures and is able to attract traditional venture capital financing. By the end of the process, most companies will have

- proven the technology,
- demonstrated the product concept and design,
- positioned the product (and the company) in the marketplace,
- developed strategic and operational plans to reflect a viable business model, and
- completed its management team.

(*continued*)

EXHIBIT 1 | Excerpts from ONSET III Investment Memorandum (*continued*)

___

The final step in the incubation process is to provide for future funding of the successful seed company. The Partnership will organize a syndicate of other venture capital funds to participate with ONSET III in funding the next stage, usually known as first-round financing. This downstream financing syndication is a critical element in the success of seed stage investing. ONSET III will typically introduce projects in their earliest stages to other major venture firms (including the more than 40 firms that have co-invested with earlier ONSET Ventures' funds) to facilitate first-round investment. Upon completion of the financing, the company will have successfully emerged from the incubation phase and established a more conventional venture capital relationship with ONSET III.

ONSET Ventures' Incubation Process

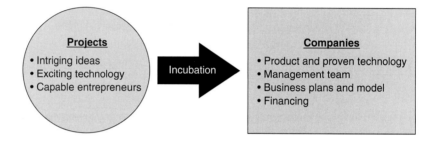

Value-added Approach

As a company transitions from the incubation phase to independent operation, the ONSET Ventures' partners will remain active on the company's board and will continue to be involved throughout the company's development. The principals of ONSET Ventures couple their past experiences as operating executives in both small and large businesses with a personal commitment to achieving success in each portfolio company.

Technology-based Industries

ONSET III will target seed investments in high-technology industries (particularly computer software and hardware, communications products and services, pharmaceuticals delivery, and medical devices and instrumentation) for several reasons. First, companies based on an advanced technology usually have significant early risks that ONSET Ventures and the project team can reduce during the incubation process, substantially increasing the companies' chances of success and value. Second, companies in technology-based industries often have many of the desired investment characteristics described above in "Seed-stage Investments." Finally, the partners have extensive investment and managerial experience in technology businesses in these areas.

Northern California and Texas Focus

Most of ONSET III's projects will be in Northern California or Texas, often initially located in ONSET Ventures' facilities in Menlo Park or Austin. The incubation process requires that the project team and the general partners work together closely on a frequent basis. Locating the project in or near ONSET Ventures' offices facilitates this interaction.

Key Success Factors

To be successful, a seed-stage venture capital fund must

- be exposed to a flow of high-quality investment opportunities,
- be selective in its investments,

EXHIBIT 1 | (continued)

- provide focus, guidance, and managerial assistance to its seed projects,
- have access to capital for follow-on company financings, and
- provide ongoing company monitoring and guidance.

ONSET III has the expertise, commitment, and structure to address these requirements.

Exposure to Investment Opportunities

ONSET III will have several advantages in exposure to high-quality investment opportunities:

- The partners of the General Partner have developed relationships with entrepreneurs and executives throughout Silicon Valley through their association with existing and prior portfolio companies, other venture capital funds, and prior employment at leading high-technology companies. In addition, the partners have established strong deal flow over the past three years in Austin, Texas, and are well positioned to take advantage of this burgeoning new center of entrepreneurial activity.
- Investment opportunities are frequently referred by Paul Gomory, a premier executive recruiter that maintains extensive contacts with entrepreneurial companies and the best executive talent.
- David Kelley, as president of IDEO, a prominent product design firm, and as a professor at Stanford University, has a broad network of entrepreneurial contacts that offer investment opportunities.
- ONSET Ventures' location in Silicon Valley, where more venture-backed companies are formed each year than in any other region, results in high exposure to entrepreneurial activity.
- ONSET Ventures' unique position as the first Silicon Valley venture firm to establish an office in Austin, Texas, positions the firm to be a leader in an environment with strong high-technology job formation and entrepreneurship, and limited early-stage capital availability.
- Fewer venture firms compete for the seed stage investments on which ONSET III will focus.

Careful Selection of Investments

Selecting which companies to invest in may seem an obvious critical factor in the success of seed stage venture capital funds. However, it requires looking beyond the conspicuous flaws and defects of seed-stage projects to understand their potential, given adequate development, for becoming successful companies. This potential is resident in relatively few opportunities. ONSET I and ONSET II both invested in less than one percent of the potential opportunities presented to them—a model of selectivity that ONSET III intends to continue.

Because uncertainties surround early-stage investments, ONSET III will often follow an incremental investment policy. That is, when a project shows promise, the Partnership will often move the project team into ONSET Ventures' incubation facility without a seed-financing commitment. The partners will then work closely with the entrepreneurs exploring the dimensions of the opportunity. When both the entrepreneurs and ONSET III are satisfied with the definition of the opportunity and have a clear understanding of what needs to be accomplished during the incubation process, the Partnership will commit to seed-round financing. Often this commitment will involve incremental funding contingent upon accomplishing agreed-upon milestones.

Focus, Guidance, and Managerial Assistance

Successful entrepreneurs generally have an overriding sense of optimism, self-confidence, drive, and creativity. They are rarely individuals of broad general-managerial background.

(continued)

EXHIBIT 1 | Excerpts from ONSET III Investment Memorandum (*continued*)

They are frequently technically oriented, possessing a particular insight. They infrequently appreciate marketing and other functional specialties necessary for company success. This is particularly true in seed-stage situations.

To increase a seed-stage company's chance of success, it is necessary to provide constructive counsel and value-added support during the early months of a new company's development. Typically, the Partnership will devote the equivalent of one full-time partner to working with each company. This intensive commitment limits the number of investments ONSET III will make each year but increases the likelihood that each investment will succeed.

Access to Capital for Follow-on Company Financings

Seed-stage companies often fail because they lack the ability to attract first-round financing after the seed investment. ONSET III's incubation approach in itself lessens this risk, but beyond this, ONSET Ventures also offers transitional support. ONSET III will introduce its projects to other venture capital firms at an early stage, often before making its own investment commitment. This facilitates first-round financing by creating an understanding of the needs and desires of the later-stage investors and recognition of the need to adjust the incubation plan accordingly The partners' knowledge of the characteristics of attractive first-round investments and the partners' contacts in the venture community lay the groundwork for a smooth transition to later financings. In fact, more than 40 different venture capital organizations have invested in the later-stage financings of ONSET Ventures–led seed stage companies.

Ongoing Company Monitoring and Guidance

Beyond the seed stage, companies still face developmental hurdles: sales ramp-up, quality manufacturing, subsequent product research and development, team building, reaching profitability, and evaluating additional financing options. ONSET III is committed to building strong boards of directors for its companies, thereby increasing the developing companies' chances of success.

ONSET III intends to maintain a significant ownership position in its companies and to contribute to their later-stage development through active participation on the boards of directors The partners have participated in the financing and later-stage guidance and monitoring of nearly 50 companies over the last 10 years.

Prior Funds

ONSET I

ONSET I is a $30 million fund formed in late 1989 for the purpose of investing in high-technology companies with a special focus on incubating seed stage investments. The general partner, ONSET Management, L.P., is managed by Rob Kuhling, Terry Opdendyk and NEA as general partners. David Kelley is a special limited partner of the general partner. The investors of ONSET I include institutions and successful entrepreneurs and other individuals. (A list of the institutional investors can be found in **Exhibit 1, Appendix D**.)

As of March 31, 1997, ONSET I had invested $22,467,635 in 20 companies. Of these companies, 8 are medical technology–related, primarily drug delivery and medical devices, and 12 are in information technology with a software focus.

ONSET I is over seven years old and the portfolio is mature, with distributions of $60,200,000 and a fund IRR of 26% at year end 1996. To date, eight companies are public, six have been acquired and several others are prospects for 1997–1998 acquisitions or IPOs.

EXHIBIT 1 | (continued)

The following table summarizes ONSET I's IRR performance since inception in 1989:

ONSET I Annualized Cumulative Internal Rate of Return								
	1989	1990	1991	1992	1993	1994	1995	1996
Fund	−38.12%	−23.67%	−12.77%	1.05%	5.10%	19.11%	26.62%	26.30%
Limited Partner	−38.12%	−23.67%	−12.77%	0.70%	3.87%	15.10%	22.26%	21.72%

ONSET II

ONSET II is a $67 million fund formed in late 1994 for the purpose of investing in high-technology companies with a special focus on incubating seed-stage investments. The general partner, ONSET II Management, L.P., is managed by Rob Kuhling, Terry Opdendyk and Tom Winter as general partners. David Kelley, Alexis Lakes, Darlene Mann and NEA are special limited partners of the general partner. The investors of ONSET II include institutions and successful entrepreneurs and other individuals. (A list of the institutional investors can be found in **Exhibit 1, Appendix D.**)

As of May 9, 1997, ONSET II had invested or reserved for investment $43,214,765 in 19 companies. Of these companies, 7 are medical technology–related, primarily medical devices and drug delivery, and 12 are in information technology with a focus on software, services and communications. ONSET II was the initial venture investor in 8 of the companies; 14 of these were at the seed/start-up stage when ONSET Ventures made its first investment. Fourteen of the companies are located in California, mostly in the San Francisco Bay Area.

The following table summarizes ONSET II IRR performance since inception in 1994. (Given the early stage of development reflected by the majority of companies represented in the ONSET II portfolio, these numbers should be viewed as highly variable and not necessarily indicative of the long-term performance of the fund.)

ONSET II Annualized Cumulative Internal Rate of Return		
	1994	1995	1996
Fund	−14.26%	−36.32%	15.49%
Limited Partner	−14.26%	−36.32%	11.69%

ONSET I vs. ONSET II Comparison

The following graph compares the annualized cumulative Internal Rate of Return (IRR) of ONSET I vs. ONSET II for the same period within each fund. Note that the ONSET II IRR was substantially greater than was the ONSET I IRR at the same point (Year 2) of the fund's life.

ONSET, a California Limited Partnership ("OLP")

OLP, a company incubator, was founded in 1984 with $3 million from three venture-fund limited partners and $2 million from 31 individual investors. OLP was structured to serve as a "feeder" fund to provide later-stage financing opportunities to the venture-fund limited partners and tax advantages to the individual investors.

While OLP was not a traditional venture fund, its focus was to establish the ONSET Ventures investment approach of creating and investing in seed-stage, high-technology companies lacking the completeness necessary to attract capital from traditional venture investors. It was in

(continued)

EXHIBIT 1 | Excerpts from ONSET III Investment Memorandum (*continued*)

OLP that the ONSET Ventures' incubation process was developed and refined (see "The Incubation Process"). At this time, the fund is inactive, with one final security awaiting liquidity.

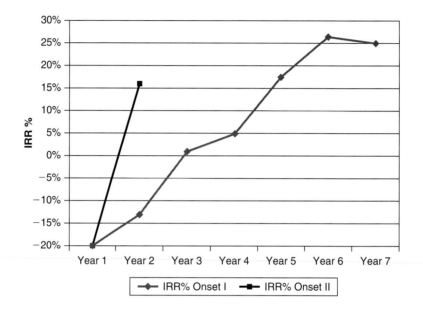

OFFERING DESCRIPTION

The Offering

ONSET III expects to raise $80 million through investment in limited partnership interests by selected investors who are capable of assuming the substantial financial risks and illiquidity of venture capital investing. The initial closing may be held when at least $60 million of committed capital has been raised. ONSET III may elect to continue this offering on the same terms and conditions for up to 12 months after the initial closing. The General Partner may increase the amount of this offering to a maximum of $95 million of Limited Partner interest.

The General Partner will contribute an amount equal to 1% of the total capital of the Partnership on the same draw-down schedule as the Limited Partners. The General Partner's capital contributions may be made either in cash or by an interest-bearing full recourse promissory note.

Allocation of Income, Gains and Losses

Generally, all income, gains and losses will be allocated 75% to all Partners based on the respective amounts of their capital commitments and 25% to the General Partner. However, if the Partnership has cumulative net realized losses, all income, gains and losses will be allocated to the Partners based on the respective amounts of their capital commitments. Distributions of securities to the Partners will be treated as sales for the purpose of calculating realized gains and losses.

EXHIBIT 1 | (continued)

Investor Committee

The Partnership will have an Investor Committee consisting of at least three members chosen by the General Partner from among the Limited Partners, which will serve at the discretion of the General Partner.

The functions of the Investor Committee will be to confer with the General Partner as to the conduct of the business generally, without advising as to the merits of Partnership investments, and to: (l) review the annual operating budget of the General Partner; (2) review certain changes in the fee paid to the General Partner and approve changes in the percentages of such fee allocated among the ONSET Ventures' partnerships; (3) review certain distributions authorized by the General Partner; (4) approve certain guarantees for the Partnership on be-half of its portfolio companies; (5) approve the values established by the General Partner for portfolio assets and liabilities; and (6) resolve questions relating to certain potential conflicts of interest between the Partnership and the General Partner or between the Partnership and ONSET I or ONSET II, including an investment by the Partnership in a portfolio company of ONSET I or ONSET II. All actions taken by the Investor Committee must be authorized by a majority of the Committee members.

EXHIBIT 1 | Excerpts from ONSET III Investment Memorandum (*continued*)

Appendix C Resumes

Robert F. Kuhling, Jr.

Work Experience

1987–Present	ONSET Ventures, Menlo Park, CA

General Partner, ONSET III (in formation)
General Partner, ONSET II
General Partner, ONSET I
General Partner, ONSET, a California Limited Partnership
Special Partner, New Enterprise Associates V, VI & VII
Special Partner, Chemicals and Materials Enterprise Associates. L.P.

1985–1987	SUN MICROSYSTEMS, Mountain View, CA

Director, Design Automation Marketing Group. Started up and managed Sun's entry into the design engineering markets. Responsible for marketing, technical support and sales development.

1983–1985	CALMA COMPANY (a General Electric Subsidiary), Milpitas, CA

Vice-President, Electronic Design Automation Products & Marketing. Responsible for Calma's $100 million electronic CAE and CAD/CAM business including Product Development (R&D), Marketing and Sales Development.
Director, Microelectronics Marketing.
Director, Business Development.

1980–1983	THE BOSTON CONSULTING GROUP, Boston, MA and Menlo Park, CA

Case Team Leader. Managed teams of consultants developing business strategies for U.S. and international corporations. Specialized in high-technology assignments.

1972-1978	THE CHARTER COMPANY, Jacksonville, FL and Houston, TX

Assistant Vice President. Worked in several Charter divisions, including real estate finance, commercial banking and petroleum exploration but primarily in commercial real estate development.

Education

1980	HARVARD BUSINESS SCHOOL

Master of Business Administration, with Distinction

1971	HAMILTON COLLEGE

A.B. with Honors, Economics

EXHIBIT 1 | (continued)

Appendix C (continued)

Darlene K. Mann

Work Experience

1996–Present	ONSET Ventures, Menlo Park, CA Venture Partner, ONSET III (in formation) Venture Partner, ONSET II
1995–1996	AVANTOS PERFORMANCE SYSTEMS, Emeryville, CA Vice President, Marketing and Sales. Managed all sales, marketing, and technical support functions for start-up software company in the Human Resources and Electronic Performance Support Systems market.
1993–1995	BROADVISION, INC., Los Altos, CA Vice President, Marketing and co-founder. Responsible for all marketing activities for next-generation electronic commerce systems provider.
1993	PARAMOUNT COMMUNICATIONS, Sunnyvale, CA Director, Product Marketing. Managed marketing staff and business planning functions for multimedia educational products representing $80M in revenue.
1989–1993	VERITY, INC., Sunnyvale, CA Director, Product Marketing. Managed product management, marketing and sales development activities during growth of business from start-up through $20 mm in revenue for recognized market leader in text retrieval applications.
1986–1989	LOTUS DEVELOPMENT CORPORATION, Cambridge, MA Product Planning Manager, Lotus Notes. Responsible for product management and market research teams for first product in the "Groupware" category. Manager, Inside Sales and Customer Support, Information Services Division. Developed and managed inside sales and customer support organizations to support lead generation and leverage performance of direct sales force.
1984–1986	DATA TRANSLATION, INC., Marlborough, MA Senior Technical Sales Representative. Managed major accounts and OEM sales at leading vendor of analog to digital conversion and image processing products.

Education

1982	UNIVERSITY OF CALIFORNIA AT SAN DIEGO, REVELLE COLLEGE Bachelor of Arts with Honors, Psychology

(continued)

EXHIBIT 1 | Excerpts from ONSET III Investment Memorandum (*continued*)

Appendix C (*continued*)

Terry L. Opdendyk

Work Experience

1984–Present	ONSET Ventures, Menlo Park, CA

General Partner, ONSET III (in formation)
General Partner, ONSET II
General Partner, ONSET I
General Partner, ONSET, a California Limited Partnership
Special Partner, New Enterprise Associates V, VI & VII
Special Partner, Chemicals and Materials Enterprise Associates. L.P.

1980–1984	VISICORP, San Jose, CA

President, Chief Operating Officer. Responsible for all company activities, organization and P&L during the growth of the business from a start-up to a $40 million leader in the personal computer software industry.

1973–1980	INTEL CORPORATION, Santa Clara, CA

Several responsibilities including:

Co-Manager of the Development Systems Business Segment. Responsible for the P&L, marketing, manufacturing and R&D of microcomputer system products.

Manager, Computer Systems Engineering. Responsible for microprocessor architecture and hardware and software systems R & D in California, Oregon, Arizona and Israel.

Manager of the Corporate Human Resources Business Segment.

1970–1973	HEWLETT-PACKARD, INC., Cupertino, CA

Project Manager/Member of Technical Staff. Responsible for design and development of systems software products. Also responsible for corporate software strategy and methodology for software management.

Education

1972	STANFORD UNIVERSITY

Master of Science. Computer Science

1970	MICHIGAN STATE UNIVERSITY, The Honors College

Bachelor of Science with High Honors, Computer Science

EXHIBIT 1 | (*continued*)

Appendix C (*continued*)

Thomas E. Winter

Work Experience

1993–Present   ONSET Ventures, Menlo Park, CA

General Partner, ONSET III (in formation)
General Partner, ONSET II
Consultant, ONSET I
Special Partner, New Enterprise Associates V11

1991–1993   BIRD MEDICAL TECHNOLOGIES INC., Palm Springs, CA

President, Chief Executive Officer and Director. Returned company to profitability, positive cash flow, re-structured bank debt and re-staffed senior management team during turnaround of this $50 million manufacturer of respiratory care equipment and disposables.

1983–1991   BURR EGAN DELEAGE & COMPANY, San Francisco & Costa Mesa, CA

General Partner of the general partner, of partnerships managed by Burr Egan Deleage & Co investing in early-stage high-technology enterprises within the information science and biomedical products fields, including Alta III, L.P., Alta IV, L.P., Alta Subordinated Debt, L.P., and Alta Subordinated Debt II.

1981–1983   BURROUGHS CORPORATION, Detroit, MI

Executive Vice President Finance and Director. Responsible for all financial and administrative activities.

1966–1981   XEROX CORPORATION, Rochester, NY and Stamford, CT

Numerous assignments combining staff and operating responsibility including:

- Vice President Operations/Information Products Group
- Corporate Controller
- Vice President Finance/Information Systems Group
- Director Distribution/Information Systems Group
- Controller & Director Planning/Research & Engineering Division
- Director Pricing & Strategy Analysis

1963–1966   AEROJET GENERAL CORPORATION, Sacramento, CA

Various engineering positions in test and project management.

Education

GEORGIA INSTITUTE OF TECHNOLOGY

1963   Master of Science, Industrial Management

1959   Bachelor of Science, Aeronautical Engineering

EXHIBIT 1 | Excerpts from ONSET III Investment Memorandum (*continued*)

Appendix D

INSTITUTIONAL LIMITED PARTNERS OF ONSET I

Ameritech Pension Trust
Computrol Limited, BVI
Crossroads Providence Limited Partnership
Delaware State Employees Retirement Fund
The Ford Family
Henry J. Kaiser Family Foundation
Hughes Aircraft Retirement Plans
The James Irvine Foundation
Kansas Public Employees Retirement System
Metropolitan Life Insurance Company
Meyer Memorial Trust
NED Delaware Co, Ltd.
Oberlin College
St. Paul Fire and Marine Insurance Company
Technology Funding Venture Partners IV
T. Rowe Price Associates

INSTITUTIONAL LIMITED PARTNERS OF ONSET II

The Casey Family Program
Computrol Limited, BVI
Delaware State Employees Retirement Fund
The Ford Foundation
Hitachi Chemical Research
Hughes Aircraft Retirement Plans
The James Irvine Foundation
Henry J. Kaiser Family Foundation
Ewing Marion Kauffmann Foundation
Meyer Memorial Trust
Nippon Enterprise Development Corp.
Oberlin College
Pratt Street Ventures IX, LLC
Prime New Ventures Management, L.P.
Scinet Development & Holdings, Inc.
St. Paul Fire and Marine Insurance Company
United States-Japan Foundation
Ziff Investors Partnership, L.P. II

EXHIBIT 2 | Summary Statistics on Venture Capital Industry—Mid-1997

Most Active Venture Firms (ranked by number of 1996 investments)

Venture Firm	1995	1996	1st Half 1997
1. New Enterprise Associates	108	105	41
2. Robertson, Stephens & Company L.P.	35	63	32
3. Norwest Venture Capital	62	58	NA
4. Oak Investment Partners	NA	52	39
5. Hambrecht & Quist Venture Partners	52	51	40
6. Sprout Group	29	51	NA
7. Accel Partners	32	49	NA
8. Sequoia Capital	NA	46	NA
9. U.S. Venture Partners	46	46	32
10. Mayfield Fund	44	45	NA
11. St. Paul Venture Capital Inc.	33	45	31
12. Institutional Venture Partners	NA	44	NA
13. Burr, Egan, Deleage & Company	58	43	NA
14. Enterprise Partners	NA	42	NA
15. Greylock Management Corporation	NA	42	NA
16. Kleiner Perkins Caufield & Byers	66	39	NA
17. Bessemer Venture Partners	30	37	29
18. Crosspoint Venture Partners	25	37	NA
19. OneLiberty Ventures	39	37	NA
20.[a] Advent International Corporation	NA	36	39
20.[a] Dominion Ventures	NA	36	NA

[a]In a tie for 20th place, both Advent and Dominion had 36 investments in 1996.
Source: *The Private Equity Analyst*, February 1997

Venture Capital Activity 1995 thru 6/30/97

		Investment[a] ($ billions)	Number of Deals	Average per Deal ($ millions)	Median Pre-Money Valuation ($ millions)
1995	Q1	1.1	276	4.0	NA
	Q2	1.8	436	4.1	NA
	Q3	1.6	407	3.9	NA
	Q4	2.1	424	5.0	NA
Total		6.6	1,543	4.3	
1996	Q1	2.3	489	4.7	12.2
	Q2	3.0	584	5.1	14.1
	Q3	2.3	519	4.4	10.9
	Q4	2.5	571	4.4	12.9
Total		10.1	2,163	4.7	
1997	Q1	2.4	586	4.1	12.0
	Q2	3.2	684	4.7	14.9
Total	1st Half	5.6	1,270	4.4	

[a]VC investment into portfolio companies.
Source: *Private Equity Analyst,* August 1997 and Venture Edge 3Q, 1997

EXHIBIT 3 | TallyUp Operating Plan—Excerpts

Seed-Round Operating Plans	
Responsibility/Task	**Deadline**
A) *Office of the President*	
Achieve Objectives for First-round Financing	Q4 97
Objectives for first-round financing, planned in October of 1997, include:	
• Hire key employees to achieve seed plan	
• Bring product to "trial" stage	
• Sign 3-5 "development partners" with expectation of installing two paying partners in target markets	
• Significant progress toward signing one key marketing partner	
• Develop and validate business model, including market size, pricing, and sales and distribution	
• Develop business plan and presentation for first-round financing	
Develop and Validate Business Model	Jun. 97
Develop Critical HR Policies & Guidelines	Feb. 97
Recruit Core Team	Ongoing
Establish Product Advisory Board	Q3 97
B) *Engineering*	
Deliver Sales Prototype	Apr. 97
Complete Product Design and Roadmap	Apr. 97
Deliver Development Partner Release	Oct. 97
C) *Marketing*	
Prove a Viable Attainable Market	Jun. 97
Complete Corporate Identity	Jan. 97
Complete Sales Collateral	Jan., Apr., Nov. 97
Assist Development with Product Direction	Mar. 97
Deliver Marketing Requirements Document	May 97
D) *Sales and Business Development*	
Sign 2 Development Partners in Key Markets	Jun. 97
Prove Sales and Distribution Model	Jun. 97
Progress Towards Signing Strategic Marketing Partner	Sep. 97
Sign 2 Strategic Marketing Partners	Q4 97
Develop Lead Tracking System	Feb. 97
Hire VP of Sales	Q4 97
E) *Finances and Operations*	
Establish Financial and Board Reporting Systems	Jan. 97
Retain Payroll, Benefit, and Audit Services	Feb. 97
Secure Office Space and Office Equipment	Mar. 97
F) *Staffing*	
Hire According to Plan	Ongoing

E Ink: Financing Growth

"We signed it!" Russ Wilcox exclaimed to James Iuliano over his cellular phone. Wilcox, E Ink's Vice President of Business Development, was referring to the meeting he had just come out of with executives from JC Penney. It was March 4, 1999 and JC Penney's managers had just agreed to test E Ink's latest prototype large-area display signs in 10 stores located in four different U.S. cities. The JC Penney deal was significant because it gave E Ink its first commercial forum in which to test its revolutionary electronic ink technology.

The timing of Wilcox's call could not have been better. Iuliano, President and CEO of E Ink, was in his Cambridge, Massachusetts office preparing for his upcoming meeting with Doug Eller, the Chief Financial Officer of Newstime Publishing. The purpose of Iuliano's meeting was to raise a portion of the $20 million needed for E Ink's second-round funding. Wilcox's accomplishment with JC Penney represented the company's first commercial deal and could only improve E Ink's attractiveness to Eller. While Iuliano was excited by the leverage Wilcox had just provided, he could not help but wonder if he was making a mistake by bringing this investment opportunity to Newstime Publishing. After all, E Ink still had $9 million in the bank from its $15.8 million first round of financing ten months earlier. Perhaps more importantly, E Ink had generated an almost unprecedented level of "buzz" regarding its electronic ink technology. Even without a released product, E Ink had already been featured in over 30 publications ranging from *Fortune*'s list of "Cool Companies 1998" to the *L.A. Times* to *Popular Science,* and interest continued to build. The excitement surrounding E Ink had created a unique financing problem for Iuliano—how to politely turn away the numerous venture capitalists, technology companies and publishers who wanted to participate in the current round of financing.

The interest in E Ink stemmed from the vast potential of the company's electronic ink technology. Iuliano, Wilcox and the rest of the E Ink team had their sights set on revolutionizing the way people viewed information. The technology would hopefully one day result in an ability to print electronic ink on virtually any surface, enabling people to change displayed information through the use of a paging-type network. If successful, E Ink's technology could be used for a seemingly endless number of applications such as embedding updateable maps on the sleeves of hiking jackets, creating more "readable" displays on cellular phones and enabling a fleet of billboards to change messages on command. E Ink's technology could alter existing information display mechanisms as well as enable information displays that did not currently exist. Despite the numerous possibilities for the technology, E Ink had fixed its sights on "radio paper," an actual book or newspaper printed with electronic ink and able to receive information wirelessly, as the company's end objective. Iuliano's upcoming meeting with publishing executive Doug Eller highlighted E Ink's commitment to creating a radio paper that would replace the traditional printed newspaper.

Background

The Idea

Electronic ink was the brainchild of Joe Jacobson, a professor at the Massachusetts Institute of Technology's (MIT) Media Laboratory. During the summer of 1995, Jacobson was enjoying the California sun at a beach near Palo Alto when he was confronted with a practical problem that formed the genesis of electronic ink. Having just completed the book he was reading, Jacobson had two choices: he could pack up and head home to get another book, or he could bake in the sun with nothing to read. This simple dilemma spurred Jacobson into action. Rather than choosing another book, he began to sketch out possibilities for creating a single book that could morph into other books by changing the ink on the page. Jacobson, having recently completed his postdoctoral work in quantum mechanics at Stanford University, commented on his early vision of electronic ink:

> The idea of an electronic book seemed like an exciting challenge. I knew it had to be done on paper or something pretty similar to paper. People are so used to reading from real paper that the whole notion of using some type of liquid crystal display didn't appeal to me. Second, it needed to use very little power so you could eliminate the need for heavy battery packs or other power sources. Lastly, it needed to be crisp in appearance—just like regular ink on paper. Taking these factors into account, I defined the parameters more narrowly. The electronic book must have 200 or more pages printed on real paper, each capable of displaying information. It must look as good as real ink. The cost per page must be comparable to traditional publishing costs. And the power required to run the book must be sufficiently low that the entire power source could be contained in the spine of the book at almost zero weight.

With rough parameters for electronic ink outlined in his mind, Jacobson turned his attention to various technologies that he could employ to meet his specifications for an electronic book:

> I had experience working with a type of vinyl that could conduct electricity. I figured if you could cover a sheet of paper with millions of two-toned conductive particles you could then create images by carefully applying an electric charge. You could, theoretically, alter the content of each page by simply adjusting the flow of electricity across the page.

The Theory of Electronic Ink

With a vision in mind of what his end product would be, Jacobson came to the MIT Media Lab seeking the best way to develop electronic ink. He formed a team of students that included J.D. Albert and Barrett Comiskey. The two MIT seniors, under the direction of Jacobson, embraced an "Edisonian Approach" in developing the technology. Unlike traditional scientific work where only one variable at a time was modified with results carefully recorded, Albert and Comiskey adopted a more ad hoc approach of changing multiple variables with great frequency in an effort to home in on a successful combination that would yield the required properties for electronic ink.

Near the end of 1996, after countless hours in the laboratory experimenting across scientific disciplines, Albert and Comiskey produced dramatic, though preliminary, results. Their efforts had yielded a technological foundation for an electronic ink that drew from two typically unrelated fields: electrophoresis and microencapsulation. Electrophoresis is the motion of a charged particle in response to an electric field. It could be used to create an electronic image display by using white particles suspended in a black liquid: when the particles are floating on top the viewer sees white, but when the particles are submerged the viewer sees black. Based on electrophoresis, an array of electrical fields such as a pixel array could move particles up and down to create white and black in a pattern. This formed the basis for making images with true black and white color. The question that remained was how to hold the liquid onto a flexible piece of paper? The answer was microcapsules: hollow shells about the size of a grain of laser toner that could be filled with the electrophoretic liquid and fabricated in bulk. The shells could then be printed onto just about any surface, just like traditional ink. A pattern of pixel electrodes could also be printed using conductive inks, completing the electronic display (see **Exhibit 1** for a schematic drawing of electronic ink). Thus, the technology allowed for fabricating thin, flexible, low cost displays with significant economies of scale.

Liquid crystal displays and cathode ray tubes (CRTs), the two most popular forms of electronic displays, suffered from numerous drawbacks that had limited their ability to displace paper for markets such as books and newspapers. The advantages of electronic ink versus traditional display technologies were dramatic. First, electronic ink would be made of the same pigments and dyes as ink on paper. As a result, it would have the superior viewing characteristics of paper such as high contrast, wide viewing angle, and a paper white background. Second, electronic ink could be printed on almost any surface ranging from plastic to metal to paper and could cover large areas inexpensively. Third, the ink was capable of holding its image even after the power was turned off, just like ink on paper, and was legible enough in low light that a backlight would rarely be needed. The team felt this would significantly extend the battery life for portable devices. Lastly, the process was highly scaleable, suggesting that electronic ink could catch up on a cost basis with more mature technologies.

Jacobson and his team dreamed of the day when they could beam digital information from a wireless transmitter directly to a sheet of electronic ink that incorporated a printed antenna and processor. This would allow people to read whatever they wanted, whenever they wanted, wherever they were. Achieving this ambitious goal would require another three to five years of well-funded R&D in both ink technology and pixel circuitry.

The Company

By early 1997, it was clear that electronic ink held strong commercial potential if sufficient resources and passion were committed. At this stage, Jerry Rubin, Chairman of the "News in the future" forum at the MIT Media Lab and a veteran of the publishing and information management industries, offered to help the team incorporate a company to pursue electronic ink and achieve the ultimate vision of radio paper. Together, Jacobson and Rubin brought Russ Wilcox, a 1995 graduate of Harvard Business School, on board to lead the effort to raise capital. By April 2, 1997 E Ink was incorporated and Wilcox was hard at work on a business plan.

Armed with a potentially revolutionary technology, Wilcox was able to quickly raise a seed round of $1.7 million in convertible debt from three local venture capitalists. In addition to the venture money, Wilcox arranged for a $2 million capital equipment credit facility with Imperial Bank. Wilcox then devoted his time to recruiting both scientists and managers while Comiskey and Albert built an R&D lab and began to move the technology forward. Wilcox also negotiated term sheets for a first equity round that would convert the $1.7 million in debt and add $14.1 million in new capital from the venture capitalists as well as four major corporations (see **Exhibit 2** for a list of equity investors). By May of 1998, the equity round was closed and by October 1998, E Ink had a team of 22 people in place focused on advancing the technology.

The surge in employees was highlighted by the arrival of Iuliano and an array of high profile scientists (see **Exhibit 3** for the management team and board of directors' biographies). With the nucleus of a team together, Wilcox assumed the role of Vice President for Business Development and Jacobson refocused on his teaching efforts at MIT while continuing to serve as a consultant to E Ink.

The technical efforts quickly produced results. By March of 1999, the scientists at the company's laboratory had increased the brightness and contrast of the display by a factor of five. Additionally, reflectivity increased from 15% to 35% while switching voltage dropped from 300 volts to 90 volts. Prototypes increased in size from 3 square inches to 25 square inches. The progress of the technology was highlighted by E Ink's production of the world's first all-printed flexible reflective display. While the technology was evolving, Iuliano moved aggressively to protect E Ink's technological progress via a series of patents. By the time of Eller's visit, Iuliano and his team had succeeded in acquiring, filing or licensing a large number of patents including a license from MIT that gave the university a small ownership stake in E Ink in exchange for rights to the patents filed by Jacobson, Albert and Comiskey.

The technological improvements had made the company's prototypes sufficiently attractive that E Ink began to receive requests for shipment from potential customers. Strong customer interest and the advancement of the technology led Iuliano to aim for commercial readiness of the technology in the form of large-area retail displays in some form by the end of 1999. The deal with JC Penney represented a significant step forward in achieving Iuliano's goal for retail displays.

The Critical Path

E Ink's founders were driven by a desire to answer a single question: How could E Ink provide all of the benefits of digital content yet retain the pleasures of reading in bed, browsing a newspaper on the subway or thumbing through a magazine on the beach? Attempting to answer this question had set the company on a course to transform one of the world's largest industries: publishing.

While radio paper was the pot of gold at the end of E Ink's rainbow, there were many other potentially distracting and/or profitable applications along the way. E Ink's technology could one day be used to replace almost any display currently in use or to create displays that had never before been possible. In fact, E Ink's original business plan mentioned applications for electronic ink ranging from sneakers that track the number of steps taken to drug dispensers that indicate remaining doses to cereal boxes that scroll during breakfast reading. The media coverage of E Ink's progress regarding the technology had already led to a flood of interest from potential partners such as JC Penney and other large corporations.

The challenge for Iuliano and his team was in pursuing only the opportunities that could generate short-term profitability while also serving to develop the technology along the path of radio paper. Iuliano explained the company's predicament:

> Our stated goal has always been to create radio paper. Having said that, we know that we
> have a long way to go technologically to make radio paper a reality. In the meantime, we
> have a consortium of investors and a continual influx of potential customers and partners
> who all have different views on the best use for electronic ink. In fact, over the past
> 45 weeks, we have had 40 well-known companies visit our offices hoping to use electronic
> ink in some way to improve their business. The challenge for us as an organization is to
> very carefully select only the applications that can advance the technology along the criti-
> cal path towards radio paper. We can't afford to veer off track by pursuing seductive appli-
> cations that have no relevance to our end goal. We really need to be creative in developing
> the technology and disciplined in applying it.

After much analysis and debate, Iuliano had chosen to set E Ink along a well-defined "critical path" towards the ultimate goal of radio paper. The path envisioned by Iuliano would begin with (1) large-area displays, followed by (2) battery-powered flat-panel displays, ending with (3) radio paper. All of these steps represented entry to successively larger markets. The relevant portion of the large-area display market exceeded $600 million. The flat-panel display industry was expected to exceed $25 billion by 2004. The U.S. publishing industry alone exceeded $135 billion in annual revenue. With this critical path in mind, Iuliano attempted to profitably steer the company through a series of obstacles in route to radio paper.

Phase I: Large-Area Displays

E Ink's first commercial venture would be in the large-area display market. Convinced that E Ink needed to produce a "single product for a single market and a single market niche," E Ink's focus would be large-area displays for retail signs, such as the prototypes developed for JC Penney. Large-area displays represented an attractive market for E Ink because the opportunity was "big but with no entrenched gorilla" and a commercially viable product could be launched quickly based on the existing state of the technology.

Technically, electronic ink offered dramatic improvements over other large-area display technologies. While other display technologies were glass-based and did not scale readily to large areas, electronic ink could be economically printed over large areas. The light weight and visual appearance of electronic ink were key advantages over existing technologies.

The market for in-store displays was both large and ripe for improvement (see **Exhibit 4** for market data on large-area displays). LEK Consulting reported that the presence of machine printed signs could raise unit sales by an average of 200% based on a study of 143 different items. Despite the impact of signs, field compliance with prescribed messages for signs was remarkably low. In fact, only 33% of in-store displays conformed to specified requirements and the average lead-time to create a point-of-purchase program and delpoy it to the field was nearly 90 days.

E Ink's ability to incorporate a wireless communications interface such as an embedded pager offered another dramatic improvement versus existing in-store display options. Electronic ink enabled signs could be changed instantly from a central location, thus ensuring field compliance and quick response times. E Ink's technology might also allow retailers and manufacturers to display more intelligent information based on factors such as time of day, demographics and sales trends. In addition to potentially delivering a higher quality product, E Ink also offered a cost advantage. A large two line LED sign would cost a retailer over $2,000 to install. The higher performing E Ink sign of similar dimensions was expected to sell for less than half the price of existing signs once production was ramped up to manufacture signs at a significant scale.

Wilcox, who headed up the Phase I effort for E Ink, estimated that the company could exceed a $20 million revenue run rate within three years. Wilcox also believed that the in-store display business could exceed $100 million in revenue by 2004 if the technology advanced to the point of offering higher resolution and color. To fully take advantage of this opportunity Wilcox estimated E Ink would need to invest $10 to $20 million.

Despite the economic opportunity available in the in-store display market, it was the advancement of E Ink's technology that interested Iuliano the most. Iuliano saw large-area displays as a building-block opportunity. He described the in-store display opportunity from a technology development perspective:

> The product requirements are right in line with our path to create electronic paper. By subjecting ourselves to marketplace demands early in our lifecycle, we can begin to build a customer and market-driven mentality that will serve us well going forward. As we enter the next phases along our critical path, the large-area display product line should be able to make use of all of the progress being made in our core technology.

Phase II: Flat-Panel Displays

Iuliano intended to make flat-panel displays the second step on E Ink's critical path to radio paper. Flat-panel displays had received pervasive acceptance in the marketplace in

FIGURE A | Global Flat-Panel Display Market of Relevance to E Ink
($4.9 billion–$6.9 billion)

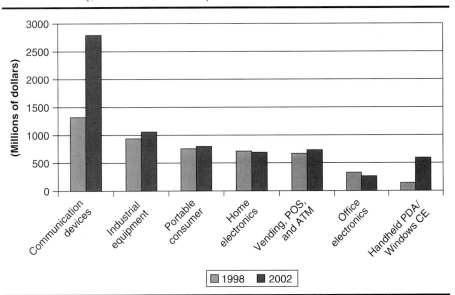

a variety of forms for a number of uses. Most consumer electronics, computers, personal digital assistants and cellular phones utilized flat-panel displays. In 1998, total flat-panel display sales were nearly $14 billion and were expected to grow rapidly to over $25.9 billion by 2004.[1]

E Ink's strategy in the flat-panel display market was to identify specific niches of the market where the attributes of electronic ink created substantial value, permitting the company to price at a premium. Within this market, Iuliano sought applications requiring a high-contrast, low-power, thin and ultra-lightweight display. Such applications covered a wide array of products including communications, portable consumer and handheld devices. The market relevant to E Ink totaled almost $5 billion in 1998 and was expected to grow to almost $7 billion by 2002 (see **Figure A** for flat-panel display market relevant to E Ink).

In researching the flat-panel display market, Iuliano and others had engaged in conversations with managers at two major handheld device companies. These managers indicated a willingness to pay a substantial price premium for electronic ink versions of the typical handheld display, which typically cost $30 for volumes over one million. The premium was due to electronic ink's greater visual appeal and lower power consumption.

Liquid Crystal Displays: The flat-panel display market was currently dominated by several large manufacturers of liquid crystal displays (LCDs). Despite the fact that Sharp, Toshiba and other makers of LCDs had significantly improved the technology

---

[1]All market-size data in this section are from "Flat Information Displays Market & Technology Trends (1998)" by Stanford Resources, Inc.

TABLE A | Electronic Ink versus LCDs

Electronic Ink	Liquid Crystal Displays
Direct color change	Requires a change in light transmission
Looks like real ink on paper	Lacks the appeal of ink on paper
Less than 1 mm thick	Significantly thicker than 1 mm
Flexible	Rigid
Easily scaled to large sizes	Significant price increase when scaled up
Holds image without power drain (bistability)	Requires significant power to hold images
Lightweight	Power supply and glass makes LCDs relatively heavy
Broad temperature range	Does not perform well in low temperatures
Readable in sunlight	Difficult to see in bright light situations
Wide viewing angle	Limited viewing angle
Does not distort under finger pressure	Distorts when pressure is applied

over time (See **Exhibit 5** for LCD technology progress), LCDs had many inherent shortcomings. Active-matrix LCD displays were costly because of the need for an ultra high-precision glass-based thin-film transistor (TFT) backplane for switching. The backlight in many LCD displays consumed significant amounts of power, while reflective LCDs tended to be dim under many viewing conditions. Also, LCDs were produced on rigid substrates.

E Ink's Flat-Panel Display Advantages: Iuliano believed that E Ink's technology offered the best combination of price and performance for flat-panel displays. When comparing the promise of electronic ink versus traditional LCDs, Iuliano pointed out a number of benefits highlighted in **Table A.**

Given the current limitations of LCDs and the large and growing market for flat-panel displays, a number of other display technologies were under development. Microdisplays, organic light emitting diodes (OLEDs), field emission displays, plasma displays, microsphere approaches and further improvements to existing LCDs were all in the works (see **Exhibit 6** for information on competing flat-panel display technologies).

Technological Hurdles: While E Ink had already made tremendous progress in developing its technology for use in large-area displays, the leap to flat-panel displays was still challenging. Specifically, E Ink's scientists needed to combine their electronic ink with a transistor backplane. The backplane would serve as the "circuitry" by which high-resolution images could be changed through the application of a charge to the ink. E Ink was aggressively pursuing several backplane technologies in parallel. E Ink's team had identified both cooperative and proprietary approaches to solving this problem and expected to demonstrate a crude working device sometime in 2000, with product shipping roughly eighteen months later. To successfully launch into the flat-panel display market, Iuliano estimated that E Ink would need an additional $30 to 50 million in financing.

TABLE B | U.S. Publishing Market Revenues in 1998

Market	1998 U.S. Revenues ($ billions)
Newspapers	$60
Professional/Educational Books	30
Consumer Magazines	18
Consumer Books	18
Business Magazines	9
Total	**$135**

Phase III: Publishing

Radio paper had been the ultimate goal at E Ink since Jacobson's reading dilemma at the California beach. The notion of radio paper captivated the minds of employees, investors and the press. If Iuliano and the rest of the team could deliver what they were aiming for, E Ink might revolutionize one of America's largest industries.

The U.S. publishing industry generated over $135 billion in revenue in 1998 (see **Table B** for detailed breakout) from a variety of sources including purchases, subscriptions and advertising. Publishing revenues were surprisingly robust despite the growth of the Internet and the digital economy. For example, even though overall newspaper circulation had been on the decline since 1987, advertising sales were growing at a rate of nearly 8% per year. The growth in advertising rates yielded a forecasted industry revenue figure of over $160 billion by 2001.

Iuliano intended to leverage technological advancements achieved during the development of large-area displays and flat-panel displays to make radio paper a reality. The possible economic rewards associated with replacing much of traditional publishing with electronic ink technology were astronomical. All sectors of publishing could benefit economically from a paper-free distribution model that required $0 for manufacturing, no inventory, and $0 for distribution. Such expenses typically accounted for 20%–40% of publishers' costs, suggesting a multi-billion problem that was E Ink's opportunity.

Newspapers: The newspaper industry was particularly ripe for an electronic ink enabled change. Nearly 65% of Americans read a daily newspaper, with 60 million daily newspapers sold on average each day and an average per-copy readership of 2.3. Thus 138 million people were reached on a daily basis. There were nearly 1,500 daily newspapers in the United States with the top 10 newspaper companies owning 325 newspapers that accounted for 43% of the total daily circulation.

The average circulation revenue per year per subscriber was $175, with an additional $600 per year in per subscriber advertising revenue. Newsprint was the single largest expense for newspapers besides labor. Newsprint prices were volatile, ranging 40% from peak to trough in the space of a single year. This instability added risk to the newspaper business and made profits hard to predict. In 1996, 11.1 million tons of newsprint were purchased by the U.S. newspaper industry at a cost totaling $7 billion. Newsprint alone represented a cost of roughly $115 per subscriber every year. Adding other variable manufacturing and distribution costs, newspapers spent roughly $350 per customer each year.

While Iuliano was unclear as to the specific business model he would employ to exploit the newspaper opportunity, it was clear that the impact of electronic ink could be dramatic (see **Exhibit 7** for economics of the newspaper industry). E Ink might one day offer consumers the ability to have one newspaper where content could be updated and customized instantaneously at the push of a button.

Books: Books represented another large segment of the publishing industry where E Ink's technology might one day become applicable. Jacobson's initial vision was centered on the ability to provide consumers with a single paper based book that could be updated with customized content through a wireless network. While newspapers had not received much attention from other display technology companies, electronic books were not a new phenomenon. In fact, in 1999 several electronic book products were scheduled to be available to consumers (see **Exhibit 8** for a description of competing electronic book products). Additionally, Microsoft was already in the process of devising an industry standard for the operating system that would enable electronic books.

E Ink hoped to differentiate, and eventually dominate, the electronic book industry by utilizing the inherently superior display technology of electronic ink. Iuliano and his team intended to comply with whatever standards were developed and believed that an early electronic ink based book could be ready in two to three years, with the ultimate radio paper version arriving in four or five years.

While the rewards associated with transforming the publishing industry were great, the investment required for success was not inconsequential. Depending on the business model Iuliano could envision needing an additional $50 million to $100 million in capital to fully exploit the publishing opportunity.

Financing

Despite still having $9 million on hand from E Ink's first round of financing, Iuliano was now in the process of raising still more capital. His upcoming meeting with Eller would hopefully yield a portion of the $20 million in funds he hoped to raise during the second full round of financing. The company was consuming nearly $500,000 in cash each month and the burn rate was forecasted to increase to nearly $1 million per month as Iuliano ramped up personnel and development efforts. Iuliano estimated that E Ink would need over $16 million to sustain progress over the next five fiscal quarters. He described his motives and strategy for the company's second-round financing:

> We are trying to revolutionize an entire industry within five years, so going slow is not an option. We have quite a bit of momentum right now in terms of the attention we are receiving and the progress we are making. This is critical and a second round of financing, despite our cash position, is integral to keeping that momentum.
>
> This round of funding will be used primarily to fund the large area display business and second generation technology development. But I can see additional fund-raising over the next few years. It will not be long before we need another $30 to $50 million to launch the flat panel display business. Shortly thereafter, we will require another infusion to grow

our radio paper business. So I intend for this current round of financing to be a mezzanine round that will allow us to prove some things and give us the ability to go public if we so choose.

Sizing a round is about more than money. I am convinced that raising capital more frequently in smaller rounds as the technology is demonstrated will minimize dilution. On the other hand, raising bigger amounts of capital may block out competitors and improve our flexibility. We need to strike the right balance.

Conclusion

Everyone involved with E Ink believed in the company's ability to achieve its end goal of radio paper. To attain this goal, Iuliano knew that he and his team of managers and scientists would need to aggressively maneuver past a series of technological, financial, marketing, manufacturing and human resource obstacles (see **Exhibit 9** for goals and responsibilities of E Ink functional areas). The pace of business for E Ink was extremely aggressive with a 1999 schedule including a move into a new facility, ramping up production of large-area displays, more than doubling the number of in-house scientists, achieving demonstrable progress in the area of transistor backplanes and raising a second round of funding.

While the critical path to success was both disciplined and well thought out, Iuliano knew there were hundreds of things that could go wrong. In particular, Iuliano was focused on choosing the right partners for both financing and technology development. As he prepared for Eller's arrival, he contemplated the journey ahead:

While we have a lot of people interested in partnering with us, we must be very careful in choosing the right partners. Financing in particular is going to be very important as we will need a lot of capital in a relatively short period of time to achieve our goals. Our current investors are very valuable, but their resources are limited and we can't count on them to finance all of our efforts.

I spend a lot of time thinking about who the right investors are for this opportunity. Venture capitalists are capable of moving very quickly, which is a positive, but it is not clear to me what new VC's will add above and beyond what our current venture capital investors provide. Corporate investors might also be attractive, but they also have drawbacks. Chemistry companies might give us valuable assistance in our R&D efforts while sign companies could speed up the development and implementation of our large area display business. Down the road, handheld device manufacturers and publishers could prove to be invaluable in achieving our Phase II and Phase III objectives. The problem with corporate investors is that they tend to move cautiously and they may want to tie their investments to specific rights and restrictions that would limit our flexibility.

Getting to radio paper is not going to be easy and there is not much room for error. We need to make the right decisions in so many areas. Who do we partner with for financing and technology development? Can we beat competing technologies to market? How will the company's culture evolve as we grow so quickly? What will our business model look like as we move along the "critical path"? All of these questions represent inflection points in the growth of this business and the repercussions of making the wrong decisions could be disastrous.

EXHIBIT 1 | Schematic Drawing of Electronic Ink

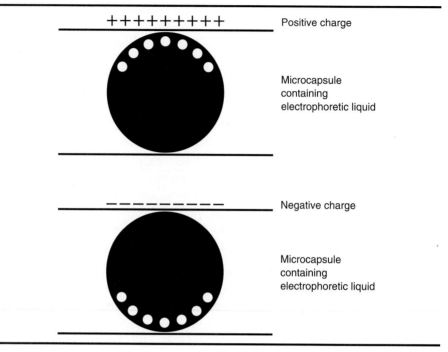

Positive charge

Microcapsule
containing
electrophoretic liquid

Negative charge

Microcapsule
containing
electrophoretic liquid

EXHIBIT 2 | E Ink's First-Round Financing as of March 1999[2]

E Ink was funded by a $15.8 million first round of equity that included the following investors:

Applied Technology*: Appled Technology, a venture capital firm founded in 1983 with more than $80 million in capital under management, maintains offices in Lexington, MA; Austin, TX; and Menlo Park, CA. Focused on early-stage high-tech companies, it offers a unique framework for maximizing investment returns by coupling an experienced management team with both corporate partners and academic experts. The Partnership is actively investing from its third fund with investments in 32 companies to date.

Atlas Venture*: Venture capital firm focusing on information technology and life sciences with offices in Boston, Menlo Park, Amsterdam, London and Munich. The firm manages over $850 million with over $400 million committed from the most recent fund formed in 1999. Since its inception in 1980, Atlas Venture has funded more than 200 companies. Of these companies, 39 have successfully completed initial public offerings, 76 have been acquired and 81 are still developing.

---

[2]Information on investors taken from the websites of the respective companies or was supplied by E Ink management.

EXHIBIT 2 | (continued)

Creavis GmbH: Headquartered in Marl, Germany, Creavis is a wholly owned subsidiary of Degussa-Huels. Degussa Huels is one of the world's largest specialty chemical companies. Creavis specializes in investing in and developing innovative products with a heavy reliance on chemistry.

The Hearst Corporation: The Hearst Corporation is one of the nation's largest diversified communications companies. Its major interests include magazine, newspaper and business publishing, cable networks, television and radio broadcasting, Internet businesses, television production and distribution, newspaper features distribution, and real estate.

Interpublic Group of Companies, Inc.: Interpublic Group specializes in advertising and communication services. IPG operating companies include McCann-Erickson WorldGroup, Ammirati Puris Lintas, The Lowe Group and Western International Media.

Motorola, Inc.*: Motorola is a global company specializing in providing integrated communications and embedded electronic solutions. Motorola is a leader in software-enhanced wireless telephone, two way radio, messaging and satellite communications products and systems. Motorola also offers networking and Internet access products.

Solstice Capital**: Solstice Capital is a private venture capital partnership formed in 1995 to invest in seed and early-stage private companies. The partnership oversees the investment of $22.75 million of committed capital and has invested in 20 portfolio companies. The basic strategy of the Fund is to identify companies which are positioned to capitalize on major change factors. Solstice believes that a number of long term trends such as concern for the environment, clean water, whole foods, and quality of life create opportunities for new companies. The primary factors which are determinants of success for investment are quality of management, technology advantage, and market positioning.

*Received a position on the E Ink Board of Directors.

**Received observer rights on the E Ink Board of Directors.

EXHIBIT 3 | E Ink Management Team as of March 1999

James P. Iuliano, President and CEO, is also a member of the board of directors. Iuliano was recruited to develop and implement the strategy for commercializing electronic ink. Prior to joining E Ink, Iuliano was president, director and CEO of Molecular Devices Corp. of Sunnyvale, CA (NASDAQ: MDCC), an analytical instrumentation company in the life sciences market. At Molecular Devices, Iuliano completed a successful turnaround, generating 20 consecutive quarters of record profits and growing revenues 300% in five years. Iuliano led Molecular Devices through a highly successful initial public offering and grew its market capitalization to nearly $250 million. In his career, Iuliano has raised over $100 million in public and private financing, negotiated several acquisitions and technology licensing deals and built worldwide market leadership positions in emerging technologies. He earned an M.B.A. from Harvard Business School and a B.S. from Boston College.

F. Javed Chaudhary, Vice President Operations, is responsible for all operational and manufacturing activities at E Ink. Most recently as Vice President and General Manager of Seagate Technology (Thailand), Chaudhary was responsible for building over 20 million assemblies annually with a P&L budget exceeding $280 million. He holds an M.S. in Engineering Management from Northeastern University and a B.S. in Mechanical Engineering from the Engineering University Lahore, Pakistan.

(continued)

EXHIBIT 3 | E Ink Management Team as of March 1999 (*continued*)

Russell J. Wilcox, Vice President and General Manager (co-founder), holds P&L responsibility for launching the large-area display business, encompassing wireless networks of billboards, signs and displays. One of the founders of E Ink, Wilcox led the company during its first ten months of operations as Vice President of Business Development. He was instrumental in recruiting the initial team, securing $18 million in debt and equity financing, licensing intellectual property and developing corporate relationships. Wilcox was previously Director of PC Products for venture-backed PureSpeech, Inc. Wilcox earned honors degrees from Harvard College in Applied Mathematics and the Harvard Business School MBA Program where he was named a Baker Scholar.

J.D. Albert, Principal Engineer (co-founder), is the lead design engineer behind the company's large-area display product line. At the MIT Media Lab, he developed novel methods of making electronic ink and flexible displays. He is an MIT graduate, with a B.S. in Mechanical Engineering.

Barrett Comiskey, Principal Scientist (co-founder), works on intellectual property, quality testing, and future technologies. Comiskey pioneered the original research at the MIT Media Lab. Comiskey graduated from MIT, earning a B.S. in mathematics. He has published several papers and holds patents on technologies related to electronic ink, digital and analog steganography and cryptography.

Dr. Paul Drzaic, Director of Display Technology, has extensive experience in both display systems and materials science. Prior to joining E Ink, Drzaic was the principal scientist leading the polymer-dispersed liquid crystal (PDLC) effort for Raychem Corporation, where he developed new materials for use in flat-panel displays. Drzaic is the author of *Liquid Crystal Dispersions* (1995).

Dr. Ian Morrison, Director of Ink Technology, leads E Ink's ongoing development of enhanced versions of electronic ink. Prior to joining E Ink, Morrison had a distinguished career at Xerox Corporation where he held a variety of high-level research and development positions. Most recently, Morrison researched electrical, rheological and optical properties of non-aqueous dispersions. Morrison holds 19 patents, and has written numerous technical articles published in scientific journals.

Tom Grant, Managing Director, Applied Technology   Tom Grant selects and manages investments for Applied Technology and serves actively on the boards of several portfolio companies. Applied Technology focuses on early-stage companies developing enabling information technologies and content.

James P. Iuliano, President and CEO of E Ink Corporation   Mr. Iuliano serves as the company's chief executive officer.

Dr. Joseph Jacobson, Assistant Professor, MIT Media Lab   Joseph Jacobson is an Assistant Professor at the Massachusetts Institute of Technology (MIT) Media Laboratory, where he initiated a program to develop electronic paper-books with pages consisting of electronically addressable, rewritable displays formed on real paper. He holds several patents and patents pending in electronic display technology. Dr. Jacobson received his Ph.D. in physics at MIT in 1992 in femtosecond laser engineering. He created the world's shortest pulse laser (in optical cycles) in 1991. He was a post-doctoral fellow at Stanford from 1992 to 1995, working on experimental and theoretical nonlinear non-local quantum systems. His theoretical work, published in the *Physical Review,* has been written up in the *New York Times* and *Physics Today.*

Jerome S. Rubin, Founder Lexis/Nexis, and Managing Director Veronis, Suhler & Associates (Chairman)   Jerry Rubin was first exposed to electronic ink while serving as Chairman of the M.I.T. Media Lab's research initiative, News in the Future. He joined M.I.T. in

EXHIBIT 3 | *(continued)*

December 1992 after retiring from the Times Mirror Company, where he was Chairman of the Professional Information and Book Publishing Group. Before joining Times Mirror in 1983, Mr. Rubin developed and brought to commercial success LEXIS, the computer-assisted legal research service (launched in 1973), and NEXIS, the on-line news research service (launched in 1978). Combined, these constitute the world's largest on-line textual information service. In 1985 the Information Industry Association inducted Mr. Rubin into its Hall of Fame for his pioneering achievements in electronic publishing. Since September 1995, Mr. Rubin has been a Managing Director of Veronis, Suhler & Associates, the foremost investment banking firm specializing in communications & media (newspaper, magazine & book publishing, radio, TV & cable, and online information systems). Mr. Rubin is a Director of several corporations besides E Ink and also of some not-for-profit organizations. Mr. Rubin holds two Harvard degrees—a bachelor's degree in Physics (1944) and a law degree (1949). He was a co-author of *Toward the Year 2000: New Forces in Publishing* (Bertelsmann, 1989) and of *Mastering the Changing Information World* (Ablex, 1992).

Larry Silverstein, Esq., Partner, Bingham Dana (general counsel)   Larry Silverstein practices as a member of the Entrepreneurial Services Group at Bingham Dana. Mr. Silverstein acts as counsel to many emerging growth, middle market and established companies, both public and private.

Christopher Spray, General Partner, Atlas Venture Capital   Christopher Spray founded Atlas Venture's US partnership in 1986. He began his international venture capital career in 1983, when he joined CINVen, a leading European venture fund based in the UK. Atlas Venture is a partnership of international venture capitalists formed to finance high-technology businesses seeking success in the global economy. Investments are concentrated in two sectors—life sciences and information technology.

John Steadman, Vice President, Motorola Messaging Systems Products Group   Mr. Steadman is currently Vice President of Motorola's Messaging Systems Products Group (MSPG). MSPG is responsible for all aspects of Motorola's paging business worldwide. Motorola's 1997 sales were $29.8 billion.

EXHIBIT 4 | Segments of the Large-Area Display Market Relevant to E Ink ($ millions)

	LED Matrix Over 2' Wide	Incandescent Bulbs	Electro-mechanical	Total ($610M)	%
General Purpose	$80	$50	$15	$145	24%
Casino & Bar	20	125	—	145	24
Government	75	35	25	135	22
Retail & Food	70	—	—	70	11
Sports	—	35	10	45	7
Transport	10	—	30	50	7
All Other	15	15	—	30	5
TOTAL:	$270	$260	$80	$610	100%

EXHIBIT 5 | Technological Progress of Liquid Crystal Displays

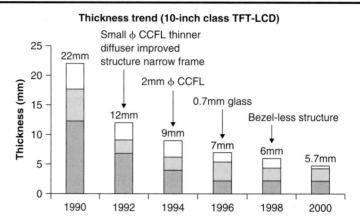

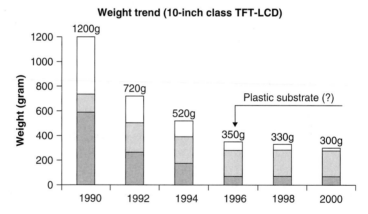

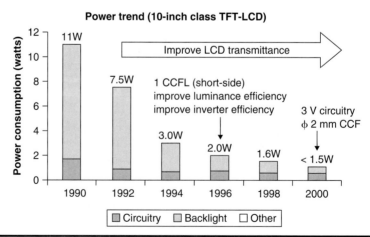

Adapted from: *Flat Panel Displays*; Toshiba America Electronic Components, Inc.

EXHIBIT 6 | Competing Flat-Panel Display Technologies

***

Enhancement of LCDs—the LCD is not a fixed technology. With hundreds of millions of dollars being spent annually on incremental improvements, the LCD is getting cheaper and better with each passing year. Enhancements include new ways of addressing passive displays, filters to improve light transmission, the development of plastic-substrate LCDs, wider viewing angles, and a sustained and massive effort by Asian display companies to drive down costs

Microdisplays—being commercialized by Kopin, DisplayTech, Colorado Microdisplay, Siliscape, and others. These devices consist of a 1-inch or smaller display, which must be magnified for the viewer to discern an image. Microdisplays are suited for virtual reality headgear, camcorders, PDA with lens attachment and projection TVs where the image can be expanded onto a distant surface.

Organic LEDs (OLEDs)—under study by over 60 companies worldwide, including most major display companies. OLEDs offer full color capability in a flexible light-emitting display (i.e., visible in the dark). This is described as a "high potential new display technology" but is still in the development stage. OLEDs are likely to achieve commercial status in the next few years.

Field Emission Displays (FEDs)—being commercialized by Candescent, Motorola, and PixTech. This technology is based on the same principle as the television, but replicated on a tiny scale with one emitter per pixel. While original prospects were strong for this technology to replace laptop screens, several years of delay have allowed LCDs to narrow the gap in price/performance.

Plasma (PDPs)—being commercialized by several Japanese companies, especially Fujitsu. Plasma displays offer a better alternative to the LCD for large displays from 40–80 inches. While starting factory prices were at $15,000 for a 42″ display in 1996, prices reached $7,000 in 1998 projected at $2,600 by 2002, according to Fujitsu. The emphasis in PDP technology has been on large-area displays, competing primarily against projection display systems.

Gyricon—Xerox, as long ago as 1977, began research of the 'Gyricon' in which half black/half white microspheres are encapsulated in a rubber sheet. This is considered a rival technology to E Ink's for creating an electronic paper. No product plans have been announced.

***

EXHIBIT 7 | Potential Radio Paper Economics versus Traditional Newspapers

Line Item	Traditional Newspapers (billion)	Radio Paper (billion)
Newspapers Per Year	22.50	22.50
Sales Per Paper	$2.18	$2.18
Operating Costs	$1.75	$1.40
Operating Margin	$0.44	$0.78
Net Income	$0.18	$0.40

Source: E Ink estimates.

Additional benefits of radio paper versus physical newspapers:
- Faster turnaround eliminates 11:30 p.m. deadlines to deliver by 5:30 a.m.
- Elimination of vulnerability to hyper-cyclical input cost of newsprint.
- No space constraints (can expand size of paper and therefore advertising space as desired).
- Ability to microsegment delivery zones.

EXHIBIT 8 | Competing Electronic Book Products

RocketBook—a small, lightweight device with medium memory but long battery life. Partnered with Sharp to help design and manufacture the device, with Levenger and Franklin Electronics to sell it by mail order and retail outlets, with many publishers to provide content, and with Barnes & Noble to sell electronic versions. Consumer focus, especially popular business books for traveling executives. Users are demanding ability to store user files and HTML on device. Sells for $499. Must buy books from barnesandnoble.com.

SoftBook—a large, heavy device with much memory and short battery life. Fewer partners. Some consumer sales but oriented to fleet sales to corporate customers who must publish many pages of documents to mobile workers. Sells for $599 or $299 with 24 months subscription at $19.95/month. Must buy books from proprietary store.

Everybook—a large, heavy device with much memory and short battery life. Focused on selling to the professional/educational market as a replacement for heavy textbooks. Full color screens with high resolution for precise book reproduction. Sells for $1000-$1500 with two full side-by-side screens. Must use proprietary store.

Librius—a small, lightweight device with limited memory and long battery life. Focused on selling romance novels to consumers. Sells for $199. Must buy novels in proprietary store; priced at 20–25% less than paper.

EXHIBIT 9 | E Ink Functional Area Objectives

Marketing

E Ink's goal is to distinguish the company as more than a component supplier. Efforts will involve both consumer marketing and industrial marketing campaigns. The company intends to develop a two-tiered strategy with a flagship E Ink brand and product line names for each major product category (large-area, flat-panel, publishing).

Near-term marketing responsibilities include corporate identity and branding, creation of sales demo kits and printed collateral, public relations and evaluating customer feedback to display designs.

Research & Development

Near-term R&D objectives include optimizing first-generation ink that can be sold, developing enhanced second-generation ink and adding additional layers of patent protection. Following the achievement of near-term objectives, R&D efforts will focus on minimizing the cost to manufacture the ink, optimizing the visual appeal of the displays, further reducing power and voltage requirements and exploring third-generation ink possibilities.

Engineering

The engineering department is primarily responsible for applying R&D technologies to products. Near-term priorities for the engineering team include designing large-area text displays, developing volume production processes, engineering custom designs for major corporate partners and building prototypes to support sales activities.

Manufacturing

E Ink's manufacturing employees will develop and control all critical manufacturing processes to commercialize electronic ink in large-area displays, portable flat panel displays and publishing applications. The manufacturing strategy consists of demonstration of process capability ready for scale up by E Ink followed by in-house pilot production of selected key process steps. Volume production of most process steps will be maintained at sub-contract supply partners and controlled by E Ink technical support staff for conformance to E Ink specifications.

Near-term manufacturing objectives include start-up of new E Ink consolidated facility and scale production of large-area displays.

Valhalla Partners Due Diligence

It was March 2002, and Art Marks was sitting around a campfire in the Blue Ridge Mountains with two friends from the venture capital world, Gene Riechers and Hooks Johnston. They'd had a few drinks. They'd told some jokes. But, like retired athletes who can't help rehashing old games, the campfire conversation kept circling back to the same place, back to the same topic, and each time they returned to it, their enthusiasm grew. The topic was: due diligence.

While the campfire appeal of a s'more or a rendition of "Kumbaya" is short-lived, the due diligence process hatched by the three partners that night in March became the foundation of a $177 million venture capital fund called Valhalla. The partners believed that they'd figured out a better way to do due diligence, one that would give them a competitive advantage in the crowded world of venture capital.

A year and a half later, in August 2003, Art Marks was sipping coffee in his office, flipping through an investment memo concerning a company called Telco Exchange (later renamed Rivermine Software). (See **Exhibit 1** for excerpts from the Telco Exchange investment memo.) Telco Exchange was the first deal that Valhalla had run through its new due diligence process.

Telco Exchange (TX) was a company that developed software to help companies strategically manage their telecom assets and reduce the cost of managing their voice and data networks. TX was seeking a $5 million Series A investment, and Valhalla was deciding whether to lead the round.

Gene Riechers, now a General Partner at Valhalla, and Scott Frederick, Partner at Valhalla, had prepared the investment memo. The memo was unusual by venture capital standards. The most obvious point of departure was the length: a hefty 22 pages, plus many extra pages of summaries from reference checks on the management team.

As Marks pored over the document, he was able to get a clear picture of the company and the challenges it faced. TX had great strengths: an innovative product in a market that was expected to grow, as well as a set of customers who had used the product

Professor William A. Sahlman and Research Associate Dan Heath prepared this case. HBS cases are developed solely as the basis for class discussion. Cases are not intended to serve as endorsements, sources of primary data, or illustrations of effective or ineffective management.

and achieved impressive ROI. The company also had big challenges, including an unproven management team and a fragmented competitive environment.

As always, learning more about the company had made things clearer and more complex at the same time. At the partners' meeting the next day, Marks would have to vote up or down on the TX deal. Valhalla made investments only with unanimous consent among the general partners, so Marks knew his vote was critical. At this point, Marks was leaning moderately toward approving the investment, but the investment memo had raised some important concerns. He wanted to find a way to address these concerns in the structure of the deal that was proposed. Finally, in the back of his mind, he wondered whether the new due diligence process was yielding dividends for Valhalla. It had taken a lot of partner time to create the memo in front of him. There was no question it was useful—but was it worth the resources expended? How much due diligence was enough? Why not half as much? Or twice as much? There were no easy answers to these questions, but then, he didn't really expect any.

Background on Valhalla Partners

Art Marks graduated from Harvard Business School in 1971 as a Baker Scholar. He worked at Baxter Laboratories for four years, then began to work for General Electric, where he would spend almost ten years. From 1975 to 1979, Marks served as the General Manager of X-Ray products in GE's Medical Systems division. From 1979 to 1984, Marks worked in the Software Products division (GE Information Services), first as Senior Vice President and subsequently as President. Marks considers his biggest career accomplishment to be a GE joint venture in Japan that he set up. The joint venture was the market leader in 2004, with $2 billion in sales.

Marks became a venture capitalist in 1984, joining New Enterprise Associates (NEA) as a General Partner. Marks had a 17-year run at NEA. Highlights of his investment record included Progress Software, Clarify, InSoft, IndusRiver Networks, and Call Technologies. He also admits to making some bad calls. "Passing on Ciena wasn't such a good idea," Marks said with a chuckle. In June 2001, Marks retired from the venture capital world, intending to fly-fish, garden, and spend more time with his family.

His retirement lasted about nine months.

In April 2002, a month after the camping excursion to the Blue Ridge Mountains, Marks and his partners—Riechers and Johnston—announced the formation of Valhalla Partners. Riechers had been, most recently, the founder and Managing Director of FBR Technology Venture Partners (FBRTVP). Johnston had also been a Managing Director at FBRTVP. The three partners had worked together on deals before and traveled in the same circles in the mid-Atlantic venture community.

Of his decision to come out of retirement, Marks said, "I thought about doing nothing, to be honest. Or not doing anything in the venture business, anyway. But my personal jollies come from working with entrepreneurs and being able to look around corners to see where the next technology is coming from. Once you get that in your blood, you're addicted."[1]

---

[1] Alistair Christopher, "Q&A: Art Marks: What Made an 18-Year Vet Come Out of Retirement?", *Venture Capital Journal*, June 2002.

It was a curious time to start a new venture fund. Owing to the collapse of the dot-coms, commitments to venture capital funds had fallen off a cliff. Commitments dropped from $82.7 billion in 2000 to $12.0 billion in 2002, the lowest level seen since 1996.

The first few fundraising meetings did not bode well. Riechers recalls an early meeting with a large endowment fund manager: "The guy just started screaming at us. He went on a tirade about the venture capital industry. He obviously wasn't irritated at us specifically—we just happened to be the guys in the room at the time."

What made Marks abandon a relaxing retirement to fight a hostile market climate in venture capital? He believed he could succeed by getting back to the basics, by returning to "old-school" venture capital principles: smaller funds, fewer partners, fewer deals, and more attention paid to each deal. "We thought the big problem during the bubble was that no one had time to do due diligence. There was too much competition, too much pressure to move fast. We said to ourselves, the key thing is to *go slow*. Do a lot of due diligence," said Marks.

When the three partners had first started talking about the VC due diligence process, they had realized a couple of surprising things. First, they realized there were no established "best practices" for due diligence—despite the fact that thousands of smart people were doling out billions of dollars in investments each year. Second, none of the partners had ever developed a "framework" for analyzing deals. They had certainly looked for many of the same elements across deals—the strength of management, the size of the market, the density of competition, etc.—but the methodology they'd used had tended to vary from deal to deal.

To the three partners, this smelled like an opportunity. According to Marks, Valhalla would have a multi-pronged strategy. First, they'd invest more time in the due diligence process. This would yield several advantages: allowing them to choose better deals, helping them craft smarter deal terms (e.g., weighing the relative merit of a higher valuation versus more board control), and helping them assess the company's operating plans. A second part of the strategy was to work more closely with management. Marks believed the payoff from a closer relationship with management would outweigh the heavier use of scarce partner time. The final element of the strategy was to focus on East Coast information technology deals, which reflected the partners' location and expertise.

Telco Exchange

Telco Exchange (TX) was based in Fairfax, a mere nine miles from the Valhalla office in Vienna. TX made a dramatic entrance onto Valhalla's radar in July 2003. In the same week, they had the deal recommended to them, independently, by a lawyer, a recruiter, and a CFO at a local company. Riechers said, "We were impressed by the serendipity. So we invited them in for a presentation." As it turns out, Riechers said with a laugh, "They'd actually orchestrated the whole thing. All three of our 'sources' were on their advisory board. I guess we should have suspected it."

When TX made a presentation to the firm on July 25, 2003, the partners were immediately interested in the deal. It fit Valhalla's target profile perfectly: early-stage, IT-oriented, based in the mid-Atlantic region. One week later, all of the partners went on a field trip to the TX office.

TX competed in the "enterprise telecommunications management" (ETM) space. "Enterprise telecommunications management" was a soporific buzzword for a real source of pain in big organizations. According to the Aberdeen Group, the average Fortune 500 company spent almost 1% of its revenue on telecommunications. This 1%—which translates to about $116mm per year—was bewilderingly hard to administer. The money was spent on everything from cell phones to giant T3 data pipes. Orders were placed by junior salesmen and CIOs and everyone in between.

Simply handling the invoices could be a Herculean task. In fact, the average Fortune 500 company processed an astonishing 15,000 telecom-related bills each year! Some bills were hundreds of pages long, arriving in their own boxes. Needless to say, it was tough for a manager to pinch pennies when it was a challenge simply to file the documents, much less scrutinize them.

Valhalla's conversations with TX's customers identified big problems that had been solved by the company's software. A sampling of the customers' comments revealed accomplishments such as:

- Dramatically reducing the number of invoices that had to be dealt with
- Identifying telecom circuits the company was being billed for that hadn't been used for years
- Generating $500,000 in savings by identifying overcharges from service providers
- Creating an inventory of telecom assets to help managers keep track of the big picture
- Streamlining the process of adding new telecom resources

As a venture deal, TX was highly atypical. For one, TX was seeking a Series A financing after having been in existence for 14 years. TX had originated as a project inside another company, CICAT Networks. CICAT, also based in Fairfax, was a company that provided outsourced telecom provisioning. CICAT had started to create TX's software in the 1990s and eventually spun out TX as a separate entity in 2001.

By the time TX approached Valhalla for investment, it was a profitable company on track to do $2mm in 2003 bookings. It had already signed up blue-chip customers such as IKON and Marriott. Most Series A ventures did not have this much of a track record.

Another atypical element to the TX deal was the CEO, Bryant Dunetz, who was almost 70 years old. Dunetz's son, Kevin, was the CTO. In the real world, an older CEO whose son worked in the business would not have been unusual. In the world of venture capital, though, it was enough to scare some firms away.

Test-Driving the New Due Diligence Process

Marks and his partners had diagrammed their new due diligence process. (See **Exhibit 2** for an overview of the process.) They were eager to try it out, and TX became the guinea pig.

The Valhalla team worried about how entrepreneurs would respond to the new process. Would entrepreneurs be spooked by the intense scrutiny Valhalla would put them through? Would Valhalla miss out on deals because entrepreneurs decided to take their deals to bigger, less analysis-intensive funds? Charles Curran, a Partner at Valhalla, said, "Some entrepreneurs have had bad experiences with venture capitalists who got involved in ways that were not productive. If those entrepreneurs perceive us as the 'Bearhug VC,' that could be a real concern."

The team was also concerned about wasting their time. Marks said, "Our model is that we're going to do a lot of work. We want to make sure we get rewarded for that." And yet there was ample opportunity for Valhalla to come up empty-handed. For instance, what if Valhalla poured a half-dozen partner-months into due diligence on one deal, only to lose the deal to another VC that offered a slightly higher pre-money valuation? Lots of partner time and no closed deals was not a recipe for success.

With these concerns—and big hopes, as well—as the context, Valhalla began to dig into TX's business. The theme of the new due diligence process was, as Marks said, "We're going to make mistakes. But one mistake we're not going to make is the 'I wish we'd discovered that earlier' mistake."

Valhalla set out to answer three key questions. The partners called these questions the "real, win, worth" framework. Marks had adapted the framework from a GE marketing course that was used to assess new product ideas. The three questions were:

1. Is it real? (I.e., is there a strong market demand and is it growing?)

2. Can they win? (I.e., does the company have a competitive advantage in the marketplace and can it sustain that advantage over time?)

3. Is it worth it? (I.e., if we assume good performance, does this turn out to be a compelling investment opportunity?)

Gene Riechers and Scott Frederick worked intensively for approximately seven weeks on the investment memo. They emerged from the process feeling confident about the investment. The customer calls had been particularly compelling. Most enterprise software companies spent a fortune on sales and marketing. Yet TX's customers had, in some cases, actually sought them out. One Fortune 500 company, which was now a satisfied customer of TX, had discovered TX's products by doing a search on Google. This was the kind of thing that brought joy to the heart of a venture capitalist.

There was one snag, however. The Valhalla team agreed that, in order to make the investment, Dunetz (the TX CEO) would have to agree to let Valhalla search for a new CEO. Marks said, "Dunetz and his son were incredibly capable, self-motivated people who had taken the company this far. But we felt we needed new management, and we didn't want there to be any misunderstanding about that. We also felt obligated to make it clear that, once a new CEO comes in, he or she would have full authority to make any personnel or strategy changes they thought appropriate." Marks summarized the situation: "Clearly, this was a very sensitive issue. And our hope was that the TX team would embrace the idea, not just 'accept' it."

Dunetz had been prepared for this possibility, and he agreed that another CEO might help the company reach the next level. He agreed to transition to the role of Chairman once a suitable replacement was located.

Unfortunately, this was not the stickiest point of negotiation. The two sides were relatively far apart on valuation. Valhalla intended to offer a $5 million pre-money valuation, but Dunetz was holding out for a $10 million valuation.

The 100-Day Plan

The Valhalla team made one crucial discovery during its inaugural due diligence effort. They realized that the due diligence efforts could be put to a secondary (perhaps primary) use. As Art Marks said, "Usually the way it works is that you do all this due diligence work, you learn everything there is to know about the company, and then you use it to negotiate. You spend five weeks arguing back and forth with the CEO about the valuation. It dawned on us that, rather than spend five weeks haggling, we could use what we'd learned and spend some real time helping the company execute on its plans."

The partners came up with a new concept: the 100-day plan. (See **Exhibit 1** for an example of a 100-day plan.) It was envisioned as a joint action plan for both the investors and the management team. Joint tasks might include recruiting new managers or board members, establishing banking and legal relationships, revising the company's financial plan, and setting timelines for product development.

The 100-day plan took place before the close of the investment but after the term sheet had been agreed to by both parties. Typically in venture capital firms, this period was used primarily for drawing up legal documents, conducting background checks on the top management, and finalizing negotiations. Scott Frederick, the co-author of the investment memo, believed that they could use this period to assess how well Valhalla would work with the TX management team.

"When you're headed towards a deal, it's easy for both sides to hear what they want to hear. Then, you show up at the first board meeting and find out you weren't on the same page at all. The 100-day plan provides a sense of transparency about what is important and what the goals are. It gives us a chance to get comfortable with each other," said Frederick.

Assessing the Trial Run

In general, the trial run of the due diligence process had been a success, according to the partners. Marks said, "The proof that it worked, to us, was that Dunetz had another term sheet before we got involved, and he had another one on the way when we submitted ours. And Dunetz told us, 'I know what you guys are like, and that means more to me than the specific terms.'"

Frederick said, "Doing this due diligence documentation is not the most fun part of our jobs. It can be laborious. But I think it's a vital exercise to put pen to paper, because it forces clarity of thought. It's easy to talk yourself into thinking that you know more than you know. When you force yourself to write a structured memo, it's easier to see the weak spots in your case. Then, you can spend time figuring out whether those weak spots are terminal."

All the partners were aware that their approach to due diligence was not costless. Curran said, "I am absolutely a believer in what we are doing. But there are potential downsides to it. Our process is tough and somewhat conservative. We think it will reduce the number of times that we strike out with a deal. But might it also keep us from hitting a home run? A shocking percentage of venture capital profits are driven by a very small number of 'mega-hit' deals, such as eBay. Would something like eBay have gotten a unanimous 'yes' vote after going through our process? We are cognizant of this risk."

The Investment Decision

This was Valhalla's first deal. The fund's limited partners would be watching carefully. Was TX the right deal?

Marks liked the picture of TX that was presented in the investment memo. It struck him as a good risk overall. However, it wasn't a good deal at any price. Marks thought about the issues raised by the memo. He started scribbling notes on a pad, marking down his assessment of TX's biggest challenges. He wanted to make sure that the risks were, if possible, reflected in the deal terms offered to TX.

He knew that, as always, there was a disagreement between the investors and the company over the proper pre-money valuation, and he wanted to offer constructive feedback to Riechers and Frederick the next day. Was TX worth the $10mm pre-money valuation that the CEO wanted?

He was also looking forward to discussing the trial run of the new due diligence process in the partners' meeting the next day. It had gone from campfire talk to reality in less than 15 months. The 22-page document in front of him was proof of concept, but not necessarily proof of success. Had this been the best use of Scott Frederick's time? Would Riechers, having invested so much time in the deal, become too attached to the investment? Tomorrow's morning would be the first installment of a long discussion about how Valhalla could improve the art of dissecting deals.

EXHIBIT 1 | Excerpt from Telco Exchange Investment Memo

To:	**Valhalla Partners**
From:	**Scott Frederick**
Subject:	**Telco Exchange—Investment Memo**
Date:	**September 8, 2003—*Finalized October 16, 2003 by Gene Riechers***

This memorandum serves as an investment proposal for Telco Exchange (TX), a Fairfax, VA-based company delivering "enterprise telecommunications management" (ETM) or "strategic communications management" (SCM) software.

Their product helps companies strategically manage their telecom assets and reduce the cost of managing their voice and data networks. Their product appears to be the most comprehensive and most highly integrated software offering available. It has three main modules:

Service Order Management: Enables an enterprise to strategically manage their procurement processes for telecom equipment and services. Module includes multi-carrier and multi-vendor product catalogs; an order processing system complete with automated interfaces and workflow for placing, approving, routing and tracking orders. Module also includes sophisticated project management functionality, so that an enterprise can easily "turn-up" or "turn-down" standardized facilities with automated circuit ordering and labor scheduling. Module also includes trouble ticket management and the ability to expedite orders. TX claims to be the only software vendor which has integrated with AT&T's provisioning systems.

Inventory Management: Enables an enterprise to maintain a dynamic, central repository of all voice and data networking assets (services, circuits and equipment). Module can be integrated with existing ERP systems (Oracle, SAP and PeopleSoft) as well as with an enterprise's general ledger to facilitate cost center accounting and the automatic issuance and termination of services. Note: They do not do automatic network discovery, so building the database requires some custom data acquisition work, but they have built tools to manage the process.

(*continued*)

EXHIBIT 1 | Excerpt from Telco Exchange Investment Memo (*continued*)

<u>Financial Management:</u> Enables an enterprise to automate the invoice management process by receiving service provider invoices electronically, validating charges against inventory, and preparing invoices for payment. Module also includes rate table and MACD order reconciliation; as well as contract management features to ensure contract and SLA compliance.

In our sector review, Valhalla identified "Enterprise Telecom Management" as a desirable target based on the inevitable increase in the complexity and rate of change of enterprise telecom networks, the potential cost savings for an enterprise, and the trend toward enterprises attempting to automate non-strategic, highly administrative business processes.

Although there are a number of service-oriented solutions on the market; no one has established a dominant technology-oriented solution. TX appears to have the most robust product offering on the market and an impressive list of satisfied customers (Agere Systems, IKON Office Solutions, Marriott, and others). The company is now focused on sales and marketing execution in order to gain market share before competitors are able to match the functionality of their solution.

We are contemplating leading a $5.0 mm Series A Preferred investment with a <u>Valhalla Partners' investment of $2.5 mm</u> along with $2.5 mm from Columbia Capital. We have given the company initial guidance on a $5.0 mm pre-money (post-expanded option pool) valuation, resulting in a Valhalla ownership position of around 25%. In making the investment, we are assuming that the company will need to raise another $5mm in the year 2005. When calculating our expected ROI, we are assuming that we contribute our pro-rata to that financing, for a total Valhalla investment of $3.75 mm. Columbia Capital is an excellent partner because we have worked with them successfully and they have significant telecom expertise (note: they have an investment in Vibrant Solutions which provides cost and revenue management software to carriers).

<u>Forecasts of a success scenario place the value of the company at $170 to $343 mm and the value of our share post an illiquidity discount at $26 to 45 mm in 2007. Assuming we invested $3.75 mm in total we would return 6.8 to 12.1 times our capital.</u>

<u>Under our more conservative forecasts, the company will reach a value of between $115 to $140 mm and will still reach profitability. Under such a scenario we estimate our share of the company post an illiquidity discount to be valued at between $17 and $23 mm, producing a 4.6 to 6.1 times return on our capital.</u>

Note: the one-time $250,000 software license assumption used in both these models leaves room for considerable up-side (as the company is currently in discussions for a 7 figure license deal, as well as term license deals which would result in larger recurring revenue streams). Also the above analysis does not take into consideration the beneficial impact of our securities being participating preferred securities.

While the management team is raw and will need significant additions, the combination of a very large untapped market, a unique and robust product offering, impressive customer traction and an attractive valuation make this an appropriate candidate for Valhalla.

INVESTMENT SUMMARY

Positives	Negatives
Company addresses a real customer pain in a new, high-growth market (where in-house development is not a viable option)	Unproven management team with significant holes
Impressive customer list with proven ROI	CEO likely to be replaced; and CEO and CTO are related (Father/Son)
Dilgence suggests TX has the most comprehensive and highly integrated software-based solution on the market	Well-funded competitors focused on administrative outsourcing can and are developing software solutions (e.g., Teldata, QuantumShift, ProfitLine and BroadMargin)
	(*continued*)

EXHIBIT 1 | *(continued)*

Positives	Negatives
AT&T is introducing TX to key accounts, as are some of the leading outsourced vendors (Note: Teldata Control expressed an interest in investing in TX).	Vendors with financial management-only solutions could use a "beach-head" strategy and develop more comprehensive and robust product offerings
TX will benefit from increasing telecom complexity and trend toward business process automation	Aberdeen* seems narrowly focused on "cost management" as opposed to "strategic management"
Valuation is attractive and <u>we can help</u>	Aberdeen* is also pushing complete "outsourced" solutions including dispute resolution services

THE FOLLOWING POINTS HIGHLIGHT THE INVESTMENT THESIS FOR TX:

- "Enterprise Telecom Management"/"Strategic Communications Management" is a fast-growing market w/ the potential for less than 12 month ROI.
- Diligence suggests that TX has the most comprehensive and highly integrated software solution on the market. They are winning in competitive situations and are being introduced to key customers by AT&T, as well as some of their expected competitors on the outsourcing side (namely Teldata Control).
- TX has an impressive list of referenceable customers (Agere Systems, IKON Office Solutions, Marriott, and others). Current deal sizes are between $100,000 and $950,000; and TX is close to signing a large deal with Circuit City.
- TX's software has been running at Agere for roughly two years and at IKON for over one year, so there is reduced technology risk.
- TX was profitable in 2002 and is currently running close to cash-flow breakeven for 2003. They appear to have developed a replicable sales process and we think the business has the ability to scale well, offering the potential for more than $50,000,000 in annual revenue within four years. Equally important, we believe they can achieve these revenue numbers in a capital efficient manner. If TX hits our revised projections, they will not need to raise more money until 2005, and they should be able to become profitable with the addition of an incremental $5 mm.

COMPANY HISTORY AND CURRENT STATUS

TX was initially incubated by CICAT Networks (CICAT). CICAT was founded in 1989 to provide enterprise customers with outsourced telecom services. CICAT specialized in circuit ordering and provisioning services, and in doing so established key relationships with the Tier 1 providers, LECs and CLECs. Equally important, through these 14 years of experience CICAT's principals developed a deep understanding of how all types of services needed to be ordered and provisioned. These experiences provided the basis for TX's service order management, inventory management and financial management modules.

In the second half of 2001, CICAT's principals launched TX as an independent software company. Sustained by a short term loan from CICAT, the founders signed Agere Systems as their first customer in August of 2001. Telesis and NEC were signed in early 2002. Then in 3Q02 IKON Office Solutions became the company's largest customer to date. In December 2002, the company signed a major international retailer as a customer and began paying back the short term loan from CICAT out of operating cash flow.

In the first half of 2003, the company signed Marriott. During this period the company was also focused on implementing at the major international retailer, moving into new office space and beginning to raise their first institutional round. A large deal with Circuit City is expected to be closed in the near term.

WHAT DO YOU HAVE TO BELIEVE?

1) Their product is currently more robust and offers a more comprehensive solution than the competition.
2) TX will be able to maintain its product advantage.

(continued)

---

*Aberdeen is a respected industry research firm.

EXHIBIT 1 | Excerpt from Telco Exchange Investment Memo (*continued*)

3) The market wants a robust and comprehensive software-based solution (as opposed to a more narrowly focused financial management/invoice processing module).

4) The market wants a robust and comprehensive software-based solution (as opposed to an outsourced solution complete with dispute resolution).

5) The market for Enterprise Telecom Management or Strategic Communications Management software will continue to grow rapidly.

6) TX will be able to replicate its initial sales success and maintain a significant average deal size. The revised forecast is reasonable. Note: The key assumptions in our revised forecast are:

   a) After a 6 month training period, each salesman will average closing 1.0 deal per quarter until 2006, after which they will be able to average 1.25 deals per quarter;

   b) The company will be able to average $250,000 in one-time software revenue per deal, plus an equivalent amount of one-time services revenue, plus an on-going 20% annual maintenance contract.

   c) *Note: this last assumption creates the potential for considerable upside. The Company is currently in discussions with potential customers quoting a seven figure software license; and they have already sold several term licenses which set up the potential for larger recurring revenue streams.*

7) The management team can execute well vs. competition. We will be able to replace the CEO with minimal disruption to the existing team.

8) We can help the company recruit additional sales resources and improve pipeline yield. We can fine tune the sales model and pricing strategy. We can help prioritize the product development process. We can help upgrade financial systems and personnel.

IS IT REAL?

Discussion drawn largely from the Aberdeen Group's* April 2003 report on Total Telecommunications Cost Management.

In March 2003, the Aberdeen Group identified telecommunications management "as one of the hottest new emerging sectors in the business process automation marketplace." They estimate that telecommunications costs—including voice, data and wireless services—are the 2nd or 3rd largest indirect expense at most large companies.

- The average Fortune 500 Company spends $116 million a year on telecom services and processes more than 15,000 telecom-related bills per year.

- The average mid-market enterprise spends $26 million a year on telecom services and processes 3,000 telecom-related bills per year.

However, few enterprises have a comprehensive and accurate way to determine what they are spending on telecom services, with whom, and why. Aberdeen research indicates that 85% of mid-market enterprises' telecom bills are paid in full and go un-audited by the enterprise. Aberdeen research also suggests that the relationship between error rates and invoice dollar size is counterintuitive. The high-volume, low-dollar invoices present the greatest opportunity for savings because error rates are lowest among high dollar items due to increased sales process scrutiny. As a result, highly manual "stare and compare" efforts are rarely effective. In addition, the procurement processes for telecom services in most large enterprises tend to be very decentralized, and handled by people who understand a T-1 in detail but don't understand or care about what a purchase order is. As a result, order compliance is poor and the cost to complete an order through manual processes is excessive. This dynamic has created a great opportunity for the creation of high value-added business process automation software focused on an enterprise's telecom assets.

The average Fortune 500 Company spends $116 mm on telecommunications. To provide perspective, the average revenue of a Fortune 500 Company in 2002 was $13.9 billion, making the annual telecom service spend 0.84% of revenue. Meanwhile the average profit of a Fortune 500 Company in 2002 was $139 million, or 1% of revenue. Thus even incremental improvement in telecom costs could have a significant improvement on profits because indirect expense cuts drop straight to the bottom line.

---

*Aberdeen is a respected industry research firm.

EXHIBIT 1 | (*continued*)

Market Drivers

As the global economy stagnates, companies continue to focus on streamlining internal processes and cutting costs. The economy has a counter-cyclical impact on the Business Process Outsourcing (BPO) and Business Process Automation (BPA) markets. Companies faced with competitive and cost pressures will be compelled to focus on core competencies and look for external help in non-core areas. After reducing head count, organizations have devoted major attention to cutting indirect costs, which represent 30% to 60% of companies' total expenditure budgets.

IT and telecom budgets are not insulated from this trend; yet few enterprises have had an easy, comprehensive way to determine what they are spending on telecom services, with whom and how. This is because, typically, many different areas of a company are purchasing telecom services. For one, an operations manager may be responsible for local and long distance service; often this can be true for each division or regional office. Second, an IT manager may be responsible for network services. Third, a marketing manager may select a preferred audio conferencing service for client calls. Finally, a sales representative may be reimbursed for wireless services through a company's travel and entertainment reimbursement process.

Organizational issues such as increased merger and acquisition activity, decentralized operating cultures and the promotion of entrepreneurial environments have contributed to procurement management challenges such as maverick buying (where buying decisions are made outside of existing purchasing contracts) and under-leveraged corporate buying power.

Additional market drivers include increasing corporate complexity and technological change. As mentioned elsewhere, the average mid-market U.S. enterprise receives more than 300 telecom-related bills per month. Enterprises, particularly those with many satellite offices, are inundated with separate bills for every location. Moreover, with new telecom services such as wireless devices becoming more widespread, enterprises are receiving still more monthly statements. In the meantime, telecom bills are growing increasingly complex—they can average more than 100 pages, chock full of indecipherable line items. At the same time, the complexion of enterprise communications technologies is rapidly changing. Underlying technologies—Internet Protocol, telephony, Ethernet Wireless Area Networks, etc.—are forcing architectural shifts in the workplaces.

CAN TELCO EXCHANGE WIN?

There are a number of companies attempting to address the invoice processing side of enterprise telecom management, either through a software solution (e.g. Stonehouse Technologies, Tangoe, TeleSoft, Formity Systems and Visionael), or through a highly manual outsourced approach (MSS Group, Teldata Control, Profitline, Broadmargin, QuantumShift). These solutions can provide significant value, but they only address the financial management piece of the puzzle, and do not adequately address service order management or inventory management. If an enterprise out-sources or purchases invoice processing software, they may be ensuring accurate and efficient invoice payment, but they are treating a symptom and not addressing the root cause of many of their problems.

TX offers a more comprehensive and highly integrated solution. As a result, TX is able to not only catch invoice errors, it is able to identify unnecessary services and equipment, prevent erroneous ordering, ensure that all the requisite elements of a circuit are disconnected when they are no longer needed, ensure contract compliance, facilitate true cost-center accounting and prevent the need for multiple re-keyings by order administrators. TX's software solves these problems by providing their customers with a holistic view of their communications infrastructure, automating the ordering process, providing a common set of data for all parties to work with, applying business rules to ensure that corporate policies are followed and that contracts are adhered to, and by integrating with an organization's existing software applications.

TX's Service Order Management and Inventory Management capabilities are important differentiators. Where their competitors focus primarily on cost management, TX is able to provide a more strategic offering and move their customers closer to the Holy Grail—complete network optimization. TX's goal is to allow an enterprise to apply the same discipline and rigor to their communications investments that they have previously applied to their customers through Customer Relationship Management (CRM), and to their production resources through Enterprise Resource Planning (ERP).

(*continued*)

EXHIBIT 1 | Excerpt from Telco Exchange Investment Memo (*continued*)

In addition, to the more narrowly focused software vendors and the complete third-party outsourcing firms, a third set of competitors could come from large, established companies that offer full-service consulting and IT services to the Fortune 500. Competitors in this space generally offer more complete business process outsourcing. These players include IBM, CSC, EDS, Accenture and Bearing Point.

A fourth set of potential competitors could come from the Enterprise Spend Management (ESM) world (e.g. Ariba and Commerce One). These companies have historically focused on office supplies; maintenance, repair and operations (MRO) materials; and computers and peripheral devices; because these areas have more universally understood attributes and pricing structures that can be effectively represented in a Web-based catalog format. However, it is certainly possible that these companies will try to move into the procurement and management of more complex business services.

A fifth set of potential competitors could come from the Network Management Providers such as HP (Openview), IBM (Tivoli) and Computer Associates (Unicenter).

However, the complexities inherent in telecommunications provisioning, billing and inventory management should provide a barrier to entry and at a minimum should place a traditional network management or ESM vendor (who is unlikely to have the in-depth, telecom specific knowledge that TX has) at a significant disadvantage.

Another company to keep an eye on is Peregrine Systems ("*the Infrastructure Management Company*"). Founded in 1981, Peregrine Systems develops and sells enterprise software to enable its 3,500 customers to manage their IT resources. One of the company's products, AssetCenter, claims to be the industry's leading IT Management software. It provides inventory, financial and contract management functionality. Peregrine Systems just emerged from Bankruptcy protection and released version 4.3 of AssetCenter in June of 2003. The latest version of the product "automates business processes for inventory reconciliation, improving the accuracy of data, while addressing growing challenges in software license management." Peregrine essentially does for software license management what Telco Exchange does for telecommunications management. However, their website also talks about a "Cable and Circuit" product which allows their customers to: "easily manage the connected infrastructure. This solution details the physical connectivity at a granular level, enabling you to manage and understand the data and voice services you provide to the rest of the organization. Cable and Circuit provides a set of best practices that reflect a lifecycle approach to managing the connected infrastructure, assisting end-users through common business practices and storing critical physical, business, financial, and contractual information about networks, into a centralized repository."

Our due diligence calls suggest that TX can compete favorably with the aforementioned companies. Our calls suggest that TX offers the most complete and most highly integrated telecommunications management solution on the market. When TX loses competitive accounts it has been because the customer has chosen (a) to completely outsource their telecommunications management, (b) to use outside analysts to manage their dispute resolution, or (c) to purchase a cheaper, more limited financial management-only solution. If a customer wants to keep management in-house and they recognize the importance of inventory management (or that you cannot do effective invoice reconciliation without an accurate circuit inventory), TX seems to compete very well.

Once purchased, customers appear very happy and the ROI is compelling.

CUSTOMER CALLS

Senior manager @ IKON:

- Runs $50,000,000 a year telecommunications budget
- Found TX via a Google search; knew he wanted an Oracle based system that could manage inventory and invoices, and which could interact with their general ledger and HR systems
- Looked closely at Teldata (but their outsourced solution would have cost in excess of $1mm a year) and ProfitLab (but they couldn't match TX's functionality). Note: it was impressive that TX beat out ProfitLab b/c ProfitLab was already IKON's audit vendor and the CEO of ProfitLab used to run a division of IKON.
- Recognized the power of TX's system and fought hard for it; he strongly believes in their vision.
- Said TX is a "godsend"; and TX has "made me a superstar within the company"

EXHIBIT 1 | (continued)

- Believes that any company with more than 1,000 cell phones should buy TX for that reason alone b/c TX helped save $100,000 a month on their Nextel bill.
- TX dramatically reduced the number of invoices they have to deal with and the inventory management system identified circuits that they were being billed for in locations that they closed four years ago.
- All told, he claims that TX will save IKON $3.3 mm this year
- Thinks team is "outstanding" and "very responsive"

Senior manager @ Agere:

- 32 veteran of AT&T; 2 years at Lucent
- He knew that Agere would need a telecommunications management system after the spin-out; and he estimated that it would have cost 2-3x what TX charged to fix Lucent's homegrown system. AT&T Solutions did a study and confirmed his cost estimates.
- Used combination of Gartner, Andersen and the web to identify provisioning and inventory tools.
- He identified 10 candidates and short-listed 4 (but, he couldn't remember their names).
- Said that TX's provisioning background and experience was a real strength; especially fact that they understood both voice and data (very different technical needs)
- Very impressed by their software; he committed 25% of his budget (including headcount) for a 5 year license. He also has a contract with Teldata Control for bill reconciliation.
- ROI "wasn't an issue"; "tool is very powerful"; "absolutely moves you to a higher level of management."
- "Currently looking to give them more business and add modules."
- Views them as "a business partner, not just a vendor."

Senior manager @ Marriott Corporation:

- Manages about 15 people
- Marriott has 2,600 hotel and remote site locations worldwide
- Three years ago, he began looking for an enterprise telecom management platform; he sent out an RFI and looked at Gartner reports. Initially narrowed their list down to MetaSolv (they originally wanted to target enterprise customers as well as carriers) and Wisor Telecom and a 3rd company he couldn't remember. Sept. 11th then devastated the hotel industry and the project was shelved.
- One year ago, he revisited the project and learned that MetaSolv was only focused on carriers. Then a Marriott affiliate (Marriott Vacation Clubs) recommended that he speak with TX.
- He also evaluated Tangoe—and while he concluded that they had a good solution for financial management, they did not have inventory tracking capabilities. Conversely, when he had evaluated MetaSolv and others, he found that they had strong inventory tracking functionality but weak financial management capabilities.
- TX was the first company he found that had both inventory management and financial management capabilities.
- The final reason he chose TX was their AT&T relationship. AT&T had recommended TX and roughly 90% of the Marriott network rides on AT&T, so the deep integration with AT&T's provisioning systems was a significant positive.
- Marriott's evaluation process lasted 9 months—the project is currently in the testing phase. He believes the project will go live in January 2004. The implementation is on schedule and in some areas (AT&T XML integration) ahead of schedule.
- He said that the value proposition was pretty easy to sell internally. By doing a high-level, cursory manual billing audit, he found $500,000 of annual savings due to overcharging by AT&T. He said the savings would be significantly larger if he took a deep look, but he did not need to do this to convince the buying authorities of the ROI.

(continued)

EXHIBIT 1 | Excerpt from Telco Exchange Investment Memo (*continued*)

- He shares the TX vision and believes there is real value in an end-to-end platform that manages all aspects of telecommunications (above and beyond mere bill reconciliation and auditing). "Innovation and Automation" are key themes to the projects he is funding.
- TX is a top 5 IT priority for Marriott
- Team at TX has been "outstanding, knowledgeable and very customer-centric"
- Future functionality they'd like to see would be integration into Siebel and HP Openview.

In conclusion, we believe TX should be able to compete well, especially with customers that fit the following profile:

- Greater than $10mm in annual telecom spend
- Multiple locations and/or frequent location churn
- Forced to deal with a heterogeneous telecom environment (e.g. multiple carriers)
- In the midst of a technical / infrastructure up-grade
- In need of tighter cost allocations
- In the midst of a BPO/BPA or cost savings initiative

IS IT WORTH IT?

Proposed Capitalization Table

The proposed fully diluted capitalization of the company is as follows:

	Pre-Money	Post-Money
Valhalla Partners		25.0%
Columbia Capital		25.0%
Current management: CEO and 3 VPs	100.0%	35.0%
Employees (Options)	0.0%	15.0%
TOTAL	100.0%	100.0%

Working from the public comparables' trading multiples, we see the following valuation scenarios:

Valhalla Ownership	25%
Total Valhalla Investment	$ 3,750,000

Company's Model	Exit Multiple	Company Exit Valuation	40% Discount	20% Discount	Post-Discount Valhalla Multiple	Valhalla Multiple (No Discount)
2007 Revenue	$ 84,700,000	2.0	$ 169,400,000	$ 101,640,000	$ 135,520,000	6.8–9.0	11.3
2007 Net Income (After-Tax)	$ 9,834,000	23.0	$ 226,182,000	$ 135,709,200	$180,945,600	9.0–12.1	15.1

Valhalla's Model (Conservative Scenario)	Exit Multiple	Company Exit Valuation	40% Discount	20% Discount	Post-Discount Valhalla Multiple	Valhalla Multiple (No Discount)
2007 Revenue	$ 57,480,000	2.0	$ 114,960,000	$ 68,976,000	$ 91,968,000	4.6–6.1	7.7
2007 Net Income (After-Tax)	$ 3,999,600	23.0	$ 91,990,800	$ 55,194,480	$ 73,592,640	3.7–4.9	6.1

* Note: Our conservative scenario reduces the Net Income estimates in the Company's model because their model resulted in unrealistic margins. * Note 2: After-Tax Net Income assumes a 33% tax rate.

EXHIBIT 1 | (*continued*)

Our forecasts result in returns that range from 3.7 to 15.1 times invested capital.

Our more conservative forecasts (based on the revisions to their financial model outlined above and assuming an illiquidity discount) result in returns that range from 4.6 to 6.1 times invested capital.

However, none of these valuation forecasts take into consideration the beneficial impact of our securities being participating preferred securities.

We also believe that there is a significant chance that exit multiples increase between now and the time at which we exit the investment.

Another significant opportunity for upside is for the company to exceed the assumed $250,000 in one-time software license revenue per transaction.

"100 DAY PLAN"

1) Identify and recruit CEO and, potentially, CFO candidates
2) Help identify sales talent
3) Help identify and recruit strong, value-add and independent Director
4) Work with company to establish appropriate revenue recognition policies
5) Work with company to establish appropriate stock-option plan
6) Work with company to develop new name and branding message
7) Work with company to establish proper analyst relationships and to articulate "strategic telecom management" message
8) Work with company on pricing strategy
   a) How should the products be packaged and priced?
   b) Multiple year licenses?
   c) Gain share opportunities?
   d) Product / services mix?
   e) Channel development and pricing
9) Introduce company to national accounting firms and appropriate banks

---

Source: Company.

EXHIBIT 2 | Overview of Valhalla Partners Due Diligence Process

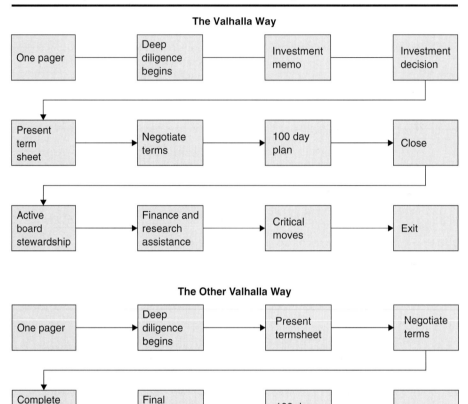

Note: The "other way" would be used in a case where Valhalla was in competition with other VC firms and needed to get a term sheet on the table quickly.

Source: Company.

MAC Development Corporation

Colleen, the bank meeting is scheduled for Thursday and we still haven't figured out how to get the $500,000 revolving line of credit we need to meet the bank's debt covenants for the $2 million construction loan. If Harwich Bank and Trust Company hadn't backed out on their commitment to provide the revolver ten days ago, we would be done with all of the financing issues and could spend much needed time on the other issues bearing down on us. The seller and I are still $75,000 apart on the final purchase price for the land and I'm unsure how to handle the required sale of the first lot. Given that we'd like to close on October 9, I don't have time to make a mistake.

Dick McCaffrey, Sunday night, September 30, 2001

Colleen McCaffrey, Dick McCaffrey's daughter, spent part of the summer between her first and second years at Harvard Business School working for MAC Development Corporation (MACD), her family's commercial real estate development organization. MACD was trying to close on a 41-acre site in Woodland, Illinois on October 9, 2001; MACD would develop the property for land sale of seven industrial properties. Dick McCaffrey had worked on the deal for two years and was eagerly anticipating completing the land purchase so they could begin and finish earthwork before winter. Before MACD could close on the land purchase, however, several issues still needed to be resolved.

The first piece of the puzzle involved the Village of Woodland, which had informally committed to contributing $4.1 million toward land development. Before the commitment could be finalized, the Village Board needed to approve both the project and the Village's financial contribution. Dick McCaffrey was concerned that the unpredictability of the local government and vocal Village residents could jeopardize the $4.1 million agreement, a key feature of the deal. McCaffrey knew that Village residents

Colleen McCaffrey (MBA '02) prepared this case under the supervision of Professor Richard G. Hamermesh. HBS cases are developed solely as the basis for class discussion. Cases are not intended to serve as endorsements, sources of primary data, or illustrations of effective or ineffective management. The identities of certain individuals and institutions have been disguised.

were concerned about several aspects of the project. First, the business park would be located near a residential area. Second, development of the property required mitigating several wetlands.[1] McCaffrey was confident that their design protected the residents and that they would gain the necessary approvals at the Village Board meeting on the evening of October 2, but worried that the residents would not see it that way.

Another piece of the puzzle involved the debt portion of the project. MACD had signed an agreement with Bank One on September 14 to provide the necessary funds for closing, in the form of a $2 million construction loan. The loan required MACD's compliance with certain covenants, two of which were causing difficulties. First, MACD needed to have a signed purchase and sale (P&S) agreement for one of the seven parcels on the 41-acre site by October 9. The Village was not satisfied with the prospective buyer of the first lot so MACD needed to find another buyer or find a way to make the prospective buyer more acceptable to the Village. Second, the bank required that MACD obtain a revolving line of credit to pay subcontractors their fees while MACD waited for the Village funds. Harwich Bank and Trust Company, which had agreed to provide the revolver, had backed out, leaving MACD without the revolver.

A third piece of the puzzle involved finalizing the transaction with the property's current owner. MACD had established a purchase agreement with the seller in January 2000, but was still negotiating the final price. At the most recent negotiation on September 27, 2001, MACD and the seller were $75,000 apart on the price. Even if they could come to an agreement before October 9, Dick McCaffrey was concerned because the seller had, on previous occasions with other buyers, failed to show up at closing to exert pressure on the buyer to renegotiate terms.

Colleen McCaffrey was unsure exactly what to tell her father and reflected:

> I've always been interested in MACD's projects, but working there over the summer and studying the details while applying tools I'd just learned in school took this interest to a whole new level. The risks on this project are high, but so are the rewards. We have been very deliberate in this project, but now events are starting to force our hand. It is important that we don't make a big mistake now.

Company Background

An entrepreneur by nature, Dick McCaffrey started his first business when he was 13 years old. He and his brother, John Pat McCaffrey, operated JP&D Blueline Service, which made blueprints of drawings for local architects. Dick McCaffrey and his brother used the profits from their business to pay their tuition at Marquette High, the local private high school.

In 1976, at age 31, Dick McCaffrey incorporated McCaffrey & Associates (see **Exhibit 1** for a description of the various McCaffrey companies) as an engineering and architectural design firm. When he discovered that engineering fees were marginal for

---

[1]Wetlands are marshes that are frequently protected by the government. Government regulations typically require developers to construct a wetland of 50% greater size within the area when plan layout requires the developer to fill in an existing wetland with soil. The process of filling in existing wetlands and constructing new wetlands is called "mitigation."

the liability risks associated with design, Dick McCaffrey decided to form a general contracting company to execute McCaffrey & Associates' designs. According to McCaffrey,

> Engineering carries more risk than contracting and earns smaller fees. We decided to enter into contracting to control the risk and make more money and found out that this design/build integration eliminates lots of problems including communication breakdowns between the designer and the contractor and the liability of having someone poorly execute your good plan or having you execute well on someone else's bad plan. Moreover, it eliminated the time and money spent on blame resolution when something goes wrong.

In 1980, Dick McCaffrey added MAC Construction Corporation to do general contracting for the projects that McCaffrey & Associates designed. To generate business, MAC Construction would frequently find land for clients, develop financial models to demonstrate the feasibility of owning a new building, and motivate the project through completion. Discovering that they were completing all the functions of a developer except project financing but were not charging for them, the McCaffreys formed MACD in 1997.

Using this structure, MACD initiated a project and then hired McCaffrey & Associates to perform project architecture and engineering and MAC Construction to manage construction through completion. On design and construction projects, McCaffrey companies would typically earn fees with gross profit equal to 15 to 20% of the project's constructed value. They also retained additional value in the form of equity on some projects.

The McCaffrey companies had two full-time employees: Dick McCaffrey and his son, Brian McCaffrey (see **Exhibit 2** for bios of company management and family members). Dick McCaffrey, age 56, had earned undergraduate and masters degrees in Civil and Structural Engineering and had worked in the industry for over 30 years. Brian McCaffrey, age 33, had earned an undergraduate degree in Business Administration and a masters degree in Architecture. He had worked with McCaffrey companies for seven years. Dick McCaffrey's wife, Jane McCaffrey, age 56, had earned an undergraduate degree in English and had worked for McCaffrey companies part time for 20 years managing the money and finding potential customers. Dick and Jane McCaffrey's three other children helped out in the business as their other employment and abilities permitted. Tim McCaffrey, age 31, was an attorney who discussed legal matters with the McCaffrey companies from time to time. Colleen McCaffrey, age 27, was a former information technology consultant and an MBA candidate at Harvard Business School who helped with strategy and finance. Jim McCaffrey, age 24, was a civil engineer who worked as a project engineer for a large construction company. Brian McCaffrey's wife, Debie McCaffrey, age 32, was a former retail buyer who also contributed in family business meetings. While they always felt connected to the family business and completed various tasks for the company in their younger years, the non-business family members also contributed time because they were owners; as a Christmas gift in 1998, Dick and Jane McCaffrey gave each of their four children 5% ownership of MACD.

To keep overhead low, the McCaffreys operated the various companies from their home in Hoffman Estates, IL. They converted three of their children's old bedrooms to offices for Dick, Jane and Brian McCaffrey and maintained drafting and printing machinery in a 250 square foot (sf) addition to the home. A local facility provided professional meeting space and a business address to receive the companies' mail on a fee-for-service basis.

Project Background

In August 1999, Dick McCaffrey's attorney referred him to a property for sale in Woodland, Illinois, a Chicago suburb. The 41-acre site was vacant land zoned for industrial use, and located near residences, a shopping mall, theater, and small industrial business park. The property was five minutes a major expressway leading to Chicago and was surrounded by thriving business communities including Schaumburg, Elgin, and Hoffman Estates.

The Leone family, who owned the parcel for sale, had at one time owned much of the land in Woodland and had developed a contentious relationship with the Village over the years. Because of this poor relationship, the Village had blocked the Leone's attempts to develop the property. The vacant land had become a dumping ground with car bodies, kids' bicycles, and steel drums littering the area (see **Exhibit 3** for photographs of the site). Numerous wetlands had formed because of prior failed attempts to develop the parcel. In addition to this difficult relationship with the Village, the Leone family group was fighting internally. These factors had led to the desire to sell the land.

Dick McCaffrey explained his deal-making philosophy: "If we're going to do business together, you name the price and I'll name the terms. If I can agree to your price, I will." He negotiated with the seller, and they agreed on a purchase price of $1.50 per square foot. Dick McCaffrey's terms required the seller to provide credits (i.e., reductions to the negotiated purchase price) for wetland mitigation, environmental clean-up, road construction, and poor soil remediation. The P&S indicated that certain of these credits would go into an escrow account[2] at closing, and that these funds would be drawn from the escrow account as needed during construction. Additionally, the contract terms of the purchase agreement stated that MACD would receive the entire 41-acre parcel but would only pay for usable land.[3] Subsequent investigation into the property revealed that 28 acres, or 1.2 million sf, were usable, bringing the total purchase price to $1.8 million. Comparable developed property in the area sold at $4.25/sf or more. In the purchase agreement, MACD's attorney included a clause requiring the seller to guarantee that the land had never been used as a dumping ground. The contract also established that if any part of the contract were untrue to the seller's knowledge, the seller would be responsible for all legal fees in the event of contract disputes. The Leones and MACD agreed to the terms and signed the purchase agreement on January 17, 2000. Under the purchase agreement, MACD paid a $10,000 deposit (which was held in escrow) for the exclusive right but not the obligation to purchase the land. The deposit was fully refundable during an eighteen-month due diligence period if the buyer

---

[2]Escrow is an account managed by an independent third party from which funds may be deducted when pre-established conditions have been met.

[3]Usable land included property not covered with wetlands or designated for streets.

decided not to purchase the land. If not exercised, this right would expire in two years. If exercised, the deposit would be applied to the land purchase.

With the purchase agreement in place, MACD began its due diligence, completing an appraisal in the spring. The appraisal established that the purchase price was considerably below the current market value for undeveloped property. The Phase I assessment was completed in July 2000 and investigated the background of the property from existing regulatory agency reports. It uncovered no significant problems with the property. Given this background work, the McCaffrey family decided to continue investing in developing the property. They named the property Phoenix Lake Business Park because the symbolism of the phoenix rising out of the ashes seemed prophetic for the site's destiny. The Phase II environmental assessment proceeded in stages and was completed in June 2001. This assessment investigated the land through digging test pits and testing soil and water samples and revealed that only the surface litter required cleanup and that the land and water appeared to be in good shape.

Property Design and Wetland Mitigation

MACD apportioned the property into seven lots for large buildings of 20,000 sf or greater. This design was based on Dick McCaffrey's experience: "economies of scale dictate that a company that wants a small building should buy a condo or lease inside a larger building." Significant fixed costs driving the economies of scale included design fees, project management, utilities, legal and accounting expenses, government approval process costs, and subcontractors' bidding costs and overhead.

The property contained seven wetlands requiring mitigation. To allow for an efficient layout, Brian McCaffrey designed the park so that the relocated wetlands would provide a buffer zone between neighboring residents and the business park of 380 feet where only 100 feet was required (see **Exhibit 4** for aerial photographs and computer-generated renderings of the design). His design ensured that the excess buffer did not come at the expense of salable land because regulations required the wetlands to be relocated rather than eliminated.

Despite these efforts to protect the residents, MACD was worried that concerns about relocating the wetlands and about traffic in the residential area would hinder the Village approvals process. Before the Village public hearings, MACD had mailed a letter to neighboring residents on May 10, 2001 explaining the project's benefits to them and the efforts being taken to protect their interests (see **Exhibit 5** for a copy of the letter). MACD hoped the letter would mitigate residents' resistance that could jeopardize the project.

Village Board Approvals

The vacant land was an eyesore and represented significant opportunity costs to the Village with regard to tax revenue and jobs. The Village was eager for the land to be developed by someone other than the Leone family. After signing the P&S agreement, Dick McCaffrey approached Village staff about the possibility of establishing the land as a Tax Incremental Financing (TIF) district. As a TIF district, the project would enjoy two benefits: the Village would contribute to the cost of developing the land because of the value to the community of putting it to productive use; and the Village would share some of the incremental tax revenue it received due to the land's higher valuation. Village staff signed an "inducement resolution" in June 2000, which committed their good faith effort to work for the approval of the business park plan and the TIF agreement.

Village staff worked with MACD to develop a program where the Village would provide a $1.5 million TIF infrastructure contribution to be paid, during the construction period, to MACD for public improvements, including road construction, utility and sewer development, and environmental clean-up. These funds would be released as MACD demonstrated that they had completed the work for which the funds were earmarked. [Indeed, it was the time lag between paying the subcontractors for this work and receiving the cash from the Village that had led the Village to insist that MACD obtain the revolver.] The Village committed another $2.6 million in TIF tax reimbursements to be paid to MACD over 12 years out of the incremental tax revenue that the Village would receive from the property's high valuation. Village staff also agreed to recommend that the Village grant a property tax abatement to companies that purchased lots from MACD for development.

To calculate how much would be received in incremental tax revenue from the development, the Village would need a base year tax assessment. Each year for the past 20 years, the property value for tax purposes had been assessed at $14,700. In year 2000, for an unknown reason, the land was assessed at $429,505 and the Leone family had neglected to challenge the assessment. With this higher base, the incremental annual taxes produced by MACD's development would be lower, making the TIF tax reimbursements less. At MACD's urging, the Leones were appealing the tax assessment, but the outcome of this appeal was not likely to be returned until November 2001. McCaffrey estimated that if this appeal was unsuccessful, the TIF tax reimbursement would fall to two thirds of the forecasted level.

The process for approving a business park plan was complex. Ordinances required Village staff and the petitioner (MACD in this instance) to present their program to the Village's Plan Commission, comprised of eight appointed village residents in a series of two public hearings culminating in the Plan Commission's vote whether to recommend the plan to the Village Board. Majority approval was required. If the Plan Commission recommended the plan, ordinances then required Village staff and the petitioner to present the program to the Village Board, comprised of six elected Trustees, the Mayor, and the Village Clerk, in a series of two public hearings culminating in the Village Board's vote to decide whether to approve the plan. Majority approval was required. Village residents were encouraged to attend all hearings and express their views to Plan Commission and Village Board members, who would vote to support or deny the plan. Although members had the option of voting against the expressed wishes of the residents, it was less likely that they would vote in favor of the plan should residents express significant concerns. Approvals for the TIF district ordinance were similarly complex.

With the June 2000 inducement resolution, MACD had initiated the Village approvals process for both the business park plan and the TIF designation. Worried about the residents' potential concerns regarding the development and influence on

Plan Commission and Village Board members, MACD mailed a letter to residents explaining the benefits to them, prepared thoroughly for the required hearings and retained their wetlands, traffic and environmental consultants as well as their attorney and broker to attend the hearings to provide support and assist in answering questions. A small crowd of residents attended the Plan Commission hearings and expressed some concerns, but residents were generally satisfied by the MACD team's responses. The Plan Commission voted in May 2001 to recommend the program to the Village Board. MACD prepared for a similar set of hearings prior to the Village Board vote and experienced a similar response. The Village Board's final vote was scheduled for October 2. With experience as their guide, MACD was careful not to "count their chickens before they hatched." If the Village Board denied the plan, whether on their own or under last-minute pressure from residents, MACD would not be allowed to proceed. If the Village Board denied the TIF agreement, the deal would fall through because the economics of the project would no longer work and MACD would choose not to proceed. Under either negative outcome, MACD would lose the time and money it had invested to date.

Property Marketing

Phoenix Lake Business Park would be developed in phases, with land development preceding building construction. Land development would include environmental cleanup, road and utility construction, and wetland mitigation. MACD would complete these public improvements before beginning work on any of the building projects. Each of the seven building projects would be completed independently on a build-to-suit basis as buyers were identified. Each building's constructed value would be approximately $4,000,000.

MACD hoped to sell lots to customers prior to or during land development so MACD could move directly into building construction. A P&S agreement for one of the lots would have to be in place prior to MACD's closing on the land, since one of the loan covenants required that the agreement be in place at the time of the closing and that the first lot actually be sold within six months of MACD's purchasing the land.

These factors combined to necessitate that the sales effort begin before MACD closed on the land. MACD interviewed five commercial real estate brokers in January 2001. Brian McCaffrey recalled the broker selection process:

> Two of the brokers seemed promising at first. To evaluate one of them, we asked the broker to investigate another MACD property and propose a market value for the property. This young broker showed up in a yellow BMW M3, was cocky, and was wearing funky sunglasses. The broker underestimated the building's appraised value by $2 million and we decided not to use them. The other promising broker asked us to submit a proposal on a different project he was working on and, in the process, unethically provided us with the competitor's bid. We decided not to use this broker either, applying the philosophy that "what someone will do for you, he'll do to you."

Eventually, MACD found a suitable team in RXC. Dick and Brian McCaffrey explained that they were impressed by the lead broker's seasoned, straightforward, and honest manner. RXC was the only firm that felt they could make a pre-sale and wasn't pushing MACD to develop a speculative building.[4] MACD contracted with RXC in April 2001 to be the exclusive selling broker for one year, and the broker created a "tear sheet" regarding the property (see **Exhibit 6** for this brochure), completed mailings to prospective customers and made follow-up calls. In the first six months of the contract, they provided few prospects and made no sales. Brian McCaffrey summarized what MACD felt to be the source of the problem:

> First, a broker isn't motivated to sell if he can't deliver and we don't own the property yet. Second, the park is designed for build-to-suit occupants, meaning that the properties will be designed and built specifically for pre-identified customers. The build-to-suit occupancy process takes at least ten months. The speculative occupancy process takes two months. Because we pay the broker at building occupancy, they're probably more motivated to sell competitors' speculative buildings because they get their commission sooner. Finally, brokers tend to reduce the sale process to price and location decisions. This minimizes the value of the property infrastructure, which is what we focus on with build-to-suit.

The poor sales response was disconcerting to MACD. They worried about paying for and developing the land only to have it remain vacant. They wondered whether there were more effective ways to structure the broker relationship or provide sales incentives or whether they should allow the contract to elapse and select another broker or try to sell the lots themselves.

Investor Financing

To complete the land purchase and development, MACD needed to raise significant capital from a bank and from investors. Dick McCaffrey's high school friend had provided $150,000 of working capital for the project in May 2000, with the promise of a 25% return and McCaffrey's personal guarantee of the loan. MACD needed to raise additional capital and hoped it would come from this friend, from a partner who had invested in a previous MACD project, and from those investors' friends.

On the basis of feedback from potential investors, Dick McCaffrey was concerned that the planned offering of a priority return totaling a fixed 25% internal rate of return (IRR) would be appealing to some of the more risk-averse investors, but unappealing to others who had indicated willingness to take on more risk in exchange for participating in the project's potential upside. An alternate plan would offer a priority return with a fixed 20% IRR, but also including a share of ongoing cash flows. MACD's accounting firm proposed that these investors should own 40% of the cash flows after their priority returns were paid.

Colleen McCaffrey was finishing her first year at HBS and had discussed the development at length with her father. MACD hired Colleen to help formulate an investor offering. She proposed that, rather than choosing one of the two alternatives, MACD should offer two classes of membership for investors with different risk profiles.

---

[4]A speculative project is designed for a hypothetical "generic" occupant and built without an owner or tenant. This requires the developer to raise project financing and assume the resulting vacancy risk.

However, before finalizing the offering to investors, she felt it was important to consider the impact of a few factors that were difficult for MACD to predict and control. These included lot sale dates, lot sale prices, and the outcome of the Leones' tax assessment appeal.

To assess these uncertainties, Colleen estimated aggressive, moderate, and conservative sets of assumptions regarding lot sale date and price, as well as the outcome of the tax appeal. She formulated every combination of the variables to create 18 scenarios for each proposed class of membership, ran them through the baseline projection (see **Exhibit 7a and 7b** for the project's baseline cash flows and cash flows to each class of investors) created by the accountants, and determined the returns under each scenario.

Using the model and sensitivity analysis to evaluate potential investment offerings, MACD settled on a two-class offering. MACD would offer ownership units for $100 each. Investors could choose Class A or Class B units. Once the bank loans were repaid, the Class A and B units would receive all of the cash flow from the project until they had reached their respective "target" returns (see below). Then, the McCaffrey family's ownership units—which were termed C units—would receive all of the cash flow until they received their target return (see below). Then, the McCaffrey family's Class C units and the Class B owners would continue to receive the ongoing cash flows from the project until its completion.

Specifically, the basic outline of these three classes of ownership was as follows:

- Investors in Class A units would receive a share of cash flow until they reached a 25% IRR, and then their ownership interests would be redeemed by the company and their participation would end.

- Investors in Class B units would share pro-rata in the cash flow with the A units until the B units had achieved a 20% IRR. Payments would then be suspended until the Class A units had achieved a 25% return, and continue suspended until Class C units had reached their target return.

- The McCaffreys' Class C units would receive all the cash flow from the project after the above two classes had received their target returns until the Class C units had achieved an 18% IRR.

- Then, the B and C units would split all remaining cash flow until the completion of the development. (This was referred to as the "residual cash flow.")

Of course, all of the proportions depended upon how many units of each class were actually purchased.

MACD needed some of the funds as working capital prior to closing and some for land development after closing. Those investors willing to allow their money to be used as working capital prior to closing would earn a bonus of 20% of their purchased units in the form of free "bonus units." If the land purchase did not close, MACD would not guarantee the return of those funds. Those investors not willing to allow their money to be used as working capital prior to closing would provide their money to be placed in escrow until closing. If the land purchase did not close, MACD would return their investment.

MACD hoped to raise up to $850,000 from investors in this offering. The project could not afford the lengthy fundraising period that could result if the returns were perceived as too low. Colleen McCaffrey hoped that the lessons she had learned in her HBS Entrepreneurial Manager and Finance classes would prove valuable for MACD. She reflected:

> I was worried that, in trying to protect MACD's returns, I had created an untenable offer for investors. MACD had already discussed a preferred return equivalent to 25% IRR with their main investor, so I knew we couldn't offer less for the fixed class, but was unsure what would be reasonable for the class with ongoing ownership. I wanted to increase our returns and thought we were giving away too much. My father pointed out that our equity return was not our only source of income from the project. He felt that we needed to make sure that investors were happy so that they would invest in building development projects once the land development was completed and so we didn't waste too much time in lengthy negotiations.

MACD sent the offering to its potential investors on June 11, 2001. By July 31, MACD had received commitments for $650,000 of investment with $150,000 designated as available for working capital. In addition to the newly available $150,000 in working capital was the $150,000 that had been previously provided by Dick McCaffrey's high school friend. Thus MACD finalized the equity financing at $800,000. Dick McCaffrey's high school friend and his partner from a previous project had both been instrumental in the fundraising process by bringing in their friends. In total, MACD had enlisted two investors directly and five more indirectly and had received all investors' checks by September 15.

Finally, the McCaffreys had to decide how many of the Class C units to allocate to themselves (of course, this was related to their notion of how much of the residual cash flows they had to leave on the table for the Class B investors). Ultimately, they decided to allocate themselves 6,250 Class C units. Dick McCaffrey explained: "We tried to value the services we had provided already, the time we had invested to date, and the time and energy we would expend over the life of the project. I thought that $625,000 was a fair value for all of this, and that equated to 6,250 units at the same $100 price other investors were paying. Of course, our units were the lowest priority return—we didn't get anything until the A and B investors had received their target returns."

By the time of the anticipated closing in early October, the forecast ownership structure[5] of the enterprise was as follows:

- Class A Units: 5,300 initially purchased, plus 300 additional to be issued as bonus units in exchange for use of cash as working capital, plus an additional bonus of 400 units to McCaffrey's high school friend for his preferred return = 6,000 Class A units.

---

[5]The project was structured as a limited liability company (LLC). A relatively new organizational form, an LLC was like a partnership in that it was not a tax-paying entity; profits and losses flowed through to the individual members or owners. However, as the name implied, an LLC offered the same protection from personal liability as the corporate form. As a result, LLCs were becoming a popular form of business organization.

- Class B Units: 2,700 initially purchased, plus 300 additional to be issued as bonus units = 3,000 Class B units
- Class C Units: 6,250 units held by the McCaffreys.

In addition to the development fees which the McCaffreys took in the form of equity, there were other fees for which they anticipated receiving cash. Specifically, their design firm was scheduled to receive approximately $160,000 in fees, and the construction firm, $600,000 in cash fees. These fees were included as part of the land development costs shown in **Exhibit 7a.**

Bank Financing

While raising equity, Dick McCaffrey was also trying to obtain bank financing; this effort had begun in May 2000. After evaluating several options, McCaffrey decided to work with Bank One. He and a loan officer at Bank One developed, over several iterations, a proposal for a $2 million loan for land purchase and land development expenses to be repaid from lot sale proceeds over two years, an additional $2 million letter of credit guaranteeing completion of the public improvements that, barring unforeseen circumstances, would not be drawn down and therefore would not need to be repaid, and finally the $500,000 revolver for construction expenses to be repaid during land development by Village TIF funds.

The required terms of the loan included a personal guarantee of the funds from Dick McCaffrey, a first mortgage interest in the property itself, and a covenant requiring Village approval of the $1.5 million TIF infrastructure contribution. In addition, the bank required—by the time of the closing on the land—a signed P&S agreement for one of the lots, with closing to occur within six months of MACD's closing on the land. A previous MACD customer had indicated strong interest in building a 10,000 sf building surrounded by a parking lot for trucks used in his operation. Although having a building smaller than the desired project size and using part of the lot as a truck parking facility were not ideal, MACD needed a signed P&S prior to its closing and was inclined to encourage this customer to build in the business park. The Village Board, unenthusiastic about the land's use, established a clause that buildings in the park must be 20,000 sq. ft. minimum. The customer agreed to sign a P&S with the understanding that he would work with MACD to design a building that met his needs and satisfied plan requirements. If they could not accomplish this, MACD would have to find a replacement customer for the lot before the six-month window elapsed. Dick McCaffrey:

> I have done two previous buildings for this prospective buyer and we have tremendous trust and respect for each other. On the one hand, we're excited he's working with us to meet the bank's covenants. On the other hand, it's a little scary to consider that we may have to replace this customer at a moment's notice to avoid default on our loan.

Bank One also required MACD to pay for a second appraisal of the land, which would be offered as collateral on the loans. Typically, a commercial property appraisal would be the market value of the land and a bank would usually lend up to 80% of the land's market value. When the appraisal was completed, it came in at $3.35 million, significantly lower than expected. In hindsight, MACD realized that the appraiser had given the land no additional value for the TIF Tax Reimbursements to be paid to MACD over twelve years by the Village and had discounted the land value to wholesale prices should MACD have to sell it off in a fire sale.

On the basis of the low appraisal, Bank One revised its commitment letter on September 4, 2001 to indicate that it would lend $2 million for the land purchase and provide the $2 million letter of credit but would not provide the $500,000 revolver and that MACD would be required to secure this from another source. McCaffrey began looking for other financing sources. On September 12, MACD received a verbal commitment from Harwich Bank and Trust Company, where it conducted everyday banking functions, that they would provide the revolver. With this commitment, MACD paid Bank One a $20,000 non-refundable loan fee and finalized the commitment letter. However, on September 20, Harwich Bank and Trust Company backed out of its agreement, stating that "Bank One had claimed all the collateral."

Dick McCaffrey needed to work quickly to solve this problem and identified several options. 1) He could seek another bank to provide the revolver. He was skeptical about his chances for success, however, as it seemed unlikely that another bank would provide financing when Bank One and Harwich would not. Also, he did not have contacts at additional banks to ease a last-minute request. 2) He could seek the financing from an investor. One had indicated that he might be willing to induce his own bank to provide the revolver with his own assets as collateral. Dick McCaffrey expected that the investor would charge approximately $50,000 for this guarantee. 3) Dick McCaffrey could induce subcontractors to accept delayed payments either to win the job or to earn interest on the deferred fees. If the bank agreed, this deferred fee arrangement would eliminate the need for a line of credit. He worried about renegotiating the commitment letter with Bank One, however, as they had proven quick to add requirements during renegotiations. Dick McCaffrey wondered which of these or other options could be concluded quickly enough to permit MACD to close on the property on October 9.

Economic Risk: September 11, 2001

After the burst of the Internet bubble in Spring 2000, the economy had reached near-recession conditions, with construction and capital investment slowing significantly. After the terrorist attacks on the World Trade Center and the Pentagon on September 11, 2001, a recession appeared inevitable and the depth of the impact to the economy was unclear, but likely to be significant.

The Chicago area was home to United Airlines, Boeing and several other hospitality industry companies including Hyatt Hotels, which were severely impacted by the terrorist attacks. Local manufacturing and high-tech service companies were MACD's target customers. Prior to September 11, it had appeared that those industries were positioned for recovery, but the terrorist attacks and war effort could easily postpone any recovery. Colleen McCaffrey considered the impact of the economy on the project:

> With lot sales already proving difficult, I'm worried that developing a commercial/industrial business park in a time of slowed economic activity and capital investment is a tough proposition. However, the economy may prove to be beneficial in that we'll be buying subcontractors' services during the recession and might obtain favorable prices. And, of course, lower interest rates reduce the cost of our debt.

Resource Planning

Dick McCaffrey explained the McCaffrey companies' past resource planning issues:

> When we were a young company, we were interested in growing as fast as we could and becoming as big as we could. When the economy collapsed in the early 80's, we collapsed along with it and I had to let everyone go. It scarred me to the point where I could not imagine hiring anybody again. Since then we've stayed so small that all our resources are devoted to developing and building a single project. When that project is completed, I have to go out and sell the next one. In the case of this Phoenix Lake project, we lost a lot of time in 2000 because I was working on another development that eventually fell through.

MACD had been productive with only two full-time employees. However, if they were able to close on the land and begin construction, it would be important for Dick McCaffrey to be developing the building projects. Brian McCaffrey would be consumed with designing the buildings. MACD would need help with construction project management. If they could develop projects at a faster rate, MACD would also need someone to complete finance and business administration work and would need additional design and project management personnel.

Anticipating this problem, MACD offered the youngest McCaffrey, Jim, a civil engineer with construction project management experience, a position with the company. The offer was contingent on closing on the property. Jim McCaffrey evaluated his options:

> I've always wanted to work in the family business, but I'm not sure whether it's too soon in my career to work for my family in such a small company with so much financial risk. I'm also not sure how working with my parents and brother will impact our personal relationships. On the bright side, Brian offered to help me deal with the issue of working out of my old bedroom and Mom promised not to give me a hug and a kiss every time I leave the office for home.

Land Purchase

With the closing date of October 9 quickly approaching, Dick McCaffrey had set up a meeting with the seller on September 27 to review the final purchase price in light of the seller's credits that had been built into the purchase agreement. Dick McCaffrey commented:

> I knew the seller was aware that the credits for wetland mitigation, environmental clean-up, road construction, and soil remediation were adding up, but I didn't think they knew just how bad it would be and I didn't want to have any surprises on closing day. As it turns out, the credits added up to $1.32 million dollars of the $1.8 million purchase price and the seller would only receive $80,000 on closing day with $400,000 more released from escrow over the next few years if we didn't have to use the contingency funds. In all honesty, the Leones had helped us out on several occasions. I wanted them to be paid more than that for their property, but I had to balance this with the obligation to get the best deal for my investors. I also knew we weren't likely to succeed by paying so little because the seller

would risk legal action rather than live with a deal like that and we couldn't afford the time that suing them would take. But, I wanted to set expectations for the meeting. When the seller heard the price in our meeting, there was a lot of yelling. This seller has a reputation for trying to create pressure on the buyer by not showing up at closing. I wanted to exert return pressure based on the site's environmental problems and the seller's poor relationship with the Village. We had maintained the confidentiality of our environmental assessments because we'd paid for them and they were proprietary. Because the results of the environmental studies were not public and because of the real uncertainty despite the positive outcome of the studies, I think that this return pressure was effective in keeping the seller at the table to renegotiate a price we could both live with. By the end of the day, I was offering them $775,000 while they were insisting on $850,000. I agreed that we would pay the entire sum at closing, eliminating the escrow account. We've agreed to talk again this Tuesday morning (October 2).

Current Situation

When they began investigating the project, the McCaffrey family had a meeting to decide whether the potential payoff was significant enough to invest $3,500 in appraising the property with the understanding that if the appraisal yielded negative results they would lose money and abandon the project. This kicked off a series of decision points with associated investments and potential payoffs. At each decision point, MACD's assessment of the potential payoff had grown, they decided to continue to pursue the project and, subsequently, their interim investments grew (see **Exhibit 8** for a list of MACD's pre-closing expenses).

By September 2001, MACD had invested two years' effort and $311,500 in expenses in pursuing the project (See **Exhibit 9** for a timeline of the project's history). MACD had negotiated with many of their service providers to accept deferred payments for work they had performed, totaling an additional $205,831 in deferred expenses. This $205,831 needed to be paid even if the deal fell through. Of the expenses that had been paid, investors supplied $191,500 cash and McCaffrey companies contributed $120,000 cash. McCaffrey anticipated paying himself back this $120,000 out of the proceeds from the closing. All of these costs were built into the cash flow projections and project financing, and were expected to be paid should the land purchase close and the project move forward as anticipated, but the investment had accumulated to the point where it had become difficult for MACD to consider any option other than to continue with the project. Nonetheless, with the Village Board meeting only two days away, no agreement on the purchase price of the land, no signed purchase agreement for the sale of the first lot, and the $500,000 revolving credit line not in place, a great deal had to be resolved for the Phoenix Lake Business Park to come to fruition. Dick McCaffrey reflected:

> We originally expected to close on the property in September 2000. Our commitments of resources and time were all made with a target date of last year. When you don't have any money and find yourself ensnared, it's either win or go bankrupt. We often wonder, if we were wealthy people, would we have risked all that money and time? Sometimes it starts to feel like the only option is to move forward.

EXHIBIT 1 | Description of McCaffrey Businesses

McCAFFREY & ASSOCIATES, INC. was formed in 1976 as an Illinois professional corporation by Richard McCaffrey to provide engineering and architectural design services. The company is an "S" corporation and reports income on a cash basis. Richard McCaffrey is licensed as an Illinois Structural Engineer and as a professional engineer in other states. He is the sole owner and only employee and is paid through a year-end profit distribution. The company's principal clients are the related companies, MAC DEVELOPMENT CORPORATION and MAC CONSTRUCTION CORPORATION.

MAC CONSTRUCTION CORPORATION was formed in 1980 as an Illinois corporation by Richard McCaffrey and Jane McCaffrey (his wife) to provide general contracting services. In 1992 the company was converted to a "C" corporation. The founders, Richard McCaffrey and Jane McCaffrey, own all the stock. Brian McCaffrey (son) is also an employee and vice-president. All construction trades are subcontracted. The firm specializes in commercial and industrial construction.

MAC DEVELOPMENT CORPORATION was formed in 1997 as a "C" corporation. The company is engaged in real estate development and management activities. The company is owned by Richard and Jane McCaffrey (40% each) and their four children, Brian, Timothy, Colleen and James (5% each).

McCAFFREY FAMILY LIMITED PARTNERSHIP is a real estate investment partnership and is owned by Richard and Jane McCaffrey (40% each) and their four children, Brian, Timothy, Colleen and James (5% each). The partnership owns 71% of Phoenix 1, LLC.

Source: MAC Development Corporation.

EXHIBIT 2 | Biographies of Management

Richard McCaffrey, S.E., P.E., President, MAC Development Corporation, MAC Construction Corporation, and McCaffrey & Associates, Inc.

Mr. McCaffrey, age 56, has been President of McCaffrey & Associates, which completes consulting engineering related to buildings, electric transmission lines, engineered products and failure analysis, since 1976. He has been President of MAC Construction Corporation, which completes general contracting for commercial and industrial buildings, since 1980. Mr. McCaffrey has been President of MAC Development Corporation, which develops commercial and industrial properties, since 1997. Prior to forming the McCaffrey companies, Mr. McCaffrey was a structural engineer completing engineering design related to buildings and large hydraulic structures for the firms Teng & Associates, Inc., Consoer, Townsend & Associates, Inc., and the Engineers Collaborative, Inc. Mr. McCaffrey has a Master of Science degree in Structural Engineering from Marquette University and a Bachelor of Science degree in Civil Engineering from Marquette University. His work has been published in the *Construction Guidebook, American Society of Civil Engineers Structural Engineering Journal,* and *American Society of Civil Engineers Transportation Engineering Journal.* Mr. McCaffrey has professional licenses in Illinois, Wisconsin, and Michigan and is affiliated with American Society of Civil Engineers, Structural Engineers Association of Illinois, National Society of Professional Engineers, Sigma Xi, the Scientific Research Society, American Concrete Institute and American Welding Society. Mr. McCaffrey is married to Jane McCaffrey and is father of Brian, Timothy, Colleen, and James McCaffrey.

(continued)

EXHIBIT 2 | Biographies of Management (*continued*)

Jane McCaffrey, Vice President, MAC Development Corporation

Mrs. McCaffrey, age 56, has been Vice President of MAC Development Corporation since 1997. She works with the McCaffrey companies part-time completing marketing, strategic planning, and financial management functions. Since 1994, Mrs. McCaffrey has been a freelance writer and speaker, with contributions to the *Chicago Tribune* and www.theknot.com. She is also a partner in a company formed to produce women's seminars. Mrs. McCaffrey graduated Cum Laude from University of Wisconsin – Milwaukee with a Bachelor of Science degree in English. Mrs. McCaffrey is married to Richard McCaffrey and is mother of Brian, Timothy, Colleen, and James McCaffrey.

Brian McCaffrey, M. Arch, Vice President, MAC Development Corporation and MAC Construction Corporation and Project Manager, McCaffrey & Associates Inc.

Mr. McCaffrey, age 33, joined the McCaffrey companies in 1994. He completes architectural design for all phases of building development and manages construction projects including jobsite supervision and quality control, implementation of safety programs, and construction administration. Prior to joining the McCaffrey companies, Mr. McCaffrey was an Information Technology Consultant with Innovative Systems Group and an Information Technology Analyst with Commonwealth Edison. Mr. McCaffrey has a First Professionals Masters degree in Architecture from the Illinois Institute of Technology and received the American Institute of Architects/AAF scholarship award for First Professional Master's degree candidates. Mr. McCaffrey has a Bachelor of Science degree in Business Administration from Marquette University. Mr. McCaffrey is married to Debie McCaffrey and is father of Alaina, Collin, and Emily McCaffrey.

Timothy McCaffrey, J.D., Associate, Winston & Strawn

Mr. McCaffrey, age 31, has been employed as an attorney by Winston & Strawn since 1996 with construction litigation as one of several specializations. McCaffrey companies have employed Mr. McCaffrey temporarily in the past. Mr. McCaffrey has a Doctoral degree in Jurisprudence from Indiana University and a Bachelor of Science degree in Business Administration from Indiana University.

Colleen McCaffrey

Ms. McCaffrey, age 27, is a candidate for a Masters in Business Administration degree from Harvard Business School in June 2002. Prior to attending graduate school, Ms. McCaffrey worked as an Information Technology Consultant for Deloitte Consulting and Andersen Consulting. Ms. McCaffrey was employed by MAC Development Corporation during Summer 2001 and has been employed by McCaffrey companies temporarily prior to that time. Ms. McCaffrey has a Bachelor of Science degree in Speech from Northwestern University.

James McCaffrey, Project Manager, Power Construction Corporation

Mr. McCaffrey, age 24, has worked for Power Construction since 1999 managing construction of large commercial buildings. McCaffrey companies have employed him temporarily in the past. Mr. McCaffrey has a Bachelor of Science degree in Civil Engineering from Northwestern University.

Debie McCaffrey

Mrs. McCaffrey, age 32, was a retail buyer for Sears Corporation for three years ending in 2000, when she left to take care of her children full-time. Prior to working for Sears, Mrs. McCaffrey was a retail buyer for Spiegel and a retail manager for Casual Corner. McCaffrey companies have employed Mrs. McCaffrey in the past. Mrs. McCaffrey has a Bachelor of Science degree in Business Administration from Marquette University. Mrs. McCaffrey is married to Brian McCaffrey and is mother of Alaina, Collin, and Emily McCaffrey.

Source: MAC Development Corporation.

EXHIBIT 3 | Phoenix Lake Business Park: Photographs

40.7 Acres
Existing Conditions

Source: MAC Development Corporation.

EXHIBIT 4 | Plans for Phoenix Lake Business Park

Phoenix Lake Business Park

BEFORE AFTER

Source: MAC Development Corporation.

EXHIBIT 5 | MAC Development Corporation Letter to Neighbors

May 10, 2001

Name

Address

City, State, Zip

Dear Neighbor:

We are preparing to purchase a parcel of property near you and want to tell you about our plans and how they will benefit you. The property is approximately 41 acres, including a segment of the pond, south of Leone Drive and west of Frances Avenue. It was originally a farm, but abandoned construction for a subdivision left behind a dangerous clay stockpile and caused the formation of several small wetlands. This, combined with unauthorized dumping over the years, has degraded the condition of the property.

We plan to renovate and renew this area by building a new business park with a heavily landscaped nature preserve to screen the homes on the west from the industrial and commercial areas to the east and south. Our proposed use matches the current zoning required by the Village (I-1 Office, Research and Restricted Industrial District).

Benefits to you include:

- Taxes: Tax revenue is projected to exceed $400,000 per year as a result of this development, without adding any burden to schools and parks. Year 2000 tax revenue was only $3,401 for the entire property.
- Nature Preserve: The newly landscaped wetland area will be surrounded by a paved walk path and will be donated to the Village. This will separate the homes to the west from the commercial and industrial areas to the east and south by ten times the required separation space.
- Traffic: The plan is designed to keep business traffic off neighborhood streets.
- Safety: The existing path through the property is a dangerous shortcut. Renovations will include development of a paved walkway connecting East Avenue on the north to East Avenue on the south without requiring walking through the business area.
- Utilities: New electric and telephone services and new sanitary sewers will improve reliability for the entire neighborhood.
- Jobs: New neighborhood businesses will bring new job opportunities.
- Property Values: These improvements will increase the value of your property.

A public meeting is scheduled (see attached notice) so that we can meet you, outline our program, answer your questions, and formally present our development plan to the Village Plan Commission. The Village staff has been studying this program with us for nearly two years and will present their opinions that evening as well.

Sincerely,

MAC DEVELOPMENT CORPORATION

Richard McCaffrey, S.E., P.E.

President

EXHIBIT 6 | Sales Brochure

New Business Park

Build to Suit for Sale or Lease
10,000 to 150,000 sq. ft.

Phoenix Lake Business Park
Woodland, Illinois

- *Attractive New Business Park*
- *Extensive landscaping with water features and nature trail*
- *Numerous amenities within walking distance*
- *Class 6 tax incentive program approved by Village*
- *Occupancy beginning Spring 2002*
- *Redundant power and Ameritech fiber available to Park*
- *Zoned I-1–manufacturing, technology and office uses*
- *Fee simple and condominium ownership available*
- *Large diverse local labor pool*

Source: MAC Development Corporation.

EXHIBIT 7a | MAC Development Corporation—Phoenix Lake Business Park—Cash Projections

	TOTALS	2001	2002	2003	2004	2005	2006	2007	2008	2009	2010	2011	2012	2013
INFLOWS														
Land Sale Gross Proceeds														
LOT 1	581,200	—	581,200	—	—	—	—	—	—	—	—	—	—	—
LOT 2	570,500	—	570,500	—	—	—	—	—	—	—	—	—	—	—
LOT 3	561,200	—	—	561,200	—	—	—	—	—	—	—	—	—	—
LOT 4	566,100	—	—	566,100	—	—	—	—	—	—	—	—	—	—
LOT 5	847,700	—	—	—	847,700	—	—	—	—	—	—	—	—	—
LOT 6	847,700	—	—	—	847,700	—	—	—	—	—	—	—	—	—
LOT 7	896,500	—	—	—	—	896,500	—	—	—	—	—	—	—	—
Total Land Sale Proceeds	4,870,900	—	1,151,700	1,127,300	1,695,400	896,500	—	—	—	—	—	—	—	—
Legal, Survey & Broker														
LOT 1	40,600		40,600	—	—	—	—	—	—	—	—	—	—	—
LOT 2	39,900		39,900	—	—	—	—	—	—	—	—	—	—	—
LOT 3	39,400		—	39,400	—	—	—	—	—	—	—	—	—	—
LOT 4	39,700		—	39,700	—	—	—	—	—	—	—	—	—	—
LOT 5	56,600		—	—	56,600	—	—	—	—	—	—	—	—	—
LOT 6	56,500		—	—	56,500	—	—	—	—	—	—	—	—	—
LOT 7	59,500		—	—	—	59,500	—	—	—	—	—	—	—	—
Total Legal, Survey and Broker	332,200	—	80,500	79,100	113,100	59,500	—	—	—	—	—	—	—	—
Land Sale Net Proceeds														
LOT 1	540,600		540,600	—	—	—	—	—	—	—	—	—	—	—
LOT 2	530,600		530,600	—	—	—	—	—	—	—	—	—	—	—
LOT 3	521,800		—	521,800	—	—	—	—	—	—	—	—	—	—
LOT 4	526,400		—	526,400	—	—	—	—	—	—	—	—	—	—
LOT 5	791,100		—	—	791,100	—	—	—	—	—	—	—	—	—
LOT 6	791,200		—	—	791,200	—	—	—	—	—	—	—	—	—
LOT 7	837,000		—	—	—	837,000	—	—	—	—	—	—	—	—
Total Net Land Sale Proceeds	4,538,700	—	1,071,200	1,048,200	1,582,300	837,000	—	—	—	—	—	—	—	—
Other Receipts														
Village TIF Infrastructure Contribution	1,500,000	—	1,500,000	—	—	—	—	—	—	—	—	—	—	—
Village TIF Tax Reimbursements	2,577,940	—		—	7,697	133,149	256,450	318,054	318,054	318,054	318,054	318,054	318,054	272,320
Total Receipts	8,616,640	—	2,571,200	1,048,200	1,589,997	970,149	256,450	318,054	318,054	318,054	318,054	318,054	318,054	272,320

(continued)

EXHIBIT 7a | MAC Development Corporation—Phoenix Lake Business Park—Cash Projections (*continued*)

	TOTALS	2001	2002	2003	2004	2005	2006	2007	2008	2009	2010	2011	2012	2013
OUTFLOWS														
Purchase Land:														
Cash to Seller	800,000	800,000	—	—	—	—	—	—	—	—	—	—	—	—
Land Development:														
Land Development costs	3,162,054	968,590	2,143,764	8,000	8,000	8,000	8,000	8,700	9,000	—	—	—	—	—
Developer's contingencies & fee	20,000	—	20,000	—	—	—	—	—	—	—	—	—	—	—
Other Costs:														
Construction Loan Interest	102,192	3,646	70,004	28,542	—	—	—	—	—	—	—	—	—	—
Line of Credit Interest	27,075	—	17,588	9,487	—	—	—	—	—	—	—	—	—	—
Bank Loan Initiation Cost	34,480	34,480	—	—	—	—	—	—	—	—	—	—	—	—
Administrative and Maintenance	55,000	—	13,000	13,000	13,000	13,000	3,000	—	—	—	—	—	—	—
RE Taxes on Unsold Lots	54,266	—	17,104	15,892	12,334	8,936	—	—	—	—	—	—	—	—
Total Disbursements	4,255,067	1,806,716	2,281,460	74,921	33,334	29,936	11,000	8,700	9,000	—	—	—	—	—
Cash Flow from Operations	4,361,573	(1,806,716)	289,740	973,279	1,556,663	940,213	245,450	309,354	309,054	318,054	318,054	318,054	318,054	272,320
FINANCING														
Total Equity Contributions	800,000	800,000	—	—	—	—	—	—	—	—	—	—	—	—
Cash Flow Before Loan Proceeds	5,161,573	(1,006,716)	289,740	973,279	1,556,663	940,213	245,450	309,354	309,054	318,054	318,054	318,054	318,054	272,320
Loan Proceeds—Principal	2,506,716	1,006,716	1,500,000	—	—	—	—	—	—	—	—	—	—	—
Net Cash Flow From All Sources	7,668,289	—	1,789,740	973,279	1,556,663	940,213	245,450	309,354	309,054	318,054	318,054	318,054	318,054	272,320
Bank loan repayments—Principal	(2,506,716)	—	(1,789,740)	(716,976)	—	—	—	—	—	—	—	—	—	—
Cash Available to Owners	5,161,573	—	—	256,303	1,556,663	940,213	245,450	309,354	309,054	318,054	318,054	318,054	318,054	272,320

Note: This scenario has been run for an assumed purchase price of $800,000. This reflects the negotiations that had transpired since the original baseline cash flows were prepared at the time of seeking investor financing.

EXHIBIT 7b | Cash Flows by Investor Class ($)

	Closing/2001	2002	2003	2004	2005	2006	2007	2008	2009	2010	2011	2012	2013
TOTAL PROJECT CASH FLOWS													
Forecast Flows (from Exhibit 7a)													
Cash Available to Owners[1]	**(920,000)**	**0**	**256,303**	**1,556,663**	**940,213**	**245,450**	**309,354**	**309,054**	**318,054**	**318,054**	**318,054**	**318,054**	**272,320**
CASH FLOWS TO A, B, C UNITS REQUIRED TO MEET TARGET RETURNS													
Series A Units (#)	6,000												
A's Share of A&B Units	66.7%												
Cash Available for A Units		0	170,869	1,037,775	626,809	163,633	206,236	206,036	212,036	212,036	212,036	212,036	181,547
Target Return	25%												
Beginning Balance[2]		600,000	750,000	766,631									
Distribution		0	170,869	958,289									
Ending Balance[2]		750,000	766,631	0									
Cash Flow to A Units	**(530,000)**	**0**	**170,869**	**958,289**	**0**	**0**	**0**	**0**	**0**	**0**	**0**	**0**	**0**
Series B Units (#)	3,000												
B's Share of A&B Units	33.3%												
Cash Available for B Units		0	85,434	598,374	940,213	245,450	309,354	309,054	318,054	318,054	318,054	318,054	272,320
Target Return	20%												
Beginning Balance[2]		300,000	360,000	346,566									
Distribution		0	85,434	415,879									
Ending Balance[2]		360,000	346,566	0									
Cash Flow to B units	**(270,000)**	**0**	**85,434**	**415,879**	**0**	**0**	**0**	**0**	**0**	**0**	**0**	**0**	**0**
Series C Units (#)	6,250												
Cash Available for C Units		0	0	182,495	940,213	245,450	309,354	309,054	318,054	318,054	318,054	318,054	272,320
Target Return	18%												
Beginning Balance[2]		625,000	737,500	870,250	844,400	56,179							
Distribution		0	0	182,495	940,213	66,291							
Ending Balance[2]		737,500	870,250	844,400	56,179	0							
Cash Flow to C Units	**(120,000)**	**0**	**0**	**182,495**	**940,213**	**66,291**							

(continued)

EXHIBIT 7b | Cash Flows by Investor Class ($) *(continued)*

	Closing/2001	2002	2003	2004	2005	2006	2007	2008	2009	2010	2011	2012	2013
CASH FLOWS TO B, C UNITS AVAILABLE AFTER TARGET RETURNS MET FOR ALL UNITS													
Cash Remaining after Target Returns Achieved to be divided by B&C Units	0	0	0	0	0	179,159	309,354	309,054	318,054	318,054	318,054	318,054	272,320
Series B Units (#)	3,000												
B's Share of B&C Units	32.4%												
B's Share Residual Cash Flow	0	0	0	0	0	58,106	100,331	100,234	103,153	103,153	103,153	103,153	88,320
Total Cash for B Units[3]	**(270,000)**	**0**	**85,434**	**415,879**	**0**	**58,106**	**100,331**	**100,234**	**103,153**	**103,153**	**103,153**	**103,153**	**88,320**
Series C Units (#)	6,250												
C's Share of B&C Units	67.6%												
C's Share Residual Cash Flow	0	0	0	0	0	121,053	209,023	208,820	214,901	214,901	214,901	214,901	184,000
Total Cash for C Units[3]	**(120,000)**	**0**	**0**	**182,495**	**940,213**	**187,344**	**209,023**	**208,820**	**214,901**	**214,901**	**214,901**	**214,901**	**184,000**

Notes: This is one possible interpretation of case facts about the cash distribution. It assumes the bank requires the McCaffrey companies to keep the $120,000 already expended in the project after closing. It assumes all cash distributions are made annually on the anniversary of the closing.

[1] Cash Available to owners from Case Exhibit 7a, the base case. The $920,000 negative cash flow is the total investment from all three classes of unit owners.

[2] "Beginning Balance" is the amount of distribution required at the beginning of a year in order to provide the target IRR. This balance is increased during the year (by the rate of return required) or decreased (by the amount of distribution actually made) to result in an "Ending Balance."

[3] Total of cash flow required to meet target return plus residual cash flow available to B and C units.

EXHIBIT 8 | Pre-Closing Expenditures

Expenses Incurred by MACD Prior to September 30, 2001

Type	Amount	
Legal fees	$ 53,229	
Accounting	43,217	
Consultants	9,537	
Surveys	20,140	
Environmental and GeoTech	58,548	
McCaffrey & Associates, Inc.	158,100	
Village fees	56,024	
Marketing	3,076	
Miscellaneous	5,530	
Closing Legal Fee and Expenses	11,552	
Financing / loan fees	98,378	($23,233 not paid)
Total	$517,331	
Of which $311,500 already paid		
$205,831 remaining to be paid at closing		

Source: MAC Development Corporation.

EXHIBIT 9 | Timeline

cat.*	DATE	EVENT	COST TO MACD	NOTE
pp	Aug-99	Identify Property		
pp	17-Jan-00	Sign Purchase Agreement	$10,000	Deposit to be applied to purchase price or refunded within due diligence period
bf	May-00	Begin Search for Bank Financing		
if	19-May-00	High School Friend Provides $150,000 Working Capital		
va	Jun-00	Sign Inducement Resolution		
pp	Jul-00	Property Appraisal	$3,500	
pp	27-Jul-00	Complete Phase I Environmental Assessment	$4,450	
pm	Jan-01	Interview Brokers		
va	Jan-01	Complete Plan Development		
pm	09-Apr-01	Retain RXC		
va	May-01	Complete Plan Commission Hearings and Vote		
va	10-May-01	Send Letter to Residents		
bf	22-May-01	Receive Bank One Proposal Letter		
pp	06-Jun-01	Complete Phase II Environmental Assessment	$54,098	
if	11-Jun-01	Send Investor Offering		
pp	12-Jul-01	End of Due Diligence Period		
if	31-Jul-01	Receive Investor Commitments and Close Offering		
bf	28-Aug-01	Receive Bank One Commitment Letter		
pm	01-Sep-01	Previous MACD Customer Offers to Sign Lot 1 Pre-Sale Contract		
va	Sep-01	Complete Village Board Hearings		
bf	04-Sep-01	Receive Bank One Revised Commitment Letter		Changes the terms as described in the Bank Financing section
bf	12-Sep-01	Receive Harwich Bank and Trust Company Verbal Commitment for Line of Credit		
bf	14-Sep-01	Pay Bank One Loan Fee and Sign Loan Agreement	$20,000	Non-refundable
if	15-Sep-01	Receive Investors' Checks		
bf	20-Sep-01	Harwich Bank and Trust Company Backs Out of Verbal Commitment for Line of Credit		
bf	26-Sep-01	Investor Offers to Back Line of Credit	$50,000	Should MACD pursue this option, the cost will be $50,000.
pp	27-Sep-01	Renegotiate with Seller		
va	02-Oct-01	*Village Board Vote*		
bf	04-Oct-01	*Bank Meeting to Finalize Details*		
pp	09-Oct-01	*Close on Property Purchase*		

*bf = Bank Financing, if = Investor Financing, pm = Property Marketing, pp = Property Purchase, va = Village Approvals. Italics = future event.

Source: MAC Development Corporation.

PART 5

Managing Growth and Realizing Value

Successful ventures face their own challenges, albeit different from those of start-ups. Once the business model has been proven, the venture can typically access a broader range of capital sources and will have an easier time attracting employees. Success provides some measure of stability. Yet, there remains an imperative to grow—investors want to maximize their return on investment; the company wants to expand its reach in the marketplace before competitors seize on its success to copy or exploit the market the company has now proven exists. This requires complicated decisions about what pieces of the business model are really key and which must be adapted to permit expansion to new customers or new markets. Once a company has a set of skills, resources, routines, it is often tempting to "exploit and leverage" those resources, rather than keeping the focus on opportunity. While some degree of exploitation is necessary, it is a dangerous trap into which many companies have stumbled. Growth also engenders a series of difficult decisions about the skills required to run a larger enterprise, and about the entrepreneur's own role in this larger setting. Finally, the question of exactly how the value created (on paper) should be monetized presents itself. Investors need to see "cash" back on their investment and often require some kind of "exit" or "liquidity event" to achieve it. Even for the entrepreneur, who may wish to continue to manage and grow the business, it is often wise to "take some chips off the table" and diversify one's holdings. This section provides an opportunity to see how these issues play themselves out in the entrepreneurial venture.

11

Managing the Growing Venture

The earlier modules of *The Entrepreneurial Manager* have focused primarily on getting into business—finding an attractive opportunity, developing a viable business model and systematically reducing the risks associated with it, attracting financial and other resources required to actually start the venture, and managing the early phase of operations.

In this module of the course we will move beyond that initial phase to a stage in the life of the venture where the original business model is arguably proven, and the concern of the entrepreneur—as well as the management team and investors—shifts to *growing* the venture. Typically, this involves expanding the scope of activities to new geographic or product markets and/or finding new groups of customers to serve. For an organization that has been focused solely on its survival, this impetus for growth represents a new—and fundamentally different—set of challenges for the entrepreneur and the organization.

The fact that many organizations fail to make the transition to a sustainable, financially successful business is well-known. Even the most successful venture capital firms rarely "make money" on much more than 50% of their investments. Firms fail for a wide variety of strategic, organizational, and execution-related reasons.

During this growth phase, many things are changing at once. The tasks of developing new products or services, as well as serving new customers in new markets, create more complexity within the firm. As the number of employees grows, the existing, largely informal organization is taxed in new ways, and typically some of the classic tools of professional management—budgets, organization charts, formalized policies and procedures—are introduced for the first time. The entrepreneur must begin to develop new ways of getting work done—and institutionalize some of what is in her head—or the task of managing the firm's day-to-day operations will become overwhelming.

In this note, we will describe a way of thinking about all of these managerial tasks and the challenges they create for the entrepreneur.

Senior Lecturer Michael J. Roberts prepared this note as the basis for class discussion.

Overview

Earlier in the course, we discussed the P-O-C-D framework as a way of thinking about entrepreneurial ventures. This is an example of a "dynamic-fit" model, in which there is no single best choice for any one of the variables, but the key factor is that these elements fit with one another, and that when one element changes, they *all* change in order to remain in alignment. The 7-S model, used in the LEAD course, is another such dynamic-fit model that is often applied to organizations in a state of flux, in order to determine both what the key elements of organizational alignment are and how change in one dimension is likely to ripple through to other dimensions of the organization. The model we will discuss in this note is similar to the 7-S model but is a bit simpler and tries to focus more explicitly on the observable activities of the organization, as well as on the entrepreneur, her role in the organization, and the specific changes that growth stimulates in her role.

Managing Growth—A Model

The model we will discuss has four components (see **Figure A**):

- *Vision and strategy*   What is the entrepreneur's vision, and what strategy has evolved to pursue it?
- *Organization, structure, and process*   How can the broad strategic and operational requirements be broken down into specific, individual tasks and jobs, and how should these tasks be structured and coordinated?
- *People*   Who will actually fill these roles and do the work in terms of their skills, background, and experience?

FIGURE A | Managing Growth

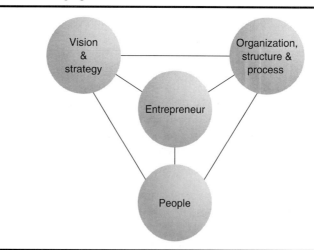

Source: Casewriter.

- *The entrepreneur* As growth changes the nature of the enterprise—and there-fore, of the entrepreneurial manager's role—the entrepreneur faces a series of crit-ical issues. What role(s) will she play in the organization as it evolves? How will responsibilities be delegated, and to whom? What new tasks must she assume, and what skills will be required to execute them successfully?

Moreover, it is important to be cognizant of the critical role of *fit* in the model; each of these elements needs to fit with and reinforce one another, and when one element changes, all must adapt. Thus, for example, we see how a strategy of growth generates increasingly far-flung operations that, in turn, create new tasks for the organization to master and often demand new and different people to perform those tasks. In addition, this set of changes pressures the entrepreneur to manage in a different way. Not all entrepreneurs succeed in making this transition. Some develop the new skills required by the new demands of the enterprise, others recognize their limitations and find a role to which they are suited, and some simply fail and bring their businesses down with them.

We will discuss each of these elements in turn and will focus on the particular set of challenges introduced by the enterprise's growth.

Vision and Strategy

Typically, most ventures begin life based upon the entrepreneur's vision for the enter-prise—a particular problem to be solved, a technology to be exploited, a market to be served. Moreover, because resources are scarce, this vision is pursued with a very focused strategy and a relatively simple set of operations to support that strategy. There is usually one central idea that animates the enterprise in the early days, and the key requirement is that the venture prove the premise behind that idea. As we know, the business model often evolves during the course of these early days through a combina-tion of conscious experimentation and simple learning from experience. In the case of Zipcar, for instance, the premise revolved around the idea that people would use and pay for a shared vehicle on an hourly basis. In the Keurig case, it is the idea that office man-agers will value the convenience and quality of the fresh-brewed coffee to bear the extra cost of the Keurig system. In the early days of the venture there is usually very little commitment to any particular operational strategy. No one knows what the right approach is, and even if they did know, the firm lacks the resources to really commit deeply to a particular operating strategy. This minimal commitment preserves flexibil-ity, enhances options, and minimizes fixed costs.

However, once the original business model is proven, it is typically easier for the firm to obtain more resources, including both its own internally generated funds as well as debt and equity from outside sources. Moreover, the impetus for growth raises the stakes in terms of really committing to a particular strategy. As the confidence level increases, it becomes increasingly attractive to invest in—and commit to—a given strat-egy. This may mean hiring a direct sales force rather than using reps, building a plant rather than using contract manufacturers, or making all sorts of other decisions that attempt to increase efficiency, usually at the expense of flexibility.

When the firm steps on this path, it becomes critical to grow—in terms of volume, revenues, and profits—in order to justify these fixed investments. At the same time, the

FIGURE B | Alternative Growth Strategies

Source: Casewriter.

enterprise may require additional, and increasingly larger, amounts of financing to make these investments. Often the providers of this later-stage financing, including the public markets, have a shorter-term time horizon and less appetite for risk. This is a further source of pressure on the firm to make its strategy generate more predictable financial results. Thus, as firms consider growing beyond the initial niche they may have carved out, they have several options, as depicted in **Figure B** above.

Generally, knowledge of markets and reputation among potential customers are precious resources, and therefore, companies typically have a much easier time selling new products to markets and customers they already know and who, in turn, know them. A riskier strategy—but one potentially offering a higher payoff—is to attempt to serve new customers with new products. In some cases, new customers may be distinguished by their geographic location (e.g., opening retail stores in a new state or selling a product overseas).

The questions that entrepreneurs, and their management teams, must answer as they confront this phase in their growth include:

- Which markets/customers will we serve, and which will we not?

- What results do we endeavor to deliver to these customers? (This is akin to answering the question "What business are we in?")

- What are the underlying dimensions of product/service that create value for the customers and markets we serve, and how will we ensure that we continue to provide that value while at the same time keeping costs at a level that allows us to earn a superior return?

- What critical operational tasks and financing requirements does the growth strategy imply, and how will we meet them?

- What resource commitments are required to pursue the strategy?

- What is the basis of the competitive advantage we have established so far, and how will we maintain/extend that advantage as we grow? That is, by what means do we increase value delivered to customers at lower costs than our competitors?

Organization, Structure, and Process

Once a firm has decided *what* its growth strategy will be and *what* operational requirements it imposes, a host of issues present themselves around *how* to organize to accomplish that growth. In the classic early days, everyone pitched in and did everything, including the entrepreneur. The firm was often small and simple enough to remain a highly informal organization with little in the way of formal process and procedure. Roles were organic, unstandardized, and usually quite general, as opposed to highly specialized. In part, the young firm had not yet learned enough to specialize and formalize. And it was still small enough, and the future uncertain enough, that it paid to preserve the flexibility that such an organization allowed. Similarly, the early employees were often "jack of all trades" types, hired more for flexibility and attitude than any specific skill set.

Growth and the complexity it brings, however, create much more work for the firm to do. The classic approach to organizing all of that work is what is termed "professional management"—some mix of delegating responsibility and using more formal coordinating mechanisms such as plans, budgets, policies, and procedures. We also find that roles become more standardized and formalized.

For example, in the early entrepreneurial phase of any business that deals with customers by phone, one employee may simultaneously deal with new-customer inquiries as well as billing and service-related questions from existing customers. As the company grows, however, it will learn that new customers have a specific set of questions and require handling in a particular way. Moreover, the same will be true of customers with billing inquiries. At some point, the firm will have sufficient call volume to hire a dedicated person—and ultimately an entire staff—to work solely with new customers and another staff to work with existing customers on billing inquiries. While the entrepreneur may be sufficiently involved in this process in the early days to trust the one employee who is giving billing credits, or perhaps to review all of the credits himself, volume will soon make that impossible. So, the firm will need other methods of ensuring that employees are not incorrectly—or dishonestly—applying credits to customer bills. Perhaps a computerized billing system will impose a ceiling beyond which a manger must review all credits. A weekly list of all credits over $10 could be produced for the entrepreneur's review. In this simple example, we see how the volume of managerial work grows as the company grows and how the entrepreneur must develop new approaches for accomplishing that work.

The values of the entrepreneur—which were so easily communicated by direct example when the firm was small—will diminish in their ability to influence the larger organization unless they are institutionalized as culture. Research suggests that when a company is small and new, it is far easier to create a strong culture than later in its life. Indeed, some would suggest that this is the only time a strong culture can be inculcated in an organization. Values and culture represent a tremendously powerful lever for influencing the behavior and performance of individuals in all layers of the organization and for driving superior performance. Moreover, culture is not only a lever of influence but also a potentially powerful source of satisfaction and reward when it is congruent both with individual employee values and with the dimensions of performance demanded by customers. So, for example, Southwest Airlines' culture of "having fun" not only provides a distinctive competitive advantage in the marketplace but also serves as an important source of employee satisfaction. Initially, "having fun" was simply a personal value of the entrepreneur-founder Herb Kelleher, but the company succeeded in institutionalizing this in its culture through hiring practices, training policies, and its reward and recognition programs.

Figure C, below, describes the set of choices faced by entrepreneurs as they attempt to coordinate a larger enterprise.

While these alternatives result from choices made by the entrepreneur, these choices have profound influences on the organization. If the entrepreneur wants fewer people reporting to her, the organization becomes more hierarchical. If the entrepreneur wants to "manage by objective," then planning, budgeting, and performance review processes become more embedded in the firm.

As the figure below describes, there are several archetypes of management, which are defined by the delegation of responsibility and the use of formal coordinating mechanisms.

FIGURE C | Alternative Managerial Approaches

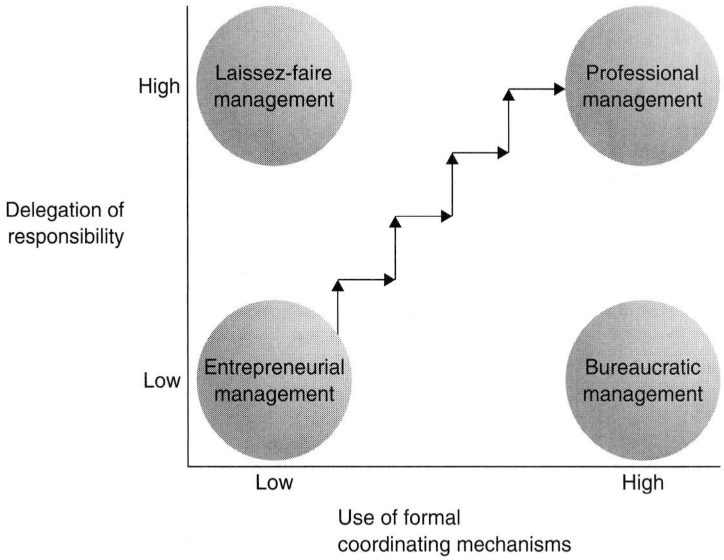

Source: Casewriter.

The entrepreneurial style of management is the term applied to the classic start-up approach to managing the venture. Professional management is used to describe a managerial approach that relies on significant delegation of responsibility and the consequent use of formal mechanisms to coordinate that activity. Two alternative managerial approaches are also highlighted: "laissez-faire" management, in which responsibility is delegated but no formal control mechanisms are put in place; and bureaucratic management, in which extensive use is made of formal control mechanisms with little delegation of authority.

The key to success here lies in migrating to the upper-right-hand quadrant in a stepwise fashion. That is, it is critical to develop more formal coordinating mechanisms prior to actually delegating responsibility. Moreover, it is important to do this slowly, so that both the entrepreneur and her subordinates can adjust to this new managerial approach. Just as entrepreneurs often have difficulty with this transition, so too do the senior managers who were used to doing things the "old" way. It is important to use this period to test and assess the senior team's ability to adapt to this new management approach.

As entrepreneurs confront the challenges of organizing a larger, more complex enterprise, they need to address a number of questions, including:

- What are the key tasks, and how can these be broken down into positions that map onto the availability of staff in the marketplace?

- What responsibilities can be delegated to the senior layer of management?

- How can I—as the entrepreneur—maintain the required degree of influence over these tasks (now that I am no longer doing them all myself), and how can I build coordinating mechanisms that will allow these activities to be coordinated without my direct involvement?

- What are the key values that must be institutionalized as culture, and how can this process be accomplished?

People

As the nature of *how* work is accomplished changes within the firm, the type of person *who* is required to do that work also changes.

As the previously informal, organic work structure is parsed into more narrowly defined, formalized, standardized tasks, it is necessary to find the right people to fill these roles. Early in the life of the enterprise, people were often selected for their energy, enthusiasm, and flexibility. This made sense, as the uncertainty surrounding the venture made it impossible to accurately predict what would be required of individuals. Moreover, had it been possible to predict the specialized skills and abilities required, it would likely have been impossible to afford to hire people with those skills. But as the firm commits increasingly heavily to its strategy and the organization falls into place to support it, this changes. It is now known what kinds of deeper knowledge, expertise, and experience are required to fill the more narrowly defined roles that are taking shape, and the firm begins to hire more people with such skills.

Moreover, as the entrepreneur herself delegates more responsibility, this has implications for the kind of person who must be in place to accept that larger role. The history of growing enterprises is full of examples of loyal lieutenants who were found wanting once the entrepreneur was forced to begin delegating real responsibility. Similarly, we know how lower-level staff often bristle as growing firms become more formalized, looking back on the "good old days" before there were policies and procedures.

As the firm grows and its requirements for people change, the entrepreneur needs to address several fundamental questions:

- What specific knowledge, skills, experience, and aptitudes are required for the set of positions that have been identified?

- How can individuals be hired, trained, evaluated, and rewarded to motivate superior performance?

- What attitudes toward customers, suppliers, and fellow employees must new hires possess if they are to fit into the culture and be effective contributors to strategic success?

The Entrepreneur

For each of the important elements of the enterprise discussed above, it should be clear that the entrepreneur both drives these dimensions and is influenced by them. For example:

- The entrepreneur's *vision* largely determines the firm's *strategy*.

- The entrepreneur's *values* drive the firm's *culture.*

- The entrepreneur's *management style* creates the features of *organization structure and process*.

Yet, as it grows, the enterprise becomes a force of its own, making demands on the entrepreneur and forcing her, in turn, to adapt to the needs of the business itself. Thus, all of these factors change, and the nature of the entrepreneur's managerial role must change as well. Early on, the entrepreneur's vision and passion animated the enterprise, and the organization changed quickly in response to her direction. The entrepreneur could make most, if not all, of the important decisions herself and could directly supervise most of the work being done. Based upon this close involvement with the daily activities of the business, there was little need for more formal control and coordinating systems, as the entrepreneur could keep directly in touch with what was going on simply through day-to-day involvement in all of the firm's key activities.

As the sheer volume of managerial work increases, however, the "bandwidth" required to perform this managerial work—in this informal fashion—quickly overwhelms the capacity of the entrepreneur to do that work. This is why we so often see entrepreneurs flail and ultimately fail at the task of managing their growing enterprise. The set of skills required to manage a small, young, informal venture is simply different than the skill set required to oversee a much larger enterprise. The kind of deep focus and involvement that is required for success in the early days can become a barrier to developing the broader managerial perspective required for success as the company grows.

For example, it is easy to imagine the difficulties faced by an entrepreneur who is accustomed to running the business in an informal manner, communicating directly with a relative handful of employees. As new facilities open and as operations move away from the entrepreneur's direct involvement, the entrepreneur must learn new ways to give direction and get information. Clearly, organizational changes—the use of budgets, plans, policies, and procedures—can help, but the entrepreneur must develop a new mental model of his job and must learn how to use these new tools.

All sorts of metaphors describe this dilemma: "moving from player to coach," "transitioning from doer to manager to leader." These all capture an essential truth about the change in role required. Thus, entrepreneurs must begin to delegate responsibility for many tasks yet at the same time develop mechanisms for keeping their fingers on the pulse of what is going on and for providing the vital coordinating link between various functions. As the entrepreneur becomes less able to influence people and activity via direct involvement, it becomes more important to develop—and learn how to use—some of the elements of organizational "glue" that are available, such as culture and values.

Of course, some entrepreneurs choose not to attempt to make this transition. Some step up to the role of chairman or chief technical officer and bring in a "seasoned" CEO; others move on to another entrepreneurial challenge.

Entrepreneurs must ask themselves the following questions as they seek to make this transition:

- What is my existing model of management, and where is it likely to "hit the wall" as we scale?

- What changes—in terms of people and organizational structure and process tools—will be required, and what do I need to do to be competent in using these tools?

- How can I get feedback on my own performance—from a board or set of advisors—that will let me know how I am doing?

- Do I even want to attempt to make this transition?

Remaining Opportunity-Driven As You Grow

Note that many of the approaches we have described above could easily inhibit the firm's ability to remain entrepreneurial and opportunity driven. As resources expand and commitments deepen, and as the venture enters a phase where investors may begin to look to harvest the value the enterprise has created, the firm comes under pressure to maximize its efficiency. As discussed above, the drive to professionalize can bring formalization, standardization, and a diminished ability to act quickly.

It is also the case that a classic response to growing complexity is to "buffer" the managerial core from the problems, issues, and changes that are going on in the environment. We discussed above how the challenges of growth lead to a series of actions designed to both shift the responsibilities for decision making and obviate the need for certain decisions to be made. Standardized polices and procedures, as well as plans and budgets, are one common example of this trend.

But by shielding senior managers from the problems, customer requests, and last-minute issues that arise in the business, firms are simultaneously cutting their senior decision makers off from the most valuable source of information about required innovations and new opportunities.

To remain opportunity-driven, it is critical that senior mangers remain in touch with the environment as well as with customers and competitors. Firms that remain entrepreneurial find ways of ensuring this, from institutionalizing a culture of spending time with customers to developing processes that ensure that these outside voices are heard.

Once an opportunity is perceived, it is critical that mangers have some resource slack to run some small experiments and learn more fully about the potential dimensions of the opportunity. The planning and budgeting cycles in larger companies can sometimes overwhelm the ability to run small experiments.

KIPP National (A) (Abridged)

On an icy January afternoon in 2000, Mike Feinberg, David Levin, and Scott Hamilton landed at Chicago O'Hare Airport. The trio had flown in from different corners of the United States to meet urgently for a day in a nearby hotel before flying home again in the morning. The purpose for the meeting was to discuss the design and potential launch of a national network of high-performing middle schools for poor and minority students. The network would be modeled on two schools, known as the KIPP academies, which had been founded by Feinberg and Levin.

Feinberg arrived from Houston, where he was the principal of the Houston KIPP Academy, a public middle school that he had launched in 1995 and which had achieved remarkable academic results with some of Houston's most disadvantaged students. Levin landed from New York where he ran the second KIPP academy, also a public middle school and the sister school to Feinberg's school in Houston. Like Feinberg, Levin had founded his school in 1995 and seen dramatic success with his students, almost all of whom lived in the impoverished neighborhoods of the South Bronx section of New York City.

Levin and Feinberg were old friends and trusted colleagues. Before opening their middle schools, the duo had met and served together in the early 1990s as Teach for America corps members in Houston's public school system. During this time, as idealistic and determined entry-level teachers in their early 20s, Feinberg and Levin cofounded the original KIPP program in a distressed Houston elementary school. From their early collaboration and experimentation as teachers in Houston, Feinberg and Levin set out in 1995 to launch two distinct public middle schools. One school would be in Houston, another in New York. Both would be named KIPP Academy, and both would serve the fifth through the eighth grades. KIPP was an acronym for Knowledge is Power Program.

Lecturer Stig Leschly prepared the original versions of this case, "KIPP National, 1999 (A): Designing a School Network," HBS No. 803-124. This version was prepared by Lecturer Stig Leschly. HBS cases are developed solely as the basis for class discussion. Cases are not intended to serve as endorsements, sources of primary data, or illustrations of effective or ineffective management.

Feinberg and Levin's schools contrasted sharply with their inner-city counterparts. For example, the KIPP academies stayed in session from 7:30 a.m. to 5 p.m. each weekday, for half the day on Saturday, and for a month each summer. Teaching in the schools, most of which was done by young and tireless teachers in the mold of Feinberg and Levin, stressed mastery of core academic subjects. Despite the statistics that normally characterized inner-city students, KIPP pupils excelled on state-administered standardized exams, maintained nearly perfect attendance records, and regularly won scholarships to the most selective private, parochial, and public high schools in the United States.

Hamilton reached Chicago from San Francisco where he worked as the managing director of the Pisces Foundation, an education-related philanthropy funded by Donald and Doris Fisher, the founders of Gap Inc. Prior to managing the Pisces Foundation, Hamilton had served as associate commissioner of education in Massachusetts where, among various job responsibilities, he oversaw the state's first wave of investments in charter schools. Hamilton had met Feinberg and Levin in the fall of 1999 and, impressed with their schools, had begun talks with the two principals about financing a national replication of their schools.

Through the fall of 1999, Hamilton, Levin, and Feinberg had communicated regularly about expansion possibilities. The threesome was interested in the possibility of demonstrating on a wider scale that poor and minority students could excel in rigorous academic settings. They believed that the KIPP schools exemplified school-design principles that, if adopted widely, could improve dramatically the academic prospects of disadvantaged children. Their early talks about expansion centered on launching hundreds of middle schools nationwide in the mold of Levin and Feinberg's schools.

The immediate goal for their meeting in Chicago was for Hamilton, Levin and Feinberg to push their initial talks toward an actionable proposal for the launch of a national network of schools. This proposal would need, at a minimum, to identify the essential attributes of Levin and Feinberg's schools and, from there, to address the rich mix of operating challenges that would accompany a national expansion.

With a written proposal in hand, Hamilton could return to San Francisco to propose an investment to the Fishers, and Feinberg and Levin could evaluate clearly the professional reorientation and personal commitment required of them in a replication effort.

The Early Years: 1992–1995

Levin and Feinberg met in the summer of 1992 in Los Angeles as enlistees with Teach for America (TFA), the legendary teacher–training program that, since its founding in 1990, had placed thousands of college graduates in two-year teaching positions in disadvantaged rural and urban schools. Levin joined TFA directly from his graduation at Yale University in 1992. Feinberg graduated in 1991 from the University of Pennsylvania and enrolled with TFA after a yearlong internship for a senator in Washington.

Like most TFA recruits, Levin and Feinberg joined out of an idealistic and urgent sense of public service. "TFA is the Peace Corps of my generation," explained Feinberg. "Every year it attracts another class of idealistic and committed young people. Many of them stay on in education after their TFA experience." Levin continued, "I needed a job out of college and had an interest in education policy. An advisor of mine told me to get teaching experience before I began working on policy."

At the close of their summer training with TFA, Levin and Feinberg shared a long car ride from Los Angeles to Houston where both had drawn teaching assignments in disadvantaged Houston elementary schools. On the desert highways from Los Angeles to Houston and fresh from their TFA initiation, the duo fashioned their first intuitions about strong teaching and effective schools. Feinberg recalled:

> We drove an old Ford Taurus across the Southwest in August of 1992. We had big ideas and big plans. We talked the whole drive about the perfect school and the perfect system and what it would take to create them. Even then, before we had taught, we had the right instincts, I think, about the nature of good teaching, the need for hard work, and the effect on kids of high expectations.

Feinberg and Levin landed hard in Houston, harder than either ever expected. Feinberg was assigned to Garcia Elementary School, a struggling primary school located in one of Houston's poorest neighborhoods. His task was to teach an English-Spanish bilingual class of fifth graders. "I walked into my first classroom in 1992," remembered Feinberg, "and, to be honest, got my ass kicked. I'm embarrassed to admit it, but I actually handed out lollipops and invited the kids to call me Mr. F in hopes of getting them to like me."

Nearby, Levin met an equally difficult task. He had been assigned to Bastian Elementary School, Houston's lowest performing elementary school, and charged with leading a self-contained class of sixth graders. "The senior teachers in the school," said Levin, "were taking bets, actual bets, on how long I would survive. They were sure that the day would come when I would simply stop showing up. It was complete chaos initially. I was lost. The kids were out of control."

In the ensuing two years, exhaustion, professional solitude, and frustration followed Levin and Feinberg as they fought to master their craft. Their persistent search for mentors and master teachers helped their cause. Harriet Ball, a fellow elementary school teacher in Houston, figured prominently in Levin's and Feinberg's development.

"Mike and I met Harriet Ball during our first year in Houston," explained Levin. "In our free periods, we would sit in on her class. She taught us almost everything we know about teaching. We adopted her use of chants and rhymes, her ways of relating to kids, and her views of discipline and community accountability." (See **Exhibit 1** for excerpts from an interview with Ball.)

In addition to Ball, Rafe Esquith influenced Feinberg and Levin. A fifth- and sixth-grade teacher in Los Angeles, Esquith had achieved standout results with poor and minority students. His approach to teaching involved a combination of extended day schooling, demanding expectations, and total commitment by teachers, students, and parents. Feinberg recalled the duo's encounter with Esquith:

> Dave and I saw Rafe Esquith speak in the fall of 1993 just as we were beginning our second year in Houston. He preached longer days, hard work, high expectations, and college entry for all kids. His fifth and sixth graders, almost all of whom were poor and spoke a language other than English as their primary language, were reading Shakespeare,

doing advanced math, and coming back year after year to study with him. Everything he described resonated with what we were beginning to learn firsthand. He was speaking right to us. Our jaws were on the floor.

Levin went on: "Rafe didn't claim he was a better teacher than anyone. He just said he worked harder than most. That was helpful to Mike and me because, however good or bad we were at the time, we knew we had stamina and grit. Over and over, he repeated that good teaching was built on simple ideas, reflected in aphorisms like, 'Work hard. Be nice' and 'There are no shortcuts.'"

The First KIPP Classroom, 1994–1995

In their second year of teaching, as they improved and deepened their insights about effective schooling, Feinberg and Levin grew increasingly dissatisfied with the common run of schools around them. They resolved to launch a self-contained classroom program for fifth graders and, in the fall of 1993, wrote a formal proposal to Houston district officials. In their proposal, Levin and Feinberg offered to coteach a fifth-grade classroom in a format that stressed high expectations and hard work. Levin and Feinberg requested permission to keep their students in class from 7:30 a.m. to 5 p.m. on weekdays, for half the day on Saturdays, and for one extra month of summer school. They would require parents and students to sign commitment contracts. To run their program, Levin and Feinberg also petitioned for freedom to manage their own materials budget and curriculum. Levin and Feinberg promised academic results to the district.

At the school district headquarters in Houston, the proposal stalled for months. "When one senior manager finally read the report," noted Levin, "she asked us why we had picked such a small font size for our document. After reading our request, another district leader didn't understand what was new about KIPP since we weren't proposing some new curriculum. Our plan was to teach harder and longer and to expect more from students. We admitted that we do it with a hodgepodge of existing materials and teaching techniques that we had lifted and modified from others."

Levin and Feinberg pushed on in the face of the district's indifference. "By April of 1994," said Levin, "our proposal had languished for seven months at district central offices. In that time, while teaching full time, Mike and I had scraped together $3,000 in donations to supplement whatever funding we might get from the district, and we had gathered significant interest from parents."

In the spring of 1994, the district finally relented and assigned the young teachers to a vacant art room in the elementary school where Feinberg was working. With a green light from central, Feinberg and Levin raced in the late spring of 1994 to enroll students and to prepare for their launch the following September. To recruit students, Levin and Feinberg walked house to house in Houston's poorest Hispanic neighborhoods. Feinberg recalled:

Here came two, tall white guys with bad Spanish. When we knocked, parents thought we had taken a wrong turn and were looking for directions back to our part of town. We'd sit in modest living rooms and talk to first-generation Hispanic immigrants about how all kids could learn, about how to succeed in America, and about how their child could climb the mountain to college. We would tell them about the work that was needed and promise them that it was worth the effort. I'll never forget those initial house calls. When you look people in the eye and make them a promise, you better honor your part of the deal.

In the summer of 1994, Levin and Feinberg opened the doors of their single classroom to 50 fifth graders, almost all of whom were poor and Hispanic and two-thirds of whom arrived from bilingual programs with limited English skills. An intense and formative year followed for Levin and Feinberg, one marked both by deep trust and collaboration and by constant and sometimes heated debate. Feinberg remembered:

> Dave and I taught our hearts out that year. We were in our mid-20s, and the district had given us our own group of kids. They were ours to teach. We were working out how to make operational the principles in which we believed so strongly. We had deep beliefs about the capacity of our kids and about the consequences of hard work and high expectations, but we were only just beginning to translate them into successful and practical teaching.

Levin continued:

> We were responsible for our own fate and had to figure out precisely how to grab and hold these kids, how to build a predictable and controlled environment around them, and how to teach them. We worked until we dropped. After the KIPPsters went home, we spent nights figuring out what we could do better. I remember one entire evening spent arguing with Mike over how best to write an equation on the board. We couldn't let up. We had asked these kids and their parents to believe, to make a commitment, and to join the KIPP family. We had painted them a picture of the mountaintop. We had to deliver.

And deliver they did. By year's end, Levin and Feinberg joined ranks with master teachers like Esquith and Ball. Half of their students began the year with failing scores on the math and English sections of the Texas Assessment of Academic Skills (TAAS), a set of state-administered standardized tests. By the summer of 1995, after a year under Levin and Feinberg's tutelage, 98% of the students passed both tests.

In testing their students and reporting their results, Levin and Feinberg purposefully claimed no exemptions for any of their students, a policy that ran counter to the common practice among principals of excluding students with special education status, bilingual status, and other learning impairments from school-level achievement reports. Levin and Feinberg maintained this stance even though a majority of their students qualified as bilingual students and even though many of their students initially exhibited behavioral patterns consistent with low-level special education diagnoses.

Feinberg and Levin succeeded with their first group of KIPP students despite continued interference from administrators. "At one point," recalled Levin, "they moved us without warning from our single classroom to two smaller, adjacent classrooms. They didn't realize or didn't care that we couldn't split the kids up. To coteach these kids, we had to keep them together and monitor them constantly. So we crammed all of our babies into one room and taught all 50 of them in one regularly sized classroom."

Planning the KIPP Schools

Energized by their success, Levin and Feinberg set their sights on launching a full middle school program. Loyalty to their students explained Levin and Feinberg's determination to develop a full school. Levin reflected:

> We didn't want to create a situation where, year after year, we sent our fifth graders back out there after just one year with us. We saw what happened to them. They sank back into apathy or, worse, into crime, gangs, drugs, and teenage pregnancy. In 1994, the elementary school that housed us fed its students to a nearby middle school where only 17% of the students progressed through high school and applied to college. Those few that applied to college had an average combined SAT score of 700. We couldn't sacrifice our kids to that future.

In late 1994, while coteaching their first KIPP classroom, Levin and Feinberg approached the district to negotiate for the expansion of their KIPP program into a full middle school from fifth to eighth grade. Levin and Feinberg proposed opening their school with a single class of fifth graders and adding a grade each year so as to reach a full middle school over several years.

Like their proposal to open their first classroom, Feinberg and Levin's pitch to start a full middle school met a cool reception at headquarters. So slow was the response in Houston that Feinberg and Levin initiated conversations with district officials in New York, Levin's hometown, about opening a KIPP middle school in the Bronx. Unlike Houston, New York seemed interested, a development that caught press coverage in a local Houston newspaper. With the press involved, the Houston school district engaged Feinberg and Levin and offered to support their middle school plan.

Consequently, by the spring of 1995, Feinberg and Levin held offers to open schools in both New York and Houston. Levin and Feinberg accepted both. "We took both deals," explained Feinberg, "because we were young and dumb. Somehow, after three years of working together, Dave and I thought we had enough momentum and confidence to step into running two schools. So that's what we did." In finalizing their negotiations in New York and Houston, Feinberg and Levin insisted on and won significant control over their schools' academic schedule, hiring and firing decisions for their classroom staff, and curriculum design.

With their approvals in place, Levin and Feinberg stepped up the pace in the spring and summer of 1995 to prepare for their school openings. Feinberg received classroom space in modular trailers stationed in the parking lot of Lee High School, in the Gulfton section of Houston. Lee High was one of Houston's most feared schools. The school had the highest ratio of English-deficient students of any school in the city, and its zip code had one of the worst juvenile crime profiles in Texas.

To recruit a fresh batch of fifth graders, Feinberg picked up where he and Levin had left off the prior summer. Walking door to door in Gulfton, Feinberg visited with immigrant families. Sharing stories of the prior year and the success he and Levin had seen, Feinberg won the confidence of almost all the families he met and, within months, had assembled a class of 72 fifth graders.

To teach them, Feinberg recruited three full-time teachers. Two of them were fellow TFA graduates. The third was the twin sister of a former girlfriend. "I didn't know anything about hiring or managing teachers, nor did I really have any time to think about it," mused Feinberg. "I hired a few and figured that if things didn't work out I would just teach all 72 kids myself and get new teachers for the next year."

In the summer of 1995, only months before opening his school, Feinberg received news that he had been evicted from his modular classrooms in the parking lot of Lee High School. The principal of Lee High School had reclaimed the space to meet an unexpected surge in enrollment. Feinberg scrambled to save his plans and was reassigned to classroom space in a school located 40 minutes by bus from Lee High School and the Gulfton neighborhood in which he had recruited most of his students. "It was hectic," remembered Feinberg. "One of the hardest parts of the move was my having to go back to my KIPPsters and convince them to ride the bus for hours every day to our new location."

At the same time, in New York, Levin worked with equal determination. Because of his teaching commitments in Houston, Levin arrived in New York in June of 1995 with less than two months to organize his school. Levin was granted space in an existing school complex in the Bronx, just north of the Harlem River. Levin shared space in the complex with several other schools.

To recruit his students, Levin resorted again to door knocking. This time, Levin's travels required him to communicate to a predominantly African-American constituency of parents and students who, unlike the first-generation Hispanic immigrants in Houston, had often endured multiple generations of poverty and racism and who harbored deep skepticism toward appeals by outsiders. To staff his school in its first year, Levin hired one full-time teacher who, like Feinberg's initial hires, had graduated from TFA.

The KIPP Academies, 1995–1999

From their launch in 1995, the KIPP academies grew steadily. By the fall of 1998, the Houston and New York schools enrolled approximately 300 and 220 students, respectively. KIPP students were almost universally poor and nonwhite. Each year from 1995 to 1999, the percentage of students in the schools who were poor and minority hovered north of 90%.

The KIPP schools were public schools. Revenue for both schools came from public funds controlled either by school districts or state agencies. Both schools admitted children by blind lottery and without regard to prior achievement, special education needs, or bilingual status. The only unusual attribute of the schools admission policy was the requirement that parents and students sign KIPP commitment forms, documents that delineated clearly the roles and responsibilities of teachers, parents, and students in KIPP schools.

From 1995 to 1999, the KIPP schools operated variously as district contract schools and as charter schools. Initially, both schools held contracts with the school districts in Houston and New York. These contracts, backed by various verbal agreements and understandings, defined the relationship between the Houston and New York districts and the schools, including the districts' obligation to fund the schools and provide various services, including food and transportation.

Later, in the late 1990s, both schools converted to charter schools. In 1998, KIPP Houston became a state charter school and, as such, received funding and oversight directly from the Texas Education Agency on the basis of state law. In 1999, KIPP New York converted to a district charter school. As a district charter school, KIPP New York was granted special financial and staffing freedoms from the superintendent's office in New York. In negotiating the various contracts and charter agreements that authorized and governed their schools, Levin and Feinberg sought to maximize their managerial freedom.

As a state charter school beginning in 1998, KIPP Houston operated independently of human resource and financial policies of the Houston school district. Moreover, since Texas did not sanction collective bargaining by teachers, Feinberg worked without the typical constraints of union contracts. Feinberg was free to dismiss teachers without compliance with lengthy legal processes, to compensate teachers as he saw fit, and to hire teachers without regard to detailed teacher-credentialing rules.

By contrast, KIPP New York, both as a contract school and a district charter school, employed teachers who were protected, at least nominally, by the district's contract with the teachers union. As a result, Levin was required technically to match the seniority-driven pay scales defined in the union contract, to hire only legally credentialed teachers, and to honor the extensive contract provisions that protected teachers identified for dismissal. In practice, though, Levin did not feel unmanageably inhibited by the union status of his school. This was so partly because of his well-developed ability to pressure underperforming teachers to self-assign out of his school.

Culture

Explicit and sustained commitments by students, teachers, and parents were the hallmark of the KIPP schools. All parents, teachers, and students signed commitment contracts that made explicit a variety of KIPP policies, notably the schools' extraordinarily long school day and year. Keeping with what they had begun in Houston, Feinberg and Levin ran their schools from 7:30 a.m. to 5 p.m. on weekdays, for several hours on Saturdays, and for a month over the summer. In the evenings, they kept their buildings open for students who preferred or needed to study away from home.

Commitment contracts asked parents to check homework every night, to read to their children whenever possible, and to accept general responsibility for the consequences, which could include expulsion, of failing to honor their contract. Students, in addition to accepting the long KIPP school day and year, agreed to help one another, to ask questions in class if they were confused, and to take responsibility for their own actions and their place in their KIPP community. Teachers promised in writing "to do whatever it takes" for their students to learn. This commitment included carrying pagers and cell phones 24 hours per day to answer homework questions from students. (See **Exhibit 2** for excerpts from KIPP contracts.)

KIPP schools exhibited unusually high levels of discipline. In both schools, when visitors entered classrooms, students remained unwaveringly focused on their work. Between classes, KIPP students walked in neat lines. Over lunch, they ate with the manners of adults. In New York, Levin barred students from wearing baseball caps, makeup, artificial nails, baggy pants, and hoop earrings.

KIPP teachers in both schools could share endless anecdotes about discipline. One teacher in Houston offered:

> The other day, an argument broke out on the school bus about a Game Boy console. One student called the other a mother f----- within earshot of the bus driver. When the kids came

off the bus, I sat them down and reminded them that they had failed to live up to the KIPP maxim, "Work hard. Be nice." I told them that they had ignored the KIPP rule for riding the bus, which is, "Sit back and enjoy the ride." I had them write essays about how to ride on the bus. I called home to talk with their parents. I suspended them both from several weekend field trips. And I porched them both.

At KIPP Houston, misbehaving students were often porched. A porched student was required, for some period of days or weeks, to wear his school uniform inside out, to refrain from any conversation with other students, and to eat and study on the porches. Porches were isolated areas of chairs and tables in each classroom and in the school lunchroom. Above each porch hung a banner that read, "If you can't run with the big dogs, stay on the porch." When porched, students were required to write individual letters of apology for their behavior to classmates in their homerooms.

In another story of student discipline, a KIPP New York teacher recalled:

Our kids know to start their work if a teacher is late. Yesterday, I purposefully waited outside my classroom after the beginning of class to see how my students would act. A few of them slacked off and talked instead of staying on task. Worse yet, when I walked in and asked the class if everyone had begun their work in my absence, one of the misbehaving students didn't volunteer that he had been talking. I called him out and explained that he had broken my trust and the trust of his peers, including his classmates who had been honorable enough to admit their mistake. I reminded him that he had the mountain of college to climb, and I told him that he would need months to win back my trust in him as an honest KIPPster.

Occasionally, transgressions required expulsion. Feinberg elaborated:

One year in Houston, we had a boy who joined the school in seventh grade. That's unusual since we don't admit many kids in the later grades. In the first few weeks of school, this boy was caught stealing a toy from another student. He eventually admitted to the theft and was given a chance to apologize to his fellow KIPPsters and to make the case for why he should stay in the KIPP family. Afterwards, I let the students vote on whether to expel him. They didn't believe he was sincere in his apology, and they believed he would steal again. They voted to expel him. So, that's what I did. I think the kids knew what was at stake for the boy and what was likely to happen to him out there. I also think they realized the effect that a bad element could have on their team. Expelling a student is extremely hard on everyone. But the good of the entire team must come first.

The KIPP schools coupled tough discipline with strong positive incentives. For example, students who completed their work and behaved well were eligible for monthly field trips to museums, sports events, and historic sites. At the end of each year, students in good standing were invited on a long-distance field trip. On this trip, fifth graders went to Washington, D.C., sixth graders to the national parks in Utah, seventh graders to the East Coast for a college and city tour, and the eighth graders to Yosemite National Park and the West Coast for a college and city tour. Moreover, KIPP students received weekly school paychecks by which they accumulated credits to purchase T-shirts, books, and other goods from KIPP school stores. The size of KIPP paychecks depended on the degree to which students mastered their weekly workload and followed KIPP rules.

To communicate the KIPP culture, Levin and Feinberg constantly promoted slogans and rhymes that captured the KIPP model. These included the original phrases "There are no shortcuts" and "Work hard. Be nice" that the duo had borrowed from Esquith. These aphorisms appeared ubiquitously on classroom walls and in hallways. They also adorned school uniforms and all official school communications. The KIPP culture was also reflected in the chants and rhymes that teachers regularly integrated into their teaching plans. KIPP students knew these chants from memory. One frequently recited rhyme ran, "How do we make good grades? We bring our tools and follow the rules. It might sound square, but we're going somewhere." (See **Exhibit 3** for selected KIPP aphorisms and rhymes.)

Teachers

KIPP teachers were, in many cases, in their 20s, unmarried, and without children. Feinberg and Levin staffed their schools heavily with recruits from the TFA alumni network. Teachers averaged less than five years of experience. In New York, where Levin had purposefully sought more senior teachers, two-thirds of the staff had more than five years' experience, and several teachers had over 20 years' experience.

Though they worked long days, often arriving at the school at 7 a.m and working into the evening, KIPP teachers invested their time heavily in professional development and preparation. In New York, for example, teachers averaged only five hours in the classroom each day. Much of the remaining time was spent on lesson planning, often supervised by Levin.

KIPP teachers earned approximately 25% more than they would in the regular public schools of New York and Houston. Extra pay resulted primarily from extended hours. Levin and Feinberg also distributed small performance bonuses to teachers. In New York, annual salaries averaged $45,000. The most senior teachers in New York, some of whom had 15 years' experience, earned $70,000. The KIPP schools funded their operating costs, almost all of which were salary related, from standard per pupil allocations that they received under their contractual and charter agreements.

By 1999, teacher turnover in the KIPP schools ranged annually from 15% to 20%. Each school maintained staffs of fewer than 20 teachers. In the opinion of Feinberg and Levin, KIPP's demanding work ethic did not cause turnover. Rather, according to the school founders, teachers often left KIPP because they did not have the skills to teach. "Some new teachers just don't have the confidence and charisma it takes to lead these kids," explained Levin. In addition, teachers occasionally left KIPP out of irreconcilable differences with Feinberg and Levin over the KIPP program.

Instruction

The KIPP academies emphasized mastery of core academic subjects, particularly reading, writing, and math. The schools' long hours were central to their academic mission. KIPP students spent approximately 66% more time in class than their peers in regular public schools. The extra time was needed, in part, to compensate for incoming students' academic deficits. Tutoring and one-on-one instruction featured prominently in the KIPP program. (See **Exhibit 4** for an overview of courses at KIPP Houston.)

KIPP teachers shared common approaches to classroom discipline and, especially in New York, followed schoolwide norms about structuring lesson plans around consistent openings and board plans. Within those parameters, however, teachers were free to develop their own instructional styles and techniques. The KIPP schools, for example, had no fixed stance on how to teach reading. Levin commented:

> If teachers approach their work coherently and show results, then they can operate freely in our classrooms. There is no religion here about this or that curriculum. We teach what works. What emerges across our classrooms is an eclectic and integrated set of techniques and instructional approaches. For example, we teach reading by combining the best elements of direct instruction, whole language instruction, and reader's workshop.

Feinberg echoed Levin, "Our curriculum is not rocket science. We lengthened the day, and we work hard. That creates more time for reading and math, and we use that time to teach in ways that work. That's the story, basically. It's not flashy."

Leadership

From their beginning, the KIPP schools reflected the relentless and passionate leadership of Levin and Feinberg. Both principals lived by the KIPP work ethic and regularly arrived at school at 6 a.m. and left close to midnight. "You can't expect people to be on time if you're not on time," summarized Levin. "You can't expect people to be consistent if you're not consistent. You can't expect people to be humble and honest and hungry if you're not honest and humble and hungry."

Levin and Feinberg tended carefully to their star teachers. One year, for example, Levin convinced a supporter of KIPP New York to donate frequent flier miles so that an exhausted teacher could take a hiking vacation in Colorado. Another year, Levin accompanied some of his teachers to Atlantic City to listen to their concerns regarding the school.

A teacher in Houston recalled a memorable episode involving Feinberg:

> By 1997, we had reached 230 students in Houston. We were running three grades and had about a dozen teachers. One day that year, Mike walked into a classroom where a couple of teachers had seventh and eighth graders watching a movie clip from *West Side Story*. I think the students had been reading the book and were watching the movie in parallel. Some of the students were talking, rather than paying attention, and the teachers weren't intervening. Mike saw this and was incredibly upset. He walked out of the room and spent the rest of the day thinking about what to do. The next day, he called the students and teachers together and, for a while, just stood quietly in front of them. The teachers and students figured out pretty quickly that something was up. After sitting in silence for a while, Mike explained to the kids that they had been merely regular students the day before, not KIPPsters, and that they had broken their promise to each other, their parents, and the school. He asked each student to write an essay for the next day about the difference between watching a movie as a regular student and as a KIPPster. The next day, one kid had blown off the assignment and turned in a three-line essay. Mike was so disappointed and angry that, in full view of the teachers, he threw a chair out the window. He then assigned the student a daily 10-page essay for two weeks.

Academic Results

From 1995 to 1999, students in Levin and Feinberg's schools excelled academically. Each year in Houston, for example, almost 100% of Feinberg's students, in all grades, passed all sections of the state-administered Texas Assessment of Academic Success. These success rates applied even to KIPP Houston's fifth graders, many of whom entered the school in need of remediation, and even during the 1995 school year, Feinberg's first as a solo principal. In 1995, only one-third of Feinberg's first incoming class of fifth graders had passed both the math and reading section of the state exams in the prior year. By the summer of 1996, more than 90% of pupils in KIPP Houston passed both halves of the test. (See **Exhibit 5** for schoolwide test results in KIPP Houston.)

In addition to monitoring performance on standardized tests, Feinberg tracked the grade-level improvement of his students. KIPP Houston's first batch of fifth graders arrived at the school in 1995 with fifth-grade math skills and approximately fourth-grade reading and writing skills. Four years later, as they completed eighth grade in the summer of 1999, these students had progressed an average of 7.3 grade levels in each major subject area. In math alone, Feinberg's first graduates had advanced 10 grade levels and were more skilled in math than an average American high school graduate. (See **Exhibit 6** for data on grade-level proficiency in KIPP Houston and **Exhibit 7** for data on KIPP Houston's performance relative to other Texas middle schools.)

Levin had also achieved strong academic results in New York. In 1999, for example, KIPP New York was selected as the best-performing public middle school in the Bronx for the second year in a row. Approximately one-third of the fifth graders admitted to his school each year met grade-level proficiency standards in reading and math. Typically, by the time these fifth graders entered seventh grade at KIPP New York, two-thirds of them were functioning at or above grade level in both math and science. That all but a third of Levin's students were fully remediated by eighth grade was notable. In adjacent Bronx middle schools, schoolwide failure rates regularly surpassed 80%. In each of KIPP New York's first four years of operation, Levin and his teaching team had improved the rate and frequency with which their students reached grade-level mastery in core subjects.

The KIPP schools excelled at more than standardized tests. For example, from 1995 to 1999, daily attendance and annual promotion rates hovered near 100% at both schools, and both schools maintained waiting lists with hundreds of students. Early data also indicated that KIPP graduates would succeed in high school. In 1999, over 95% of Levin's first graduating class in New York gained admission to top New York parochial and magnet schools. High school admission results were equally impressive in Houston. KIPP graduates often earned scholarships to attend selective private and parochial schools. The 1999 graduating class in Houston, for example, had earned more than $1 million in academic scholarships to private, parochial, and boarding schools. (See **Exhibit 8** for a sample of high schools attended by graduates from KIPP Houston. See **Exhibit 9** for national data on the effect of family, community, and school variables on student outcomes.)

The KIPP schools flourished from 1995 to 1999 despite ongoing school district intransigence and neglect. For example, in its first four years, KIPP Houston moved five times. At one point, Feinberg set up school in unused administrative offices at district headquarters, a situation that required him and his team to use kitchenettes as classrooms.

By 1999, school-wide student attrition at the KIPP Academies in Houston and New York had stabilized at approximately 3% per year. Accordingly, approximately 12% of students in an entering cohort of 4th graders left the schools before graduation 4 years later. Feinberg and Levin testified that, with the exception of an occasional expulsion, attrition occurred primarily in situations where families needed to move away from Houston and New York.

The National Spotlight and New Aspirations

As Levin and Feinberg developed their schools from 1995 to 1999, public interest in their work grew steadily. During this period, for example, every major newspaper in the United States covered KIPP. Some publications, including *The New York Times,* the *Los Angeles Times*, and *The Washington Post* repeatedly wrote about the program. Journalists as far away as Japan, Mexico, and France had picked up KIPP.

Politicians from both sides of the ideological spectrum embraced KIPP. By 1999, for example, the Children's Defense Fund had honored the KIPP schools. Concurrently, Texas Governor Bush had visited KIPP Houston in 1998 and mentioned it by name in his first campaign speech for president in September 1999.

In the spring of 1999, CBS television journalist Mike Wallace visited the Houston and New York schools to film a segment on KIPP for the program *60 Minutes.* When the piece aired in September 1999, Levin, Feinberg, and their KIPP schools became subjects of national interest. Feinberg remembered the aftermath of his and Levin's prime-time television debut:

> Press coverage and public interest in KIPP had been building for some time. But when the *60 Minutes* piece ran in the fall of 1999, the lid blew off. The phones were ringing all day long in our offices. I was taking calls from foundations, reporters, superintendents, and politicians. You name them. They were calling. One day, I picked up my cell phone, and it was the superintendent of a California school district. He said, "Mr. Feinberg, please, I want to order 15 KIPP schools for next year."

Independent of their newfound celebrity, Levin and Feinberg had been pondering for some time the possibility of national expansion. Both were ready again for a new challenge.

Scott Hamilton and the Rendezvous in Chicago

In the fall of 1999, the two principals met Hamilton, an introduction that would speed them on their way to national expansion. Hamilton was the managing director of the Pisces Foundation, an education-related philanthropy in San Francisco. Funded by Donald and Doris Fisher, the founders of Gap Inc., the foundation made strategic investments in education reform.

Hamilton visited Feinberg's school in Houston in the fall of 1999 and, soon thereafter, paid Levin a visit in New York. His reaction was immediate, and he quickly sought out Feinberg and Levin about the possibility of the Pisces Foundation investing in the national expansion of the KIPP schools. Levin recalled, "We were approached by a variety of investors and sponsors in the fall of 1999, but most had little idea about what it takes to build a school, much less a series of schools. Scott, on the other hand, immediately understood the KIPP schools, and he had deep experience with start-up schools. We were also intrigued by working with the Fishers who, from building the Gap, understood how to replicate an organization."

Through the fall of 1999, Levin, Feinberg, and Hamilton communicated regularly about a national strategy for the KIPP academies. With a growing sense of progress, the threesome agreed to convene in Chicago for an intense working session. Their aim would be to push their talks toward a finite proposal, one to which Feinberg and Levin could consider committing and one which Hamilton could present formally to the Fishers. The proposal would include, at a minimum, the rationale for expanding nationally and a first draft of an implementation plan.

From their informal talks through the fall, Hamilton, Levin, and Feinberg shared a common strategic outlook. For example, all three were interested in long-term and lasting reform. Whatever shape their school network might take, Levin, Hamilton, and Feinberg sought meaningful, national impact. They were particularly interested in demonstrating nationally the academic potential of poor and minority students and in promoting a wider understanding of the essential attributes of successful schools. Each of the trio had an approximate sense that their ambitions required rolling out hundreds of schools across the country over a decade or more.

The threesome also agreed that the core attributes of Levin and Feinberg's schools would serve as a starting point for expansion and as a constant in their work. They had generated a list, titled the "KIPP five pillars," of the defining attributes of their schools. These five features were more time on task for students, strong principals with the power to lead, high expectations of students, a school culture focused on objective measures of success, and clear commitments from students, parents, and teachers. (See **Exhibit 10** for details on the KIPP five pillars.)

The Challenges of Scale

These points of clarity aside, Feinberg, Levin, and Hamilton faced a variety of open issues related to the proposed expansion. For starters, to move forward, the threesome would need to develop a clearer view of the role and reach of the national office that would orchestrate the national expansion. The trio agreed that the national office would be located in San Francisco, near the headquarters of the Gap and the Pisces Foundation, and that its primary purposes would be to recruit, train, place, and support principals who would operate KIPP schools. These recruits would need to share Feinberg and Levin's unusual talent for teaching and leading. Exactly how this recruitment and training program would function and how likely it would be to succeed were topics of considerable debate.

Also unclear was the degree to which the national office would take responsibility for the mundane but critical operating challenges of opening and sustaining schools. For example, the trio would need to discuss their approach to winning approvals for new KIPP schools. These schools would presumably be a mix of state charter schools and district contract schools.[1] Hamilton, Levin, and Feinberg appreciated the difficulty of negotiating into district contracts and state charter agreements the financial, regulatory, and personnel autonomy that KIPP schools required.

Facilities issues, especially in the context of charter schools, also ranked high on the trio's list of implementation issues. Charter school operators faced notoriously intractable challenges in locating, financing, and improving leased or owned building space for their schools. The national office would face a choice of how heavily to invest in supporting school leaders in their facilities efforts.

Funding questions were also sure to arise in Feinberg, Levin, and Hamilton's working session. From Levin and Feinberg's experience as principals, the trio had accurate cash flow forecasts for new KIPP schools. These schools, once opened, would collect cash from public sources (i.e., school districts, state legislatures, and the federal government) and from charitable contributions, and they would use cash primarily on teacher salaries and materials. While KIPP schools would receive all manner of technical assistance from the KIPP national office and while KIPP national would seek to retain certain control rights over the schools (e.g., the right to revoke the use of the KIPP brand name and the right to veto a new principal appointment), they would operate as distinct legal entities governed by local boards of trustees and would not receive significant direct cash subsidies from KIPP national. (See **Exhibit 11** for a model KIPP school budgets.)

The cashflow model of the national office was heavily dependent on philanthropy. To push their conversations on this point, the trio had drafted a financial forecast for a national office stretching to 2012. This scenario contemplated opening 235 KIPP schools, at a pace of 25 per year, and called for approximately $150 million in cash. Most of this cash would be used to recruit and train principals, conduct outreach to win district contracts and state charters for KIPP schools, and support sitting KIPP principals. Headcount in the national office, under this scenario, would stabilize at 60 within a few years of launch.

One-third of the $150 million needed at KIPP national would come from fees assessed to KIPP schools once they matured. The remaining two-thirds would come from foundations, notably the Pisces Foundation. Hamilton had briefed the Fisher family on the size of the investment that would likely be required to launch and support a national chain of KIPP schools. From this information, the Fishers were not deterred in their potential role as lead investors. That said, the Fishers had cautioned Hamilton, in partnership with Levin and Feinberg, to deliver a thoughtful implementation plan and to articulate opportunities to stage investment, look for partner investors, and reassess operating plans and financing requirements as events unfolded. (See **Exhibit 12** for details on the financial model of KIPP national.)

---

[1]Charter schools were sanctioned by state law, and state education agencies (or their nominees) usually approved, funded, and regulated charter schools. State charter school statutes generally funded the operating costs of charter schools without any subsidies for facilities or capital investments. By the end of 1999, 37 states had passed charter school statutes, and 1,700 charter schools served some 350,000 children (less than 2% of US public school students). District contract schools were operated on the basis of contracts issued by public school districts. These contracts typically set districts' per-pupil funding obligations to contract schools, clarified districts' role in providing non-financial assistance to contract schools (for facilities, busing, food services, etc.), and enumerated the degree to which contract schools would by exempt from traditional district oversight and labor contracts.

The question of who would lead KIPP national would also surface in the trio's deliberations. Feinberg and Levin were, on the one hand, obvious candidates to lead the expansion. They had conceived of and built the flagship KIPP schools. On the other hand, neither had run non-school organizations, neither lived in San Francisco, and neither could predict for sure whether they would enjoy leading KIPP national.

Finally, Hamilton, Feinberg, and Levin would need to discuss the path by which they hoped to influence national education reform. That influence would be hard to acquire even under the rosiest of scenarios. The public bureaucracies that operated US public schools and the maze of legal regulations that governed them were profoundly resistant to change. This reality had already led the trio to an uncompromising view that each new KIPP school would need to rival the academic results of KIPP Houston and KIPP New York. Anything short of an undiluted record of break-through success would, in the trio's opinion, expose their efforts to criticism and politicized attack.

Feinberg summarized with his characteristic candor:

> If we want to have national impact, if we want to KIPP-notize the country, then we have to answer the "yes buts." People always say, "Yes, that might work over there, but it won't work here." They make excuses for themselves to avoid making change. There are no excuses. To get that message across, we need to show that we can lead kids up the mountain to college in many places and under many circumstances just as we have in Houston and New York.

EXHIBIT 1 | Harriet Ball, Excerpts from Comments on Teaching, 1999

Topic	Comments
On Learning	There's always a label that says they [disadvantaged students] can't. But you can take these kids above grade level. The thing is to get them to think that they're not in school, that they're doing what they love to do. They love to sing. They love to rap. It crosses all color lines. They forget they're in class. They're having fun. The fear is out.
On Teaching	I tried so hard that first month in Houston, because the kids knew nothing. They couldn't do numbers, and I couldn't get the second graders to read. There were seasoned teachers there, but they wouldn't help me do my lesson plans. So I wove my own method. I got them singing. I'd get the most popular songs, and change the words and set objectives to rhyme. "Sing the song, I can't go wrong. When you're working to music, you forget you're working." Eliminate all the education terms. Show them how to get through and find the answer. I teach them to find the answers through patterns, verbalization, memory cues, codes, chants, and acting.
	You have to train them how to listen and see things. They listen by singing. If you just talk, they will not hear you. Give it to them in a beat: Give them a stomp, stomp, clap. Have some competition in it. Put it into a game format. You could start with a $2 pack of flashcards from the store. Sing them at the beginning. Then get them to beat the clock. See who can do all of the tables in 50 seconds. Sometimes I'll write something on the board and then say, "I'll bet you can't remember what I just wrote." Just say, "I'll bet you can't," then erase it. They'll remember it every time.
	Just listen to the kids. They'll tell you everything you need to know. I started to watch them on the playground to see what they were doing. They were dancing, so I brought those moves into the classroom and used them to teach about latitude and longitude.
On Discipline	I tell them: When you see that one of your teammates is weak, it's your duty to make sure that you get your teammate over the river. Row the boat. You can't just sit in the boat. You must move.

Source: Excerpted with permission from "A Conversation with Harriet Ball" by Gail Russell Chaddock. Reproduced with permission from the April 13, 1999 issue of *The Christian Science Monitor* (www.csmonitor.com). © 1999 The Christian Science Monitor. All rights reserved.

EXHIBIT 2 | KIPP Academies, Excerpts from Commitment to Excellence Contracts

Contract	Excerpts
Teacher Commitment Contract	• We will arrive at KIPP every day by 7:25 a.m. (Monday to Friday). • We will remain at KIPP until 5 p.m. (Monday to Thursday). • We will come to KIPP on appropriate Saturdays at 9 a.m. and remain until 1 p.m. • We will teach at KIPP during the summer (July 17 to August 4). • We will always teach in the best way we know how, and we will do whatever it takes for our students to learn. • We will always make ourselves available to students, parents, and any concerns they might have. • We will always protect the safety, interests, and rights of all individuals in the classroom. • Failure to adhere to these commitments can lead to our removal from KIPP.
Parent Commitment Contract	• We will make sure our child arrives at KIPP every day by 7:25 a.m. (Monday to Friday). • We will make arrangements so our child can remain at KIPP until 5 p.m. (Monday to Thursday) • We will make arrangements for our child to come to KIPP on appropriate Saturdays at 9 a.m. and remain until 1 p.m. • We will ensure that our child attends KIPP summer school (July 17 to August 4). • We will always help our child in the best way we know how, and we will do whatever it takes for him/her to learn. This also means that we will check our child's homework every night, let him/her call the teacher if there is a problem with the homework, and try to read with him/her every night. • We will always make ourselves available to our children, the school, and any concerns they might have. This also means that if our child is going to miss school, we will notify the teacher as soon as possible, and we will read carefully all the papers that the school sends home to us. • We will allow our child to go on KIPP field trips. • We will make sure our child follows the KIPP dress code. • We understand that our child must follow the KIPP rules so as to protect the safety, interests, and rights of all individuals in the classroom. We, not the school, are responsible for the behavior and actions of our child. • Failure to adhere to these commitments can cause my child to lose various KIPP privileges and can lead to my child's expulsion from KIPP.
Student Commitment Contract	• I will arrive at KIPP every day by 7:25 a.m. (Monday to Friday). • I will remain at KIPP until 5 p.m. (Monday to Thursday). • I will come to KIPP on appropriate Saturdays at 9 a.m. and remain until 1 p.m. • I will attend KIPP during summer school (July 17 to August 4). • I will always work, think, and behave in the best way I know how, and I will do whatever it takes for my fellow students and me to learn. This also means that I will complete all my homework every night. • I will call my teachers if I have a problem with the homework or a problem with coming to school, and I will raise my hand and ask questions in class if I do not understand something. • I will always make myself available to parents, teachers, and any concerns they might have. • I will always behave so as to protect the safety, interests, and rights of all individuals in the classroom. This also means that I will always listen to all my KIPP teammates and give everyone my respect. • I will follow the KIPP dress code. • I am responsible for my own behavior. • Failure to adhere to these commitments can cause me to lose various KIPP privileges and can lead to my expulsion from KIPP.

Source: Organization documents.

553

EXHIBIT 3 | KIPP Academies, Selected Chants, Rhymes, and Aphorisms

Topic	Words
School Culture (1)	*If there's a problem, we look for a solution.* *If there's a better way, we try to find it.* *If we need help, we ask.* *If a teammate needs help, we give.* *There are no shortcuts. It's not a KIPP thing. It's a life thing.* *Knowledge is power. Power is freedom. And I want it.* *Work hard. Be nice.*
Academics (2)	*The more that you read,* *The more things you will know.* *The more you learn,* *The more places you'll go.* *This is the room* *That has the kids* *Who want to learn* *To read more books* *To build a better tomorrow!*
	No need to hope *For a good-paying job* *With your first-grade skills* *You'll do nothing but rob* *You got to read, baby, read!* *You got to read, baby, read!* *How do we make good grades?* *We bring out the tools and follow the rules.* *It might sound square, but we're going somewhere.*
Discipline (3)	*If you can't run with the big dogs, stay on the porch.*

Notes: (1) Statements of culture were continually repeated by staff, displayed ubiquitously inside of the KIPP schools, repeated on school uniforms, and promoted on all KIPP correspondence.

(2) Teachers integrated chants and rhymes in daily teaching plans, often at the beginning of teaching sessions, to captivate and focus students.

(3) The "If you can't run with the big dogs, stay on the porch" slogan hung above the "porches" in KIPP Houston's cafeteria and classrooms, areas where misbehaving students would eat and study alone and in forced silence while wearing their T-shirts inside out.

Source: Organization documents.

EXHIBIT 4 | KIPP Houston, Course Offerings

Courses (1)		Grade 5	Grade 6	Grade 7	Grade 8 (2)
English	English	X	X	X	X
	Independent Reading Workshop	X	X	X	X
	Study Skills	X	X		
	Verbal SAT classes			X	X
History	U.S. History	X			
	Ancient Civilizations		X		
	Current Events	X	X		
	American History (pre-1865)			X	
	American History (post-1865)				X
Math	Math Survey	X			
	Thinking Skills	X			
	Technology	X	X		
	Pre-Algebra		X	X	
	Algebra 1 (A)			X	X
	Algebra 1 (B)				X
	Math SAT classes			X	X
Science	General Science	X			
	Earth Science		X		
	Life Sciences			X	
	Physical Science				X
Spanish	Native Spanish			X	X
	Non-Native Spanish			X	X
Other (3)	Music	X	X		
	Band			X	X

Notes: (1) KIPP Houston graduation requirements included four years of English, history, math, and science and two years of Spanish and art.

(2) In some cases, KIPP schools offered a postgraduate year for students who, after finishing eighth grade, needed another year of study and maturity before advancing to a college preparatory high school. During this year, postgraduates studied, among other courses, biology, geometry, and world history.

(3) In addition to the courses listed here, KIPP Houston offered daily enrichment classes (such as dance, drama, yearbook, baseball, basketball, technology, and ultimate Frisbee) and Saturday enrichment classes (such as chess club, guitar lessons, swimming, self-defense, ballet, and computers).

Source: Organization documents.

EXHIBIT 5 | KIPP Houston, Texas Assessment of Academic Skills (TAAS)

	Schoolwide Percentage of Students Passing TAAS (1)			
	1995	1996	1997	1998
Math	96%	95%	97%	99%
Reading	93%	98%	96%	98%
Writing	n/a	n/a	n/a	100%
Science	n/a	n/a	n/a	100%
Social Studies	n/a	n/a	n/a	96%

Notes: (1) In computing these passing rates, KIPP Houston claimed no exemptions for students with learning disabilities or English deficiencies.

Source: Organization documents.

EXHIBIT 6 | KIPP Houston, Improvement in Grade Level Proficiency, Class of 1999

	Grade Level Proficiency for Graduating Class of 1999 (1)				
	Entering 5th Grade, Summer of 1995	Entering 6th Grade, Summer of 1996	Entering 7th Grade, Summer of 1997	Entering 8th Grade, Summer of 1998	At Graduation, Summer of 1999
Reading	4.8	7.0	8.4	9.7	11.7
Math	5.3	7.3	11.4	13.3	15.3
Writing	4.1	5.6	6.3	9.2	9.7

Notes: (1) KIPP Houston tracked grade-level proficiency progress by students' scores on the Woodcock-Johnson test of grade-level proficiency. KIPP Houston administered the test each summer.

Source: Organization documents.

EXHIBIT 7 | Texas Middle Schools, 1999 (1)

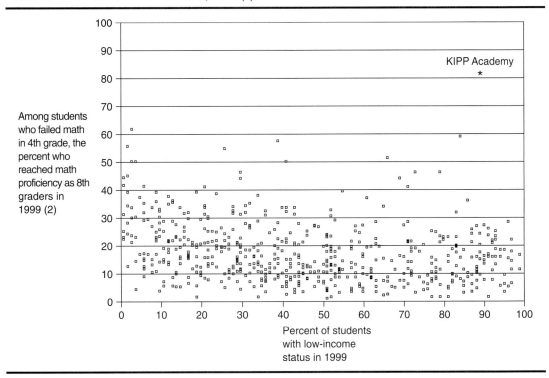

Among students who failed math in 4th grade, the percent who reached math proficiency as 8th graders in 1999 (2)

Percent of students with low-income status in 1999

Notes: (1) The sample includes Texas middle schools that had at least 200 students in 1999, that had less than 15% of their students classified as special education students in 1999, and that had at least 15 8th graders in 1999 who had been in the school for two or more years and who had failed math in 4th grade.

(2) The percentage on this axis is equal to the number of 8th graders in a school who reached proficiency in math in 1999 after failing math in 4th grade divided by the number of students in a school who failed math in 4th grade. Failure is defined as a math score of 69 or less on the Texas Learning Index (TLI), an index derived from scores on the math section of the Texas Assessment of Academic Skills (TAAS). Proficiency is defined as a TLI math score of 85 or more.

Source: Adapted from Chrys Dougherty, "Mathematics Proficiency of Texas Public Schools Students," Houston Mathematics Workshop, January 24, 2000.

EXHIBIT 8 | KIPP Houston, Selected High Schools Attended by Graduates

Type	Location	Name
Public Schools	Houston, TX	Bellaire Foreign Language Magnet High School
	Houston, TX	DeBakey Health Professions Magnet High School
	Houston, TX	High School for Performing and Visual Arts
	Houston, TX	YES College Preparatory High School
Private Schools	Houston, TX	Duchesny Academy
	Houston, TX	The Kinkaid Academy
	Houston, TX	St. John's School
	Houston, TX	Strake Jesuit College Preparatory
	Houston, TX	The Awty International School
	Houston, TX	St. Thomas High School
	Houston, TX	St. Agnes Academy
Boarding Schools	MA	Phillips Andover Academy
	MA	St. Mark's School
	MA	Concord Academy
	CT	The Hotchkiss School
	CT	Pomfret School
	NH	Phillips Exeter Academy
	RI	St. Andrews School
	TX	Chinquapin
	TX	Hockaday School
	TX	Saint Mary's Hall
	TX	Texas Military Institute
	CA	Thatcher School
	CA	Cate School
	TN	Baylor School
	NC	The Asheville School
	VA	Foxcroft School
	PA	George School
	IL	Lake Forest Academy

Source: Organization documents.

EXHIBIT 9 | Variations in Student Outcomes

	Percentage of Variation Explained By:		
	Family Variables	**Neighborhood Variables**	**School Input Variables**
Variations in 12th Grade Math Scores	93.4%	3.8%	2.8%
Variations in Income at Age 33	89.8%	6.3%	3.9%
Variations in Education Attainment at Age 33	91.5%	4.8%	3.7%
Illustrative Variables	Parental education level, family income, number of siblings, family ethnicity, parental attendance at school events, parental knowledge of graduation requirements, number of books at home, family visits to museums.	Mean household income and other household income measures, income inequality index, ethnicity of population, education level of adult population.	Per-pupil spending, average class size, teacher salary measures (minimums, maximums, and average), teacher attributes (specialization level, education level, experience level).

Note: Hoxby analyzed data from the National Educational Longitudinal Survey, which began following 25,000 eighth graders in 1988, and data from the National Longitudinal Survey of Youth, which began following 13,000 teenagers in 1979. Neighborhood variables refer variously to census regions, school districts, and metropolitan areas.

Source: Adapted by casewriter from Caroline Hoxby, "If Families Matter Most, Where Do Schools Come In," in *A Primer on America's Schools,* edited by Terry Moe (Stanford, CA: Hoover Institution Press, 2001).

EXHIBIT 10 | KIPP Academies, Five Pillars

Pillar	Explanation
More Time	KIPP schools know that there are no shortcuts when it comes to success in academics and life. With an extended school day, week, and year, students have more time in the classroom to acquire the academic knowledge and skills that will prepare them for competitive high schools and colleges, as well as more opportunities to engage in diverse extracurricular experiences.
Choice and Commitment	Students, their parents, and the faculty of each KIPP school choose to participate in the program. No one is assigned or forced to attend these schools. Everyone must make and uphold a commitment to the school and to each other to put in the time and effort required to achieve success.
Power to Lead	The principals of KIPP schools are effective academic and organizational leaders who understand that great schools require great school leaders. They have control over their school budget and personnel. They are free to swiftly move dollars or make staffing changes, allowing them maximum effectiveness in helping students learn.
High Expectations	KIPP schools have clearly defined and measurable high expectations for academic achievement and conduct that make no excuses based on the background of students. Students, parents, teachers, and staff create and reinforce a culture of achievement and support through a range of formal and informal rewards and consequences for academic performance and behavior.
Focus on Results	KIPP schools focus relentlessly on high student performance on standardized tests and other objective measures. Just as there are no shortcuts, there are no excuses. Students are expected to achieve a level of academic performance that will enable them to succeed in the nation's best high schools, colleges, and the world beyond.

Source: Organization documents.

EXHIBIT 11 | KIPP Model School Budget

	Entire School				Per Student	
	Year 1		Year 5		Year 1	Year 5
Number of Students	80		320			
Revenues						
Local Funds (1)	$ 415,840	56%	$ 1,663,360	72%	$ 5,198	$ 5,198
Federal Funds (2)	191,280	26%	365,120	16%	2,391	1,141
Grants (3)	130,000	18%	275,000	12%	1,625	859
Total Revenues	737,120	100%	2,303,480	100%	9,214	7,198
Expenses						
Salaries and Benefits						
Instructional Staff	280,440	39%	1,011,211	44%	3,506	3,160
Administrative Staff	24,600	3%	86,100	4%	308	269
Extended Time	38,192	5%	152,767	7%	477	477
	343,232	47%	1,250,078	54%	4,290	3,906
Instruction						
Supplies and Materials	91,170	13%	122,530	5%	1,140	383
Motivators and Rewards	44,000	6%	130,000	6%	550	406
Extended Time Materials	18,263	3%	39,810	2%	228	124
	153,433	21%	292,340	13%	1,918	914
Other						
Administration	48,560	7%	48,480	2%	607	152
Insurance	25,000	3%	55,000	2%	313	172
Food Service	84,480	12%	337,920	15%	1,056	1,056
Rent	54,000	7%	283,179	12%	675	885
Building Operations	19,659	3%	29,459	1%	246	92
	231,699	32%	754,038	33%	2,896	2,356
Total Expenses	728,364	100%	2,296,456	100%	9,105	7,176
Surplus	8,756		7,024		109	22

Notes: (1) Local funds are per-pupil revenues received by schools under their contracts and charter agreements with districts and states.

(2) Federal funds include receipts under various federal education programs paid directly to schools, including aid for schools with high concentrations of poor students.

(3) Grants include funding from foundations and other donors.

Source: Organization documents.

EXHIBIT 12 | KIPP National, Cash Flow and Operating Projections, 2002–2012 ($ millions)

	2002	2003	2004	2005	2006	2007	2008	2009	2010	2011
Sources of Cash										
Support from schools (1)	$0.02	$0.6	$1.5	$2.7	$4.0	$5.3	$6.6	$7.9	$9.2	$10.6
Donations and grants (2)	13.6	15.1	14.7	12.4	11.6	10.3	9.0	7.8	6.5	5.3
Total Sources	**13.6**	**15.7**	**16.2**	**15.1**	**15.6**	**15.6**	**15.7**	**15.7**	**15.8**	**15.8**
Uses of Cash										
Leadership Development										
Selection and Training	1.3	1.6	1.6	1.6	1.6	1.6	1.6	1.6	1.6	1.6
Guides and Other	2.3	2.5	2.5	2.5	2.5	2.5	2.5	2.5	2.5	2.5
Subtotal	3.6	4.1	4.1	4.1	4.1	4.1	4.1	4.1	4.1	4.1
School Development										
Trailblazing and Recruiting (3)	1.7	1.9	1.9	1.9	1.9	1.9	1.9	1.9	1.9	1.9
Other	.8	1.2	1.4	1.6	1.8	1.8	1.9	1.9	2.0	2.0
Subtotal	2.5	3.1	3.3	3.5	3.7	3.7	3.8	3.8	3.9	3.9
National Office										
National Staff	0.8	0.8	0.8	0.8	0.8	0.8	0.8	0.8	0.8	0.8
Office Rent and Equipment	1.3	1.2	1.3	1.3	1.3	1.3	1.3	1.3	1.3	1.3
Finance and Development	0.6	0.6	0.7	0.7	0.7	0.7	0.7	0.7	0.7	0.7
Other	0.9	1.2	1.2	1.2	1.2	1.2	1.2	1.2	1.2	1.2
Subtotal	3.6	3.9	4.0	4.0	4.0	4.0	4.0	4.0	4.0	4.0
Other										
School Evaluation	1.5	1.5	1.8	0.9	0.9	0.9	0.9	0.9	0.9	0.9
Fellow Compensation (4)	1.2	1.5	1.5	1.5	1.5	1.5	1.5	1.5	1.5	1.5
Annual Operating Reserve	1.2	1.6	1.6	1.2	1.5	1.4	1.5	1.5	1.5	1.5
Subtotal	4.0	4.6	4.9	3.6	3.9	3.9	3.9	3.9	3.9	3.9
Total Uses of Cash	**13.6**	**15.7**	**16.2**	**15.1**	**15.6**	**15.6**	**15.7**	**15.7**	**15.8**	**15.8**
Operating Forecasts										
# of fellows in training (5)	20	25	25	25	25	25	25	25	25	25
# of school in 1st year	10	20	25	25	25	25	25	25	25	25
Total # of schools (6)	15	35	60	85	110	135	160	185	210	235
Total students (7)	1,920	4,560	9,200	15,600	23,200	31,200	39,200	47,200	55,200	63,200

Notes: (1) Schools contribute 1% of school revenues in year 1 and 3% of school revenue per year subsequently. Accordingly, in fiscal year 2011–12, 25 new schools contribute 1% of revenues and 215 other schools contribute 3% of revenues.

(2) Donations and grants are primarily from the Fisher family and their foundation, the Pisces Foundation.

(3) Trailblazing staff complete early preparation work for launching KIPP schools, including developing relationships with district and state education leaders, negotiating contracts and charter agreements, locating facility sites, and establishing community relationships.

(4) During their training year, fellows receive $60,000 in salary and benefits.

(5) This forecast anticipates 20 principals in training from September 2002 to September 2003.

(6) The calculation of total number of schools includes the two original KIPP schools and 3 new schools opened in 2001-02, and it assumes no school closures.

(7) Total students served by KIPP schools = [number of new schools * 80 students] + [number of 2nd-year schools * 160 students] + [number of 3rd-year schools * 240 students] + [number schools in 4th or later year * 320 students].

Source: Organization documents.

Innocent Drinks

Richard Reed was walking across the green AstroTurf floors of Innocent Drinks toward the Acorn Room, the office conference room. It was 10 am on a Wednesday (September 29, 2004), which meant that it was time for the weekly meeting between Reed and the other two founders of Innocent. The three of them were old friends from college, so the atmosphere of the meetings was usually light. Today, though, there was a bit more anxiety in the air than usual. The problem on the table was success.

In 1998, the three founders—Reed, Jon Wright, and Adam Balon—started Innocent, a London-based company selling prepackaged smoothies and juices to customers via channels such as grocers and convenience stores. (See **Exhibit 1** for background on the founders.) In 2004, they were expected to hit £16 million in revenue. (**Exhibit 2** shows Innocent's revenue growth.)

The founders had raised £235,000 to get started and not another dime since. They had managed to exceed the projections in their initial business plan, which, in the entrepreneurial world, was a rarity on par with sighting a bald eagle. With a winning Lotto ticket in its beak. Things had gone well so far for Innocent. And now, with expectations raised by success, they had to figure out what to do next.

Having grown at a compounded rate of 63% over the preceding four years, Innocent had earned a 30% share of the UK smoothie market, eclipsing the former leader, PJ. But the UK smoothie market was small—estimated at £50 million annually. For Innocent to continue its spectacular growth, they needed a market with more headroom.

One option for Innocent was to extend its brand, which had gained a devoted following in the UK, to other product lines such as ice cream or yogurt. Another option was to expand internationally, either to continental Europe or to the United States.

Richard Reed, vice-president of marketing, started the meeting: "We all know that for the last year, we've been trying to do everything—develop ice cream, open markets in Europe, expand the market here. I don't think it's working. I don't think we're

Professor William A. Sahlman and Research Associate Dan Heath prepared this case. HBS cases are developed solely as the basis for class discussion. Cases are not intended to serve as endorsements, sources of primary data, or illustrations of effective or ineffective management.

making progress fast enough. I think we need to choose one option for growth and focus on it."

Over the next two hours of discussion, the other founders' positions became clear. Jon Wright was in favor of pursuing expansion in Europe. Adam Balon thought they should be patient and continue to do both. He said, "Once we start generating revenues in both markets, we'll know more about which option to pursue." There were other viable options that didn't involve growth. Innocent had attracted acquisition interest from other beverage companies. Was it time to sell? In addition, Innocent was capable of generating strong cash flow. The founders knew that, if they chose, they could put the brakes on growth and start harvesting some of the value they had created.

Reed was torn. He wanted to do everything. He hated closing off options but knew it was the right thing to do. The question was: Which options should be closed off?

Company Background

Reed, Balon, and Wright met at Cambridge during their first week of school. The three became instant friends. Reed and Balon were roommates during school, and it apparently worked out, because the two would spend ten years as roommates.

After graduating from Cambridge, the three of them moved to London and started their careers. Reed spent four years at the advertising agency BMP DDB Needham. Balon spent two years at McKinsey and two years at Virgin Cola. Wright, who had earned a masters in manufacturing engineering, spent three years at Bain.

Despite the diverging career paths, the three friends stayed in touch and constantly bantered about starting a company together. In a sense, they had already worked together: They had organized events, both in college and afterward. In 1997 and 1998, for instance, Reed and Balon had organized a music festival in West London called Jazz on the Green, which drew over 20,000 attendees.

In March 1998, the three of them planned a weekend trip to France for skiing and snowboarding. As they drove through the Chunnel, the topic came up again: Wouldn't it be great to work on something together?

Jon Wright said, "We'd had this conversation so many times. Finally, on the way to France, we said to ourselves: 'We're going in circles here. Let's either figure out something to do or forget about it and be happy with our jobs.' Everyone said, 'Great.' Then, we realized the problem: We weren't sure what we were qualified to do."

Their first idea was to start a "strategic marketing consultancy," which built directly on the experience of the three. The idea was scrapped, according to Wright, after they concluded that they lacked the necessary experience, desire, and clients. This seemed conclusive. On to the next idea.

They began to discuss the things in life that frustrated them. Wright said, "We thought that people were prepared to pay for things that make life a little bit better and a little bit easier." They had almost unconsciously made the leap to consumer products.

The first brainstorm involved bathing. Wasn't it a pain, the founders thought, to get a bath to the right level and the right temperature? What if you could just press a button and have your bath drawn exactly the way you preferred? This idea, too, was nixed.

Balon did not want to be a bath salesman, and Wright preferred not to work on a product that mixed electricity and water.

A second brainstorm that didn't make the cut involved keyless door entry systems—applying security card technology to home users. No one seemed passionate about the concept.

The third brainstorm paid off. They talked about their lifestyles in London—working hard and playing hard. They had a desire to be healthier but didn't have much time to act on it. What about healthier food or drinks? They talked about their habit of buying juice on the way to work in the morning—a little thing that made them feel a bit healthier. They were shocked that none of them could remember the names of the brands they were buying.

The pitch, as it evolved, was simple. According to Wright, "We thought that if we could come up with a more memorable brand, and with juice that tasted a bit better, that it could be a good business opportunity. No one could think of a reason that it couldn't work. We put it to the Snowboarding Test—we said if we're still excited about this idea on the way home, let's do something about it."

The strategic marketing consultancy had transmogrified into a juice company.

The Juice and Smoothie Market

The market for smoothies was considered to be a subset of the much larger market for juices. Smoothies were blends of fruit that included the fruit's pulp and sometimes included dairy products such as yogurt. (For instance, the ingredients in one of Innocent's best-selling smoothies were: $1^1/_2$ freshly squeezed oranges, 1 crushed banana, and $^1/_4$ pressed pineapple.) Smoothies tended to be thicker and fresher than regular juice. (See **Exhibit 3** for a list of Innocent's product line in fall 2004.)

Some smoothies were made on demand at a juice bar, such as Smoothie King or Jamba Juice in the U.S. Innocent did not compete in this market, but rather in the market for prepackaged smoothies. The UK prepackaged smoothie market was divided into two segments: premium and standard. Premium smoothies contained no water or added sugar and commanded a higher price point. Standard smoothies were made with water and added sugar and were closer in price to ordinary juice.

Most prepackaged smoothies were sold through three channels:

- grocery stores
- cafes and sandwich shops
- impulse retail (e.g., convenience stores and gas station minimarts)

In all three channels, smoothies were packaged in individual serving sizes ranging from 250mL to 330mL. Juice and smoothie buying patterns were distinct. A customer shopping at a grocer might buy a liter of orange juice to take home for the family and, while in the store, pick up a 250mL smoothie to drink on the way home. (In 2004, Innocent introduced a larger-volume take-home product, but the great majority of sales still came from individual servings.)

Competition

Adam Balon estimated the size of the UK smoothie market in 2004 to be £50 million. The pie was carved into four pieces, with rough market share figures as follows:

- Innocent: 30% market share
- PJ Smoothies: 25% market share
- Store own-brands: 25% market share
- All others: 20% market share

PJ had essentially created the smoothie market in the UK. When Innocent entered the market in 1999, PJ was the only branded premium smoothie player in the market. Only in 2004 did Innocent begin to eclipse PJ's market share. Innocent benefited from a higher-qualiity product and the customer perception of a hipper brand.

Store own-brands were tougher to compete against. Chains such as Prêt a Manger, a popular sandwich shop, formulated their own smoothies and were able to lock out the competition.

In the U.S., the smoothie market was more mature and the competition was fiercer. The size of the U.S. smoothie market was estimated to be $300 million. Odwalla, the largest competitor, was bought by Coca-Cola in late 2001 for $180 million.

Juice buying patterns across different countries, even countries similar demographically, were surprisingly idiosyncratic. (See **Exhibit 4** for a comparison of juice buying patterns.) Germans, for instance, bought large amounts of juice per capita but had no true market for smoothies. Italians, on the other hand, bought very little juice, period.

Market Sizing

The smoothie market was small compared to the overall juice market in the UK, which was an estimated £1.3 billion in 2004. However, the smoothie market had been growing rapidly—30–40% annually for the three-year period from 2002 to 2004.

There were internal debates within Innocent about the "ceiling" of the UK smoothie market. How big was the market? How big could it get? It depended on how you defined the market. There was no question that Innocent could encroach on the traditional juice market, for instance by introducing larger-volume take-home products. Yet smoothies were, perhaps fundamentally, a niche product. The price per milliliter of a smoothie could be five times the price per milliliter of Tropicana orange juice. Switching from juice to smoothies was simply not an affordable option for many families.

Early Developments and Decisions at Innocent

Having agreed on a company concept in March 1998, the three founders spent the next five months investigating the idea and developing the business plan. Early on, they divided up roles. Reed, with his ad agency experience, took charge of marketing. Balon, with recent experience marketing Virgin Cola, wanted to take over sales. Wright, the manufacturing engineer, handled operations. They agreed that, rather than select one of them to serve as CEO, the three of them would jointly serve as leaders of the company.

Conducting a Pilot Test

Their homework on the smoothie concept led up to a crucial test run in August 1998. It took place at the Jazz on the Green Festival, which had been organized by Reed and Balon. The three founders set up a smoothie booth at the festival in order to gauge demand for the product. They squeezed the fruit themselves, borrowed bottles from a guy who made carrot juice, printed up 2000 labels, and set up a stand on some bales of hay.

They thought up a gimmick that doubled as market research. Next to their smoothie stand, they set up two trash bins, one labeled "Yes" and one labeled "No." Above the bins was a question: "Should we quit our day jobs and start a smoothie company?" The "Yes" bin overflowed. This would become the oft-told founding story of Innocent.

Pricing the Smoothies

In the four months following the jazz festival, the founders made three key decisions that, in retrospect, proved pivotal.

First, the company had a challenge with pricing. The founders were emphatic that Innocent smoothies would not be made from concentrate, unlike the other alternatives on the market at that point. They believed freshness and quality would be a critical differentiator in the marketplace and the key to Innocent's positioning against its competitor, PJ.

In 1998, PJ was the only important competitor in the smoothie market. PJ sold a line of 330mL smoothies made from concentrate. PJ smoothies were priced at £1.99, which was a premium price.

Innocent planned to beat PJ on quality and taste by making a fresher, more natural product. Freshness came at a price, however. After talking to potential suppliers, Wright learned some disturbing news about ingredient costs. For Innocent to make a reasonable margin on a 330mL product, they would have to charge over £2.50. This was considered a non-starter. There was simply no evidence that such a high price point could exist in the beverage market.

Wright said, "We were depressed. We thought, 'This is it, isn't it? The model just doesn't make sense." The three founders agreed that £2.00—matching PJ's price—was the highest they could go. They also agreed that they couldn't give on the freshness issue. There was only one variable left to adjust: volume.

A London design shop came up with an idea for a 250mL bottle that impressed the Innocent team. They decided to run with it. It was a risky move: Innocent planned to match PJ's retail price while offering a third less juice. Balon said, "We were wavering. We didn't know if we could get such a premium price. But our financial model told us we HAD to get that amount, so we stuck to our decision. At the time, we were scared. In retrospect, the price may have actually helped our growth by sending a signal that our drinks were something different."

Finding a Manufacturer

The second key decision made in late 1998 involved manufacturing. At the time, there were no British manufacturers set up to create the fresh smoothies that Innocent wanted. The manufacturers were certainly willing to adapt to earn a large account, but Innocent wasn't a large account. What manufacturer was going to make a big investment in new technology for a risky startup offering puny product volumes?

Wright said, "Nothing was coming together. Out of frustration, we started talking about building our own factory. We just felt like we needed to bring this issue under our control."

In November 1998, Wright met with a small supplier in a rural area. The supplier was relatively dependent on a few key supermarket customers, so he liked the idea of diversifying his client base. More importantly, perhaps, he got along well with the Innocent team. He agreed to take a risk on them.

Wright said, "If we'd made it to Christmas without a supplier, I am sure we would have started building a factory. And I think it would have been a disaster. All the energy we put into the brand might have gone into reinventing ways to squeeze fruit."

Raising Investment Capital

The final important decision was whether to raise money and, if so, how much to raise. Initially the founders had thought they could grow the business organically. When they began to run projections, they quickly realized that it would be impossible.

They considered small business loans, but found the paperwork terrifying. Also, banks were reluctant to lend to them due to a lack of assets. They pursued venture capital firms. They met with perhaps 12 investors and never got a second meeting. Said Wright, "They had no interest whatsoever. They'd say, 'You're selling a drink?! Isn't that one of the world's most competitive marketplaces? And, on top of that, it's a chilled drink. Isn't that a nasty distribution problem?'"

With no leads and mounting personal debt, they threw a Hail Mary. They sent an email to all their friends and acquaintances, asking if they knew anyone who was rich. A few responses trickled back. Wright had a friend at Bain who had worked with a man named Maurice Pinto, who had been an angel investor in other deals.

The team met with Pinto in October 1998. Wright remembers being surprised by Pinto's approach to the meeting. "He didn't ask detailed questions about our plan. He asked about our lifestyle, about how we'd make decisions, about where we were headed as people and as a team." They learned later that Pinto had made search fund investments in the past and felt it important to evaluate individuals rather than products.

After more discussions, Pinto sicced two business students on Innocent, who grilled the founders about their assumptions and forecasts. In the end, an investment offer was extended: £235,000 for 20% of the company. The team accepted, and the investment was closed in January 1999. Three months later, the company received its first pallet of smoothies from the manufacturer. (See **Exhibit 5** for a timeline of selected events.)

The Innocent Brand

In the summer of 1999, Dan Germain was back in London after a stint teaching English in Thailand and Indonesia. He called up the Innocent founders, whom he had known since he was 18. He thought their juice business sounded fun, so he deferred a masters program he had been planning to start in the fall. He started by delivering juice to retailers in Innocent's vans.

Germain and the founders were checking out the packaging of other beverages and someone commented on how boring labels were. The labels were dominated by minutiae. Why not make labels fun to read, like cereal boxes for kids?

They came up with the idea to print offbeat messages on the smoothie labels. One of the earliest messages, written by Richard Reed, was: "We're not saying that there's anything wrong with having a gym workout, it's just, you know, all bit of an effort really, isn't it? If I were you, I'd just have an Innocent smoothie instead. They're 100% pure fruit, they're made with fresh rather than concentrated juice and they contain no additives whatsoever. As a result they taste good and do you good. And you don't need to take a communal shower afterward."

The messages on the packaging became one of the hallmarks of the Innocent brand. The tone was offbeat, honest, irreverent, and often self-deprecating. It was non-corporate. For a company with very little money to spend on marketing, it became an effective way to create a buzz and earn customer loyalty. As the company grew, Germain began to take over as the unofficial voice of the Innocent brand—writing most of the messages on the labels, as well as the company newsletter and other customer communications.

Another example of the company's guerrilla marketing tactics involved the company's delivery vans. Like package labels, delivery vans were usually boring and generic. Innocent covered one of its vans with fake grass and dressed up another one to look like a cow (symbolic of the yogurt in the company's dairy-based smoothies). (See **Exhibit 6** for a photo of an Innocent delivery van.)

The press began to get interested in the Innocent story. In the fall of 1999, BBC Food & Drink called Innocent the "UK's best smoothie." The company, with its distinctive voice and innovative marketing, became a darling of the press.

Germain said, "I'd like to say that the witty labels and such were part of our master plan to dominate the industry. But I think the main reason we did those things is that the three founders and I were friends. We were doing things to make each other laugh. I think our customers could smell the fact that we were having fun."

The labels, which may have started as a lark, have become an institutionalized part of the company's marketing plan. In 2004, keeping up with the labels had become a major responsibility. For each product (e.g., the strawberry and banana smoothie), there were 10 labels in circulation at any given time. That way, people buying two smoothies from the same store would likely receive two different messages. In addition, the messages were cycled four times per year. Across about 20 different products, this yielded an astounding 800 labels per year in circulation. (See **Exhibit 7** for sample communications from the company's labels.)

Adam Rostom, Innocent's Marketing Manager, said, "It's very expensive and difficult to deal with. The obvious 'corporate' answer is to standardize them. But these messages are important to our brand. Standardizing them would send a very clear and very negative signal to our customers."

Hats for Bottles

In the summer of 2004, Innocent was preparing to launch seasonal beverages for the fall and winter. For the winter drinks, a graphic designer had added a winter hat to the artwork on the labels. Rostom thought: Why not use real hats instead? Something to cover the caps of the bottles "to keep the drinks warm in cold weather," he said. The quirkiness of the idea appealed to him and seemed consistent with the Innocent brand.

Rostom said, "In trying to figure out if this was a viable idea, I was wondering, 'Where do we get the hats?' We could source them from China, but what's the point of that? So we decided to have English grannies knit them." (See **Exhibit 8** for a photo of the smoothie with a knit cap.)

The company mentioned the idea in its customer email newsletter, which has a circulation of 5,000. Within a few weeks, they had signed up 40 grannies. The grannies agreed to knit the caps for free, in exchange for a 20p donation, per cap sold, to charities trying to keep the elderly warm.

Traditional Marketing versus Guerrilla Marketing

As the company grew, it incorporated more traditional marketing approaches, such as bus and subway advertisements. Rostom, who was recruited from Unilever in April 2003, said, "I think of our marketing approach as a 'see-saw.' On one side is Big Brand and on the other side is Little Brand. We've got to balance Big Brand stuff, like bus ads, with Little Brand stuff, like the knit caps. We may have a row of shelf space in a big supermarket chain, which looks like Big Brand. But then next door at the café, there is an Innocent fridge covered with fake grass. That's Little Brand."

One of the challenges with non-traditional marketing approaches was that it made it difficult for the company to track what was working and what wasn't. As an example, in August 2003, Innocent created Fruitstock, a "free festival for nice people." The company spent one-third of its marketing budget on the event, which was held in a public London park and included outside food vendors and live music. By the time of the second event in Aug 2004, it was attracting over 80,000 attendees.

Richard Reed said, "This event cost about £200,000 to put on. At this point, I can't prove that it was a good investment. From a hard numbers perspective, maybe we'd have been better off hiring new salespeople. But we are doing things that are hard to quantify. From a hard numbers perspective, why waste time on labels? There are important secondary benefits to things like Fruitstock: We had customers in the 'VNP[1] area' having a great day with their families. Employees could come with their family and friends. It's not just about advertising—it helps with recruiting, PR, and other areas."

The Growth Options

In 2003, as Innocent's sales continued to grow sharply, investor Maurice Pinto gave the founders some advice. He felt it was time for the Innocent team to start thinking about opportunities for growth. As Reed recalls, he said, "You guys should think like a chef. You may spend most of your time working on the main dish, but you've always got something cooking, some kind of side dish, on the back burners."

The founders agreed that the three best growth options were (1) taking the Innocent product line to Europe; (2) expanding into the U.S.; or (3) extending the Innocent brand to other products in the U.K.

---

[1]"Very Nice People"

Expanding to Europe

The Innocent team believed that its prospects in Europe were strong. The motivation to pursue continental Europe was so strong internally that an informal mission statement had caught on among employees: Innocent would be "Europe's favorite little juice company."

The case for expansion into Europe was simple: Find more customers for the same juice product, while keeping the supply chain intact. The founders believed that they could expand into a new country with only a small sales and marketing team on the ground.

An early experiment in Ireland had gone well. By the end of 2004, 7% of Innocent's revenue came from Ireland with only a couple of employees working in the country. In fact, on a per capita basis, Ireland was more successful than Britain.

However, Europe was, of course, a collection of very different markets. In Germany and Italy, for instance, most of the juice sold was "ambient," meaning it was non-refrigerated with a long shelf life. Selling premium refrigerated smoothies into such a marketplace would be no small feat. In some European markets, Innocent would have to establish the smoothie category, as PJ did for Innocent in the UK.

Will Hartley, international sales manager and a former employee of Odwalla in the U.S., said that Innocent's target markets within Europe would be locations with big urban populations, high disposable income levels, strong demand for eating and drinking outside the home, and strong demand for juice (though not necessarily smoothies specifically). According to Hartley, the countries that best fit these criteria were Sweden, Denmark, Norway, the Netherlands, and France. (See **Exhibit 9** for the size of the juice market in selected countries.)

With the exception of France, however, these markets were significantly smaller than the UK market. And the company's progress in achieving a presence in France had been disappointingly slow.

In thinking about the opportunity in Europe, the founders analyzed the size of the chilled juice market in three promising countries—the Netherlands, Belgium, and France. (The chilled juice market is a small subset of the overall juice market.) Then, they applied Innocent's market share growth from the U.K. to the new countries. They thought that the chilled juice market was a good proxy for the smoothie market, since not all countries tracked smoothies as a separate category.

Using this approach, the founders estimated that the project to expand into Europe could yield over £10,000,000 in revenue by the third year. (See **Exhibit 10** for the founders' analysis.) The costs were relatively low, with the bulk of the investment coming from the salaries of several employees on the ground in each country. One cost that was difficult to forecast was the price of advertising. If the Innocent brand could spread by word of mouth, as it did in the U.K., advertising cost might be quite low. On the other hand, if the brand did not translate well, or if the smoothie concept did not grow as quickly as in the U.K., then Innocent might have to make a substantial investment in each market.

Another cost that was difficult to calculate was the distraction of management attention. (This cost also applied to the product line expansion.) New ideas, with prospects for new growth, naturally drew the attention of the top performers in the organization. Could Innocent, having just eclipsed the smoothie market leader, afford to lose focus?

Expanding into the United States

The United States was easily the world's largest market for smoothies. The smoothie category in the U.S. was well-established, having been pioneered by Odwalla about a decade earlier.

The team's concern about the U.S. was not the market size, it was two other factors: (1) intense competition; and (2) the need to build an entirely new supply chain. The juice and smoothie market was crowded with competition, and unlike the U.K., much of the competition had long been offering fresh juices.

The founders knew it was feasible to build a supply chain in the U.S., but they were daunted by the amount of management attention it would consume. For a small company to build a distribution network in one of the world's largest countries, from 3000 miles away, it would be a challenge.

In the summer of 2004, the three founders had traveled to Las Vegas for Richard Reed's bachelor party. They used the opportunity to meet with some key potential partners while in the U.S. They were taken aback by the positive response. Buyers from some of the U.S.'s most prestigious national retail chains expressed strong interest in carrying Innocent smoothies. The founders were torn: The U.S. market was a tough one to enter, but could they walk away from interest by such marquee companies?

Other Product Lines

"Europe's best little juice company" was one vision for the future. Another vision was a U.K. "natural brand for healthy lifestyles." In this vision, Innocent would extend its brand into other categories, such as ice cream or soup, much as Odwalla (U.S.) eventually added nutrition bars and bottled water.

The ice cream business was their first target. Lucy Ede, Innocent's Head of Recipes, had been leading the effort to develop an ice cream product. Her team had made substantial progress in the past year, but because they needed to devote most of their time to new smoothie flavors and seasonal changes, they had not yet completed the ice cream development.

The lure of other product lines was clear: Customers loved the Innocent brand. It was the company's biggest asset. Reed wondered, "When we talk about expanding into Europe, we are emphasizing our product over our brand. No one in Europe has heard of Innocent. And I think our brand is an enormous asset."

Jon Wright was the least excited of the three founders about this vision. He said, "Yes, we get to keep our customers. But we'll need a whole new supply chain, and we may have different buyers at the retail level. For me, I want to keep things simple, keep things the same, and just scale them up. We do certain things well, let's do more of that. But I know the argument isn't quite that easy. I think what we do well is distribute chilled drinks. But the other guys argue convincingly that what we do well is give customers a feeling of healthiness."

The founders worked on a rough analysis of the market opportunity in their first two target categories: ice cream and frozen yogurt. If they were able to launch the products in early 2005, they believed they could grow the business to £8 million by the third year. (See **Exhibit 10** for their analysis.) The founders agreed that the ice cream and yogurt products were, in a lot of ways, riskier than the European expansion. They simply could not guarantee that demand for their product would be there.

However, they considered the move into ice cream a first test of the "healthy lifestyles" vision. It had value as an indicator for the overall strategy. It would also be powerful evidence to a potential acquirer that the Innocent brand was a valuable asset with room to grow.

Financial Issues Related to Growth

Adam had spoken extensively with James Davenport, the financial controller. From a finance perspective, the two options were remarkably similar. Adam gave the overview to Richard and Jon:

> From a "cash needs" perspective, the options aren't too different. Looks like it will cost us roughly £500,000 up front to pursue either option—that's made up mostly of salaries and a bit of marketing. Cap ex is not a big issue: in Europe we'd use our existing infrastructure, and with the ice cream and yoghurt products, we'd outsource the manufacturing. As for working capital, we'll need to invest a bit in either scenario for extra inventory in the system, but that is built into my £500,000 figure.
>
> Margins are tougher to forecast. In Europe, we know what our cost structure will be, but we don't know what price we'll be able to achieve—particularly without the benefit of having PJs there ahead of us to set the expectations. With ice cream, we know our costs will be higher than Ben & Jerry's and the others, and we'll have to give the retailers a bit more cash margin. So, again, it will come down to price—can we set a price that is above the "super-premium" category leaders like Ben & Jerry's?
>
> Net net, there aren't any glaring differences from a cash needs or margins perspective. In my opinion, it boils down to pricing, market sizes, likelihood of success—and figuring out what kind of business we want to run.

Harvest Options

Innocent had already drawn the attention of large beverage companies in the U.S. and the U.K. None of the suitors had put specific offers on the table, but if Odwalla was used as a comparable data point, then Innocent might expect to be valued at twice sales. (See **Exhibit 11** for a list of selected M&A transactions in the beverage industry and **Exhibit 12** for valuation data on public beverage companies.) Given that the founders still owned almost 80% of the company, this was potentially a large sum of money for each of them.

None of the founders were particularly keen to sell the business right away, but they also didn't want to be naïve. Reed said, "This isn't a charity. We are not opposed to making money. And as the three of us move into our mid-thirties, our interests are going to diverge naturally. We'll have families; we'll have other business ideas. At some point, we need to figure out a way to create financial options for ourselves."

Another option was to scale back the company's growth efforts and focus on improving profitability in the U.K. market. The company would still, inevitably, grow organically, but it would not focus on additional markets or products. Wright estimated that, if the company was run for cash, the business could generate £3 million in dividends to shareholders annually.

The founders knew that both of these options would be unpopular among the Innocent employees. As Wright said, "We've always been a growth business. We're always thinking about new ideas. People join up and agree to drive a delivery van because they know two years later they'll be managing a team. If we lose that momentum, it could be a dangerous thing." Balon agreed: "We've built a certain momentum here, and people want to continue to see that growth. We are constantly celebrating milestones internally—like the biggest sales week ever and so forth. If we lost that, I think the culture would lose some of its value."

The employees were also instinctively against an acquisition. They valued the independence and creativity of the Innocent brand, and they feared that its spark would be slowly extinguished by a multinational parent.

A Final Complication

The debate continued in the Acorn Room. The three founders were very comfortable debating each other, with relative civility and rationality, for hours on end. They believed that this inclination to analyze an issue, to talk it out exhaustively, had been a key to Innocent's success. As Maurice Pinto said of the founders, "They tend to worry an issue to death. Their decision-making takes ages to accomplish—grinding through it, talking through it, trying to reach consensus. But their hit rate of good decisions versus bad decisions is absolutely extraordinary."

In the back of their minds, however, the three friends wondered whether this model of leadership was sustainable. In times of high ambiguity, when a bad decision could kill the company, a model of careful deliberation and consensus decision-making seemed to work well. But what about now, when the company needed speed?

Of course, the other point of view was "If it ain't broke, don't fix it." Pinto said, "The co-CEO arrangement has worked brilliantly. In my 40+ years of operating and investing, this is the most effective management team I have come across." And it was almost unthinkable that after knowing each other for 13 years, and after building the company as equals, that one of them would step up and become "the boss."

The Decision

None of the issues on the table were ambiguous: Each founder understood the other, and the advantages of each strategy—pro and con—were relatively clear. The frustrating thing was that all of their choices were wrapped in uncertainty. It was an important decision, potentially a decision that could make or break the company. And it looked as if they'd have to make it primarily on instinct.

Reed felt strongly that the company should focus. He thought their attempts to do everything had cost them time. But he was not devoted to a single option. Wright was leaning toward the European expansion. Balon thought they could continue to keep both projects moving forward, if they were smarter about it. All three of them were uncomfortable putting the American market on hold, but they felt it might be too much to handle too soon.

Wright joked, "Looks like you're breaking the tie, Rich." Reed nodded and said, "No pressure, though, right?"

EXHIBIT 1 | The Background of Innocent's Founders

Adam Balon, Head of Sales
- Educated at St. John's College, Cambridge after Latymer Upper, London
  - *Graduated with a 1 in Economics in June 1994*
- 1 year on the Arthur Andersen Scholarship Programme
- 2 years at McKinsey & Company as a Business Analyst
  - *Worked in a variety of sectors including financial services and, more importantly, grocery retailing. Spent 7 months in South Africa running 2 client teams during the major restructuring of one of South Africa's big four banks.*
- 2 years at Virgin Cola
  - *Most recent role: Marketing Manager. Ran UK marketing for Virgin Cola, developing the brand strategy, coordinating the 10 person department and controlling the £5m budget. Had extensive experience of dealing with impulse and grocery multiples to drive listings.*
  - *Previous roles: Brand Manager; Logistics and Production Planning*
- Earned a place in the Harvard MBA program in 1998

Richard Reed, Head of Marketing
- Educated at St. John's College, Cambridge after Batley Grammar, Leeds
  - *Graduated with a 2.1 in Geography in June 1994*
- 4 years at advertising agency BMP DDB Needham
  - *Most recent role: Account Director on the agency's Volkswagen business. Responsible for devising and implementing new marketing strategies to double VW's market share and also to exploit new revenue streams for the agency by developing new services, including macro-planning and retail communications.*
  - *Previous roles: Business Director for BMP's Interactive Marketing Consultancy; New Business Director for the agency*
- Together with Adam Balon, responsible for West London's music festival, Jazz on the Green

Jonathan Wright, Head of Operations
- Educated at St. John's College, Cambridge after Winchester College, Hants
  - *Graduated with a 2.1 in Engineering in June 1994*
  - *Masters in Manufacturing Engineering in June 1995*
- ESSO Petroleum Bursary, including 12 months in Plant Technical Services at Fawley Refinery, Southampton
- 3 years at Bain & Company
  - *Joined as Associate Consultant, promoted to Senior Associate in June 1997 and to Consultant (post-MBA level) in June 1998*
  - *Worked across a range of industries including manufacturing, financial services, and media in the UK, the US, and Asia. Projects have included developing startup plans for established companies setting up new ventures overseas, business cases for corporate parents to invest/dispose of their business units, and negotiating strategies as part of subsequent disposals. Also heavily involved in internal operations including IT and recruiting.*

Source: Company.

EXHIBIT 2 | Innocent Actual and Forecasted Revenue Growth, 1999–2005

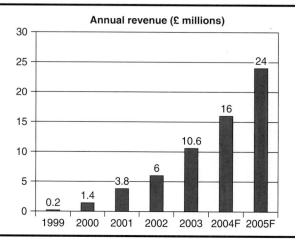

Source: Company.

EXHIBIT 3 | Innocent's Product Line, Fall 2004

Smoothies	Super Smoothies	Thickies	Really Lovely Juices	Juicy Waters
Seasonal: Blackcurrants and gooseberries	Natural vitamin C	Yoghurt, vanilla bean, and honey	Oranges, mangoes, and limes	Blackcurrants
Cranberries and raspberries	Natural detox	Seasonal: Yoghurt, figs, and honey	Nothing but oranges	Cranberries and limes
Strawberries and bananas	Fruit and veg			Lemons and limes
Blackberries and blueberries				Mangoes and passion fruits
Oranges, bananas, and pineapples				
Mangoes and passion fruits				
Pineapples, bananas, and coconuts				

Source: Company.

EXHIBIT 4 | Juice Consumption Patterns in Selected Countries
(liters per capita/year)

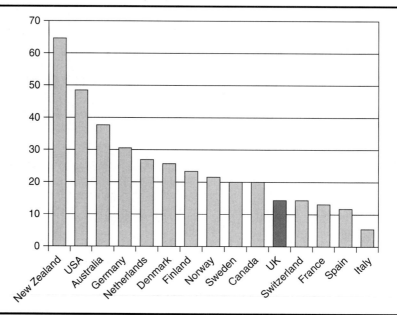

Source: Adapted from A.C. Nielsen data.

EXHIBIT 5 | Timeline of Selected Events

1998

Feb	Road trip to France, discussion of business ideas
August	Pilot smoothie test at jazz festival
October	First meeting with investor Morris Pinto
November	Juice supplier found

1999

January	Investment closed with Pinto
April	Started trading selling 24 bottles on day 1
October	BBC Food & Drink calls Innocent "UK's Best Smoothie"

2000

July	The team relocates to a larger office space (the "Fruit Towers")
November	Launch of "thickies" (smoothies with yogurt)

2001

December	Release of Innocent's *Little Book of Drinks* cocktail recipe book

EXHIBIT 5 | *(continued)*

2002
January	Madonna orders in Innocent smoothies for a party she is hosting
September	Closed deal to sell 750mL bottles in large UK grocer Sainsbury's

2003
June	Launch of Juicy Water drinks with deal to supply Starbucks UK stores
Aug	First Fruitstock attracting c40,000 people
December	Reed, Wright, and Balon named E&Y Young Entrepreneurs of the Year

2004
Feb	Became #1 smoothie brand in Sainsbury's
August	Second Fruitstock held attracting over 80,000 people
September	Founders' meeting

Source: Company.

EXHIBIT 6 | One of the Innocent Delivery Vans

Source: Company.

EXHIBIT 7 | Copy from Selected Innocent Labels

"Life is like your dressing gown—you wake up in the morning and it's there. Of course, it's easy to take both of them for granted, but then where would you be without them? Naked on the doorstep when you're getting the milk in, that's where. So treasure your life, treasure your dressing gown, and feel free to even treasure this little bottle stuffed full of fruit, because life consists of many beautiful things, and some of them are made out of towelling."

"It's our right as normal people to say what we're thinking. So, we think that 'nuggets' made out of reconstituted chicken, water and additives are a bit wrong. We think that using concentrates to bulk out fruit juice is a bit cheeky. We think that living your life simply and naturally is an admirable thing. And we think that someone should invent a manual cheese grater that doesn't graze your knuckles every time you want some parmesan on your spaghetti (please send details to cheeseease@innocentdrinks.co.uk if you know of such a thing)."

"Life is simple. Get born, mess about with wax crayons, do some kissing, go to work, play bingo. So why do people make things all complicated?

Why make burgers and pies that don't have proper meat in them? Why confuse us by adding concentrates and preservatives to some tasty fruit juice? Why make us do loads of sums at school when we'd rather be playing kiss chase? It's all a bit confusing, so we'll just stick to putting lots of fruit in our bottles and learning how to tie our laces.

Under, over, loop and knot."

Source: Company.

EXHIBIT 8 | Innocent Winter Smoothie with Protective Headgear

Source: Company.

EXHIBIT 9 | Estimates of Growth Opportunities

	1998	1999	2000	2001	2002	2003
Fruit/Vegetable Juice—Retail Volume (million liters)						
Western Europe (total region)	8,156	8,540	8,728	8,980	9,169	9,752
Belgium	186	191	197	202	207	216
France	1,141	1,174	1,193	1,209	1,199	1,214
Germany	2,983	3,072	3,024	3,002	2,995	3,319
Ireland	43	45	49	53	55	56
Italy	491	530	567	617	641	709
Netherlands	318	325	346	373	415	454
Spain	435	464	544	597	622	644
United Kingdom	1,177	1,295	1,291	1,299	1,342	1,377
USA	9,728	10,051	10,266	10,324	10,502	10,575
Carbonates—Retail Volume (million liters)						
Western Europe (total region)	19,065	19,664	20,245	20,611	20,972	21,544
Belgium	776	790	783	797	815	846
France	1,421	1,437	1,481	1,513	1,538	1,622
Germany	3,768	3,889	4,101	4,231	4,324	4,373
Ireland	304	321	339	354	356	360
Italy	1,521	1,537	1,570	1,582	1,606	1,731
Netherlands	955	1,010	1,046	1,082	1,121	1,167
Spain	2,503	2,649	2,743	2,783	2,784	2,816
United Kingdom	3,753	3,807	3,933	4,029	4,086	4,164
USA	39,573	39,846	40,055	40,323	40,649	40,372

EXHIBIT 10 | Estimates of Growth Opportunities

EXPANSION INTO EUROPE

Key assumptions:

- Entry into France, Belgium, and the Netherlands only
- Market share estimates modeled on experience in the U.K.

	2005	2006	2007	2008
Total value of chilled juice markets	£270,000,000	£282,000,000	£296,000,000	£302,000,000
Projected market share	0.25%	1.00%	3.85%	5.00%
Value to Innocent	£675,000	£2,820,000	£11,400,000	£15,100,000

EXPANSION INTO OTHER PRODUCT CATEGORIES

Key assumptions:

- New ice cream and yoghurt products ready to launch in early 2005
- Revenue estimates based on internal analysis of market opportunity

	2005	2006	2007
Revenue from ice cream	£825,000	£2,900,000	£4,000,000
Revenue from yoghurt	£420,000	£2,500,000	£4,200,000
Total new product revenue	£1,245,000	£5,400,000	£8,200,000

Source: Company.

EXHIBIT 11 | Selected Beverage Industry M&A Transactions

Date annc'd	Acquired Company	Acquirer Name	Business Description	Value ($mil)	LTM Sales ($mil)	Value/ LTM sales
10/08/93	Hillside Coffee of California	Gourmet Coffee of America Inc	Produce coffee	42	28	1.5
11/02/94	Snapple Beverage Corp	Quaker Oats Co	Produce, wholesale soft drinks	1,703	700	2.4
01/04/95	Dole Food Co–Juice Business	Seagram Co. Ltd.	Produce, wholesale juice beverages	285	325	0.9
06/27/95	Mistic Beverage Co.	Triarc Cos. Inc.	Produce soft drinks	94	150	0.6
11/22/95	Wine World Estates	Investor Group	Produce wine	350	210	1.7
09/19/96	Hansen Juices Inc.	Fresh Juice Co. Inc.	Produce, wholesale juice	8	11	0.7
06/14/00	Bass Brewers	Interbrew	Produce, wholesale beer	3,450	2,654	1.3
10/30/00	South Beach Beverage (SoBe)	Pepsi-Cola North America	Produce, wholesale soft drinks	337	250	1.3
11/05/01	Odwalla Inc.	Coca-Cola Co.	Produce smoothies and juices	181	94	1.9
03/18/02	Molson Brazil	Heinken	Produce, wholesale beer	220	79	2.8

Source: Company.

EXHIBIT 12 | Selected Data on Public Companies

Company	Ticker	Mkt Cap 11/04	+ Debt	− Cash	− Joint Vntrs	Ent Val	2003A EBITDA	2004E EBITDA	EV/ EBITDA 03	EV/ EBITDA 04	2003 sales	Gross Profit '03	Op Margin '03
Concentrate Companies													
Coca-Cola Co.	KO	100,257	7,658	5,520	700	101,695	7,451	7,751	13.6	13.1	21,044	67.20%	24.80%
PepsiCo Inc.	PEP	88,440	2,662	2,753	800	87,549	6,913	7,502	12.7	11.7	26,971	58.10%	18.50%
Bottlers													
Coca-Cola Enterprises	CCE	10,376	11,110	131	0	21,355	2,513	2,528	8.5	8.4	17,330	47.70%	9.10%
The Pepsi Bottling Group	PBG	7,441	4,720	257	−100	12,004	1,517	1,567	7.9	7.7	10,265	54.70%	9.30%
Midcap Beverages													
Jones Soda Co.	JSDA	76	0	1	0	75	0	1	n/a	54.2	20	35.50%	1.80%
Constellation Brands (wine)	STZ	5,166	1,994	10	−110	7,260	629	684	11.5	10.6	3,552	30.30%	14.60%
Specialty Foods													
Dreyer's Grand Ice Cream Holdings, Inc.	DRYR	7,309	168	2	0	7,475	15.6	−10.1	479.2	n/a	1,190	19.90%	—
CoolBrands	COB.A	308.4	27.9	21.7	0	315	42.7	n/a	7.4	n/a	258.0	41.80%	15.20%

Source: Hoovers, Kanter Equity Research.

Shurgard Self-Storage: Expansion to Europe

There are 300 million people in the U.S. and Canada served by more than 25,000 storage facilities. In Europe, there are 500 million people served by fewer than 200 facilities.

Dave Grant, President, Shurgard Europe, 1998 Annual Report

Dave Grant, president and chief executive officer of Shurgard Europe, returning from a meeting in July 1999 with bankers in London, glanced out the airplane window. As the Brussels Zaventem Airport drew closer, he thought of the company's nearby facility with its trademark lighthouse tower. Shurgard Storage Centers, Inc. (Shurgard USA), based in Seattle, Washington, had been offering self-storage services to relocating U.S. consumers since the 1970s. In 1994, Shurgard became a publicly traded real estate investment trust. The company was one of the largest owners and operators of U.S. self-storage facilities, with 980 employees and 348 managed properties, representing 20 million rentable square feet (1.86 million square meters), located in 20 states. Fiscal 1998 had been the best in the company's 25-year history, with total revenues at $159 million, store-level profit margins at 72%, and market capitalization at $1.28 billion. (See **Exhibits 1a** to **1f** for Shurgard 1994 to 1998 financial statements.)

Seeking new growth in an increasingly fragmented industry, Shurgard USA decided to expand to Europe and in 1994 established regional headquarters in Brussels, Belgium. Grant, a U.S. expatriate, moved to Brussels from Seattle in 1996 to lead the management team, which he built over the next several years by hiring a mix of restaurant site developers from McDonald's Europe and real estate professionals. Despite unexpected challenges in adapting the American self-storage concept to European consumer lifestyles, by July 1999 Grant's team had opened 17 operating facilities in Europe (nine in Belgium, five in Sweden, and three in France), with another 18 in development/construction, at a

---

Professor Richard G. Hamermesh and Indra A. Reinbergs, Manager Research Staff Development, prepared this case. HBS cases are developed solely as the basis for class discussion. Cases are not intended to serve as endorsements, sources of primary data, or illustrations of effective or ineffective management.

cost of €120 million to its U.S. parent and joint-venture partners. Shurgard had grown to over 100 employees and 4,000 self-storage customers across Europe.

Now, Grant felt that European operations had stabilized enough to speed up the rate of expansion to reach between 133 and 170 operating facilities by December 2003. This strategy, however, would require considerable capital, and Shurgard's U.S. parent company was not willing to fund this plan on its own. Therefore, throughout the spring of 1999, Grant had been working with several financial institutions, trying to negotiate the terms of a capital infusion. The deal he had just reviewed in London seemed the most promising he had seen so far. It included a €262 million investment—€122 million in equity for 43% of the company and a €140 million credit facility. As Grant reviewed the term sheet, he realized that not only would the deal take a large piece of equity but also contained important provisions that Shurgard Europe would have to share many decisions with an investor-dominated board, and that could force the sale of Shurgard Europe after five years. Did it make sense to accept these conditions and valuation in return for such a large capital infusion? Should his team instead scale back the expansion and wait before seeking additional funding? And, most importantly, could the self-storage business model deliver the returns in Europe that Grant was projecting to his potential investors?

Development of the Self-Storage Industry and Shurgard

Growth of Industry and Shurgard USA

The self-storage industry was born in the 1970s, as the increasingly affluent and mobile American consumer lifestyle created a demand for extra or temporary storage space. Households became cluttered with affordable, mass-produced appliances and electronics, while frequent relocations for work or study became commonplace. Demographic changes—increasing divorce rates and an aging population—fueled this trend. Grant commented, "We are a change-driven business, and change is constant in people's lives."

As an alternative to expensive, full-service relocation or warehousing services, oil industry entrepreneurs in Texas began renting out extra warehouse space directly to consumers. An owner/operator (usually, but not always the same company) of a self-storage facility would rent out single units to customers, who signed a rental agreement similar to an apartment lease. The customers had to pack and transport their goods to/from the facility themselves. In contrast to traditional warehouses, whose operators had to inventory and insure stored goods on behalf of customers, in a self-storage facility the tenants, not the owner/operators, carried primary legal responsibility for the *care, custody, and control* of their stored goods. Self-storage customers received their own unique keys to their units and were encouraged to insure their goods. The facility owner/operators bore only limited legal and financial liability for the goods that customers stored in their facilities and in situations where customers' goods were stolen or damaged by fire or water due to the company's negligence.

Capitalizing on this business opportunity, in 1972, Charles (Chuck) Barbo, a real estate entrepreneur, founded Shurgard in Seattle. At the time, Barbo was studying for a doctorate in history at the University of Washington. Barbo recalled, "I realized that my competitive advantage in life was not in academics. I got involved in the real-estate business sort of by accident. A friend of mine told me about the storage industry down in Texas, and so we decided to try it in Seattle. We built one that worked and we've been building them every since."[1] By the end of the 1970s Shurgard had 25 storage facilities in the Seattle, Washington area.

Over the next 30 years, three generations of U.S. self-storage facilities evolved. Initially, single-story facilities, containing 400 rental units on 45,000 square feet (ft^2) (4,180 m^2), were constructed in rural, industrial-park settings, with manual gates and chain-link fences.[2] Listed in the *Yellow Pages* as having the "lowest prices in town," these modest, "mom-and-pop" operations were usually managed by married couples who lived in a small apartment on-site, similar to operators of roadside motels. Commented Grant, "The husband-and-wife team was a good division of labor between people with different skill sets. The wife typically minded the store and interacted with customers, while the husband was fixing and cleaning storage units. The problem was that rarely were both spouses equally good at their jobs."

Soon Shurgard was competing not only with individual mom-and-pop operators but larger corporations such as Public Storage, U-Haul, and Storage USA. Barbo explained, "Everyone realized that you could rent a storage space for the same price per square foot as an apartment, but at only a third to a half of the cost." In another interview, he elaborated, "It's a fairly simple business model. . . . We are a very low maintenance business. When someone moves out, we don't have to . . . repaint, we just sweep it out and rent it to the next guy. So the margins are very high, about 70% gross margins."[3]

In the 1980s, branding and retail chain management experience became increasingly important. To distinguish itself from competitors, Shurgard came up with a new architectural feature—a lighthouse tower in which the manager's office was located. The design director, a Swedish-American architect, commented, "The lighthouse is an internationally recognized symbol of safety, and its appearance and height is unusual enough for a customer to think 'What was that?!' while driving by on the highway." To attract more sophisticated consumers, self-storage operators improved facility locations (closer to major highways or shopping areas), appearance ("fortress" design, glass doors, wrought-iron fences), and security (access-control gates, cameras). Commented Grant, "From Chuck's first foray into the business, he believed that you could differentiate the product. Many people view it as a commodity, but I think we've clearly demonstrated that if you provide a premium product, you can get higher rates." In the 1980s Shurgard began to change the profile of its store managers and migrated away from married couples to professional store managers (starting salary $27,000) and assistant store managers, 20% of whom were college educated. Because the staff assumed both

---

[1]Beverly Shuch, "Shurgard Storage Centers—CEO," *CNNfn: Business Unusual,* July 21, 1999.

[2]R.K. Kliebenstein, "The Face of Change: Technology's Hand in Self-Storage Operations," *Inside Self-Storage Magazine,* January 2002. Accessed October 25, 2003 at http://www.insideselfstorage.com/articles/211feat4.html.

[3]Beverly Shuch, "Shurgard Storage Centers—CEO," *CNNfn: Business Unusual,* July 21, 1999.

sales/billing and facility-upkeep responsibilities, only one to two people were necessary to run a large facility. Within two years, a successful store manager could be promoted to a regional team trainer, then a district manager in charge of 10 facilities.

From Seattle, Shurgard expanded to the Midwest (Michigan) and then the East Coast. To get a better sense of the markets his company was going into, in the mid-1980s the enthusiastic Barbo moved to Philadelphia and "spent a year driving down every road from Richmond, Virginia to northern Connecticut, between the mountains and ocean, to see how self-storage customers lived. It was an amazing year." By 1988, with Barbo back in Seattle, Shurgard had 100 facilities across the United States. Continued Barbo, "For 30 years, I've had the vision that we're going to be this national and global company, and we're going to dominate this business. I never acted like we were a company without money or with only a small portfolio. This is very different than the typical person who came into our industry, apartment builders who liked having a small business."

The third generation of storage facilities (*stores*) of the mid-1990s, between 60,000 ft^2 to 85,000 ft^2 (5,575 m^2 to 7,900 m^2) in size, addressed customers' increased desire for security—stricter access-control gates, more prevalent video surveillance with digitized backups, and motion-sensor lighting. According to Grant, "Security was not such a large issue in the industry's early days, but then criminals became aware of the goods stored in our facilities. Now controlling access is very important." Using a digital access code to the facility and a physical key to their unit, Shurgard's U.S. customers could usually access their units from 6 a.m. to 10 p.m., seven days a week, even when the manager's office was closed. Third-generation units, many built as multistoried units, also had computerized, zoned climate control and a brightly lit 600 ft^2 (55m^2) retail space, where customers could buy packing materials and often rent trucks. (See **Exhibit 2** for photograph of Shurgard's typical U.S. facility.)

From several thousand self-storage facilities in the early 1980s, by 1999 the U.S. self-storage market, with $10 billion in total revenues, had grown to 30,000 facilities (8 million storage units).[4] The industry was very fragmented—the top 10 U.S. self-storage operators controlled only 18% of the total industry square footage. Industry observers questioned whether the industry, where price competition had become common, could be reaching a point of saturation.[5]

By 1999, Shurgard managed 348 self-storage properties, representing 20 million rentable ft^2 (1.86 million m^2), located in 20 U.S. states. Over the years, 60% of Shurgard's U.S. growth had been through acquisitions of existing facilities. The remaining 40% had been built new from the ground up. Grant commented, "Our experience with acquisitions in the mid-1980s is the reason we ended up wanting to develop more of our own portfolio. Because other developers were going to own a facility for a short period of time, they tended to take construction shortcuts that just showed up as deferred maintenance issues for us." (See **Exhibit 3a** for industry growth, 1992–1998, and **Exhibit 3b** for Shurgard's competitors' 1998 performance.)

---

[4] "'It's Not Clutter': Self-storage Industry Grows as Americans Hoard," *The Independent,* August 19, 2000. Accessed October 25, 2003 at http://www.theindependent.com/storeies/08200/fea_store20.html.

[5] Analyst report on Shurgard Storage Centers (SHU), Morgan Stanley Dean Witter, February 8, 1999, p. 1.

Customers, Operations, and Pricing

Most U.S. self-storage facilities were located on the outskirts of cities, close to high-ways, where large plots of land were available on which to build many garage-type storage units, popular with American customers because they could drive up, park, and unload their goods directly into the unit. Shurgard's typical U.S. facility, a one-story construction with 80% externally accessible units, required four acres (1.6 hectares) of land. For its facilities, Shurgard aimed to purchase real estate sites in "dominant locations"—visible, accessible locations within a 3- to 5-mile (4.8 kilometers to 8 kilo-meters) retail corridor. When entering a market, Shurgard preferred building its pres-ence to a critical mass of 10 to 15 stores before moving to the next city. Barbo explained, "Clustering stores increases brand awareness, maximizes advertising effectiveness, and creates managerial efficiencies." For each new facility, Shurgard handled the facility design and financing in-house but subcontracted the actual construction out to a third party.

Thanks to 30 years of lobbying by Barbo and his industry colleagues, the construc-tion and operation of self-storage facilities were regulated by a network of national leg-islation, individual self-storage acts in each state, and local-building zoning ordinances that contained language specific to self-storage facilities. Maintaining good relations with local communities was important—each time a self-storage operator sought a building permit for a new facility, residents might object that a warehouse-type facility would bring down neighborhood property values, or local authorities might fear that self-storage tenants would store illegal or dangerous goods in the units.

The self-storage industry estimated the market potential of an area by the number of residents and the average amount of self-storage space (in square feet) that each per-son in the area was likely to rent. In the 1970s and 1980s, the early years of the industry's development, Shurgard and its competitors used active marketing campaigns to explain the notion of self-storage to the U.S. population. However, by the late 1990s, this was no longer necessary, as all 280 million U.S. residents were characterized as "aware of self-storage," and a "5% rule" was usually applied to calculate the percentage of the population that would become active self-storage customers at any one time. The number of customers was then multiplied by the size of the average rental space, which ranged from 80 to 100 square feet, to determine market potential.

Shurgard had 175,000 U.S. tenants, averaging 500 to 600 customers per facility, typically split between 75% residential and 25% commercial tenants but with up to 80% commercial clients at some facilities. Barbo commented, "When we started this business, we could never have guessed the crazy things that customers would do with the space." For corporations, storage units offered a flexible place to store inventory (off-season greeting cards) and product samples (pharmaceuticals) or to use as an inter-mediate distribution point (local newspapers). For small-business and home-based craftspeople, storage units offered an extra workspace. For example, at a Seattle facility close to Lake Union, we (the casewriters) saw narrow, long, coffin-shaped units that local apartment dwellers used for storing racing kayaks. By the drive-up units, in one unit we saw an antique Ford automobile, whose owner kept it parked there, in another the local Red Bull microbrewery truck, complete with beer-product samples that were distributed in the neighborhood for promotional purposes. In one unit, a cabinetmaker was assembling furniture; in another, a fruit merchant was unpacking bananas for delivery. To accommodate customers' needs, Shurgard developed various size units, features, and services. For commercial customers, Shurgard offered dedicated salespeople, centralized billing, and air conditioning.

The minimum length for a Shurgard unit rental was one week, with an average rental for 10 months. "We are like a hotel, we don't have many long-term tenants and our price structure discourages it. That being said, we do have some customers who have been renting with us in the Seattle area since we opened over 25 years ago," commented Grant. Instead of fixed prices, Shurgard had a flexible, airline-type, demand-based pricing system that charged higher prices for popular features and size units or at full facilities. In 1999, the average U.S. industry occupancy rate was 86.9%.[6] Every month, between 7% and 10% of Shurgard's tenant base moved out, with more fluctuation in the summer.

Rents were due, in advance, at the beginning of each month. If a customer did not pay on time, in addition to charging late fees, Shurgard had the legal right to foreclose the contract and sell a customer's goods to recover some of the lost revenue. In the United States, if a customer's rent was more than 30 days overdue and Shurgard had notified the overdue customer by mail, then Shurgard could begin selling the goods within 45 to 60 days after the last rent payment, without a court hearing. Only 15% of Shurgard's customer base failed to pay by the fifth of the month, and the company wrote off less than 2% of revenues.

Financial Issues

Although the self-storage business was relatively easy to enter, because the business concept was very different from the standard real estate investment, obtaining financing to grow had proven a constant challenge for Barbo. In 1985, Barbo gave a recruiting presentation to the MBA students of the Young Entrepreneurs Club at Harvard Business School. Recalled Barbo, "As soon as they found out I was in the storage business, they were off going in another direction. It was clear that self-storage wasn't people's dream career." Self-storage was a capital-intensive, long-term business, requiring investment for several years before a store would *rent up* (reach a high enough occupancy rate to generate a stable cash flow). When a store reached an 85% occupancy rate (usually after two years in the United States), Shurgard considered the store stabilized. Grant explained:

> Self-storage is the most stable real estate business—as an industry, except for the 1988 recession, we've had steady, solid growth. A self-storage facility breaks even [before financing charges] at approximately 35% occupancy. It has a low-risk cost structure and doesn't require much maintenance. But real estate investors require long-term tenant leases for five years into the future. So when we show them just week-long rental contracts, the investors freak out.

---

[6] "'It's Not Clutter': Self-storage Industry Grows as Americans Hoard," *The Independent,* August 19, 2000.

In its first 20 years of existence, from 1972 to 1992, Shurgard funded its growth through 24 separate, limited real estate partnerships, in which 80,000 individuals invested $600 million. Barbo added, "In the 1970s we were building properties with money we raised through private limited partnerships—each deal had its own financing. In the 1980s we followed the lead of our competitor Public Storage and created public partnerships to fund our expansion. We raised money in so many different ways that we came to refer to it as 'just-in-time financing.' " In the early 1990s, Barbo decided to *roll up* (consolidate) the limited partnerships into one company, incorporated as a real estate investment trust (REIT).[7] Commented Barbo, "At the time, the political climate for roll-ups of limited partnerships in the United States was not favorable. I had to go to Washington, D.C. and repeatedly testify before the Senate before we got approval to do the roll-up." In 1994, Shurgard was able to consolidate most of its partnerships and went public as a single REIT on NASDAQ. In 1995 Shurgard moved its stock listing (SHU) to the New York Stock Exchange.

Shurgard Expansion to Europe

As the U.S. self-storage industry became increasingly saturated and competitive, Barbo began to look elsewhere for opportunities. In 1985, he graduated from the Owner/President Management Executive Education Program[8] at Harvard Business School and several years later traveled to Monte Carlo to attend a class reunion. Barbo, whose grandparents had emigrated from Norway, reminisced:

> It was my first trip to Europe. On a whim, I asked the desk clerk at my hotel for a phone book and looked through the Yellow Pages for the words "self-storage." We couldn't find any listings. When I thought about the possibilities to expand our business into Europe, I thought I was living my life all over again. If the *per capita* demand propensity for self-storage in western Europe is even half that of the United States, then I can see about 25,000 self-storage facilities developing there in 20 years.

However, at the time, combining the many partnerships and going public were taking all of Barbo's time and resources. In 1992, Michael Fogelberg, a Swedish undergraduate business student at Seattle University, was moving back to Europe for a year to work in his family business and needed a place to store his belongings. Michael recalled:

> So I went around to a couple of self-storage companies in Seattle, including Shurgard, and they were full. But Shurgard called around and found me another Shurgard location. My Norwegian friend, an MBA who was helping me move, said, "This is just a fantastic idea that

---

[7]A real estate investment trust (REIT) is a publicly traded company whose assets are primarily made up of real estate properties, offering shareholders liquidity and diversification. REITs do not pay corporate tax on net earnings distributed to shareholders. Indeed, REITs are *required* to distribute at least 95% of their taxable earnings to shareholders in the form of quarterly dividends. As a result, REITs are often valued based on their dividends or as a multiple of EBITDA.

[8]Harvard's Owner/President Management Program (OPM) was aimed at owners/chief executive officers of businesses with annual sales ranging from five million to several hundred million dollars. Participants attended sessions for a total of nine weeks over a three-year period.

doesn't exist in Europe." We went back out to the car, and stayed up all night researching, and wrote a paper for class the next day on how we were going to develop self-storage in Europe.

Michael's father, Åke Fogelberg, a civil engineer and real estate investor, was looking for ways to invest abroad. He had moved his family from Sweden to Seattle in 1984 to form a real estate consortium with several Swedish banks. Then in 1987, he moved back to Europe, to Belgium. In 1990, the European real estate market collapsed, and Åke formed Grana International, a holding company, with Patrick Metdepenninghen, a Belgian tax lawyer. Åke explained, "Our company's mission was to help Swedish banks clean up and get out of investments down here in Brussels. Patrick could help them solve their problems." In 1992, Åke sold off his last building.

Åke recalled when 22-year-old Michael arrived back in Brussels, enthusiastic about the self-storage opportunity, "We were out of real estate, we were looking for new businesses. Of course we knew what self-storage was, but Michael was so enthusiastic. I gave Michael one year to prove this business concept." Through a connection at the Norwegian Chamber of Commerce in Seattle, Michael's friend met Barbo, and soon the Fogelbergs and Shurgard, whose executives had been eyeing Europe, were talking. In September 1993 Shurgard USA and Grana International formed a joint venture, SSC Benelux & Co SCA (Shurgard Europe). The Fogelbergs would do the lion's share of the work to develop the self-storage business in Europe and have 90% of the equity. Shurgard USA would contribute its name, knowledge, and licenses for 10% of the equity.

After spending some months learning the business working at Shurgard's stores in Seattle, Michael returned to Brussels, where his research revealed promising market potential for self-storage in Europe. The European population size was comparable with that of the United States, and on the Continent, self-storage was virtually nonexistent. Most Continental Europeans used the furniture-storage services of 35 moving companies like Allied van Kamp (Holland). However, moving companies did not give customers direct access to their goods, offered only one-size-fits-all containers, and required advance notice to retrieve goods from their warehouse. The second option for Continental Europeans was more expensive specialty movers, whose "moving consultants" managed the packing and storage of corporate office contents and fragile goods. In the United Kingdom, there were 50 established self-storage facilities around greater London, owned by both small mom-and-pop operators and one or two corporate players. These facilities, usually rough, low-technology buildings converted from industrial uses, were in run-down, inconvenient locations with limited opening hours. The Fogelbergs concluded that the Shurgard product—defined as "conveniently located, well designed and functionally flexible, accessible by the customer at all times, secure, and climate controlled"—would be superior to European offerings in quality, service, and price.

Nonetheless, the unfamiliarity of the self-storage concept in Europe was a mixed blessing. While it could give Shurgard a preemptive, first-mover advantage in the European markets, it also made European banks, already shaken by the real estate bust, reluctant to lend the Fogelbergs money. Metdepenninghen, executive director, capital markets, was talking to the banks while Michael was conducting market research:

> We thought it would be easy to raise money and leverage the business, because we had
> banking relationships with Belgian, Dutch, and Swedish banks. In the late 1980s, Swedish

deals had 90% debt, so we thought we'd need only 10% to 15% equity. But the banks' reaction was "Who will ever use this? If this were a real product, a real need, it would have obviously happened here." So we realized we'd require much more equity than we had hoped.

By 1994 Barbo was becoming impatient "to get Europe going." Finally, in February 1994 both sides renegotiated the terms of the venture, reversing the equity split— Shurgard USA agreed to put up 90% and the Fogelbergs 10% of the equity capital for SSC Benelux & Co. Grant commented, "For Shurgard USA this was a serious commitment. In 1994 we decided to invest in Europe even though the cost of the money was high and we only recently had become a public company and were still expanding rapidly in the United States." Between 1995 and July 1999, Shurgard USA and its other joint-venture partners invested a total of €120 million in the European joint venture, with the first three Shurgard facilities in Europe 100% equity funded.

Shurgard in Belgium

Forest and Molenbeek: The Fogelbergs and Metdepenninghen decided to locate Shurgard's European headquarters and first country operations in Brussels, Belgium, where Grana International was based. Besides convenience, the Fogelbergs also felt that Brussels would be a good starting point because of its central location and relatively mobile, cosmopolitan European Community staff. Commented Metdepennighen, "I originally thought self-storage was a simple business. But if you really want to execute well, it isn't that simple."

In planning Shurgard's first three properties in Belgium, the joint-venture partners encountered an important philosophical difference. Instead of building or acquiring new self-storage sites, as was Shurgard's standard practice in the U.S., the Fogelbergs planned to convert existing industrial real estate, which was plentiful and reasonably priced. Commented Grant, "What you're seeing in the first few stores is the European/American debate. Our position was that they don't have enough drive-up spaces—but Europeans think it's cheaper not to buy as much land. We decided to try both models." Not knowing which approach would work, the joint-venture partners agreed to follow the "European" approach in the first two stores and the "American" design in the third.

Shurgard's first two Brussels facilities—Shurgard Forest, opened in April 1995, and Shurgard Molenbeek, opened in September 1995—were conversions of brick industrial facilities (one a parking garage) in densely populated, lower-income, immigrant neighborhoods on the outskirts of Brussels. A train regularly clattered by the Molenbeek facility, and the Forest store stood next to a highway exit ramp. Both facilities were within walking distance of apartment buildings and local merchants.

Both facilities were multistory buildings with four levels, elevators, and a loading dock that the Fogelbergs thought would be good for drive-up customers. To minimize the risk of having the wrong *unit mix* (how many units of which size a facility contained), according to standard U.S. practice, Shurgard delayed construction of self-storage units in half of the facility until the first half rented up. Instead of a three-dimensional lighthouse tower, the Shurgard trademark, both stores had only a flat lighthouse painted on their exterior wall. Customers could access their facilities from 10 a.m. to 6 p.m. during the workweek and from 10 a.m. to 4 p.m. on Saturdays.

However, the conversion strategy turned out more expensive than planned ("both Forest and Molenbeek were way over budget," explained Grant), and the stores did not rent up as quickly as anticipated. (See **Exhibit 4** for European facility performance data.)

Waterloo Experiment: To boost the European expansion team, in January 1996, Grant, a U.S. expatriate, moved from Seattle to Brussels to take over as president of European operations. Grant, with bachelor's degrees in business and accounting, was a former Touche Ross consultant who had joined Shurgard USA in 1985 as director of real estate investment and had been traveling over to Brussels since 1995, when the first stores were being built.

For its third Belgian store Shurgard Europe decided to do things by the U.S. book—build from scratch. An empty plot of land in Waterloo, a well-to-do suburb about 15 minutes' drive out of Brussels with a high concentration of American expatriates, was purchased. The real estate site was located across from a major shopping center but not directly by a highway. On the land, adjoining Napoleon's battlefield, Shurgard built a new, modern-looking facility modeled after Shurgard's typical U.S. store design, with a "real" Shurgard lighthouse tower. The square footage of the facility was much larger than that of the Forest and Molenbeek stores combined. One innovation over U.S. construction methods was the use of Belgian prefabricated concrete parts, which the Fogelbergs turned to after discovering that U.S. self-storage materials were not familiar to European installers. The floors/ceilings of the facility were from concrete, with walls/doors of corrugated iron. However, as Grant commented, "We overengineered our Waterloo design to follow European building codes so much that, although it was within budget, the facility ended up costing more than U.S. facilities would."

The Waterloo store, which opened in October 1995 along with the Molenbeek store, took 34 months to rent up to stable occupancy. After renting up in August 1998, however, it remained a high 96% to 98% occupied. After conducting focus groups, Grant learned the reason for the lukewarm response: the outside, drive-up units, so popular among U.S. customers, were perceived as unsafe and unappealing to Europeans. To 70% of Shurgard's Belgian customers interior units signified luxury, compared with 30% of U.S. customers who felt that way.

Furthermore, the focus groups revealed that the lukewarm Belgian response to self-storage was not surprising. For Europeans, Belgians had large houses, with less need for self-storage; they were known as slow to adopt new products, and the dual languages, French and Flemish, made advertising and promotions difficult. Wim Van Beveren, Benelux country manager, explained, "Among American companies in Europe, there's the consensus that if you can make it in Belgium, you can make it anywhere. But on the flip side, just because a new product fails in Belgium doesn't mean it can't succeed elsewhere in Europe. For example, McDonald's does much worse in Belgium than elsewhere in Europe."

As Shurgard Europe was learning, not only did rent-up periods last longer in Europe due to product-awareness issues, but European customers also exhibited a different price elasticity than U.S. customers. To speed up the initial rent-up, in 1997 Shurgard cut rental charges at all three Belgian stores (Forest, Molenbeek, and Waterloo) by over 50%. Once the three facilities had reached stable occupancy rates in 1998, Shurgard raised the rates back up to the original level and continued raising them by 15% to 20%, with no impact on occupancy.

Multistory Facilities: After the Waterloo experience, Shurgard switched its standard European facility design to a compromise—a modern, compact, multistory building with a gated courtyard accessible by car (*interior drive-through*) and interior units accessible by elevator, with some exterior units. This design was first used in the fourth European facility, Brussels Zaventem, near the airport, and opened in October 1996. (Because local authorities were worried that incoming pilots would become confused by Shurgard's lighthouse tower, they required Shurgard to lower the tower's height.) Commented Grant, "Zaventem is the result of the European/American compromise—where we finally got our facility design, location, and unit mix right." By this time, Shurgard's simpler design also made more efficient use of the prefabricated concrete materials, speeding up construction time. By Shurgard's sixth Belgian store, the first opened close to a major highway, in Aarstselaar in May 1997, Shurgard was finally getting some name recognition. (See **Exhibit 5** for photographs of Shurgard's European facilities.)

Multiple-story facilities with a smaller unit mix had several advantages. In the expensive European real estate market, multiple-story facilities, which required only 1.5 acres of land, economized on land costs and opened up the possibility of using more downtown locations. They were also more visible from the highway and served as an important consumer education and marketing tool. The design director commented, "Using cutaway marketing, we design our buildings with some transparent windows and units on the ground and upper floors. So if you are walking by on the street or driving by on the highway, you'll see oversized, sample crates and belongings—or paintings of them—visible through a window. Our European managers' offices also have small, sample storage units. It's important to show Europeans what self-storage can be used for; just seeing a facility doesn't mean anything to them."

Europe Phase II

France, Human Resources, and Regulation: In September 1997, Shurgard Europe expanded into France by taking advantage of a competitor's bankruptcy. A French mom-and-pop operator had opened a self-storage facility, in Nice, when it ran out of money. The bank took over the project and was in the middle of constructing two facilities in Paris when it was approached by Shurgard Europe. By assuming the existing 70% debt on the facilities, Shurgard was able to buy the three facilities at a very good price from the bank during the foreclosure process. The design director explained, "Building from scratch gives us more control over the cost and image of a building— but if we are forced to choose, then location is our first priority. In fact, our Paris Varlin facility isn't the most upscale—it's inside the city, not outside—but because of its central location in a space-starved city, we command a good occupancy rate and one of our highest rental rates anywhere."

In France, Shurgard began to learn that not only was the ideal unit mix of a European facility different from that of a typical U.S. facility but that there were significant variations within Europe. While Belgians rented self-storage units of a similar size to those of Americans (110 ft^2 to 120 ft^2/unit), in France and other European countries Shurgard found that consumers preferred smaller, 70 ft^2 to 90 ft^2 units on average. In downtown locations, the French wanted even smaller units. While Shurgard could charge more for the small units, they also required Shurgard to attract more customers per facility to generate the same amount of business. Explained Grant, "We initially made the mistake of focusing on the square feet, not the number of customers we could get at a facility."

Over time, Shurgard Europe developed a thorough site-selection process, involving the market's real estate development team, the board of Shurgard Europe, and the Real Estate Committee. In this process, one of the challenges was the unfamiliarity of European regulators with the self-storage concept and lack of any specific legislation. To help educate French authorities about self-storage, Shurgard's executives would show U.S. building codes as well as pictures and tours of existing European facilities. Nevertheless, Shurgard found that in Europe many legal processes took longer or were more complicated.

With operations in two countries, Grant began devoting more time to human resources issues. Because self-storage expertise in Europe was nonexistent, to head up country operations, Grant hired several country managers from an American brand with similar real estate characteristics—McDonald's. For example, Van Beveren had been responsible for the launch of 70 McDonald's stores across Europe. While the skills were transferable, he saw important differences: "The biggest problem I see for Shurgard in Europe is that the awareness of the self-storage product is not there. Furthermore, a McDonald's generates cash flow immediately, whereas a self-storage facility takes a while to rent up, so it's harder to get financing. Finally, the McDonald's brand has instant name recognition, while the Shurgard name is unknown."

Grant's approximately 140 employees were divided into three functional groups: store operations, new-store development, and finance and accounting. Because of the entrepreneurial nature of launching Shurgard self-storage in Europe, the European store manager position attracted more qualified individuals (all bilingual, 80% with a university degree) than their U.S. counterparts. The high European unemployment rate also helped to produce good candidates. However, European labor regulations also made it harder to hire (or fire) employees or rotate them between stores, a common U.S. Shurgard training practice. For example, French labor regulations required a company to renegotiate the labor contract of employees required to commute more than 25 kilometers from their original office location. Cultural and linguistic differences also created challenges. For example, because the term "self-storage" did not exist in any Continental European language and attempts at literal translations produced awkward results, Shurgard had decided to use the English term "Shurgard Self-Storage" throughout Europe to create a new product category and unified company brand identity. However, when Shurgard entered France, the French staff insisted that French consumers would be more welcoming if the term were "de-Americanized." In France, Shurgard therefore compromised and used the name "Shurgard Self-Stockage" on all its facilities and signs.

Sweden and Marketing: By the time Shurgard entered its third European country, Sweden, in May 1998, it had learned several lessons from its Belgian and French experiences. Michael Fogelberg, who had been acting as the Belgium country manager, moved back to Sweden to lead the expansion. Whereas almost 48 months passed between the opening of the first and fifth Belgian stores, in Sweden Michael opened five stores around greater Stockholm in eight months. Because land prices were not as high in Sweden and, like Americans, the Swedes valued drive-up convenience, there Shurgard reverted to a slightly more American mix of one-story external and multistory internal units.

Shurgard's Swedish experience confirmed that preemptive marketing was essential to a quick rent-up of a European facility. Commented the European marketing director: "Until Europe, Shurgard operated on the U.S. real estate mentality, in other words—if you build it, they will come. This works fine in a country where everyone knows what self-storage is. In Europe we have become much more marketing focused, because we have to create basic awareness and demand for the product." During the initial Belgian launch, Shurgard had not done much marketing besides distributing local flyers and dressing staff in lighthouse costumes at store openings. By contrast, in Sweden, Michael launched two national campaigns right away, taking out full-page ads in a national newspaper and creating a humorous radio spot that suggested that a Shurgard storage unit was a good place to put a mother-in-law. (See **Exhibit 6** for sample Shurgard advertising campaign.) Both campaigns greatly boosted Shurgard's name recognition.

Future Expansion: Once the product-awareness problem in an area was solved, Shurgard's European and U.S. self-storage consumers were very similar in their storage needs, demographic profile, and average length of stay, with a slightly higher mix of commercial (30%) to residential (70%) customers in Europe. (See **Exhibit 7** for European vs. U.S. consumer profile.) However, whether the same level of total market penetration could be expected was still debatable. Arguments in favor of self-storage in Europe included the higher population density and smaller houses in Europe. A marketing study conducted for Shurgard Belgium in July 1996 had revealed that the "5%" U.S. market potential rule did apply in Brussels, that is, that 5% of Belgians who were aware of the self-storage product might become active customers. However, Europeans were a less mobile population: only 10% of Europeans moved every year, compared with 20% of Americans. Simple proximity was one reason that Europeans moved less often. Grant explained, "A Belgian can commute to work in Brussels from anywhere in Belgium." Furthermore, road-safety laws made it harder for Europeans to rent trucks to move their own belongings, as compared to the booming U-Haul business in the United States.

As Shurgard was learning, there were important cost differences in running a self-storage business in the United States and Europe. In the United States, Shurgard ran a relatively lean operation, with corporate functions located in Seattle and approximately 1,000 employees for 350 open stores, or a ratio of fewer than three staff (including corporate functions) per store. In Europe, this ratio was almost double the U.S.

ratio—cultural/regulatory differences between countries required Shurgard to duplicate corporate functions such as accounting between Brussels regional headquarters and country operations. "For what we spend on overhead costs in Europe, we could run three times more stores in the United States," commented a U.S. operational executive. Furthermore, each time Shurgard entered a new country, it had to bear the staff and construction costs until facilities were rented up. New self-storage facilities in Europe took Shurgard up to two years to plan and build (12 to 18 months for the initial site search and permitting, and then six months for the actual construction of the facility). The average Continental facility cost $4 million to $5 million, with 75% going to construction and 25% to land purchase. On top of that, depending on the speed of expansion, the upfront overhead costs to hire and train country staff could run from between 7% and 8% of the development cost. Once a facility was open, it could take several more years until it was generating a profit.

Decision Time

By late 1998, Shurgard's European managers were convinced they had made enough progress and that the major challenge facing the business was to rapidly expand in Europe. As a result, they prepared a detailed five-year growth plan. (See **Exhibits 8a** to **8d** for Shurgard Europe 1999 to 2003 projections.) The plans called for expanding the number of stores from the 11 at the end of 1998 to between 133 and 170 stores by the end of 2003 and for entering two new countries, the United Kingdom and the Netherlands. By June 1999, the Shurgard Europe team had opened 17 self-storage facilities, with 4,000 active customers, and was developing or constructing another 18 stores, including five projects in the United Kingdom and one in the Netherlands. Shurgard was optimistic that its product was better than existing U.K. competitors' and that the space-starved, easygoing Dutch would give Shurgard a warmer reception than the Belgians had. Grant sent experienced Belgian staff to start up Holland and hired an experienced U.K. developer to start up operations in the United Kingdom.

Shurgard Europe's expansion plan would require over €500 million in investment by the end of 2003. Finding sources of these funds was a challenge. Because Shurgard USA and its European joint-venture partners had already invested €120 million into the European operations, much of it coming in late 1998 and early 1999 to fund the accelerated pace of development, they now had little capacity or appetite for additional investment. Barbo explained:

> I'm still tremendously excited by our opportunities in Europe and believe that in time our returns in Europe will be higher than in the U.S. But as a public REIT, we have to dividend out 95% of our profit and thus have limited internally generated cash available for investment. Our shareholders want steady returns and don't understand why we would invest in Europe rather than continue to pursue the U.S. market. It would be nice to issue more equity, but right now the whole REIT sector is out of favor. The average EBITDA multiple for U.S. self-storage REIT is now 9.5, down considerably from a few years ago. Investors want Internet-type returns and, within the REIT sector, self-storage is poorly understood. (See **Exhibits 9a** and **9b** for stock-price data on publicly traded REITs.)

As a result, late 1998 and early 1999 found Grant and Metdepenninghen making numerous presentations to potential investor groups in London. Unlike in 1995, when they could find virtually no investor interest, this time there were interested investors, but they had steep terms and conditions. Grant noted, "The question is, have we really proven that Europeans will go for self-storage and that our business model will work? We obviously think so, but potential investors are more skeptical." One potential investor, Fred Zarrilli of Fremont Realty Capital, explained:

> We are an opportunity real estate private equity firm, looking for special high-return situations that will earn our investors at least 20% on their money. Last year we made our first investment in Shurgard U.S. and have been very pleased. So far I have already made nine trips to Europe, doing due diligence and getting myself convinced that this will work and that the returns will be there.

By July 1999 a group consisting of Deutsche Bank, Fremont, AIG, and Credit Suisse First Boston (CSFB) had emerged with the most promising offer. The group was offering to make an equity investment of €122 million in return for 43.3% of Shurgard Europe. In addition, a €140 million credit facility (at LIBOR plus 175 basis points) from CSFB had been arranged. Both the equity and debt would be made available as Shurgard Europe needed the funds. The investors would hold a full-liquidation preference. The investors also insisted on some important governance conditions. Shurgard Europe's board would have nine members. Each of the equity investors would have a board seat. The other five directors included three from Shurgard USA and Åke Fogelberg and Metdepenninghen.

Grant explained his concerns: "In the U.S., Chuck Barbo has put together a great outside board, and they represent the shareholders' interests. We all have a lot of trepidation about working with this large a board representing so many separate investors, especially because our biggest challenge is going to be to move quickly." For example, the investor group wanted to review the investment in each new store. Grant wanted to limit approvals, which would require a super majority, to overall spending levels within certain key parameters. Other decisions requiring super-majority approval included senior executive hires, all salaries over $120,000, and the annual and five-year plans. Finally, based on a previous bad experience, Grant wanted to be absolutely certain that the investors would have no possible way of reneging on their full financial commitments.

The equity investors were also concerned about their liquidity. An initial public offering (IPO) after a few years, at a high valuation, would be ideal but could not be counted on. Thus, the investors' terms also included a long stop clause that entitled any investor, after five years, to trigger a process by which the company would get valued and any investor could buy out the others at that price. But if no investor were willing to do so, an outside offer would be solicited and investors could sell as long as the offer was for at least 95% of Shurgard Europe's valuation.

So as Grant's plane began its descent, he knew that a decision needed to be made soon. Should he accept all of the investors' terms in return for the €262 million capital infusion? Could he operate effectively with the governance structure the investors wanted? And most importantly, had the self-storage concept in Europe been sufficiently proven to justify such a large bet? Grant commented:

> Our entry into Europe has been a real learning experience. We've hit some bumps along the way, but we've managed to figure things out. Having the right partner—the Fogelbergs—was critical. Now we are at an important juncture. We have already stepped up our rate of expansion and will be opening 12 new stores in 1999. This is very expensive in terms of development costs and early operating losses. We could cut our overhead, grow at a much slower pace, and not face these issues. Or we can try to take advantage of what we have put in place here and push for market leadership in Europe. The opportunities for growth are enormous, and in the long run Europe may turn out to be more profitable than the United States. But it is going to take a lot of capital, and unfortunately that capital has steep terms and conditions.

EXHIBIT 1a | Shurgard U.S. Income Statement, 1994–1998 (in $000s except per share)

Year Ended December 31	1998	1997	1996	1995	1994
Rental revenues	$158,989	$137,746	$103,784	$92,397	$66,697
Other real estate investments income (loss)	(1,628)	225	3,371	1,396	224
Property management	1,893	2,463	3,244	2,978	—
Total revenue	**$159,254**	**$140,434**	**$110,399**	**$96,771**	**$66,921**
Operating expenses	46,421	40,278	30,889	24,851	15,799
Depreciation and amortization	33,644	28,243	21,199	17,410	11,373
Real estates taxes	13,195	11,295	8,898	7,596	5,840
General, administrative and other	4,578	3,956	4,351	6,179	6,548
Total expenses	**$ 97,838**	**$ 83,772**	**$ 65,337**	**$56,036**	**$39,560**
Income from operations	61,416	56,662	45,062	40,735	27,361
Nonoperating income (expense)	(19,645)	(15,615)	(12,225)	(10,912)	(9,540)
Minority interest	2,963	1,264	(52)	(251)	—
Net income	**$ 44,734**	**$ 42,311**	**$ 32,785**	**$29,572**	**$17,821**
Net income per share	1.39	1.40	1.39	1.43	1.05
Cash dividend per share	1.96	1.92	1.88	1.84	1.76
Avg. shares outstanding	28,724	27,999	23,570	20,661	16,984
Closing stock price (high)	29.56	29.94	29.625	27.00	23.00
Closing stock price (low)	24.38	26.00	23.25	24.75	17.75

Source: Shurgard Storage Centers annual reports. Some 1994 data *pro forma*. Some line items consolidated.

EXHIBIT 1b | U.S. vs. European Store Performance (year ended December 31, 1998)

($000s)	Same Stores	New Stores	European Stores	Total
Rental revenue	146,138	21,579	4,243	171,960
Operating expenses	(41,025)	(9,167)	(2,545)	(52,737)
Net operating income (NOI)	105,113	12,412	1,698	119,223
Total assets	673,164	275,467	90,664	1,039,295

Source: Shurgard Storage Centers 1998 Annual Report.

EXHIBIT 1c | Shurgard U.S. Same-Store Results, 1994–1998

Year Ended December 31	1998	1997	1996	1995	1994
Rental revenue ($000s)	146,138	105,551	92,334	79,616	75,307
Property operating expenses ($000s)	(41,025)	(30,936)	(28,031)	(24,002)	(23,383)
Net Operating Income ($000s)	**105,113**	**74,615**	**64,303**	**55,614**	**51,924**
Avg. annual rent/sq. ft. ($)	10.08	9.68	9.22	8.87	8.31
Avg. sq. ft. occupancy (%)	88	88	89	88	89
Total net rentable square feet (million)	15.3	11.5	10.9	9.4	9.4
No. properties	232	172	169	134	134

Source: Shurgard Storage Centers 10-K SEC filings. 1994 *pro forma* results taken from 1995 report. "Same Stores" defined as existing facilities acquired prior to January 1 of the previous year, as well as developed properties that have been operating for a full eight quarters as of the beginning of the fourth quarter. Shurgard projects that new properties will reach stabilization in an average of 21 to 24 months.

EXHIBIT 1d | Shurgard European Same-Store Operating
Results, 1997–1998

Year Ended December 31	1998	1997
Rental revenue ($000s)	2,018	1,220
Property operating expenses ($000s)	897	780
Net Operating Income ($000s)	**1,121**	**440**
Avg. annual rent/sq. ft. ($)	11.00	9.50
Avg. sq. ft. occupancy (%)	86	75
Total net rentable sq. ft.	234,000	234,000
No. properties	4	4

Source: Shurgard Storage Centers 1998 Annual Report.

EXHIBIT 1e | Shurgard U.S. Balance Sheet, 1994–1998 (in $000s)

(As of December 31)	1998	1997	1996	1995	1994
Storage centers:					
Land	212,154	168,076	142,127	105,224	88,532
Buildings and equipment, net	751,258	636,168	538,180	404,329	362,332
Construction in progress	81,043	49,484	32,531	20,942	532
Total storage centers	1,044,455	853,728	712,838	530,495	451,396
Other real estate investments	33,057	38,522	29,436	21,407	15,104
Cash and cash equivalents	9,474	7,248	3,239	5,683	13,162
Restricted cash and investments	6,864	7,028	6,814	5,551	2,766
Other assets	60,057	48,962	52,156	47,258	12,162
Total assets	1,153,907	955,488	804,483	610,394	494,590
Accounts payable and other liabilities	41,201	31,150	29,964	29,770	10,138
Lines of credit	95,028	57,477	140,997	10,905	42,000
Notes payable	331,109	239,494	131,794	131,935	125,137
Total liabilities	467,338	328,121	302,755	172,610	177,275
Minority interest in other real estate investments	34,759	18,675	3,217	3,288	470
Total shareholders' equity	651,810	608,692	498,511	434,496	316,845
Total liabilities and shareholders' equity	1,153,907	955,488	804,483	610,394	494,590

Source: Shurgard Storage Centers annual reports. Some line items consolidated.

EXHIBIT 1f | Shurgard Europe 1998 Income Statement and Balance Sheet (in €000)[a]

Total revenue	4,310
Operating expenses	5,841
Real estate taxes	124
General admin. & other	1,379
Depreciation & amort.	1,858
Net loss from operations	(4,892)
Net interest expense	(2,194)
Net loss before taxes	(7,086)

Storage centers:		Accounts payable and other liabilities	6,480
Land	5,423	Liabilities under capital leases	2,057
Buildings and equipment, net	35,065	Lines of credit	10,618
Construction in progress	29,865	Loan payable	54,217
Total storage centers	71,253	Total liabilities	73,372
Cash and cash equivalents	1,291	Shareholders' interests	15,687
Deferred taxation	3,350	Accumulated losses	(7,715)
Other assets	5,450	Total shareholders' equity	7,972
Total assets	81,344	Total liabilities and shareholders' equity	81,344

[a]In July 1999, 1USD = 0.97EUR, 1EUR = 1.03USD.

Source: Shurgard Europe financial filings.

EXHIBIT 2 | Photographs of U.S. Self-Storage Facilities

Exterior Drive-Up Units

Source: Company presentation.

EXHIBIT 3a | U.S. Self-Storage Industry Trends, 1992–1998

	1992	1993	1994	1995	1996	1997	1998
Total No. Facilities	19,438	21,291	22,966	23,979	25,180	26,272	27,535
Average Units/Facility	371	330	325	324	327	331	331
Total Units (million)	7.21	7.03	7.46	7.77	8.23	8.70	9.11
Avg. Square Footage/Facility	43,425	40,494	759	36,234	38,354	38,650	38,650
Total Square Footage (million)	840	862	759	869	966	1,015	1,064
Avg. Sq. Footage/Person	3.39	3.59	2.93	3.31	3.64	3.81	3.81
Most Facilities in State	2,671	2,675	2,809	2,816	2,823	2,873	2,967
Least Facilities in State	31	40	41	40	37	39	41
Most Sq. Ft./Person in State	8.98	10.89	9.53	10.62	10.94	11.27	12.18
Least Sq. Ft./Person in State	1.11	1.27	1.01	1.14	1.06	0.89	1.04
Most Facilities in Metro Area	467	472	491	1,049	1,049	1,062	509
Most Sq. Ft./P in Metro Area	7.97	8.91	6.7	8.13	8.33	8.87	9.06
Avg. Occupancy Rate (%)	84.8	88.5	89.9	89.9	88.3	85.1	85.1

Source: *1998–1999 Self-Storage Almanac* (Phoenix, AZ: MiniCo.), pp. 113–120. Annual MiniCo. survey.

EXHIBIT 3b | U.S. Self-Storage Industry 1998 Profile

		Operating Data (May 1998)				Financial Data (December 31, 1998)				
Rank	Firm Name	No. Facilities	No. Units (000s)	Square Footage (million)	Square Footage (% Total)	Total Revenues ($000s)	Net Income ($000s)	Funds from Operations ($000s)	Total Assets ($000s)	Total Liabilities ($000s)
1	Public Storage, Inc (NYSE: PSA)[a]	1,145	656	67.8	6.4	582,151	227,019	336,363	3,403,904	145,239
2	Storage USA (SUS)	456	280	29.5	2.8	222,713	60,398	85,655	1,705,627	847,872
3	U-Haul (Amerco)[b] (UHAULQ)	897	307	26.1	2.5	1,551,932	62,509	NA	3,087,503	2,471,478
4	**Shurgard Storage Centers, Inc. (SHU)**	**340**	**218**	**22.1**	**2.1**	**159,254**	**44,734**	**71,900**	**1,153,907**	**467,338**
5	Storage Trust Realty[a]	231	107	12.2	1.2	Acquired	NA	NA	NA	NA
6	Sovran Self Storage, Inc. (SSS)	192	96	11.0	1.0	69,360	23,540	33,932	490,124	203,439
7	U-Store-It (Amsdell Co.)	120	65	6.5	0.6	Private	NA	NA	NA	NA
8	Storage Inns, Inc.	100	NA	5.0	0.5	Private	NA	NA	NA	NA
9	Derrel's Mini Storage, Inc.	35	43	4.7	0.5	Private	NA	NA	NA	NA
10	Morningstar Group	49	28	3.9	0.4	Private	NA	NA	NA	NA
	Total Top 10 Companies	**3,565**	**1,801**	**188.9**	**17.8**					
	Total Top 20 Companies	4,040	2,069	218.9	20.6					
	Total Top 30 Companies	4,378	2,249	238.1	22.4					
	Total Top 40 Companies	4,584	2,364	251.4	23.6					
	Total Top 50 Companies	4,750	2,550	261.2	24.6					
	1998 U.S. Total	**27,535**	**9,114**	**1,064.2**	**100.0**					

[a]Public Storage acquired Storage Trust Realty assets as of December 31, 1998. Storage Trust Realty was a publicly traded real estate investment trust (REIT) from 1994 to 1998. Storage Trust Realty financial results not reflected in reported 1998 Public Storage results.

[b]U-Haul financial data not fully comparable with that of other pure-play self-storage operators. U-Haul is a private subsidiary of Amerco (Ticker: UHALQ), a holding company that also owns real estate and insurance businesses. The financials reported in table for U-Haul are Amerco's consolidated totals. In the fiscal year ended March 31, 1999, Amerco's Moving and Storage Operations (U-Haul) generated total segmental revenues of $1,224,372 and had identifiable assets of $1,339,312 (in $000s).

Funds from operations (FFO) defined as net income plus depreciation of real estate assets and amortization of intangible assets, exclusive of deferred financing costs.

Source: Operational data, 1998–1999 Self-Storage Almanac (Phoenix, AZ: MiniCo.), p. 126. Based on May 1998 survey. Financial data from individual company 1998 annual reports (all for 1998 fiscal year ended December 31, 1998, except for U-Haul/Amerco, whose fiscal year ends March 31. For U-Haul/Amerco, reported data is for 1999 fiscal year, ended March 31, 1999).

EXHIBIT 4 | Shurgard Europe Store Performance (for 17 existing stores as of June 30, 1999)

Country/Store	Open Date	Rentable Sq. Meters	Development Cost (EUR Mil) Total	Development Cost (EUR) Cost/m2	Occupancy Rate (% Units) Jan–Jun 98	Occupancy Rate (% Units) Jan–Jun 99	Rental Rate/m2 (EUR) Jan–Jun 99	Rental Rate/m2 % increase	Gross Store Revenues (EUR 000s) Jan–Jun 99	Gross Store Revenues % inc.	Net Operating Income (Euro 000s) Jan–Jun 99	Net Operating Income % inc.
BELGIUM												
Forest	May-95	4,328	3.5	807	75	89	120	24	212.4	40	118.5	165
Molenbeek	Oct-95	2,840	2.3	798	90	87	136	17	148.0	15	78.5	98
Waterloo	Oct-95	7,762	4.7	605	84	90	129	22	419.7	36	326.0	60
Zaventem	Oct-96	6,579	4.7	720	69	88	125	19	331.4	50	230.8	107
Machelen	Apr-97	6,060	3.1	507	55	85	108	24	190.6	84	112.6	1987
Aartselaar	May-97	6,517	4.4	668	51	73	117	18	259.1	85	168.7	338
Same-store subtotal/average		34,086	22.6	663	69	85	122	20	1,561.2	48	1,035.0	133
Ghent	Dec-98	6,769	3.6	532	NA	17	124	NA	46.4	NA	(29.3)	NA
Overijse	Feb-99	5,916	2.8	480	NA	22	128	NA	28.3	NA	(48.9)	NA
Leuven	Feb-99	5,916	3.9	667	NA	11	120	NA	23.8	NA	(50.0)	NA
Country subtotal/average		52,687	33.0	626			124		1,659.7		124	
FRANCE												
Mountrouge	Sep-97	5,500	3.1	568	53	74	214	6	351.2	27	114.5	148
Paris Varline	Sep-97	2,230	0.3	133	49	98	225	2	186.4	47	(23.0)	72
Nice St. Isidore	Sep-97	3,929	3.1	795	93	94	198	1	326.6	–2	207.1	2
Country subtotal/average		11,659	6.5	562	66	85	211	3	864.3	18	298.6	80
SWEDEN												
Kungens Kurva	May-98	6,557	4.1	630	NA	51	161	NA	204.1	NA	48.9	
Taby	Jun-98	5,485	4.2	771	NA	55	164	NA	207.7	NA	66.3	
Jakobsberg	Dec-98	5,545	3.4	605	NA	36	155	NA	113.5	NA	(14.7)	
Uppsala	Mar-99	5,814	4.2	718	NA	13	149	NA	16.2	NA	(94.4)	
Rissne	Jan-99	6,146	4.8	784	NA	27	174	NA	72.1	NA	(44.4)	
Country subtotal/average		29,547	20.7	701.00		36	161		613.6		(38.3)	
Europe Total/Average		93,893	60.3	642.00					3,137.6		1,167.1	

Notes: "Same Stores" defined as existing stores acquired prior to January 1 of the previous year and developed properties operating for a full two years as of October 1 of the current year. Stabilized occupancy rate defined as 85% units for stores larger than 5,000 sq. meters and 90% units for smaller stores.

Development costs are capitalized costs pursuant to June 30, 1999 interim balance sheet, including development fee. Exclude lease-up deficits.

Gross store revenues and net operating income given for half year. Percentage increase compared with that of January–June 1998 half year.

Source: Company documents.

EXHIBIT 5 | Photographs of Shurgard European Facilities: France and Sweden

Source: Company presentation.

(continued)

EXHIBIT 5 | Photographs of Shurgard European Facilities: France and Sweden (*continued*)

Inside Drive-Through Access

Inside Heated Units

Source: Company presentation.

EXHIBIT 6 | Shurgard 1999 Advertising in Sweden

Text of Radio Advertisement: "The Mother-in-Law"

[Daughter-in-law]: "It was an incredible change to be married and to get to know Nils-Åke's family, especially his mother. Nils-Åke's mother is really very special. She came by, bringing curtains and embroidered sofa cushions and candle sticks and . . . well, yes, in the end she was practically living at our place, so I felt I had to call Shurgard and rent a unit.

"Nine square meters, practical and easy accessible, and my mother-in-law is better off there. It is heated and there is an alarm system, and then Nils-Åke can go visiting her and really take care of her, all on his own."

[Voice-over]: *Do you have more things than square meters? Rent a safe and secure unit at Shurgard. From 1 to 50 square meters on short- or long-term basis. Call 020-510-500. Shurgard—we give you more space!*

Source: Company documents. Translated from Swedish by company executive.

EXHIBIT 7 | 1998 Shurgard Customer Breakdown (Swedish vs. U.S. customers)

(% Total Customers)	Sweden	USA			Sweden	USA
1. What event prompted your need for storage?				**5. How often do you visit your storage unit?**		
Moving	36	49		Monthly	26	25
Too much stuff	26	20		Twice a month	21	18
Death in family	6	3		Every 2 months	20	10
Divorce	6	1		Only to move in/out	15	NA
Marriage/joining households	5	3		Weekly	14	20
Remodeling	4	2		Every 2–6 months	NA	9
Expanding business	2	5		Daily	3	5
Other (incl. seasonal business)	15	17		Other	1	13
	100	100			100	100
2. What alternatives to self-storage did you consider?				**6. How did you first contact Shurgard?**		
None	21	84		Called the store	57	48
Conventional/containerized storage	31	NA		Went directly to the store	31	45
Storing at home, cellar, garage	17	5		Called the main office	12	NA
With family/relatives	16	3		Called the 1-800 tel. number	NA	2
Selling/disposing goods	10	1		Other	NA	5
Other (incl. summer house)	5	7			100	100
	100	100		**7. Do you use your storage space for personal or business?**		
3. How did you become aware of Shurgard?				Personal use	72	76
Drove by store	38	51		Business use	17	14
Newspaper advertisement	19	NA		Both	11	9
Yellow Pages (Telephone book listing)	16	20		Other	NA	1
Saw sign at store	12	5			100	100
Word of mouth	11	11		**8. What will you do with your things when you move out?**		
Other	4	13		Take/move to new home	58	66
	100	100		Move to another place for storage	14	3
4. Why did you choose Shurgard?				Sell	13	6
Security	20	6		Throw away	6	10
Location	13	62		Give away	3	2
Climate-controlled units (heat/cool)	10	2		Other	6	13
Service, management	7	2			100	100
Price	4	9				
Easily accessible	22	NA				
Access/opening times	10	NA				
Flexibility/leasing time	8	NA				
Unit sizes	6	NA				
Other	NA	19				
	100	100				

Source: Company documents. Excerpted from internal 1998 surveys of Swedish and U.S. customers. Lump "other" category used to account for slightly different questions in both countries and for cases when U.S. responses did not exactly add up to 100%.

EXHIBIT 8a | Shurgard Europe Five-Year Expansion (Store Opening) Plan, 1999 to 2003

(Open Stores)	Existing	1999	2000	2001	2002	2003	Total
MINIMUM PLAN							
Belgium	9	1	3	4	4	5	26
Netherlands	0	1	4	5	7	7	24
Scandinavia	5	4	4	6	6	6	31
United Kingdom	0	4	3	5	5	5	22
France	3	1	5	6	7	8	30
Total	17	11	19	26	29	31	133
TARGET PLAN							
Belgium	9	1	6	6	4	4	30
Netherlands	0	1	7	8	9	9	34
Scandinavia	5	3	7	9	8	6	38
United Kingdom	0	4	4	7	7	7	29
France	3	0	9	9	9	9	39
Total	17	9	33	39	37	35	170

Note: Target plan represents objective management considers reasonable and attainable. Aggressive expansion planned in France (Paris), United Kingdom (London), and Netherlands. In Sweden, expansion planned in Stockholm and move into Gotenburg. Denmark proposal as of January 2000. In Belgium, moderate expansion across country, some in-fill.

Source: Company documents.

EXHIBIT 8b | Generic Store *Pro Forma* Assumptions

	Belgium	Sweden	U.K.	France	Netherlands
Operating Margin (%)					
Year 2 (2000)	40.6	46.6	47.8	47.0	39.7
Year 3 (2001)	66.3	63.6	70.6	64.7	69.3
Year 4 (2002)	66.6	63.9	70.8	65.0	69.6
Year 5 (2003)	66.8	64.2	71.0	65.3	69.8
Development Cost (EUR/m2)					
Site acquisition	165	137	458	263	213
Preconstruction	9	18	30	36	9
Hard costs	363	455	611	466	392
FF & E	5	—	6	5	5
Start-up costs	—	2	—	—	—
Capitalized interest	12	13	27	18	14
Lease-up deficits	46	45	67	44	54
Development fee	32	37	66	46	37
Total	**632**	**708**	**1,265**	**879**	**724**
Development Yield (%)					
(Stabilized—Year 3)					
On DPC only	15.2	15.0	14.9	14.8	15.2
+ Pre-open cap. costs	14.8	14.7	14.5	14.5	14.9
+ Lease-up deficits	13.7	13.7	13.7	13.7	13.7
+ Dev. fee	13.0	13.0	13.0	13.0	13.0

Source: Company documents.

EXHIBIT 8c | Projected Shurgard Europe Income Statement (Minimum Plan—133 Stores)—As of June 30, 1999

(EUR millions)	2H1999	2000	2001	2002	2003
Store Level:					
Total Revenues	4.26	14.05	29.24	55.10	88.44
Operating Expenses	(2.54)	(9.20)	(16.30)	(24.15)	(32.40)
Management Fee	(0.26)	(0.84)	(1.75)	(3.31)	(5.31)
1 **Store Level EBITDA:**	**1.46**	**4.01**	**11.19**	**27.64**	**50.73**
Corporate/Country Level:					
Management Fee	0.26	0.84	1.75	3.31	5.31
Dev. fees, cap. int., start-up	1.11	12.45	18.06	19.50	17.21
Total Corporate Revenues	1.37	13.29	19.81	22.81	22.52
Ground/capital rent expense	(0.32)	(0.64)	(0.64)	(0.64)	(0.64)
Country Overhead	(6.32)	(12.96)	(13.74)	(14.47)	(14.95)
Head Office Overhead	(2.01)	(4.21)	(4.37)	(4.54)	(4.72)
Capex Overhead	(0.70)	(0.90)	(0.40)	(0.20)	(0.20)
Total Corporate Expenses	**(9.35)**	**(18.71)**	**(19.15)**	**(19.85)**	**(20.51)**
2 **Corporate/Country EBITDA**	**(7.98)**	**(5.42)**	**0.66**	**2.96**	**2.01**
1 + 2 = 3 Consolidated EBITDA	(6.52)	(1.41)	11.85	30.60	52.74
4 Interest Expense	(0.82)	(6.27)	(13.07)	(20.79)	(28.93)
3 + 4 = 5 **Consolidated EBT**	**(7.34)**	**(7.68)**	**(1.22)**	**9.81**	**23.81**
6 Development Cost to Fund	(32.32)	(152.89)	(155.75)	(173.19)	(123.55)
Proceeds from Land Sales	1.07	8.12	0.00	0.46	0.00
Deal Closing/IPO Costs	(1.00)	0.00	0.00	0.00	0.00
5 + 6 = 7 **Cash flow prefunding**	**(39.59)**	**(152.45)**	**(156.97)**	**(162.92)**	**(99.74)**
Funded By:					
Equity	10.00	51.45	49.43	43.15	9.44
Debt	44.63	100.24	107.54	119.77	103.07
8 **Total external funding**	**54.63**	**151.69**	**156.97**	**162.92**	**112.51**
Difference funded by					
7 + 8 = 9 working capital	15.04	(0.76)	0.00	0.00	12.77

EBITDA = earnings before interest, taxes, depreciation, and amortization. EBT = earnings before taxes.

Source: Company documents. Some discrepancies due to rounding.

EXHIBIT 8d | Projected Shurgard Europe Balance Sheet (Minimum Plan—133 Stores)—As of
June 30, 1999

(EUR millions)	2H1999	2000	2001	2002	2003
Assets:					
Cash with capital facility	0.89	15.75	15.00	15.00	15.00
Storage centers:					
Finished Assets	65.40	65.40	89.92	231.85	412.46
Stores in Development	13.05	49.50	177.87	191.70	184.27
Freehold in Ownership	16.13	16.13	16.13	16.13	16.13
Total CSFB Collateral	94.58	131.03	283.92	439.68	612.86
Pre-ownership	1.16	1.16	1.16	1.16	1.16
Total Investment	95.75	132.20	285.09	440.84	614.03
HO Fixed Assets	2.68	2.68	2.68	2.68	2.68
Other Assets	10.86	10.86	10.86	10.86	10.86
Total Assets	110.18	161.49	313.63	469.38	642.57
Liabilities:					
CSFB/Other Loans	—	44.63	144.86	252.41	372.18
Other Liabilities	9.82	9.82	9.82	9.82	9.82
Total Liabilities	9.82	54.44	154.68	262.22	382.00
Equity:					
Shurgard Equity	100.37	100.37	100.37	100.37	100.37
Cumulative NOI	—	(3.32)	(2.87)	(4.09)	6.17
Investors and other equity	—	10.00	61.45	110.89	154.04
Net Equity	100.37	107.04	158.95	207.16	260.57
Liabilities and Equity	110.18	161.49	313.63	469.38	642.57
Undrawn Committed Equity	122.00	112.00	60.55	11.11	—

NOI = net operating income.

Source: Company documents.

EXHIBIT 9a | U.S. REIT vs. General Stock Market Index Performance (through June 30, 1999)

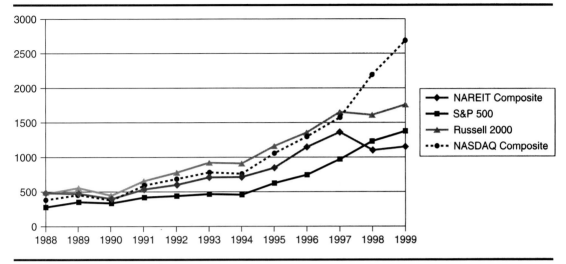

Note: Chart gives annual, period-ending equity market index levels through June 30, 1999.

Source: Adapted from *REIT Watch,* July 1999, http://www.nareit.com/researchandstatistics/reitwatch.cfm, accessed December 15, 2003.

EXHIBIT 9b | U.S. REIT vs. General Stock Market Historical Returns—As of June 30, 1999

(% Compound Annual Rates)	1-Year	3-Year	5-Year	10-Year	15-Year	20-Year
NAREIT Composite Index	(10.18)	8.66	9.59	8.75	8.70	11.09
S&P 500	21.07	26.97	25.31	15.75	15.74	13.83
Russell 2000	1.50	11.22	15.40	12.39	12.64	14.15
NASDAQ Composite	41.77	31.36	30.64	19.96	NA	NA

Note: National Association of Real Estate Investment Trusts (NAREIT) Composite Index includes all real estate investment trusts (REITs) that trade on the New York Stock Exchange, American Stock Exchange, and NASDAQ National Market List.

Source: Adapted from *REIT Watch,* July 1999, http://www.nareit.com/researchandstatistics/reitwatch.cfm, accessed December 15, 2003.

Kendle International Inc.

We looked at the competitive landscape and, based on what was happening, knew we were either going to sell Kendle, grow or disappear.

It was May 1997, and Candace Kendle, the chairman and chief executive officer of Kendle International Inc. (Kendle), and her husband, Christopher C. Bergen, the president and chief operating officer, were reviewing the strategic options for their Cincinnati, Ohio based company. Kendle, a business they had founded over 15 years previously, conducted clinical trials for pharmaceutical and biotechnology companies to test the safety and efficacy of their new drugs. The company had grown successfully to $13 million of sales and had attracted significant business from major pharmaceutical and biotechnology companies. Kendle was competing, however, with several larger contract research organizations (CRO), many of which had an international presence that allowed them to do clinical studies outside the United States and gave them an advantage when competing for major projects.

To compete more effectively, Candace and Chris had embarked on a plan to grow through acquisition, particularly internationally, and to finance this growth through a public offering of equity. Toward this end, by the spring of 1997 Kendle had lined up two potential European acquisitions—U-Gene, a CRO in the Netherlands with 1996 sales of $12.5 million, and gmi, a German-based CRO with $7 million in sales. To finance these acquisitions, Kendle had worked out possible debt financing with Nationsbank and was working with two investment banks on an Initial Public Offering (IPO) that would repay the bank debt if successful and provide the equity base for future acquisitions. It was now time to decide whether to go ahead with the full program of two acquisitions, a large debt financing and an equity issue.

Research Associate Indra A. Reinbergs prepared this case under the supervision of Professors Dwight B. Crane and Paul W. Marshall as the basis for class discussion rather than to illustrate either effective or ineffective handling of an administrative situation.

Kendle History

Candace and Chris met in 1979 while working at The Children's Hospital of Philadelphia. Candace had received her doctorate in pharmacy from the University of Cincinnati, then taught in North Carolina and Pennsylvania. Her scientific specialty was virology. At the Children's Hospital, Candace was serving as the director of pharmacy, working as an investigator on a study of an antiviral drug for the pharmaceutical company Burroughs Wellcome. Chris, a Wharton MBA, was a senior administrator at the hospital.

Looking for something new, Candace and Chris began to discuss the idea of going into business together. One day in early 1981 Candace received an unexpected visit from a new physician, replacing the usual medical monitor for her project with Burroughs Wellcome. This physician was a pioneer in the contract clinical research business. As he described how his business worked, Candace became more and more intrigued. When he left that day, she immediately called Chris and said, "I've got a business idea!" The concept was to set up a small research consulting firm that would take on outsourced research and development (R&D) work on a contract basis from large pharmaceutical and biotechnology companies. Based on the positive response she received from potential clients, Candace left her job at the hospital in June 1981 and Chris left his job in December 1981.

Kendle International Inc. was incorporated in Cincinnati, Ohio in 1981, with Candace taking 55% of the shares, and Chris 45%. Candace had strong ties to the Cincinnati area. Her grandfather, a coal miner, had moved there from Appalachia, and the clan had grown to about 140 members, including Candace's two sons from a previous marriage. By January 1982, Candace and Chris were working from Candace's parents' home.

Kendle started as a small company with a few contracts, and business grew slowly through referrals from professional colleagues. Kendle suffered the usual bumps of a start-up business, particularly in the late 1980s when it suffered a loss for two years and ran up $1 million in bank debt on a $250,000 line of credit. Afraid that its bank would call the loan, the company went through a bankruptcy scare. Fortunately, Kendle succeeded in attracting business from a new client, the pharmaceutical company G.D. Searle & Co. (Searle). By the early 1990s, the company was turned around and it generated annual sales of about $2.5 million. Candace and Chris were married in 1991.

The Pharmaceutical Lifecycle

The clinical research process was influenced by government regulations that required drugs to pass through a series of steps before they could be marketed for public use. In the United States, the Food and Drug Administration (FDA) regulated pharmaceuticals. To receive FDA approval, a drug had to meet *safety* and *efficacy* standards for a specific *indication* (medical diagnosis). A drug for hypertension, for example, would have to lower blood pressure by a certain statistically significant amount without producing unacceptable side effects. The entire FDA approval process could take from 8 to 15 years and involve several thousand patients.[1]

---

[1] Robinson Humphrey Co. analyst report on Covance, Inc., July 7, 1997.

After a pharmaceutical company discovered a new drug and completed pre-clinical testing on animals in the laboratory, an Investigational New Drug application was filed with the FDA. The drug then passed through three phases of clinical testing on humans. Before beginning each subsequent phase, the drug company had to submit additional regulatory information to the FDA.

- **Phase I** Phase I studies were primarily concerned with assessing the drug's safety. This initial phase of testing in humans was done in a small number of healthy volunteers (20 to 100), such as students, who were usually paid for participation.

- **Phase II** Once Phase I testing had proven the drug's safety, Phase II tested its efficacy in a small number of patients (100 to 300) with the medical diagnosis. It was specifically designed to determine the likely effective dose in patients.

- **Phase III** In a Phase III study, the drug was tested on a larger patient population (1,000 to 3,000) at multiple clinical sites. The purpose was to provide a more thorough understanding of the drug's effectiveness, benefits, and the range of possible adverse reactions. Most Phase II and Phase III studies were *blinded* studies in which some patients received the experimental drug, while *control* groups received a placebo or an already approved drug. Once a Phase III study was successfully completed, a pharmaceutical company requested FDA approval for marketing the drug by filing a New Drug Application, which averaged about 100,000 pages.

- **Phase IV** Post-marketing testing (of at least 300 patients per trial) was sometimes conducted for high-risk drugs to catch serious side effects (liver toxicity) and monitor them for long-term effectiveness and cost-effectiveness.

The pharmaceutical companies traditionally designed and conducted their own clinical trials. They selected the research sites and recruited investigators to conduct the trials of the new drug. Investigators were often medical school professors at teaching hospitals, but they could also be professional investigators who conducted clinical trials at dedicated centers or occasionally regular physicians who ran trials, particularly Phase IV trials, out of their private practices. These investigators then recruited patients, sometimes with the help of the pharmaceutical company, to participate in the study.

After patients were recruited, there was a considerable amount of data collection by the investigators, monitoring of the process and data retrieval by the pharmaceutical company, and analysis of the data to determine whether the statistical criteria for safety and efficacy were met. Finally, there was the complicated process of compiling the data and preparing the long report for the FDA.

The Contract Research Business

In the 1970s, large pharmaceutical concerns in the United States began to look for ways to outsource their clinical testing work as their R&D budgets grew. At the beginning, contract research was a small cottage industry and the work was awarded on a piecemeal basis. As Chris recalled, "For years, there had been companies conducting animal testing and Phase I, but there was no one managing the entire research and development process. The acronym 'CRO' (contract research organization) did not exist, pharmaceutical companies gave out only small contracts, and did not have much confidence in for-profit research managers."

The growth of the CRO industry was stimulated by pricing pressures on drug companies that led them to try to transfer the fixed costs of clinical research into a variable cost through outsourcing. As Chris described,

> The general problem that drug companies face is balancing a variable workload with a fixed workforce. The problem is that you don't know when the guy in the white lab coat will come running down the hall, beaker in hand, shouting, "Eureka, I've got it, it's going to cure disease X." When he does that, you know your workload is going to spike. Your workload is impacted by the rate of discovery, the number of projects killed in vitro and, subsequent to that, how many studies get cancelled due to safety or efficacy problems in human testing.

Pure CROs like Kendle derived their income solely from the outsourced portion of the R&D budget of pharmaceutical clients. In theory, any part of the clinical testing process could be outsourced. While most pre-clinical discovery was conducted in-house by drug companies, the trend in the 1990s was for CROs to receive contracts to manage the entire clinical research piece, especially Phases II and III. The whole process was an incredible race against time, as every day for which FDA approval was delayed could cost the pharmaceutical client over $1 million in lost revenues. Pharmaceutical contracts ranged in duration from a few months to several years. For multi-year contracts involving clinical trials, a portion of the contract fee was paid at the time the trial was initiated, with the balance of the contract fee payable in installments over the trial duration, as performance-based milestones (investigator recruitment, patient enrollment, delivery of databases) were completed.

Contracts were bid by CROs on a fixed-price basis, and the research was a labor-intensive business. The contract bids depended on careful estimation of the hourly labor rates and the number of hours each activity would take. The estimation process involved statistical algorithms, which took into account the length of the study, frequency and length of site visits, the number of sites involved, the number of patients involved, and the number of pages per report form. A premium would be added for more complicated therapeutic testing. As the chief financial officer, Tim Mooney, described the business,

> The way that Kendle makes money is like any professional service firm—We focus on maximizing labor utilization, especially at the operational level. We assume a 65% to 70% utilization rate, so profit margins are higher if we have a higher utilization rate of personnel. We have the same assumed profit margin on all levels of people, but we can charge higher rates for contracts where we have specific therapeutic expertise that is in demand. Margins can also be higher on some large projects when we can share overhead costs across more sites.

The business of contract research entailed several types of business risk. With contracts running at an average of $1 million for companies of Kendle's size, client dependence was a major risk. Project cancellation by the client and "change orders" to reduce project costs were also increasingly frequent in the CRO industry, as healthcare cost pressures intensified. On the other hand, product liability for medical risks was borne by the pharmaceutical company.

Competition in the 1990s

By the mid-1990s, contract research had evolved into a full-service industry, recognized by both the pharmaceutical/biotech industries and the financial community. In 1995, worldwide spending on R&D by pharmaceutical and biotechnology companies was estimated at $35 billion, with $22 billion spent on the type of drug development work that CROs could do. Of the $22 billion, only $4.6 billion was outsourced to CROs in 1995. While R&D spending by pharmaceutical companies was growing at 10% a year, CROs were growing at twice that rate.[2] Specialized CROs could manage increasingly complex drug trials—in the previous decade, the number of procedures per trial and average number of patients per trial had doubled—far more efficiently than their pharmaceutical clients.[3]

Kendle participated in this growth in clinical research. Its net revenues grew 425% from $2.5 million in 1992 to $13 million in 1996. From a loss of $495,000 in 1992, its net income rose to $1.1 million by 1996. By 1996, Kendle had conducted clinical trials for 12 of the world's 20 largest pharmaceutical companies. Kendle's three largest clients were G.D. Searle, Procter & Gamble, and Amgen, which generated 48%, 19%, and 13% of Kendle's 1996 revenues, respectively. (See **Exhibits 1** and **2** for Kendle's income statements and balance sheets.)

The contract research industry was very fragmented, with hundreds of CROs worldwide. In the 1990s, in response to the increased outsourcing of pharmaceutical R&D, and a demand for global trials, consolidation among the CROs began. A few key players emerged and went public, creating a new industry for Wall Street to watch. Many CRO start-ups were founded by former drug company executives who decided to form their own operations. After a period of internal growth, some of the start-ups began growing through a financial "roll-up" strategy. An industry publication listed 18 top players in North America, with total contract research revenues of $1.7 billion. The top five public companies, ranked by 1996 revenues, were Quintiles Transnational Corp. ($537.6 million), Covance Inc. ($494.8 million), Pharmaceutical Product Development Inc ($152.3 million), ClinTrials Research Inc. ($93.5 million), and Parexel International Corp. ($88 million).[4] (See **Exhibit 3** for recent sales and profit data on CROs.)

With its talent pool of scientists at the Research Triangle and U.S. headquarters of the pharmaceutical giants Glaxo and Burroughs Wellcome (later merged as Glaxo Wellcome), the state of North Carolina quickly became the center of the burgeoning CRO industry. Two of the "big five" companies, Quintiles and Pharmaceutical Product Development, were started there by academic colleagues of Candace's. Quintiles

[2]J.C. Bradford & Co. analyst report, January 15, 1998, pp. 5–6.

[3]*The Economist,* "Survey of the Pharmaceutical Industry," February 21, 1998, p. 4.

[4]"Annual Report: Leading CROs," *R&D Directions,* September 1997, pp. 28+.

Transnational was considered to be the "gold standard of the industry." Quintiles was founded in 1982 by Dennis Gillings, a British biostatistician who had worked at Hoechst and was a professor at the University of North Carolina, where Candace completed her postdoctoral work. After raising $39 million in a 1994 IPO, Quintiles went on an acquisition spree, adding other professional service businesses. For example, the firm provided sales and marketing services to support the launch of new drug products. By the end of 1996, Quintiles was the world's largest CRO, with 7,000 employees in 56 offices in 20 countries. A typical clinical study managed by Quintiles was conducted at 160 sites in 12 countries, involving 10,000 patients. Quintiles was more diversified than many of its CRO competitors, with about 65% of revenues derived from the core CRO business and 35% from other services.[5]

Pharmaceutical Product Development (PPD) was founded in 1989 by Fred Eshelman, a colleague of Candace's from the postdoctoral program in pharmacy. Like the founder of Quintiles, Eshelman had worked in drug research for several pharmaceutical firms, including Glaxo and Beecham. PPD's revenues jumped 500% between 1990 and 1994, based on such work as multi-year contracts for AIDS research for the National Institutes of Health. PPD conducted a successful IPO in March 1996, with its stock jumping from $18 per share to $25.50 per share on the first day of trading. PPD bought a U.K. Phase I facility in November 1995, and in September 1996 merged with another leading CRO. Their combined net revenues exceeded $200 million.

Kendle at the Crossroads

To Candace and Chris, it was clear that certain competitive capabilities were necessary for companies of Kendle's size to compete successfully with the major CROs:

- **therapeutic expertise** (in specific medical areas)
- **broad range of services** (pharmaceutical companies wanted to work with fewer CROs, with each offering a wide range of services across multiple phases of the R&D process);
- **integrated clinical data management** (the ability to efficiently collect, edit and analyze data from thousands of patients with various clinical conditions from many geographically dispersed sites);
- **international, multi-jurisdictional presence** (to speed up drug approval, tests were being launched in several countries at once);

With the exception of international presence, Candace and Chris felt comfortable with their ability to meet these criteria. Kendle's staff had scientific expertise in multiple therapeutic areas, including cardiovascular, central nervous system, gastrointestinal, immunology, oncology, respiratory, skeletal disease and inflammation. The company also had broad capabilities, including management of studies in Phases II through Phase IV. It did not consider the absence of Phase I capabilities to be an issue, since this activity was quite separate. (See **Exhibit 4** for a comparison of CRO geographical locations.)

---

[5]William Blair & Co. LLC analyst report, *Quintiles Transnational Corp.,* June 20, 1997, p. 3.

To build an integrated clinical data management capability, Chris had directed the development of TrialWare®, a proprietary software system that allowed global data collection and processing and the integration of clinical data with clients' in-house data management systems. TrialWare® consisted of several modules including a database management system that greatly reduced study start-up costs and time by standardizing database design and utilizing scanned image technology to facilitate the design of data entry screens, the point-and-click application of edits from a pre-programmed library, and workflow management (parallel processing). Other modules included a system that coded medical history, medication and adverse event data and a touch-tone telephone system that was used for patient randomization, just-in-time drug supply and collection of real-time enrollment data.

Against the backdrop of a changing industry, Candace and Chris felt the need to develop additional business skills and focus Kendle's strategy. To clarify their management roles, Candace and Chris switched their existing responsibilities. Chris pointed out, "Candace became CEO as we realized that her focus was long-range and I took over as Chief Operating Officer to focus on the short-range. In addition, the marketing strength of our competitors was propelling them further and further ahead of Kendle. Candace brought her science background and entrepreneurial skills, while I brought my management. The problem was that we were relatively weak in sales and marketing." To broaden their skills, Candace went off in 1991 to the Owner/President Management Program (OPM), an executive education program run by Harvard Business School for three weeks a year over three years. Chris followed her to OPM in 1994.

After completing the OPM program, Candace assessed the situation,

> We have to be big enough relative to our competitors to take on large, international projects. When Searle was looking for CROs for international work, all we could do was possibly subcontract it out to small shops. In contrast, Quintiles had six overseas offices of its own. Furthermore, when Searle calls and says, "I just got off the phone, Quintiles will cut their price by a million dollars," if you're too small, you're not going to be able to respond to that.

Candace and Chris realized that Kendle could not grow fast enough internally to keep up with its peers and did not have the cash for acquisitions. They entertained the thought of selling Kendle, and were approached several times about a sale. But by nature, they were a competitive, athletic couple. Chris got up to play squash every morning at 7 AM, and Candace was an avid rower, recently winning a gold medal in a Cincinnati regatta. Perhaps not surprisingly, Candace and Chris decided to grow the firm and take it public rather than sell. As Candace described their motivation, "We were not driven to be a public company as such, but primarily to be bigger, and for this, we needed public financing to succeed in the new competitive landscape. The whole target was not to let the big guys get too far out ahead of us."

Preparations for Growth

By 1994, Kendle had grown to $4.4 million in revenues. Candace, the driving force throughout the IPO process, sought advice from an old college friend, a well-known

Cincinnati businessman. He advised her, "before you go public, practice being a public company." Candace therefore formulated a plan for Kendle to go public in 1999.

Kendle began hiring key managers to build up functional units. Between 1994 and February 1997, new directors of clinical data management, information technology, biostatistics, finance, mergers and acquisitions, regulatory affairs, and human resources were hired. As Chris described, "the plan was to put this infrastructure in place to look and act like a public company—communications, IT, finance. The idea was hire at the top and they'll fill in their organization." Many of these new managers had previously worked together at other companies.

To prepare for Wall Street scrutiny, Kendle began issuing internal quarterly financial statements and sharing them with employees in an open-book management style. Candace and Chris tried to make the growing number of employees feel like "part of the family" in other ways, too. The Kendle "photo gallery" displayed professional portraits of employees with their favorite hobbies. In 1995 Chris led the development of a corporate mission statement and a document on strategic plans that was shared with all employees.

Kendle was organized in a matrix fashion (see **Exhibit 5** for organizational chart). Each department was treated as a strategic business unit (SBU) with a director who established standards and carried profit responsibility. At the same time, each research contract was managed by a project manager who assembled a team from across the various SBUs.

Clinical trials involved five functional SBUs at Kendle:

1. **Regulatory Affairs** recruited investigators, helped them with FDA registration forms, and obtained approval from ethics boards. Regulatory Affairs maintained a database of 5,000 investigators.

2. **Clinical Monitoring** sent clinical research associates (CRAs) out to the testing sites (every 4 to 6 weeks) to enforce Good Clinical Practice regulations. The CRAs were typically young, single health care professionals who spent a significant amount of their time on the road. The CRA would collect data from investigators, resolve queries generated by **Clinical Data Management**, and promote patient enrollment.

3. **Clinical Data Management** produced a "locked" database that could be submitted to the FDA. Data from case report forms were input into a computer system and "cleaned" through a manual review of the forms and an automated check of the databases. The challenge was to lock a database quickly while maintaining data quality.

4. **Biostatistics** would "unblind" the locked database and analyze it to determine if the data confirmed that the test results met the criteria for safety and efficacy. Biostatistics also defined the scope of new studies.

5. **Medical Writing** generated "the truckload of paper submitted to the FDA" for a New Drug Application, including a statistical analysis, a clinical assessment, preclinical and clinical data, a description of the manufacturing process, and the supporting patient documentation.

1996: The Celebrex™ Study, Filing Preparations, and European Acquisitions

1996 was a busy year for Candace, Chris, and Kendle's new management team. They simultaneously began conducting a major drug study, working with underwriters on IPO preparations, and looking for overseas acquisition targets. In 1996 Kendle managed 62 clinical studies at 4,100 sites involving approximately 20,000 patients.

Celebrex™ Study

In January 1996, Kendle began working on a major drug called Celebrex™ (celecoxib). Its client Searle was engaged in a neck-and-neck race with Merck, the largest U.S. drug company, to be the first to market a COX-2 inhibitor. A COX-2 inhibitor was a new type of anti-inflammatory drug that promised low incidence of bleeding ulcers in long-term, high-dosage users such as arthritis patients. The Searle-Merck race was closely followed in the business press.

Searle awarded the international portion of the Celebrex™ contract to another CRO, since Kendle only had facilities for testing in the United States. However, Kendle did win the contract to conduct all the U.S. Phase II and III trials. The Celebrex™ contract was a "huge feather in our cap," recalled the chief financial officer. "In order to beat Merck, we worked very hard and kept compressing the timelines."

To head the Celebrex™ project, Kendle hired Bill Sietsema, PhD, as assistant director of clinical research. A therapeutic expert in skeletal diseases and inflammation, Sietsema had worked at Procter & Gamble for 12 years. While Sietsema served as overall program director, Chris acted as the operational project manager, meeting with his Searle counterpart in Chicago on a monthly basis. In early 1997, Kendle also set up a new regional office in Chicago, close to Searle headquarters.

For Kendle, the Celebrex™ project was a chance to "show what we could do and to develop a reputation as a leader in the field of skeletal disease and inflammation." Kendle actively helped investigators recruit arthritis patients, running television advertisements, directing interested volunteers to a call center. Three hundred investigators enrolled over 10,000 patients, producing over one million pages of case report forms.

Most importantly, through close integration of information systems with Searle, Kendle was able to beat an industry standard. Instead of taking the typical six months to one year, the time span between the last patient in Phase II and the first in Phase III, which began in June 1996, was only 22 days.

Preparation for SEC Filing

By the time the Celebrex™ program rolled around, Candace and Chris felt that they might have to go public earlier than intended because of the competitive landscape. The new chief financial officer, Tim Mooney, took a leading role in the preparations. Prior to joining Kendle in May 1996, Mooney had worked as CFO at The Future Now, Inc., a computer reseller and Hook-SupeRx, a retail drugstore chain. At Kendle, Mooney replaced the controller with an audit manager from Coopers & Lybrand to beef up his staff. Mooney also led the building of many of the other financially related departments at Kendle.

To act as the lead underwriters on the IPO, in August 1996 Mooney chose two regional investment banks, Chicago-based William Blair & Company, L.L.C., which had handled the 1995 IPO of Kendle's competitor Parexel, and Wessels, Arnold & Henderson from Minneapolis. William Blair began putting Kendle through the paces of preparing to file a preliminary prospectus with the U.S. Securities and Exchange Commission (SEC). The process of going public generally took from 60 to 180 days. One of the key steps in the process was the conversion of Kendle from a subchapter S corporation to a C corporation at the time of the IPO. (Subchapter S corporations were entities with 35 or fewer shareholders that were treated like partnerships for tax purposes. Corporate income tax was passed through tax-free to the owners who then paid personal income taxes due.)

U-Gene

In October 1996 Mooney hired Tony Forcellini, a former colleague, as director of mergers and acquisitions (M&A). Tony had worked at Arthur Andersen in the tax department, and then as a treasurer at Hook-SuperRx with Mooney. The search for European acquisition targets was mainly conducted by Candace and Tony Forcellini, with back-up support by Tim Mooney and Chris. All the while, Chris and Bill Sietsema were working away on the Celebrex™ program.

Forcellini's first decision was easy—whether to pursue an offering memorandum that landed on his desk shortly after he arrived. The company for sale was U-Gene Research B.V. (U-Gene), a CRO based in Utrecht, the Netherlands. U-Gene was represented by Technomark Consulting Services Ltd. (Technomark), a London-based consulting firm uniquely specializing in the healthcare industry. Technomark had an extensive database on European CROs and was primarily in the business of matching its pharmaceutical company clients' trials with appropriate European CROs, but it also had a small investment banking division.

U-Gene, a full-service CRO, was an attractive target for Kendle. The venture capitalist owners were actively looking for buyers. With a 38-bed Phase I facility in Utrecht and regional offices in the United Kingdom and Italy, U-Gene could increase both Kendle's service offering and geographic presence. Since its founding in 1986, U-Gene had served more than 100 clients, including 19 of the world's largest pharmaceutical companies. In 1996, U-Gene participated in 115 studies at approximately 500 sites involving approximately 4,700 patients and recorded net revenues of $12.5 million, a 37% increase over the prior year, and operating profit of $1.3 million, a 47% increase over the prior year. Because of its U.K. and Italian offices, U-Gene viewed itself as on the way to becoming a pan-European CRO. (See **Exhibit 6** for U-Gene financial statements.)

With momentum building, in November 1996, Forcellini seized upon U-Gene as Kendle's possible entry into Europe and submitted a bid, offering cash and private stock. Unfortunately, Kendle lost out on this bid to a competitor, Collaborative Clinical Research, Inc, as U-Gene's owners either wanted a full cash deal or stock from a public company. Collaborative was a competitor slightly larger than Kendle ($25.7 million in revenues) that had gone public in June 1996 and had established a software partnership with IBM. Although it had access to investigators outside the United States, Collaborative also viewed U-Gene as the establishment of a European presence. On February 12, 1997 Collaborative announced that it had signed a letter of intent to acquire U-Gene in exchange for 1.75 million newly issued shares.

While this put Kendle out of the picture, the prospects of a deal were not completely killed. On the same day, February 12, 1997, Collaborative also announced that its first-quarter 1997 earnings would be significantly below expectations. On the next day, on analyst speculation that a major client contract had been lost, their stock fell by 27.3%, closing at $9.00.[6] This put Collaborative's U-Gene deal in jeopardy.

Underwriter Concerns

About two weeks after Collaborative's announcement, on February 25, 1997, another CRO, ClinTrials, also suffered a drop in stock price. ClinTrials' stock lost more than half its market value, dropping 59%, to $9.50 per share. The fall began when an analyst from Wessels Arnold downgraded the ClinTrials stock to "hold" from "buy," citing a number of key management departures, and continued after ClinTrials announced that its first-quarter earnings would be half its year-earlier profit. The reason for the unexpected earnings decline was the cancellation of five projects totaling $37 million, with the possibility of even lower earnings due to an unresolved project dispute with a client.[7] ClinTrials' negative performance began to affect other CRO stocks, including that of Quintiles.[8]

With client concentration an issue in ClinTrials' stock performance, William Blair developed doubts about the timing of Kendle's IPO. Although Kendle was close to filing its preliminary prospectus, on the day after ClinTrial's stock dropped, William Blair analysts had a meeting with Kendle's management and told them that they had decided to withdraw as lead underwriters in the IPO.

Candace was resolved to keep going. She said, "There's no way out of the concentration issue. We can't buy our way out of it, because we can't do M&A deals until we have a public currency, and every day Searle is bringing us more work, we won't tell them no." She then asked Mooney to find new investment bankers, and he thought, "what am I going to do now?"

Hoping for a lead, Mooney called up a former security analyst from Wessels Arnold who had gone to work at Lehman Bros. Although Kendle was smaller than Lehman's usual clients, Lehman agreed to underwrite Kendle's IPO, with the reassurance that "we think we can sell through the client concentration issue." After an agreement with New York-based Lehman was reached, Mooney searched for a regional firm because, as he decided, "I didn't want two New York-size egos. J.C. Bradford, based in Nashville, Tennessee, had a good reputation in the industry, and struck us as a nice regional bank. They were more

[6]Donald Sabath, "News Depresses Stock of Collaborative Clinical," *The Plain Dealer,* February 14, 1997, p. 2C.

[7]"ClinTrials Predicts Sharply Lower Profit: Shares Plunge 59%", *The Wall Street Journal,* February 26, 1997, p. B3.

[8]David Ranii, "Investors Avoiding Quintiles," *The News & Observer, Raleigh, NC,* February 27, 1997, p. C8.

retail-oriented than institutional-oriented, so they wouldn't directly be competing with Lehman in types of clientele." Bradford had managed the IPO of the first large CRO to go public (ClinTrials, in 1993) and Lehman had led the IPO of PPD in January 1996.

gmi and U-Gene Revisited

At the same time, Forcellini was moving ahead on the acquisition search. In January 1997 he tasked Technomark with using its CRO database to generate a list of possible European acquisition targets that met the following criteria: "ideally a CRO with United Kingdom headquarters; $5 million to $7 million in revenues; no Searle business; certain types of therapeutic expertise; strong in phases II through IV; and certain country locations." The initial list had 50 European CROs, which Kendle narrowed down to 14 prospects. Technomark then contacted these 14 prospects to sound out their willingness to sell, bringing the number down to five candidates: three CROs in Germany, two in the United Kingdom, and one in the Netherlands (not U-Gene). To assess the prospects, Kendle used information from Technomark on comparable M&A deals.

Candace and Tony Forcellini then traveled around Europe for a week visiting the five companies. They decided to further pursue two companies: a small, 15-person monitoring organization in the United Kingdom and one in Germany. The U.K. prospect was quickly discarded because of an aggressive asking price and accounting problems.

Kendle then moved on to the German target, a company named gmi. Its full name was GMI Gesellschaft fur Angewandte Mathematik und Informatik mbH. Founded in 1983, gmi provided a full range of Phase II to IV services. gmi had conducted trials in Austria, the United Kingdom, Switzerland and France, among other countries, and had experience in health economic studies and professional training programs. In 1996, gmi participated in 119 studies at multiple sites and recorded net revenues of $7 million, a 32% increase over the prior year, and operating profit of $1.4 million, a 16% increase over the prior year. At March 31, 1997, gmi's backlog was approximately $9.6 million. gmi considered itself to be especially good at Phase III trials. (See **Exhibit 7** for gmi financial statements.)

While Candace and Forcellini were narrowing down European targets, Mooney was hunting for cash. In February 1997 Kendle met at a special lunch with its existing bankers, Star Bank (later renamed Firstar), in Cincinnati. Mooney recalled the conversation vividly: "After Candace and Chris described their plans, Star Bank's CEO made a proposal, 'If you keep Kendle a private company and avoid the hassles of being public, we'll lend you the money you need for acquisitions.'"

With the financing in hand, Candace and Forcellini visited gmi in Munich. While gmi's owners were willing to talk, they did not have much interest in selling. As Mooney described it, "gmi was a classic case of having grown to a certain size, had a comfortable level of income, but weren't interested in putting in the professional systems to grow beyond that level." After several conversations in March, it was not clear that Kendle and gmi's owners would be able to reach a mutually agreeable price.

At this point in early April 1997, the possibility of U-Gene as an acquisition candidate heated up. After the U-Gene deal with Collaborative Research began to collapse, Kendle had initiated a carefully structured inquiry about U-Gene's interest in renewed discussions. This inquiry led to further discussions and a request in April for Kendle to meet in Frankfurt to try to reach an agreement. With the gmi deal in doubt, Kendle agreed to try to reach closure with U-Gene. After some discussion, both sides agreed on a price of 30 million Dutch guilders, or about US$15.6 million, $14 million of which would be paid in cash, and the remaining $1.6 million would be in the form of a promissory note payable to the selling shareholders. U-Gene wanted to complete the transaction within the next several weeks, so it would have to be financed at least initially by borrowings. Even if Kendle went ahead with an IPO, the equity financing would not be completed until the end of the summer.

Discussions with gmi continued through this period since Kendle was confident about its ability to obtain financing from Star Bank. Ultimately, Kendle's team was able to agree upon a price with gmi. The owners were willing to accept a price of 19.5 million Deutsche marks, or about US$12.3 million, with at least $9.5 million in cash. They would accept shares for the remaining $2.8 million, if Kendle successfully completed an IPO. The owners were willing to hold off the deal until the IPO issue was resolved.

Closing the Deals and IPO Decision

To complete both the U-Gene and gmi deals, Kendle would need to borrow about $25 million to $28 million, so financing became critical. Mooney went back to Star Bank to take the bankers up on their promise. He described their reaction: "Star Bank said they couldn't lend $28 million to a company that only has $1 million in equity. Nobody did that. They might be willing to finance one acquisition, with the help of other banks, but there was no way that they would provide $28 million."

Mooney was quite angry, but had no choice but to look for other sources of financing. He first tried to get bridge financing from Lehman and Bradford, but they refused, saying that they had "gotten killed on such deals in the 1980s." There was also a possibility of financing from First Chicago Bank, but this did not materialize.

Finally, in late April 1997, Mooney contacted NationsBank, N.A., which was headquartered in Charlotte, North Carolina and provided banking services to the CRO industry. Nationsbank expressed interest, but only in a large deal. Even $28 million was a small amount to Nationsbank. In a few short weeks, Nationsbank ended up structuring a $30 million credit for Kendle, consisting of a $20 million, three-year revolving credit line and $10 million in five-year, subordinated notes. The interest rate on the credit line was tied to a money market base rate plus 0.50% (currently totaling 6.2%), and the subordinated debt carried a 12% rate. "So NationsBank stepped up in a pretty big way. They could have ended up with Kendle as a private company, with $30 million in debt." Because of the risk, Nationsbank would also take warrants giving the bank the right to purchase 4% of Kendle's equity, or up to 10% if the IPO was delayed and Kendle had to borrow the full amount to do both acquisitions.

Lehman Brothers was confident about an IPO. The underwriters felt Kendle could raise $39 million to $40 million at a price between $12 and $14 per share, and that Candace and Chris could sell some of their shares as well. Premier Research Worldwide Ltd., a CRO with $15.2 million in 1996 revenues, had raised $46.75 million from its recent IPO in February 1997. Kendle felt they had a much better track record than Premier.

Kendle now faced some difficult decisions. It could do the full program, including both acquisitions, taking the $30 million Nationsbank deal, and planning for an IPO in late summer. The successful acquisitions of gmi and U-Gene would establish Kendle as the sixth largest CRO in Europe, based on total revenues, and one of only four large CROs able to offer clients the full range of Phase I through Phase IV clinical trials in Europe. The pricing on the two acquisitions of 8 to 10 times EBITDA seemed in line with recent CRO deals (see **Exhibit 8**). And, once the IPO was completed, Kendle would have both a cash cushion and stock as a currency to help finance future growth and acquisitions. Assuming an IPO of 3 million new shares at a price of $13.00, Kendle would have a cash position of about $14 million and no debt in the capital structure. (See **Exhibits 9** and **10** for pro forma income statements and balance sheets showing the impact of the acquisitions and the IPO.)

A related issue was how many of their shares Candace and Chris should sell if an IPO were done. Their current thinking was to sell 600,000 shares. Thus, a total of 3.6 million shares would be for sale at the time of the IPO, including a primary offering of 3 million shares and a secondary offering of 600,000 shares. This sale would reduce holdings controlled by Candace and Chris from 3.65 million shares (83.1% of the shares currently outstanding) to 3.05 million shares (43.4% of the new total outstanding).

Doing the full IPO and acquisition program, however, was unprecedented among Kendle's peers. "Nobody does this combination all at once—an IPO, senior- and sub-debt financing, and M&A deals," as Mooney described the situation. Furthermore, the stock prices of public CROs had been falling since last February (see **Exhibits 11** and **12** for stock market valuation and price information). If Kendle bought into the full program and the market crashed or the IPO was unsuccessful, the company would have almost $30 million of debt on its books with a very modest equity base. Perhaps it would be better to do just the U-Gene acquisition and use Star Bank to finance it. After completing this acquisition, it could then pursue the IPO. This approach was safer, but of course Kendle might miss the IPO window and miss the opportunity to acquire the second company. Indeed, instead of discouraging Kendle from doing an IPO, the fall in CRO stock prices might be taken as a signal that Kendle should forge ahead before the window closed completely.

List of Exhibits

Kendle International Inc. and CRO Industry
Exhibit 1   Kendle International Inc. Financial Data
Exhibit 2   Kendle International Inc. Balance Sheets
Exhibit 3   Kendle vs. CRO Industry Sales and Net Income Data
Exhibit 4   Geographic Presence of Kendle vs. CRO Industry
Exhibit 5   Kendle International Inc. Organizational Chart (mid-1997)

European Acquisitions and Valuation
Exhibit 6   U-Gene Summary Financial Statements
Exhibit 7   gmi Summary Financial Statements
Exhibit 8   Valuation of Proposed Kendle International Acquisitions

Valuation of Kendle with Acquisitions
Exhibit 9   Kendle Pro Forma Income Statements after Acquisitions and IPO
Exhibit 10   Kendle Pro Forma Balance Sheets after Acquisitions and IPO
Exhibit 11   Market Valuation of CRO Industry
Exhibit 12   CRO Industry Stock Prices

EXHIBIT 1 | Kendle International Inc. Financial Data

(in thousands)	Years Ended December 31,					1st Qtr 3/31/97
	1992	1993	1994	1995	1996	
INCOME STATEMENTS						
Net revenues	$ 2,468	$ 2,555	$ 4,431	$ 6,118	$ 12,959	$ 5,962
Cost and expenses:						
Direct costs	1,689	1,548	2,760	3,564	8,176	3,375
Selling, general and administrative	1,158	603	1,067	1,776	3,278	1,893
Depreciation and amortization	81	111	127	168	316	150
Total costs and expenses	2,928	2,262	3,954	5,507	11,770	5,418
Income (loss) from operations	(460)	293	477	610	1,189	543
Other income (expense):						
Interest income	—	—	24	6	15	12
Interest expense	(72)	(61)	(43)	(69)	(65)	(31)
Other	37	20	—	—	(4)	5
Net income	$ (495)	$ 252	$ 458	$ 547	$ 1,134	$ 529
Memorandum Items:						
Capital contribution by shareholders	n.a.	n.a.	366	—	—	—
Distributions to shareholders	n.a.	n.a.	(304)	(379)	(535)	(216)
EBITDA	$ (379)	$ 404	$ 604	$ 778	$ 1,505	$ 693
BALANCE SHEET DATA						
Working capital (deficit)	$ (972)	$ (492)	$ (208)	$ (139)	$ (294)	(294)
Total assets	832	2,181	1,874	2,432	8,623	9,847
Total debt	278	173	139	151	761	1,155
Total shareholders' equity (deficit)	$ (827)	$ (343)	$ 177	$ 345	$ 944	1,257

Note: Since Kendle was a subchapter S corporation, it paid no corporate income taxes. As a C corporation, state and federal taxes would have been about 40%.

Source: Kendle company documents.

EXHIBIT 2 | Kendle International Inc. Balance Sheets

(in thousands)	December 31, 1995	December 31, 1996	1st Qtr 3/31/97
ASSETS			
Current assets:			
Cash and cash equivalents	$ 15	$ 2,047	$ 14
Accounts receivable	1,655	3,583	4,379
Unreimbursed investigator and project costs	88	981	2,610
Other current assets	38	13	137
Total current assets	1,797	6,624	7,140
Property and equipment:			
Furnishings, equipment and other	770	1,177	1,447
Equipment under capital leases	472	1,588	2,072
Less: accumulated depreciation	(617)	(931)	(1,078)
Net property and equipment	625	1,835	2,441
Other assets	10	164	266
Total assets	$ 2,432	$ 8,623	$ 9,847
LIABILITIES AND SHAREHOLDERS' EQUITY			
Current Liabilities:			
Notes payable and bank overdraft	$ 320	—	1,164
Current portion of capital lease obligations	129	360	342
Trade payables	254	913	1,923
Dividends payable	—	250	—
Advance billings and advances against projects	1,120	5,080	3,535
Accrued compensation and related taxes	79	251	405
Other accrued liabilities	33	63	64
Total current liabilities	1,935	6,918	7,434
Obligations under capital leases, less current	112	761	1,155
Deferred rent	39	—	—
Total liabilities	2,086	7,679	8,590
Shareholders' equity:			
Common stock	75	75	75
Additional paid-in capital	270	270	270
Retained earnings	—	599	912
Total shareholders' equity	345	944	1,257
Total liabilities and shareholders' equity	$ 2,432	$ 8,623	$ 9,847

Source: Kendle company documents.

EXHIBIT 3 | Kendle vs. CRO Industry Sales and Net Income Data

(in thousands)	1993	1994	1995	1996	CAGR %
NET SALES					
Quintiles	$ 61,704	$ 195,900	$ 337,006	$ 601,126	113.6
Covance	289,697	319,501	409,174	494,828	19.5
PPD	20,835	192,105	209,778	197,796	111.7
Parexel	65,294	69,646	79,928	125,053	24.2
ClinTrials	35,284	42,874	57,846	94,719	39.0
Premier	10,245	12,910	12,064	15,283	14.3
Total	$ 483,059	$ 832,936	$ 1,105,796	$ 1,528,805	46.8
Kendle	**$ 2,555**	**$ 4,431**	**$ 6,118**	**$ 12,959**	**71.8**
NET INCOME					
Quintiles	$ 3,842	$ 9,047	$ 16,068	$ 9,664	36.0
Covance	16,811	19,645	24,226	12,716	(8.9)
PPD	3,572	8,257	(17,150)	(3,507)	(199.4)
Parexel	(2,157)	2,423	(10,630)	6,655	n.a.
ClinTrials	1,041	2,153	3,601	6,425	83.4
Premier	(177)	580	341	1,070	n.a.
Total	$ 22,932	$ 42,105	$ 16,456	$ 33,023	12.9
Kendle[a]	**$ 151**	**$ 275**	**$ 328**	**$ 680**	**39.1**
NET INCOME MARGINS (%)					
Quintiles	6.2	4.6	4.8	1.6	
Covance	5.8	6.1	5.9	2.6	
PPD	17.1	4.3	(8.2)	(1.8)	
Parexel	(3.3)	3.5	(13.3)	5.3	
ClinTrials	3.0	5.0	6.2	6.8	
Premier	(1.7)	4.5	2.8	7.0	
Average	4.7	5.1	1.5	2.2	
Kendle	**5.9**	**6.2**	**5.4**	**5.3**	

[a]Kendle net income is adjusted for 40% tax rate on corporate income.

Source: Disclosure, Kendle company documents.

EXHIBIT 4 | Geographic Presence of Kendle vs. CRO Industry

	Quintiles	Covance	Parexel	PPD	ClinTrials	Kendle
North America	Canada	Canada	Canada	Canada	Canada	
	U.S.	U.S.	U.S.	U.S.	U.S.	U.S.
	Mexico					
South America	Argentina	Argentina			Chile	
	Brazil			Brazil		
UK, Ireland	England	England	England	England	England	
	Ireland	Ireland		Ireland		
	Scotland			Scotland	Scotland	
Western Europe	Belgium	Belgium		Belgium	Belgium	
	Netherlands		Netherlands			
	France	France	France	France	France	
	Germany	Germany	Germany	Germany	Germany	
	Italy		Italy	Italy	Italy	
	Finland		Norway			
	Denmark	Switzerland				
	Sweden	Sweden	Sweden	Sweden		
	Spain	Spain	Spain	Spain		
	Austria					
Central/East Europe	Bulgaria	Czech Rep.	Czech Rep.	Czech Rep.		
	Hungary		Hungary	Hungary		
		Poland	Poland	Poland	Poland	
			Lithuania			
	Russia		Russia			
Asia	Japan	Japan	Japan	Japan	Japan	
	China	China				
	Singapore	Singapore				
	India					
	Taiwan	Taiwan				
Rest of World	Australia	Australia	Australia	Australia	Australia	
	South Africa	South Africa		South Africa		
	Israel		Israel		Israel	
	New Zealand					

Source: Cleary Gull Reiland & McDevitt Inc. analyst report, December 3, 1998.

EXHIBIT 5 | Kendle International Inc. Organizational Chart (mid-1997)

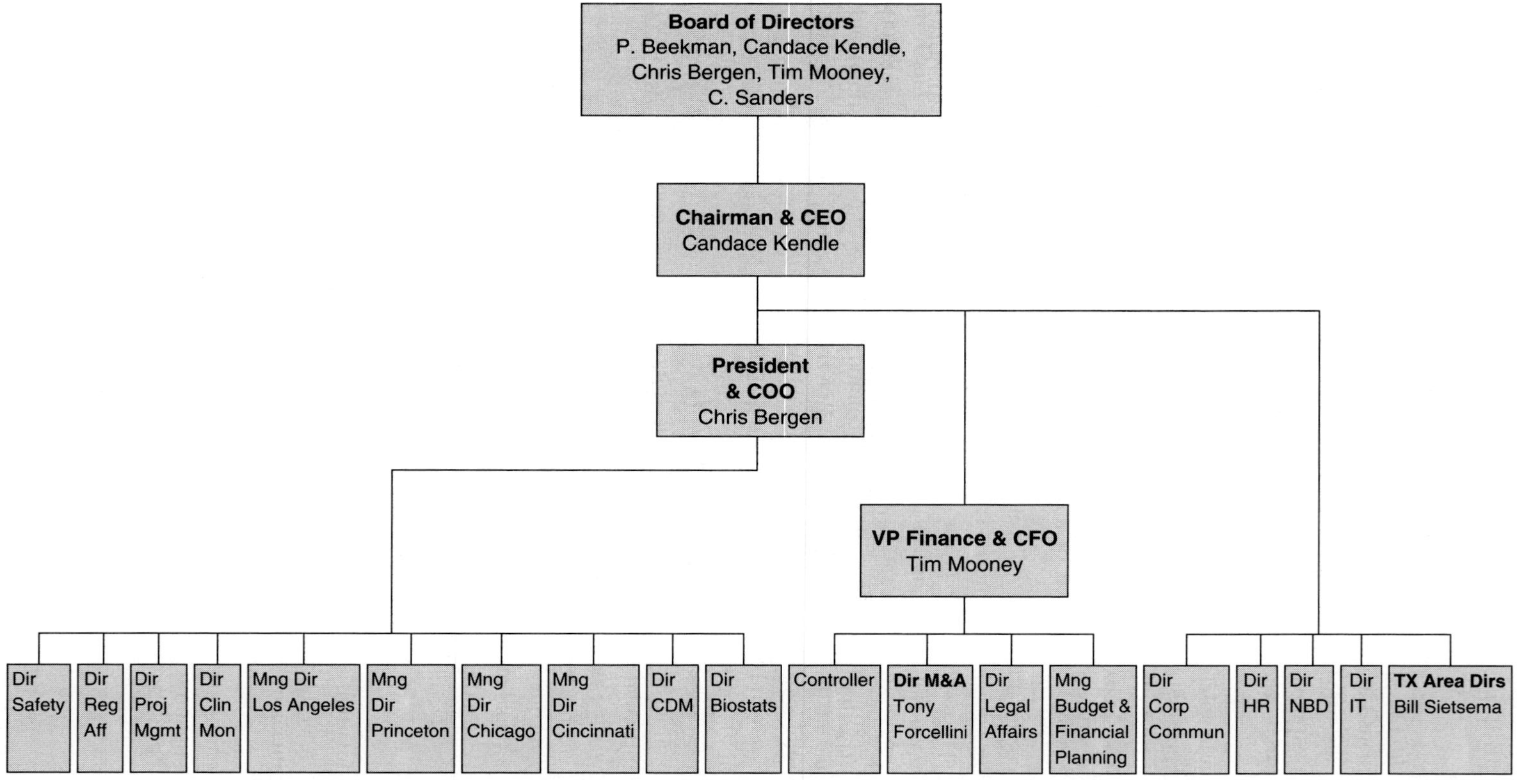

Board of Directors
P. Beekman, Candace Kendle,
Chris Bergen, Tim Mooney,
C. Sanders

Chairman & CEO
Candace Kendle

President & COO
Chris Bergen

VP Finance & CFO
Tim Mooney

Dir Corp Commun

Dir HR

Dir NBD

Dir IT

TX Area Dirs
Bill Sietsema

Controller

Dir M&A
Tony Forcellini

Dir Legal Affairs

Mng Budget & Financial Planning

Dir Safety

Dir Reg Aff

Dir Proj Mgmt

Dir Clin Mon

Mng Dir Los Angeles

Mng Dir Princeton

Mng Dir Chicago

Mng Dir Cincinnati

Dir CDM

Dir Biostats

EXHIBIT 6 | U-Gene Summary Financial Statements

(in thousands)	Years Ended December 31,		1st Qtr
	1995	**1996**	**3/31/97**
INCOME STATEMENTS			
Net revenues	$ 9,115	$ 12,508	$ 3,273
Costs and expenses	8,234	11,211	2,863
Income from operations	881	1,297	410
Interest income	6	7	11
Income before tax	887	1,304	422
Tax on income	303	465	148
Net income	$ 584	$ 838	$ 273
Distributions to Shareholders	$ (285)	$ (276)	$ —
Earnings Retained	300	563	—
Memo Item: EBITDA	$ 1,159	$ 1,617	$ 495
BALANCE SHEETS			
Assets			
Current assets	$ 4,058	$ 5,327	$ 4,805
Deferred tax asset	24	93	73
Net property and equipment	728	1,118	1,073
Total assets	$ 4,810	$ 6,538	$ 5,951
Liabilities and Shareholders' Equity			
Current liabilities	$ 3,831	$ 5,013	$ 4,253
Pension liabilities	96	171	175
Total liabilities	3,927	5,184	4,428
Shareholders' equity	883	1,355	1,522
Total liabilities and shareholders' equity	$ 4,810	$ 6,538	$ 5,951

Note: For U.S. dollar reporting purposes, assets and liabilities have been translated from Dutch guilders to U.S. dollars at year-end rates and revenues, costs and dividends have been translated at average rates for the year. Gains and losses resulting from this translation are accumulated in shareholders' equity.

Source: Kendle company documents.

EXHIBIT 7 | gmi Summary Financial Statements

(in thousands)	Years Ended December 31, 1995	Years Ended December 31, 1996	1st Qtr 3/31/97
INCOME STATEMENTS			
Net revenues	$ 5,294	$ 6,996	$ 1,995
Costs and expenses	4,092	5,596	1,124
Income from operations	1,202	1,400	871
Interest and other income	25	45	5
Income before taxes	1,228	1,445	876
Income taxes	623	658	412
Net income	$ 604	$ 786	$ 464
Distributions to shareholders	$ (279)	$ (399)	—
Earnings retained	325	387	—
Memo. Item: EBITDA	$ 1,346	$ 1,505	$ 891
BALANCE SHEETS			
Assets			
Current assets	$ 2,872	$ 3,497	$ 4,248
Net equipment	160	170	149
Total assets	$ 3,032	$ 3,667	$ 4,397
Liabilities and Shareholders' Equity			
Current liabilities	$ 2,067	$ 2,623	$ 2,969
Deferred tax liability	239	—	—
Total liabilities	2,306	2,623	2,969
Shareholders' equity	727	1,044	1,428
Total liabilities and shareholders' equity	$ 3,032	$ 3,667	$ 4,397

Note: For U.S. dollar reporting purposes, assets and liabilities have been translated from Deutsche mark to U.S. dollars at year-end rates and revenues, costs and dividends have been translated at average rates for the year. Gains and losses resulting from this translation are accumulated in shareholders' equity.

Source: Kendle company documents.

EXHIBIT 8 | Valuation of Proposed Kendle International Acquisitions

Data on Comparable CRO Acquisitions

Date	Acquiror	Target	Payment (%) Stock	Payment (%) Cash	Value ($m)	Ratio of Deal Value to Sales	Ratio of Deal Value to EBITDA	Ratio of Deal Value to EBIT
Apr-95	IBRD	MCRC (UK)	—	100	$11.1	1.2	17.8	27.9
Apr-95	Quintiles	Benefit (France)	73	27	16.0	3.2	n.a.	n.a.
Apr-95	Quintiles	SDCRA (US)	100	—	3.4	0.7	n.a.	n.a.
Aug-95	PPD	Gabbay (UK)	—	100	0.5	0.5	5.6	8.6
Aug-95	APBI	LCRC (UK)	—	100	4.2	1.2	4.6	6.0
Sep-95	Quintiles	GDRU (UK)	—	100	9.2	1.2	9.6	13.9
Jan-96	Collaborative	GFI Pharm. (US)	33	67	6.8	1.1	15.2	22.8
Apr-96	Clintrials	Bio-Res. (Can)	—	100	59.5	2.4	20.4	28.5
Apr-96	Quintiles	Lewin Health (US)	—	100	$30.0	1.3	n.a.	n.a.
Averages					**$15.6**	**1.4**	**12.2**	**18.0**

Proposed Kendle International Acquisitions

Date	Acquiror	Target	Payment (%) Stock	Payment (%) Cash	Value ($m)	Ratio of Deal Value to Sales	Ratio of Deal Value to EBITDA	Ratio of Deal Value to EBIT
May-97	Kendle	U-Gene (NL)	—	100	$15.6	1.2	9.8	12.0
Jul-97	Kendle	gmi (Germany)	23	77	$12.3	1.8	8.2	8.8

Source: Technomark Consulting Services Ltd. (for comparable acquisition); Kendle company documents, casewriter calculations (for proposed Kendle acquisitions).

EXHIBIT 9 | Kendle Pro Forma Income Statements after Acquisitions and IPO

(in thousands, except EPS)	For the Year Ended December 31, 1996					1st Qtr
	Actual Kendle	Actual U-Gene	Actual gmi	Pro Forma Adjustments	Consolidated Pro Forma	3/31/97 Pro Forma
Net revenues	$ 12,959	$ 12,508	$ 6,996	—	$ 32,463	$ 11,230
Costs and expenses:						
Direct costs	8,176	8,108	4,894	—	21,178	6,437
Selling, general and administrative	3,278	2,783	597	—	6,658	2,714
Depreciation and amortization	316	320	105	965	1,706	496
Total costs and expenses	11,770	11,211	5,596	965	29,542	9,647
Income from operations	1,189	1,297	1,400	(965)	2,921	1,583
Interest expense	(65)	—	—	—	(65)	(31)
Other income	10	7	45	—	62	33
Income before income taxes	1,134	1,304	1,445	(965)	2,918	1,585
Income taxes		465	658	210	1,333	686
Net income	$ 1,134	$ 839	$ 787	$ (1,175)	$ 1,585	$ 899
Shares outstanding	3,653	—	—	3,803	7,457	7,481
EPS	—	—	—	—	$ 0.21	$ 0.12
Memorandum Item						
EBITDA	$ 1,505	$ 1,617	$ 1,505	—	$ 4,627	$ 2,079

Note: The pro forma income statements assume that U-Gene and gmi were acquired on January 1, 1996.

In the pro forma adjustments, amortization was increased by $965 to reflect the 30-year, straight-line amortization of goodwill from the two acquisitions.

Income taxes were increased to reflect the shift of Kendle to a taxable C Corporation.

Shares and share-equivalents outstanding were increased to reflect:

3,000 new shares issued in the IPO;

218 shares issued to sellers of gmi;

154 warrants issued to NationsBank as part of the acquisition financing; and

432 options exercised at the time of the offering.

Source: Kendle company documents, casewriter estimates.

EXHIBIT 10 | Kendle Pro Forma Balance Sheets after Acquisitions and IPO

(in thousands)	Actual Kendle	Actual U-Gene	Actual gmi	Pro Forma Adjustments	Consolidated Pro Forma
			As at March 31, 1997		
ASSETS					
Current assets:					
Cash and cash equivalents (overdrafts) (a)	$ (1,150)	$ 879	$ 2,560	$ 10,379	$ 12,668
Receivables—trade	4,379	3,540	1,597	—	9,516
Unreimbursed project costs	2,610	—	—	—	2,610
Other current assets	137	386	91	—	614
Total current assets	5,976	4,805	4,248	10,379	25,408
Net property and equipment	2,441	1,073	149	—	3,663
Other assets	266	73	—	400	739
Goodwill	—	—	—	24,960	24,960
Total assets	$ 8,683	$ 5,951	$ 4,397	$ 35,739	$ 54,770
LIABILITIES AND SHAREHOLDERS' EQUITY					
Current Liabilities:					
Capital lease obligations (current portion)	$ 342	$ —	$ —	$ —	$ 342
Trade payables	1,923	1,508	831	—	4,262
Dividends payable	—	140	—	—	140
Income taxes payable	—	—	1,160	(400)	760
Accrued liabilities	471	1,051	796	—	2,318
Billings in excess of costs and advances	3,535	1,555	182	—	5,272
Total current liabilities	6,271	4,254	2,969	(400)	13,094
Capital lease obligations, less current	1,155	—	—	—	1,155
Pension obligation	—	175	—	—	175
Note payable to U-Gene owners	—	—	—	1,560	1,560
Deferred taxes	—	—	—	25	25
Total liabilities	7,426	4,429	2,969	1,185	16,009
Shareholders' equity (b)	1,257	1,522	1,428	34,554	38,761
Total liabilities and shareholders' equity	$ 8,683	$ 5,951	$ 4,397	$ 35,739	$ 54,770

Note: The pro forma consolidated balance sheet as of March 31, 1997 assumes that U-gene and gmi were acquired on that date.

Source: Kendle company documents.

EXHIBIT 10 | Kendle Pro Forma Balance Sheets after Acquisitions and IPO

Explanation of Significant Pro Forma Adjustments (in thousands)

(a) Cash and Cash Equivalents:		(b) Total Shareholders' Equity:	
Net proceeds from IPO	$ 35,000	Net proceeds from IPO	$ 35,000
Cash component of U-Gene acquisition	(14,040)	Shares issued to gmi owners	2,827
Cash component of gmi acquisition	(9,483)	Exercise of warrants	1,502
Costs of temporary debt financing	(398)	Purchase of U-Gene equity	(1,522)
S Corporation distribution to Kendle owners	(700)	Purchase of gmi equity	(1,428)
	$ 10,379	Write-off of unamortized debt discount	(1,100)
		S Corporation distribution	(700)
		Deferred tax from shift to C Corporation	(25)
			$ 34,554

EXHIBIT 11 | Market Valuation of CRO Industry

(millions except per share and ratios)	Quintiles	Covance	PPD	ClinTrials	Parexel	Premier
Income Statement Items: 1996						
Sales	$ 537.6	$ 494.8	$ 197.8	$ 93.5	$ 88.0	$ 15.3
EBITDA	77.4	90.5	25.4	12.7	8.8	2.2
Net Income	$ 5.2	$ 12.7	$ (3.5)	$ 6.8	$ 4.6	$ 1.1
Common Shares Outstanding	66.3	57.1	21.6	17.9	15.6	4.4
EPS	$ 0.08	$ 0.22	$ (0.16)	$ 0.38	$ 0.29	$ 0.24
Balance Sheet Items: Dec 31, 1996						
Cash	$ 99.7	$ 25.4	$ 36.0	$ 38.1	$ 46.4	$ 1.5
Total Assets	518.0	451.0	181.5	157.0	102.4	5.7
Total Liabilities	373.7	340.3	66.2	31.6	41.2	3.2
Total Long Term Debt	168.7	163.0	1.4	–	0.4	–
Total Stockholders' Equity	$ 144.3	$ 110.7	$ 115.3	$ 125.4	$ 61.2	$ 2.5
Liabilities/Stockholders' Equity	2.59	3.07	0.57	0.25	0.67	1.28
LT Debt/Total Capitalization	0.54	0.60	0.01	–	0.01	–
Market Data: April 30, 1997 (a)						
Stock Price	$ 25.44	$ 14.75	$ 16.75	$ 7.75	$ 28.00	$ 9.63
Market Value	$ 1,686.5	$ 841.7	$ 362.2	$ 138.4	$ 437.5	$ 42.4
Stock Price Beta (b)	1.04	n.a.	n.a.	1.16	1.32	n.a.
Valuation Multiples:						
Value/1996 Net Income	323.6	66.2	(103.3)	20.3	95.1	39.6
Value/1996 Sales	3.1	1.7	1.8	1.5	5.0	2.8
Value/1996 EBITDA	21.8	9.3	14.3	10.9	49.5	19.1

Notes: (a) U.S. Treasury interest rates: 1-year = 6.0%; 10-year = 6.9%; and, 30-year = 7.1%.

(b) The stock price beta is based on monthly data from the date of the company's IPO through February 2000.

Source: Standard & Poor's Compustat, Bloomberg, casewriter calculations.

EXHIBIT 12 | CRO Industry Stock Prices

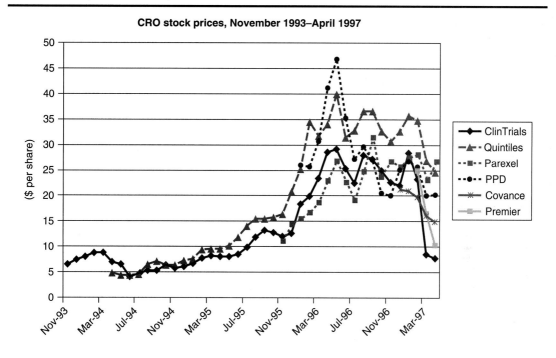

CRO stock prices, November 1993–April 1997

Initial Public Offerings

Offer Date	Issuer	Offer Price	Shares Offered (mil)	Gross Proceeds ($mil)
23-Nov-93	ClinTrials	$9.00	2.00	$18.00
20-Apri-94	Quintiles	19.50	2.00	39.00
22-Nov-95	Parexel	15.00	2.18	32.73
24-Jan-96	PPD	18.00	2.00	36.00
10-Jun-96	Collaborative	13.50	3.00	40.50
03-Feb-97	Premier	$17.00	2.75	$46.75

Source: Securities Data Corporation.

RightNow Technologies

Unlike most case protagonists, Greg Gianforte, founder and CEO of RightNow Technologies, was not sitting at his desk and was not staring out the window. There was no point in looking outside—in Bozeman, Montana in December, the forecast was pretty reliable: Bright, cold and snowy. Instead, Gianforte was playing with his kids. It was the only way he could stop himself from obsessing about a bit of good news RightNow had received. The previous week, a large software company had made him a very attractive acquisition offer. If he accepted it, Christmas would come early in the Gianforte household.

Six years earlier, in 1997, Gianforte had come up with an idea for a software product that would help companies respond to their customers' emails. He founded RightNow with $5,000 of his own money. By the end of 1997, the company had booked about $20,000 in revenue. By December 2003, RightNow's annual revenues had grown to over $35 million.

Between 1997 and 2003, RightNow had experienced a lot of ups and downs, but mostly ups: There had been a period of clever bootstrapping. Then a round of venture capital. Continued customer adoption. A failed IPO attempt. Another round of venture capital. A major strategic shift. Rapid expansion. An influx of experienced management. And now came the next key decision for Gianforte: Was it time for an exit?

As Gianforte saw it, there were three viable options for RightNow:

1. Accept the acquisition offer, pocket a lot of money, and work to grow RightNow's products within a larger organization.

2. Plan for an IPO in 2004—with no guarantee that the markets would be receptive to a software offering.

3. Put aside thoughts of an exit for the time being and focus on continuing the company's strong record of growth.

Professor William A. Sahlman and Research Associate Dan Heath prepared this case. HBS cases are developed solely as the basis for class discussion. Cases are not intended to serve as endorsements, sources of primary data, or illustrations of effective or ineffective management.

There was debate within the board of directors and the senior management team about which option to pursue. RightNow's senior team felt strongly that the company had an enormous opportunity to grow: Customers liked RightNow's solution and there were plenty more customers in the market. There was mixed opinion, though, about the best way to grow. Some felt that RightNow would be strongest as an independent company, while others felt that RightNow stood to gain more from the resources of a larger parent.

Structurally, RightNow was a benevolent dictatorship. Through the years, Gianforte had managed to keep a 60% equity stake in the company. This made his opinion rather important. Before he could contemplate the matter any further, his daughter poked him on the leg, irritated by his momentary distraction from playtime. He promised himself that he would postpone any further consideration of the issue until after the weekend was over. Or at least until his daughter was in bed.

RightNow Background: From Hoboken to Bozeman

Gianforte was a technology guy. (See **Exhibit 1** for biographies of the management team.) He graduated with a degree in electrical engineering and a masters degree in computer science from Stevens Institute of Technology. In 1986, three years after he graduated, he founded a company called Brightwork Development. Brightwork developed network management applications.

After spending eight years building Brightwork, Gianforte sold the company to McAfee in 1994 for about $10 million. McAfee retained Gianforte to direct the unit's North American sales operations. In 1995, having earned enough money to retire, Gianforte left McAfee and relocated to Bozeman, Montana. Gianforte had become enamored with Montana on a junior-high-school backpacking trip, and he thought it would be a good place to raise his 4 kids.

His retirement did not last long. He fished and hiked and skied, but it was not enough to hold his attention. He was antsy. Gianforte said, "After selling Brightwork, I had the 'money box' checked off. But I didn't want my tombstone to say, 'He caught a lot of fish.'" He resolved to start another software company.

Montana was an unlikely spot for a software startup. It is safe to say that Montana was not on most entrepreneurs' short-lists of high-tech hot spots. For one thing, Montana averaged only 6 inhabitants per square mile. And it had a lot of square miles. As a thought experiment, imagine that you gathered all the people from the 10 most-attended college football games in the U.S. on a given weekend, and then scattered them over a region the size of Germany. That was Montana.

Bozeman had only 27,500 people, most of whom were associated with Montana State University. Gianforte was not deterred by the geographic limitations. He believed he could find the employees he needed from the educated local workforce. He also thought he could attract others based on the town's natural beauty. He set a goal for himself: to add 2,000 high-paying tech jobs to the community.

In early 1997, Gianforte started trying to decide what kind of company to start. Given the times, it was inevitable that the Internet would play a role in the decision. He mapped out the landscape of available software, hoping to find a gap that he could fill.

Eventually, he thought he had discovered an opportunity: to provide software that would help companies deliver customer service over the Internet, a growing need as the Internet became more widely adopted.

The Art of Bootstrapping

Having successfully sold Brightwork, Gianforte would have had no trouble raising venture capital to fund his idea. As he said, "The knee-jerk approach to starting a company is to write a business plan. Then, you raise a bunch of money and pitch the money on a bonfire, hoping that a company turns up before you run out of money." Gianforte was determined to bootstrap his new company.

An article in *Inc. Magazine* described Gianforte's bootstrapping approach, once he had identified the idea for a customer-service product:

> [He] started trying to sell that nonexistent product. Armed with a data sheet outlining what such a product might do, Gianforte sat in a spare bedroom and cold-called customer-support managers at hundreds of companies. After talking them through the sheet, he told them that the product would be released in 90 days and asked whether they would use that type of software on their web sites. If someone said no, he asked why. Sometimes the potential customer needed a feature that Gianforte hadn't thought of. If he thought that he could deliver it in 90 days, he added it to the data sheet.
>
> Some might say that Gianforte was peddling vaporware—the much-criticized practice of hyping the imminent release of new software that is far from ready. Gianforte disagrees. The key is not to promise anything that can't be delivered within the specified time frame. "You never want to lie to your customers," he says. What he did, he says, is "really sales as a method of market research. It allows you to determine very quickly, without much money, if you have a viable business idea."[1]

Gianforte aggregated the feedback he got from his customer calls, using it to create a spec sheet for his first software product. Then, he locked himself away for six weeks, coding a product that he admits was "very minimal, bare bones."

With a product in hand, he began to sign up customers. He tried to take price out of the equation by offering bargain-basement deals—a few thousand dollars for a two-year lease, for instance. Sometimes he gave the product away for free. With no expenses— he was the only employee and was operating out of an extra bedroom—Gianforte could afford to go slow on revenue. He was less interested in large-revenue deals than in finding out whether customers would embrace the product.

From fall 1997 to spring 1998, Gianforte closed deals with about 40 customers. He was still the only person in the company. He said, "Some entrepreneurs don't like sales very much. They do it only because they have to, and as soon as they can, they hire someone else to do the selling. They may even feel that there's something a little bit sleazy about calling up strangers for money. Yes, sales can be hard work. No one likes making cold calls. But sleazy? On the contrary, I think sales is actually the noblest part of business. It's the part that brings the solution together with the customer's need."

---

[1]Emily Barker, "Start with Nothing," *Inc. Magazine* (February 2002), http://www.inc.com/search/23855.html

Convinced by the 40 adoptions that his business model was viable, Gianforte was ready to start hiring. Over the next few months, he hired five employees. All five were sales reps. The hiring pattern was not a coincidence. Gianforte said, "I really believe that sales is the only job that has to be done well in building a business. To this day, I keep a sign on my desk in my office that says, 'Nothing happens until somebody sells something.'"

Early-Stage Product Development

In August 1998, Mike Myer became employee #8. He was recruited to RightNow from Lucent Technologies in New Jersey and became RightNow's Vice-President of Development.

Myer was the guy who had to build the products that the RightNow sales team was selling. "One of the frustrations in the early days came from Greg's philosophy, 'Don't confuse selling with shipping.' We'd get ourselves in situations where we had to develop a product in response to something we sold. At times that was a challenge. The hard part was staying focused on building the product we wanted to build, while also taking care of the customer-specific features that were getting us our sales."

The first generation of the product was described as a "self-service knowledge base." People who came to a company's web site could search on the knowledge base and get relevant answers returned to them—potentially saving the company from paying for the costs of a customer service interaction. From the beginning, RightNow was an application service provider (ASP). This meant that customers were buying software that was hosted remotely and provided to them over the Internet. The ASP model of software delivery was a sharp departure from the norm in the software industry. The norm was for completed software products to be burned onto disks, shrink-wrapped, shipped, and then installed locally on a company's intranet.

Before the Internet, the ASP model would have been technologically impossible. In 1998, the ASP model had become feasible, but customers were skeptical of the concept. Software was perceived as a product—something that should be owned. RightNow, and other ASP vendors, were proposing a huge paradigm shift: Software would be provided as a *service,* something that could be leased by the month. At the time, it was as peculiar as the idea of leasing one's music collection.

Myer said, "In those days, there were no significant ASP-based companies. Most of the ASP experiments involved taking existing applications and putting them on the network. The problem was that those applications weren't designed to share a lot of customers on the same system. It was a completely different approach to software architecture."

The ASP model faced ingrained customer resistance, but it also offered huge advantages to a startup such as RightNow. First, since the software was hosted on RightNow's own servers and delivered over the Internet, it created a bias internally toward open-source solutions. Myer believed this gave RightNow a lot of development advantages, such as more flexibility and a greater ability to leverage existing tools.

Second, the model allowed RightNow to show rather than tell. The product could be demonstrated to any customer with a browser. This, in turn, made telesales possible, eliminating the huge expense of a field sales force. Gianforte would pay Montana State

University students $8 an hour to customize the demo so that it had the look and feel of the prospect's own web site. For less than $20 and the cost of a phone call, the product could be demonstrated anywhere in the country. Even better, if a deal was closed, the service could be activated very quickly.

Third, the ASP model enabled RightNow's development team to iterate the software design much faster than is possible in the shrink-wrap model. Myer said, "In the shrink-wrap-and-ship model, you do an incredible amount of quality assurance testing. You do beta tests. You observe the product in use at its site. You have to do these things because you lose control of it once it's installed. With the ASP model, you can launch sooner and fix problems on the fly based on real time customer feedback."

Rapid Growth and Financing Needs

From the fall of 1998 to the fall of 1999, RightNow experienced enormous internal growth, increasing the size of the company from 8 employees to 80. Business had been doubling in sales every quarter. RightNow desperately needed management help in finance.

Gianforte found a candidate named Susan Carstensen, who had been the CFO of Powerhouse Technologies, a publicly-traded $200 million diversified gaming technology company. Powerhouse had recently been sold, and Carstensen was looking for a new opportunity. Carstensen and Gianforte began talking in August 1999, and her first day was October 14, 1999.

Looking back on her to-do lists from October and November 1999, Carstensen had to laugh. "Here's what Greg needed to get done: Hire accountants, bankers, and lawyers. Get audits done. Change hosting operations. Put in place new financial systems. Implement benefit systems. Set up revenue recognition policies. Develop cash reporting and forecasting process. And prepare for an IPO. I said, 'Oh, is that all?'"

Talk had begun internally about an IPO. Though RightNow was doing only $2 million in revenue in 1999, it was the heyday of the Internet bubble. Companies were going public with much less to show for themselves. Carstensen said, "Our competitors at the time, such as eGain and Kana, were going public. Everybody was going public. It was the way to get the visibility we needed. There was enthusiasm all around."

But RightNow needed money for growth sooner than an IPO would allow. Gianforte was finally ready to take some investment. On the basis of previous experience, he knew he wanted to work with Roger Evans at Greylock Capital. Gianforte needed to raise at least $5 million, which would be used to open up European offices and further expand the sales force. Greylock, though, was not interested in a round that small.

Eventually, a deal was struck. In December 1999, RightNow closed a $16.4 million round, led by Greylock. Summit Partners also participated. The post-money valuation was $100 million.

The 2000 IPO Attempt

A month later, investment banks were flying to Bozeman to pitch their services. Gianforte and Carstensen eventually selected Credit Suisse First Boston (CSFB). By April 2000, the company had filed its S-1. Then, the market tanked. The NASDAQ index fell by 25% in one week. In this environment of panic, the IPO had to be postponed.

By the end of August, the NASDAQ had almost recovered to its pre-crash level. The team thought that its new window would be in October. They restarted the road show, visiting investors in Europe and the Midwest U.S. The timing once again proved inhospitable. By the end of September, the NASDAQ had slipped back down by 15%.

Carstensen said, "We met with investors, they liked us, and they liked the story, but there was just too much chaos in their world. There was an investor in Chicago; he looked at us and said, 'You guys are great, but you're like a really good house in a bad neighborhood. You shouldn't be doing this right now.' Greg and I could see the writing on the wall."

Gianforte remembered the moment the IPO was postponed indefinitely: "We were sitting on the tarmac in Kansas City. We could feel that it wasn't working. We had a conference call with our bankers, and we told them, 'Listen, we're not going on to San Francisco, we're going back to Bozeman.' It's done." On November 21, 2000, the company filed its request for withdrawal of the IPO with the SEC.

Looking back, Carstensen was grateful that the company did not make it public. She said, "In reality, our financials didn't support being a public company at that stage. We were too small. I think there would've been a negative side to going public so early, with only a couple million dollars in revenue. As all the market caps continued to go down, we would have become a microcap. There would have been the perception of a busted IPO. We would have had all the distractions of being a public company without any of the positive visibility that we wanted in the first place."

Having withdrawn its IPO, the company faced another problem: It was running out of cash. Carstensen said, "The only problem with taking venture capital is that you're supposed to spend it. Fortunately, we had not spent it quite as fast as some would have liked. But we still needed another round."

One year and one day later after its first round of venture capital, RightNow closed on a $16 million Series B round, led by Summit Partners. The post-money valuation was $129 million. The step-up in valuation was underwhelming, given the company's explosive growth in 2000: Revenues had exploded from $2 million in 1999 to $11.3 million in 2000. (See **Exhibit 2** for selected financial data on RightNow.)

However, the NASDAQ's see-sawing had spooked venture capitalists. Now, the valuation from the Series A round looked generous in retrospect. All things considered, Gianforte and Carstensen were pleased to have an influx of cash with good terms and a minimum of management distraction.

A New Strategic Focus

With money in the bank and the distraction of an IPO eliminated, the management team entered 2001 with a focus on the basics: winning customers and improving the product. By the summer of 2001 there was new anxiety internally. The company's strategy had not been thoughtfully examined since the fall of 1997. The board knew that the company had executed well on the company's original vision of five years ago, but this was high technology, where whole markets can come and go within 18 months. The question on the board members' minds was: Are we still pursuing the right vision?

The board felt it was time to bring in someone who could bring a new focus to the company's strategy. A consummate networker, Greg Gianforte began working through his Rolodex and connected with Sean Forbes. At the time, Forbes was a Vice President at Trilogy software, running their Automotive Business Unit alongside one of Trilogy's founders.

Forbes (HBS 1996) was initially skeptical whether he should pursue the opportunity. He was not sure that his background was a fit with the marketing position, and he had concerns about Bozeman. Making the decision to join more challenging was Forbes' discovery that RightNow's board had appointed and then fired two other senior marketing executives within the last 12 months. And, in the same period, a third hire into the position had quit after just one day on the job. "There was an open question in my mind if *any* company officer carrying the marketing title wasn't predestined for failure at RightNow," said Forbes.

However, after taking a closer look at RightNow, and spending time with Greg and his family, Forbes eventually signed on. He explained: "What I saw in Greg and the company he'd founded was a fundamentally better approach to software. Both from a perspective of delivery model, and an unwavering insistence on high ethical standards that had been driven to the core of the company's culture. It wasn't hard to see the writing on the wall across the rest of enterprise software. My team at Trilogy had just completed a deal with a major auto manufacturer worth nine figures against competition in the final rounds from Oracle. That customer and the rest of my business unit's installed base were clearly signaling they were at the end of their rope with any engagement that didn't include demonstrating solution capability in minutes or days as opposed to quarters or years."

Forbes joined RightNow in the fall of 2001 and was given six months to perform a technical and operational due diligence, come up with a new strategic direction, new business plan, and alignment around both across the executive team and board of directors.

At the beginning of the process, Forbes got both the board and executive team to agree that any new strategy and associated operational plan must be able to:

4. Drive leadership in the space (#1 or #2 market share as measured by revenue)
5. Deliver 50–99% year-over-year revenue growth
6. Achieve profitability within 18 months after the restart

Achieving early consensus on these goals would prove critical to success. The high bar set by the three criteria effectively eliminated many potentially contentious discussions around less promising opportunities. Time was short. Forbes was all too aware of the fate of his three predecessors. He said, "Given the previous turnover and cross-territorial sensitivity of the questions needing to be addressed, agreement on the framing of the problem was critical, or you were going to be set up for a high-profile professional failure."

In April 2002, Forbes and the management team presented the proposal to the board. Gianforte started the meeting by saying, "Guys, we've put this presentation together over

almost six months. It takes 45 minutes. I'm not allowing any questions until the end."
Looking back at his presentation, Forbes summarized the message he delivered:

> To date, we have built and sold an ancillary piece of web self-service software. I am
> proposing that we move into fully-featured customer service software and then use that as
> a beachhead to move across to the other two segments of CRM [customer relationship
> management]: marketing automation and sales force automation. CRM is where the best
> market opportunity is for our company's capabilities and where on-demand software is
> going to go. We will be picking a fight with big competitors, like SAP, Siebel, and Oracle.
> But, with the right execution, we can beat them. They have a long track record of over-
> promising and under-delivering—and in doing so they have built an incredible repository
> of discontent.
>
> Our ultimate target customer is in the upper mid-market. There is a latent demand
> there that lies just below the full enterprise application level. And, it's a market that the big
> guys can't afford to pursue with their $500,000 per year Armani-clad sales guys.

One hundred and thirty pages of detailed plans—translating the strategy into an operations plan—backed up the presentation. The board was impressed. Roger Evans, not
known for effusive praise, reacted with a sentiment that was shared across the board of
directors: "This is the single most important and best piece of work I've seen."

Strategic Transition and a New Sales Operation

By June of 2002, RightNow had returned to generating positive cash flow after a year
and a half of outflows. Gianforte, pleased with the company's financial position and the
new strategic and operational direction, gave Mike Myer the green light to double the
size of the engineering team.

To implement the new strategy, Myer would essentially have to rewrite the software
from the ground up. The development was staged so that, as each new layer of the product
was developed, it could be sold into RightNow's increasingly large customer base.

In addition to the changes in the product, the strategy and operations plan called for
quickly transforming the company's traditional product-selling sales force into a solutions-
selling direct channel. There would be less telesales and more field sales, more focus on
sales of professional services, larger average selling prices, and longer sales cycles.

Gianforte began the recruiting process while serving as temporary head of sales. He
set three ironclad requirements for the candidate: He/she (1) needed to have built a
sales organization of at least a half-billion dollars, and preferably over a billion dollars;
(2) must want to do it again, with all the work that entails; (3) must have the same
commitment to integrity that Gianforte believed existed within the organization.

Gianforte reviewed over 400 candidates. He flew 50 candidates to Bozeman for
interviews and, astonishingly, made no offers. Fortunately, after an exhausting 18-month
search, he found the right candidate: Peter Dunning, who had built SAP's Global
Accounts Group over an eight-year period to a 1,200 person team that had accounted
for over $1 billion in revenue. Dunning signed on in August 2003.

Meanwhile, during these internal transitions, the company continued to grow. In
2002, the company did $26.9 million in revenue, and in 2003, the company was on track

to do about $35 million. This was fast growth but slower than the company had experienced during the dot-com boom.

By late 2003, optimism was high internally. The new, full CRM solution suite was headed toward release. The sales operation had new leadership. Analysts were beginning to take serious notice of RightNow. Together with SalesForce.com, a competitor in the on-demand CRM space, RightNow had helped to re-legitimize the ASP space. And then, in December, Gianforte received a phone call.

The Offer and the Options

The call was from the top executive at a software company. The company was much larger than RightNow, and it stood to lose from RightNow's continued success advancing the on-demand model. The executive was impressed by RightNow's assault on his company's traditional territory and felt that the combination of the two companies would be powerful. He was not shy about proposing an acquisition.

As talks developed, Gianforte began to get a sense of the value of the offer. It would be an all-stock deal. No specific number was laid out at the time, but valuation metrics were discussed, which helped Gianforte estimate the potential price range. The acquirer talked about a multiple of many times sales, which was appropriate for comparable market-leading software companies at that time. (See **Exhibit 3** for valuation data on selected public software companies and **Exhibit 4** for data on recent software M&A transactions.) It sounded as though the acquirer was willing to pay this multiple on RightNow's revenue run rate—approximately $50 million—rather than the company's trailing 12-month sales of $35 million. (See **Exhibit 5** for RightNow's internal financial forecasts for 2004.)

Another benchmark was related to the venture capitalists in the deal. It would be difficult to get their consent on an acquisition without a step-up of at least 2–3 times the last round's post-money valuation. Without such an increase in value, the VCs might be tempted to gamble on an IPO. The acquirer knew this and was comfortable that they could meet or exceed the expectation range.

When delivered, Gianforte and Carstensen were impressed by the offer. As Carstensen said, "From a financial standpoint, when compared to relevant public company comparables and transactions, it was a fair offer. From a current market perspective, I would have no trouble advising that we take it. But the strategic perspective is harder to assess in quantitative terms."

The board and the senior management team wrestled with those strategic issues. Forbes offered, "The debate was one about wealth creation—one about how much potential value in the market we could create with the resources at our disposal under various liquidity scenarios. A related question was how quickly we were likely to capture that value before competitive pressures began, starting the process of commoditization that all markets eventually evolve through. There were varying beliefs about these questions. And, there was one nine digit and multiple other eight digit personal wealth creation events at stake."

With equity control of the company, Gianforte knew the decision would ultimately rest on his shoulders. He evaluated the strengths and weaknesses of the three options available to him.

Option 1: Accept the Acquisition and Grow within a Larger Organization

RightNow's competitors were vastly larger. Siebel, for instance, had over 40 times RightNow's revenue. RightNow had not yet created a market-wide fight in the CRM space. It might take years—or, pessimistically, decades—for RightNow to achieve the kind of scale its competitors had.

Achieving quick scale was one of the most attractive features of an acquisition. Gianforte said, "Our biggest challenges are achieving market-leading solution breadth, securing widespread distribution, and enhancing our visibility. An acquisition would immediately contribute to all three. In an acquisition scenario, we'd potentially no longer have those problems. We'd be plugged into a vast resource pool."

The offer itself was also attractive. It was a credible, fair offer, which spoke well of the acquiring company. While everyone in the management team believed RightNow could achieve enormous growth, there was another issue that nagged at them: valuation. Being valued at a market-leading multiple of sales was attractive indeed. What if they could not take this valuation metric for granted? What if the company stayed independent and achieved spectacular revenue and profit growth—but its valuation did not change much, as valuation metrics became less generous? Warren Buffett, for instance, would not have valued any company at the revenue multiples implied in the offer.

Option 2A: Reject the Acquisition and Plan for an IPO in 2004

Some members of the management team bristled at the idea of accepting the embrace of "the enemy." The consensus strategic view among top management was as follows: The CRM market was moving toward on-demand solutions—the day of the $100 million contract with a 3-year installation period was over. RightNow was in the pole position for on-demand CRM. They would grow, and their competitors would shrink. The management team believed that, in this new space, the advantage would go to the new entrants rather than the incumbents.

Once the competitors resolved to attack the on-demand space, some members of RightNow's management team believed it might be too late for them to make up the lost ground. Specifically, Gianforte believed that there were four key factors that would keep them from competing well in the on-demand CRM space:

1. They'd have to rewrite their software from scratch for the needs of the on-demand environment.

2. The ease of implementation of the on-demand model would obviate the need for the layers of consultants that surrounded the big CRM players. These consultants would fight a business model change with everything they had.

3. A switch to on-demand would make it hard for the big CRM players to keep Wall Street happy. As they abandoned big up-front contracts for an annuity revenue stream, there would be a "gap period" where the numbers would appear to be terrible. Would they have the fortitude to ignore the pressure to hit their quarterly numbers?

4. The on-demand model, with its emphasis on renewals, would require a culture shift from "closing deals" to "ongoing customer satisfaction." Given the size of the organizations, this could be a wrenching change.

There was also an element of quasi-religious fervor in the RightNow culture. Some CRM competitors were routinely referred to as "evil"—only half-jokingly. Gianforte spoke of "returning respect and legitimacy to the enterprise software space." What would happen to morale if the acquirer's offer was accepted?

There were two other practical concerns with respect to the offer. First, an all-stock deal would mean that RightNow was betting on the currency of its acquirer. If traditional enterprise software was in decline, would RightNow—after its absorption—be enough to keep the stock price strong?

Second, there was a critical data point forthcoming in the next nine months. Sales-Force.com had filed for an IPO. (See **Exhibits 6 and 7** for an excerpt and selected financial data from SalesForce.com's S-1.) SalesForce.com was the company most comparable to RightNow in the on-demand space. RightNow moved into CRM from a strength in customer service. (See **Exhibit 8** for a screenshot from RightNow's customer-service software. The screenshot shows what the software would look like from a service agent's perspective.) SalesForce.com was moving into CRM from a strength in sales force automation. SalesForce.com had spent on the order of 50 times what RightNow had spent on marketing since inception and consequently, it had achieved greater brand visibility than RightNow.

Carstensen discussed the value of waiting for SalesForce.com's IPO: "The other player with a very similar business model in our space is SalesForce.com. They are due to go public within a few months. We don't know how the market is going to value a real, on-demand company. We have been testing the theory of the on-demand business model—with high visibility and recurring revenues—on analysts and investors for years. The feedback has always been positive and encouraging, but to date, companies have not been rewarded for the model with higher multiples. Realistically, there have been no legitimate test cases. Will the market value the business model more like an Internet subscription company—with higher multiples—or like a traditional 'software & services' firm? In other words, will SalesForce.com be perceived more like Siebel or like eBay? The ramifications for us are enormous. After working for six years on this business, is it wise for us to make a decision before seeing this data point?"

Talk had begun internally about a second attempt at an IPO. Investment banks were salivating to get RightNow's business. But the market for tech IPOs was still depressed, and there were not many optimistic signs in the marketplace. SalesForce.com had generated enormous buzz over the years, which would help it overcome the market's inertia. It was unclear whether RightNow could go public alone without the same brand cachet.

Option 2B: Reject the Acquisition Offer and Continue to Grow Organically

The arguments for rejecting the acquisition offer were the same as in the IPO scenario. But there was also a debate about whether an IPO was the next logical step for the company.

Gianforte was a proselytizer for bootstrapping. In fact, he was working on a book about bootstrapping. (See **Exhibit 9** for a "bootstrappers' quiz" from Gianforte's book.) Part of him thought that he should keep his head down and focus on the core business of pleasing customers. Selling the business—to an acquirer or to the public—could come later. The scars from the 2000 IPO attempt had not fully healed.

And RightNow did not really need the cash infusion from an IPO. It was cash-flow positive and had been for some time. Furthermore, there were costs to being a public company. Some costs were very tangible, such as the costs of complying with the Sarbanes-Oxley legislation. Gianforte ballparked these costs at about $1 million per year—not chicken feed, given the size of the company.

Another cost was management distraction. Inevitably, top management would have to spend more hours worrying about investors' needs and fewer hours worrying about customers' needs. This bothered Gianforte and seemed inconsistent with his relentless focus on customer satisfaction and selling.

On the other hand, if visibility was one of RightNow's biggest problems, then the IPO would presumably help address it. As Gianforte said, "Our customers read the business press: *Forbes, Fortune,* and the *Wall Street Journal.* These publications don't generally write about private companies. We need to raise our financial profile, to be taken more seriously. As a public company, we'll get more coverage. Customers can see our balance sheet and feel confident about our stability." In essence, in Gianforte's mind, the IPO was another form of marketing.

Gianforte's Decision

The Bozeman winter was conducive to reflection, since it was often too cold to function outside. Gianforte thought about his pledge to create 2,000 jobs in Bozeman. At the moment, he was about 1,600 jobs short, but he wasn't finished. Not by a long shot.

He believed he had a chance to create one of the next great software companies. He could envision a RightNow with hundreds of millions—perhaps billions—in sales and thousands of employees. He was also aware, though, that technology changed rapidly. Markets changed rapidly. He could make a lot of good people rich—today, with no risk—by accepting the acquisition offer. Or he could bet their wealth—and his—on the notion that RightNow could grow faster and better on its own.

Gianforte was not much of an agonizer. He had a strong bias toward action. Having analyzed the issues in his head for a week, and having debated them with the board and his top management team, he felt he knew enough to make a decision. He had made up his mind. He called his board to tell him the conclusion he had reached.

EXHIBIT 1 | Biographies of RightNow Management Team

Greg Gianforte, CEO, President, Chairman and Founder

Greg's work leading RightNow builds on 15 years of success in the computer/Internet industry, including 11 years with Brightwork Development and McAfee Associates. Greg founded Brightwork, a developer of network management applications, in 1986. With 75 employees and software installed on more than 150,000 Novell systems nationwide, Greg sold the company to McAfee Associates in 1994. Retained by McAfee, he grew the company's North American sales operation from $25 million in revenues to more than $60 million in under a year. During Greg's tenure, McAfee was selected by *Fortune Magazine*—based primarily on its Internet selling approach—as one of the "10 Coolest Companies in America."

In June of 2003, Ernst & Young awarded Greg the Pacific Northwest 2003 Entrepreneur of the Year for the software category. A panel of independent judges evaluated the excellence and extraordinary success of outstanding entrepreneurs in such areas as innovation, financial performance, and personal commitment to their businesses and communities. Greg holds a BE in electrical engineering and an MS in computer science from Stevens Institute of Technology.

Susan Carstensen, CFO, Vice President of Finance and Administration, Treasurer

Susan is a 19-year veteran of corporate financial management. At RightNow she oversees the company's Finance, Information Technology and Human Resource organizations and serves on the company's executive management team. She joined RightNow in 1999 following 5 years at Powerhouse Technologies, a $200 million publicly traded diversified gaming technology company. At Powerhouse, Susan held various positions in finance and audit, advancing to chief financial officer in 1997. She was a key player in the organization's financial turnaround, culminating in the 1999 sale of the company. Susan's earlier experience includes 3 years in financial management with Martin Marietta Astronautics Group and 6 years with Ernst & Young. Ms. Carstensen, CPA, holds a BS in Business and a BA in Political Science from Montana State University.

Peter Dunning, Executive Vice President for Worldwide Field Operations

Peter has a proven track record with more than 29 years of rapidly growing revenues for a variety of established and private companies. At RightNow Peter oversees the worldwide sales, pre-sales, channels, professional services and customer service organizations and is a member of the company's executive management team. As EVP of SAP's Global Accounts Group, Dunning led a 1,200-person team that accounted for over $1 billion in revenue. He was then recruited by Oracle as SVP Worldwide Applications and Vertical Markets to lead a 2,500-person team. Dunning helped grow the applications business from zero to 25% growth rate. Dunning also ran 50% of Oracle's global vertical markets. Prior to RightNow, he was EVP and General Manager with S1 Corporation, a $280 million publicly traded financial services software provider headquartered in Atlanta, Georgia. Mr. Dunning holds a Bachelor of Business Administration degree with the University of Georgia.

Sean Forbes, Vice President of Marketing and Business Development

Sean joined RightNow in 2001 and runs the company's strategy, marketing, product management and business development efforts. He leads the company's cross-departmental planning operations and serves on the executive management committee. Sean comes to RightNow from Trilogy, where he was a vice president of business development. Before Trilogy, Sean was a consultant with Bain & Company's Private Equity Group in Boston and Moscow. Sean is a decorated veteran of the United States Navy. He received his MBA from Harvard and his BS in Mechanical and Aerospace Engineering from Cornell.

Mike Myer, Vice President of Development

Mike leads the company's product design, development and quality assurance efforts and serves on the executive management team. Mike brings to RightNow extensive experience in computer research and product development gained at AT&T/Lucent Technologies/Bell Labs. At Bell Labs Research, which he left in 1998 to join RightNow, Mike developed a first-generation DSL System, a breakthrough for high-speed consumer Internet access over existing phone lines. At Lucent, Mike was a lead developer in the redesign of AUDIX, the company's highly successful voice-messaging product. He also took part in the introduction of several innovations in voice-message networking topologies. At AT&T, he was a principal architect for an operations support system (the world's largest at the time) designed to accommodate 1,000 support technicians simultaneously. Mike has an MS degree in Computer Science from Rutgers University.

Source: Company web site.

EXHIBIT 2 | RightNow Technologies, Selected Financial Data

	(in thousands)					
	1998	**1999**	**2000**	**2001**	**2002**	**2003**
Consolidated Statements of Operations Data:						
Revenue:						
Software, hosting and	$ 279	$ 1,806	$ 10,549	$ 18,998	$ 23,338	$ 29,300
Professional services	0	219	758	2,009	3,603	6,579
Total revenue	279	2,025	11,307	21,007	26,941	35,879
Cost of revenue:						
Software, hosting and	3	378	3,306	4,636	4,279	5,263
Professional services	0	11	485	1,335	2,156	3,740
Total cost of revenue	3	389	3,791	5,971	6,435	9,003
Gross profit	276	1,636	7,516	15,036	20,506	26,876
Operating expenses:						
Sales and marketing	279	3,017	20,756	22,050	15,939	20,809
R&D	74	603	3,639	4,584	4,117	5,915
G&A	86	493	3,375	3,973	2,842	3,518
Total op. expense	439	4,113	27,770	30,607	22,898	30,242
Income (loss) from operations	−163	−2,477	−20,254	−15,571	−2,392	−3,366
Interest and other income (exp), net	0	32	607	229	−357	−215
Income (loss) before income taxes	−163	−2,445	−19,647	−15,342	−2,749	−3,581
Provision for income taxes	—	—	—	—	—	−539
Net income	−163	−2,445	−19,647	−15,342	−2,749	−4,120

	1999	**2000**	**2001**	**2002**	**2003**
Consolidated Balance Sheet Data:					
Cash and cash equivalents	$ 14,183	$ 17,128	$ 6,258	$ 8,038	$ 8,360
Working capital (deficit)	13,114	9,033	−6,553	−6,082	−9,024
Total assets	17,349	28,741	18,625	23,102	29,386
Deferred revenue	4,165	17,160	18,875	24,683	35,553
Long-term debt, less current portion	7	—	1,185	940	484
Redeemable convertible preferred stock	16,120	31,075	32,340	32,373	32,398
Total stockholders' deficit	−3,980	−23,345	−38,683	−41,291	−45,254

Source: SEC filings.

EXHIBIT 3 | Selected Data on Comparable Public Companies

Company	Ticker	11-7-2003 price	Mkt. Cap.	CY Rev 03	CY Rev 04	Growth 03/02	Growth 04/03	MCap/ Rev 03	MCap/ Rev 04	P/E 03	P/E 04	Cash	Debt	EV*	EV/ 03 Rev	EV/ 04 Rev
Siebel Systems	SEBL	13.84	7,364.7	1,337.3	1,406.2	−18.2%	5.2%	5.5	5.2	115.3	49.4	2,027.0	10.3	5,348.0	4.0	3.8
E.Piphany, Inc.	EPNY	7.43	547.8	93.5	104.0	11.5%	11.3%	5.9	5.3	Nm	Nm	255.9	0.0	291.9	3.1	2.8
Kana Software	KANA	3.30	92.7	60.2	69.0	−23.9%	14.6%	1.5	1.3	Nm	Nm	35.7	3.4	60.4	1.0	0.9
Chordiant Software	CHRD	4.52	295.5	67.7	82.8	−8.4%	22.4%	4.4	3.6	Nm	41.1	32.7	2.1	264.9	3.9	3.2
SAP	SAP	38.55	47,906.1	7,912.0	8,540.0	−4.5%	7.9%	6.1	5.6	37.8	33.2	2,115.0	0.0	45,791.1	5.8	5.4
PeopleSoft, Inc.	PSFT	22.47	8,028.6	2,254.5	2,836.7	15.7%	25.8%	3.6	2.8	35.7	25.5	1,648.6	0.0	6,380.1	2.8	2.2

*EV = Enterprise value.
Source: Pacific Growth Equities report, November 7, 2003.

EXHIBIT 4 | Data on Selected M&A Transactions in the Software Industry

				($ Millions)		
Announce Date	Buyer	Seller	Seller Description	Adjusted Price	Seller Revenue*	Adjusted Price/Revenue
11/18/03	CHINADOTCOM CORP (CDC SOFTWARE HOLDINGS INC)	PIVOTAL CORP	Provides customer relationship management solutions.	$ 43.7	$ 56.1	0.78x
10/27/03	SYMANTEC CORP	ON TECHNOLOGY CORP	Provides remote software and content management solutions.	$ 82.1	$ 34.6	2.37x
10/7/03	MELITA INTERNATIONAL INC	CONCERTO SOFTWARE INC	Provides contact center software solutions.	$ 107.0	$ 103.3	1.04x
8/6/03	INTERWOVEN INC	IMANAGE INC	Develops collaborative content management software products that enable document, collaboration, workflow and knowledge	$ 136.7	$ 42.7	3.20x
7/21/03	EASTMAN KODAK CO	PRACTICEWORKS INC	Provides practice management software applications, e-commerce services and electronic data interchange services.	$ 420.4	$ 111.9	3.76x
7/18/03	BUSINESS OBJECTS SA	CRYSTAL DECISIONS INC	Provides business intelligence software and services including enterprise resource planning and customer relationship management.	$ 741.9	$ 270.0	2.75x
4/21/03	DENDRITE INTERNATIONAL INC	SYNAVANT INC	Provides customer relationship management and e-business applications, interactive marketing and server and database management.	$ 37.7	$ 166.4	0.23x
3/25/03	BMC SOFTWARE INC	IT MASTERS INTERNATIONAL SA	Provides enterprise management solutions that allow customers to model and visualize IT infrastructure components.	$ 42.0	$ 10.0	4.20x
12/19/02	COGNOS INC	ADAYTUM INC	Provides enterprise performance planning	$ 159.3	$ 57.0	2.79x
9/22/02	BMC SOFTWARE INC	PEREGRINE SYSTEMS INC (REMEDY ASSETS)	Provides best practice service management applications, including IT service management and customer service and support solutions.	$ 350.0	$ 250.0	1.40x
3/12/02	ASCENTIAL SOFTWARE CORP	VALITY TECHNOLOGY INC	Provides enterprise data quality management software used in applications such as enterprise resource planning applications.	$ 92.0	$ 21.2	4.34x

*Trailing 12 months.
Source: Broadview.

EXHIBIT 5 | Internal RightNow Forecasts for 2004

Consolidated Statements of Operations Data:	2004
Revenue:	
Software, hosting and support	$ 48,000
Professional services	12,000
Total revenue	60,000
Cost of revenue:	
Software, hosting and support	8,400
Professional services	5,880
Total cost of revenue	14,280
Gross profit	45,720
Operating expenses:	
Sales and marketing	32,000
Research and development	6,500
General and administrative	5,000
Total operating expenses	43,500
Income (loss) from operations	2,220

Note: These numbers have been disguised—they differ somewhat from actual company projections for reasons of confidentiality.

Source: Company.

EXHIBIT 6 | Excerpt from SalesForce.com S-1, Filed 12/18/2003

SECURITIES AND EXCHANGE COMMISSION

FORM S-1

REGISTRATION STATEMENT

salesforce.com, inc.

Salesforce.com is the leading provider of application services that allow organizations to easily share customer information on demand. We provide a comprehensive customer relationship management, or CRM, service to businesses of all sizes and industries worldwide. By designing and developing our service to be a low-cost, easy-to-use application that is delivered through a standard Web browser, we substantially reduce many of the traditional expenses and complexities of enterprise software implementations. As a result, our customers incur less risk and lower upfront costs. Our service helps customers more effectively manage critical operations including: sales force automation; customer service and support; marketing automation; document management; analytics; and custom application development. We market our services on a subscription basis, primarily through our direct sales efforts and also indirectly through partners. From the introduction of our service in February 2000 through October 31, 2003, our customer base had grown to approximately 8,000 subscribing customers, with an aggregate of over 110,000 paying subscribers in approximately 70 countries.

The pervasiveness of the Internet, along with the dramatic declines in the pricing of computing technology and network bandwidth, have enabled a new generation of enterprise computing in which substantial components of information technology, or IT, infrastructure can be provisioned and delivered dynamically on an outsourced basis. This new computing paradigm is sometimes referred to as utility computing, while the outsourced software applications are referred to as on-demand application services. On-demand application services enable businesses to

(continued)

EXHIBIT 6 | Excerpt from SalesForce.com S-1, Filed 12/18/2003 (*continued*)

subscribe to a wide variety of application services that are developed specifically for, and delivered over, the Internet on an as-needed basis with little or no implementation services required and without the need to install and manage third-party software in-house. The market for on-demand application services is projected to grow from $425 million in 2002 to $2.6 billion in 2007, which represents a compounded annual growth rate of 44 percent, according to a May 2003 report by International Data Corporation, or IDC, an independent market research firm.

We believe that the CRM applications market, which was approximately $7.1 billion in 2002 according to a July 2003 report by IDC, is one of the first to benefit from on-demand application services. CRM applications are intended to enable businesses to automate sales, customer service and support and marketing. Despite the significant potential benefits that can be attained from CRM, many enterprises have failed to successfully deploy the CRM applications that they have purchased for a variety of reasons including the difficulty and relatively high cost of implementing and maintaining enterprise applications, as well as the historically low rates of user adoption and lack of ubiquitous access that have contributed to lower returns on investment in CRM deployments.

From inception, our service has been specifically designed to provide customers with robust CRM solutions on an outsourced basis through our proprietary, scalable and secure multi-tenant application architecture. Key benefits of our solution include:

Rapid deployment.   Our service can be deployed rapidly and provisioned easily, since our customers do not have to spend time installing or maintaining the servers, networking equipment, security products or other infrastructure hardware and software necessary to ensure a scalable and reliable service.

Enable high levels of user adoption.   We have designed our service to be easy-to-use and intuitive. Since our service contains many tools and features recognizable to users of popular websites such as those of Amazon.com, eBay and Yahoo!, it has a more familiar interface than typical CRM applications. As a result, our users do not require substantial training on how to use and benefit from our service.

Lower total cost of ownership.   We enable customers to achieve significant savings relative to the traditional enterprise software model. Our service enables customers to automate sales, customer service and support and marketing processes without having to make large and risky upfront investments in software, hardware and implementation services and additional IT staff.

Extensive features, functionality and configurability.   We offer a comprehensive array of CRM capabilities across sales, customer service and support and marketing that meet the needs of businesses of any size. We also enable customers to tailor important characteristics of our service to meet their unique requirements without the use of significant IT resources.

Secure, scalable and reliable delivery platform.   We built and maintain a multi-tenant application architecture that has been designed to enable our service to scale securely, reliably and cost-effectively to tens of thousands of customers and millions of users.

Ease of integration.   We have developed a set of application programming interfaces, or APIs, which we provide on a platform we call sforce, that enable customers and independent developers to integrate our service with existing third-party, custom and legacy applications and write their own application services that integrate with our service.

Our objective is to be the leading provider of on-demand application services for businesses worldwide. To achieve this objective we intend to:

- continue to lead the industry transformation to on-demand application services;
- strengthen and extend our service offering;
- pursue new customers and new territories aggressively;
- deepen relationships with our existing customer base; and
- encourage the development of third-party applications on our sforce platform.

EXHIBIT 7 | Selected Financial Data from SalesForce.com S-1, Filed 12/18/2003

	Fiscal Year Ended January 31,		
	2001	2002	2003
Consolidated Statement of Operations:			
Revenues:			
Subscription and support	$ 5,022	$ 21,513	$ 47,656
Professional services and other	413	896	3,335
Total revenues	5,435	22,409	50,991
Cost of revenues(1):			
Subscription and support	1,730	3,718	7,199
Professional services and other	1,692	2,329	3,164
Total cost of revenues	3,422	6,047	10,363
Gross profit	2,013	16,362	40,628
Operating expenses(1):			
Research and development	3,366	5,308	4,648
Marketing and sales	25,392	25,234	33,145
General and administrative	6,855	8,317	12,958
Lease abandonment (recovery)	—	7,657	—
Total operating expenses	35,613	46,516	50,751
(Loss) income from operations	−33,600	−30,154	−10,123
Interest income	1,715	755	572
Interest expense	−42	−272	−178
Other income (expense)	63	8	98
(Loss) income before provision for income taxes and Provision for income taxes	−31,864 —	−29,663 —	−9,631 —
(Loss) income before minority interest	−31,864	−29,663	−9,631
Minority interest in consolidated joint venture	193	425	292
Net (loss) income	$ −31,671	$ −29,238	$ −9,339

	As of January 31,			
	2000	2001	2002	2003
Consolidated Balance Sheet Data:				
Cash, cash equivalents and short-term marketable securities	$ 12,609	$ 22,200	$ 11,709	$ 16,009
Working capital	12,053	20,163	5,867	1,310
Total assets	14,196	37,047	29,084	39,421
Convertible preferred stock	17,156	59,852	61,137	61,137
Accumulated deficit	−5,452	−37,123	−66,361	−75,700
Total stockholders' deficit	−3,878	−29,329	−51,977	−56,127

Source: SEC filings.

EXHIBIT 8 | Screenshot of RightNow's Customer Service Product

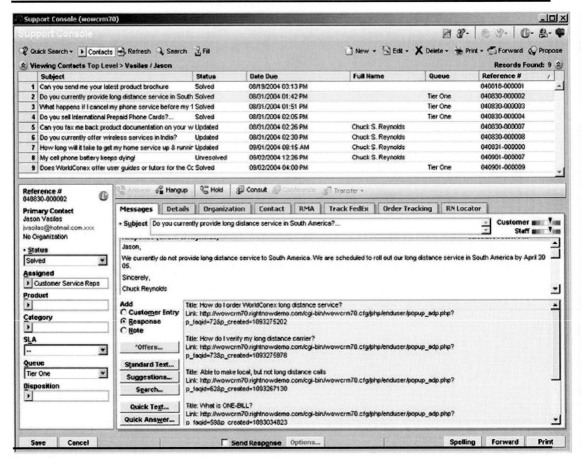

Source: Company.

EXHIBIT 9 | Quiz: Test Your Bootstrap Ability

1. **What should you do first?**
   A. Write a business plan and then try to raise money.
   B. Call lots of people to understand the issues in your market.
   C. Develop a prototype of your product idea.
   D. Hire a marketing consultant.

2. **You have an idea. What next?**
   A. Implement the business plan.
   B. Rent office space and buy used office furniture.
   C. File for a patent.
   D. Fax or email your idea to 300 people and then call them.

3. **You have a good product. Next?**
   A. Find a good intellectual property lawyer to protect your idea.
   B. Build a prototype and you personally start selling.
   C. Try to raise money.
   D. Hire a salesperson to sell your product.

4. **You find a prospect. Next?**
   A. Explain that you would like to have them join your beta-test program.
   B. Try to get them to place an order.
   C. Tell them you don't have the product available yet.
   D. Tell them all about the features you are going to add to the product.

5. **Your product does not do everything a prospect wants. You should?**
   A. Tell them it won't do those things.
   B. Get them to pay for the enhancements.
   C. Take the order and tell them it will ship in 4 weeks.
   D. Explain why those things are difficult to do and convince them to buy the current product.

6. **A major publication calls, saying they are writing a big article about your product and they want you to buy an ad in the same issue of their magazine. You have enough money for the ad, but not much more. You should:**
   A. Buy the ad.
   B. Tell them your advertising budget is already committed.
   C. Tell them you don't have enough money.
   D. Tell them to get lost.

7. **You are still getting started and Dun & Bradstreet is asking for company info and detailed financial data. You should:**
   A. Give them the information they are asking for.
   B. Politely decline.
   C. Refer them to your accountant.
   D. Don't return their call.

(continued)

EXHIBIT 9 | Quiz: Test your Bootstrap Ability (*continued*)

8. **A major prospect says they want to fly out to visit you, but you are still working out of your house. You should:**
   A. Tell them you are just getting started and don't have an office that will accommodate a visit.
   B. Rent office space prior to the visit and get your family and friends to occupy all the desks.
   C. Tell them you will be traveling the week they want to visit.
   D. Borrow your accountant's office and hang your shingle over theirs the day of the visit.

9. **You are the only person working full time in the business and you are asked how many employees you have. Tell them:**
   A. We have 50 employees.
   B. We have 20 employees.
   C. I'm the only one.
   D. We have 5 people involved in the business.

10. **You've just made your first sale and generated your first monthly profit. You should:**
   A. Give yourself a raise.
   B. Get that bigger office you have wanted.
   C. Throw a party.
   D. Hire a consultant.

Gianforte's answers:

(1) B; (2) D; (3) B; (4) B; (5) B or C; (6) B; (7) B; (8) A; (9) D (involved includes spouse, accountant, printer, lawyer, insurance agent, and yourself); (10) C (and enjoy it!)

Score yourself:

Number correct	Classification
0	Bureaucrat—think about public office.
1	
2	
3	
4	Find a big company and call it home.
5	
6	
7	You can work in a startup.
8	
9	
10	Bootstrapper. You've got what it takes.

Source: Company.

Jamie Dimon and Bank One (A)

On a personal level, I've actually been having the time of my life because I'm thrilled to be back at work. This will probably be my last real professional job because I don't want to ever do this again, but I am actually pretty comfortable we're going to make this a great company.

Jamie Dimon, Chairman and CEO Bank One[1]

It is unclear whether even Hercules could turn around the company by himself—this is not an easy turnaround story.

CSFB analyst[2]

Jamie Dimon, Chairman and CEO of Bank One, the fifth largest bank in the United States, reviewed the outline of the Board presentation he would deliver in a few weeks. Over the past three months, since the Bank One Board of Directors had hired Dimon to resurrect the beleaguered bank, Dimon had tirelessly immersed himself in Bank One's operations to understand the challenges facing the company. Now, in late June 2000, Dimon felt he needed to synthesize his findings and deliver an action plan to the Board.

When Dimon arrived at Bank One in March 2000, he discovered a bank that had very serious problems. A number of mergers had not been fully integrated and political infighting was rampant throughout the company. Overhead spending was not under control and morale among the 83,000 employees was low. Loan quality, a key measure of a commercial bank's health, was extraordinarily weak. Moreover, First USA—Bank One's credit card unit—had lost millions of customers who had grown increasingly dissatisfied with poor customer service and relatively high interest rates. Finally, Dimon discovered IT and accounting systems that needed improvements in order to upgrade service levels, manage customer profitability, and improve management accountability.

---

[1] 2Q00 investor meeting, July 19, 2000.

[2] Michael L. Mayo and David A. Hendler, Credit Suisse First Boston, March 27, 2000.

Professor Paul W. Marshall and Research Associate Todd Thedinga prepared this case. HBS cases are developed solely as the basis for class discussion. Cases are not intended to serve as endorsements, sources of primary data, or illustrations of effective or ineffective management.

While he had expected to find significant operational challenges, the extent of Bank One's problems surprised even Dimon, a seasoned veteran of financial services company turnarounds. As a longtime protégé of Sandy Weill, now Chairman of Citigroup, Dimon had helped turn around Commercial Credit Corp., and build the company through acquisitions into Citigroup, the world's largest financial services firm. But now that he was out from under the shadow of Weill, some cynics questioned how a "New York banker" like Dimon was going to save a severely distressed, regional Midwestern bank. However, the stock market had been very positive about Dimon's appointment. By the day after he joined the company the market capitalization jumped $6 billion, more than 20%. But by late June, the stock had given back those gains and was hovering in the high $20s, down from a high of $55 less than a year before. In keeping with his philosophy that leaders "should eat their home cooking," Dimon purchased two million shares of Bank One at a cost of $57 million.

As Dimon prepared to flesh out his turnaround plan which he would present to the Board in a few weeks, he began to prioritize the action items he had outlined. Dimon, a very hands-on manager, wanted to build another world-class financial services firm. He knew that many people, including Bank One employees and Wall Street investors, had a lot at stake. As one of Bank One's largest individual shareholders, now Dimon did too.

Background—Bank One[3]

Bank One began in 1870 as City National Bank (CNB) in Columbus, Ohio. CNB was run as a family business, and in 1958 John G. McCoy became president following his father's death. John G.'s mission was "to provide financial services to people," whom he believed chose a bank solely based on convenience. John G. insisted that approximately 3% of earnings were set aside for R&D in hopes of identifying ways that technology could improve convenience, efficiency and customer service. In 1966, CNB was the first bank to offer credit cards outside of California by introducing the City National BankAmericard (now VISA). In 1969, the company introduced the forerunner of the automated teller machine (ATM).

In the late 1960s and throughout the 1970s, CNB grew rapidly through acquisitions. The company acquired 22 small Ohio banks, each under $100 million in assets, within a holding company that eventually became Banc One. In 1984, John G. retired and his son, John B., became CEO and president. The leadership transition came at a time when state banking laws were changed to allow bank holding companies to acquire banks in other states. In 1985, Bank One began rapidly acquiring banks, first in Indiana, and then in Kentucky, Wisconsin, Texas, Arizona, and Louisiana. These acquisitions were much larger than those previously undertaken in Ohio.

In June 1997, Banc One acquired credit card giant First USA Inc. for $7.9 billion. The company proceeded to aggressively grow the credit card portfolio through acquisitions, but began to experience increased customer attrition in 1999.

---

[3]Portions of this section were excerpted from the 1982 HBS case: "Banc One Corporation and the Home Information Revolution," No. 682-091, originally prepared by Dr. Karen Freeze and Professor Richard Rosenbloom; and the 1990 HBS case: "Banc One Corporation 1989," No. 390-208, originally prepared by Professor Rosabeth Moss Kanter and Paul S. Myers.

In October 1998, Banc One consummated the largest transaction in its history, the $18.9 billion merger with First Chicago NBD, itself the result of a 1995 merger between First Chicago and Detroit's NBD Bancorp (see **Exhibits 1a** and **1b** for Banc One and First Chicago NBD's acquisition history from 1993 to 1998). First Chicago NBD had a reputation for being conservative, a stark contrast to the entrepreneurial culture of Banc One. However, the consensus was that the long-term benefits to consumers would outweigh the short-term challenges to culture clashes between Banc One and First Chicago NBD in the new Bank One. Bank One spokesman Tom Kelly said at the time: "Customers don't immediately need new checks. They go to the same branches, the same ATM machines that they always did. The merger will be completed, but it won't make a difference in the world to customers in the short-run."[4] John McCoy became the CEO of the merged bank, which was headquartered in the former First Chicago NBD offices in Chicago. The Board of Directors was comprised of 22 directors, 11 from each of the former banks.

By mid-1999, Bank One had over $260 billion in assets, making it the fifth largest U.S. bank behind Citigroup, Bank of America, Chase, and J.P. Morgan. Despite the company's large size, however, it remained primarily a regional bank with a strong presence in the Midwestern and Southwestern U.S. (See **Exhibit 2** for a map of Bank One's footprint).

However, Bank One began to have problems. On August 24, 1999, Bank One announced earnings would be $500 million pretax less than expected. In November, the company told analysts that 1999 earnings would be still lower. The company attributed the problems to ongoing difficulties at the First USA credit card unit.

Michael Mayo, CSFB equity analyst, predicted that Bank One's management would continue to destroy shareholder value in 2000 and 2001 (see **Exhibit 3** for Mayo's estimate for Bank One's return versus its cost of capital). Indeed, the increasing consensus on Wall Street was that Bank One's troubles foreshadowed more bad news. As one analyst put it: "Bank One has weakened significantly over the past several months, primarily because of bad news at First USA—and we think there could be more bad news to come. In our opinion, management credibility—at a low before the latest earnings guidance—has sunk even further, and we think credibility cannot be restored in the near term."[5]

In the last three months of 1999, four top executives left the company, including head of commercial banking, head of consumer banking, head of consumer finance and head of credit cards. In December, John B. McCoy stepped down as Chairman and CEO and the company notified Wall Street that they were searching for another CEO. Meanwhile, the current Bank One President and former First Chicago NBD Chairman and CEO Verne Istock—who was told he would be considered a candidate for the permanent CEO position—was named interim CEO and Bank One director John Hall was named interim Chairman. On January 11, 2000, the company announced it was discontinuing the traditional biannual stock dividend and taking a $725 million restructuring charge to

---

[4]Cliff Edwards, "First Chicago NBD, Banc One Merger Forms Nation's Fifth-Largest Bank," *AP Newswire,* October 1, 1998.

[5]Thomas H. Hanley and Jennifer A. Thompson, "Bank One," Warburg Dillon Read, November 22, 1999, p. 1.

TABLE A | Special Charge-Offs

Special Pretax Charges 4Q 1999 ($ millions)	
Charge-offs and consumer reserve additions resulting from FFIEC[6]	197
FirstUSA asset impairment	187
Indirect auto lease residual value	80
Restructuring and other charges	261
Total	725
Per share	$0.42

Source: Company reports.

fix First USA and other areas of the company (See **Table A** for a breakdown of the restructuring charge). The company also said that already-delayed system conversions for Michigan and Louisiana would be delayed by another year.

The deteriorating performance at Bank One led to increasing divisiveness within the Board. John Hall recalled the rising tensions:

> The legacy Banc One directors thought the legacy First Chicago NBD directors were too slow moving. In contrast, the legacy First Chicago NBD directors thought the legacy Banc One directors were a bunch of cowboys. Also, the legacy First Chicago NBD directors favored a tightly controlled organization versus the decentralized style developed under the old Banc One model. Each side blamed the other for the company's problems. The board's size made it that much harder to bridge the gap and move forward.

Background—Jamie Dimon

Dimon grew up in New York City, with an older brother, Peter, and a fraternal twin brother Ted (see **Exhibit 4** full bio). Dimon's early interest in financial services could be traced to his father and grandfather, both top stock brokers at the brokerage firm Shearson. Dimon worked at Shearson one summer while on break from Tufts College and learned the securities industry up close.

In addition to an education in the securities industry, Shearson provided Dimon with a good vantage point from which to study Sandy Weill, the successful financial services entrepreneur. Several years earlier, Weill's firm, CBWL, had acquired the brokerages Hayden Stone and Shearson. Dimon's parents, who had become friends of Sandy and Joan Weill, at one point gave Sandy a copy of an economics term paper that Dimon had written on the Shearson takeover by CBWL Hayden Stone. Weill was impressed and he sent Dimon a note: "Terrific paper. Can I show it to people here?" Dimon wrote back to Weill: "Absolutely. Can I have a summer job?"[7]

---

[6]The Federal Financial Institutions Examinations Council (FFIEC) is a regulatory body that provides oversight to depository and other financial services firms. In order to comply with FFIEC uniform code, Bank One was required to maintain certain levels of reserves.

[7]Monica Langley, *Tearing Down the Walls: How Sandy Weill Fought His Way to the Top of the Financial World . . . and Then Nearly Lost It All* (New York: Simon & Schuster, 2003), p. 50.

After graduating from Tufts, Dimon worked in management consulting for two years before entering Harvard Business School, where he spent the summer at Goldman Sachs. In 1982, when he was about to graduate Harvard Business School as a Baker Scholar, Weill asked Dimon to work for him at American Express, where Weill had become Chairman of the executive committee following American Express' acquisition of Shearson. Dimon, who had offers from Goldman Sachs, Morgan Stanley, and Lehman Brothers, seized the opportunity to be Weill's apprentice.

In 1985, about three years after Dimon joined Weill at American Express, Weill was forced out of the company. Dimon had the option to continue at American Express, join another Wall Street firm, or work for Weill, whose plans were unclear. Although Dimon and his wife Judy—whom Dimon had met when they were classmates at Harvard Business School—had just had their first daughter, they decided that Dimon should pursue the relatively riskier option of working for Weill. Weill and Dimon set out to find a financial services firm in need of a turnaround. It took more than a year for them to identify Commercial Credit Corp., a troubled consumer-lending subsidiary of Control Data Corporation, and then convince Control Data to spin off Commercial Credit in an initial public offering.

Building a Financial Services Empire[8]

Weill and Dimon, the Chief Financial Officer, began to drastically cut costs at Commercial Credit, reducing headcount and benefits and replacing guaranteed bonuses with stock options. Weill and Dimon quickly developed a turnaround approach that they would implement in subsequent deals: Fix the company's balance sheet, cut costs, hire talented managers, and motivate the workforce to behave like owners, rather than employees.

With the Commercial Credit turnaround under way, Weill and Dimon began to look for the next acquisition. In August 1988, they acquired Primerica, another "Middle-America" financial services firm, which included the prestigious Smith Barney brokerage franchise. A year later they acquired sixteen Drexel, Burnham & Co. branches and 221 BarclaysAmerican/Financial branch offices. In 1990, Dimon was named President of Primerica. In 1992, Primerica announced it was investing $722 million for a 27% stake in the insurance giant Travelers.

In 1993, Weill and Dimon purchased Weill's former company, Shearson, from American Express. The combined Smith Barney Shearson brokerage had 11,400 brokers and almost 500 branches.[9] Later that year, Weill and Dimon took on their largest turnaround to date, buying the remainder of Travelers, and Dimon became President and Chief Operating Officer of Travelers Group. As in the case of many previous mergers and acquisitions, Weill and Dimon adopted the takeover candidate's name for the combined company. They also continued to reduce costs and to increase revenues through aggressive cross-selling: for example, Smith Barney brokers were encouraged to sell Traveler's insurance products to their customers.

---

[8]Much of this section is based upon *Tearing Down the Walls: How Sandy Weill Fought His Way to the Top of the Financial World . . . and Then Nearly Lost It All* (New York: Simon & Schuster, 2003).

[9]Ibid., p. 211.

By the end of 1997, Weill and Dimon had created a financial services giant under the Travelers' umbrella. They had recently acquired Salomon Brothers, and Dimon became the Chairman and co-CEO of Salomon Smith Barney with former Salomon head Deryck Maughan.

In April 1998, Travelers and Citibank announced the $70 billion merger of their companies, at the time the largest in history. Weill and Citibank CEO John Reed would be co-CEOs of the combined company, now called Citigroup. Along with Deryck Maughan and Citibank executive Victor Menezes, Dimon was named co-CEO of the global corporate and investment banking divisions. Dimon also took on the title of Citigroup President.

Then, in the fall of 1998, Weill fired Dimon at a weekend executive retreat. After receiving the news, Dimon addressed the executive team: "I've been with this company fifteen years. I put my heart and soul into it. I want to tell you it's a fabulous place. Keep making yourself proud."[10] The following day, as he left the Citigroup building for the last time, Dimon reiterated his feelings to a colleague, "Look what we've all built together. It still goes on, and I'm proud of that."[11]

Year in Exile

Dimon spent the remainder of 1998 and 1999 without full-time employment, spending a lot of time traveling and reading. He took up boxing, drove across country visiting friends, and spent six weeks in Europe with Judy and their three daughters. Meanwhile, the 42-year-old Dimon considered his next move. Some observers expected Dimon to go into semi-retirement—helping to build the Citigroup empire had left Dimon wealthy and he certainly didn't need to go back to work. Dimon spent time doing non-profit work and thought about what challenges he wanted to take on next. As he recalled:

> I thought a lot about what I should be—an investor, a merchant banker, an executive? Did I want to work at a big or small company? Did I want to return to financial services, or try something new? The more I thought about it, I loved the challenges of a big company, especially a company that needed a lot of improvement. But I didn't want to just preside over a liquidation. I wanted a fixable problem.

Dimon was approached by Home Depot, WebVan, Amazon.com, Starwood Hotels and Resorts, and many financial services companies, but nothing seemed to be the right fit. By his own admission, Dimon knew that "he was a financial services guy" and he thought that the next opportunity would be in that industry. Still, as 1999 wore on, Dimon began to wonder whether the right opportunity would ever come along.

Hiring Jamie Dimon

In January 2000, the Bank One Board formed a search committee consisting of three directors from legacy Banc One and three directors from legacy First Chicago NBD (see **Exhibit 5** for Board of Directors and Search committee composition). As interim

---

[10]Ibid., p. 319.

[11]Ibid., p. 321.

Chairman and member of the search committee John Hall recalled, the Bank One Board viewed their task as "no less than to find the best person in the United States to lead us back to the top."[12]

At the beginning of the search process, Bank One hired a consulting company to conduct a study of the company's culture. The findings revealed a divide between the legacy Banc One and the legacy First Chicago NBD employees. The study concluded that someone from the outside would have a better chance than an internal candidate of bridging the cultural gap among the workers and successfully turning around the bank.

The search firm Russell Reynolds, which was hired to manage the search process, pared an initial list of 150 candidates down to 25 finalists. Then the search committee reviewed the candidates, and interviewed 15 of them in detail. Verne Istock, the interim CEO, was automatically considered as a finalist.

James Crown, a legacy First Chicago director, recalled how Jamie Dimon stood out from the other candidates: "Jamie met with the Board and made a very convincing presentation about where he would focus his energy in the beginning. It was clear he had seen this movie before. He had the experience of cutting costs and bringing organizations together, something we clearly needed."

Dimon recalled one of the final interviews with the directors:

> I told them how I think a company should be run. I went through a whole litany of issues, including how I thought my first 100 days as CEO would play out. I thought it was very important that we all understood what needed to be done, and how it would get done. It's kind of like getting married. If they didn't think I was the right person for the job, that was fine. But I didn't want to deceive them about who I really was in the hopes that it would get me the job.[13]

In March 2000, the Board of Directors met to decide between the two finalists, Verne Istock and Jamie Dimon. John Hall asked each director to share who they considered to be the better candidate. A passionate debate ensued. Several legacy Banc One directors pointed to the culture study and the merits of bringing in a leader from the outside, while some of the legacy First Chicago NBD directors argued in support of Istock, who already had extensive knowledge of the organization and its challenges.

On March 27, Bank One announced the decision to hire Jamie Dimon. "Jamie's fresh perspective and his ability to galvanize employees also set him apart from an exceptional field of candidates from around the country," John R. Hall told reporters.[14]

The analysts, however, were not convinced Dimon was the best candidate. Michael Mayo of CSFB commented: "Mr. Dimon has limited commercial banking experience, still 27% of earnings and an area at Bank One with undifferentiated competitive positioning. He also has less experience with large credit card operations since Travelers had a small presence. A mitigating factor is his likely ability to attract capable managers who can handle the situation."[15]

---

[12]John R. Engen, "Hiring a Celebrity CEO," *Corporate Board Member Magazine,* Winter 2000.

[13]Ibid.

[14]Anita Raghavan and Jathon Sapsford, "Embattled Bank One Names Dimon as Its Chairman, CEO," *The Wall Street Journal,* March 28, 2000, p. C1.

[15]Michael L. Mayo and David A. Hendler, *Credit Suisse First Boston Equity Research,* March 27, 2000.

The press release announcing his appointment also said that he had bought two million shares of Bank One at $28.38 a share, or a total of $57 million. Buying a significant stake in Bank One stock was important to Dimon since "I was going to give it my all, and this was going to be my new family." According to some estimates, Dimon would have nearly one-half his net worth tied up in the fate of Bank One.[16]

Dimon's First Hundred Days

One of Dimon's early decisions at Bank One was where to situate his office. He decided to take a relatively understated middle office along a row of other senior executives and next to a conference room, instead of the wood-paneled corner office belonging to the former CEO McCoy. Dimon wanted to be accessible and visible, and he wanted to be "in the middle of the action." Dimon also halted progress on renovations of the executive floor, resulting in a floor that was half-finished. Verne Istock remained in another corner office at the end of the hallway. Upon Dimon's arrival, Istock took the title of President and he remained a member of the Board.

Dimon called the initial phase of his turnaround plan "boot camp," emphasizing the early focus on tactics and execution. He planned to spend the bulk of boot camp—the first 100 days or so—learning the business, understanding the company's problems, strengthening the balance sheet and improving the operating margins. Longer-term strategic vision would take place in subsequent phases.

Dimon's first objective was to understand Bank One's lines of businesses, and he felt the best way to do that was to spend a lot of time meeting and listening to employees. Dimon recalled the process:

> I wanted to totally immerse myself. I knew a lot about financial services, and although I had read a lot of analyst reports about Bank One prior to my arrival, I wanted to start fresh. I really didn't know what to expect. The first thing I did was meet with lots of people— breakfast, lunch, and dinner, and in between. I would say to them, "Give me the information you're looking at."

Dave Donovan, who Dimon named co-head of capital markets three weeks after arriving, recalled Dimon's management style:

> Jamie met with me and capital markets co-head Dave Schabes every day for the first three weeks. He would spend 1 to 2 hours each time, going through items. What is this derivative? How do you price it? What's the risk? Literally, hundreds of questions. He was testing to see if we knew the details, and if we were honest enough to admit it when we didn't. He wouldn't hold it against you if you didn't know. He just wanted to make sure you would deal with problems and move on. Finally, after three weeks he said, 'We don't have to meet every day from now on.'
>
> Jamie is a unique manager—he is both a charismatic leader and a very hands-on, detailed person. He is also highly energetic. People know that he is up at five and continues to work very late with employees. That behavior continues to push employees to work harder under Jamie.

---

[16]John R. Engen, "Hiring a Celebrity CEO," *Corporate Board Member Magazine,* Winter 2000.

    In addition to meeting with employees throughout the day, Dimon began to analyze in detail the company's financial and operating data. He found that Bank One had a relatively poor efficiency ratio, the industry's definition for costs divided by revenue, and a weak balance sheet (see **Exhibit 6** for select financials and **Exhibit 7** for a financial comparison to industry competitors). In addition to the macro problems, Dimon began to analyze a variety of problems that were specific to each line of business— Commercial Banking, Investment Management, Retail Banking and First USA. He devoured as much data as he could gather from each business unit, and he began to compile a list of action items on a folded sheet of paper he called his "follow-up list." He carried this piece of paper around with him wherever he went.

Commercial Banking

Bank One's commercial banking division was the leading player in the Midwestern market primarily serving middle-market and corporate customers (**Exhibit 8** shows select business line data estimated by an equity analyst and **Exhibit 9** shows business line data reflecting organizational changes). Despite the company's regional dominance in commercial banking, however, Dimon felt the division was unnecessarily fragmented into "fiefdoms," a legacy of the previous mergers. James Boshart, who would later join the bank as head of capital markets and eventually all of commercial banking, recalled how dysfunctional the division was:

> The commercial banking division was a collection of loosely affiliated lending groups. There were no synergies at all, no concept of a unifying brand. Everyone was focused on legacy. "Where are you from?" people would frequently ask. They still thought of themselves as NBD, First Chicago, Banc One. It filtered down to the customers too—thousands of First Chicago customers had no idea they were really customers of Bank One. Also, each region had different business models and overlapping coverage maps. They were singularly focused on growing their loan book, regardless of customer profitability.

    Dimon was concerned that an unrestrained focus on lending had resulted in bad loans and a weak balance sheet. He questioned whether the loan loss reserves were adequate, but poor loan documentation and management reporting hampered the ability to get an accurate risk assessment. Bank One's credit system was developed internally, and they did not rely on Moody's, S&P or other credit rating agencies. Some managers complained that installing a new credit system would be too bureaucratic and interfere with their ability to evaluate credit. Moreover, many loan officers argued that Bank One would risk losing longstanding customers—particularly a few who were currently in financial trouble—if they focused on current credit-worthiness.

    Dimon also discovered that certain loan loss provisions were accounted for at the corporate parent. He thought this was a bad practice because it didn't charge the commercial bank the true cost of writing bad loans.

Investment Management

Investment management was one of the most profitable areas for the bank, but it accounted for only about 10 percent of earnings. Investment management sold a range of products and services, including private wealth management, mutual funds, insurance products, annuities, and a series of retirement plans. This was the area that felt the most familiar to Dimon, given both his professional experience and family background in the securities industry. If there were any problems, Dimon saw a lack of cross-selling into the bank's other areas. For example, he wanted to get more commercial banking clients to use the bank for investment management business.

Retail Banking

Bank One's retail presence began with the corporate Chicago headquarters, whose entire lobby was filled with rows of tellers. This was a leftover practice from old Illinois banking laws which originally limited the number of branch offices any bank could have. Bank One's Chicago predecessor, the First National Bank of Chicago, was forced to house literally a city's worth of tellers under one roof.

By 1999 the bank's retail presence fanned out from the Chicago headquarters, with branches across 14 Midwestern and Southwestern states, utilizing four main distribution channels. There were roughly 1,800 branches, 5,100 ATMs, 2,200 telephone bankers, and two Internet platforms, bankone.com and Wingspan.com. Retail had over 7 million household and 500,000 small business customers.

The first observation Dimon had about the retail business was that, similar to the commercial banking division, there was very poor documentation across all retail lines, including auto leases, home equity loans, and other consumer credit loans. Bad documentation made it difficult to get an accurate picture of the risk profile of the consumer loan portfolio, but one thing that was clear to Dimon was that the auto lease portfolio was particularly troubled.

Bank One's fourth quarter charge had included $80 million for the loss in residual value of auto leases in the first quarter.[17] Part of the problem was an overall trend of declining used car prices. Dimon didn't like the auto leasing business since it involves competing with car companies, which don't necessarily need to make a profit on the leasing. Dimon considered selling part of the car lease portfolio or taking further write-downs of the auto leases in the next quarter. There were signs that there could be a further deterioration in used car prices and more impairment to the auto lease portfolio.

During the first couple of months Dimon spent time visiting tellers, loan officers and customer service representatives. He continually asked people what problems they saw and what resources they needed to do a better job. As he toured many branches and several call centers, he became increasingly committed to the idea, however difficult, of maintaining headcount amongst the "employees who faced the customer."

Dimon had a reputation for taking an interest in the details of the business's operations, which was rare for a large company CEO. He recalled one visit to a call center:

> I walked into a call center and asked one of the employees how long the average response time was per in-bound call. The answer was around forty seconds. I remember almost pulling my hair out when I heard that. I had spent a lot of time in call centers during the early

---

[17]Residual value is the implied value of the car when the lease matured, and lower residual values impaired the value of the auto leases.

days of Commercial Credit and Primerica, and I knew that forty seconds was unacceptable. I stayed on the call center managers' case until they cut the response time in half.

Next Dimon turned to the Internet channels, Wingspan Bank and bankone.com. Bankone.com was the portal for all Bank One customers. Wingspan.com, launched in June of 1999, was an ambitious Internet-only bank. At the time, John McCoy had suggested the online business might be so successful that Bank One would never acquire another bricks-and-mortar branch.[18] Dimon, however, questioned the rationale of maintaining two expensive platforms. Indeed, early estimates showed that integrating the platforms could save $30 million. However, he also realized combining the systems would be expensive and it was unclear whether they could afford to combine the businesses in the near-term.

First USA

At the beginning of 1999, First USA was the second largest credit card issuer in the nation, trailing only Citigroup. At the end of 1999, First USA had more than 55 million cardmembers, 1,500 marketing partners, and $69 billion of receivables, but had recorded no growth in the second half of the year.

The biggest problem First USA faced was significant customer defections, which rose far above 10% after remaining steady below that for several years prior. The reasons included payment processing problems, low customer satisfaction, a shortening of the late-fee grace period for some customers, and a very competitive low-interest/zero percent solicitation.

First USA began changing the date after which late fees could be assessed on some accounts. This meant that customers had fewer days to pay their balance before incurring a late fee. Eventually customer wrath ensued and attrition increased. The result was declining net interest margin, the key profitability measure of the credit card business.

IT Systems

Bank One faced an enormous obstacle with its IT infrastructure. Technology decisions were currently handled by each technology group within each division. Very little centralized technology planning occurred.

Dimon, a staunch proponent of technology as a way to gain competitive edge in the financial services industry, had to decide what to do about Bank One's seven deposit networks (DDA systems), eleven loan systems, three teller platforms, and five wire-transfer arrangements. The proliferation of systems was the result of the company's past mergers and prior management's reluctance to invest in new technology or consolidating systems. The effect was an environment where it was difficult to deliver adequate customer service and it was expensive to operate. Dimon recalled the problems:

> Seven DDA systems meant that every time a customer called up, the Bank One representative had to ask what state they were from. That was so they could pull up the right system for that customer. Of course, many of our business customers did business in several states.

---

[18]Julie Johnsson, "Taking Flight with Wingspan: The Strategy behind McCoy's Mega-Marketing Push," *Crain's Chicago Business,* August 2, 1999, p. 3.

That created the even bigger issue that customers would have to keep separate accounts because we couldn't service them on a single technology platform. I knew it was going to be expensive in the short run, and it was going to take a significant portion of my time, but I was committed to moving to a single platform.

Dimon spent almost a quarter of his time during the first three months with the IT team, planning the conversion of the various systems. Immediately it became clear that many employees only wanted to preserve the IT system that was left over from their legacy bank. So when it was time to discuss converting the DDA systems, Dimon called the managers and the IT team together and spent several days discussing what functionality they needed. They generated a list of more than 100 functional requirements of the new system, and they highlighted the 20 or so that were the most important.

If Dimon was going to go ahead with the system conversion to single platform, he would have to make two major decisions. First, he would have to decide whether to use the old Banc One platform or the First Chicago platform, or start from scratch entirely. More customers were on the Banc One platform, but it had less functionality. Moreover, the Banc One system was at least $10 million more expensive to convert than the First Chicago system. Second, Dimon had to decide whether they would convert the systems all at once—the "Big Bang approach"—or follow a phased conversion plan across geographical regions. If the latter, Dimon would have to decide which regions should convert first.

First Impressions

Dimon described the first month as "performing triage and making priorities." He felt that he "couldn't take major action until he really knew what was going on." Current management reporting systems were severely hampering that effort. Meanwhile, Wall Street analysts and other observers were eagerly waiting for Dimon to articulate his turnaround plan, and analysts were calling him daily. But Dimon told Bank One's investor relations staff that he would be silent until early July, when he would put a stake in the ground and publicly reveal his plan.

Shortly after Dimon's arrival, the CFO announced he was resigning. Dimon, however, did not rush to fill the position immediately. The reason was he wanted to "advertise that he was waiting for the best people to fill those positions, even if it meant acting as the interim CFO, in addition to Chairman and CEO."

Subsequently, on May 1, Michael Cavanagh arrived as Head of Strategic Planning. Cananagh had worked for Dimon at Citigroup and he was excited to rejoin his former boss at Bank One. Cavanagh recalled his initial impression:

Jamie had told me that I was walking into a challenging situation. Jamie's attitude is "If you can track, track it," so my first job was dissecting the internal management mayhem and getting the right information. Jamie and I went through the balance sheet line by line to see exactly what our strength of capital was. The balance sheet set the tone. We also needed to understand the accounting systems. And we knew we had our own accountability. We had a few months to get everything straight before it was on our watch and we owned what happened.

Shortly after Cavanagh's arrival, Charlie Scharf joined Bank One as CFO. Scharf had started off in the financial services industry 14 years earlier as Jamie Dimon's assistant at Commercial Credit. Like Cavanagh, Scharf was excited to rejoin his mentor, and the challenging circumstances made it that much more interesting. Scharf recalled the lack of expense control he saw at Bank One:

> The senior management of the company didn't have the exposure to the expenses that you'd want to have if you were running your business with your own money. So someone who worked for me could spend four and a half million dollars and I wouldn't even know about it. There are also other items such as T&E, where the company had self-approval and I'd never seen self-approvals of anything in a company. And you can imagine what happens when you have self-approval of things.[19]

Everywhere they looked, Dimon, Cavanagh and Scharf were struck by how much waste they saw. Bank One had eight million vacant square feet of real estate around the country, which they were actively looking to sublet. There were thousands of unused phone lines.

Meanwhile, Dimon cut expenses wherever he saw them. He canceled subscriptions to the *Wall Street Journal,* telling employees they could buy it on their own if they wanted. Dimon also significantly cut outsourcing contracts which he viewed largely as a waste. "The vendors are taking this company for a ride," he complained to his management team. Bank One Director Jim Crown recalls Dimon's hands-on involvement to reduce the company's outsourcing fees:

> Jamie reviewed the outsourcing contracts with our vendors, which were supposed to be "most favored nation" deals. He evaluated our service and benchmarked our cost to other alternatives. He finished that analysis convinced that Bank One was not being well served, and personally called the CEOs of our vendors to demand better service and pricing. This also launched us on our path to abandon outsourced solutions where we could do it better and cheaper internally.

Perhaps most troubling to Dimon was the overall low employee morale and the upper management rifts that still existed between previous fiefdoms—Banc One versus NBD versus First Chicago versus First USA (See **Exhibit 10** for the upper management team as of July 2000). Dimon was also concerned about the compensation system, especially for top managers, which incorporated the most lavish perks from each merger. Still, Dimon knew there was an argument that now was not the time to "rock the boat" and change the compensation system.

There was one last decision facing Dimon: whether or not to cut next quarter's dividend, and if so, by how much (See **Exhibit 11** for Bank One's dividend history). He knew that any cut in the dividend would likely be perceived by Wall Street as a sign of corporate weakness, yet he also knew that the company needed all the cash it could get. Part of the dividend decision was related to the second-quarter earnings reduction that Dimon anticipated in the $3 billion range before taxes. Dimon recalled his decision process underlying the dividend cut and the earnings write-down:

> I knew how negatively Wall Street reacts to dividend cuts, but I also knew we had to live within our means. Bank One had had to revise its earnings expectations in 1999 and I

---

[19] 2Q00 investor meeting, July 19, 2000.

didn't want to have to cut the dividend twice. Still, there were a lot of large shareholders who were going to take some tough convincing that a dividend cut was the right thing to do in the long-term.

Presentation to the Board

Dimon looked down at the folded $8^{1}/_{2} \times 11$ sheet of paper he carried around with him in his breast pocket. The host of issues on the sheet reinforced for Dimon that Bank One was deeply troubled. Dimon began to identify the priorities and action items he would present to the Board of Directors. How should he go about cutting costs and increasing revenues? How could he restore strength to Bank One's balance sheet? How much should he write-down assets and increase reserves? Should he cut the dividend, and by how much? What should he do about the disparate IT system platforms? Finally, how could he motivate employees to work harder and more efficiently, and how should be communicate operational changes to employees, customers and investors?

EXHIBIT 1a | Banc One Acquisition History, 1993 to 1998 ($ in millions)

Seller	State	Completion Date	Deal Value	Assets Acquired
Colorado Western Bcp	CO	11/01/93	$17.3	$74.2
Central Banking Group	OK	12/31/93	104.8	544.1
Croghan & Associates	CO	01/03/94	0.4	0.5
Nebraska Capital Cp	NE	02/14/94	N.A.	95.0
First Tier Financial	NE	02/14/94	698.0	3,014.9
Parkdale Bank	TX	03/07/94	9.5	68.1
Capital Bancorp	UT	05/02/94	17.3	119.6
Mid States Bancshares	IL	06/09/94	32.7	192.5
Liberty National Bcp	KY	08/15/94	842.0	4,847.1
American Holding Co.	IL	12/31/94	31.5	237.6
1st Bank	TX	03/10/95	13.4	116.0
DHI Computing Service	UT	05/16/95	N.A.	N.A.
Premier Bancorp	LA	01/02/96	696.0	5,494.2
First Data Corp. (receivables)	NJ	12/31/96	N.A.	N.A.
Liberty Bancorp, Inc.	OK	06/02/97	526.8	2,905.4
First USA Inc.	TX	06/27/97	7,912.1	N.A.
Delphos International	DC	07/15/97	N.A.	N.A.
Fitzgerald, Davis	IL	12/15/97	N.A.	N.A.
BankBoston Corp. (receivables)	MA	06/01/98	N.A.	N.A.
First Commerce Corp.	LA	06/12/98	3,477.5	9,495.0
Chevy Chase (cards)	MD	09/03/98	N.A.	4,900.0
First Chicago NBD	IL	10/02/98	18,912.4	119,781.0
Total			**$ 33,291.7**	**$ 151,885.1**

Source: Michael L. Mayo and David A Hendler. "Bank One: Repositioning." *Credit Suisse First Boston Equity Research*. January 21, 2000. p. 31.

EXHIBIT 1b | First Chicago NBD Acquisition History, 1987 to 1998 ($ in millions)

Seller	State	Completion Date	Deal Value	Assets Acquired
Beneficial National Bank USA	DE	07/01/87	$ 258.0	$ 1,100.0
Society for Savings (cards)	CT	03/31/89	272.6	229.8
Ravenswood Financial	IL	11/01/89	N.A.	N.A.
Hampton Park Corp.	IL	06/17/94	7.0	41.4
Lake Shore Bancorp	IL	07/08/94	306.9	1,236.4
NBD Bancorp, Inc.	MI	12/01/95	6,096.8	48,501.6
Barrington Bancorp	IL	06/06/96	18.2	69.7
DuPont Co. (centrifuge business)	DE	07/01/96	N.A.	N.A.
Roney & Co. (brokerage)	MI	05/11/98	95.0	N.A.
Total			**$ 7,054.5**	**$ 51,178.9**

Source: Michael L. Mayo and David A Hendler. "Bank One: Repositioning." *Credit Suisse First Boston Equity Research*. January 21, 2000. p. 32.

EXHIBIT 2 | Bank One Market Area

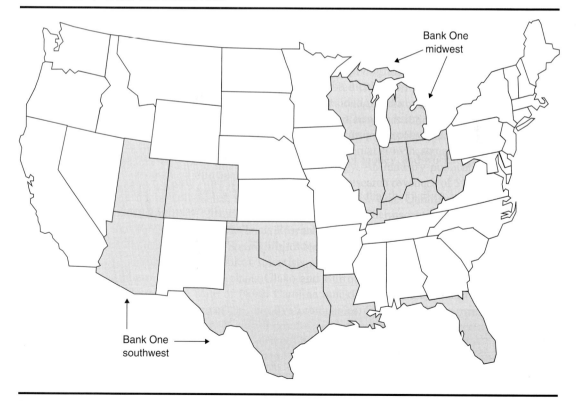

Source: Bank One.

EXHIBIT 3 | CSFB Analyst's Estimate of Bank One's Return on Invested Capital (ROIC) versus Weighted Average Cost of Capital (WACC)

Source: Michael L. Mayo and David A Hendler. "Bank One: Repositioning." *Credit Suisse First Boston Equity Research*. January 21, 2000. p. 35.

EXHIBIT 4 | Jamie Dimon's Biography, March 2000

Jamie Dimon became Chairman and Chief Executive Officer of Bank One Corporation in March 2000. Bank One is the nation's sixth-largest bank holding company, with assets of nearly $300 billion. It offers a full range of financial services to large corporate and middle market commercial customers as well as consumers.

Mr. Dimon was President of Citigroup Inc., the global financial services company formed by the combination of Travelers Group and Citicorp in 1998. In addition, he served as Chairman and Co-Chief Executive Officer of Salomon Smith Barney Holdings Inc., the investment banking and securities brokerage subsidiary.

At Travelers, Mr. Dimon was President and Chief Operating Officer for seven years. He was named Chairman and Chief Executive Officer of its Smith Barney Inc. subsidiary in January 1996, having previously been the firm's Chief Operating and Chief Administrative Officer. In November 1997, with the merger of Smith Barney and Salomon Brothers, he became Co-Chairman and Co-CEO, of the combined firm.

Mr. Dimon was a key member of the team that launched and defined the strategy for Commercial Credit Company in October 1986, when the consumer lending company was spun off from Control Data Corporation. He served as the company's Chief Financial Officer and an Executive Vice President, and then President. In the ensuing years, a completely restructured Commercial Credit made numerous acquisitions and divestitures, substantially improving its profitability. Most significantly, in 1987, it acquired and changed its name to Primerica Corporation, which in 1993 acquired The Travelers Corporation and was renamed Travelers Group.

He began his professional career at American Express Company, where he was Assistant to the President from 1982 until 1985.

A summa cum laude graduate of Tufts University, Mr. Dimon holds an MBA degree from the Harvard University Graduate School of Business, where he was a Baker Scholar. He serves on the Board of Directors of The National Center on Addiction and Substance Abuse (CASA), Yum! Brands, Inc., the University of Chicago, Harvard Business School, the United Negro College Fund, the Clearing House, and the Economic Club of Chicago as well as on the Civic Committee of the Commercial Club of Chicago. He is also a member of the World Economic Forum, the Financial Services Forum, and the Council on Foreign Relations, and serves on the board of the Mount Sinai-NYU Medical Center and Health Systems.

Mr. Dimon and his wife, Judy, have three daughters.

Source: Bank One.

EXHIBIT 5 | Bank One Board of Directors, April 2000

Name	DOH	Legacy	Affiliation	Age	Shares Owned
William Boardman	1999	Banc One	President of FirstUSA, Bank One	58	182,416
John Bryan	1982	First Chicago	CEO Sara Lee	63	13,534
Siegfried Buschmann**	1991	NBD	CEO Budd Div of Thyssen	62	4,689
James Crown**	1991	First Chicago	GP Henry Crown (Investment Firm)	46	9,031,940
Bennett Dorrance**	1996	Banc One	Private Investor	54	16,930
Maureen Fay	1985	NBD	Pres Mercy College	65	5,624
John Hall**	1987	Banc One	Retired CEO Ashland Oil	67	48,255
Verne Istock	1985	NBD	President Bank One	59	912,088
Laban Jackson Jr.	1993	Banc One	CEO Clear Creek Properties	57	26,672
John Kessler**	1986	Banc One	Chr New Albany Real Estate	64	26,992
Richard Manoogian**	1978	NBD	CEO Masco	63	15,619
William McCormick Jr.	1985	NBD	CEO CMS Energy Corp	55	20,884
Jamie Dimon	1983	—	Chairman & CEO Bank One	44	2,035,242
Thomas Reilly	1995	First Chicago NBD	CEO Reilly Industries (Chemicals)	60	221,145
John Rogers	1998	First Chicago NBD	Founder Ariel Capital Mgmt (Investment Firm)	42	3,607
Thekla Shackelford	1993	Banc One	Founded School Selection Consulting	65	202,992
Alex Shumate	1993	Banc One	Partner, Squire, Sanders & Dempsey	49	6,633
Frederick Stratton	1988	Banc One	CEO Briggs and Stratton	61	41,619
John Tolleson	1997	Banc One	CEO Tolleson Group (Investment Firm)	51	1,031,768
Robert Walter	1987	Banc One	CEO Cardinal Health Care	54	106,050

**Member of search committee.

Note: Four directors, including John McCoy, stepped down in 1999. Bill Boardman joined the Board at the time McCoy stepped down, decreasing the total from 22 to 19.

Source: Public filings, April 2000.

EXHIBIT 6 | Select Financial Data

In millions, except ratios and per share data	1995	1996	1997	1998	1999
Net interest income—tax-equivalent basis	$ 8,042	$ 9,417	$ 9,619	$ 9,469	$ 9,142
Provision for credit losses	1,067	1,716	1,988	1,408	1,249
Non-interest income	5,478	5,994	6,694	8,071	8,692
Merger-related and restructuring charges	267	—	337	1,062	554
Operating expense	7,948	8,681	9,403	10,483	10,936
Net income (a)	2,675	3,231	2,960	3,108	3,479
Per Common Share Data:					
Net income, basic	$ 2.17	$ 2.64	$ 2.48	$ 2.65	$ 2.97
Net income, diluted	2.12	2.57	2.43	2.61	2.95
Cash dividends declared	1.13	1.24	1.38	1.52	1.68
Book value	15.28	16.64	16.03	17.31	17.34
Balance Sheet:					
Loans	$138,478	$153,496	$159,579	$155,398	$163,877
Deposits	145,343	145,206	153,726	161,542	162,278
Long-term debt	12,582	15,363	21,546	22,298	35,435
Total assets	228,298	225,822	239,372	261,496	269,425
Common stockholders' equity	17,345	18,856	18,724	20,370	19,900
Total stockholders' equity	18,143	19,507	19,050	20,560	20,090
Performance Ratios: (%)					
Return on assets	1.19	1.43	1.29	1.30	1.36
Return on common equity	15.7	17.5	15.8	15.9	17.1
Net interest margin	4.07	4.70	4.75	4.52	4.09
Efficiency ratio	60.8	56.3	59.7	65.8	64.4
Credit Quality: (%)					
Net charge-offs to average loans	0.59	1.04	1.21	0.97	0.77
Allowance for credit losses to loans outstanding	1.76	1.75	1.77	1.46	1.39
Nonperforming assets to related assets	0.55	0.4	0.42	0.53	0.71
Common Stock Data:					
Average shares outstanding, basic	1,198	1,199	1,176	1,170	1,168
Average shares outstanding, diluted	1,248	1,254	1,213	1,189	1,178
Stock price, year-end	$ 31.10	$ 39.09	$ 49.37	$ 51.06	$ 32.00
Stock dividends (%)	—	1	—	10	—
Dividend payout ratio (%)	40	38	61	58	57

(a) Net income figures include the effect of taxes.

Source: Public filings.

EXHIBIT 7 | Industry Comparisons, 1999

PROFITABILITY (% except where noted)	Bank One	BAC	BCS	C	FB	NCC	STI	USB	WB	WFC
Pretax Profit Margin	19.41	23.71	18.84	19.45	17.15	26.14	22.25	21.99	21.88	27.29
Net Profit Margin	13.58	15.30	13.47	12.19	10.20	17.10	14.75	13.63	14.59	17.19
Return on Assets	1.29	1.24	0.69	1.37	1.04	1.61	1.18	1.20	1.27	1.70
Return on Equity	17.42	17.75	20.74	20.61	13.59	24.64	14.74	13.87	19.29	16.98
Return on Investment	6.26	7.51	10.98	10.51	5.77	9.23	8.33	7.73	7.00	11.28
Net Interest Margin	4.09	3.47	3.40	@NA	4.23	3.99	3.88	4.09	3.79	5.66
DIVIDENDS										
Dividend Payout	56.48	40.55	42.41	18.53	51.38	47.71	39.20	59.10	56.48	34.83
Dividend Yield	5.25	3.69	2.83	0.97	3.19	4.47	2.01	2.19	5.71	1.94
Dividends per Share ($)	1.68	1.85	0.81	0.41	1.11	1.06	1.38	0.46	1.88	0.79
One Year Total Return	−34.80	−13.95	31.67	70.10	−19.79	−32.49	−8.19	−30.27	−43.50	3.23
BALANCE SHEET										
% of Total Assets										
Reserve for Loan	0.85	1.08	0.78	@NA	1.30	1.11	0.91	0.98	0.69	1.45
Total Deposits	60.23	54.90	66.11	35.78	60.25	57.47	63.01	71.28	55.74	60.85
Shareholder's Equity	7.46	7.02	3.33	6.93	8.03	6.57	8.00	8.67	6.60	10.15
Total Debt	27.97	28.88	10.96	30.16	22.79	34.43	25.36	18.33	32.44	23.91
Total Nonperforming Assets ($MM)	59.98	57.52	44.56	42.71	61.47	67.99	68.28	68.57	52.88	53.32

Note: BAC = Bank of America; BCS = Barclays Plc; C = Citigroup Inc.; FBF = FleetBoston Financial Corp; NCC = National City; STI = SunTrust Banks; USB = US Bancorp; WB = Wachovia Corp.; WFC = Wells Fargo & Co.

Source: Public filings.

EXHIBIT 8 | Bank One Corp., Income Statement Breakdown, 1999–2000E Q2 ($ millions)

	1999A				2000E	
	1Q	2Q	3Q	4Q	1Q	2Q
Income Statement[a]						
Average Earning Assets	$ 217,909	$ 220,505	$ 223,205	$ 232,380	$ 234,000	$ 235,000
Net Interest Margin[b]	4.30%	4.26%	4.04%	3.79%	3.75%	3.72%
Net Interest Income[b]	$ 2,309.0	$ 2,341.0	$ 2,271.0	$ 2,221.0	$ 2,193.8	$ 2,185.5
Loan Loss Provision	281.0	275.0	277.0	240.0	315.0	325.0
NII After Llp	2,028.0	2,066.0	1,994.0	1,981.0	1,878.8	1,860.5
Noninterest Income						
Fiduciary and Investment Management Fees	$ 179.0	$ 197.0	$ 201.0	$ 216.0	$ 220.0	$ 223.0
Service Charges and Commissions	690.0	723.0	671.0	701.0	705.0	710.0
Mortgage Banking						
Credit Card Fees	952.0	920.0	907.0	747.0	740.0	750.0
Trading Account Profits	67.0	33.0	30.0	21.0	30.0	45.0
Equity Securities Gains	96.0	133.0	86.0	100.0	115.0	110.0
Other Income	194.0	182.0	197.0	186.0	190.0	195.0
Extraordinary Gains	360.0	0.0	0.0	0.0	0.0	0.0
Total Noninterest Income	$ 2,538.0	$ 2,188.0	$ 2,092.0	$ 1,971.0	$ 2,000.0	$ 2,033.0

Noninterest Expense

Salaries and Benefits	$ 1,147.0	$ 1,073.0	$ 970.0	$ 1,081.0	$ 1,080.0	$ 1,090.0
Net Occupancy and Equipment	241.0	219.0	220.0	244.0	240.0	245.0
Depreciation and Amortization	175.0	169.0	167.0	164.0	165.0	165.0
Outside Services	406.0	420.0	458.0	459.0	465.0	475.0
Marketing and Development	315.0	302.0	341.0	230.0	240.0	250.0
Communication and Transportation	200.0	208.0	205.0	216.0	208.0	208.0
Other Expenses	293.0	270.0	296.0	278.0	285.0	290.0
Nonrecurring Charges	164.0	145.0	56.0	725.0	0.0	0.0
Total Noninterest Expense	$ 2,941.0	$ 2,806.0	$ 2,713.0	$ 3,397.0	$ 2,683.0	$ 2,723.0
Pretax Income[b]	$ 1,625.0	$ 1,448.0	$ 1,373.0	$ 555.0	$ 1,195.8	$ 1,170.5
Normalized Tax Rate[b]	31%	33%	33%	26%	33%	33%
Normalized Taxes[b]	$ 507.8	$ 478.1	$ 451.9	$ 145.3	$ 400.6	$ 392.0
IBST	$ 1,117.2	$ 969.9	$ 921.1	$ 409.7	$ 794.9	$ 778.2
Net Inv. Sec. Transactions	33.8	22.1	3.9	1.3	2.0	5.0
Net Income	$ 1,151.0	$ 992.0	$ 925.0	$ 411.0	$ 796.9	$ 783.2
Operating Earnings—Diluted	$ 0.88	$ 0.93	$ 0.86	$ 0.78	$ 0.69	$ 0.67
Net Income per Share—Diluted	$ 0.96	$ 0.83	$ 0.79	$ 0.42	$ 0.69	$ 0.68
Cash Flow per Share	$ 0.85	$ 0.91	$ 0.82	$ 0.82	$ 0.68	$ 0.67
Book Value per Share	$ 17.68	$ 17.73	$ 16.87	$ 17.24	$ 17.46	$ 17.67

Note: (A = Actual; E = Estimate).

[a]Dollars in millions, except per share data.

[b]Fully taxable equivalent.

Source: Adapted from Diane B. Glossman. "Bank One: Working Out the Kinks." *Lehman Brothers Equity Research*, Feb. 2, 2000, p. 16.

EXHIBIT 9 | Line of Business Data Reflecting Reorganization, January 1, 2000

1999 ($MM)	Commercial Banking	Credit Card	Retail	Other Activities	Unallocated	Managed Business Segment Results
Net interest income	3,027	6,895	4,389	28	118	14,457
Provision for credit losses	437	3,593	415	—	(107)	4,338
Noninterest income	2,298	1,858	1,719	420	178	6,473
Noninterest expense	2,917	3,444	4,004	193	60	10,618
Net income	1425	1135	1118	170	228	4076
Return On equity	20%	18%	24%	—	—	20%
Efficiency ratio	55%	39%	66%	—	—	51%
Average loans	83.1	69.0	66.2	0.3	—	218.6
Average managed assets	117.9	75.3	72.8	36.2	—	302.2
Average common equity	7.2	6.2	4.7	0.8	14.0	20.3

1998 ($MM)	Commercial Banking	Credit Card	Retail	Other Activities	Unallocated	Managed Business Segment Results
Net interest income	2,841	6,457	4,293	144	93	13,828
Provision for credit losses	404	3,274	457	—	(221)	3,914
Noninterest income	1,990	1,628	1,920	388	144	6,070
Noninterest expense	2,902	3,054	4,214	113	33	1,036
Net income	1109%	1177%	1024%	276%	283%	3869%
Return On equity	15%	21%	22%	—	—	20%
Efficiency ratio	60	38	68	—	—	52
Average loans	77.0	60.5	62.2	0.2	—	199.9
Average managed assets	113.1	65.7	67.5	32.6	—	278.9
Average common equity	7.3	5.6	4.6	0.6	1.4	19.5

Source: 1999 10-K.

	Investment Management (1998)	Investment Management (1999)
Total Revenue	1799	1523
Noninterest expense	1065	1016
Net income	485	335

Note: Results for Investment Management are fully attributed to the other lines of business in the above table.

Source: 1999 10-K.

EXHIBIT 10 | Senior Management Team, July 1, 2000

Name	Title	Legacy
Jamie Dimon	Chairman and CEO	Joined March 2000
Verne G. Istock	President	First Chicago NBD
William P. Boardman	Vice Chairman and Head of Credit Card Services	Banc One
Marvin W. Adams	Chief Technology Officer	Banc One
David P. Bolger	Head of Corporate Banking	First Chicago NBD
Christine A. Edwards	Chief Legal Officer and Secretary	Hired in 2000
David J. Kundert	Investment Management	Banc One
Richard R. Wade	Chief Risk Management Officer	First Chicago NBD
Timothy P. Moen	Human Resources	First Chicago NBD
Robert A. O'Neill Jr.	General Auditor	Banc One
Charles W. Scharf	Chief Financial Officer	Hired in 2000
Kenneth T. Stevens	Retail Banking	Banc One
Geoffrey L. Stringer	Corporate Investments	First Chicago NBD
R. Michael Welborn	Middle Market Banking	Banc One

Source: Bank One.

EXHIBIT 11 | Cash Dividend Payout History

Declaration Date	Cash Payment Date	Dividend Amount
4/18/2000	7/1/2000	$0.42
1/18/2000	4/1/2000	$0.42
10/19/1999	1/1/2000	$0.42
7/20/1999	10/1/1999	$0.42
4/20/1999	7/1/1999	$0.42
1/19/1999	4/1/1999	$0.42
10/20/1998	1/1/1999	$0.38
7/21/1998	9/30/1998	$0.38
4/21/1998	6/30/1998	$0.38
1/20/1998	3/31/1998	$0.38
10/21/1997	1/2/1998	$0.35
7/15/1997	9/30/1997	$0.35
4/15/1997	6/30/1997	$0.35
1/20/1997	3/31/1997	$0.35
10/15/1996	1/2/1997	$0.31
7/16/1996	9/30/1996	$0.31
4/16/1996	6/28/1996	$0.31
1/23/1996	3/29/1996	$0.31
10/17/1995	1/2/1996	$0.28
7/18/1995	9/29/1995	$0.28

(continued)

EXHIBIT 11 | Cash Dividend Payout History (*continued*)

Declaration Date	Cash Payment Date	Dividend Amount
4/18/1995	6/30/1995	$0.28
1/24/1995	3/31/1995	$0.28
10/18/1994	1/2/1995	$0.26
7/18/1994	9/30/1994	$0.26
4/19/1994	6/30/1994	$0.26
1/25/1994	3/31/1994	$0.26
10/19/1993	1/2/1994	$0.23
7/20/1993	9/30/1993	$0.23
4/21/1993	6/30/1993	$0.21
1/19/1993	3/31/1993	$0.21
10/20/1992	1/2/1993	$0.19
7/21/1992	9/30/1992	$0.19
4/21/1992	6/30/1992	$0.17
1/22/1992	3/31/1992	$0.17
10/15/1991	1/2/1992	$0.16
7/17/1991	9/30/1991	$0.16
4/16/1991	6/30/1991	$0.16
1/15/1991	3/29/1991	$0.16
10/16/1990	1/2/1991	$0.14
7/18/1990	9/28/1990	$0.14
4/17/1990	6/30/1990	$0.14
1/17/1990	3/31/1990	$0.14
10/17/1989	1/2/1990	$0.13
7/18/1989	9/30/1989	$0.13

Source: Bank One.

Case Index

The Aravind Eye Hospital, Madurai, India:
In Service for Sight, 17

Beta Golf, 191
Business Plan for Room for Dessert™: Adding Unique
Ingredients to Life's Balancing Act, 343

Crunch, 257

E Ink: Financing Growth, 465
Endeavor—Determining a Growth Strategy, 73

Innocent Drinks, 563

Jamie Dimon and Bank One (A), 667
Jim Sharpe: Extrusion Technology, Inc.
(Abridged), 389

Kendle International Inc., 617
Keurig, 233

KIPP National (A) (Abridged), 537

MAC Development Corporation, 499

NanoGene Technologies, Inc., 331

ONSET Ventures, 435

RightNow Technologies, 645
R&R, 45

Sheila Mason & Craig Shepherd, 315
Shurgard Self-Storage: Expansion to Europe, 585

Valhalla Partners Due Diligence, 483
Vermeer Technologies (A): A Company Is Born, 63

Walnut Venture Associates (D): RBS Deal Terms, 379

Zipcar: Refining the Business Model, 213

Subject Index

Page numbers followed by *n* indicate footnotes.

A. C. Nielson, 125
Abacus Direct, 125, 126
Abrams, Jonathan, 173
Accounts receivable, 299, 300
Action orientation, 7
Administrative practices, 11
Advertising
  costs of, 155
  fees related to, 153, 159
Airlines, 128–129
Angel investors, 293–294
Anthony, Robert, 154*n*
Anti-dilution provisions, 312
Arbitrage businesses, 127
Arbitrary marks, 287
ASK Computer Systems, 123
Asset-based financing, 298–299
Assets, 300
Avid Technology, 143

Bain Capital, 144
Barley, Lauren, 169*n*
Bay Networks, 141
Bhidé, Amar, 293
Biotechnology companies, 121
Bootstrap approach, 293
Bottom-up valuation, 164
Bower, Joseph, 125
Break-even, 142
Buffett, Warren, 126
Burge, David A., 285*n*, 290
Business
  attributes of successful, 117–118
  understanding nature of, 306–307
Business models
  cost drivers and, 150, 154, 155
  cost structures and, 154–156, 160
  critical success factors and, 150, 158–159
  definition of, 149–150
  evaluation of prospective, 171, 176,
    180–181, 186
  framework for analysis of, 150–151
  investment size and, 150, 156–158, 161
  revenue streams and, 150–153
Business plans
  competition and, 127–128
  context and, 133
  deals and, 133–139

due diligence and, 143–144
financial projections and, 141–143
function of, 116, 144–145
opportunity and, 120–132
people and, 118–120
risk/reward management and, 139–141
  (*See also* Risk/reward management)
role of, 115, 118
translation glossary for, 148
Business practice
  commitment to opportunity in, 7–8
  commitment to resources in, 8–10
  management structure in, 12–13
  resources control in, 10–11
  reward philosophy in, 13, 15
  strategic orientation in, 5–7

Cantillon, Richard, 4
Capital allocation systems, 10
Capitalization tables, 166, 167
Capital markets, 3
Cash flow
  analysis of, 123
  components of, 306–307
  lending against, 298, 308
  positive, 156
  timing of, 158
Cash flow diagrams
  evaluation of, 156
  examples of, 128–132
  for medical device venture, 161
  for new venture, 161
Cash flow financing, 298
C corporations, 426–427, 431–434
Change, 11
Chase, Robin, 421
Chief executive officers (CEOs), 178, 181
Christensen, Clayton, 125
Cisco, 122, 141
Clarus, 181–182
Coined marks, 287
Commercialization skills, 127
Commitment
  nature and timing of, 423–424
  to opportunity, 7–8
  to resources, 8–10
Common stock, 311
Compaq Computer, 122

Compensation
   incentive, 10
   philosophy regarding, 13, 15
Competition
   on business plans, 127–128
   compensation and, 15
Confidential business information, 288–289
Confidentiality, 296
Conner Peripherals, 121
Conscious experiments, 422–423
Consulting firms, 157
Control, 312
Convertible securities, 311
Copyrights, 284, 286–287
   explanation of, 286–287
Corporate partners, 297
Cost centers, 155
Cost drivers
   analysis of, 155
   case example of, 155–156
   explanation of, 150
   types of, 154–155
Cost structures, 154–156, 160
Critical success factors
   analysis of, 158–159
   explanation of, 150, 158
   by revenue model, 159
Customers, 172

Dauppe, V. A. F., 290
Deals
   alternative structures for, 310
   business fundamentals and, 306–307
   business plans and, 133–135
   characteristics of, 138
   entrepreneur's needs and, 309–310
   example of term sheet for, 310–312
   factors that drive, 306
   financier needs and objectives
      and, 307–309
   nature of, 305, 312–313
   principles for structuring, 136–137
   valuation of, 138–139
Debt capital, 297–298
Decision process, 8
Descriptive marks, 287
Design patents, 284, 286
Disk drive business, 120–121,
      125, 130
Dividends, 311
Doerr, John, 134, 173
Doriot, George F., 122n
Dougherty, Heather, 151n
Draper, Tim, 186

Due diligence
   business plans and, 143–144
   customers and, 172
   industry, 172
   for potential venture opportunities, 171–172, 176–177,
      181–182, 186–187
Dynamic-fit model, 528

Eastway, N. A., 290
EMC, 121
Employee rights, 289
Entrepreneurial management, 12–13, 532–533
Entrepreneurial ventures. *See also* Ventures
   business model and, 420–421
   commitment management and, 423–424
   components of, 116
   conscious experiments and, 422–423
   cost strategy and, 423
   flexibility and, 424
   overview of, 417–418
   risk and uncertainty in, 418–420
   size and, 421–422
   stage financing and, 424
Entrepreneurs
   aspects of, 4–5, 10
   issues facing, 9
   as managers, 12–13, 533–535
   needs of, 309–310
   traits of, 7, 139–140
   values of, 531–532
Entrepreneurship
   as behavioral phenomenon, 5
   commitment to opportunity by, 7–8
   commitment to resources in, 8–10
   control of resources by, 10–11
   definitions of, 4–5, 417
   increasing interest in, 3–4
   management structure in, 12–13
   perspective on, 14, 15
   reward philosophy in, 13, 15
   strategic orientation of, 5–7
   supply-side, 4
   in teams, 170
Equipment, 299
Equity capital
   explanation of, 292
   private investors and, 293–294
   public equity markets and, 296–297
   venture capital and, 294–296
Equity markets, 296–297
Equity/subordinated debt, 300
Exit routes
   for investors, 434
   for potential venture opportunities, 174, 178, 184, 188

Ferguson, Bruce, 145
Fidelity, 122
Financial analysis, 173, 177, 183, 187–188
Financial projections, 141–143
Fit
    concept of, 116, 146
    degree of, 116–118
    management of, 8, 147
Fixed costs, 154, 423
Flexibility
    increased, 11
    as risk-reducing strategy, 424
Flight Safety, 129n
Formal planning systems, 10
Freear, B., 294n
Fuel Tech, 127
Funding decisions, 172–173, 177, 182–183, 187
Future value, 165

Gallafent, R. J., 290
Gates, Bill, 145
General partnerships, 427
Giarman, Keith, 181
Gillette, 126
Globalization, 150
Government secured loans, 299
Grateful Dead revenue model, 153, 159
Gupta, Mahendra, 154n

Hamermesh, Richard G., 149n, 420n
Haney, William, 127
Hart, Myra, 119–120
Harvesting, 141
Hawkins, David, 154n
Helyar, John, 294n
Hoel, Sonja, 174–178
Hybrid financing, 299–300

IBM, 120–121
Implied valuation, 164
Inc. magazine, 124
Incentive compensation, 10
Industry due diligence, 172
Innovation, types of, 4
Integration. *See* Fit
Intellectual property
    confidential business information and, 288–289
    copyrights and, 286–287
    employees' rights regarding, 289
    issues related to, 283–284, 289–290
    legal issues and, 284
    patents and, 284–286
    trademarks, service marks and trade dress and, 287–288
    trade secrets and, 288

Interdependent revenue streams, 151
Internal rate of return (IRR), 163
International business, 10
Internet Profiles, 125
Internet Wicked Ale, Inc. (IWA), 115, 119
Intrepreneurship, 3
Intuit, 124–125
Invention, 126
Inventory
    cost of, 154
    financing based on, 299
Investment size
    for business models, 150, 156–158, 161
    case example of, 157–158
    examples of, 157
Investors. *See also* Venture capital firms
    compensation and demands of, 15
    equity capital and private, 293–294
    needs and objectives of, 307–309
    preferences of, 166
Iomega, 126
IPOable, 141

Jefferson, Elana Ashanti, 153n
Johnston, Donald F., 290

Kent, Calvin, 4
Kleiner, Perkins, 134
Kroc, Ray, 5
Kurtzig, Sandra, 123

Letter-of-credit financing, 299
Levin, Richard, 124n
Licensing fees, 153
Lietman, Alan, 290
Limited liability companies (LLCs), 428, 431–434
Limited partnerships, 427–428, 431–434
Line-of-credit financing, 298
Long-term debt, 298
Loss leaders, 151–152
Lynch, Peter, 122

Magazine publishing, 124
Magellan Fund (Fidelity), 122
Management
    archetypes of, 532–533
    entrepreneurial, 12–13, 532–533
    of fit, 8
    role of, 118
    turnover in, 10
Marketing costs, 155
Marshall, Paul W., 149n, 420n
McCraw, Thomas, 155n
MCI Telecommunications, 127

Medical device venture, 157–158, 161
Memorex, 121
Merchant, Kenneth, 154n
Miller, Michael W., 120n
Molten Metals, 127
Mooradian, Mark, 151n
Morse, Kenneth P., 294n
Multiple revenue streams, 151

Narasimhan, Chakravarthi, 154n
Nintendo, 126
Nippon Electric Company, 156
Niraj, Rakesh, 154n
Nomura Research Institute, 156
Non-recurring costs, 154

Obsolescence, 11
OEMs (Original equipment manufacturers), 121
Opportunities
    assessment of, 128–132
    in business plans, 120–128
    commitment to, 7–8
    in context, 133
Orbital Sciences Corporation, 145
Organizational culture, 13
Organizations
    C corporation, 426–427, 431–434
    choosing form of, 428–430
    comparison of forms of, 431–434
    partnership, 427–428, 431–434
    S corporation, 428, 431–434
    sole proprietorship, 426
    tax issues and, 429, 431
    types of, 425–426

Participation rights, 311
Partnerships, 427–428, 431–434
Patents
    design, 286
    explanation of, 285
    plant, 286
    potential venture opportunities and, 170, 179
    types of, 284
    utility, 285–286
Payroll-centered costs, 154
Per share approach, 165
Personally secured loans, 299
Pirmohamed, Taz, 149n
Plant patents, 284, 286
P-O-C-D framework, 528
Potential venture opportunities
    business model and, 171, 176, 180–181, 186
    due diligence and, 171–172, 176–177, 181–182, 186–187
    evaluation of, 170–171, 174–176, 178–180, 184–186

exit routes and, 174, 178, 184, 188
    financial analysis and, 173, 177, 183, 187–188
    funding decisions and, 172–173, 177, 182–183, 187
    risk and, 174, 177–178, 183, 188
Priam, 121
Pricing, 123
Private investors, 293–294
Proportional ownership approach, 165

Quantum, 121
Quicken, 124–125

Razeghi, Andrew, 153n
Real estate, 299
Redemption rights, 312
Reiss, Bob, 423, 424
Rent costs, 154
Resource intensity, 10
Resources
    commitment of, 8–10
    control of, 10–11
Retail businesses, 157
Retained earnings, 300
Revenue models
    analysis of, 152–153
    case example of, 153
    examples of critical success factors by, 159
    types of, 152
Revenue streams
    analysis of, 152
    for business models, 151–153
    explanation of, 150
Reward philosophy, 13, 15
Risk
    cash flow analysis and, 131
    nature of, 134
    of potential venture opportunities, 174, 177–178, 183, 188
Risk bearing, 5
Risk management, 8
Risk reduction, 8, 10
Risk/reward management
    business models and, 420–421
    business plans and, 139–141, 144
    commitment management and, 423–424
    conscious experiments and, 422–423
    cost strategy and, 423
    flexibility and, 424
    model of, 140
    nature of, 417–418
    opportunities and, 128
    risk and uncertainty and, 418–420
    size and, 421–422
    stage financing and, 424

Risk-to-reward ratio, 174
Roberts, Michael J., 163*n*, 169*n*, 283*n*,
 291*n*, 294*n*, 305*n*, 417*n*, 425*n*, 527*n*
Rock, Arthur, 122, 134–135
Rosen, Ben, 122

Sabre Corporation, 129*n*
Sahlman, William A., 115, 138*n*, 139*n*
Salesforce.com model, 180–181
Say, Jean Baptiste, 4
Scherlis, Daniel R., 139*n*
Schumpeter, Joseph, 4
Science Technology case (Harvard Business School), 136
S corporations, 428, 431–434
Seagate, 121
Semi-variable costs, 154
SEMS (systematic emerging market selection)
 process, 175, 177
Sensitivity analysis, 158
Service marks, 287
Seven-Eleven Japan, 155–156, 160
7-S model, 528
Sevin, L. J., 122, 135
Shaw, George Bernard, 145
Short-term debt, 298
Shumacher, E. F., 9
Siegelman, Russell, 169–174
Simon, Robert, 184–188
Single revenue streams, 151
Social needs, 9
Societal norms, 15
Software businesses, 157
Sohl, J., 294*n*
Sole proprietorships, 426
Space costs, 154
Staples, 121, 144
Start-ups, 3
Stemberg, Tom, 121, 144
Stevenson, Howard H., 3*n*, 135, 291*n*,
 294*n*, 305*n*, 425*n*
Stock options, 165–166
Strategic orientation, 5–7
Strategy
 for managing growing ventures, 529–531
 negotiation of, 8
Subscription/membership fees, 153, 159
Suggestive marks, 287
Suppliers, 300
Supply-side entrepreneurship, 4
Syndication fees, 153

Taxes
 investors and, 308
 organization forms and, 429, 431, 433

Teams, 170
Technological advances, 150
Term sheets, 310–312
Thompson, David, 145
3M, 141
Tokyo Electric Company, 156
Trade dress, 288
Trademarks, 286, 287
Trade secrets, 288
Transaction fees, 153, 159

Unit-based fees, 153
Unprotectable terms, 287
US Air, 126
Utility patents, 284–286

Valentine, Don, 122
Valuation
 explanation of, 163
 implied vs. bottom-up, 164
 inherent rate of return and, 163–164
 origin of, 164–165
Value
 extraction of, 118
 future, 165
 growth in, 121–122
Vanderbilt, Nicole, 151*n*
Variable costs, 154, 423
Venture capital
 decisions regarding, 134–136
 explanation of, 294–295
 funding flows from, 302
 model in, 120
 rate of return for, 295
 statistics regarding, 296
 timing of, 171
Venture capital firms. *See also* Investors
 capital committed to, 3
 issues of concern regarding, 296
 projected financials and, 173
 structuring deals with, 137–139
 term sheets from, 310–312
Venture financing
 alternative sources of, 303
 asset-based, 298–299
 bootstrapping and, 293
 cash flow, 298
 corporate partners and, 297
 debt capital and, 297–298
 equity, 292
 hybrid, 299–300
 implications of choices in, 301
 internally generated, 300–301
 methods for obtaining, 291–292

outside equity capital and, 293–297, 302
views regarding, 134
Venture leasing, 300
Venture management
    entrepreneurs and, 534–535
    individuals involved in, 533–534
    maintaining momentum in, 535–536
    model of, 528–529
    organization, structure, and process of, 531–533
    phases in, 527
    vision and strategy for, 529–531
Ventures. *See also* Entrepreneurial ventures;
    Potential venture opportunities
    analysis of, 117
    evaluation of, 121–124
    fit of, 116–118
    role of context in, 133

role of deals in, 133–139
role of opportunities in, 120–132
role of people in, 118–120
size of, 421–422
Volume-based fees, 153
Voting rights, 311

Wang, Fred, 178–184
Watson, Thomas, 5
Webster, Scott, 145
Wetzel, W. E., 294*n*
White, Herbert S., 290
Working capital, 300

Yeager, Chuck, 124

Zip Drive (Iomega), 126